To
GLORIA, ALLISON, KRISTIN
and
LINDA

CHAPTER CONTRIBUTORS

CHARLES CLIFTON, JR., *Associate Professor of Psychology, University of Massachusetts*

WILLARD W. HARTUP, *Professor and Associate Director, Institute of Child Development, University of Minnesota*

EILEEN MAVIS HETHERINGTON, *Professor of Psychology, University of Wisconsin*

WENDELL E. JEFFREY, *Professor of Psychology, University of California, Los Angeles*

HOWARD A. MOSS, *Chief, Section on Parent-Infant Behavior, Child Research Branch, National Institute of Mental Health*

HARRY OSSER, *Associate Professor of Psychology, San Francisco State College*

HAROLD W. STEVENSON, *Professor and Director, Institute of Child Development, University of Minnesota*

MY GEMS
William M. Harnett
National Gallery of Art, Washington, D.C.
Gift of the Avalon Foundation

Paula and Thomas Green

PERSPECTIVES IN CHILD PSYCHOLOGY

Research and Review

McGRAW-HILL SERIES IN PSYCHOLOGY

Consulting Editors

NORMAN GARMEZY, RICHARD L. SOLOMON,
LYLE V. JONES, HAROLD W. STEVENSON

Edited by

THOMAS D. SPENCER

Associate Professor of Psychology
San Francisco State College

NORMAN KASS

Professor of Psychology
San Diego State College

Panama   *Mexico*   *Sydney*   *London*

PERSPECTIVES
IN
Research and Review
CHILD
PSYCHOLOGY

McGRAW-HILL BOOK COMPANY

New York   San Francisco   St. Louis   Toronto

This book was set in Fototronic Elegante and Galaxy Medium by Graphic Services, Inc., and printed on permanent paper and bound by The Maple Press Company. The designer was Janet Bollow. The drawings were done by Mark Schroeder. The sculptures were created by Sue Sellars and photographed by William Skeahan. The editors were Walter J. Maytham and Michael A. Ungersma. Charles A. Goehring supervised production.

PERSPECTIVES
IN
CHILD
PSYCHOLOGY
Research and Review

Printed in the United States of America.

Library of Congress catalog card number: 78-95833

1234567890   MAMM   79876543210

60194

PREFACE

In the early stages of his studies in child psychology, a student is typically exposed to the subject matter of the course through "general" textbooks or books of readings. Each of these formats has its advantages. Traditional textbooks provide the student with a summary survey or overview of the field allowing him to experience some appreciation of the diverse facets of the discipline. Books of readings have the advantage of putting the student in direct contact with original research reports including, many times, classic studies as well as current ones. In addition, books of readings help reduce traffic on overtaxed library sources and in the process, provide the student with the convenience of having his own copy of each research study to read at his leisure. In recent years, a number of good textbooks and books of readings have been published, making it possible for instructors to organize their courses using either source or a combination of them as reading materials.

An alternative approach to a general survey course in child psychology is to involve the student in more concentrated studies of selected subject areas in the field. Such an approach is becoming useful not only because of the rapidly growing literature on child behavior, but also because many instructors find it quite attractive and stimulating to both their students and themselves. With this more concentrated approach in mind, the editors of the present volume set out to compile a series of "perspectives" on selected topics in child psychology. Each of these perspectives should provide the student with an integrated review of research on the topic as well as expose him to individual research studies. This "selected topics" organization is a new approach, and should see considerable use in the future.

The book is organized into seven sections or subjects areas that generally reflect present interests and concerns in child psychology and in which substantial amounts of research are currently underway. Each section consists of an original "review chapter" and three or four reprinted journal articles. The review chapters have been written by individuals who are actively engaged in research in the respective areas. By drawing upon a selected sample of recent research studies, authors of the chapters have attempted to present current perspectives on their topics. In spite of being confronted, in many cases, with diverse and voluminous literatures, the review authors have skillfully selected, interpreted, and integrated the subject matter of their areas. Their efforts have produced clear, concise, and up-to-date chapters. The "articles," which appear after each chapter, were selected as illustrative of the source materials upon which the research review was based. The findings of the studies have been integrated into the chapters themselves.

It is our hope that by reading each review chapter along with its accompanying articles, the student will not only gain some general familiarity with the subject area but will also develop an appreciation for the way in which research and experimentation become integrated into bodies of knowledge. Hopefully, the book will provide the student with a reasonably sophisticated understanding of child psychology as a scientific discipline. Instructors should find *Perspectives in Child Psychology* with its combined advantages of a text and a reader appropriate either as a basic source for their courses or as a strong supplement to other materials they may choose to use.

The editors wish to extend their gratitude to a number of people whose contributions have made the publication of this book possible. First, we express our appreciation to the seven review authors who have given a great deal of time, energy, and thought in producing well organized, readable, and stimulating chapters. A special thanks is due Harold Stevenson, who not only authored one of the chapters but also encouraged us and offered helpful suggestions throughout the preparation of the volume.

In addition, we extend our thanks to the authors and publishers of the journal articles for their permission to reproduce these studies in the book. In some cases, articles have been edited by us with a view toward simplifying some of the more technical aspects of research design or statistical analyses. We have used the customary conventions of ellipses and brackets to indicate all deletions or insertions.

The chapter openings are illustrated by photographs of original sculptures created especially for the book by Sue Sellars. In these sculptures, the artist has attempted, in a most unique manner, to capture the central meaning of each chapter.

Acknowledgement must also be given to Carol Baltz, Cheryl Logan, and Gary Schoessler for their efforts with the clerical aspects of manuscript typing and library research. The editors extend a special thank you to Gloria Spencer who gave continuous support and encouragement and whose patience, compulsiveness, and grammatical know-how were most valuable in assisting with the proofreading.

Thomas D. Spencer

Norman Kass

CONTENTS

VII

PERSPECTIVES IN CHILD PSYCHOLOGY

Research and Review

EARLY ENVIRONMENTAL EFFECTS: MOTHER-CHILD RELATIONS

Howard A. Moss

A long-standing assumption in developmental psychology is that infantile experience is of major importance in determining adult character and personality formation. The meaningfulness of early experience for adult functioning is especially emphasized by those psychological theories that conceptualize the ontogenesis of behavior in terms of developmental stages. These theories claim that the quality of adaptive behavior at each stage is contingent on the degree of success that is achieved in the resolution of issues associated with preceding stages. Psychoanalytic theory has been particularly influential in promulgating this point of view. Some of the specific contentions made by psychoanalysts are that schedule feeding, early and/or abrupt weaning, severe toilet training, and the failure to breast-feed are circumstances that result in maladaptive adult behavior. Evidence for many of these contentions consists of reconstructions, from adult interviews, of the probable events that took place during infancy. These reconstructions are often made to fit the theoretical model for explaining the current psychological status of the individual.

3

Yet the empirical data reported in the literature have been either ambiguous or unsupportive of most of the propositions concerning the enduring effects of early experience. Orlansky (1949), after completing a thorough and incisive review of the literature of this matter, concludes that the evidence does not warrant the importance that is ascribed to infantile experience. He states that ". . . the rigidity of character structure during the first year or two of life has been exaggerated by many authorities, and that the events of childhood and later years are of great importance in reinforcing or changing the character structure tentatively formed during infancy . . . (p. 38)." The position taken by Orlansky may or may not be valid. His evaluation was based mainly on an analysis of highly specific theoretical assumptions and a critical review of studies, many of which seem inadequate for testing the developmental hypothesis of the long-term effects of early experiences.

The fact that infantile experiences have been found to have little relationship to later behavior can be accounted for in two ways. First, many of the investigations concerning infancy have relied on retrospective reports by adults, particularly parents, on what took place during infancy. However, a series of recent investigations has cast doubt on the validity of such an approach. That is, what parents report as having taken place during infancy often does not accurately depict what occurred. Furthermore, maternal reports concerning events during infancy tend to change in follow-up interviews. Yarrow, Campbell, & Burton (1964) coded data available on mother-child relations from the records of a research nursery. They also interviewed the mothers from this sample when their children were between the preschool years and young adulthood and made codings from these interviews on the same dimensions coded from the nursery-school records. These investigators found a median correlation of $+.37$ between initial and recall data for variables dealing with infant personality characteristics, relations with peers, early traumatic experiences, and parent-child interaction. Such a correlation is not very satisfactory when one considers using parental-recall data as a substitute for direct observation. In terms of the nature of the shifts that occurred, the mothers saw themselves as more nurturant, warmer, closer to the child, and recalled the father being absent from the home more than was indicated from the earlier evidence. Also during the interview, the child was remembered as happier, easier to manage, and walking earlier than was reported in the nursery-school record.

Another fundamental limitation of much of the work on infancy is that it has been oriented more toward determining the origins of childhood and adult behaviors than elucidating the actual nature of early development. The behaviors of the human infant and the adult are strikingly different, and other than the fact that the infant has the structural potential of the mature organism, there is little empirical or theoretical basis for knowing if and how a given adult characteristic relates to infantile experience. Viewing the infant in terms of how this organism can inform us about later development may actually hinder our ability to gain a direct understanding of infancy. That is, regarding infants in terms of adult characteristics imposes a conceptual structure that undoubtedly competes with identifying the potentially relevant phenomena and dimensions that actually characterize infancy.

There has been a recent trend in developmental psychology to directly study the determinants and ontogeny of infantile functioning, and this trend has resulted in a shift in the behaviors that are studied and the types of concepts that are formulated. Thus, rather than focusing on feeding and toilet training experiences (developmental issues emphasized in psychoanalytic theory as affecting adult behavior), the trend has been to consider such phenomena as the role of stimulation, the emergence of attachment behavior, modes of establishing contact with the environment, the development of responses such as smiling and vocalizing, and the nature of mother-infant interaction. Much of the most provocative work in these areas of study has been conducted by ethologists and those studying animal behavior. Studies of infant development using animals probably have been able to make better headway than similar investigations with humans, because the investigators are not bound to any theory of adult functioning while designing their research. Animal investigations are more able to monitor efficiently the whole stage of infancy, since for most species, this stage covers a much shorter span of time than it does for humans. Other difficulties that exist for studies on the human infant are the obvious restrictions on the types of experimental manipulations that can be done and the desires of the parents to maintain privacy and avoid disruptive intrusions when they have a new child. Consequently, it seems that ethological and animal research has led the way and provided many of the guidelines for similar research on the early environmental experience of the human infant.

Prior to reviewing some of the recent studies dealing with

mother-infant interaction, it would be helpful for the reader to become familiar with a point of view recently advanced by Bell (1968). Bell notes that much of the research conducted on early development has been influenced by the prevailing social philosophy which maintains that the individual is largely a product of his environment. This philosophy is derived from the democratic spirit and supports the position that what an individual becomes is determined by his experience and the treatment he has received.

Bell contends that this value orientation has resulted in a strong environmentalist bias in many of the studies and theories of child development. As a result, investigations of mother-infant relations have focused mainly on ways the mother affects the child with little attention given to the effects the child (through his congenital makeup) may have on the mother. Yet many of the findings reported in the literature could just as easily be interpreted either way. For example, the finding that aggression in children is associated with a greater incidence of physical punishment by parents tends to be taken as evidence that parental punishment has led to the aggressive behavior. However, one could easily conjecture that the cause and effect were reversed; that is, the existing aggressive tendency in the children elicited the observed parental behavior. Bell summarizes a large number of research findings where an explanation was based on a parent effect but where a child effect was equally tenable for interpreting the results. He makes the supposition that characteristics such as assertiveness, an orientation toward people, and an orientation toward objects could derive from congenital predispositions present in the infant and that manifestations of these behaviors could release different parental behaviors. According to Bell, parents have a repertoire of potential responses toward their infants, and the particular response that occurs is a function of the infant's predominant characteristics. Some of the parent behaviors are aimed at stimulating and others at controlling respective infant behaviors. A hierarchical order exists for the parental repertoire of reponses, and as various responses are unsuccessful in achieving a desired outcome, responses further along the hierarchy are progressively employed. As an illustration of this paradigm, parents are more likely to exhibit stimulating behavior toward a lethargic child, whereas they are more apt to be restrictive with a hyperactive child. There is evidence that infants differ in a number of characteristics at birth. These differences may be potentially important determinants of parental behavior. It is difficult and often impossible to discern the cause-effect sequence from many studies on mother-infant relations. But for such studies it is important to recognize that either member of the dyad could have instigated or shaped the behavior of the other.

The remainder of this chapter is devoted to reviewing representative studies of mother-child relations during the first year of life. Although the focus is on the human infant, the animal literature is also considered where it amplifies or complements the research and thinking concerning the early environmental and social experiences of the human infant. In discussing material on early behavior, the chapter considers ways in which characteristics of the infant influence maternal behavior as well as how environmental factors contribute to the infant's functioning. Topics will be discussed in the following order: pregnancy, delivery, mother-infant interactions (the forming of attachments), separation and stranger anxiety, and stimulation. These topics were selected since they are the focus of recent research interests and because they relate to important facets of development over the first year of life. There is some unavoidable overlap among these areas. Nonetheless the separate topics are retained in order to provide some focus on the salient factors in early development. Pregnancy and delivery are included since the intrauterine environment and the medication absorbed by the fetus during labor and delivery could conceivably affect the alertness, viability, and emotionality of the newborn, at least during the early days of life, and this in turn could influence the mother's initial reactions toward her infant.

Under the topic of mother-infant interaction the chapter deals with some of the specific infant behaviors that bind the mother and infant to one another such as protesting, tactile contact, visual regard, smiling and vocalization. These are behaviors that usually compel the mother to respond to her infant and consequently provide the basis for a mutual attachment. For example, the infant's protests draw the mother to the infant and evoke responses from her that are oriented toward comforting and quieting her offspring. The infant's smiles and vocalizations involve channels of communication whereby the mother and infant can interact. Frequently mothers report increased pleasure with their infants once the babies begin to smile and vocalize on a regular basis. The forming of meaningful attachments to others, and parenthetically, learning the social responses that facilitate establishing these bonds, is probably one of the major developmental tasks during the first year of life. Once the child has formed an attachment to his mother and other significant adults, he becomes much more amenable to socialization since he will tend to conform to the desires and values of those to whom he is attached in order to retain their approval. Therefore, the importance of attachment behavior is further enhanced because of the potential relevance of this behavior to later socialization.

Stranger and separation anxiety involve acute emotional reactions which occur at a peak intensity level for most infants during the second half of the first year of life. Both of these reactions denote the infant's ability to recognize and discriminate among individuals in his environment, not only in regard to physical characteristics, but in terms of the variations in interpersonal significance that these individuals hold for him. These discriminations and their concomitant affective reactions reflect a highly important developmental step forward for the infant. Separation anxiety is a particularly complex reaction. It requires not only the ability to distinguish among others, but also to symbolically observe that a significant person is missing. Separation anxiety is directly related to attachment behavior, since the child must obviously be attached to someone in order for him to experience distress when separated from that person. As a matter of fact, the occurrence of separation protest in the infant is often regarded as evidence that he has formed an attachment.

The final topic to be considered involves the stimulation to which the infant is exposed. The auditory, visual, tactile, proprioceptive, vestibular, etc., stimulation that the infant experiences has important consequences for early development. For example, the patterning and intensity of stimulation may contribute to the efficacy of learning and help shape cognitive functioning. This learning can occur by orienting the child toward a stimulus configuration, creating expectancies about events associated with certain patterns of stimulation, and providing training for the process of differentiation. Furthermore, stimulation helps modulate the state of the infant. There is also evidence that children tend to become most attached to those who provide them with stimulation.

PREGNANCY   Old wives' tales say that certain events that occur during pregnancy, such as being frightened by a barking dog, result in specific defects in the fetus. These tales are now passé. However, there is accumulating evidence of a more scientific nature supporting the theory that events associated with pregnancy do have important effects on early development. The emotional state of the expectant mother, stress during pregnancy, complications of pregnancy and delivery, and the type and quantity of medication used during delivery all seem to bear on the subsequent developmental status of the infant.

McDonald, Gynther, & Christakos (1963) studied the relation of maternal anxiety assessed during pregnancy to obstetrical complications (at delivery) and to labor time. They administered the IPAT Anxiety Scale and a repression-sensitization questionnaire to eighty-six white lower-class women during the last trimester of pregnancy. These women were later assigned to either a normal or abnormal subgroup on the basis of pregnancy, delivery-room, and postpartum records. Cases with evidence of a disorder during pregnancy, physical abnormality of the infant at birth, or complications of delivery formed the abnormal group. This group consisted of forty-four cases. The remaining cases constituted the normal group. Examples of some of the criteria used for placing a subject in the abnormal group were prematurity, third-trimester bleeding, breast abscess, prolonged labor, death in utero, and a subnormal Apgar rating.[1] Following delivery each case was classified as normal or abnormal according to these criteria. Comparisons between the two groups showed that the cases classified as abnormal had a significantly higher mean score than the normal group on the IPAT Anxiety Scale and the Repression-Sensitization Scale administered during pregnancy. A correlation of $+.61$ ($p < .01$) was obtained between the anxiety scores and labor time for all cases. This correlation indicates that the more anxious women spent more time in labor. The two groups did not differ as to age, intelligence, or the number of previous pregnancies. (One unexpected finding in this study was that there was a significantly greater number of male offspring in the abnormal group—thirty-one males to thirteen females.)

No adequate explanation exists as to what causes anxiety during pregnancy to relate to later obstetrical complications and birth anomalies. One possible interpretation of this relation is that the conditions leading to the abnormalities occurring at or around delivery were already present (but not detected) during

---

[1]The Apgar test represents the obstetrician's judgment of the infant's condition at birth on several dimensions. The infant is rated from 0 to 10 based upon his color, reflex instability, respiration, heart rate, and muscle tones. All of these dimensions may be indicative of trauma.

the pregnancy when the anxiety scores were obtained. Thus, the forebodings of the women in the abnormal subgroup, based on realistic but vague signs of turbulence in the pregnancy, could have elevated their anxiety scores.

There is evidence that complications in pregnancy have long-range effects on the offspring. Pasamanick, Rogers, & Lilienfeld (1956) contend that certain childhood-behavior disorders are due to "minimal brain damage" in which neurological signs are not evident. They furthermore hypothesize that injury to the brain sufficient to contribute to these behavior disorders can occur through adverse prenatal conditions. In order to test this hypothesis, they obtained the records of all the people with behavior disturbances referred to the Baltimore Department of Education after 1939. Intelligence test scores and a description of the type of disorder were available for all these cases. This sample was in turn matched with a control sample on age, sex, race, and socioeconomic status. The birth certificates of these children (those with disorders and the controls) listed the hospital where the delivery took place. From the hospital records the relevant pregnancy and delivery information was obtained. The final sample consisted of 1,151 cases for those with childhood behavior disorders and 902 controls. Comparisons between the two groups showed that there was a significantly higher incidence of complications in pregnancy and birth anomalies among the behavior-problem cases than among their matched controls. The investigators further analyzed the specific types of maternal complications involved and observed that those complications that appear to be more highly associated with behavior disorder are the nonmechanical difficulties such as toxemias and hypertensions of pregnancy. The mechanical aspects of parturition such as the type of presentation, the use of forceps, and other operative procedures tended to be unrelated to later behavior problems.

Since the original experimental group included many cases where social and psychological conditions obviously contributed to their being classified as behavior problems, Pasamanick, Rogers, and Lilienfeld screened those cases where brain damage was more likely to exist. They accomplished this by selecting from the behavior-disorder group those children described in the department of education records as confused, disorganized, and hyperactive—characteristics considered to be indicative of brain injury. A large proportion of this revised group consisted of males. When they applied this more restrictive criterion in selecting their cases, they found an even greater frequency of pregnancy complications in the history of the children with behavior disorders as compared with the controls.

Ferreira (1960) attempted to ascertain whether certain emotional attitudes of the pregnant mother were prenatally conveyed to the fetus and subsequently reflected in "upset" or deviant behavior in the newborn. A sample of 163 baby-mother pairs was studied at a military prenatal clinic. Every woman in her last four weeks of pregnancy was asked to fill out the Parent Attitude Research Instrument (PARI) as well as an additional scale devised to measure rejection of pregnancy. The investigator hypothesized that mothers scoring high on the Fear of Harming the Baby Scale (FHB scale) (from the PARI) and the Rejection of Pregnancy Scale would be more likely to have infants exhibiting deviant behavior. Every baby born to these mothers was rated for each of the first five days of life on five parameters: (1) amount of crying, (2) amount of sleep, (3) degree of irritability, (4) bowel movements, and (5) feedings. Through daily interviews with the pediatric nurses who had been instructed to act as observers, an observational impression of each baby's behavior for the preceding twenty-four-hour period was obtained and rated in terms of each of the above parameters. A three-point rating scale was used: (1) normal, (2) somewhat deviant, and (3) markedly deviant. A deviant day was defined as any of those five days in the nursery in which the newborn displayed "somewhat" or "markedly" deviant behavior on any of the five parameters under consideration. A deviant baby was then defined as any baby who had two or more deviant days out of the first five days of life in the nursery. From this procedure the infant sample was divided into 28 deviant and 135 nondeviant babies.

The results showed that the mothers of deviant babies had significantly higher scores on the Fear of Harming the Baby Scale. This finding may be in part an artifact of social-class status, since the less well-educated mothers scored higher on the FHB scale, and it is known that the incidence of birth complications is greater among less well-educated subjects. Consistent with the two previous studies, Ferreira found that the deviant group contained significantly more male than female infants. In addition, expectant mothers with extreme scores (high or low) on the Rejection of Pregnancy Scale had more infants rated as deviant.

Ferreira maintains that a high score on the FHB scale during pregnancy reflects "unconscious hostility" toward the unborn infant, and it is this maternal attitude that is transmitted in utero to the fetus and leads to the later deviant behavior. This appears to be rather naïve theorizing, since there is no scientific basis for expecting maternal attitudes to be transmitted to the fetus. Ferreira minimizes postnatal contact with the mother as being a factor in the deviancy, since the mother and infant were together for a maximum of only ten hours during the first five days of life. This is also a dubious assumption on his part. Ten hours of exposure to the mother during the early days of life would seem to provide ample opportunity for the mother to influence the smoothness or disruptiveness of the infant's initial functioning.

Perhaps the most important point made in the studies by McDonald et al. (1963), Pasamanick et al. (1956), and Ferreira (1960) is that in the samples where complicated births and deliveries are present and where deviant behavior is observed in the infant, there are more male than female infants. Males are more vulnerable organisms, and their lack of hardiness is manifest shortly after conception. Serr & Ismajovich (1963) estimated that there are 150 males to every 100 females conceived. Yet by the time of birth, due to miscarriages and spontaneous abortions, the ratio is reduced to 106 males born to 100 females. Stechler (1964b) has obtained data which show that significantly more male than female infants fail to initiate respiration by $2\frac{1}{2}$ minutes or longer after birth, a condition which is likely to result in brain damage. It seems plausible that those findings which show a relationship between anxiety or attitudes during pregnancy and postpartum complications are in part a function of the sex of the infant. Perhaps pregnant women who are carrying a male child may more often experience certain unpleasant symptoms as a reaction to a poorly functioning or less viable fetus. These women may in turn experience increased anxiety because of severe symptoms or unusual signs associated with their pregnancy. Thus, the poor functioning of the fetus (which is later seen as a poorly functioning newborn) could be creating the anxiety rather than the anxiety leading to the complications.

Studies dealing with the effects of human prenatal conditions are limited in the information they yield, since with these subjects it is not ethically possible to impose the type of experimental controls and manipulations that are necessary in pregnancy research for establishing precise and unequivocal relationships. In this instance, animal studies can provide a useful supplement to human research because of the greater feasibility of using animals for experimental manipulations of factors associated with the prenatal environment. In a pregnancy study using animals,

Hockman (1961) investigated the effects of prenatal maternal stress in the rat on the emotional behavior of the offspring. A group of female rats was assigned to either an experimental or control condition. When conception was established, pregnant experimental animals were subjected to a previously conditioned stress situation at regular intervals until the birth of the litters. When the offspring were born, they were cross fostered in various ways so as to control for postnatal influences (see Hockman's study which is reprinted following this chapter).

The results of this study showed that the stress experienced by experimental animals during pregnancy was significantly associated with higher emotionality (disturbed behavior) among their offspring early in their lives. However, the effects of the experimental treatment interacted with the cross-fostering procedure. Only the experimental animals who had been reared by a foster mother showed higher emotionality scores. This condition held whether the foster mother was from the control group or had been subjected to the experimental stress condition. Somehow, being raised by their own mother offset the effects of the stress so that an emotionality level in offspring comparable to the control group's was maintained in the experimental group. There were no observable differences among groups as the offspring grew older; therefore, in this case the effects of the prenatal stress seem to attenuate with age.

Returning to studies with humans, there is evidence that the type and amount of anesthetic administered during labor affects the level of alertness in the newborn. Although these effects are temporary, they do potentially contribute to the mother's initial reaction toward her infant. This reaction could influence a chain of events in the developing mother-infant interaction. For instance, it has been found (Brazelton, 1961) that infants whose mothers were heavily medicated during labor remained disorganized for a longer period of time after birth, were slower in starting to gain weight, and were less effective in breast-feeding than infants where milder levels of medication were used.

DELIVERY

Stechler (1964a) studied the effects of certain medications during labor on the attentiveness of the newborn. His sample consisted of twenty healthy full-term infants from two to four days of age. The degree of attention was assessed in these newborns by means of their total fixation time to three visually presented stimuli. The three stimuli were presented in random order for a duration of one minute each. The presentation was repeated

3 times with a different random order each time. There were a total of nine presentations. All infants were quiet and awake at the start of this procedure. An observer recorded the time spent by the infant looking at the nine stimulus presentations. The total looking time was used as the measure of attentiveness. The observer, at the time of visual testing, did not have any knowledge of the medication used on the mother, so that he remained unbiased in assessing the infant's attention. The drugs studied consisted of various depressants. Two analyses were performed in testing the relation between medication used during labor and the newborn's visual attention. For the first analysis the mothers were divided into two groups, one in which a depressant drug was administered within $1\frac{1}{2}$ hours of the delivery, and another in which no drug was administered during that period. The mean looking time was significantly greater for the newborns where the mothers did not have the drug within $1\frac{1}{2}$ hours of delivery than where mothers had the drug. For the second analysis a weighted score was assigned to each case in terms of both the dosage of medication and the length of time between administration of the drug and delivery. The results showed that the larger the dosage combined with the recentness at which it was administered was associated with shorter looking time to the visual stimuli. Thus, both analyses showed a significant relationship between the use of depressant drugs in labor and visual attention in infants during the early days of life.

EARLY MOTHER-INFANT INTERACTION

Birth, by definition, involves biological separation of the infant from the mother. At first the two of them are complete strangers with no existing psychological bond or basis for responding as unique beings to one another. Over the ensuing months of life, the infant somehow becomes psychologically attached to the mother so that she gradually acquires special importance and meaning for him. How this attachment develops is a crucial question for developmental psychology. In particular, it is necessary to determine the specific behaviors that bind the infant to his mother and to discover how these behaviors work to produce this effect.

Bowlby (1958), in a carefully thought through and provocative paper, presents a theoretical schema for explaining how the infant's attachment to the mother occurs. He first describes the following four prevailing theories on attachment (which he regards as inadequate) and then presents his own conceptualization (p. 350).

1   Secondary Drive—"The child has a number of physiological needs, particularly for food and warmth, which are handled by the mother, and gradually the baby learns that she is the source of gratification."
2   Primary Object Sucking—"There is in infants an in-built need to relate themselves to a human breast, to suck it and to possess it orally. In due course the infant learns that, attached to the breast, there is a mother and so relates to her also."
3   Primary Object Clinging—"There is in infants an in-built need to be in touch with and to cling to a human being."
4   Primary Return-to-Womb Craving—"Infants resent their extrusion from the womb and seek to return there."

Bowlby feels that these theories explaining how the child becomes tied to his mother are unsatisfactory for a variety of reasons. He proposes, instead, that there are five instinctual responses in the behavior repertoire of the infant which bind him to his mother: sucking, clinging (physical contact), following (not letting the mother out of sight or "earshot"), crying, and smiling. These responses fall into two classes. Sucking, clinging, and following achieve their end mainly through the active initiation of the infant with only a minimal response from the mother being necessary; whereas crying and smiling "depend for their results on their effect on maternal behavior." In the course of development the five responses "become integrated and focused on a single mother figure" and constitute the basis for attachment behavior. Although these responses are eventually modified through learning, they initially occur as unlearned response tendencies that mature at different rates over the first year of life and become manifest under special conditions. Bowlby regards the five postulated responses as species specific to man for forming attachment, and he maintains that they have evolved through natural selection because of their survival value for the human infant. For instance, the cry has a powerful effect in releasing maternal behaviors such as feeding, varying the stimulus input of the environment, or alleviating dangerous or painful conditions that may arise. The smile, which is nonsocial at first (it can easily be elicited by nonhuman stimuli from six to eight weeks of life), nonetheless has a powerful influence on the mother. "Can we doubt that the more and better an infant smiles the better is he cared for? It is fortunate for their survival that babies are so designed by nature that they beguile and enslave mothers."

Sucking, clinging, and following

The need to cling to or maintain physical contact with the mother is a phenomenon that has been observed in infants across a wide range of species. Since this does appear to be such a pervasive phenomenon, it is important to determine the theoretical implications of contact-seeking behavior for the development of early relationships.

In what has now become a classic series of studies, Harlow (1960) has demonstrated the importance of "contact-comfort" in the development of the infant rhesus monkey. He provided a group of infant monkeys with two surrogate mothers. Both mothers were constructed of wire mesh shaped in cylindrical form and propped up at about a 45 degree angle. For one of these mothers, the wire was covered with a soft terry-cloth material. The infants were separated from their actual mothers at birth and individually placed in a cage which contained both a cloth and a wire surrogate mother. Bottles were affixed to these simulated mothers so that the infant could cling to them and nurse. One group of four monkeys was nursed only by the cloth mothers, and another group of four monkeys was nursed only by the wire mothers, although both surrogate mothers were available in the cage of each infant monkey. Harlow found that, regardless of which surrogate nursed the infant, all the monkeys spent considerably more time clinging to the cloth mother than the wire mother. This finding is regarded as a very strong case for the importance of contact-comfort, since the satisfactions ordinarily associated with nursing evidently were insufficient to create a bond when pitted against the satisfactions of contact-comfort fulfilled by the terry-cloth mother. When Harlow controlled for contact-comfort by providing two cloth mothers, only one of which nursed, he found that the infants under these conditions did show a preference for the nursing mother. However, this preference subsided by eighty to one hundred days of age even though nursing continued for 180 days. On the other hand, the bond provided through contact-comfort proved to be much more durable, since tests made at thirty-day intervals showed that the monkeys still spent considerably more time on the cloth mother up through eighteen months of age. It was further demonstrated that the cloth mothers were able to provide the infant monkeys with a sense of security. When a frightening mechanical toy resembling a large beetle was placed in the cage, the monkey first froze and then ran to the cloth surrogate mother and clung tightly to her. After a few minutes the monkey was able to notice-ably relax, leave the cloth mother, and even explore the me-chanical object.

Differences have been observed among human infants as to the degree of satisfaction they exhibit over physical contact with the mother. Some infants are highly receptive to being held close, whereas others actively resist this type of treatment. Schaffer & Emerson (1964a) attempted to establish whether the variations among infants in their acceptance of contact was associated with the nature of the psychological attachment they formed with the mother. They divided a sample of infants into a group of "cuddlers" and a group of "noncuddlers" on the basis of inter-view material obtained from the mothers when the infants were twelve and eighteen months of age. The noncuddlers did not object to all forms of physical contact, but were mainly distin-guished by active struggles, protests, and efforts to break free when their bodies were restrained in a cuddling position. Schaffer and Emerson assumed that the amount of physical contact re-ceived by the noncuddlers was likely to be considerably reduced because of their resistance to situations involving cuddling. They studied whether this presumed reduction in physical contact for the noncuddlers was associated with differences between the two groups in the ways social attachments were formed. Attachment was studied in terms of the age of onset, intensity, and the num-ber of people toward whom attachments were formed. Informa-tion on the infant's attachment behavior was based on maternal reports from a series of interviews held every four weeks up to twelve months of age and on one additional interview conducted when the infants were eighteen months old. Attachment was determined by the amount of protest shown by an infant in a variety of situations when separated from significant adults. Schaffer and Emerson found that the two groups of infants did not differ as to the age of onset or the number of people toward whom attachments were directed, but that the cuddlers did show significantly more intensity in their attachments over the first twelve months of life. However by eighteen months, the cuddlers and noncuddlers no longer differed on the intensity measure.

In addition to studying the social consequence of cuddliness, some of the factors that might account for why certain infants became cuddlers and others noncuddlers were investigated. Ma-ternal characteristics, such as the mother's preferred mode of interacting with her infant, tended to be unrelated to whether the child objected to or accepted restrictive physical contact.

There was a trend for the cuddlers to make greater use of soft toys such as "security objects," to exhibit more autoerotic activity, and to be less active than the noncuddlers. On the other hand, the noncuddlers showed significantly greater resistance to situations involving motor restraint (being dressed and put into bed), slept less, were more advanced in the motor skills of sitting, standing, and walking, and obtained a higher developmental quotient on the Cattell Infant Scale than the cuddlers. From these findings, the investigators conclude that a congenital factor seems to underly the infant's receptiveness to being cuddled.

There has been increasing interest among behavioral scientists in the role of visual functioning in early development (Walters & Parke, 1965). Attention has been given both to the way maternal handling facilitates visual behavior in the infant, and also to the contribution of the visual mode for establishing a bond with the mother. Korner & Grobstein (1966) sought to determine whether holding a crying infant close with his head facing over the shoulder effectively soothed him and increased his level of visual alertness and his tendency to scan the environment. The investigators contend that alert scanning ordinarily occurs at a very low frequency for neonates. If being held on the shoulder facilitates this behavior, it has important developmental implications for the infant's earliest learning. In the Korner and Grobstein study (reprinted at the end of this chapter) testing was done under four different conditions which were initiated only when the infants (all girls) were crying: (1) being picked up and held on the left shoulder, (2) being picked up and held on the right shoulder, (3) being picked up and held in a sitting position, and (4) being left lying on the back (control condition) These investigators found that the conditions of placing the crying infant to either the left shoulder or the right shoulder were significantly more effective in soothing the infants, getting them to open their eyes, and increasing their visual scanning behavior than were the other two conditions

Moss & Robson (1968) investigated whether the visual interaction between mother and infant related to antecedent maternal attitudes and to the development of social visual behavior in the infant. Fifty-four women were interviewed during the last trimester of their first pregnancy. From these interviews the prospective mothers were rated on "the degree to which they saw babies in a positive sense" and their expressed "interest in affectionate contact toward infants." After the birth of the infants (twenty-seven males and twenty-seven females), naturalistic observations were conducted in the home. These observations took place at one and three months of age. By means of a time-sampling procedure, codings were made during the home observations of the frequency with which the mother and infant looked at one another's faces. This variable, called "vis-à-vis," is considered to have particular significance for the mother-infant interaction, since it represents one of the earliest channels of communication available to the dyad. Moreover, early vis-à-vis is important, since it is from this context that later and more complex social responses, such as smiling and talking, emerge. After the completion of the last home observation, when the infants were an average of $3\frac{1}{2}$ months of age, they were brought into a laboratory where their visual behavior was studied. For the visual study, the infant was placed in an infant seat and presented with two-dimensional visual stimuli. The measure of visual behavior used was the total amount of time spent looking at different stimuli. Two series of these stimuli were presented. The first series consisted of three checkerboards that varied in the number and size of the squares (geometric series), and the second series consisted of three pictures of variations of the face (social series). The data for this study were analyzed separately for males and females. It was found that the maternal attitudes assessed from the pregnancy interviews were positively related to the amount of vis-à-vis between mother and infant at one month of age for both sexes, and at three months for girls alone. In turn, the three-month vis-à-vis scores for females were strongly related to their total looking time for the social, but not for the geometric stimuli. These results are interpreted to show that the amount of mutual visual regard between mother and infant reflects maternal attitudes, and that the vis-à-vis experience, at least for girls, involves early social learning as manifest by the behavior in the visual study.

Crying and smiling

Studies concerning the implications of the cry for early development have been conducted with both humans and animals. In one study, Moss (1967) investigated the effect of irritability (fussing and crying) in the human infant on the mother-infant relationship. A sample of first-born children and their mothers was studied by means of direct observations in the home. An observer recorded a number of behaviors on a printed form including activities of the mother as well as those of the infant. Examples of some of the coding categories used for the mother were: (1) holds infant close, (2) feeds infant, (3) affectionate contact (toward infant), and (4) imitates vocalizations of infant. Most of the infant behaviors coded consisted of arousal or activity-level variables such as: (1) crying, (2) sleeping, (3) awake passive, and (4) awake active.

One of the findings of the Moss study (reprinted following this chapter) was that male infants exhibited significantly more irritable behavior than females. Moreover, most of the maternal behaviors that were observed occurred with a greater frequency for males. One might properly inquire whether the greater amount of irritability exhibited by the male infants led to the finding that mothers interacted more with them than they did with the female infants. This indeed seems to be the case. When a control was used to eliminate the influence of the infant's crying and fussing on maternal behavior, maternal treatment became essentially the same for both sexes.

Although infant irritability partially accounts for the amount of maternal contact that occurs, we know that some mothers are likely to respond more or faster than others, and these differences in responsiveness probably reflect differences in maternal attitudes. Interview ratings were available for most of these mothers from an assessment of their marriage conducted at an average of two years prior to the birth of the infant. Ratings on "acceptance of the maternal role" and "the degree that babies are seen in a positive sense" were significantly correlated with the later maternal-responsiveness scores. Thus, maternal attitudes as well as the irritability level of the infant are predictive of the amount of contact the mother has with her child.

The distress call of animals is equivalent to the cry of the human infant. In addition to the Moss research, there is ample evidence from the animal kingdom that the distress call of the young is an effective stimulus for getting the mother to approach her offspring. Furthermore when the mother is close, these calls occur considerably less often than when she is distant, indicating that the young effectively use this signal system for maintaining the proximity of the mother. Hoffman, Schiff, Adams, & Searle (1966) sought to answer a related but more specific question. They attempted to determine if the frequency of distress calls during the mother's absence increased as a function of how contingently she ordinarily responded to these calls. In order to test whether the distress calls of the young are reinforced by the mother's contingent response to them, these investigators first imprinted eighteen ducklings to a moving stimulus (a white plastic bottle mounted on a model-train engine). This moving stimulus in a sense served as a mother substitute. All of the ducklings received 4 forty-five-minute imprinting sessions with this stimulus during the first forty-eight hours of life. In testing for the effects of imprinting, the experimenters found that the ducklings emitted a high rate of distress calls when the imprinted moving stimulus was removed, and these calls decreased significantly when the moving stimulus was returned.

On the day following these test sessions, subjects were paired, with one member of each pair being randomly assigned to either an experimental or control condition. When the experimental subjects emitted a distress call, it was immediately followed by the presentation of the moving imprinted stimulus for five seconds, whereas the calls of the control subjects had no bearing on the presence or absence of the imprinted stimulus. Each pair of experimental and control animals were yoked together so that each time the experimental partner emitted a distress call a moving stimulus was produced for both members of the pair. This procedure insured that both experimental and control subjects received the same number of presentations in the same sequence. However, for the experimental subjects, presentation of the imprinted stimulus was contingent upon distress calls, while for the control partners no response contingency existed. This paradigm resulted in the experimental subjects emitting a greater number of distress calls than their paired controls. The procedure was reversed in a subsequent session where the controls were given the experimental condition; the control subjects showed a significant increase from their previous level in distress vocalizations. From these results, the investigators concluded that the contingent appearance of the imprinted stimulus had a reinforcing effect on the distress calls of the ducklings.

Etzel & Gewirtz (1967) conducted a study with human infants which also demonstrated the effectiveness of reinforcement for controlling crying behavior. They selected two infants (one six weeks and one twenty weeks of age) from a children's hospital where it was established that crying was reinforced regularly in the nursery. They were able to successfully extinguish crying in these babies by means of nonreinforcement of crying responses combined with reinforcement of smiling, a response that is incompatible with crying.

As mentioned earlier, Bowlby (1958) stated that the smile was one of the instinctual responses of the infant that required a reciprocal response from the mother in order to produce the desired effect of forming a bond between mother and infant. In this respect, it would be of interest to determine whether maternal reactions to the infant's smile strengthened that response and, if so, to further ascertain the nature of the learning conditions that best favored this particular outcome. Brackbill (1958) has provided some evidence that bears specifically on this issue. She took a group of infants between $3\frac{1}{2}$ and $4\frac{1}{2}$ months of age and studied the effects of "operant conditioning"[2] on the rate and maintenance of the smiling response. As an initial step, an experimenter observed the base rate at which the smiling response naturally occurred for the infant prior to an experimental manipulation of this response. For the conditioning procedure, each infant was placed on his back in a crib. When the infant smiled, the experimenter smiled in return, picked the infant up, talked, patted, and jostled him for a thirty-second period before returning him to the crib. This reinforcement from the experimenter resulted in a significant increase in the rate of smiling over the infant's original base level.

One-half of the subjects in this study were given an additional treatment. After the frequency of their smiling responses had reached a maximum rate for ten consecutive five-minute trials (criterion), they were switched to a reinforcement schedule where their smiling responses were only intermittently reinforced. The other half of the subjects continued to receive reinforcement for every smiling response for additional trials after they had reached the above specified criterion. Brackbill then tested to see if the intermittent and regular-reinforcement groups differed in their resistance to extinction.

The extinction procedure consisted of several trials where the experimenter stood in front of the infant, but did not provide the reinforcement when he smiled. This procedure resulted in a decrease in the smiling rate for all subjects. However, infants who received the intermittent-reinforcement series were significantly more resistant to extinction than those in the regular-reinforcement group. That is, their smiling responses decreased at a slower rate and never got as low as those infants who had previously received regular reinforcement. These data thus show that the smile, even though it initially can be released by nonsocial stimuli, quickly comes under the control of social reinforcements.

Wahler (1967) conducted an experiment similar to the one by Brackbill. The main difference between the two studies is that

[2]Classical and operant conditioning procedures, reinforcement schedules, and extinction of behaviors are clarified in Chapter VI.

Wahler had two experimental sessions with each infant. The reinforcement to the infant's smiling response was provided by the mother during one session and by a female stranger (selected from students in an undergraduate psychology course) during the other session. Wahler found that the mothers were significantly more effective than the strangers in conditioning the infants' smiling responses. He regards this as evidence that the infants by $3\frac{1}{2}$ months of age already had formed attachments to their mothers. Although this is an interesting study, there is a problem with the methodology which makes the results ambiguous. Namely, it is difficult to know if the mothers were more effective as reinforcers because of the infants' attachment to them, or whether the mothers, through $3\frac{1}{2}$ months of experience with their own infants, were more skillful in presenting the reinforcements.

Similar conditioning results have been found in studies on the vocal behavior of infants. Rheingold, Gewirtz, & Ross (1959) and Weisberg (1963) demonstrated that contingent social reinforcements are highly effective in influencing the rate of vocalizations in the infant. These two studies are discussed in some detail in later chapters, and the Weisberg article is reprinted following Chapter III. The results of these studies suggest that the principles of operant conditioning function in much the same way with infant vocalizations as was previously observed for the smiling response.

The studies discussed under the topic of mother-infant interaction provide a picture of some of the major factors that bind the mother and infant to each other and thus contribute to the forming of a mutual attachment. For example, the protest responses of the infant compel the mother to respond and engage in caretaking activities, and in turn, contingent maternal responsiveness can lead to an increase in protesting behavior. The infant's smiles, vocalizations, and visual behavior are important modes for interacting which are also subject to modification through social learning. Thus, the mother's and infant's instigation and reciprocal shaping of one another's social behaviors are two of the primary factors that contribute to establishing attachment behavior.

SEPARATION AND STRANGER ANXIETY

The term "separation anxiety" generally is used to refer to separation reactions that are relatively sustained and lead to disruption in normal functioning. The basis for separation anxiety is in a sense derived from attachments, since an infant first has to develop an attachment to someone before separation from that person can have any meaning to him. Bowlby (1960) noted that when children between fifteen and thirty months of age were hospitalized, and thus separated from their mothers, they tended to go through a predictable sequence of behavior. First they protested, then they went through a period of despair, and finally they exhibited a quality of detachment. Each of the phases in this sequence is regarded by Bowlby as a reflection of anxiety specifically associated with separation from the mother. He states that protest, despair, and detachment do not occur as discrete phases, but tend to merge into one another. The protest phase is manifest by an active effort on the part of the child to regain his mother. He may cry loudly, resist the attention of others, and demand the return of the mother. This phase may last from a few hours to a week or more. Despair follows protest and is largely characterized by a sense of hopelessness. The child becomes subdued, withdrawn, apathetic, and "appears to be in a state of deep mourning." To the casual observer, the child may appear to have recovered during the stage of detachment, since in this phase he shows a renewed interest in his environment, his mood seems satisfactory, and he cooperates as well as ever with those around him. However, when his mother visits, he seems strangely impersonal in his behavior toward her and shows little reaction to her leaving. It is as if the child is in the process of undoing his attachment to his mother. Bowlby adds, if a child loses a succession of mother figures, his capacity to form attachments is diminished, and he becomes increasingly egocentric and shifts his interests from people to material things.

Many children, after they have matured sufficiently so that they are able to distinguish among people, show an anxious reaction toward strangers. When a stranger approaches, they may freeze, turn away, or cry and cling to the mother or to any other familiar person who is available. There are two different points of view regarding the origin of stranger anxiety. Some investigators consider the avoidance of strangers as a manifestation of an innate fear response that is released by exposure to stimuli that are unfamiliar or that violate existing expectancies. Such innate fear responses are common among the young of a number of species. In many instances this fear has real survival value for the young by initiating flight responses from dangerous predators. A different explanation of stranger anxiety is that it represents the infant's fear of losing the person to whom he has become attached. Supporting this view is the observation that stranger anxiety occurs shortly after attachments are formed, and a common response to strangers is that the infant will seek out and cling to the person to whom he is attached.

Morgan & Ricciuti (1968) traced the development of stranger anxiety during the first year of life by studying differences in reactions to strangers among five groups of infants at $4\frac{1}{2}$, $6\frac{1}{2}$, $8\frac{1}{2}$, $10\frac{1}{2}$, and $12\frac{1}{2}$ months of age. Each of these groups consisted of sixteen infants, eight males and eight females. These investigators also obtained some evidence concerning the meaning of stranger anxiety by testing for it under different conditions. The infants were studied in a laboratory setting with the mother present. The procedure for testing stranger anxiety consisted of an experimenter (playing the part of the stranger) moving progressively closer to the infant in four graduated steps. For the first step, the stranger sat smiling silently about 6 feet from the infant. By the final step, he was kneeling in front of the infant while touching and talking to him. For each step, which lasted ten seconds, an observer coded the infant's behavior according to how fearful or upset he became. This procedure was repeated twice for each infant, once while held on the mother's lap and once while seated in a feeding table located about 4 feet from the mother. A male stranger was used for one administration and a female stranger for the other administration of the procedure. In order to control for sequence effects, half of the infants in each age group were first exposed to the male stranger and half to the female stranger. Likewise, the order for the two locations of the infant (mother's lap or feeding table) were counterbalanced.

In addition to the human strangers, a Halloween mask of a smiling woman's face and a papier-mâché mask of a distorted face were used as stimuli. These masks were attached to a pole and held in front of the infants. Morgan and Ricciuti found that stranger anxiety increased with the age of the child. "The younger infants reacted very positively towards the strangers by smiling, cooing, and reaching out, but the older infants, especially those in the twelve months group, were often very negative: frowning, crying, and turning away." Moreover, the younger infants tended to become more positive and the older infants more negative as the stranger approached. The older subjects also were more affected than the younger ones by being separated from the mothers. The younger infants behaved about the same toward the stranger regardless of whether they were on their mother's lap or in the feeding table. The older infants became considerably more negative when in the feeding table. In general the infants responded positively toward the masks, especially the distorted one. The results of this study tend to support the importance of attachment behavior as a determinant of stranger anxiety. The older infants, with presumably the stronger attachments, showed more of this anxiety, particularly when separated from the mother.⟩

Although there is an apparent developmental course to stranger anxiety, striking individual differences can be observed among infants as to the timing and severity of this reaction. Evidence exists that individual differences in stranger anxiety can in part be explained in terms of early experiences. Levine & Mullins (1966) report that rats who were handled in infancy show a less extreme reaction to novel stimuli than nonhandled rats. From these results, they hypothesize "that one of the major consequences of handling in infancy may be the endowment of the organism with the capacity to make responses more appropriate to the demands of the environment, including appropriate responses to stress."

Collard (1967) conducted a study with kittens showing the effects of handling on the fear of strangers. She subjected three groups of five-week-old kittens to different treatments. One group of kittens was handled by and given the opportunity to play with a different person each day on five consecutive days for a four-week period (five-person groups). The second group of kittens was given the same treatment, but with a single experimenter (one-person group), and the last group received no special handling or play experience during the four-week experimental period. A "stranger test" was conducted at the end of each five-day period. The test consisted of recording the number of escape attempts made by the kittens when held for a one-minute period by a stranger and also by the experimenter. Collard found that the kittens handled and played with by the experimenter alone attempted to escape significantly more often from the strangers than from the familiar experimenter. The kittens who had experience with five-person treatments showed less fear of strangers than the kittens who received the one-person or no-person treatments. The number of escape attempts did not increase over the four-week period of the study for the five-person kittens, but the number did increase for the kittens in the other two groups. Since the kittens in the one- and five-person groups had a comparable amount of human contact, it would appear that the opportunity to adapt to the novelty of strangers experienced by the five-person kittens accounts for their lowered fear-of-stranger reaction.

Moss, Robson, & Pedersen (1969) studied the effects of maternal stimulation of the human infant at one and three months of age on the degree of fear shown toward a stranger at 8 to $9\frac{1}{2}$ months of age. Maternal stimulation was assessed from behavioral codings made during home observations. Fear of strangers was rated from the child's reactions during a testing procedure when approached in graduated steps by a stranger. It was found that stimulation of the infant by the mother at three months of age, particularly of the distance receptors (visual and auditory), was significantly related to less avoidance and fearfulness of a stranger at 8 to $9\frac{1}{2}$ months of age. Distance-receptor stimulation consisted of such things as placing a radio next to the infant, seating the infant in front of a television set, shaking a rattle or mobile in the infant's visual field, etc. The results of this study and the one by Collard show that although there is a particular developmental course for stranger anxiety, this reaction is influenced by the number of social contacts and the amount of stimulation the infant experiences.

STIMULATION

One of the conditions that tends to favor optimal growth in the infant is that where moderate levels of stimulation are maintained. For instance, there is evidence that the occurrence of moderate stimulation enhances the infant's responsiveness toward the external environment. This responsiveness, in turn, appears to facilitate the development of social attachments and to maximize early learning. The responsibility for maintaining an optimal level of stimulation for the infant falls largely on the mother, since the infant himself is relatively helpless in regulating the flow of stimulation that he experiences. Not only the intensity, but the tempo of stimulation to which the infant is exposed, must be modulated by the caretaking environment. The mother generally provides the infant with moderate stimulation through rocking, patting, caressing, and moving him about as well as by introducing auditory and visual patterns to his immediate surroundings. The infant at first is unable to recognize and communicate in the usual ways, but is responsive to variations in stimulation. The mother, by being the mediator of much of this stimulation, has a means for relating to and forming a bond with her infant. Some recent studies show the bearing stimulation has on the infant's functioning.

Birns & Blank (1965) studied the effects of different forms of stimulation on soothing irritable infants, and they also evaluated whether infants were similar and consistent in terms of how easily they were soothed. They studied a sample of newborns over the first few days of life. Their procedure consisted of administering a series of four soothing stimuli to an irritable infant and then rating the infant's reaction to these stimuli on a behavioral scale ranging from a placid, quiet state to one of extreme agitation. The soothing stimuli consisted of (1) a loud, continuous sound, (2) a sweetened pacifier inserted in the baby's mouth, (3) gentle rocking of the bassinet, and (4) immersing the infant's foot in warm water. Each stimulus was applied three times in a predetermined order for a sixty-second period. In order to determine the stability of the infant's responsiveness to stimulation, this procedure was repeated on the following day for a portion of the sample. The experimenters found that all four stimuli were equally effective in soothing an irritable infant, that the infants varied considerably in their ability to be soothed, and that the infants were consistent in their response to these stimuli on successive days.

In addition to the soothing effect of stimulation, an assumption held by many developmental psychologists is that the stimulation an infant experiences also acts to increase his responsiveness and interest in the external environment. White & Castle (1964) studied the effects of additional handling on the amount of visual attention shown by a group of infants who ordinarily receive very little handling. Their sample consisted of eighteen control and ten experimental subjects drawn from an institutional population. White and Castle state that the handling of infants in the institution was generally limited to what was necessary for carrying out routine caretaking functions. The procedure of only receiving basic care was modified for the experimental group so that beginning with the sixth day of life and continuing for the next thirty days, these infants were given 2 ten-minute periods of extra handling daily by the nursing staff. These sessions consisted of picking up the infant and holding him close against the chest while rocking him for ten continuous minutes in a rocking chair. White and Castle assumed that some of the crying that occurred during the early weeks of life reflected a need for "tactual, vestibular, and kinesthetic stimulation." Therefore whenever possible, they attempted to have the handling sessions occur as a response to an episode of crying. However, if an experimental infant did not cry within a designated period of time, he was still picked up and given the ten minutes of continuous handling. The control infants, on the other hand, were given the standard institutional care. Starting at one month and continuing to four months of age, the visual attention of both groups was assessed every two weeks. The amount of time an infant spent visually exploring his environment was recorded during a three-hour evaluation period while awake, alert, and lying in a supine position. "An infant was judged visually attentive if his eyes were more than half open and their direction of gaze shifted within thirty seconds." The results showed that the handled infants exhibited significantly more visual attention than the control infants, although this difference between groups diminished for the later assessments. The groups did not differ on other measures used in this study of overall development, health, weight gain, and visually directed reaching.

Schaffer & Emerson (1964b) studied the development of attachment behavior over the first eighteen months of life and, in so doing, evaluated the degree to which stimulation of the infant, as well as other maternal behaviors, contributed to the formation of attachments. Their methodology was the same for this research as was used in their work on cuddling behavior. That is, from interviews with the mothers spaced every four weeks over the first year of life and again at eighteen months, they evaluated attachment behavior in the child from the degree of protest he exhibited when separated from the mother. The interviews were structured so as to cover the amount of protest seen by the mother for each of seven commonly occurring and representative separation situations. This provided a standard basis for evaluating the separation protest of all infants for each point in time. The following are two examples of the separation situations they used: (1) the infant is left alone in a room, and (2) the infant is put down after being held in the adult's arms or lap. From the interview material, Schaffer and Emerson studied the relationship of different maternal practices to the intensity of the attachment the child manifested toward his mother. They found that both the amount of time the mother spent with her child and the number of caretakers that shared in the maternal responsibility were generally unrelated to the intensity of the child's attachment toward the mother. They also observed that in a great many instances, the infant showed stronger attachments to persons other than those who directly cared for his basic needs. This is an important finding since it is contrary to the popular view which maintains that the child develops the strongest bond toward those who are instrumental in satisfying his need for food and physical comfort.

Variables that were predictive of the infant's attachments to the mother at eighteen months of age were the degree of maternal responsiveness to the infant's crying and the amount of stimulation the mother provided for her offspring. The maternal responsiveness scores were based on a rating scale ranging from not responding to responding immediately to the infant's cries. Evidence for this rating consisted of the interview records and observational notes of the mother's behavior made at the time of each of the home interviews. The maternal stimulation variable also was assessed by means of a rating scale. The lowest point on the scale was defined in terms of the mother initiating minimal interaction with her infant, whereas the highest score was given where the mother described herself as providing "continuous stimulation of the infant, often of a rather intense form."

Schaffer and Emerson further attempted to determine if the type of stimulation the mother provided for the infant had any bearing on his attachment to her. Consequently maternal stimulation was categorized into the use of physical contact, stimulation of the distance receptors, and instances where the mother used impersonal means such as presenting toys and objects to the infant. They found that the mode of stimulation did not matter, but that the intensity of the infant's attachment behavior toward the mother was simply a function of the quantity of stimulation that he received from her. From these results, the authors suggest the possibility "that the infant's need for the proximity of other people is not primary but arises, in the course of development, from his need for stimulation in general," and that his attachment to humans is facilitated, since "the most interesting object in his environment is the human object, with its high arousal potential and most varied stimulation propensity."

In addition to the above findings, Schaffer and Emerson noted that the majority of infants form their initial attachment to a specific person somewhere between six and nine months of age. At first, the separation protest is most prevalent for situations where physical contact is interrupted, but as the child gets older, his protests occur more when the person to whom he is attached moves out of visual range.

Yarrow (1963) studied mother-infant interaction among a group of infants placed in foster and adoptive homes. By using foster mothers as subjects, correlations between maternal practices and infant behaviors can be explained quite convincingly in terms of environmental influences, since hereditary factors have been naturally controlled. Also, since it is a common practice of adoption agencies to place infants in foster homes at different ages and to shift a child from home to home, some estimate can be made of when attachments are formed by observing the age at which infants first show a disturbed separation reaction. The circumstances of the foster child can thus be put to good use in designing what might be called a "natural experiment."

Through a series of home observations with mother-infant pairs, Yarrow found that the infant's developmental progress during the first six months, based on IQ scores, appeared to be highly influenced by both the amount and quality of maternal stimulation. An additional finding of Yarrow's study (reprinted following this chapter) was that those infants who were shown spontaneous expressions of positive feelings by the substitute mothers tended to exhibit a greater degree of social initiative. In a separate analysis, Yarrow studied the emotional reactions of children who experienced separation from foster homes when placed for adoption at ages ranging from six weeks to twelve months. This analysis revealed that when separation occurred as early as three months, a few infants exhibited disturbed behavior; when a change in mothers was experienced at six months, the majority of infants manifested disturbances; and, that all those infants who were separated after seven months had severe emotional reactions. One reason the separation reaction occurred earlier among these children than those studied by Schaffer and Emerson may be that the separation the foster and adoptive children experienced was more sustained and permanent.

A highly interesting and important aspect of the work by Yarrow is the observation that the foster mother's behavior can be influenced by characteristics of the infants, so that the same mother may exhibit grossly different behaviors toward different infants. This supports the point of view advanced by Bell (1968) concerning the effects the child may have on the mother.

The material covered in this chapter is intended to provide the reader with a perspective of some of the major issues and the areas of investigation currently under study on early development. Much of the recent developmental research has been directed toward trying to understand the functioning of the infant and the factors that affect his well-being rather than toward learning what aspects of infantile experience produce particular adult characteristics. Studies of infants have made increasing use of direct observation instead of relying on retrospective reports.

SUMMARY

This method has begun to provide important dividends in furthering our understanding of early development. Direct observations of the infant in his natural setting have helped sharpen our focus on highly important determinants of overall functioning, such as the quantity and quality of the stimulation that is experienced and the role of various infant characteristics in the formation of attachment behavior. Observations of the transactions between mother and infant also have increased our sensitivity to the ways the infant influences the mother and vice versa. This recognition of infant effects has contributed to investigators noting the importance of congenital differences among infants. Investigations of prenatal influences have become a scientifically respectable area of inquiry, and the evidence suggests that the infant's behavior is already being shaped by external factors before he first sees the light of day.

BIBLIOGRAPHY

Bell, R. Q. A reinterpretation of the direction of effects in studies of socialization. *Psychological Review*, 1968, **75**, 81–95.

Birns, B., & Blank, M. The effectiveness of various soothing techniques on human neonates. Paper presented at the meeting of the Society for Research in Child Development, Minneapolis, April 1965.

Bowlby, J. The nature of the child's tie to his mother. *International Journal of Psycho-Analysis*, 1958, **39**, 350–373.

Bowlby, J. Separation anxiety. *International Journal of Psycho-Analysis*, 1960, **41**, 89–113.

Brackbill, Y. Extinction of the smiling response in infants as a function of reinforcement schedule. *Child Development*, 1958, **29**, 115–124.

Brazelton, T. B. Psychophysiologic reactions in the neonate. II. Effect of maternal medication on the neonate and his behavior. *Journal of Pediatrics*, 1961, **58**, 513–518.

Collard, R. R. Fear of strangers and play behavior in kittens with varied social experience. *Child Development*, 1967, **38**, 877–891.

Etzel, B. C., & Gewirtz, J. L. Experimental modification of caretaker-maintained high-rate operant crying in a 6 and a 20-week-old infant (infans tyrannotearus): Extinction of crying with reinforcement of eye contact and smiling. *Journal of Experimental Child Psychology*, 1967, **5**, 303–317.

Ferreira, A. J. The pregnant woman's emotional attitude and its reflection on the newborn. *American Journal of Orthopsychiatry*, 1960, **30**, 553–561.

Harlow, H. F. Primary affectional patterns in primates. *American Journal of Orthopsychiatry*, 1960, **30**, 676–684.

Hockman, C. H. Prenatal maternal stress in the rat: Its effects on emotional behavior in the offspring. *Journal of Comparative and Physiological Psychology*, 1961, **54**, 679–684.

Hoffman, H. S., Schiff, D., Adams, J., & Searle, J. L. Enhanced distress vocalization through selective reinforcement. *Science*, 1966, **151**, 352-354.

Korner, A. F., & Grobstein, R. Visual alertness as related to soothing in neonates: Implications for maternal stimulation and early deprivation. *Child Development*, 1966, **37**, 867-876.

Levine, S., & Mullins, R. F. Hormonal influences on brain organization in infant rats. *Science*, 1966, **152**, 1585-1592.

McDonald, R. L., Gynther, M. D., & Christakos, A. C. Relation between maternal anxiety and obstetric complications. *Psychosomatic Medicine*, 1963, **25**, 357-363.

Morgan, G. A., & Ricciuti, H. N. Infants' response to strangers during the first year. In B. M. Foss (Ed.), *Determinants of infant behavior*. Vol. IV. London: Methuen, 1968.

Moss, H. A. Sex, age, and state as determinants of mother-infant interaction. *Merrill-Palmer Quarterly*, 1967, **13**, 19-36.

Moss, H. A., & Robson, K. S. Maternal influences in early social visual behavior. *Child Development*, 1968, **39**, 401-408.

Moss, H. A., Robson, K. S., & Pedersen, F. Determinants of maternal stimulation of infants and consequences of treatment for later reactions to strangers. *Developmental Psychology*, 1969, **1**, 239-246.

Orlansky, H. Infant care and personality. *Psychological Bulletin*, 1949, **46**, 1-48.

Pasamanick, B., Rogers, M. E., & Lilienfeld, A. M. Pregnancy experience and the development of behavior disorder in children. *American Journal of Psychiatry*, 1956, **112**, 613-618.

Rheingold, H. L., Gewirtz, J. L., & Ross, H. W. Social conditioning of vocalizations in the infant. *Journal of Comparative and Physiological Psychology*, 1959, **52**, 68-73.

Schaffer, H. R., & Emerson, P. E. Patterns of response to physical contact in early human development. *Journal of Child Psychology and Psychiatry*, 1964, **5**, 1-13. (a)

Schaffer, H. R., & Emerson, P. E. The development of social attachments in infancy. *Monographs of the Society for Research in Child Development*, 1964, **29**(3, Serial No. 94). (b)

Serr, D. M., & Ismajovich, B. Determination of the primary sex ratio from human abortions. *American Journal of Obstetrics and Gynecology*, 1963, **87**, 63-65.

Stechler, G. Newborn attention as affected by medication during labor. *Science*, 1964, **144**, 315-317. (a)

Stechler, G. A longitudinal follow-up of neonatal apnea. *Child Development*, 1964, **35**, 333-348. (b)

Wahler, R. G. Infant social attachments: A reinforcement theory interpretation and investigation. *Child Development*, 1967, **38**, 1079-1088.

Walters, R. H., & Parke, R. D. The role of the distance receptors in the development of social responsiveness. In L. P. Lipsitt & C. C. Spiker (Eds.), *Advances in child development and behavior*. Vol. 2. New York: Academic Press, 1965. Pp. 59-96.

Weisberg, P. Social and nonsocial conditioning of infant vocalizations. *Child Development*, 1963, **34**, 377–388.

White, B. L., & Castle, P. W. Visual exploratory behavior following postnatal handling of human infants. *Perceptual and Motor Skills*, 1964, **18**, 497–502.

Yarrow, L. J. Research in dimensions of early maternal care. *Merrill-Palmer Quarterly*, 1963, **9**, 101–114.

Yarrow, M. R., Campbell, J. D., & Burton, R. V. Reliability of maternal retrospection: A preliminary report. *Family Process*, 1964, **3**, 207–218.

PRENATAL MATERNAL STRESS IN THE RAT: ITS EFFECTS ON EMOTIONAL BEHAVIOR IN THE OFFSPRING[1]

Charles H. Hockman

That experiences early in life affect the subsequent behavioral development of the organism is well documented (Beach & Jaynes, 1954). However, there have been relatively few studies concerned with the effects of prenatal influences on behavior.

There seems to be little doubt that a great many constitutional defects in both human and infrahuman organisms are directly traceable to prenatal influences. Sontag (1941) and Fraser and Fainstat (1951) review evidence which strongly supports this assertion.

If the developing fetus can be affected by stressor agents, it does not seem unreasonable to suppose that these agents might influence the behavioral development and subsequent adjustment of the organism. This hypothesis has been favored by an accumulation of evidence from many disciplines, including population biology (Christian, 1959), teratology (Baxter & Fraser, 1950), clinical medicine (Strean & Peer, 1956), and experimental psychology (Thompson, 1957; Thompson & Sontag, 1956).

Thompson and Sontag (1956) subjected albino rats to massive audiogenic seizures during gestation. The offspring from these animals were tested at 39 days of age and again at 60 days of age. In a water maze, the nonseizure controls took significantly fewer trials to reach criterion and made fewer errors.

Using hooded rats, Thompson (1957) found that offspring of "stressed" mothers showed startling behavioral differences when compared with the offspring of the controls. He tested the offspring at 30 to 40 days of age and again at 130 to 140 days of age. When compared with the controls, the offspring of the "stressed" mothers showed "high emotionality" at both early and late testing periods. In a later unpublished study using albino rats, Thompson obtained results which gave some support to his earlier findings.[2]

[1] This paper is based on a thesis submitted by the author to the Psychology Department of Brown University in partial fulfillment of the requirements for the MS degree. This investigation was supported by a PHS research grant, 3-B-9019, from the National Institute of Neurological Diseases and Blindness to the Institute for the Health Sciences at Brown. The author wishes to express his appreciation to Harold Schlosberg for his generous advice throughout the execution of this research.

[2] This work was reported at an AAAS symposium in 1957.

From C. H. Hockman. Prenatal maternal stress in the rat: Its effects on emotional behavior in the offspring. Journal of Comparative and Physiological Psychology, *1961,* **54,** *679–684. (With permission of the author and the American Psychological Association.)*

The present study attempts to replicate Thompson's exploratory experiment using similar apparatus and procedure but with a larger sample of animals and their litters and more rigid control.

METHOD

Subjects

Thirty-two female hooded rats (Long-Evans) were selected in the following manner: 44 female rats of approximately three months of age were placed individually in an open field for a 10-min. period on each of three consecutive days, and their activity was recorded. The 12 animals with extreme scores, high and low, were discarded. The remaining 32 rats were randomly assigned to the experimental and control groups—16 animals to each group. The 5 male rats that were used for mating were similarly selected from a group of 19 animals. This selection procedure was used to minimize activity differences between the experimental and control parents.

During the preliminary phase of the experiment, one animal from each group had to be discarded. . . . During the actual study, the experimental group was further reduced to 9 (6 animals were lost). These losses will be described in the Results section as they constitute possible differential effects of the experimental treatments. In the final analysis, there were 15 control and 9 experimental mothers. There remained a total offspring numbering 166 (98 control and 68 experimental animals).

Apparatus

The apparatus consisted of a two-compartment shuttlebox and a rectangular open field. The shuttlebox was 36 in. long, 7 in. wide, and 12 in. high. The back and side panels were of wood and the front of glass. A center panel divided the box into equal compartments: the white compartment had a grid floor, and the black compartment a wooden floor. The rat could open a small door in the center panel by the depression of a lever. A strong electric shock, which elicited frantic jumping and squealing, was delivered through the grid floor of the white compartment.... A damped 110-v. buzzer attached to the outside end of the stock compartment was used as a conditioned stimulus.

The open field was a rectangular box 40 in. long, 32 in. wide, and 18 in. high. The floor was divided into 8-in. squares and covered with a piece of $\frac{1}{4}$-in. plate glass. Seven photocells were attached to the rectangular field in such a manner as to form a grid with 20 squares. The movement of an animal interrupting a beam could be recorded on either of two mechanical counters. Preliminary testing proved the photocell arrangement unstable over long periods of time. Furthermore, some animals, while remaining stationary, would bob their heads up and down in such a manner as to activate the counters. It was, therefore, decided to use a hand-operated counter to record all activity in the open field, with observations made through a one-way-vision screen. . . .

Procedure

Table 1 lists the sequence of the operations that will be described below.

TABLE 1   Successive phases of experimental treatment

Phase	Operation	Period
1	CS paired with US	Days 1 to 7
2	Escape training	Days 8 to 10
3	Avoidance training	Day 11 to criterion
4	Mating	
5	Application of stress	From conception to parturition
6	Early test of offspring	30–45 days of age
7	Late test of offspring	180–210 days of age

On Days 1 to 7, the escape door was locked, and each experimental animal received 10 paired classical conditioning trials per day, i.e., the [Conditioned Stimulus] CS was on for 5 sec. accompanied by unavoidable shock during the last second. These trials were separated by 10-sec. intervals. On Day 8 the door to the safe side was opened, and the animals were given three days of escape training. The same [Conditioned Stimulus-Unconditioned Stimulus] CS-US interval was used in this phase of the experiment, but the intertrial intervals were 1 min. On Day 11 avoidance training began. Animals could avoid shock by depressing the lever that opened the door in the center panel and running to the safe side before the onset of the [Unconditioned Stimulus] US. Each daily session consisted of 10 trials. Avoidance training was to a criterion of 10 successive responses.

During avoidance training, vaginal smears were taken daily in order to establish each animal's estrus cycle. The criteria by which the rat's cycle is divided into 5 stages are described by Nicholas (1949).

When criterion was reached in the avoidance situation, this phase of the experiment was terminated. The animals were then mated. Usually one or two days intervened between the cessation of avoidance training and mating, as all animals, both experimentals and controls, were mated in Stage I of their cycle, which is approximately 12 hr. before ovulation. Using the vaginal smear technique, we were able to establish conception within 48 hr. after mating. When conception was thus established, the experimental animals were subjected to ''stress'' three times daily at approximately 8-hr. intervals. The stressful event consisted of placing the pregnant experimental animal in the shock compartment and of presenting the CS *alone* for 10 trials with a 10-sec. interval between trials. On the first trial of each session, the animal was permitted to, and did, cross into the safe compartment at the onset of the CS. During the remaining 9 trials of each session, the door leading to the safe compartment was locked. Each pregnant experimental animal was subjected to ''stress'' until the birth of its litter. Throughout the experiment all control animals were given equivalent daily handling.

During the stress phase of the experiment, blood samples were taken from the tail of each animal, at rest and immediately following a stressful session. Differential blood counts were then made in order to test for ''emotional lymphocytosis.'' These counts were made at different stages of gestation for different animals. Blood samples were also taken from controls in order to compare resting baselines in both groups.

Possible postnatal influences were controlled by cross-fostering in such a way as to yield a design with six cells with two main variables, namely, prenatal and postnatal treatment. Experimental litters were thus raised from birth by either their own mothers, other experimental mothers, or control mothers; and control litters were raised from birth by either their own mothers, other control mothers, or experimental mothers. All offspring were weighed at birth and then immediately cross-fostered. There was *no* further handling until testing was initiated in the early series. All litters were limited to 8 animals: offspring in excess of this number were discarded.

The offspring of both the experimental and control animals were tested in the open field at 30 to 45 days of age and again at 180 to 210 days of age. The two test series, designated as "Early" and "Late," consisted of a 10-min. test in the open field on each of three successive days. On each daily test, in both series, each animal was placed in what was arbitrarily designated as the starting corner. Activity was measured in terms of squares or lines crossed during the 10-min. Latency to leave the starting corner and defecation in the field were also recorded.

RESULTS

Fifteen animals were conditioned, mated, and then subjected to the stressful experience. During this phase, the number of experimental animals was reduced to 9 (1 animal died on Day 15 of pregnancy; 3 [animals gave birth to dead litters]; 1 animal refused to raise her litter; and 1 animal aborted on Day 12 of gestation). All 15 control mothers bore live and healthy offspring. Compared with the controls, this decrease in experimental litters is [statistically] significant. . . .

Although each experimental animal received in excess of 500 "extinction" trials, the avoidance response remained at high strength throughout this phase of the study. During all extinction trials, all animals exhibited agitated behavior, which included squealing, jumping, chewing at the lever, and frequent defecation.

There were no significant differences in birth weight between the experimental and control offspring. Although all mothers appeared to be disturbed when their offspring were removed for purposes of weighing and cross-fostering, only one animal refused to raise her foster offspring. In all other respects there were no noticeable differences in the mothers' rearing behavior.

Handling of all animals proved difficult on the first day of testing, especially during the ear-clipping operation.

The major data of the experiment are concerned with the mean number of lines crossed in the open field during a 10-min. period on 3 successive days on the Early Series of tests. These data are illustrated in Figure 1. The curves show the differences in activity between the experimental and control offspring. An analysis of [the data] shows a [significant difference between the experimental and control offspring in the number of lines crossed and also a significant difference in activity level across the 3 days of testing] . . . Figure 1 also shows, for purposes of comparison, the activity level for the Late Series of tests. There were no significant differences between the experimentals and controls on this Series.

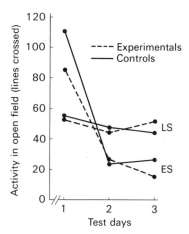

FIG. 1   Activity scores in open field on Tests 1, 2, and 3 in both Early (ES) and Late (LS) Series.

The data were further analyzed in terms of the postnatal "mothering." The experimental offspring had 3 types of mothers: (*a*) experimental, own; (*b*) experimental, foster; and (*c*) control, foster. The control offspring were divided into corresponding subgroups. The analysis shows that the only offspring to show a clear loss of activity were the experimental [offspring] that were cross-fostered. The experimental offspring reared by their own mothers were similar to all control subgroups. The mean activity (lines crossed) for the experimental offspring raised by control mothers was 73.59, and for the control offspring raised by experimental mothers it was 113.08. The difference between these means is significant. . . . The mean activity of the experimental offspring raised by foster experimental mothers was 81.8, and for control offspring raised by foster control mothers, 118.57. The difference between these means is also significant. . . . Experimental offspring raised by their own mothers showed a mean of 104.63, and control offspring raised by their own mothers showed a mean of 105.47. All control subgroups showed an activity level which was statistically comparable to that of the experimental offspring raised by their own mothers. On Test 2, both subgroups which showed a significant depressed activity level on Test 1 had a lower activity level than their comparison control subgroups; however, it did not reach significance. Again the experimentals raised by their own mothers showed an activity level comparable to the control subgroups. On Test 3 the pattern resembled that of Test 2 with one exception: the experimental offspring raised by control mothers showed a mean activity level of 10.34, and the control offspring raised by experimental mothers showed a mean of 26.0. The difference between these means is significant. . . .

A similar analysis of the data for the Late Series of tests showed no differences between the experimental and control offspring.

Further analysis of the highly significant days effect shows that the significant drop in activity for both experimental and control groups is from Test [Day] 1 to Test [Day] 2. The decrease from Test [Day] 2 to Test [Day] 3 is not significant. . . .

The experimental animals regardless of postnatal treatment excreted significantly more boluses than did the controls on Day 1 of the Early Series. . . . There were no significant differences on this measure on the remaining two days of the Early Series nor on all three tests of the Late Series.

The results of the differential blood counts on the mothers showed an increase of about 12% in lymphocytes immediately following stress. This figure agrees with that reported by Farris (1938) for "emotional lymphocytosis" in both the rat and man. It was also noted that the resting baseline of control animals was comparable to that of the experimentals before "stress." In a count of 100 white cells made between Day 15 and Day 20 of pregnancy, the lymphocyte means for the experimental animals immediately before and after "stress" were 64.8 and 77.3, respectively. A [statistical] test indicated this difference to be significant. . . .

DISCUSSION

Implicit in the hypothesis tested was the assumption that the offspring of the "stressed" mothers would show a lower activity level than would the offspring of the controls. The results on the first test of the Early Series confirmed this assumption. However, the treatment effect did not appear to be so striking nor so clear-cut as in Thompson's (1957) exploratory study. The experimental offspring raised by foster mothers were significantly less active than the controls on the Early Series; however, the experimental offspring raised by their own mothers were comparable to the controls. There were no differences in activity between the control subgroups. It appears that the "stress" applied during gestation is not, by itself, sufficient to noticeably affect the offspring, but must be supplemented by the cross-fostering experience. This unexpected finding raises some interesting questions which may be answered in future studies.

The analysis of [the data] showed a striking Days effect which is significant for both groups only from Test [Day] 1 to Test [Day] 2. This big drop in activity may be attributed to the "traumatic" events of the first test. The animals had never been handled before this test, so they were difficult to catch when removed from the open field, at which time their ears were clipped for identification purposes. They were also separated, for the first time, from their mothers (or foster mothers). It is thus not surprising to witness this striking drop in activity on the second test. The same traumatic events might also explain activity levels of both groups on Days 2 and 3 of the Early Series. Unfortunately the paucity of evidence in this area does not permit assessment of the possible importance of these factors.

Thompson found differences in activity between experimentals and controls on both Early and Late Series of tests. In the present study there were no differences between groups on the Late Series. In the present experiment, the animals were approximately four months older than in the Thompson study when late testing was initiated. This age difference is conceivably an important factor.

There is an indication that stress might have been more severe than in the Thompson study, as six experimental litters were lost during the "stress phase" of this experiment as compared with no losses in the control group. Although the specific causes of death are unknown, the significance of mortality as a possible differential treatment effect deserves further investigation.

The two other measures used as indices of emotionality were: latency to leave the starting corner in the open field and defecation in the same situation. There were no significant differences between the latencies of the experimental and control animals in either the Early or Late Series of tests.

As to the defecation measure, this index of emotionality was significant *only* on Test 1 of the Early Series. On Tests 2 and 3 of this series, both experimental and control *S*s excreted approximately the same number of boluses. Granting Hall's (1934) suggestion that defecation is a sensitive index of emotionality, we might assume that the above-mentioned traumatic events similarly affected both groups by lowering their threshold to a level at which this physiological response is maximal.

The findings in the present study tend to support Thompson's suggestion that prenatal maternal stress does have some effect on the emotional behavior of the offspring; however, the effect is not a simple one. Future research must investigate the combined effects of both prenatal and postnatal treatment in terms of stress applied at distinct stages of fetal development. Future research in this area must also inquire into the possible mechanisms by which the effects of "stressful" events are transmitted from the mother to the fetus. Presumably hormones such as cortisone, ACTH, and others, which are normally released into the bloodstream during stress, might, either directly or indirectly, produce fetal changes at certain critical stages of development. A recent study in which Strean and Peer (1956) examined 228 children with cleft palate lends strong support to this belief.

SUMMARY

This study tested the hypothesis that stress undergone by female rats during pregnancy can affect emotional behavior of the offspring. Thirty-two female hooded rats were randomly assigned to two groups: 16 experimentals and 16 controls. During pregnancy, the experimental mothers were exposed to a stressful situation. In order to control for possible postnatal effects, the offspring of both experimental and control mothers were cross-fostered.

The offspring of both groups were tested in an open field between 30 and 45 days of age and between 180 and 210 days.

The major results of the experiment showed that the overall activity of the experimental litters was significantly lower than that of the controls on the Early Series of tests; however, there were no differences between groups on the Late Series of tests. Further analysis indicated that the effect failed to appear in the offspring raised by their own mothers. In other words, there appeared to be an interaction between prenatal treatment and postnatal separation experience. Another highly significant finding, in terms of differential treatments, was the high mortality in the experimental group during the "stress phase" of the experiment. The only other measure which yielded a significant difference between the experimental and control animals was the defecation in the open field on the first test of the Early Series.

These findings are explained tentatively in terms of biochemical changes due to the increased secretion of endocrine substances under maternal stress.

REFERENCES

Baxter, H., & Fraser, F. C. The projection of congenital defects in the offspring of female mice treated with cortisone: A preliminary report. *McGill Medical Journal*, 1950, **19**, 245–249.

Beach, F. A., & Jaynes, J. Effects of early experience upon the behavior of animals. *Psychological Bulletin*, 1954, **51**, 239–263.

Christian, J. J. The roles of endocrine and behavioral factors in the growth of mammalian populations. In A. Gorbman (Ed.), *Comparative endocrinology proceedings*. New York: Wiley, 1959. Pp. 71–97.

Farris, E. J. Emotional lymphocytosis in the albino rat. *American Journal of Anatomy*, 1938, **63**, 325–348.

Fraser, F. C., & Fainstat, T. D. Causes of congenital defects. *American Journal of Diseases in Children*, 1951, **82**, 593–603.

Hall, C. S. Emotional behavior in the rat: Defecation and urination as measures of individual differences in emotionality. *Journal of Comparative Psychology*, 1934, **18**, 385–403.

Nicholas, J. S. Experimental methods and rat embryos. In E. J. Farris & J. Q. Griffith (Eds.), *The rat in laboratory investigation*. Philadelphia: Lippincott, 1949. Pp. 51–67.

Sontag, L. W. The significance of fetal environmental differences. *American Journal of Obstetrics and Gynecology*, 1941, **42**, 996–1003.

Strean, L. P., & Peer, L. A. Stress as an etiologic factor in the development of cleft palate. *Plastic and Reconstructive Surgery*, 1956, **18**, 1–8.

Thompson, W. D., & Sontag, L. W. Behavioral effects in the offspring of rats subjected to audiogenic seizure during the gestational period. *Journal of Comparative and Physiological Psychology*, 1956, **49**, 454–456.

Thompson, W. R. Influence of prenatal maternal anxiety on emotionality in young rats. *Science*, 1957, **125**, 698–699.

VISUAL ALERTNESS AS RELATED TO SOOTHING IN NEONATES: IMPLICATIONS FOR MATERNAL STIMULATION AND EARLY DEPRIVATION

Anneliese F. Korner and Rose Grobstein

Observations incidental to a study of behavior genetics in neonates (Korner, 1964) suggest that when babies cry and are picked up to the shoulder, they not only stop crying, but they frequently become visually alert, and they scan the environment. We were struck by several implications of this observation: If generally true, this type of soothing would induce a state which is otherwise quite rare in the neonate and which is considered by some to be the optimal state for the infant's earliest learning. According to P. H. Wolff's (1965) observations, this state of alertness occurs spontaneously [only] 8 to 16 percent of the time in the first postnatal week, and it . . . very gradually increases over subsequent weeks. The infant thus spends only a very minor part of his day in alertness. Yet, in terms of his locomotor helplessness, visual prehension is one of the few avenues at his disposal to make contact and to get acquainted with the environment. If regular soothing of this type induces a state of alertness, it follows that a baby picked up for crying will have earlier and many more opportunities to scan the environment than an infant left crying in his crib.

In a recent symposium entitled "The Crucial Early Influence: Mother Love or Environmental Stimulation," Fantz (1966), referring to his findings that infants discriminate from birth among visual stimuli, concluded that perceptual experiences play a crucial role in early development. In fact, he could distinguish babies reared at home from institutional infants through their visual responses by the second month of life. While Fantz stressed the importance of perceptual experiences through environmental stimulation, he also stated that the effects of early stimulation would be better understood "if one could pin down the specific kinds of sensory stimulation and perceptual experience often provided optimally by a loving mother." Our observation that babies, when picked up for crying, frequently become visually alert may thus capture one important pathway by which maternal ministrations may inadvertently provide visual experiences.

This investigation was supported by Public Health Service grants HD-00825-01 and HD-00825-02 from the National Institute of Child Health and Human Development. The authors wish to thank Dr. Helena Kraemer for her helpful advice and for performing the statistical analyses of the data. We also wish to thank the nursing staff of the Palo Alto-Stanford Hospital for their helpful cooperation.

*From A. F. Korner & R. Grobstein. Visual alertness as related to soothing in neonates: Implications for maternal stimulation and early deprivation. Child Development, 1966, **37**, 867–876. (With permission of the authors and the Society for Research in Child Development, Inc.)*

43

In this study we set out to investigate how frequently soothing of the type described elicited visual alertness. With the design used to study this problem, it was possible to explore an additional hypothesis. Bell (1963) suggested that infants born to primiparous mothers may, for a number of reasons, respond differently to tactile stimulation than infants of multiparous mothers. We explored the relation between parity and visual alertness in response to soothing by including both types of infants.

SAMPLE

The sample consisted of 12 newborn, breastfed baby girls; six were born to primiparous mothers and six to multiparae. Boys were excluded because it was quite apparent that the comfort derived from being picked up and put to the shoulder was offset by the discomfort of being held close within hours of a circumcision. The babies ranged from 45-79 hours in age; the average was 55 hours old. All were Caucasian. Their birth weights ranged from 6 pounds 8 ounces to 8 pounds 13 ounces. They all had normal vaginal deliveries, received Apgar scores of 8 and above at birth, and they were found to be healthy newborn infants on physical examination.

METHOD

The infants were tested in a treatment room adjoining the nursery. Temperature and illumination approximated conditions in the nursery. The infants were tested individually after being brought to the treatment room in their own bassinets. They were dressed in shirts and diapers. To facilitate pickups, the infants were placed on the mattress underneath the plastic bassinet usually used for diapering and dressing infants. Since we were interested in soothing crying babies, they were all tested within $1\frac{1}{2}$ hours before a feeding. Occasionally, we had to rouse a sleepy baby by moving her or by flicking her foot. The tests described below were initiated only when the baby was crying. Minimum time between experiments was 1 minute. Since we were interested in comparing each infant with her own tendencies in the various experimental positions, it was of little consequence whether some infants cried harder than others at any given trial. Also, enough trials were given to each infant to randomize the degree of agitation over all the trials.

Diapers were changed before the experiments were started irrespective of need. All infants were tested in four positions:
1. Six trials on the left shoulder.
2. Six trials on the right shoulder.
3. Six trials sitting up.
4. Six control trials in which the baby lay on her back without intervention by the observers.

The "situp" experiments were introduced because it was noted that handling and the upright position alone frequently induced alertness. It was noted, for example, that many babies are alert when they are carried out to their mothers for feeding. In addition to the handling and the upright position, the experience of being put to the shoulder involves warmth, containment, the sense of smell, and the opportunity to establish mouth contact with the shoulder. Differential effects of the two positions could thus be studied.

To insure comparability of handling, the same person did all the interventions. When picked up, the baby's head was supported, and her hands were kept out of reach of her mouth. The same was done in sitting up a baby. Trials in the various positions were done at random.

For 30 seconds following an intervention, alert and scanning behavior was recorded. During the control experiments, the same was done for 30 seconds without an intervention. When the infant opened her eyes during the 30-second experimental period, the trial was scored as "yes." In each instance, the same was done for scanning behavior. Babies varied a great deal in the degree of alertness. Some drowsily opened their eyes; others actively looked around, lifting the head and exploring the experimenter. Some had brief, others had sustained periods of alertness. Since visual pursuit can be elicited even in drowsy babies (see Wolff, 1966), and since it is difficult to equate several brief periods of alertness with one sustained period, the degree and the duration of alertness were not considered in the ratings. "Yes" was scored when the infant opened her eyes and when she scanned the environment at any one time during the 30 seconds of observations. In addition to these observations, the number of spontaneous alert and scanning episodes between experiments was noted for 10 of the 12 subjects.

OBSERVER RELIABILITIES

Reliabilities between two observers were calculated on the basis of dividing the number of agreements by the combined number of agreements and disagreements. Percentages of agreement were as follows:
1.   Opening eyes during "situps" and during controls: 96 percent.
2.   Opening eyes between experiments: 98 percent.
3.   Scanning during "situps" and during controls: 97 percent.
4.   Scanning episodes between experiments: 95 percent.

Reliability ratings for opening of eyes and scanning during "pickups" would have required a third observer. Since there was very little disagreement between what constituted alerting and scanning behavior during "situps" and controls and between experiments (the percentages of agreement ranging from 95 to 98), it was felt to be unnecessary to introduce a third observer to rate alert and scanning behavior during "pickups."

RESULTS

Incidence of alerting in response to soothing

Our data confirmed the observation that, when crying infants were put to the shoulder, they not only stopped crying, but each of them also opened her eyes and alerted in the large majority of trials. Table 1 summarizes the raw data for "primips" and "multips."[1] The figures above the totals represent the number of trials out of six in which each baby opened her eyes in each position. The figures below the totals represent the percentage of trials in which alerting occurred in each position.

An analysis [of the data] was performed. The difference between "primips" and "multips" was not found to be significant. By contrast, the difference of reactions to the various positions was found to be significant. . . .

---

[1] The terms "primips" and "multips" will be used for convenience henceforth to refer to the offspring of primiparous and multiparous mothers, respectively.

TABLE 1 Frequency of eyes opened in response to soothing

Subject	Controls	Situps	Left	Right
"Multips"				
M1	2	0	6	6
M2	2	5	6	6
M3	0	2	3	4
M4	0	1	4	6
M5	3	4	6	3
M6	0	0	5	6
Totals	7	12	30	31
% of trials	19	33	83	86
"Primips"				
P1	1	0	6	6
P2	1	0	6	6
P3	0	0	6	6
P4	5	3	6	6
P5	4	5	6	6
P6	1	0	2	4
Totals	12	8	32	34
% of trials	33	22	89	94

The results suggest that handling and the upright position alone did not result in the infant's opening her eyes significantly more often than when no intervention was made.

Incidence of scanning in response to soothing

Since the degree of alertness varied when an infant opened her eyes, active scanning probably was a better measure for testing the effect of soothing on visual alertness. Table 2 demonstrates that, even with this more stringent criterion for alertness, each baby in this sample alerted and scanned when put to the shoulder, and most did in the majority of the trials.

An analysis [of the data] was performed. Even though, in absolute terms, the "primips" scanned more, the difference was not statistically significant. By contrast, the difference of reactions to the various positions was again significant. . . .

Spontaneous alerting and scanning between experiments

Spontaneous alerting and scanning between experiments was recorded only in 10 out of 12 cases. The incidence among babies of these episodes varied greatly. The average number of times the "primips" opened their eyes between experiments was 7.8; for "multips," the average was only 3.2. The "primips" scanned on the average of 6.5 times, the "multips" only 3 times. These differences between "primips" and "multips" did not reach significance, probably because of the small number of observations. It is of interest, however, that there is a consistent trend among the three types of observations: In each instance, the "primips" alerted and scanned more frequently than the "multips." This suggests that differences may exist in arousal levels

TABLE 2   Frequency of scanning in response to soothing

Subject	Controls	Situps	Left	Right
"Multips"				
M1	1	0	5	4
M2	0	1	4	5
M3	0	0	2	1
M4	0	0	3	5
M5	2	3	5	3
M6	0	0	5	6
Totals	3	4	24	24
% of trials	8	11	66	66
"Primips"				
P1	0	0	6	6
P2	1	0	4	4
P3	0	0	6	5
P4	4	3	6	6
P5	4	4	6	6
P6	0	0	0	1
Totals	9	7	28	28
% of trials	25	19	77	77

between "primips" and "multips." Our data on crying, not reported here, which shows highly significant differences between "multips" and "primips," would support this hypothesis.

Individual differences

As Tables 1 and 2 demonstrate, there were marked differences among babies in their tendency to alert and scan. . . . There also were marked differences in the capacity to sustain alertness. In some babies these episodes were fleeting; in others they were maintained for long periods of time.

There were particularly marked differences among the infants in their proneness to alert and to scan between experiments. Some babies never did alert and scan, others did very rarely, and a few did quite frequently . . . . By contrast, those infants who alerted and scanned most between experiments were not necessarily the same babies who had the highest frequency of these behaviors when picked up. Very probably, the amount of handling during the entire experimental session affected babies differently, arousing some, not affecting others. One may infer from this that there may be individual differences among babies in the ease with which the state of arousal is changed through manipulation.

DISCUSSION

Visual alertness in the neonate has become the concern of many studies (e.g., Fantz, 1958, 1966; Ling, 1942; White, 1963; Wolff, 1965, 1966; Wolff & White, 1965).

This concern on the part of some investigators stems from the observation that visual alertness is not as reflex as most neonatal behavior and, to a large extent, qualitatively resembles the later capacity of attentiveness. In terms of psychoanalytic theory, visual alertness is probably the clearest example of a primary autonomous ego function observable in the newborn. In view of the neonate's locomotor helplessness, visual prehension is one of the infant's few avenues for learning and for getting acquainted with the environment.)

Our experiments show that this state of visual alertness, so important for learning, can readily be induced by picking up a crying newborn and putting him to the shoulder. It was possible to do this without difficulty even at a time when, according to Wolff's (1965) findings, the newborn is least likely to be alert, namely, when he is hungry. Wolff's observations demonstrated that during the first week of life his subjects spent, on the average, only 11 percent of the time in the state of alert inactivity and that 86.4 percent of this 11 percent occurred within the first hour after a feeding.

One can only speculate about the causes of the association between this kind of soothing and visual alertness. Neurophysiologically, what may occur is that the soothing action of this intervention lowers the infant's state of arousal, with the result that the infant goes from crying into the next lower state on the continuum of states and arousal.[2] Waking activity, the next lower state on this continuum, was prevented by the motor restraint imposed by being held to the shoulder. This restraint may have lowered the infant's state of arousal one step further, resulting in the state of alert inactivity. In fact, by preventing the distracting effects of the infant's motor activity, the physical restraint may have enhanced the likelihood of alert behavior. Wolff and White (1965) found this relation to hold: They increased the infants' capacity for attentive behavior by inhibiting motor activity through the use of a pacifier.

In psychological terms, the association of soothing and visual alertness may involve the prototype of a reaction which may hold true throughout life: By reducing the intensity of internal needs, the organism can turn outward and attend the external world. Descriptively, this corresponds well with the sequence of events as we observed them.

Our data did not suggest that handling or the upright position alone induced a state of alertness. This was true because, in most cases, handling alone did not lower the infant's state of arousal sufficiently to reduce crying to the point of alertness. The observation that many infants are quietly alert when brought to a feeding suggests that handling and the upright position are more successful in inducing alertness in noncrying or sleepy infants. In those states of arousal, the stimulation of touch, motion, and positional change are rousing rather than soothing. In an intense form, labor and birth which entail extreme stimulation of this type may have arousing effects with similar results. Brazelton (1961) observed that, for a few hours after delivery and before going into a relative state of disorganization, all of his subjects were alert and responsive. They fixed and followed a red ring visually for several minutes at a time. They also attended and often visually followed auditory stimuli. Brazelton's observations of the alertness of the newly delivered baby are easily confirmed by casual observation. All one has to do is to watch babies as they are admitted to the newborn nursery from the delivery room: Most of them have their eyes wide open and are highly alert.

[2] For a definition of states of arousal, see Wolff (1959).

Of relevance to the alertness-producing effects of both soothing and handling are the numerous studies dealing with the effects of handling and early stimulation on both animals and infants. For the most part, these studies show the importance of early stimulation for the growth and development of the young organism. The specific factors which account for the more favorable development of the ''handled'' group are usually not spelled out. Levine (1962), noting profound psychophysiological effects of infantile stimulation in the rat, concluded that the sensory routes and mechanisms underlying these effects are not known. He suspects that proprioceptive and kinesthetic stimulation may indicate the sensory routes of effective stimulation. Casler (1961) and Yarrow (1961), in reviews of maternal deprivation studies, concluded that early tactile stimulation appears necessary for normal human development. Our own observations suggest that tactile stimulation may activate visual behavior. Activation of the visual modality through tactile stimulation may thus be one of the pathways through which early stimulation takes effect. We find support of this hypothesis in White and Castle's (1964) study which demonstrated that institution-reared infants given small amounts of extra handling during their first weeks of life later showed significantly more visual interest in their environment than nonhandled controls.

In the earliest days of life, infant care, for the most part, invites soothing rather than rousing interventions. It is the handling involved in soothing rather than rousing which may make the difference in the neonates' earliest opportunities for visual experiences. Infants in institutions, while usually given adequate physical care, generally are not picked up and soothed when they cry. This may be partly responsible for their earliest deficit.

Mothers of home-reared infants differ, of course, in their readiness to soothe their crying newborn. Our observations suggest that picked-up infants will have many more opportunities to get acquainted with the environment than babies left crying in their cribs. In particular, they will have many more occasions to explore their mothers. Their visual explorations will occur when comforted. This may lower their stimulus barrier under conditions which minimize the danger of being overwhelmed.

Fantz's (1966) findings suggest that visual and perceptual experiences during the neonatal period have lasting developmental effects. With this in mind, our observations raise a host of developmental questions. For example, do babies who are carried around a great deal learn to rely more heavily on the visual modality in their exploration of the environment than babies who do not have this experience as much? How does the development of the infant of another culture who is constantly carried around by his mother differ in this respect? With the added opportunities of exploring the mother, are there differences in time and depth in the infant-mother bond formation and in the development of differentiating self from nonself? Also, are there differences in the onset and strength of stranger and separation anxiety? As Benjamin (1959) has shown, babies who rely heavily on the visual modality will experience stranger and separation anxiety earlier and more severely.

Our observations have not only experiential implications. We also found organismic differences among the infants. Babies differed greatly in their capacity for alert behavior. This finding is confirmed by our larger study (Korner, 1964) involving a bigger sample of neonates and much longer observations. It is reasonable to believe that varying opportunities for visual experiences will affect babies differently depending on their own disposition. Thus an infant with high sensory thresholds may demonstrate the effects of maternal neglect or sensory deprivation more acutely than the infant more capable of providing visual experiences for himself.

REFERENCES

Bell, R. Q. Some factors to be controlled in studies of the behavior of newborns. *Biologia Neonatorum,* 1963, **5**, 200–214.

Benjamin, J. D. Prediction and psychopathological theory. In L. Jessner & E. Pavenstedt (Eds.), *Dynamic psychopathology in childhood.* New York: Grune & Stratton, 1959. Pp. 6–77.

Brazelton, T. B. Psychophysiologic reactions in the neonate. II. Effect of maternal medication on the neonate and his behavior. *Journal of Pediatrics,* 1961, **58**, 513–518.

Casler, L. Maternal deprivation: A critical review of the literature. *Monographs of the Society for Research in Child Development,* 1961, **26**(2, Serial No. 80).

Fantz, R. L. Pattern vision in young infants. *Psychological Record,* 1958, **8**, 43–47.

Fantz, R. L. The crucial early influence: Mother love or environmental stimulation? *American Journal of Orthopsychiatry,* 1966, **36**, 330–331. (Abstract)

Korner, A. F. Some hypotheses regarding the significance of individual differences at birth for later development. *The psychoanalytic study of the child.* Vol. 19. New York: International Universities Press, 1964. Pp. 58–72.

Levine, S. Psychophysiological effects of infantile stimulation. In E. L. Bliss (Ed.), *Roots of behavior.* New York: Harper, 1962. Pp. 246–253.

Ling, B. C. A genetic study of sustained visual fixation and associated behavior in the human infant from birth to six months. *Journal of Genetic Psychology,* 1942, **61**, 227–277.

White, B. L. The development of perception during the first six months of life. Paper presented at the meeting of the American Association for the Advancement of Science, Cleveland, December 1963.

White, B. L., & Castle, P. W. Visual exploratory behavior following postnatal handling of human infants. *Perceptual and Motor Skills,* 1964, **18**, 497–502.

Wolff, P. H. Observations of newborn infants. *Psychosomatic Medicine,* 1959, **21**, 110–118.

Wolff, P. H. The development of attention in young infants. *Annals of the New York Academy of Sciences,* 1965, **118**, 815–830.

Wolff, P. H. The causes, controls and organization of behavior in the neonate. *Psychological Issues,* 1960, **5**(1), 1–105.

Wolff, P. H., & White, B. L. Visual pursuit and attention in young infants. *Journal of the American Academy of Child Psychiatry,* 1965, **4**, 473–484.

Yarrow, L. J. Maternal deprivation: Toward an empirical and conceptual re-evaluation. *Psychological Bulletin,* 1961, **58**, 459–490.

SEX, AGE, AND STATE AS DETERMINANTS
OF MOTHER-INFANT INTERACTION[1]

Howard A. Moss

A major reason for conducting research on human infants is derived from the popular assumption that adult behavior, to a considerable degree, is influenced by early experience. A corollary of this assumption is that if we can precisely conceptualize and measure significant aspects of infant experience and behavior we will be able to predict more sensitively and better understand adult functioning. The basis for this conviction concerning the enduring effects of early experience varies considerably according to the developmental model that is employed. Yet there remains considerable consensus as to the long term and pervasive influence of the infant's experience.

Bloom (1964) contends that characteristics become increasingly resistant to change as the mature status of the characteristic is achieved and that environmental effects are most influential during periods of most rapid growth. This is essentially a refinement of the critical period hypothesis which argues in favor of the enduring and irreversible effects of many infant experiences. Certainly the studies on imprinting and the effects of controlled sensory input are impressive in this respect (Hess, 1959; White & Held, 1963). Learning theory also lends itself to support the potency of early experience. Since the occurrence of variable interval and variable ratio reinforcement schedules are highly probable in infancy (as they are in many other situations), the learnings associated with these schedules will be highly resistant to extinction. Also, the pre-verbal learning that characterizes infancy should be more difficult to extinguish since these responses are less available to linguistic control which later serves to mediate and regulate many important stimulus-response and reinforcement relationships. Psychoanalytic theory and behavioristic psychology probably have been the most influential forces in emphasizing the long-range consequences of infant experience. These theories, as well as others, stress the importance of the mother-infant relationship. In light of the widespread acceptance of the importance of early development, it is paradoxical that there is such a dearth of direct observational data concerning the functioning of infants, in their natural environment, and in relation to their primary caretakers.

Observational studies of the infant are necessary in order to test existing theoretical propositions and to generate new propositions based on empirical evidence. In addi-

[1] Presented at The Merrill-Palmer Institute Conference on Research and Teaching of Infant Development, February 10–12, 1966, directed by Irving E. Sigel, chairman of research. The conference was financially supported in part by the National Institute of Child Health and Human Development. The author wishes to express his appreciation to Mrs. Helene McVey and Miss Betty Reinecke for their assistance in preparing and analyzing the data presented in this paper.

From H. A. Moss. Sex, age, and state as determinants of mother-infant interaction. Merrill-Palmer Quarterly, *1967,* **13***, 19–36. (With permission of the author and the Merrill-Palmer Institute.)*

tion, the infant is an ideally suitable subject for investigating many aspects of behavior because of the relatively simple and inchoate status of the human organism at this early stage in life. Such phenomena as temperament, reactions to stimulation, efficacy of different learning contingencies, perceptual functioning, and social attachment can be investigated while they are still in rudimentary form and not yet entwined in the immensely complex behavioral configurations that progressively emerge.

The research to be reported in this paper involves descriptive-normative data of maternal and infant behaviors in the naturalistic setting of the home. These data are viewed in terms of how the infant's experience structures potential learning patterns. . . .

A sample of 30 first-born children and their mothers was studied by means of direct observations over the first 3 months of life. Two periods were studied during this 3-month interval. Period one included a cluster of three observations made at weekly intervals during the first month of life in order to evaluate the initial adaptation of mother and infant to one another. Period two consisted of another cluster of three observations, made around 3 months of age when relatively stable patterns of behavior were likely to have been established. Each cluster included two 3-hour observations and one 8-hour observation. The 3-hour observations were made with the use of a keyboard that operates in conjunction with a 20-channel . . . event recorder. Each of 30 keys represents a maternal or infant behavior, and when a key is depressed it activates one or a combination of pens on the recorder, leaving a trace that shows the total duration of the observed behavior. This technique allows for a continuous record showing the total time and the sequence of behavior. For the 8-hour observation the same behaviors were studied but with the use of a modified time-sampling technique. The time-sampled units were one minute in length and the observer, using a stenciled form, placed a number opposite the appropriate behaviors to indicate their respective order of occurrence. Since each variable can be coded only once for each observational unit, a score of 480 is the maximum that can be received. The data to be presented in this paper are limited to the two 8-hour observations. The data obtained with the use of the keyboard will be dealt with elsewhere in terms of the sequencing of events.

The mothers who participated in these observations were told that this was a normative study of infant functioning under natural living conditions. It was stressed that they proceed with their normal routines and care of the infant as they would if the observer were not present. This structure was presented to the mothers during a brief introductory visit prior to the first observation. In addition, in order to reduce the mother's self-consciousness and facilitate her behaving in relatively typical fashion, the observer emphasized that it was the infant who was being studied and that her actions would be noted only in relation to what was happening to the infant. This approach seemed to be effective, since a number of mothers commented after the observations were completed that they were relieved that they were not the ones being studied. The extensiveness of the observations and the frequent use of informal conversation between the observer and mother seemed to contribute further to the naturalness of her behavior.

The observational variables, mean scores and sample sizes are presented in Table 1. These data are presented separately for the 3-week and the 3-month observations. The inter-rater reliabilities for these variables range from .74 to 1.00 with a median

TABLE 1 Mean frequency of maternal and infant behavior at 3 weeks and 3 months

Behavior	3-week observation		3-month observation*	
	Males† (N = 14)	Females (N = 15)	Males† (N = 13)	Females (N = 12)
Maternal variables				
Holds infant close	121.4	99.2	77.4	58.6
Holds infant distant	32.2	18.3	26.7	27.2
Total holds	131.3	105.5	86.9	73.4
Attends infant	61.7	44.2	93.0	81.8
Maternal contact (holds and attends)	171.1	134.5	158.8	133.8
Feeds infant	60.8	60.7	46.6	41.4
Stimulates feeding	10.1	14.0	1.6	3.6
Burps infant	39.0	25.9	20.9	15.3
Affectionate contact	19.9	15.9	32.8	22.7
Rocks infant	35.1	20.7	20.0	23.9
Stresses musculature	11.7	3.3	25.8	16.6
Stimulates/arouses infant	23.1	10.6	38.9	26.1
Imitates infant	1.9	2.9	5.3	7.6
Looks at infant	182.8	148.1	179.5	161.9
Talks to infant	104.1	82.2	117.5	116.1
Smiles at infant	23.2	18.6	45.9	46.4
Infant variables				
Cry	43.6	30.2	28.5	16.9
Fuss	65.7	44.0	59.0	36.0
Irritable (cry and fuss)	78.7	56.8	67.3	42.9
Awake active	79.6	55.1	115.8	85.6
Awake passive	190.0	138.6	257.8	241.1
Drowsy	74.3	74.7	27.8	11.1
Sleep	261.7	322.1	194.3	235.6
Supine	133.7	59.3	152.7	134.8
Eyes on mother	72.3	49.0	91.0	90.6
Vocalizes	152.3	179.3	207.2	207.4
Infant smiles	11.1	11.7	32.1	35.3
Mouths	36.8	30.6	61.2	116.2

*Four of the subjects were unable to participate in the 3-month observation. Two moved out of the area, one mother became seriously ill, and another mother chose not to participate in all the observations.
† One subject who had had an extremely difficult delivery was omitted from the descriptive data but is included in the findings concerning mother-infant interaction.

reliability of .97. Much of the data in this paper are presented for males and females separately, since by describing and comparing these two groups we are able to work from an established context that helps to clarify the theoretical meaning of the results. Also, the importance of sex differences is heavily emphasized in contemporary developmental theory and it is felt that infant data concerning these differences would provide a worthwhile addition to the literature that already exists on this matter for older subjects.

The variables selected for study are those which would seem to influence or reflect aspects of maternal contact. An additional, but related consideration in the selection of variables was that they have an apparent bearing on the organization of the infant's experience. . . . Wolff (1959), . . . Brown (1964), and . . . Escalona (1962) have described qualitative variations in infant state or activity level and others have shown that the response patterns of the infant are highly influenced by the state he is in (Bridger, 1965). Moreover, Levy (1958) has demonstrated that maternal behavior varies as a function of the state or activity level of the infant. Consequently, we have given particular attention to the variables concerning state (cry, fuss, awake active, awake passive, and sleep) because of the extent to which these behaviors seem to shape the infant's experience. Most of the variables listed in Table 1 are quite descriptive of what was observed. Those which might not be as clear are as follows: *attends infant*—denotes standing close or leaning over infant, usually while in the process of caretaking activities; *stimulates feeding*—stroking the infant's cheek and manipulating the nipple so as to induce sucking responses; *affectionate contact*—kissing and caressing infant; *stresses musculature*—holding the infant in either a sitting or standing position so that he is required to support his own weight; *stimulates/arouses infant*—mother provides tactile and visual stimulation for the infant or attempts to arouse him to a higher activity level; and *imitates infant*—mother repeats a behavior, usually a vocalization, immediately after it is observed in the infant.

The sex differences and shifts in behavior from 3 weeks to 3 months are in many instances pronounced. For example, at 3 weeks of age mothers held male infants about 27 minutes more per 8 hours than they held females, and at 3 months males were held 14 minutes longer. By the time they were 3 months of age there was a decrease of over 30% for both sexes in the total time they were held by their mothers. Sleep time also showed marked sex differences and changes over time. For the earlier observations females slept about an hour longer than males, and this difference tended to be maintained by 3 months with the female infants sleeping about 41 minutes longer. Again, there was a substantial reduction with age in this behavior for both sexes; a decrease of 67 and 86 minutes in sleep time for males and females, respectively. What is particularly striking is the variability for these infant and maternal variables. The range for sleep time is 137–391 minutes at 3 weeks and 120–344 minutes at 3 months, and the range for mother holding is 38–218 minutes at 3 weeks and 26–168 minutes for the 3-month observation. . . . The finding that some of the infants in our sample slept a little over 2 hours, or about 25% of the observation time and others around 6 hours or 75% of the time, is a fact that has implications for important developmental processes. The sum crying and fussing, what we term irritability level of the infant, is another potentially important variable. The range of scores for this behavior was from 5-136 minutes at 3 weeks and 7-98 at 3 months. The fact that infants are capable through their behavior of shaping maternal treatment is a point that has gained increasing recognition. The cry is a signal for the mother to respond and variation among infants in this behavior could lead to differential experiences with the mother.

Table 2 presents *t* values showing changes in the maternal and infant behaviors from the 3-week to the 3-month observation. In this case, the data for the males and females are combined since the trends, in most instances, are the same for both sexes. It is not surprising that there are a number of marked shifts in behavior from 3 weeks to 3 months, since the early months of life are characterized by enormous growth and change. The maternal variables that show the greatest decrement are those in-

TABLE 2   Changes in behavior between 3 weeks and 3 months ($N = 26$)

Maternal variables	t-values†	Infant variables	t-values
Higher at 3 weeks:		*Higher at 3 weeks:*	
Holds infant close	4.43****	Cry	2.84***
Holds infant distant	.56	Fuss	1.33
Total holds	4.00****	Irritable (cry and fuss)	1.73*
Maternal contact		Drowsy	9.02****
(holds and attends)	.74	Sleep	4.51****
Feeds infant	3.49***		
Stimulates feeding	3.42***		
Burps infant	3.28***		
Rocks infant	1.08		
Higher at 3 months:		*Higher at 3 months:*	
Attends infant	5.15****	Awake active	2.47**
Affectionate contact	2.50**	Awake passive	5.22****
Stresses musculature	3.42***	Supine	1.75*
Stimulates/arouses infant	2.63**	Eyes on mother	3.21***
Imitates infant	4.26****	Vocalizes	3.56***
Looks at infant	.38	Infant smiles	6.84****
Talks to infant	2.67**	Mouths	3.69***
Smiles at infant	4.79****		

*$p < .10$
**$p < .05$ Significance levels
***$p < .01$
****$p < .001$

[† The t-test is a statistical method for comparing differences between the means of two groups.]

volving feeding behaviors and close physical contact. It is of interest that the decrease in close contact is paralleled by an equally pronounced increase in attending behavior, so that the net amount of maternal contact remains similar for the 3-week and 3-month observations. The main difference was that the mothers, for the later observation, tended to hold their infants less but spent considerably more time near them, in what usually was a vis-à-vis posture, while interacting and ministering to their needs. Along with this shift, the mothers showed a marked increase in affectionate behavior toward the older infant, positioned him more so that he was required to make active use of his muscles, presented him with a greater amount of stimulation and finally, she exhibited more social behavior (imitated, smiled, and talked) toward the older child.

The changes in maternal behavior from 3 weeks to 3 months probably are largely a function of the maturation of various characteristics of the infant. However, the increased confidence of the mother, her greater familiarity with her infant, and her developing attachment toward him will also account for some of the changes that occurred over this period of time.

By 3 months of age the infant is crying less and awake more. Moreover, he is becoming an interesting and responsive person. There are substantial increases in the total time spent by him in smiling, vocalizing, and looking at the mother's face, so that the greater amount of social-type behavior he manifested at 3 months parallels the increments shown in the mother's social responsiveness toward him over this same period. The increase with age in the time the infant is kept in a supine position also should facilitate his participation in vis-à-vis interactions with the mother as well as provide him with greater opportunity for varied visual experiences.

. . . Correlations between the 3-week and the 3-month observations for the maternal and infant behaviors [also] . . . reflect the relative instability of the mother-infant system over the first few months of life. Moderate correlation coefficients were obtained only for the class of maternal variables concerning affectionate-social responses. . . . The few infant variables that show some stability are, with the exception of vocalizing, those concerning the state of the organism. Even though some of the behaviors are moderately stable from 3 weeks to 3 months, the overall magnitude of the correlations . . . seem quite low considering that they represent repeated measures of the same individual over a relatively short period.

. . . [A] comparison [was made] between the sexes for the 3-week and 3-month observations. A number of statistically significant differences were obtained with, in most instances, the boys having higher mean scores than the girls. The sex differences are most pronounced at 3 weeks for both maternal and infant variables. By 3 months the boys and girls are no longer as clearly differentiated on the maternal variables although the trend persists for the males to tend to have higher mean scores. On the other hand, the findings for the infant variables concerning state remain relatively similar at 3 weeks and 3 months. . . .

In general, these results indicate that much more was happening with the male infants than with the female infants. Males slept less and cried more during both observations and these behaviors probably contributed to the more extensive and stimulating interaction the boys experienced with the mother, particularly for the 3-week observation. In order to determine the effect of state we selected the 15 variables, excluding those dealing with state, where the sex differences were most marked and did an analysis . . . with these variables, controlling for irritability and another analysis . . . controlling for sleep. These results [indicate that] . . . when the state of the infant was controlled for, most of the sex differences were no longer statistically significant. The exceptions were that the [differences] . . . were greater, after controlling for state, for the variables "mother stimulates/arouses infant" and "mother imitates infant." The higher score for "stimulates/arouses" was obtained for the males and the higher score for "imitates" by the females. The variable "imitates" involves repeating vocalizations made by the child, and it is interesting that mothers exhibited more of this behavior with the girls. This response could be viewed as the reinforcement of verbal behavior, and the evidence presented here suggests that the mothers differentially reinforce this behavior on the basis of the sex of the child.

In order to further clarify the relation between infant state and maternal treatment, . . . correlations were computed relating the infant irritability score with the degree of maternal contact. The maternal contact variable is based on the sum of the holding and attending scores with the time devoted to feeding behaviors subtracted out. These correlations were computed for the 3-week and 3-month observations for the male and female samples combined and separate. At 3 weeks a [significant] correlation of .52 . . . was obtained between irritability and maternal contact for the total sample. However, [this relationship was significant only for the females with a correlation of .68]. . . . Furthermore, a somewhat similar pattern occurred for the correlations between maternal contact and infant irritability for the 3-month observation. . . . A statistically significant difference was obtained . . . in a test comparing the difference between the female and male correlations for the 3-month observation. In other words maternal contact and irritability positively covaried for females at both ages; whereas for males, there was no relationship at 3 weeks, and by 3 months the mothers tended to spend less time with the more irritable male babies. It should be emphasized that these correlations reflect within group patterns, and that when we combine the female and male samples positive correlations still emerge for both ages. . . . That is, in terms of the total sample, the patterning of the males scores is still consistent with a positive relationship between irritability and maternal contact.

From these findings it is difficult to posit a causal relationship. However, it seems most plausible that it is the infant's cry that is determining the maternal behavior. Mothers describe the cry as a signal that the infant needs attention and they often report their nurturant actions in response to the cry. Furthermore, the cry is a noxious and often painful stimulus that probably has biological utility for the infant, propelling the mother into action for her own comfort as well as out of concern for the infant. Ethological reports confirm the proposition that the cry functions as a "releaser" of maternal behavior (Bowlby, 1958; Hinde, et al., 1964; Hoffman, et al., 1966). Bowlby (1958) states:

It is my belief that both of them (crying and smiling), act as social releasers of instinctual responses in mothers. As regards crying, there is plentiful evidence from the animal world that this is so: probably in all cases the mother responds promptly and unfailingly to her infant's bleat, call or cry. It seems to me clear that similar impulses are also evoked in the human mother. . . .

Thus, we are adopting the hypothesis that the correlations we have obtained reflect a causal sequence whereby the cry acts to instigate maternal intervention. Certainly there are other important determinants of maternal contact, . . . yet it seems that the effect of the cry is sufficient to account at least partially for the structure of the mother-infant relationship. We further maintain the thesis that the infant's cry shapes maternal behavior even for the instance where [a] negative correlation was noted at 3 months for the males. The effect is still present, but in this case the more irritable infants were responded to *less* by the mothers. Our speculation for explaining this relationship and the fact that, conversely, a positive correlation was obtained for the female infants is that the mothers probably were negatively reinforced for responding to a number of the boys but tended to be positively reinforced for their responses toward the girls. That is, mothers of the more irritable boys may have learned that they could not be successful in quieting boys whereas the girls were more uniformly responsive (quieted by) to maternal handling. There is not much present in our data to bear out this contention, with the exception that the males were significantly more irritable than the girls for both observations. However, evidence that suggests males are more subject to inconsolable states comes from studies (Serr & Ismajovich, 1963; McDonald, Gynther, & Christakos, 1963; Stechler, 1964) which indicate that males have less well organized physiological reactions and are more vulnerable to adverse conditions than females. The relatively more efficient functioning of the female organism should thus contribute to their responding more favorably to maternal intervention.

In summary, we propose that maternal behavior initially tends to be under the control of the stimulus and reinforcing conditions provided by the young infant. As the infant gets older, the mother . . . gradually acquires reinforcement value which in turn increases her efficacy in regulating infant behaviors. Concurrently, the earlier control asserted by the infant becomes less functional and diminishes. In a sense, the point where the infant's control over the mother declines and the mother's reinforcement value emerges could be regarded as the first manifestation of socialization . . . Thus, at first the mother is shaped by the infant and this later facilitates her shaping the behavior of the infant. . . . According to this reasoning, the more irritable infants (who can be soothed) whose mothers respond in a contingent manner to their signals should become most amenable to the effects of social reinforcement and manifest a higher degree of attachment behavior. The fact that the mothers responded more contingently toward the female infants should maximize the ease with which females learn social responses.

This statement is consistent with data on older children which indicate that girls learn social responses earlier and with greater facility than boys (Becker, 1964). Previously we argued that the mothers learned to be more contingent toward the girls because they probably were more responsive to maternal intervention. An alternative explanation is that mothers respond contingently to the girls and not to the boys as a form of differential reinforcement, whereby, in keeping with cultural expectations, the mother is initiating a pattern that contributes to males being more aggressive or assertive, and less responsive to socialization. Indeed, these two explanations are not inconsistent with one another since the mother who is unable to soothe an upset male infant may eventually come to classify this intractable irritability as an expression of "maleness."

The discussion to this point has focused on some of the conditions that seemingly affect the structure of the mother-infant relationship and influence the reinforcement and stimulus values associated with the mother. Next we would like to consider. . . one particular class of maternal behaviors that has important reinforcing properties for the infant. This discussion will be more general and depart from a direct consideration of the data. There has been mounting evidence in the psychological literature that the organism has a "need for stimulation" and that variations in the quantity and quality of stimulation received can have a significant effect on many aspects of development (Moss, 1965; Murphy, et al., 1962; White & Held, 1963). Additional reports indicate that, not only does the infant require stimulation, but that excessive or chaotic dosages of stimulation can be highly disruptive of normal functioning (Murphy, et al., 1962). Furthermore, there appear to be substantial individual differences in the stimulation that is needed or in the extremes that can be tolerated. As the infant gets older he becomes somewhat capable of regulating the stimulation that is assimilated. However, the very young infant is completely dependent on the caretaking environment to provide and modulate the stimulation he experiences. It is in this regard that the mother has a vital role.

The main points emphasized in the literature are that stimulation serves to modulate the state or arousal level of the infant, organize and direct attentional processes, and facilitate normal growth and development. Bridger (1965) has shown that stimulation tends to have either an arousing or quieting effect, depending on the existing state of the infant. Infants who are quiet tend to be aroused, whereas aroused infants tend to be quieted by moderate stimulation.

Not all levels of stimulation are equally effective in producing a condition whereby the infant is optimally alert and attentive. Excessive stimulation has a disruptive effect and according to drive reduction theorists the organism behaves in ways aimed at reducing stimulation that exceeds certain limits. Leuba (1955), in an attempt to establish rapprochement between the drive reduction view and the research evidence that shows that there is a need for stimulation, states that there is an optimal level of stimulation that is required, and that the organism acts either to reduce or to increase stimulation so as to stay within this optimal range.

The mother is necessarily highly instrumental in mediating much of the stimulation that is experienced by the infant. Her very presence in moving about and caring for the infant provides a constant source of visual, auditory, tactile, kinesthetic and proprioceptive stimulation. In addition to the incidental stimulation she provides, the mother deliberately uses stimulation to regulate the arousal level or state of the infant and to evoke specific responses from him. However, once the infant learns, through conditioning, that the mother is a source of stimulation he can in turn employ existing responses that are instrumental in eliciting stimulation from her. Certain infant behaviors, such as the cry, are so compelling that they readily evoke many forms of stimulation from the mother. It is common knowledge that mothers in attempting to quiet upset infants, often resort to such tactics as using rocking motion, waving bright objects or rattles, or holding the infant close and thus providing warmth and physical contact. The specific function of stimulation in placating the crying infant can be somewhat obscured because of the possibility of confounding conditions. In our discussion so far we have indicated that stimulation inherently has a quieting effect irrespective of learning but that crying also can become a learned instrumental behavior which terminates once the reinforcement of stimulation is presented. However, it is often difficult to distinguish the unlearned from the learned patterns of functioning, since the infant behavior (crying) and the outcome (quieting) are highly similar in both instances. Perhaps the best means for determining whether learning has occurred would be if we could demonstrate that the infant makes anticipatory responses, such as the reduction in crying behavior to cues, prior to the actual occurrence of stimulation. In addition to the cry, the smile and the vocalization of the infant can become highly effective, and consequently well-learned conditioned responses for evoking stimulation from adult caretakers. Rheingold (1956) has shown that when institutional children are given more caretaking by an adult they show an increase in their smiling rate to that caretaker as well as to other adults. Moreover, for a few weeks after the intensive caretaking stopped there were further substantial increments in the smiling rate, which suggests that the infant after experiencing relative deprivation worked harder in attempting to restitute the stimulation level experienced earlier.

It seems plausible that much of the early social behavior seen in infants and children consists of attempts to elicit responses from others. We mentioned earlier that it has been stressed in recent psychological literature that individuals have a basic need for stimulation. Since the mother, and eventually others, are highly instrumental in providing and monitoring the stimulation that is experienced by the infant, it seems likely that the child acquires expectancies for having this need satisfied through social interactions and that stimulation comes to serve as a basis for relating to others. Indeed, Schaffer and Emerson (1964) have shown that the amount of stimulation provided by adults is one of the major determinants of infants' attachment behavior. Strange as well as familiar adults who have been temporarily separated from an infant often attempt to gain rapport with the infant through acts of stimulation. . . .

The learning we have discussed is largely social since the infant is dependent on others, particularly the mother, for reinforcements. This dependency on others is what constitutes attachment behavior, and the specific makeup of the attachment is determined by the class of reinforcements that are involved. The strength of these learned attachment behaviors is maximized through stimulation, since the mother is often the embodiment of this reinforcement as well as the agent for delivering it. The social aspect of this learning is further enhanced because of the reciprocal dependence of the mother on the infant for reinforcement. That is, the mother learns certain conditioned responses, often involving acts of stimulation, that are aimed at evoking desired states or responses from the infant.

In conclusion, what we did was study and analyze some of the factors which structure the mother-infant relationship. A central point is that the state of the infant affects the quantity and quality of maternal behavior, and this in turn would seem to influence the course of future social learning. Furthermore, through controlling for the state of the infant, we were able to demonstrate the effects of pre-parental attitudes on one aspect of maternal behavior, namely, the mother's responsiveness toward her infant. Many investigators, in conducting controlled laboratory studies, have stressed that the state of the infant is crucial in determining the nature of his responses to different stimuli. This concern is certainly highly relevant to our data, collected under naturalistic conditions.

REFERENCES

Becker, W. C. Consequences of different kinds of parental discipline. In M. L. Hoffman & L. W. Hoffman (Eds.), *Review of child development research*. Vol. 1. New York: Russell Sage Foundation, 1964. Pp. 169–208.

Bloom, B. S. *Stability and change in human characteristics.* New York: Wiley, 1964.

Bowlby, J. The nature of a child's tie to his mother. *International Journal of Psycho-analysis*, 1958, **39**, 350–373.

Bridger, W. H. Psychophysiological measurement of the roles of state in the human neonate. Paper presented at the meeting of the Society for Research in Child Development, Minneapolis, April 1965.

Brown, J. L. States in newborn infants. *Merrill-Palmer Quarterly*, 1964, **10**, 313–327.

Escalona, S. K. The study of individual differences and the problem of state. *Journal of Child Psychiatry*, 1962, **1**, 11–37.

Hess, E. H. Imprinting. *Science*, 1959, **130**, 133–141.

Hinde, R. A., Rowell, T. E., & Spencer-Booth, Y. Behavior of living rhesus monkeys in their first six months. *Proceedings of the Zoological Society, London*, 1964, **143**, 609–649.

Hoffman, H. S., Schiff, D., Adams, J., & Searle, J. L. Enhanced distress vocalization through selective reinforcement. *Science*, 1966, **151**, 352–354.

Leuba, C. Toward some integration of learning theories: The concept of optimal stimulation. *Psychological Reports*, 1955, **1**, 27–33.

Levy, D. M. *Behavioral analysis.* Springfield, Ill.: Charles C Thomas, 1958.

McDonald, R. L., Gynther, M. D., & Christakos, A. C. Relation between maternal anxiety and obstetric complications. *Psychosomatic Medicine*, 1963, **25**, 357–363.

Moss, H. A. Coping behavior, the need for stimulation, and normal development. *Merrill-Palmer Quarterly*, 1965, **11**, 171–179.

Murphy, L. B. *The widening world of childhood: Paths toward mastery.* New York: Basic Books, 1962.

Rheingold, H. L. The modification of social responsiveness in institutional babies. *Monographs of the Society for Research in Child Development*, 1956, **21**(2, Serial No. 63).

Schaffer, H. R., & Emerson, P. E. The development of social attachments in infancy. *Monographs of the Society for Research in Child Development*, 1964, **29**(3, Serial No. 94).

Serr, D. M., & Ismajovich, B. Determination of the primary sex ratio from human abortions. *American Journal of Obstetrics and Gynecology*, 1963, **87**, 63–65.

Stechler, G. A longitudinal follow-up of neonatal apnea. *Child Development*, 1964, **35**, 333–348.

White, B. L., & Held, R. Plasticity in perceptual development during the first six months of life. Paper presented at the meeting of the American Association for the Advancement of Science, Cleveland, December 1963.

Wolff, P. H. Observations on newborn infants. *Psychosomatic Medicine*, 1959, **21**, 110–118.

RESEARCH IN DIMENSIONS OF EARLY MATERNAL CARE[1]

Leon J. Yarrow

For some time, research and theory have been preoccupied with the significance of experiences during early infancy and their effects on intellectual and personality development. Although unanimity is far from complete on the *extent* or the *persistence* of the effects of early experiences, there is an overwhelming theoretical consensus that the most significant influence in the early environment is the infant's relationship with its mother. The conclusions regarding the role of maternal influences have been very general; often limited to assertions about the harmful effects of trauma—separation, deprivation—or the positive effects of "good" maternal care. On the whole, surprisingly little research attention has been given to analysis of specific interactional variables occurring during the earliest months of life.

The early environment of the infant has usually been examined in terms of a limited number of variables of maternal care. Most often, the environmental conditions studied have been severely traumatic events; the environment has frequently been characterized simply in terms of a restricted number of child-rearing practices, such as methods of feeding, weaning and toilet training. The variations in the mother's handling of these practices have most often been analyzed on a few standard dimensions, such as rigidity or flexibility, harshness or gradualness. The choice of variables seems to have been dictated by theories derived from retrospective evidence rather than by direct study of mother-infant interaction. During the earliest period of life—theoretically the most impressionable—many of the standard child-rearing variables clearly are not applicable. Many dimensions of the infant's early environment are of much greater significance than weaning or toilet training.

[1] The data discussed in this paper are part of the findings of a longitudinal study of the personality development of adopted children. This research has been supported by the National Institute of Mental Health, USPHS Grant 3M-9077. We are indebted to the six social agencies which cooperated in the project: Family and Child Services of Washington, D.C.; Jewish Social Service Agency; Alexandria (Virginia), Department of Public Welfare; District of Columbia, Department of Public Welfare; Fairfax County (Virginia), Department of Public Welfare; Family Service of Montgomery County, Maryland. We are grateful to Mr. John Theban, Executive Director of Family and Child Services, who assumed administrative responsibility for the project.

I wish particularly to acknowledge the valuable contributions of Mrs. Marion S. Goodwin in the data collection and in the development of the codes for the analysis of the family environment. I am grateful to Mrs. Hadassah Davis for her work on coding and analysis of these data.

From L. J. Yarrow. Research in dimensions of early maternal care. Merrill-Palmer Quarterly, 1963, 9, 101–114. (With permission of the author and the Merrill-Palmer Institute.)

In this report, I will raise some questions about the choice of variables for the study of the early environment, and point up these issues with data based on analyses, as yet incomplete, of the relationship between specific dimensions of maternal care during early infancy, and the personal-social and intellectual characteristics of infants during the first six months.[2]

In choosing variables for study of the effective environment for the infant during the first six months, one fundamental consideration is the sensitivity of the infant. To what kinds of stimuli—in which modalities, and of what intensity—are infants sensitive and responsive? There are rather extreme differences in points-of-view on this question, ranging from the conviction that the young infant is aware of subtle shades of attitudes and feelings expressed by the mother, to the view that the young infant is a vegetable on whom there is little psychological impact during the first months. The adherents of the former viewpoint assume the existence of a subtle process of communication between mother and infant, and an esoteric sensitivity on the part of the infant. Data on infant learning are beginning to identify more precisely the kinds and levels of stimuli to which infants are responsive (Gewirtz, 1961; Rheingold, Gewirtz, & Ross, 1959), and recent studies with mothers and their newborn infants are beginning to elucidate this process of communication which has hitherto been in the realm of the mystical (Blauvelt & McKenna, 1961).

In developing categories for assessing the impact of the early environment on infant behavior, we were guided by consideration of infant sensitivities as well as by an empirical analysis of the basic functions and activities involved in "mothering." Selection of the maternal variables was influenced by a recent analysis of the concept of maternal deprivation (Yarrow, 1961), in which three major maternal functions were distinguished: the mother as (a) a source of social and sensory stimulation, (b) an agent of need-gratification, and (c) as mediator of environmental stimuli.

Finally, the variables chosen in this study were limited to simple and definable modes of mother-infant interaction which did not require elaborate assumptions about infant sensitivities or modes of communication.

On the basis of these considerations, the following classes of variables were selected for study: (a) those dealing with need-gratification and tension reduction, (b) those concerned with stimulation and conditions of learning, and (c) finally those involved in affectional-emotional interchange between mother and infant.

Within the category of need-gratification and tension-reduction, four variables were included: two dealing with the quantitative aspects of physical care—amount of physical contact,[3] speed of response to the infant's expressed needs[4]—and two dealing

---

[2] These data were obtained in the course of a longitudinal study of personality development in adopted children. This research has focused on the impact of a change in mother-figures during infancy, with specific concern with the critical period hypothesis in relation to maternal separation.

[3] The amount of physical contact was measured in terms of the amount of time during the day and the number of different situations in which the child was held by the mother.

[4] Speed of response was a simple measure of how quickly the mother responds to the child's expression of needs with appropriate need-reduction activities.

with the qualitative aspects of physical care—the degree of soothing,[5] and the degree of physical closeness and adaptation to the infant's rhythms.[6]

The second class of variables, dealing with stimulation and conditions of learning, includes such components of maternal care as the amount of stimulation, the extent to which stimulation was adapted to the child's developmental and individual capacities, and the extent to which the mother responded to the child's communications—vocalizations, physical activity—with rewarding behavior. The five variables in this group were achievement stimulation,[7] social stimulation,[8] communication or responsive interchange,[9] stimulus-adaptation,[10] and positive-affective expression.[11] Consistency[12] of the mother's behavior, which might be considered an index of the predictability of the environment for the infant, in a broad sense, belongs under learning conditions. But, since this variable deals with a different aspect of the environment than the amount and type of stimulation, it was not grouped with the other stimulation-learning variables.

The third class, affectional-emotional interchange, dealt with several aspects of interpersonal relationships: emotional involvement,[13] acceptance-rejection,[14] and degree of individualization of the infant.[15]

[5] Soothing was a measure of the extent to which the caretaker's response to the infant was effective in reducing tension.

[6] Physical closeness was a rating of the characteristic way in which the mother handled the child—the degree of closeness to her body, and the extent to which her manner of holding the child represented an adaptation to the child's characteristics and rhythms.

[7] Achievement stimulation—the amount of stimulation by the mother, oriented towards developmental progress, and the extent to which the environment provided the appropriate materials.

[8] Social stimulation—amount of stimulation oriented to eliciting social responses, amount of time spent in social interaction with the child.

[9] Communication stimulation—responsive interchange—the extent to which the infant's attempts to express his needs, by vocalizations or physical activity, are encouraged and facilitated by the mother.

[10] Stimulus-adaptation was rated in terms of the extent to which materials and experiences given to the infant were adapted to his individual capacities.

[11] Positive-affective expression—the frequency and intensity of expression of positive feelings by the mother, father and others in the environment.

[12] Consistency—two aspects of response to the infant were distinguished: spontaneous consistency, and consistency in response to the infant. Predictability of the environment was analyzed in terms of the timing of events in the child's daily life, as well as in terms of the consistency of behavior patterns, *e.g.*, whether the mother always picked up the baby when she passed him in his crib, or whether the father invariably chucked him under the chin when he cooed.

[13] Emotional involvement—the extent to which the mother was identified with the child. This identification expressed through warmth, sensitivity and individualization, and intensity of involvement in the child's future.

[14] Acceptance-rejection—the extent to which the child's characteristics, abilities and disabilities, and natural background are accepted without question.

[15] Individualization—the extent to which the mother shows awareness of the unique characteristics and sensitivities of the child, and adapts her behavior towards the child to his individual characteristics.

In addition to these major categories of maternal care, each home was rated on another dimension thought to be of significance for the issue of "single vs. multiple" mothering—the exclusiveness of maternal care. This represented a simple rating of the extent to which the child was cared for predominantly by one person—the mother—or shared by grandmother, older daughters, the father, helpers, or neighbors.

The dependent variables were infant "personality" characteristics and developmental functions assessed at six months of age.[16] Although a large number of infant characteristics were studied as part of the larger longitudinal study of maternal separation, this report shall consider only a selected number, which deal with the infant's social behavior, handling of objects—exploratory and manipulative behavior—capacity to cope with frustration and stress, adaptability to environmental change, and capacity to respond selectively to environmental stimulation.

These data come from observations of infants in interaction with mothers and from interviews with the mothers. Children who remained only in one home during the first six months of life were included in this analysis. Of the 40 cases to be reported, 21 were direct placements in adoptive homes, 19 were in foster homes.

Several variables of maternal care are highly related to developmental progress, exploratory and manipulative behavior, social responsiveness, and effectiveness in coping with stress during infancy. Correlation coefficients showing relationships between some selected variables of maternal care and some aspects of infant functioning during the first six months are presented in Table 1.

The environmental variables which show consistently high relationships with many aspects of infant behavior are stimulus-adaptation, achievement stimulation, social stimulation, communication, and positive-affective expression. Other variables show more selective relationships with specific infant characteristics. For example, the variables of affectional-emotional interchange—emotional involvement, acceptance-rejection, respect for individuality—are highly related to the infant's capacity to cope with stress, with correlations ranging from $+.57$ to $+.65$, but are less significantly related to developmental progress and exploratory and manipulative behavior (correlations range from $+.43$ to $+.55$). The variables grouped under need-gratification and tension-reduction—physical contact, soothing, immediacy of response—which refer primarily to physical care show an even more selective relationship, *i.e.,* moderately high relationships with some variables and low relationships to others. For example, physical involvement shows a high relationship to handling stress $(r = +.66)$, and much lower relationship to IQ $(r = +.40)$.

Perhaps the most striking finding is the extent to which developmental progress during the first six months appears to be influenced by maternal stimulation. The amount of stimulation (achievement and social), and the quality of stimulation (stimulus-adaptation) are highly related to IQ (correlations range from $+.65$ to $+.72$). These data suggest that mothers who give much and intense stimulation and encouragement to practice developmental skills tend to be successful in producing infants who make

---

[16] These were based on ratings derived from observations of the infants in developmental test situations, in structured social interaction situations, and interviews with the mothers.

TABLE 1 Relationship between maternal care during first six months and infant characteristics at six months

Maternal variable	Infant characteristic					
	IQ	Hand-ling stress	Exploratory manipula-tive behavior	Social initi-ative	Auton-omy	Adapt-ability
A. Need-gratification and tension-reduction						
Physical contact	+.57	+.53	+.48	+.50	−.15	+.17
Soothing	+.36	+.57	+.45	+.45	−.17	−.08
Immediacy of response	+.24	+.37	+.33	+.41	−.39	+.17
Physical involvement	+.40	+.66	+.48	+.08	−.31	—
B. Stimulation-learning conditions						
Achievement stimulation	+.72	+.53	+.54	+.23	−.15	+.08
Social stimulation	+.65	+.51	+.45	+.37	−.06	—
Positive-affective expression	+.55	+.55	+.38	+.53	−.18	+.01
Communication	+.59	+.64	+.51	+.39	−.17	—
Stimulus-adaptation	+.69	+.85	+.65	+.56	−.24	+.16
C. Affectional interchange						
Individualization	+.55	+.62	+.46	+.51	−.09	−.13
Emotional involvement	+.55	+.65	+.53	+.47	−.16	—
Acceptance-rejection	+.43	+.57	+.40	+.44	−.18	−.18
D. Consistency	+.19	+.17	+.14	+.005	−.16	−.02
E. Exclusiveness of mothering	+.11	+.17	+.12	+.19	−.07	−.08

r of .39 significant at 1 percent level.

rapid developmental progress. The high relationship between stimulus-adaptation and IQ ($r = +.69$) suggests that it is not simply the amount of stimulation, *per se,* that influences developmental progress but the appropriateness of the stimulation to the child's individual and developmental characteristics.

These data would tend to reinforce the conclusions from studies on institutional care that stimulus deprivation in early infancy is an etiological factor in developmental retardation. The most impressive aspects of the institutional environment are the low level of stimulation toward achievement, and the lack of individualized care. The findings on stimulus-adaptation would suggest that the lack of individualized stimulation might be as significant in the etiology of the institutional syndrome as sheer stimulus deprivation.

Another aspect of infant behavior which is significantly affected by maternal behavior is the infant's response to stress. Highly related to the infant's capacity to maintain equilibrium and avoid disorganization under stress is the quality of relationship with the mother, as reflected in the following variables: emotional involvement, physical involvement, sensitivity, adaptation to the individuality of the infant, and acceptance.

The differential effects of maternal care on infant behavior are seen more clearly when we consider the three broad categories of maternal care in relation to IQ and capacity to handle stress. There is a high relationship between IQ and the variables measuring stimulation and learning conditions; and a positive but lower relationship to IQ of the variables concerned with need-gratification ($r = +.39$) and affectional interchange. On the other hand, both need-gratification and affectional interchange are highly related to the infant's capacity to handle stress. These data lend some support to the hypothesis that the development of security and trust derived from a close and satisfying relationship with the mother in infancy strengthens the capacity to cope effectively with frustration and stress situations. They also suggest that the capacity to handle stress, at least in infancy, is not strengthened by frustration. Infants who are gratified much of the time and who experience tension infrequently tend to be more capable in handling stress than infants who are subjected to large doses of frustration.

One might expect that the amount of social stimulation would be the most significant environmental factor in the development of social responsiveness in infancy. Contrary to expectations, we found a low-positive relationship ($r = +.37$) between social stimulation and social initiative—a measure of the child's freedom in initiating social interaction—and an even lower relationship with social responsiveness ($r = +.25$). More highly related to social initiative than the amount of direct social stimulation given by the mother is the level of positive emotional expression ($r = +.53$). These findings suggest that infants who, during their first six months, are in an environment characterized by frequent and exuberant expressions of positive feelings, tend to develop a high degree of social initiative. It would appear that direct efforts to elicit social response are not as effective in developing outgoing social behavior as an atmosphere charged with a high level of positive-affect.

We tend to think of consistency as an highly important attribute of maternal behavior on the assumption that consistency in the mother's behavior is associated with the infant's perception of a stable, ordered, and predictable environment. We found, however, generally low-positive relationships between maternal consistency and such aspects of infant behavior as developmental progress, social initiative, and the capacity to handle stress. One might speculate that there may be a minimal level of consistency necessary in order for the infant to be able to relate, with some degree of integration, to his environment. After this minimal level of consistency is reached, other factors, such as the quality of contact, become more significant. A complete and monotonous predictability from day to day may not be a desirable characteristic of the environment for young infants.

The category, exclusiveness of mothering (a measure of the degree to which care was concentrated in one mother figure) was not significantly related to any aspect of infant behavior; a finding which suggests that this variable in itself may not be important during the first six months. However, since the range of scores was limited, one cannot draw any firm conclusion about the significance of this particular variable.

Several infant personality characteristics seem to be clearly unrelated to environmental influences. Autonomy and adaptability show consistently low-positive, or negative relationships with all of the environmental variables. Autonomy is a measure of the degree of selectivity in response to environmental stimuli and the degree of resistance to environmental coercion. Adaptability reflects the infant's capacity to handle change of various kinds, for example, routines, scheduling or new situations. Perhaps the lack of relationship between these variables and environmental variables is an indication that these are basic response predispositions which have constitutional determinants.

These data, based on an early stage of analysis, are presented mainly to indicate the value of analyzing the early environment in terms of discrete variables rather than broadly defined child-rearing practices, where the specific stimuli operating on the infant are not clear. We have ignored the question of how the mother's personality and her motives influence the infant's characteristics and development. It remains an interesting theoretical question whether, in analyzing determinants of infant behavior, it is sufficient to specify the measurable characteristics of maternal stimulation, such as intensity and quality, or whether it is necessary to specify the underlying bases for the mother's choice of her behavior patterns.

We are faced with an even more difficult and complex level of analysis when we move from the stimulus-response level to an interactional framework. Although these data point to significant relationships between selected aspects of maternal care and the infant's behavior and personality characteristics, it is a gross oversimplification to interpret them simply in terms of antecedent-consequent relationships. Although the transactional viewpoint, with its emphasis on the mother-child interaction, enjoys a certain popularity, the tendency is strong to look at maternal stimulation solely in terms of the mother's impact on the child. This is especially so when we are dealing with maternal attitudes on self-evaluation questionnaires. We tend to look at the mother's behavior and her practices in a hypothetical vacuum, in a psychological field in which no infant or child exists. Some of the limitations in this approach were brought out sharply in the course of study of foster mothers at two different points in time.

After studying a foster mother, and analyzing the types of stimulation she provided in her relationship with one infant, we assumed we had the significant dimensions of her interactions with infants well characterized. Several months later when another infant was placed in this foster home, the environment of this infant was assessed on the same variables of maternal care that had been used with the first infant. We were impressed by the significant differences in the environments of these two infants.

The first infant, a girl, was given much physical contact and handled with great warmth. The mother showed a high degree of sensitivity to the child's individualized character-istics and needs. She had a basically positive attitude toward this child's idiosyncratic attributes. The infant was valued as a child who knew what she wanted and insisted on getting it. The foster mother was very protective toward the infant and attempted to shield her as much as possible from normal frustrations in the environment. The second child, a month-old boy, was placed in the same home a few months after the girl had left for an adoptive home. He was a tense, irritable, demanding infant. The foster mother consistently expressed negative feelings about him. In contrast to her flexibility in scheduling with the first infant, she arranged the child's feeding on the basis of her own convenience. The child's crying was often ignored; long delays in responding to him were characteristic. He was held very little and high levels of tension were allowed to build up. In this environment, the infant continued to become more irritable and demanding. The basis for a very disturbed mother-infant relationship had been established.

Although we had been alerted to the possibility of the existence of different inter-personal relationships between the same foster mother and different infants at different points in time, we were even more impressed at a later time when we studied two infants of the same age and sex in a foster home at the same time. Not only was the basic character of relationship with the foster mother different for these two infants, but the physical environment differed. Although the gross physical environment was the same, these two infants, in reality, were exposed to different kinds and intensities of physical stimulation.

The one infant, Jack, was, from early infancy, a passive baby, with a low activity level and a generally low level of responsiveness to environmental stimuli. He usually accepted environmental frustrations without overt protest. He tended to wait quietly if he was not fed immediately when hungry. Even at three months, much of his day was spent in sleeping. He was not much interested in food, ate without much zest. By three months, he could be encouraged to respond socially with a smile or a mild increase in activity, but only after very strong stimulation. At five months he still showed no initiative in social interaction. He did not reach out toward people or make approach responses. He enjoyed his thumb, and when awake spent much of his time in a state of passive contentment, sucking his fingers or thumb.

In marked contrast to Jack, George was a vigorously active infant. He ate with great zest and sucked on the bottle with exceptional vigor. By three months, he was showing much initiative in attempting to handle and master his environment. He actively went after objects, expressed his needs directly, was very forceful in demanding what he wanted, and persisted in his demands until he was satisfied. By six months, he was showing a high degree of persistence in problem situations. George was highly responsive to social stimulation and took the initiative in seeking social response from others.

On only one dimension of the maternal rating scale—routine physical care—was the home environment comparable for these two infants. To some extent, there may have been differences even in this aspect of the environment, inasmuch as George's greater forcefulness in making his needs known probably resulted in more immediate response. On most other dimensions, the environment was markedly different for these two infants. George received a great deal of physical stimulation, not only from the foster mother, but from all members of the foster family. He was very much a part of this family; they related to him as a family member. He was held and played with a great deal by the foster mother, the foster father, and all the children.

On all aspects of physical contact, social stimulation, and relatedness to the family, Jack's environment was markedly different. He spent much of his time lying on the floor of the playpen. The playpen was in an isolated corner of the dining room, outside of the main stream of family traffic. The life of the family tended to flow on past him.

He demanded very little and received very little stimulation. This pattern of isolation and stimulus deprivation started very early. Even at seven weeks, the foster mother referred to him as "the other one," and talked about him as the "poor little thing." By three months, the foster mother came around to verbalizing basic feelings of rejection toward this infant. Her evaluations of him were consistently negative. It seemed as if he possessed no characteristics which were seen as desirable. He slept too much; he was not interested in anything. The one positive [characteristic] was that he had a nice smile—*when* he smiled. Whereas, she spontaneously made many projections about George's future development, there was little investment in Jack's future. With regard to the quality of physical contact, the foster mother reported how the members of the family fought for the privilege of holding George for his feedings because they enjoyed his "cuddly" qualities. On the other hand, they were all reluctant to take care of Jack for his feedings because of his restlessness and apparent discomfort in being held. As a result, his bottle was often propped.

These are only a few of the dimensions on which the environment of these children differed significantly. If one had rated this mother solely in terms of her responses on a questionnaire or in an interview about attitudes towards infants, one would have little understanding of the significant aspects of the environment of these two infants.

Although we can point to some fairly direct relationships between some aspects of the maternal environment and infant characteristics, it has become increasingly clear that we must also take into account what the infant imposes on his environment. There is a complex interactive relationship between the mother's behavior towards the infant and the infant's basic response patterns, predispositions, and individual sensitivities and vulnerabilities. These case examples certainly emphasize the difficulty in specifying antecedent conditions. It is difficult to establish the point of the beginning of the circle.

The previous analysis of the early infant environment indicates that variations in patterns of maternal care within the normal range are reflected in the behavior and development of infants during the first six months of life. However, these relationships are neither simple nor direct, even in normal situations. In studying the effects of traumatic events in infancy, the difficulties in establishing clear-cut relationships are even greater. Some case data from our research on maternal separation point up some of these complex issues.

Much of the literature on maternal separation has dealt with rather complicated conditions preceding, concurrent with, or consequent to separation, such as death or illness of a parent, extreme neglect or rejection, illness or hospitalization of the child. In this research, we are concerned with a relatively pure separation situation involving a change in mother-figures in infancy. Our major research questions derive from the critical period concept, *i.e.,* whether there are critical developmental periods during or after which a change in mother-figures is most traumatic. One hypothesis based on a broader intepretation of the critical period concept is that the degree of vulnerability and the effects of a separation experience will vary at different developmental periods. This hypothesis assumes that some vulnerability to separation may be present throughout infancy, but the functions affected by separation will vary with the characteristics of the developmental stage, *e.g.,* separation before object relationships are formed would have a different impact than if it occurred during the height of stranger anxiety.

The subjects of this analysis were 96 children, who were studied during infancy and early childhood. All were placed in adoptive homes during infancy. The control group consisted of 21 infants who did not experience a change in mothers during infancy. They went into adoptive homes immediately after leaving the hospital, usually at six days. The experimental group consisted of 75 children who experienced separation during infancy. For analysis, they were divided into eight groups according to age at time of separation, which ranged from 6 weeks to 12 months. All the infants in the separation groups were studied before the separation experience to provide a baseline from which to measure the immediate reactions to this experience.

Analyses of the reactions of these infants immediately after a change in mother-figures suggest that this is an event which can be considered traumatic; it is associated with immediate disturbances in behavior, such as blunted social responsiveness, excessive clinging to the mother, excessive crying, unusual apathy, disturbances in adaptation to routines, sleep, and feeding, and developmental regression, *e.g.,* a drop in IQ or loss of abilities previously present.

With regard to the question of critical period, the analysis shows that the severity and pervasiveness of disturbance increases with increasing age. A few infants show disturbance as early as three months; 86 percent of the infants who experienced a change in mothers at six months of age showed definite disturbances in behavior. Every one of the children placed at or after seven months reacted with marked disturbance.

Analyses are not yet complete on the long-term effects on personality development. We are now analyzing data on these children at five years of age, relating personality characteristics to a number of independent variables: age of separation, characteristics of the early maternal environment, depth of relationship with the mother prior to separation, infant characteristics and sensitivities, and the infant's experiences and relationship in the adoptive homes. Some of the difficulties in arriving at simple conclusions regarding direct relationships between a specific traumatic event and later personality development and adaptation are illustrated by two cases, where the break in a close relationship with a foster mother resulted in severely traumatic experiences.

Ray was devoted to his foster mother, and had established a positive relationship with the entire family. He was the first foster child in this home, and everyone from the foster father to the ten-year-old daughter lavished affection on him. When he was eight months old, Ray left this family and went into an adoptive home. The first child placed in this adoptive home, three years earlier, was part of the research sample. She was a pretty and easy-going infant, who apparently fulfilled her adoptive mother's fantasies about what a proper baby girl should be. She thrived in the home.

Ray, on the other hand, at eight months was a large and husky boy who was very different from the adoptive mother's concept of a sweet and helpless infant. He did not arouse in her the warm maternal feelings which Sally had aroused. She had difficulty in relating to him, and he in turn was not only very disturbed by the break in the close relationship with his foster mother but reacted to the separation and the new situation with disturbance in a great variety of functions. The area of greatest disturbance was in his ability to relate to the new mother. He literally withdrew from her touch, ignored her when she spoke to him and seemed, in effect, to be denying her existence. This behavior on his part had the effect of reinforcing her own difficulty in relating to him. This initial rejection and counter-rejection set the pattern for the subsequent relationship between this mother and child. At five years of age, this boy is still in constant conflict with the mother. He is a hyperaggressive child, destructive of property, with marked accident proneness and some psychosomatic disturbance. In this case, reactions to separation cannot be clearly differentiated from the effects of subsequent maternal rejection.

Our second case, Barbara, for whom separation was equally traumatic, showed a very different course of development. This girl, too, had a close and intimate relationship with the foster mother, followed by an initially rejecting experience in the adoptive home. The adoptive mother was much more restrained than the foster mother in expressing affection. She was quite firm in her expectations that the child should fit in with the demands of the new household. Barbara reacted with initial withdrawal and some loss in developmental functions. She maintained some distance from the adoptive mother initially, although her reserve was never so extreme as the rejection that Ray had shown toward his adoptive mother. In other respects, she accepted the demands of the new environment well, being neither hostilely resistant nor passively compliant. After a few months, Barbara quietly began to assert her own individuality and began to manage capably to handle the people in her environment, including the mother. She gradually won over the adoptive mother, who, by the time Barbara was three, began to identify with her, pointing out the basic similarities in temperament, *e.g.*, in their stubbornness, which she characterized as firmness in imposing their wills on the environment. At five, Barbara is a socially competent, extremely poised girl who relates very well to adults and children. On our ratings of ego variables, she is characterized as a child who is able to handle capably most difficulties posed by her environment. She has a very positive self-image, shows excellent reality orientation and adequate impulse control.

These cases suggest that the effects of an early potentially traumatic experience may be influenced by constitutional factors as well as by experiences preceding and subsequent to the potentially traumatic event. The infant behavior data on Barbara indicates that the "ego strength" she shows at five years may have constitutional bases. Her basically good capacity for withstanding stress and coping with her environment in infancy undoubtedly was strengthened by excellent mothering in the early infancy period. With this combination of constitutional strength and an early supporting environment, she was able to handle constructively a potentially traumatic experience.

The findings on the relationship between experiences in infancy and infant behavior reinforce our convictions about the importance of early experiences. These data indicate that variables of maternal care and the loss of a mother-figure do have an immediate impact on the infant. The extent to which these variables influence later personality development is not known. Clearly, it is not meaningful to formulate research questions in terms of the persisting effects over a long period of time of a single environmental variable or traumatic event.

Much research is needed to clarify the components of early maternal care and of traumatic experiences to determine the immediate effects on infants and young children of varied kinds of stimulation, deprivation, or trauma. After these relationships are clarified, further research might then concentrate on the role of later events in reinforcing, ameliorating, or reversing such effects, and on the identification of individual characteristics which may mitigate or aggravate the impact of later experiences.

REFERENCES

Blauvelt, H., & McKenna, J. Mother-neonate interaction: Capacity of the human newborn for orientation. In B. M. Foss (Ed.), *Determinants of infant behavior.* New York: Wiley, 1961. Pp. 3–29.

Brody, S. *Patterns of mothering: Maternal influence during infancy.* New York: International Universities Press, 1956.

Gewirtz, J. L. A learning analysis of the effects of normal stimulation, privation and deprivation on the acquisition of social motivation and attachment. In B. M. Foss (Ed.), *Determinants of infant behavior.* New York: Wiley, 1961. Pp. 213–290.

Orlansky, H. Infant care and personality. *Psychological Bulletin,* 1949, **46**, 1–48.

Rapaport, D. The structure of psychoanalytic theory; A systematizing attempt. *Psychological Issues,* 1960, **2** (2), 1–158.

Rheingold, H. L., Gewirtz, J. L., & Ross, H. Social conditioning of vocalizations in the infant. *Journal of Comparative and Physiological Psychology*, 1959, **52**, 68–73.

Sears, R. R. *Survey of objective studies of psychoanalytic concepts, Bulletin 51.* New York: Social Science Research Council, 1943.

Sears, R. R., Maccoby, E. E., & Levin, H. *Patterns of child-rearing.* Evanston, Ill.: Harper & Row, 1957.

Sewell, W. H. Infant training and the personality of the child. *American Journal of Sociology,* 1952, **58**, 150–159.

Yarrow, L. J. Maternal deprivation: Toward an empirical and conceptual re-evaluation. *Psychological Bulletin,* 1961, **58**, 459–490.

II

PERCEPTION, ATTENTION, AND CURIOSITY

Wendell E. Jeffery

Perception, attention, and curiosity are, in some ways, inseparable aspects of the process of obtaining information from the environment. One does not perceive without attending or attend without curiosity. The importance of attention and curiosity with respect to perception was put quite dramatically by William James when he wrote almost eighty years ago: "Millions of items of the outward order are present to my senses which never properly enter into my experience. Why? Because they have no interest for me. *My experience is what I agree to attend to.*" His explicit implication of volition with attention, however, was undoubtedly detrimental to the acceptance of attention in the scientific approach to the study of behavior that subsequently became popular. Behaviorism sought to relate its concepts solely to external events. Motivation, in most instances, was identified with conditions such as thirst, hunger, or pain, which could be readily manipulated. Therefore, it was convenient and possible either to ignore or to deny any motivational concepts with a volitional flavor.

For much of the basic research on perception in either animals or adult human subjects, the need for the concepts of attention and curiosity is avoided by careful control of the experimental situation. In the case of animals, attention and curiosity are likely to be ensured by rather severe deprivation of food or water and by highly restricted stimulus conditions. In the older human subject, attention and curiosity are elicited and directed quite easily by instructions. However, as psychologists have tried to apply what has been learned at a basic level to a wider range of behaviors and to more generalized behavioral situations (e.g., children learning to read), the need for additional concepts has become obvious. By observing the development of behavior in more generalized situations, the effects of the interaction of variables like attention and curiosity with perception and learning can be seen and, thus, may gain researchers new insights into some of the more complex psychological processes.

PERCEPTION It has been fairly well established that most senses are functional at birth or shortly thereafter. There continues to be some question, however, about the degree of organization of the infant's perceptual world. Some researchers have suggested that perceptual organization comes only as the result of the infant's interaction with the environment (empiricism). Others assume that perceptual organization is innate and is therefore either present at birth or appears with subsequent maturation (nativism). Before pursuing this broader issue, research concerning some of the simpler aspects of perception will be presented.

Audition in infancy

In 1893 Preyer reported his observations of the auditory development of a child from birth to thirty-six months. Kidd & Kidd (1966) summarize this research as follows:

> He found the child "deaf" for the first three days but that such sounds as hand clapping were heard on the 4th. The child quieted upon hearing his father's voice and responded to whispering on the 11th and 12th days, blinked at the sound of a quiet voice on the 26th day, and showed fear of a loud voice on the 30th. During the 5th and 6th weeks the baby did not sleep if people walked or talked near him, and he showed a startle response to noises. During the 7th and 8th weeks he began to show pleasure at musical sounds such as the playing of a piano, and he attended to a watch's ticking during the 9th. He oriented his head toward a sound at 11 weeks, turned his head toward a sound

with the certainty of a reflex at 16 weeks, and enjoyed the sound he made when he himself crumpled paper during the 19th week. By the 11th month he responded to a whispered "shhh," and on the 319th day he distinguished between the sound of a spoon on a plate held by a hand and the sound when the plate was not held by hand. By the 15th month the child laughed at new sounds, and at the 16th held a watch to his ear to hear the ticking. At 30 months the baby covered his ear with his hand while a kettle of water boiled beside him and he noticed the decrease in sound. At 36 months the child was unable to name the notes "C," "D," and "E" despite teaching by his parents (p. 118).

This report should produce many questions for the reader. Setting aside for the moment that the research was done on only one child, what about the statement that the infant is deaf during the first three days of life? It is to be presumed that Preyer's child made no observable response to any auditory stimulation, but what response could the child be expected to make? Can he be expected to orient his head toward the stimulus, that is, to show auditory localization? Probably not during the first few days of life. For one thing, the child's head at that age is reflexly locked into a general postural adjustment called the "tonic neck reflex" and as a part of this general posture, he tends to keep his head more on one side than the other. There are data, however, indicating that the infant may show auditory localization through eye movements. Did Preyer fail to observe these? Did he also look at the so-called "aural-palpebral reflex," a reflex squinting of the eye to sound? The chances are he utilized only a startle response to indicate the perception of sound by the infant. When only this criterion is used, there is considerable variation in the age at which sound perception is first observed.

There is some reason for questioning the hearing of the neonate because at birth the middle ear contains a gelatinous fluid that might restrict the movement of the ossicles and could thus raise the auditory threshold. Differences in the rate of re-sorption of this fluid may well account for the individual differences that are observed in infant auditory sensitivity. Some investigators have insisted that the newborn must hear because experiments have demonstrated fetal motor responses to loud sounds. These responses, however, may be elicited by muscular contractions of the mother rather than by sound. That is, part of the mother's response to the sound may be an abdominal contraction that stimulates the fetus to move. On the other hand, infants born prematurely and studied a week or more after delivery, but several weeks before their normal term, have been shown to respond to sounds of relatively mild intensities. Thus there is strong evidence that the auditory system is capable of operation at least by the seventh to eighth month of gestational age.

Even when an infant shows a startle reaction to sound, this says very little about what he hears or how well the ear operates. Preyer's account notes that the child responded to whispers on the eleventh and twelfth days and showed fear of a loud voice by the thirtieth day. Did Preyer observe differences in perception or only the maturation of response systems? Such a question is the very heart of the nativism-empiricism issue, and an answer is not easy to obtain. In order to make more precise statements about auditory perception, techniques are required that do not depend upon or await development of motor capabilities of the infant.

Pavlovian conditioning would appear to be an obvious technique for testing auditory perceptions were it not for the fact that conditioned responses in neonates have proved, for the most part, to be too unstable for such testing. Papoušek (1967), however, has been able to show that three-month-old children can learn to discriminate between a bell and a buzzer. He has used a fairly elaborate procedure involving a combination of Pavlovian conditioning and instrumental learning in which he first reinforced an infant's head turning by pairing the sound of a bell with reinforcement (milk) every time the infant turned to the left. After this response was well established, another conditioned stimulus (buzzer) was added. The buzzer was paired with reinforcement for right head turning. Through this experimental procedure, Papoušek was able to train infants to turn their heads to the left for one auditory stimulus and to the right for the other.

With the recent advances in equipment for measuring electrophysiological activity, a number of investigators have attempted to utilize various physiological measures as indices of infant perception. Pavlov first identified a pattern of responses he called the "investigatory" or "what is it" reflex. Subsequently, he also used the term "orienting reflex," a term that Sokolov (1963) has made prominent through his research. This reflex, which might better be called a reaction than a reflex, includes responses of three general types: (1) There are responses of an overt nature that in general orient the senses for more adequate reception of the stimulus. In addition, ongoing activity is likely to cease and general muscle tonus rises; (2) There are a number of measurable changes that reflect activity of the autonomic nervous system. The pupils of the eyes dilate, palmar skin resistance is reduced, heart rate is altered, and blood vessels of the head dilate, whereas those in the limbs contract; and (3) There are changes in electroencephalogram (EEG) patterns that are typically identified with alerting. At the cerebral cortex, the primary change is from relatively low-frequency high-voltage activity to high-frequency low-voltage activity.

These responses are, in general, indications of arousal or alerting that have been identified with curiosity, but which Sokolov includes as an aspect of attention. Of particular importance is the fact that these responses are independent of the development of the gross skeletal musculature of the infant. Thus, it is not surprising to find considerable research with infants using various measures of the orienting reaction as an index of attention and perception.

Bridger (1961) utilized a measure of heart rate to study pitch perception in newborn infants. After establishing that there was an increase in heart rate when pure tones were presented to the infant, he continued to present a tone until cardiac acceleration

Pitch or auditory-frequency discrimination in a two-day-old infant. **FIGURE 1**
Tones were presented for forty seconds at half-second intervals. The heart-rate response is indicated by the level of heart rate reached during the first five seconds of stimulation. The trials indicate the number of consecutive stimulus applications necessary for complete habituation. Three additional trials were given after habituation occurred and before the switch to the novel stimulus. (After Bridger, 1961)

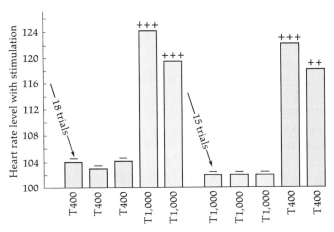

no longer occurred.[1] With no break in the procedure, he then presented a *new* tone of different frequency. Under such conditions the new tone would elicit an orienting reaction (heart-rate acceleration) if it were perceived as different from the tone to which the infant was habituated (see Figure 1). Bridger found one infant who was capable of distinguishing between 200 and 250 cycles per second although a few infants failed to show any habituation and therefore could not be tested. Nevertheless, the fact that heart-rate acceleration was observed indicates at least minimal ability to hear. Thus, the orienting reaction, and particularly habituation of the orienting reaction, shows considerable promise as a basis for measuring auditory thresholds and might be an equally useful technique to use in tests of visual perception.

Vision in infancy

The phenomena of vision are varied and complex. Studies of "visual acuity" range across such dimensions as brightness, color, movement, depth, form, and size. Fantz (1965) was one of the first in recent years to study form perception in infancy. He used a preference measure of attention. The infant was presented with two stimuli, and if he tended to look at one stimulus more than the other, regardless of its position, it was concluded that a difference between the stimuli was perceived. Fantz has found consistent preferences for patterned stimuli over unpatterned and for certain colors or brightness levels among unpatterned stimuli. Based upon an additional finding that vertical black and white stripes were preferred to a plain gray card of the same overall brightness, it became obvious to Fantz that by presenting a graded series of striped cards, he could test for visual acuity. This could be done by finding the finest stripes that could be differentiated from gray, i.e., would be preferred to gray.

Using this procedure, Fantz, Ordy, & Udelf (1962) found that at six months infants were able to see $\frac{1}{64}$-inch stripes at a distance of 15 inches. This is comparable to $\frac{20}{70}$ vision by the more familiar terms used in clinical testing. Newborns and infants of one week, however, showed much poorer acuity ($\frac{1}{8}$-inch stripes at 10 inches). Fantz concludes that the fact that infants do show preferences for relatively fine lines refutes the notion that the young infant is lacking in pattern vision and can see only vague masses of light and dark. He feels that although there may be

---

[1]Response decrements with repetition of stimulation are frequently referred to as "habituation."

continuous improvement in form perception with age, the evidence indicates that all parts of the visual system are functioning to some degree soon after birth. The response of the infant to the patterned stimulus in this study may be said to be innate, since neither visual learning nor motor maturation were necessary for preference discrimination to take place. This contrasts with the empiricist's view that pattern-form perception necessarily requires some experience with the environment.

Fantz's data should not be accepted uncritically inasmuch as differential responsiveness to patterns does not require the infant to perceive the total pattern or form, but only some part of it, or possibly only a brightness difference in some portion of the stimulus. For example, photographs of the eye movements of infants observing triangles do not indicate the kind of scanning that would be required for complete appreciation of the triangle's form. In addition, there is evidence that at ages less than one month, the infant's eye is unable to focus well on targets at distances other than approximately 8 inches. This does not mean that it is impossible to see patterns, but only that they are likely to appear somewhat fuzzy or out of focus except within a relatively narrow range. Other data indicate that in some situations, visual exploration is relatively unsystematic until five or six years of age.

Movement has been thought to be a particularly potent visual stimulus. Preyer, whose work on audition was discussed earlier, noted that an infant's eyes could follow slowly moving objects by about the third week. More recently, Haith (1966) has shown that infants are responsive to visual movement by at least the second day after birth. He used reduction in sucking rate on a pacifier as a measure of attention or responsiveness to a stimulus. The results of his study indicated that nonnutritive sucking was clearly suppressed by the movement of a visual stimulus (sequential illumination of a matrix of light bulbs).

Depth perception has received only limited attention in young infants. Gibson & Walk (1960) have devised a particularly effective way of testing depth perception in infants of several species. A so-called "visual cliff" was constructed by placing a pane of glass across two surfaces, one of which was immediately under the pane while the other surface was several feet below the glass (see Figure 1 on page 99). A wide plank was placed on top of the glass at the transition point between the two surfaces. An infant was placed on the plank and coaxed to cross the glass on the "deep" side. The reluctance of the infant to step onto the glass over the "deep" side was taken as an indication of the perception of depth. By the time infants are able to crawl there is little doubt that they can respond to depth. Inasmuch as an infant would have had considerable motor experience with his environment before he was able to crawl, this test could not answer the nativism issue for human infants. Gibson and Walk have investigated various depth cues separately and have shown, for example, that the "size" of the pattern used on the two surfaces in the visual-cliff situation as well as "motion parallax" (nearer objects moving across the field of vision more quickly than far away objects) act individually as depth-discrimination cues. The Walk (1966) monograph, reprinted at the end of this chapter, summarizes much of the research on the development of depth perception.

If an infant can perceive depth at such an early age, perhaps he is also able to recognize the absolute size of objects regardless of their distance from him. This visual phenomenon is referred to as "size constancy." An example of size constancy would be the case in which the automobile down the block does not appear as a midget or toy automobile, but as a full-sized car, in spite of the difference in the size of its representation on the retina when compared with a nearby automobile. Of course with such a familiar object as an automobile, there is good reason for assuming it is not a toy. Nevertheless, the adult human also makes

FIGURE 2 *Size constancy was investigated with cubes of different sizes placed at different distances from the infants. The conditioned stimulus was 30 centimeters on a side and 1 meter away, test stimuli 30 or 90 centimeters on a side and 1 or 3 meters away. The chart shows how test stimuli were related to the conditioned stimulus in various respects. (After Bower, 1966)*

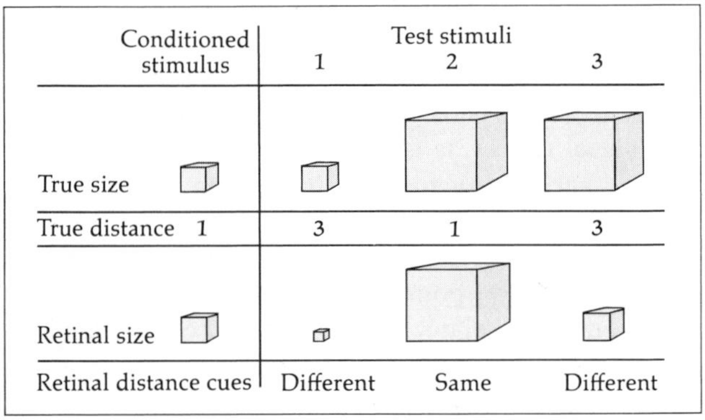

Conditioned stimulus	Test stimuli		
	1	2	3
True size			
True distance 1	3	1	3
Retinal size			
Retinal distance cues	Different	Same	Different

very good estimates of the size of unfamiliar objects at a distance, too. To do this, the organism is presumed to be able to judge depth and to compute, or at least estimate, the size of the projection on the retina that is appropriate for the distance at which the object is seen. It is legitimate to ask whether this ability is built into the organism or whether it develops only as the result of experience with objects at various distances.

Bower (1966) has attempted to answer this question by using six- to eight-week-old infants in an operant discrimination procedure. Each infant, in turn, was placed in an infant seat on a table. To begin the experiment, whenever the infant turned his head slightly, the experimenter rose from beneath the table to say "peek-a-boo" and to otherwise amuse the infant. This reinforcement increased the frequency of the head-turning response. After the rate of the response became stable, reinforcement was given only when the head turning occurred in the presence of a particular stimulus, i.e., the infant was trained to respond only in the presence of a cube 30 centimeters on a side at a distance of 1 meter. A test of generalization was then given during which the training cube was presented at 3 meters, and on interspersed trials a cube of 90 centimeters on a side was presented at both 1 and 3 meters. As indicated in Figure 2, the 90-centimeter cube produced the same size retinal image at 3 meters as the 30-centimeter training cube at 1 meter. If the infant responded at a high rate to the 90-centimeter cube at 3 meters, but not to the 30-centimeter cube at 3 meters, this would have provided evidence for a lack of size constancy, and such a finding would support the empiricist's position. If the infant responded with a high rate only to the original stimulus, even though the retinal size was reduced by one-third with the stimulus now placed at 3 meters, the nativist position would be supported. Bower found that the infants did respond only to the stimulus to which they were originally trained, regardless of its distance, and thus his results support the nativist position.

Although Bower's data do not indicate the accuracy of size-constancy judgments in infants, research with subjects from around five years of age on through adulthood generally shows improvement in constancy with age. There are some exceptions, and one study even reports a decrease in constancy after adolescence. All in all the changes in either direction are not large. Furthermore, the poorer performance of the younger subjects may have resulted from their lower motivation and greater distractibility in experimental situations not always well tailored to obtain optimal performance from children.

Altogether the Fantz (1965), Gibson & Walk (1960), and Bower (1966) research presents substantial support for the notion of a more highly developed visual system than the empiricist would have thought likely. It seems rather clear that to make adequate statements regarding perceptual functioning, researchers must be certain that their measurements of perception do not reflect the inadequate motor development of the infant or the inadequate control of attention in the experiment.

Object permanence

Piaget (1954) notes that, "Observation and experimentation combined seem to show that object concept, far from being innate or given ready-made in experience, is constructed little by little (p. 4)." He proposes that there are six stages which correspond to those of intellectual development:

> *During the first two stages . . . the infantile universe is formed of pictures that can be recognized but that have no substantial permanence or spatial organization. During the third stage . . . a beginning of permanence is conferred on things by prolongation of the movements of accommodation (grasping, etc.) but no systematic search for objects which have been removed is yet observable. During the fourth stage . . . there is searching for objects that have disappeared but no regard for their displacements. During a fifth stage (about twelve to eighteen months old) the object is constituted to the extent that it is permanent individual substance and inserted in the groups of displacements, but the child still cannot take account of changes in position brought about inside the field of direct perception. In a sixth stage (beginning at the age of sixteen to eighteen months) there is an image of absent objects and their displacements (p. 4).*

Piaget's observations represent, for the most part, anecdotal accounts of the development of his own children. Furthermore, search behavior may be a conservative measure of object permanence at eight months because of its dependence on the development of motor skills. Nevertheless, Charlesworth (1966) obtained data in support of Piaget's assertion regarding stage-four object permanence in a more systematic study that utilized various manifestations of "surprise" when an object vanished after being covered by the experimenter's hand. The response of surprise might be expected to provide a relatively sensitive measure of the concept of object permanence.

Research by Escalona & Corman (1967), however, indicates

considerable variation in the reactions of infants to a variety of tests that were thought to be appropriate to each of Piaget's stages. That is, although the infant may be said to be at a particular stage in the development of object permanence on one test, he might appear to be at a lower stage on another test. It is not unlikely that the interest or attention-getting value of a stimulus may affect the degree to which the infant attempts to interact with or search for the vanished stimulus, and that this would be the source of some error in such measurements. Even if the infant's performance on test items derived from Piaget's theory does fall in the predicted sequence, such results, although developmentally interesting, do not require one to accept Piaget's contentions regarding the infant's view of the world at each stage. Therefore, to propose that the "infantile universe is formed of pictures . . . that have no . . . permanence or spatial organization," as Piaget suggests, is a risky assertion at best. Neither should the alternative mistake be made, i.e., assume that the perceptual world of the newborn is completely unorganized just because it is difficult to prove that it is not.

As more sensitive measures of perception have been developed (e.g., change in heart rate), it has been repeatedly established that the perceptual abilities of infants are more advanced than previously suspected. The fact that Bower's infants responded to the cube to which they were originally trained, even when it was presented at a greater distance, and that they did not respond to a cube that at the greater distance subtended the same area on the retina as the training cube in its original position, strongly suggests that what was being discriminated was a cube in space rather than a picture without spatial organization.

Memory and object permanence

Obviously the development of memory is very relevant to object permanence and perception. While there is little relevant empirical information available, it appears that young infants have poor memories. Habituation represents at least one kind of memory. Sokolov (1963) assumes that as a consequence of repeated presentations of a stimulus, a mental model or concept of the stimulus is built up. As the model becomes similar or identical to the incoming stimulus pattern, the orienting reaction no longer occurs and attention declines. This decrement in response is seen as evidence of habituation. Bridger (1961) obtained habituation in neonates if he used a very brief intertrial interval

(0.5 second), whereas with a thirty-second intertrial interval, Lewis (1967) obtained only slight habituation with three-month-old infants. Differences in the complexity of the stimuli would undoubtedly also be a relevant factor. A model for a simple stimulus would be expected to build up more quickly than a model of a complex stimulus.

Data that indicate slow habituation do indeed suggest a rather impermanent world for the newborn infant. It must be remembered, however, that development is very rapid over the first few weeks and months of life, and little information exists regarding the effect of prolonged and repeated presentations of stimuli on the development of a mental model that might account for habituation. For example, mother's face is presented to the baby repeatedly and for relatively long periods of time. This fact, without doubt, contributes to the early development of a model for a face. At the same time, the young infant apparently does not discriminate between various adult faces at this early age. So what kind of mental model does the child have? What does he see when he sees mother's face? It is possible that his ability to make fine discriminations among faces is not very different from the problem of the adult Caucasian who has difficulty telling apart very different Orientals until he becomes more familiar with them. There are obviously numerous complexities of perception at this level that deserve a great deal of additional study.

ATTENTION AND PERCEPTION

Attention has become a very popular concept in psychology. It suffers, however, from the lack of a precise definition as it is commonly applied to several aspects of behavior. Perception is studied using various "attentional measures" which may include the orienting reaction as well as observations of receptor adjustment and stimulus preference. Inferences regarding perception from such measures must be made with caution. For example, when an infant does not show a preference for one or the other stimulus in a paired presentation of stimuli, it does not necessarily imply an inability to differentiate between them. With regard to this point, Saayman, Ames, & Moffett (1964) have found that although a pair of stimuli elicited equal fixation times, a differential reaction could be demonstrated by familiarizing the subject with one of the two stimuli. After presenting one stimulus alone for a period of time, when the two stimuli were paired again, the fixation time for the unfamiliarized stimulus stayed the same or went up from the first test to the retest, whereas attention to the familiarized stimulus was reduced. This habituation technique proved to be a somewhat more sensitive measure than Fantz's preference technique in that stimulus pairs not differentially preferred prior to familiarization were differentiated following the familiarization or habituation procedure.

In a series of studies (Kagan & Lewis, 1965), the effects of auditory and visual stimulation on attention were investigated using such diverse measures as cardiac deceleration, arm-movement suppression, vocalization, and fixation time. In general, all of these measures show habituation over trials: fixation time becomes briefer, cardiac deceleration decreases, and arm movements and vocalizations increase.

Kagan has speculated that various measures of attention may reflect differing aspects of the process of forming a model (schema), or what might be called a mature "object concept." Fantz had found that by three months of age infants preferred a three-dimensional face to a schematic face. Kagan, Henker, Hen-Tov, Levine, & Lewis (1966) went on to compare various reactions of infants to very realistic three-dimensional faces of differing degrees of completeness. In addition, they contrasted a complete face with features arranged in a bizarre (scrambled) fashion. (The Kagan study is reprinted following the chapter.) Fixation times increased with completeness of the faces, but the fixation times to the regular and scrambled faces were equal, indicating no differential attention. Smiling, on the other hand, was three times as frequent to the regular face as to the scrambled face. Thus, these results provide another instance of fixation time not providing a particularly sensitive measure of perceptual differentiation.

Individual differences and attention

Marked individual differences in alertness and irritability are apparent in the neonate and become even more obvious by the time he is two or three months old. It is also a frequent observation that very young infants have difficulty disengaging their attention from a stimulus, whereas older infants are more capable of active exploration of their environment. Lewis (1967) measured habituation of attention to repeated visual stimulation in a cross-sectional study utilizing infants from three to eighteen months of age, and he found that the rate of habituation of both fixation time and cardiac deceleration increased with age. On the assumption that habituation reflects the development of the central nervous system, Lewis hypothesized that infants who may have suffered some trauma to the central nervous system would show less habituation, on the average, than infants with no indications of such trauma. To test this hypothesis, he divided a group of infants according to their scores on the Apgar test (previously discussed on page 9). Infants having a perfect score of 10 were compared with those having a score of less than 10, but not less than 7. At twelve weeks of age there were clear differences between the two groups on the rate of habituation of both fixation time and cardiac deceleration. The infants with the lower Apgar scores showed less rapid habituation.

Reasoning that central neural development, as indicated by faster habituation, is also associated with cognitive growth, Lewis set out to test the frequently posed hypothesis that cognitive growth is facilitated by mother-infant interaction. To obtain a measure of mother-infant interaction, the mother and her twelve-week-old infant were left alone for thirty minutes in a room filled with an assortment of furniture, cribs, and current popular magazines. She was told that it was necessary to wait for the equipment to warm up. During this waiting period a hidden observer recorded the mother-infant interaction on a checklist. The checklist was concerned with such behaviors as whether the mother looked at, smiled at, vocalized, or touched the infant. The state of the infant in terms of eyes open or closed, crying, or other vocalizing was recorded, as was the latency of the mother's reactions, if any, to large body movements and to crying or vocalization of the infant. Interobserver reliability for these observations was reported to be high.

The results of the Lewis study, in general, support the conclusion that the rate of habituation is related to the proportion of times the mothers responded to the infants, relative to the number of opportunities to respond. Thus, the rate of habituation is apparently independent of the activity level of the infant.

ATTENTION AND CURIOSITY

Once the child is over one year of age, his general capabilities make it appear possible to use the research methods that have proved fruitful with animals and older humans. There are many problems, however, that have severely limited the quantity of such research. First, the child of this age is neither in the hospital nor at school and, therefore, is not generally available for research. He is not likely to be brought to the pediatrician's office or the well-baby clinic with any regularity following the first year. A second, and possibly even more critical variable, is the highly dependent nature of the one- and two-year-old child. They do not leave their mothers nor adapt to new situations readily, and although they are quite curious (explore their surroundings), they are also shy and must get acquainted with a situation at their own speed, a speed that typically overtaxes the patience of the experimenter.

The age period from one to three years is nevertheless a very important period for perceptual and cognitive development. During this time, the child achieves a new level of mobility and also begins to use words. Thus, he becomes capable of much greater interaction with his world, i.e., exploration (curiosity) becomes extensive.

In his book, *Conflict, arousal, and curiosity,* Berlyne (1960) has treated the topic of curiosity rather thoroughly and has presented a terminology that has proved useful. Berlyne has insisted on the importance of recognizing that organisms respond to many situations in ways not readily related to the arousal or reduction of such drive states as hunger, thirst, and pain. Therefore, it might be appropriate to propose a curiosity or exploratory drive. Berlyne, for instance, assumes that the motivation for exploration arises out of conflict produced by certain properties of stimuli, such as novelty or complexity, that cause the arousal of incompatible response tendencies. Exploration follows as a means of reducing the conflict.

In contrast with Berlyne's conflict theory, it might simply be proposed that any stimulus that elicits an orienting reaction will control attention until the orienting reaction (curiosity) habituates to all components of the stimulus. It may be that the internal mechanisms involved in exploratory behavior are less critical than a clear understanding of the characteristics of the controlling stimuli themselves. Only the controlling stimuli can be manipulated directly.

Although Berlyne notes that such stimulus properties as novelty, complexity, uncertainty, surprisingness, and incongruity are quantitative properties, they are primarily psychological rather than physical dimensions. While there are difficulties in defining these variables, the stimulus properties do indeed reflect themselves in differences in the behavior of children. A neonate spends more time observing a checkerboard of only 4 squares than one with 16 or 144 squares. Slightly older infants prefer the more complex checkerboards.

It has been proposed that a preference would be shown for some optimum amount of complexity or novelty, and that when stimuli are properly scaled, an inverted U-shaped curve would be found to relate preference to complexity or novelty. Cohen (1969) demonstrated such a relationship for two- to six-month-old infants with one, four, eight, or sixteen lights that flashed in sequence. He found that looking time was greatest to four lights when each of the light stimuli were presented individually. However, when one and sixteen lights were presented simultaneously for a series of trials, attention to one light habituated, and sixteen lights became the preferred stimulus. When one light and four lights were presented simultaneously there was no change in fixation time to one light, but fixation time to four lights decreased.

Cohen interpreted these results as providing additional support for the inverted U-shaped function. When presented individually, four lights was the preferred stimulus. When the stimuli were paired and presented simultaneously, fixation times increased to sixteen lights, but not to one light. In addition, habituation occurred to four lights. These results suggest the occurrence of a general shift in the inverted U-shaped function, with sixteen lights becoming more preferred as the result of experience with fewer lights.

PERCEPTION, ATTENTION, AND CURIOSITY IN OLDER CHILDREN

Although the discussion so far has concentrated primarily on research with infants, there has been considerable investigation with children of nursery-school age and older. Particularly relevant is some research by Munsinger & Kessen (1966). They were interested in the degree to which subject's preferences for stimuli were influenced by the complexity of the stimuli. They found that subjects from five to twenty-two years of age showed highly similar preferences for random-shaped figures of approximately ten independent turns as compared with figures varying from five to forty independent turns. Examples of these stimuli can

FIGURE 3   *Sample stimuli of four, ten, and sixteen turns as used by Munsinger & Kessen (1966).*

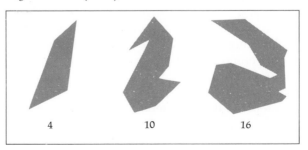

4	10	16

be seen in Figure 3. When Munsinger and Kessen attempted to change preferences by giving experience with figures of slightly greater complexity than those that were originally preferred, they were only partially successful. Although this finding is in apparent conflict with Cohen's results that showed a shift in preference with experience, there were a number of differences between the two studies that may account for this discrepancy. Probably most important are the qualitative differences in the stimuli, i.e., variation in the number of lights flashing in series versus random shapes of varying degrees of jaggedness.

In an earlier study Munsinger, Kessen, & Kessen (1964) had found a developmental difference in preference among strings of letters which varied in several stages from high redundancy through meaningful words to completely random strings. In this instance, the third-graders preferred slightly more redundant strings of letters than did the sixth-graders or adults.

In a novel experiment, reprinted following this chapter, Charlesworth (1964) used "surprise" as a measure of curiosity. In a situation somewhat similar, but more elaborate, than the experiment on object permanence referred to earlier, a discrepancy was created between the child's expectation and the actual occurrence. Violations of the expectancies of the child produced "surprise" and maintained attention and persistance to a greater degree than the novel or familiar stimuli.

Cantor & Cantor (1964) found that novelty or unfamiliarity exercises considerable control over the time six-year-old children choose to look at new stimuli as compared with stimuli presented for fifty familiarization trials. Of particular interest is the fact that the familiarization effects persisted so that the novel stimuli were still preferred two days after the familiarization treatment.

When one is concerned with perception and attention in children, as opposed to infants, it becomes exceedingly difficult to define and delimit the material to be covered. Whereas with infants, one is necessarily concerned with relatively basic aspects of perception, there is almost no limit to what may be considered to involve perception and attention in older children. Indeed, perception and attention are basic to the behaviors identified by such labels as discrimination learning, transfer, problem solving, concept formation, or cognitive development. These topics are given detailed consideration in Chapters VI and VII.

A very common research procedure for children of nursery-school age follows the instrumental learning paradigm. The child is required to utilize certain cues as the basis for making a choice.

For example, two cues are presented, and the child is reinforced for picking up or touching one of the cues or for pressing a lever in front of or below one of the cues. With such a task, three-year-old children will invariably make more errors over a series of trials than will five-year-old children. If the stimuli are highly discriminable, such as black and white cards, it is sometimes assumed that the difference in error rate between the three- and five-year-old children reflects a difference in learning ability. If the stimuli are light gray and dark gray cards, it might be assumed that there is a difference in perceptual ability. If the stimuli differ along a more abstract dimension, such as relative size, the difference will likely be considered one of cognitive abilities.

In spite of the apparent general verbal and motor ability of three-year-old children, their motivation is considerably more difficult to control than that of four- or five-year-old children. Because of this difficulty, younger children may attend to entirely different features of the experimental situation than the experimenter or older children. Alterations in the experimental situation that take account of these variables have been found to modify or completely eliminate some developmental functions. Thus, as researchers perfect their methods for studying perception in infancy, they will undoubtedly find the results from such studies in conflict with results obtained from nursery-school-age children because of the inadequacy of some of the procedures used with older children.

Indeed, there is mounting evidence that learning in many discrimination situations does not involve learning to make differential responses to the cues, but learning to attend to the appropriate cues; attention is the critical variable. Once the subject attends to the appropriate cues, he has little difficulty associating the reinforced response with the specific "correct" cue. Any training, instruction, or technique that ensures attention to the appropriate cues typically reduces the problem-solution period to a very few trials. Thus attention, which is so obviously the *sine qua non* of infant perception, is no less important for the evaluation of perception in older children. Researchers have frequently overlooked the importance of attention either by assuming that the child will necessarily attend to the cues that are so obvious to the researcher, or else by expecting attention to be controlled by instructions.

When objective measures are available on the degree to which three- and four-year-old children understand instructions, it sometimes appears that they understand very little. Furthermore, it is clear that in many instances, even when it is possible to direct his attention to an appropriate cue, the child may have difficulty maintaining his attention to that cue because some alternate cue is more dominant for him. In order to modify this behavior, special effort must be taken to enhance the salience of the appropriate cue.

Research on visual illusions has tended to focus on identifying underlying mechanisms of perception. Interestingly enough, some illusions become greater and some smaller with age. Piaget and his colleagues have attempted to demonstrate that these differences can be accounted for in terms of developmental changes in the child's manner of scanning visual stimuli. Pollack (1969) has recently challenged this hypothesis, and he proposes that those illusions that decrease with age involve integrative processes related to intelligence, whereas those that increase involve the development of physiological processes.

Much of the research in this area of investigation is concerned with little more than identifying differences in perception with age. Such differences, however, are sufficiently slight as not to be of overwhelming interest, or else they are equivocal when the results of various investigators are compared (Pick & Pick, 1969; Wohlwill, 1960). There are seldom findings in any direction that could not be accounted for in terms of greater attention to appropriate cues or better motivation on the part of the younger children. Thus, attention remains a critical factor in judgment as well as learning situations.

It should be clear by now that the extraction of information from the environment represents a dynamic interaction between curiosity, attention, perception, and also learning. This is true whether the subject is adult, child, or infant. This chapter has covered little of learning except as a technique for the study of perception, but it should be noted that although perception is essential to learning, it is also modified by learning. Even though there is considerable evidence that learning may not play as major a role in the development of perception as once presumed, many subtleties of perceptual development must depend on the types of interactions with the environment that are typified by learning situations. Speech, writing, and facial expression are good examples of perceptual situations where meaning is such an obvious part of the percept and in which perception depends so clearly on learned relationships. There are many other instances where our perceptions may be similarly enhanced or altered as the result of experience.

Information processing (perception) is fundamental to the

interaction of the infant or child with his environment whether in a problem-solving or social situation. It is necessary to recognize that the ability to direct and modify a child's behavior depends on the ability to identify and utilize those stimuli to which he can or will respond. Understanding perception, attention, and curiosity is indeed basic to any more general understanding of behavior development.

SUMMARY   Perception, attention, and curiosity are discussed as representing the total process of obtaining information from the environment. The infant and child provide excellent opportunities to study this process in its primitive forms and to observe the variables that influence its development. Critical questions as to whether or not the senses are operative at birth have been generally answered in the affirmative. The more important question has to do with the specific details of the child's perceptual abilities. With regard to questions of perceptual sensitivity, the evidence suggests that there is often continual improvement with age. Questions arise, however, over the degree to which apparent poor perception in younger children may be accounted for in terms of the difficulty of obtaining measures of their perceptual abilities.

Recent interest in the processes of attention and curiosity has led to research on measures of attention that have provided relatively passive indices of perception. This research ranges from observations of eye fixation to measures of changes in heart rate. Techniques utilizing such indices have produced more precise information on perception than has been previously available, and these techniques have indicated that the infant is frequently quite responsive to relatively small differences within a dimension. One technique has proved particularly sensitive and useful: habituating attention to one stimulus prior to the presentation of a second stimulus, on the assumption that a response to the second stimulus can occur only if it is perceived as different.

The difficulties of establishing the perception of spatial organization have permitted two extreme viewpoints to coexist for some time. The nativist assumes that the perception of spatial organization is innate, i.e., it is present at birth, or it develops later, but independently of experience. The empiricist, on the other hand, assumes that spatial organization results from the infant's interaction with his environment. Recognizing that at one level it is impossible to establish precisely what an individual perceives, the data provided by some of the newer and more sensitive techniques indicate that the perceptual world of the infant may be fairly well organized spatially even though not necessarily highly differentiated. Most specifically, depth perception occurs considerably earlier than the empiricist would suggest if its development depended on the type of interaction with the environment that the empiricists have proposed.

Research on attention and curiosity has focused on various ways of measuring attention, on the phenomenon of habituation of attention, and on external variables that control attention and exploratory behavior. Such variables as novelty and complexity have proved important determiners of curiosity and attention, and it was noted that these variables change as a function of experience with specific sets of stimuli.

Studies of perceptual development in children from three to ten years of age or older tend to show that young children frequently do more poorly than older children or adults on most tests of perception. It has been suggested that attention is as important a variable with children as it is with infants, and frequently the poor performance of the younger child may be attributed to his failure to attend to the appropriate cues and to inadequate control of his motivation in the experimental situation.

BIBLIOGRAPHY

Berlyne, D. E. *Conflict, arousal, and curiosity.* New York: McGraw-Hill, 1960.

Bower, T. G. R. The visual world of infants. *Scientific American*, 1966, **215**, 80–92.

Bridger, W. H. Sensory habituation and discrimination in the human neonate. *American Journal of Psychiatry*, 1961, **117**, 991–996.

Cantor, J. H., & Cantor, G. N. Observing behavior in children as a function of stimulus novelty. *Child Development*, 1964, **35**, 119–128.

Charlesworth, W. R. Instigation and maintenance of curiosity behavior as a function of surprise versus novel and familiar stimuli. *Child Development*, 1964, **35**, 1169–1186.

Charlesworth, W. R. Development of the object concept: A methodological study. Paper presented at the meeting of the American Psychological Association, New York, September 1966.

Cohen, L. B. Observing responses, visual preferences, and habituation to visual stimuli in infants. *Journal of Experimental Child Psychology*, 1969, **7**, 419–433.

Escalona, S. K., & Corman, H. H. The validation of Piaget's hypothesis concerning the development of sensory-motor intelligence: Methodological issues. Paper presented at the meeting of the Society for Research in Child Development, New York, April 1967.

Fantz, R. L. Visual perception from birth as shown by pattern selectivity. *Annals of the New York Academy of Sciences*, 1965, **118**, 793–814.

Fantz, R. L., Ordy, J. M., & Udelf, M. S. Maturation of pattern vision in infants during the first six months. *Journal of Comparative and Physiological Psychology*, 1962, **55**, 907–917.

Gibson, E. J., & Walk, R. D. The "visual cliff." *Scientific American*, 1960, **202**, 64–71.

Haith, M. M. The response of the human newborn to visual movement. *Journal of Experimental Child Psychology*, 1966, **3**, 235–243.

Kagan, J., Henker, B. A., Hen-Tov, A., Levine, J., & Lewis, M. Infants' differential reactions to familiar and distorted faces. *Child Development*, 1966, **37**, 519–532.

Kagan, J., & Lewis, M. Studies of attention in the human infant. *Merrill-Palmer Quarterly*, 1965, **11**, 95–127.

Kidd, A. H., & Kidd, R. M. The development of auditory perception in children. In A. H. Kidd & J. L. Rivoire (Eds.), *Perceptual development in children*. New York: International Universities Press, 1966. Pp. 113–142.

Lewis, M. Infant attention: Response decrement as a measure of cognitive processes, or what's new baby Jane? Paper presented at the meeting of the Society for Research in Child Development, New York, April 1967.

Munsinger, H., & Kessen, W. Stimulus variability and cognitive change. *Psychological Review*, 1966, **73**, 164–178.

Munsinger, H., Kessen, W., & Kessen, M. L. Age and uncertainty: Developmental variation in preference for variability. *Journal of Experimental Child Psychology*, 1964, **1**, 1–15.

Papoušek, H. Conditioning during early postnatal development. In Y. Brackbill & G. G. Thompson (Eds.), *Behavior in infancy and early childhood*. New York: Free Press, 1967.

Piaget, J. *The construction of reality in the child*. (Translated by M. Cook). New York: Basic Books, 1954.

Pick, H. L., Jr., & Pick, A. D. Sensory and perceptual development. In P. Mussen (Ed.), *Manual of child psychology*. New York: Wiley, 1969.

Pollack, R. H. Implications of ontogenetic changes in perception. In J. Flavell & D. Elkind (Eds.), *Studies in cognitive development: Essays in honor of Jean Piaget*. New York: Oxford University Press, 1969.

Saayman, G., Ames, E. W., & Moffett, A. Response to novelty as an indicator of visual discrimination in the human infant. *Journal of Experimental Child Psychology*, 1964, **1**, 189–198.

Sokolov, E. N. *Perception and the conditioned reflex.* New York: Macmillan, 1963.

Walk, R. D. The development of depth perception in animals and human infants. In H. W. Stevenson (Ed.), Concept of development. *Monographs of the Society for Research in Child Development,* 1966, **31**(5, Serial No. 107). Pp. 82-108.

Wohlwill, J. F. Developmental studies of perception. *Psychological Bulletin,* 1960, **57**, 249–288.

THE DEVELOPMENT OF DEPTH PERCEPTION IN ANIMALS AND HUMAN INFANTS

Richard D. Walk

The concept of development in space perception has always been closely tied to an old issue in psychology, the nature-nurture issue or the heredity-environment issue. In brief, do we learn to see the world about us, or do we see the world in all its complexity innately, without any learning? Hochberg (1962) has reviewed this issue in visual perception elsewhere. I shall review some research on it briefly, as it applies to space perception, before devoting my discussion to recent research that further illuminates the topic.

The nature-nurture issue in visual perception has often acted as an either-or issue, with a way of congealing opinion and narrowing vision. Lewin, in his brilliant introductory chapter to *A Dynamic Theory of Personality* (1935), referred to this type of either-or thinking as Aristotelian, and contrasted it with the Galileian type of thinking in which continuous gradations are more possible.

Unfortunately, it may take years of research to dispose of Aristotelian or either-or concepts as possibilities. What follows is a certain strategy of research as the nature-nurture issue becomes more and more susceptible to decision by experiment. If we end up, as I hope we will, with a slightly more Galileian approach to the topic, it is only because a series of experiments has made the Galileian, rather than the Aristotelian, way of thinking inevitable.

The human infant, "mewling and puking in the nurse's arms," as Shakespeare put it (*As You Like It*, Act II, Scene 3, Line 143), is a charming creature but a difficult subject with which to answer a question on the origin of space perception. The infant does not crawl until it is 6 to 12 months old, nor talk well enough to answer an experimental question for many years. The fact that the human infant, like another baby celebrated by Joel C. Harris, "don't say nothin' " has not inhibited speculation on what he sees. William James wrote a fascinating section on the visual world of the infant and his perceptual world of a "big blooming buzzing confusion" that, through the slow, sure, and steady accretions of experience, gradually becomes the stable perceptual world of the adult.

James's approach, while better literature than any of us can aspire to, has its limitations. We have recently been able to return to the human infant with some degree

The research reported here was supported by grants from the National Science Foundation. I am grateful to my graduate and undergraduate student colleagues in research for their assistance: Donna Beach, Thomas Curtis, Jean Eisenstein, Susan Finan, Bernard Z. Karmel, Thomas Quinta, Larry M. Raskin, Samuel Trychin, Jr., and Sue D. Turner.

From R. D. Walk. The development of depth perception in animals and human infants. Monographs of the Society for Research in Child Development, *1966, 31(5, Serial No. 107). Pp. 82–108. (With permission of the author and the Society for Research in Child Development, Inc.)*

of success, but animal research has, on the whole, yielded better answers on the nativism-empiricism issue than has research with children. . . .

DEPTH PERCEPTION OF ANIMALS: BACKGROUND

In 1873, Spalding conducted the first reasonably well-controlled observations of distance perception in animals. He kept a chick in a black flannel bag, after it was hatched, to occlude vision, and then watched the animal run to its mother and avoid the obstacles in its path. As a control, to make sure the animals were relying on vision, he made some chicks deaf; they still avoided objects by vision.

In 1934, Lashley and Russell tested hooded rats, which had been reared in the dark for three months, on an apparatus that measured the force of the animal's jump across increasingly wider gaps. Even without visual experience, the animals exerted more force in jumping for distant pedestals than for closer ones. Lashley and Russell concluded that depth perception in the hooded rat is innate.

This experiment was repeated by Walk, Gibson, and Tighe in 1957 using a visual cliff apparatus that had been devised to test animals without previous visual experience almost immediately upon their emergence from the dark. The apparatus is illustrated in Figure 1. The animal was placed on a center board that was on top of a piece of glass. On one side of the center board, a textured surface was just beneath the glass. On the other side of the center board, there was no textured surface under the glass, but the animal could see a textured surface some distance below. The descent of these dark-reared animals from the center board was like that of light-reared controls, predominantly to the side where the textured surface was just beneath the glass, what we have called the "shallow" side, rather than to the side with the textured surface some distance below the glass, the "deep" side. . . .

Research on . . . depth perception that is related to the nature-nurture question has been carried out on many species. [In general, the findings indicate:]
1. Some animals appear to have an innate appreciation of depth. The chick perceives depth at 1 day of age; the rat discriminates depth adequately even though it is kept in the dark from birth to 90 days of age. Other animals (ducklings, the ungulates) probably fit in here, but they are not crucial to the development of the thesis. The rhesus monkey, more important since it is closer phylogenetically to man, probably discriminates depth at birth, though more research may be indicated.
2. All seeing animals kept in the dark long enough lose their capacity to discriminate depth visually (evidence reviewed more fully in Walk, 1965). Light stimulation is thus necessary to maintain visually guided behavior.
3. More research is needed on the *development* of depth perception before one can assess whether some species have to "learn to see." . . .

RECENT RESEARCH ON PERCEPTUAL DEVELOPMENT OF ANIMALS

This section presents research on the development of normal depth discriminatory behavior in two animal species: the albino rabbit and the kitten. The developmental research is compared to research with animals reared in the dark. . . .

The *albino rabbit,* like the cat, discriminates depth well at 4 weeks of age. In fact, the albino rabbit is such a perfect "machine" for depth perception that a 6- to 8-

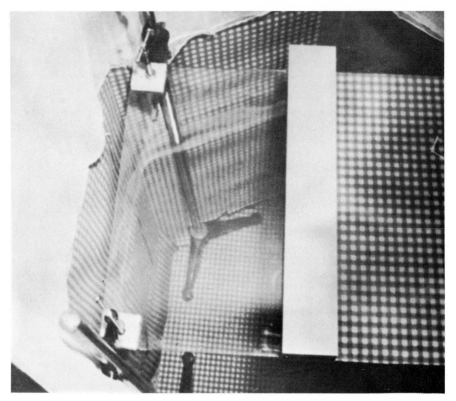

FIG. 1   The first model of the visual cliff. The clear side, with the pattern some distance below, is the "deep" side. The larger textured side is also covered by glass and is the "shallow" side.

week-old animal can be used in a class demonstration where students can ask the instructor to manipulate the stimulus in ways that interest them (Walk, 1964). . . . Like the cat, the eyes of the rabbit open at 7 to 11 days of age. . . .

[Several studies] have included [rabbits] raised in the light and studied longitudinally until depth perception developed, but not beyond 30 days. A summary of [these test findings] is shown in Figure 2. As can be seen, soon after the eyes first opened, there was no discrimination of depth; the animals went equally to the shallow and deep sides of the visual cliff on days 12 to 14 of life. There was gradual improvement over days 15 to 20, averaging about 70 percent choice of the shallow side. On days 21 to 25, 86 percent chose the shallow, and almost all choices (97 percent) were to the shallow on days 26 to 30. The albino rabbit, thus, has its eyes open by around 10 to 11 days of age but requires another 10 to 12 days before depth perception is reasonably stable. Locomotion is fairly adequate before depth perception is completely developed.

Dark-reared animals were studied also. Would dark-reared Ss, about 4 weeks old, discriminate depth? . . . All were removed from the dark at 28 to 29 days of age. Most animals . . . refused to descend from the center board on the first day of testing. . . . The trend [was thus] toward some innate depth discrimination in the rabbit.

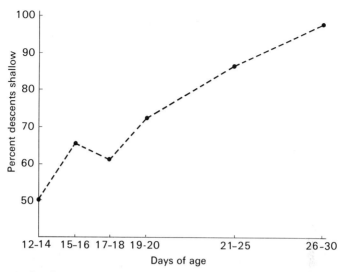

FIG. 2 Percentage of descents to shallow side by albino rabbits tested from soon after eyes were open until 30 days of age.

One can look at these data in two ways. The animals that move at all on emergence from the dark show a trend toward some discrimination of depth. This would argue for innate factors. On the other hand, the 4 weeks in the dark obviously grossly affected the animals. Even when allowed 1 to 2 hours of light a day, recovery was slow and not obtained in all animals until they were allowed to remain in the light for the normal diurnal cycle.

In summary, the albino rabbit shows, again, the tremendous importance of adequate light stimulation for visual-motor behavior. The innate-learned dichotomy is over-shadowed by this important fact. . . .

Visual depth perception of *kittens* reared in the light was studied in six different litters, a total of 28 kittens. The data reported here are from Karmel and Walk (1965).

The eyes of the kitten open at about 9 days of age, and the blink response to light and the pupillary reaction to light are both present at that time. The kittens had adequate enough locomotion to descend from the ³⁄₄-inch-high center board by 2 weeks of age, but choice of the shallow side was at a chance level. . . . Locomotion gradually improved, but depth discrimination on the visual cliff remained at a chance level until about day 23 to 24, when it rose to 74 percent shallow responses and then to over 90 percent shallow responses on days 27 to 28.

Our study, thus, showed visual cliff reactions appearing between days 23 and 24, or 14 to 19 days after the eyes opened and a week or 10 days after fairly good locomotion—locomotion as good, comparatively, as that of the human infant at 10 months of age. The 2 weeks or more of light stimulation interacted with other maturing processes. . . . Gibson and Walk's (1960) dark-reared kittens were at the 80 percent level in choice of the shallow side after 2 days in the light. Thus, while light stimulation seems to be necessary for these depth indicants to appear, other processes seem to mature independently of light stimulation and are more ready to ''trigger'' the depth responses in the older cat.

The developmental study of kittens, when . . . related to other research, appears to show that the depth response in the kitten does not appear innately, without prior practice, as it does in the chick and in the rat, but is dependent on appropriate patterned light stimulation. Animals reared from birth in the light gradually develop the responses to depth while those reared for about 4 weeks in the dark and then given light stimulation develop them rapidly. . . . There is, thus, an interaction of environmental (light stimulation) and innate (maturational) factors in the kitten. Each is important, but light stimulation is necessary to elicit the depth behavior.

From the animal studies, three main conclusions follow:
1. Depth perception is innate in some species (chick, rat).
2. Depth perception must be maintained by light stimulation in all species.
3. The development of depth perception in some species (the kitten and, to some extent, the rabbit) is dependent on an interaction of innate factors and environmental stimulation.
These possibilities have implications for the study of depth perception in human infants, to be considered next.

THE DEVELOPMENT OF DEPTH PERCEPTION OF HUMAN INFANTS

The first studies of the depth perception of human infants on the visual cliff were carried out at Cornell University in collaboration with Dr. Eleanor J. Gibson. The infants tested discriminated well on the visual cliff. Since 1960, research on infants has been carried out at George Washington University. We have tested over 600 infants on the visual cliff apparatus there. . . . The present focus of discussion is on the relation of the chronological age of the child to his behavior, in particular his behavior when the stimulus for perception is changed or varied.

The visual cliff apparatus for infants is illustrated in Figure 3. It is like a large glass-topped table 6 feet × 8 feet and 40 inches high, enclosed by an 8-inch-high border

FIG. 3   A large model of the visual cliff for testing larger organisms (rabbits, kittens, human infants).

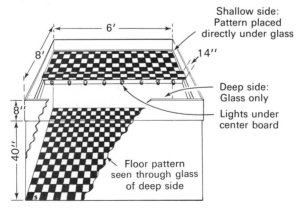

Shallow side:
Pattern placed
directly under glass

6'

8'

14''

Deep side:
Glass only

Lights under
center board

8''

40''

Floor pattern
seen through glass
of deep side

to keep the child from falling off. The deep side is enclosed for better control of the stimulus and the lights mounted under the center board roughly equate illumination on the two sides. A bank of lights above the visual cliff shines through white cotton sheeting to diffuse illumination evenly. Recently, curtains have been placed around the cliff to equate room cues.

The baby was placed on the center board, and the mother called to him. She always called him to cross both the deep and the shallow sides, using a pinwheel to attract his attention, although other details of procedure varied. The place on the cliff (east or west end of the center board) where the child was placed varied so that about half of the infants were placed on each end.

The infant often took a while to orient himself in the room, so the first trial was slow. On the first trial, in most of the studies, the child was called across the shallow side prior to being called across the deep side. This procedure insured that the child could get off the center board before he was called from the deep side. If he took over 2 minutes to reach the mother, he was usually replaced on the center board and called again from the shallow side to obtain a more rapid descent before being called from the deep side for a maximum of 2 minutes. Some of our early studies showed that babies called first across the shallow side were more likely to cross the deep side, later on, than children called first from the deep side. This was, we inferred, because those called first from the shallow side were more familiar with the testing situation by the time they were called from the deep side. These studies, where visual stimulation was varied, showed that only 13 percent crossed to the mother at the deep side on Trial 1, whereas between 30 and 40 percent crossed on later trials (Trials 2–4). The present procedure was adopted, then, both to maximize successful crawling by the child and to maximize the possibility that the child would cross the deep side. Another procedure was to have the child called from the center board opposite him, at the bisection of shallow and deep sides. This was another procedure that maximized successful crawling. After the child reached the mother there, he was called from the shallow and deep sides.

A few remarks are in order on the sample of infants and how they were obtained. A want ad was placed in the personal columns of local newspapers and $3.00 was paid to each child tested. The mothers who responded tended to be biased in favor of the upper socio-economic and more educated groups; they were interested in their children and in helping science. . . . All races have been tested, but the sample was predominantly white. The nonwhite children tended to come from the same educational and socio-economic group as the whites. In the course of the project, lasting over five summers now, many mothers have brought us more than one infant; the maximum has been three different pregnancies, and more than one mother is represented among them. Many twins have been tested and one set of triplets. . . .

Patterns and depth perception

There are many stimulus factors that influence the depth behavior of the human infant: the pattern on the deep side, the pattern on the shallow side, and the distance of the pattern below the glass on the deep side.

1. *Baseline.*— Baseline behavior may be established by a definite pattern on the shallow side, a definite one on the deep side, and a depth of 40 inches below the glass for the pattern on the deep side. The first Cornell study represented

this condition: A green linoleum pattern was on the shallow side and also on the deep side; the deep side was "exposed" so the child could see the trunk and legs of his mother below the glass and also objects around the room. Of 35 babies so tested, 27 went to the mother on one side or the other, 27 to the shallow side, and 3 to the deep side (11 percent). At George Washington University, with the deep side enclosed and painted a homogeneous gray, a $\frac{3}{4}$-inch checked pattern was put under the shallow side and on the deep side. Two of 19 subjects (11 percent) crossed to the mother. This study was repeated later, and 2 of 28 subjects crossed to the mother (7 percent). If one places 3-inch checks on the deep side, the projected density of the $\frac{3}{4}$-inch checks on the shallow side and the 3-inch checks on the deep side is roughly equated, assuming that the infant's head is about 12 inches above the board ($\frac{3}{4}$ inch is to 12 inches as 3 inches are to 48 inches). With the definite pattern on both sides creating an "equal density" condition, 4 of 45 infants or 9 percent crossed to the mother. In sum, with definite patterns on both sides a depth of 36 to 40 inches on the deep side, and adequate illumination, 9 of 119 subjects or 8 percent crossed the deep side when called by the mother. This is a baseline against which to assess changes in the infant's behavior with other patterns.

2. *Gray on the deep side.*—A gray pattern was used on the deep side, and the distance of the deep side below the glass was varied. Under these conditions, many more children crossed to the mother: 37 percent of the 197 infants tested. Here, the depth of the deep side below the glass varied from 40 inches up to a gray pattern directly under the glass. Yet, "depth" was not a significant variable. . . . An indefinite pattern, therefore, can influence the discriminatory behavior of the children. Many more will venture across the glass at the 40-inch depth then than when the pattern is definite. On the other hand, few also venture across when the gray is close to the glass of the deep side. Here, then, is a condition in which it is difficult for the infant to respond appropriately.

3. *Small checks on shallow side.*— By placing small $\frac{1}{4}$-inch checks on the shallow side and a large or 3-inch checked pattern on the deep side 36 inches below the glass, a less dense pattern is projected (larger retinal angle) to the infant's eye than by the pattern on the shallow side (about three times larger). This is sometimes called a "competing cue" experiment since gross textures might impel the infant to cross the deep side while motion parallax would lead him toward the shallow side. Here, 19 of 59 subjects, 32 percent, crossed the deep side. Was it competing cues that placed the child on the deep side or some inadequacy in the $\frac{1}{4}$-inch pattern? With the $\frac{1}{4}$-inch pattern under the shallow side and the $\frac{3}{4}$-inch one at the deep side (36 inches below), the more distant pattern projects a slightly smaller density. The number crossing to the mother was 9 of 24 tested, or 37 percent. Hence, it must have been some inadequacy of the $\frac{1}{4}$-inch pattern. The infants with the $\frac{1}{4}$-inch pattern under the shallow side all responded similarly despite patterns on the deep side ($\frac{3}{4}$ inch or 3 inch) that were identical with those on the deep side in the conditions in which a definite pattern ($\frac{3}{4}$-inch checks) was on the shallow side and less than 10 percent of the infants crossed to the mother.

4. *Depth of the deep side.*—It has been reported before that with a depth of 40 inches and a definite pattern on the deep side, about 8 percent crossed to the mother. For the purposes of the present discussion, to insure comparability, only those infants tested with the $\frac{3}{4}$-inch pattern on the shallow side and the $\frac{3}{4}$-inch pattern on the deep side will be considered. Here, it will be remembered, 4 of 47 subjects crossed to the mother ($8\frac{1}{2}$ percent). When the $\frac{3}{4}$-inch checks were

brought up to 20 inches below the board, 14 of 51 (27 percent) infants crossed to the mother. When the checks were 10 inches below the glass on the deep side, 20 of 53 infants (38 percent) crossed to the mother. The depth of the pattern, thus, influences the behavior of the infants. The closer the pattern is brought, the more infants cross to the mother. However, even at a depth of 10 inches, less than half venture across the deep side. . . .

Chronological age

1. *Age per se.* — If we group together all the studies in which the stimulus was manipulated in relation to depth perception, there were 541 infants tested on a variety of conditions. The total does not add up to 600 because there are little bits of studies, false starts or erroneous procedures that are difficult to assess. Grouping together infants without regard for experimental condition, one finds that of babies less than 10 months of age (to 299 days old; $N = 199$), 43 percent of those that got off the center board crossed to the mother at the deep side. Of those over 300 days of age, 22 percent ($N = 267$) crossed to the mother at the deep side. (There were 75 infants classified as "no go's"; they remained on the center board throughout the testing session.) The results, grouped into age levels, are shown in Figure 4. Chronological age is thus a highly significant factor in behavior on the visual cliff. But it has already been shown that there are some stimulus conditions (definite stimulus) in which practically no infants crossed to the mother. How does chronological age interact with stimulus condition?

2. *Age and stimulus condition.* — When there were few cues on the deep side, with a gray pattern there without regard for depth, 52 percent of the Ss under 300 days of age crossed to the deep side, whereas 29 percent of those over 300 days of age did. With an indefinite pattern on the shallow side (the $\frac{1}{4}$-inch checks), 49 percent of the "young" Ss crossed the deep side to the mother while 20

FIG. 4   Percentage of infants that go only to the shallow side as a function of chronological age. Stimulus conditions are combined here (total $N = 466$, with "no go" infants not included).

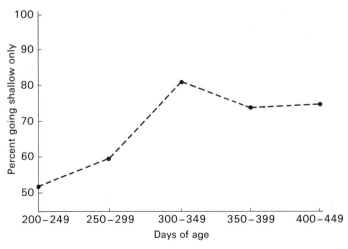

percent of the older *S*s did. These two types of patterns might be described as "acuity" patterns: they were hard to see. The younger *S* might have crawled more often to the mother because his vision was not as good as the older *S*'s.

When depth below the glass varied, the younger *S*s also went more often to the mother at the deep side. The only thing varied here was depth; patterns were constant on both sides. At the 10-inch depth, 68 percent of the younger *S*s crossed to the mother compared to 23 percent of the older ones; at 20 inches, 32 percent as compared to 22 percent; and at 40 inches, 9 percent of the younger *S*s and 8 percent of the older ones. Obviously, acuity cannot be a factor since at the greatest distance (least acuity) both groups behaved the same. Rather, it would seem to be some fault in motion discriminating mechanisms.

3. *Can younger Ss discriminate depth?*—When it became evident that the stimulus patterns affected behavior, the natural question arose: Granted that the younger *S*s discriminate depth with the more definite patterns, how well can they discriminate depth with the less definite ones? As a pilot study, infants were called by the mother from the center board opposite the child. The deep side, 40 inches below the glass, was an indefinite gray, and the shallow side was the regular $\frac{3}{4}$-inch checks. Of 20 infants, 18, or 90 percent, crawled to the mother by leaving the center board and going to the shallow side on their way to her, one straddled the board the whole way, and one went to the deep side. Yet, later, over 30 percent were coaxed by the mother across the deep side. In the procedure that has been carried out with most of the recent babies tested, the mother stood at the narrow end of the board and beckoned to the infant who had been placed on the wide end. To get to the mother, the child almost had to leave the center board on either the shallow or the deep side. A baby that could not be coaxed in this way was later coaxed to the shallow side by his mother. After the baby got to her, he was coaxed from the deep side. Many infants were later coaxed across the deep side, but infants that made a choice (a few straddled) went overwhelmingly to the shallow side: 96 percent went shallow, 4 percent deep, of those that made a choice. . . .

In summary, the center-board studies show that infants of all ages discriminate depth under all conditions tested to date. They go overwhelmingly to the shallow side even though, under some stimulus conditions, many of them are later coaxed over the deep side. . . .

Summary on human infants so far

The human infant discriminates depth well. From a theoretical "innate-learned" point of view, he discriminates depth as soon as he can be tested. But his visual mechanisms are still maturing. He discriminates depth better when there is a definite pattern under both the deep and shallow sides than when either one is in any way indefinite, and as long as the depth or distance is far enough. This lack of discrimination is reflected in the fact that he can be coaxed across the deep side under some conditions, but not under others. While all *S*s respond by crawling more often across the deep side in the presence of the inadequate patterns of stimulation, it is the infants less than 300 days of age that are particularly affected.

Let us reiterate this. It is not that the younger infant necessarily "loves his mother" more or is less adequate in motor coordination. These could be factors, but they would mask the important fact: His behavior is controlled by the visual stimulation. He responds to his mother by crawling to her over the deep side when the visual stimulation is inadequate, but he will not respond if it is adequate enough. He discriminates depth, as the center-board studies show, even in these inadequate situations, but his behavior is more labile. We have been observing, thus, the development of perceptual behavior. As he gets older, he discriminates more and is, therefore, showing his perceptual development or, in Gibson and Gibson's (1955) terminology, his stimulus "differentiation" or "perceptual learning."

Other factors in human infant behavior

It has been shown that the visual stimulus controls the infant's behavior in the sense that he will cross the glass to his mother under "impoverished" visual conditions, not under "definite" ones. Chronological age was found predictive of whether he would cross the deep side; younger infants cross more than older ones. But chronological age, alone, is an unsatisfactory explanation. Other research in psychology has stressed that it is not chronological time per se but what happens in time that is important. The infant's visual mechanisms are developing and improving as he gets older. . . .

A sample of 100 infants was drawn, composed of half who had crossed the deep side to the mother and half who had not. Of those chosen, roughly half were "young" infants, well below 300 days, and roughly half were over about 325 days, if possible. Each "crossing" baby was matched with a "noncrossing" baby of about the same age, tested on the same stimulus conditions. Because of the difficulty of finding older infants that crossed the deep side, the sample ended with 28 matched pairs of infants well below 300 days of age and 22 matched pairs of infants well above 300 days of age. Of course, no "no go" infants were included. The following were examined: sex of child, age when infant started to crawl, a rating of adequacy of locomotor behavior, and a response to a query about falling accidents. In the last two categories— rating of adequacy of locomotor behavior and the query about falling accidents—the information was somewhat sparse.

This pilot project, however, showed that of 55 males tested, 54 percent crossed to the deep side, and of 44 females, 43 percent crossed to the mother at the deep side. . . . This difference is not significant, and whatever tendency there was for males to cross the deep side more than females was contributed by infants over 10 months of age.

The ratings of adequacy of locomotor behavior were almost exactly the same for both "crossers" and "noncrossers," although, of course, older infants had better ratings for adequacy of locomotor behavior than did younger ones.

The time when the child started to crawl was an estimate given to us by the mother and was fraught with pitfalls. Many almost helpless infants were tested whose mothers claimed that the child had been crawling for several months. Its extreme is illustrated by the answer from one mother: She said that the child had been crawling since the first week of life! Mothers often feel that a baby is "smart" if he crawls early, and a little proud maternal fudging is probably natural enough, though it does muddy up an attempt to assess the start of crawling behavior. Anyway, based on this measure, there is some estimate of when the child started to crawl, and this estimate, like the account of falling accidents, was secured before the baby was tested.

Using, first, a measure of the time gap between the start of crawling and the time when tested, the older "crossers" had less experience than the older "noncrossers." This difference was significant at the 10 percent level. Younger children did not differ on this dimension; in fact, the tendency was slightly in the opposite direction. Further analysis of the younger children showed that they were not matched well on chronological age; despite my best efforts, the young crossers were a month and a half younger than their controls. Evidently, a young child who can crawl well enough will just go ahead and cross the deep side when visual stimulation is inadequate because his own visual mechanisms are not well enough developed. . . . Older children, on the other hand, were well matched on age, and the "crossing" children tended to be late crawlers. Seven of the 22 in the "crossing" group crawled at 9 to 11 months of age as against 3 of 22 in the "noncrossing" group. This tendency, in view of the trouble in obtaining good data from the mothers, seemed worth following up.

The next step was to go over the entire 1963 and 1964 list of babies tested and pull out the late crawlers, those that crawled at 9 to 11 months of age. There were only 24 late crawlers that were not "no go" babies. These were matched with all others of their age that had been tested on the same stimulus conditions. Of the 24 late-crawling infants, 11, or 46 percent, crossed to the mother at the deep side, whereas, of 56 similarly aged children, 11, or 20 percent, crossed to the mother there. This [difference] was statistically significant. . . .

The tentative hypothesis, based on these late crawlers, has some theoretical importance. The trend is toward those with more crawling experience to discriminate depth the best. This finding agrees with theories that emphasize the role of action in space in the development of visual-motor behavior. The better discrimination of older infants as compared to younger ones also favors visual experience, but the late-crawling infants further contribute by showing more than maturation may be involved and that, even with an organism exposed to as much diverse stimulation as the human infant, it may be possible to delineate further the kinds of experiences that influence depth perception.

The last possibility of individual differences was that of falling accidents. The 100 children had only 71 on whom some estimate was made by the mother of falling accidents. Infants were included in the "accident" group if the mother reported two or more accidents or one very severe one; the "no accident" group had zero or one falling accident reported. The tendency in the sample of 71 was for the infants with two or more accidents to be more cautious. This was true in both younger and older samples, but rather pronounced in the group that averaged about 12 months of age. (With two or more accidents reported, 2 of 12 subjects [14 percent] crossed to the mother, and among mothers reporting 0–1 accidents, 7 of 15 [47 percent] crossed to the mother.) The results were far from statistically significant, but they seemed worth following through. Infants with two or more accidents (or one severe one) were picked from the 1963 and 1964 studies. Of the 40 such infants so identified, 10 were "no go" and 6 of the remaining 30, or 20 percent, crossed to the mother. This included the previous Ss, but was now a larger sample. Controls were matched on stimulus condition, age, and crawling experience, so far as was possible. The results were disappointing. Only 8 of the 30 matched controls, or 27 percent, crossed to the mother. The "falling hypothesis," therefore, received little support, although the nonsignificant tendency is enough to keep falling accidents as a measure in future studies of depth perception of crawling infants.

In sum, a more detailed investigation of the infants that crossed the deep side of the visual cliff as compared to those who did not cross shows only one strong hypothesis that is based on the lack of crawling experience of late crawlers and their subsequent careless performance on the visual cliff. At the moment, then, an explanation of the behavior of the infants on the visual cliff would be based on a combination of rate of maturation of visual mechanisms and visual-motor experience. Other factors, if such can be identified, and more precise understanding of the ones cited above, are a challenge for future research. . . .

DISCUSSION

[A number of studies] show that gross discrimination of depth is present as soon as children can be tested. Thus, there is no disagreement with studies that suggest depth perception in children younger than those tested on the visual cliff. Fantz (1961) showed that infants 1 to 6 months old preferred to fixate a solid sphere rather than a flat circle. This would mean they demonstrated some discrimination of the three-dimensional objects. Bower (1964) conditioned "premotor" infants 70 to 85 days old to a 12-inch cube and found generalization to the same 12-inch cube at a distance, but little generalization to a 36-inch cube at the greater distance that paralleled the same visual angle as the 12-inch cube during training. This, again, showed some depth perception in very young infants.

But the study reported here does contend that complete development of spatial behavior in some species, particularly the "higher" ones, is dependent on adequate visual-motor experience in a well-articulated visual environment. . . .

In the monograph on depth perception (Walk & Gibson, 1961), [it was] emphasized [that] reactions of species to depth perception [are] correlated with "way of life." That the chick discriminates depth early, or that the lamb has a marked aversion to depth while the aquatic turtle is relatively indifferent to it, was seen as related to adaptation of the species for survival in its environment. The present emphasis is on the interaction of the species with the environment, of the environment as necessary for full development of the perception of space in the "higher" species. . . .

SUMMARY

An attempt has been made in this paper to discuss some developmental factors in depth perception. Not all are understood, but depth perception would seem to improve, after onset of locomotion, in such species as the rabbit and the kitten, as well as in the human infant. Without visual stimulation, depth perception in the kitten and the rabbit is grossly impaired. The human infant may discriminate depth as soon as he can crawl, and perhaps before, but as he gets older depth discrimination improves. It is "perceptual learning"; the visual stimulus is discriminated more adequately. The perceptual learning in all of these species—rabbit, kitten, human infant—seems to be dependent upon both maturation of visual mechanisms and interaction with the environment.

Thus, we are on the threshold of discarding old stereotypes and discovering the interaction of organism and environment in space perception.

REFERENCES

Bower, T. G. R. Discrimination of depth in premotor infants. *Psychonomic Science*, 1964, **1**, 368.

Fantz, R. L. The origin of form perception. *Scientific American*, 1961, **204**, 66–72.

Gibson, E. J., & Walk, R. D. The "visual cliff." *Scientific American*, 1960, **202**, 64–71.

Gibson, J. J., & Gibson, E. J. Perceptual learning: Differentiation or enrichment? *Psychological Review*, 1955, **62**, 32–41.

Hochberg, J. E. Nativism and empiricism in perception. In L. Postman (Ed.), *Psychology in the making: Histories of selected research problems.* New York: Knopf, 1962. Pp. 255–330.

Karmel, B. Z., & Walk, R. D. The development of visual perception in the kitten. Paper presented at the meeting of the Eastern Psychological Association, Atlantic City, April 1965.

Lashley, K. S., & Russell, J. T. The mechanism of vision. XI. A preliminary test of innate organization. *Journal of Genetic Psychology*, 1934, **45**, 136–144.

Lewin, K. *A dynamic theory of personality: Selected papers.* New York: McGraw-Hill, 1935.

Spalding, D. A. Instinct, with original observations on young animals. *Macmillan's Magazine*, 1873, **27**, 282–293. (Reprinted in *British Journal of Animal Behaviour*, 1954, **2**, 2–11.)

Walk, R. D. Class demonstration of visual depth perception with the albino rabbit. *Perceptual and Motor Skills*, 1964, **18**, 219–224.

Walk, R. D. The study of visual depth and distance perception in animals. In D. S. Lehrman, R. H. Hinde, & E. Shaw (Eds.), *Advances in the study of behavior.* Vol. 1. New York: Academic Press, 1965. Pp. 99–154.

Walk, R. D., & Gibson, E. J. A comparative and analytical study of visual depth perception. *Psychological Monographs*, 1961, **75**(15, Whole No. 519).

Walk, R. D., Gibson, E. J., & Tighe, T. J. Behavior of light- and dark-reared rats on a visual cliff. *Science*, 1957, **126**, 80–81.

INFANTS' DIFFERENTIAL REACTIONS TO FAMILIAR AND DISTORTED FACES

Jerome Kagan, Barbara A. Henker, Amy Hen-Tov, Janet Levine, and Michael Lewis

The dramatic increase in investigations of visual perception and attentional phenomena in the human infant has produced a proliferation of concepts and methods that requires careful analysis. The popular strategy in studies of distribution of attention to visual inputs rests on two assumptions: (*a*) length of fixation is an index of degree of preference, and (*b*) equivalent fixation times to two stimuli imply lack of differentiation between the stimuli (Fantz, 1964, Hershenson, 1964; Hershenson, Munsinger, & Kessen, 1964; Kagan & Lewis, 1965; Spears, 1964). This paper considers the validity of these two assumptions.

Most overt behaviors are ambiguous in meaning, for a single act often serves more than one need or motive and can be elicited by more than one class of stimuli. This proposition is readily accepted by those who work with older children and adults. Students of infant behavior, however, have been somewhat reluctant to accommodate to this assumption, perhaps because they viewed the infant as a very simple organism. There are a variety of classes of visual stimuli that will elicit a long fixation. It is suggested that two such classes are those that represent recently formed, familiar schema (i.e., emergent schema) and those that are a moderate violation of familiar schema. But it is neither necessary nor desirable to assume that the infant prefers both patterns to an equal degree. If "preference" is synonymous with "long fixations," there is no need to use the word, for it does not add any information. There is, however, the hidden assumption that "preference" has a surplus meaning of "liking" or "inducing pleasure." A long fixation to a violation of a familiar schema (e.g., a disordered face) may not reflect the desire to gaze at a pleasing pattern but, rather, an attempt to reduce uncertainty. Adults gaze at colorful, graceful birds out of preference; they stare at wingless flying objects because they wish to categorize them and reduce the uncertainty created by violation of a familiar schema. A long fixation, without additional information from other response modes, does not allow one to determine which of these two incentives is eliciting the sustained attention.

If there is more than one psychological determinant of a fixation, then similarities in fixation time cannot be used to imply lack of differentiation between stimuli. It seems

This research was supported, in part, by research grants MH-8792 from the National Institute of Mental Health, U.S. Public Health Service, and HD-00868 from the National Institute of Child Health and Development, U.S. Public Health Service. The assistance of Leslie Pearson, Lois Welch, and Marion Cleveland is acknowledged.

From J. Kagan, B. A. Henker, A. Hen-Tov, J. Levine, & M. Lewis. Infants' differential reactions to familiar and distorted faces. Child Development, *1966,* **37**, *519–532. (With permission of the authors and the Society for Research in Child Development, Inc.)*

reasonable, however, to search for other responses, occurring continguously with a fixation, that might yield evidence of differentiation between familiar and moderately uncertain patterns. The infant often smiles and vocalizes when he fixates visual patterns, and these responses might provide evidence of differentiation between stimuli that elicit equally long fixations. The aim of this first study was to test the hypothesis that familiar facial patterns would elicit long fixations and frequent smiles, whereas moderate violations of facial patterns would elicit long fixations but minimal smiling. No firm prediction was made for vocalizations.

STUDY 1

Subjects

The Ss were 17 boys and 17 girls, Caucasian, 4 months of age at time of testing. Fifteen percent were first-born, 32 percent second-born, and 53 percent occupied ordinal positions 3 through 10. All infants lived in the Boston-Cambridge area and came from lower-middle- and middle-class family backgrounds.

Procedure

Each S came to the laboratory with his mother, and no infant was tested if he was sleepy, hungry, or upset. The S lay supine in a crib with a stimulus holder 18 inches from the plane of his face. A blue-gray canopy surrounded the infant and provided a homogeneous visual background. The stimuli, four different three-dimensional sculptured faces painted flesh color, are illustrated in Figure 1. These four faces were called regular (R), scrambled (S), no eyes (N), and blank (B).

A high-intensity light was directed at the stimulus area which was directly above the child's face. . . . After presentation of an initial buffer stimulus (a white plastic form), each of the test stimuli was presented one at a time in random order. Each test stimulus was presented a total of four times, but no stimulus appeared more than once in any block of four consecutive trials. Two presentation sequences were used to control for order effects. Each stimulus was presented for 30 seconds, with a 15-second rest interval occurring between presentations.

Two observers viewed the infant through one-way portholes and independently coded the following variables on an event recorder: fixation of the stimulus, smiling, and vocalization. A continuous record of both incidence and duration of each of the infant's reactions was obtained. The interrater reliabilities for the variables were satisfactory ($r = .98$, .86, and .71 for fixation time, number of smiles, and vocalization time, respectively). . . .

Results

. . . Table 1 presents the average scores for [the variables of total fixation time, first fixation time, number of smiles, and number of vocalizations for all four trials combined].

The most dramatic finding was that smiles were markedly more frequent to the regular than to the other three faces. The average number of smiles to the regular face was three times the number displayed to the scrambled face. . . . [This difference was

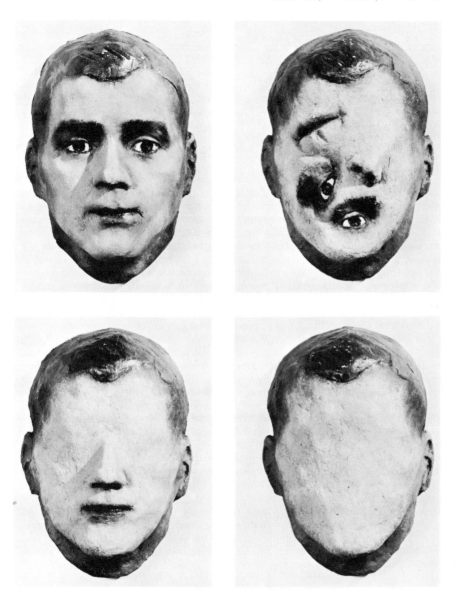

FIG. 1   The four facial patterns displayed to the infant.

highly significant.] Sixty percent of the infants smiled one or more times to the regular face, in contrast to 25 percent to the scrambled face, and 70 percent of the Ss displayed more smiles to the regular than to the scrambled face. However, both total- and first-fixation-time scores were essentially equivalent for the regular and scrambled faces. If fixation time alone had been measured, the data would have suggested that the 4-month-old infant was not differentiating between the regular and scrambled facial

TABLE 1   Mean scores across four trials to regular (R), scrambled (S), no eyes (N), and blank (B) faces

	Boys				Girls			
	R	S	N	B	R	S	N	B
Total fixation time	26.5	25.9	23.1	20.8	21.0	19.3	18.2	14.8
First fixation	16.9	15.1	11.2	8.2	9.8	9.0	6.9	3.9
Smiles	2.0	0.6	0.4	0.1	1.2	0.5	0.6	0.1
Vocalizations	2.9	2.6	1.7	2.7	2.2	1.6	1.2	1.0

patterns. The differential occurrence of smiles allowed unequivocal rejection of this null hypothesis. The vocalization scores also failed to differentiate between regular and scrambled faces. However, the form of the vocalization curves differed from that obtained for fixation time. Vocalizations increased over trials, whereas fixation times decreased over trials. Informal observations suggested that vocalizations covaried with level of excitement, and the infants became excited to both the familiar and irregular facial patterns as the experiment proceeded. Vocalization in a 16-week-old infant seems to be a general index of arousal, but this response does not provide any specific information as to the basis for the excitement.

Length of total and first fixation was [significantly] longer for boys than for girls for all four faces. . . . A reasonable interpretation of this sex difference is that the girls are maturationally ahead of the boys, despite the fact that their chronological ages are identical. Eight-month-old infants have markedly shorter fixation times to these stimuli than do 4-month-olds. Moreover, it is generally true that when stimuli remain constant, fixation times decrease with age (Kagan & Lewis, 1965). The more mature child assimilates the stimulus faster and habituates more rapidly. The boys' longer fixation times suggest a cognitive lag behind girls. This notion is supported by the data on smiles. Gewirtz (1965) and Laroche and Tcheng (1963) have reported that after 5 months of age the occurrence of smiles to human faces declines markedly, the maximal likelihood for smiles falling between 3 and 5 months of age. The higher frequency of smiles among boys than girls suggests that the more mature girls begin to extinguish the tendency to display smiles in advance of the boy.

The facial patterns that contained eyes (i.e., regular and scrambled faces) elicited [significantly] longer fixations than did the two patterns without eyes. . . . However, the child must have been responding to the presence and regular arrangement of nose and mouth components alone, for there were more smiles and longer first fixations to the face with no eyes than to the blank face. [This difference was also significant.]

STUDY 2

The data from the first study indicated that, although fixation times were equivalent to the regular and scrambled faces, smiling was dramatically more frequent to the former than to the latter. Since the scrambled face is a violation of the infant's schema for the human facial form, it seemed reasonable to postulate that the smile to the regular face reflected the fact that the regular face was, for most children, structurally similar to the face schema the infant had acquired. . . . We shall call this class of schema "emergent." This assumption prompted us to search for other indexes of assimilation, and degree of heart-rate deceleration seemed to be a good candidate. Previous work (Kagan & Lewis, 1965) indicated that 6- and 13-month-old infants display a clear cardiac deceleration to selected classes of visual and auditory stimuli. Motor quieting facilitates cardiac deceleration, and motor activity inhibits cardiac deceleration. It seemed reasonable, therefore, to predict that potentially assimilable stimuli would elicit greater deceleration than patterns that were violations of familiar schema because the former would be more likely to produce quieting.

Subjects and procedure

The Ss were 32 four-month-old infants (14 boys and 18 girls) who were not part of the first investigation. The Ss were shown the four faces in an administration that was identical to that described earlier. In addition to fixation-time scores, continuous cardiac records were obtained during the entire 16-stimulus episode. The degree of cardiac deceleration was obtained by subtracting the mean of the three lowest heart beats during the first fixation from the mean of the three lowest heart beats during the 3 seconds just prior to the onset of the first fixation.

The infant typically initiated his first fixation soon after the stimulus was presented and the major deceleration—if one appeared—usually occurred within 3 seconds of the first fixation. Despite the fact that most infants continued to look at the stimulus for an additional 15 to 20 seconds, clear cardiac decelerations usually did not occur after the first early drop in heart rate. Moreover, the magnitude of the cardiac deceleration dropped markedly after the first four presentations (i.e., one exposure to each of the four faces). The order of presentation for these 32 Ss was constant, and the order for the first four trials was no eyes, scrambled, blank, and regular. Since early appearing stimuli are more likely to elicit larger decelerations, this specific order favored larger decelerations to the scrambled than to the regular face.

Results

Magnitude of cardiac deceleration was greater to the regular than to the scrambled face for girls, but not for boys. Among girls, the average deceleration to the first presentation of the regular face was nine beats, in contrast to five beats to the scrambled face. More impressive, however, was the fact that 14 of the 18 girls showed [significantly] larger decelerations to the regular than to the scrambled face. . . . However, length of the first fixation to each of the two faces was equivalent (15 versus 14 seconds).

A second test for differences in deceleration among the four faces involved evaluation of the single stimulus presentation (out of the total of 16) that was associated with the largest deceleration for each S. This analysis revealed that 35 percent of the infants showed their largest deceleration to the regular face and that 35 percent showed their single largest deceleration to the scrambled face. Only 15 percent of the Ss showed their largest deceleration to either no eyes or the blank face. In sum, the girls' data supported the original hypothesis that stimuli matching emergent schema would elicit greater deceleration than stimuli that were more serious violations of acquired schema.

There are two interpretations of this finding. We favor the idea that cardiac deceleration is likely to occur when a stimulus matches an emergent schema, when a stimulus is potentially assimilable and elicits a distinct recognitory reaction. An alternative interpretation states that cardiac deceleration occurs to stimuli that have acquired reward value. A regular face has been associated with parental nurturance, whereas a scrambled face has not. As a result, deceleration might be expected to occur to the former pattern. Additional data on 58 eight-month-old infants (29 boys and 29 girls) support the contention that the deceleration is tied more closely to the assimilation status of the stimulus than to its acquired reward value.

The typical 8-month-old infant should have progressed to a point where the scrambled face has become the emergent schema and the regular face an easily and quickly recognized pattern. If this is the case, the scrambled face at 8 months should behave like the regular face did at 4 months. Verification of this prediction would support the notion that cardiac deceleration is selectively associated with stimuli that match emergent schema (i.e., stimuli that are at the frontier that separates a completely articulated schema from one that is in the process of becoming articulated).

These 8-month-old infants were shown the four faces in the same procedure and order used with the 4-month-old subjects. First fixation times were reduced considerably (mean of about 6 seconds), and there was no significant difference in fixation times among the four patterns. However, magnitude of cardiac deceleration was greatest to the scrambled face for both sexes. On the first presentation of each of the faces the median decelerations were five beats to the scrambled and three beats to the regular face. On the second round of stimulus presentation the median decelerations were three beats to the scrambled and zero beats to the regular face. These differences just missed statistical significance. However, on each trial the direction of the difference was the reverse of that found at 4 months. The analysis that produced a reliable difference asked about the single stimulus presentation (any one of the 16 presentations) that produced the largest cardiac deceleration. Fifty-six percent of the girls and 50 percent of the boys produced their largest deceleration (about 11 beats) to the scrambled face. Only 30 percent of the girls and 18 percent of the boys produced their largest deceleration on a trial when the regular face was presented. The corresponding proportions for the face with no eyes or the blank face were 9 and 5 percent for girls and 22 and 10 percent for boys. The difference between the proportion of Ss showing the largest deceleration to the scrambled versus regular face (53 versus 24 percent) was significant. . . .

Direct comparison of the data from the 4- and 8-month samples revealed that the proportion of Ss showing their largest deceleration to the regular face dropped from 35 percent at 4 months to 24 percent at 8 months. The corresponding proportions for the scrambled face increased from 35 to 53 percent. There was, therefore, a clear tendency for larger decelerations to occur to the scrambled face at 8 months and to the regular face at 4 months of age. However, the fixation times to the regular and scrambled faces were equivalent at each of the two ages.

CONCLUSIONS

[Fixation times to the regular and rearranged face were equivalent, but smiling and large decreases in heart rate were significantly more frequent to the regular face.] The major implication of these data is that multiple-response indexes are helpful in experiments aimed at understanding cognitive functioning. A long or short fixation of a stimulus is ambiguous in meaning, and inferences about perceptual differentiation should combine fixation time with other response variables. One way to conceptualize cognitive growth is to regard classes of stimuli as falling along a continuum from very familiar to very novel (i.e., a stimulus for which a well-articulated schema has existed for a long time, through one for which a schema is emergent, to one for which no schema exists). Magnitude estimates of different response variables seem to bear different relations to this continuum, running from extreme familiarity to novelty. Fixation time is apt to be low to very familiar and very novel patterns but equally high for a band of stimuli representing recently formed schema as well as moderate violations of these schema. The regular human face is probably a newly acquired schema for a 4-month-old infant, and fixation-time parameters are equivalent to both the newly formed schema and the moderate violation. Smiling and cardiac deceleration, however, appear to be specifically elicited by stimuli representing the recently formed, emergent schema rather than violations of these schema.

Thus at 4 months cardiac deceleration tends to be greatest to the regular face, but at 8 months deceleration is greatest to the scrambled face. This is intuitively reasonable, for cognitive development is characterized by the continual creation of schema for new patterns. A stimulus that violates an existing schema at one time will be a familiar and easily assimilated pattern days, weeks, or months later. It appears that a wise combination of fixation patterns, cardiac deceleration, and smiling may allow one to explore the degree of articulation of varied schema in the infant and facilitate differentiation among stimuli that represent familiar, emergent, and novel schema. Future research will judge the wisdom of this suggestion. In any case, the methodological lesson to be taken from this work is clear. Investigations of infant and child behavior should resist resting inferences on single behavioral variables. Nature has given each response a plurality of meanings to carry, and a sensitive combination of response patterns is mandatory if we are to discern from the tangle of observable behavior the laws that describe the relations among stimulus, schema, and act.

REFERENCES

Fantz, R. L. Visual experience in infants; Decreased attention to familiar patterns relative to novel ones. *Science*, 1964, **146**, 668–670.

Gewirtz, J. L. The course of smiling by groups of Israeli infants in the first eighteen months of life. *Scripta Hierosolymitana*, 1965, **14**, 9–58.

Hershenson, M. Visual discrimination in the human newborn. *Journal of Comparative and Physiological Psychology*, 1964, **58**, 270–276.

Hershenson, M., Munsinger, H., & Kessen, W. Preference for shapes of intermediate variability in the newborn human. *Science*, 1964, **147**, 630–631.

Kagan, J., & Lewis, M. Studies of attention in the human infant. *Merrill-Palmer Quarterly*, 1965, **11**, 95–127.

Laroche, J. L., & Tcheng, F. *Le sourire du nourrisson*. Louvain: Publications Universitaries, 1963.

Spears, W. C. Assessment of visual preference and discrimination in the four-month-old infant. *Journal of Comparative and Physiological Psychology*, 1964, **57**, 381–386.

INSTIGATION AND MAINTENANCE OF CURIOSITY BEHAVIOR AS A FUNCTION OF SURPRISE VERSUS NOVEL AND FAMILIAR STIMULI[1,2]

William R. Charlesworth

The role novel stimuli play in instigating and reinforcing curiosity behavior has been amply demonstrated in the experimental literature (Berlyne & Slater, 1957; Butler, 1953; Montgomery & Segall, 1955). Surprise stimuli, although generally included under what is meant by novel stimuli, have been viewed by Berlyne (1960) as being independent of the latter and worthy of consideration in their own right as having reinforcing and possibly motivational properties.[3] Charlesworth (1963) and Hunt (1963) have discussed the possibility that the surprise reaction resulting from an incongruity between an expectation of an event and the fact that it does not materialize may generate covert stimuli that are directly responsible for the instigation of curiosity behaviors. Charlesworth (1963) further speculated that (a) surprise stimuli under certain conditions were more effective in instigating and reinforcing curiosity behavior than novel stimuli and (b) the more precise and concrete the expectation, the greater the surprise reaction and hence curiosity motivation.

The purpose of the present experiments was to test the above notions by varying surprise and novelty independently as well as the concreteness of the expectations

[1] The author wishes to thank the administrators and teachers of the Wilder Nursery School, St. Paul, and of the Morris Park Elementary school, Minneapolis. Gratitude is also extended to Dr. Herbert Pick for critically reading the manuscript, Mr. Mervyn Bergman who built the apparatus, Mr. Alvin Price, Mrs. Ruth Eisenklam, and Miss Lynn Gometz, who helped test subjects, and the author's daughter, Erika, whose unexpected persistence in "playing the game" later used in the experiment was directly responsible for initiating this study. The writing of this manuscript was supported in part by a Summer Research Grant from the Graduate School of the University of Minnesota.

[2] Parts of this study were presented in the Symposium on Mechanisms in Cognitive Development at the Society for Research in Child Development, Berkeley, April 1963.

[3] Berlyne (1960) notes that a novel stimulus may "be surprising," thus implying "the existence of an expectation with which the stimulus disagrees." In the present study all novel stimuli are viewed as having expectations, but it is assumed that these expectations are less precise and less vivid than those preceding the surprising event. Furthermore, it is felt that surprise is best conceived of as the totality of covert and overt responses that are produced when an event fails to confirm an induced expectation. This definition requires knowledge of, and consequently allows maximum experimental control over, the expectation as well as the stimulus.

From W. R. Charlesworth. Instigation and maintenance of curiosity behavior as a function of surprise versus novel and familiar stimuli. Child Development, 1964, 35, 1169–1186. (With permission of the author and the Society for Research in Child Development, Inc.)

concerning certain contrived events. Surprise was produced by violating, by means of a trick, the law governing conservation of substance. The expectancy that physical substances—marbles in the present case—are not changed in color and number by merely shaking them in a container is known, on the basis of Piaget's (1954) work, to be already present in the preschool child. It was assumed that if such a violation was observed to occur, the subject would be surprised since such an event would contradict his expectations. The surprise reaction would then instigate him to demand to see the event again as well as possibly to make some form of inquiry into the reasons behind it. Novelty was introduced into the experiment by varying the color, number, and order of marbles from trial to trial. The precision of the expectancy was controlled by allowing S to see or not see the marbles before they were put into the container for shaking.

EXPERIMENT I

The experimental conditions consisted of four separate instances in which the relation between expectancies and outcomes was represented in terms of marbles placed into and poured from a trick container which allowed E to manipulate outcomes without S's knowledge. . . . The hypothesis of this experiment states that if a person is surprised by an unexpected event, he will be instigated to repeat the event more frequently, and demonstrate more curiosity about it, than if he is exposed to an event which confirms his expectations, or an event for which he has no precise expectation. Furthermore, being surprised will be more effective in instigating and maintaining curiosity behavior than being exposed to events that are defined as novel, or events that lack both surprise and novelty.

In the surprise condition (. . . Sur . . .) output marbles always varied in color and sometimes in number from the input marbles. This discrepancy between input and output was calculated to produce surprise since there was no visible means by which [this] could be achieved. . . . Novelty was achieved in this condition by using different combinations of marbles on each trial. A precise expectation of outcome was obtained by allowing S to see the marbles that were put into the container.

In the no-surprise condition (. . . NoSur . . .) output marbles always equaled input marbles in color, number, and order. This one-to-one relation between input and output . . . was calculated to produce no surprise.[4] Different combinations of marbles were used on each trial to maintain novelty. A precise expectation was obtained in the same fashion as in the Sur condition.

In the indeterminate expectancy condition (. . . IndetExp . . .) input marbles were hidden from S's sight, thus giving him an imprecise expectation on the basis of which he could only make a guess about the outcome. Novelty was achieved in the same fashion as in the preceding two conditions.

---

[4] The possibility that surprise would result when S became aware that output and input were always equal trial after trial was minimized, if not completely eliminated, in the first experiment by using Ss who, according to Charlesworth (1962) and Piaget and Inhelder (1951), are at the age when concepts of chance and probability are absent. In other words, the preschool child is insensitive to low-probability events (e.g., input *always* equaling output) and, in fact, has been observed in isolated instances to be surprised when the order of output marbles, holding color and number constant, is different from the input after vigorous shaking.

In the repeated confirmation condition (. . . RepConf . . .) output marbles always equaled input marbles. In contrast to the preceding conditions, the same marbles were used from trial to trial to eliminate novelty. A precise expectation was obtained in the same fashion as in the Sur and NoSur conditions. . . .

Curiosity motivation under each condition was measured by the number of trials S chose to stay and "play the game," the assumption being that having the opportunity to play the game longer allowed S to express his curiosity in the form of observing the unexpected event repeatedly occur. Facial, verbal, and vocal responses, rated in terms of the extent to which they manifested surprise, were also recorded as dependent variables.

It was predicted that Ss who were surprised (Ss in the Sur condition) would (a) take longer to satiate, i.e., play the game longer and (b) show a greater frequency of observable facial, verbal, and vocal surprise responses than Ss in the other conditions. The inevitable decline of the curiosity motive under the surprise condition is seen as a function both of fatigue factors and of an assumed decrease in the precision of the expectancies preceding each event. Since S soon learns that it is impossible to predict correctly on the basis of the information given him, he generates his own predictions or expectancies, but they are neither as concrete nor as precise as those presented to him in the memory aid and bolstered by his own concept of conservation of substance. Hence the strength of the motive ultimately declines in the same fashion as in the IndetExp condition. However, the decline is slower than in the latter condition because of the hypothesized initial motivating effects of surprise.

It was further hypothesized that Ss in the NoSur condition would satiate at approximately the same rate as those in the IndetExp condition. The consequences of having expectations consistently reinforced would, it was thought, be equally as effective in maintaining behavior as the effects of observing events that were impossible to anticipate with accuracy and hence had low surprise value, if any. In addition, it was predicted that Ss in the RepConf condition would satiate earlier than Ss in the two preceding conditions because of the relative absence of novelty.

Method

Subjects Ss were 92 normal white and Negro preschool children between 37 and 70 months with a mean age of 56 months. Roughly three-fourths of the Ss were from lower-class families who sent their children to one of three day nurseries in the area. The remaining children were from professional or middle-class families who sent their children to the University of Minnesota Institute of Child Development Nursery School. Ss were matched for age and sex and assigned randomly to experimental groups.

Apparatus   The apparatus (Figure 1) consisted of a container mounted on a horizontal pivot which allowed the container to be tipped to one side. A short input tube on the right of the container allowed S to insert marbles into it; a short output tube on the left allowed the marbles to be poured out when the container was tipped. When dumped, the marbles rolled into a receiving trough mounted adjacent to a similar trough containing marbles that served as a memory aid for the marbles put into the container. The container itself was built in such a way that marbles put into it by S would roll silently through a tube system to a receiving pad behind the apparatus where E was situated. Another tube system, leading from E to the container's output tube, allowed E to return any marbles he wished to the container without being seen.

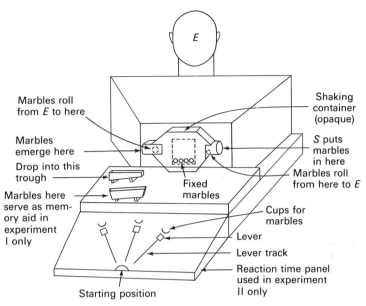

FIG. 1   Apparatus.

A mechanical device for shaking the container was also situated behind the screen. By pushing a button, E could shake the container automatically for a fixed number of shakes lasting a total of $1\frac{1}{2}$ seconds. Four marbles were placed permanently in the container to give S the impression that the marbles he put into the container were rattling inside when the container was shaken. The noise of the shaking device itself masked some of the rattling, so that it was impossible to know exactly how many marbles were inside.

Procedure   After establishing rapport with S on the way from the nursery school playroom, E introduced S to the game by pointing out where the marbles in the troughs were to be inserted into the container and where they would emerge after the container was shaken. S was informed that when playing the game he would always take the marbles from the receiving trough to place in the container and leave the other marbles, which were exactly like the latter, in the memory aid trough. In the IndetExp condition the marbles were contained in two opaque tubes, one for each trough, in order that S could not see them. The tubes could be easily handled when pouring marbles into the container.

When S indicated that he knew how the game was to be played, E told him to start playing and while doing so to keep his eyes on the marbles when they went into the container and especially when they came out. Each trial consisted of S putting one set of marbles into the container, E automatically shaking the container, then tipping it to dump the marbles out in view of S and waiting five seconds during which S's reaction to the output was recorded. At the end of the five-second period E removed both sets of marbles from both troughs and immediately replaced them with two new sets according to a predetermined plan. S then started the next trial by putting the latter marbles into the container.

The above procedure held for the first three trials. However, at the end of the third trial, after *E* placed the new set of marbles into the trough, *E* said, "From now on you may play the game as long as you want to. If you want to stop now you may, or if you want to play again, you may. You may do whatever you want to do. It doesn't matter to us what you do. Now, what do you want to do—stop or keep playing?" The Institute of Child Development *S*s were asked the question on each trial. This was subsequently discovered to be unnecessary; hence, the remaining seven groups of *S*s were asked the question on every third trial. *E* made a special effort to present the question in as neutral a tone as possible. *S*'s first reply to the question was final. If *S* stated a desire to continue *E* said, "All right. Put those marbles in the container." If *S* stated he wished to stop playing, *E* said, "All right. That's the end of the game. Thank you for playing."

Six groups of *S*s were allowed to play the game for a maximum of 20 trials; the other three groups were allowed 40 trials.

Any comments or questions made by *S* during the game were responded to with silence, or, if necessary, in a nondirective fashion. Special care was taken to minimize social reinforcement. Two different male *E*s were used at various times. The alternate *E* served both as an observer as well as a monitor of the participating *E*'s behavior as he conducted the experiment. At three of the four nursery schools a female observer served as a second monitor and rater, in addition to the male observer. The presence of the female observer had no appreciable effect on the *S*s' behavior as results later indicated.

Observers rated *S*'s facial, verbal, and vocal responses on a five-point scale with zero as the lowest value. All behavior was rated with special attention paid to responses— e.g., mouth movements, raising of eyebrows, exclamations, questions—that were agreed upon to be indicative of surprise. Brief descriptions of the surprises—e.g., whether there was perplexity, uneasiness, or mild shock—were recorded whenever possible. . . . During a judge training session, as well as during the experiments themselves, a total of 558 facial, 549 vocal, and 558 verbal responses were rated for surprise by at least two of a total of five judges who participated in the training session or in the study itself. Because of the nature of the experimental setting, it was frequently impossible to prevent the observer from knowing the experimental condition *S* was in since *S* often made remarks concerning the game. The average [interjudge reliability] values for each class of response were: (a) facial, .639, (b) verbal, .812, (c) vocal, .736. . . . The relatively moderate values obtained here, plus the rater's knowledge of *S*'s experimental condition, warrant caution in interpreting conclusions from the ratings.

Results

As predicted, the mean number of trials to satiation (Table 1) is higher for *S*s in the Sur condition . . . than any other condition. Three out of the four comparisons between *S*s in the Sur condition and *S*s in the other conditions are significant. . . . The Institute Nursery test falls short of significance . . . , but performance is clearly in the predicted direction.

Ratings of facial, verbal, and vocal responses in terms of surprise justify the methods used to produce the surprise and nonsurprise conditions. In all instances the facial

TABLE 1   Mean number of trials to satiation and number of Ss according to experimental condition and nursery

Condition	Institute*		Wilder I*		Wilder II†		Wilder III*	
	N	Mean	N	Mean	N	Mean	N	Mean
Surprise	10	12.6	—	—	12	32.7	10	16.6
No surprise	10	6.2	—	—	—	—	10	8.1
Indeterminate expectancy	—	—	9	12.9	12	19.8	—	—
Repeated confirmation	—	—	9	11.0	10	15.1	—	—

*Maximum number of trials to satiation equals 20.
† Maximum number of trials to satiation equals 40.

response was the most discriminating response (Table 2). All four comparisons of facial responses . . . involving surprise and nonsurprise conditions were significant and in the direction predicted. Ss who were presented with a discrepancy between input and output expressed facial changes indicative of surprise more frequently and intensely than Ss who were presented with a congruency between input and output, or an output without knowledge of the input (IndetExp condition).

Verbal responses, most of which were in the form of interrogatives, discriminated between Ss in the Sur and IndetExp conditions as well as between Ss in the latter condition and Ss in the RepConf condition. Why there were no other instances of significant differences in verbal responses between Ss in surprise conditions and Ss in nonsurprise conditions is puzzling. It was expected that Ss in the Sur condition in general would ask more questions than they did. Many seemed to take the surprising event for granted and were far more intent upon repeating it than inquiring into its

TABLE 2   Mean ratings of facial, verbal, and vocal surprise responses for first three trials according to experimental condition and nursery

Responses	Institute	Wilder I	Wilder II	Wilder III
Sur condition				
Facial	6.23	—	3.91	3.50
Verbal	3.02	—	2.75	1.25
Vocal	3.34	—	1.17	1.05
NoSur condition				
Facial	2.88	—	—	1.30
Verbal	1.20	—	—	0.00
Vocal	0.95	—	—	0.00
IndetExp condition				
Facial	—	2.33	2.55	—
Verbal	—	1.67	0.17	—
Vocal	—	0.78	0.25	—
RepConf condition				
Facial	—	1.67	1.00	—
Verbal	—	0.00	0.60	—
Vocal	—	0.11	0.30	—

nature. Other Ss appeared surprised, but too shy to say anything. Ss in Wilder Day Nursery 1, IndetExp condition, asked more questions than Ss in the RepConf condition, suggesting that the former may have been formulating hypotheses about the contents of marbles in the tube that were put into the container and then asking why the output did not confirm them. In the RepConf condition there was no need to ask questions or comment because the same thing occurred trial after trial.

The expectation that the IndetExp condition would produce stronger motivation to remain in the game than the RepConf condition was not borne out, although there is a tendency in this direction (Table 1, Wilder Day Nurseries I and III). The role of novelty, as defined by a change of marbles from trial to trial, appears negligible under the present conditions.

Comparisons between the NoSur condition and the IndetExp and RepConf conditions could not be tested because of limitations on sample sizes from particular nursery schools. However, a cursory comparison across Wilder Nursery Schools I and III, which were not apparently different in composition, indicates no sizeable difference between groups in mean number of trials to satiation.

The findings in general support the hypothesis that a surprising event can serve to instigate and maintain curiosity behavior as manifested in the tendency to repeat interesting and unexpected events, and can do so more effectively than novel events, events with imprecise expectations, and events that occur repeatedly in the same fashion.

EXPERIMENT II

[A second experiment] was designed to replicate most aspects of the previous experiment with older Ss [first and third graders] and under slightly different conditions. Reaction times were included as an additional dependent variable. . . .

DISCUSSION AND CONCLUSION

In both experiments the main hypothesis [was] supported. A surprising event, as defined operationally in this study, appears directly responsible for instigating and maintaining a form of curiosity behavior that repeatedly exposes the subject to the event. The consequences of not having precise expectancies confirmed have been demonstrated to be more effective in prolonging curiosity behavior than the consequences incurred when expectancies are confirmed or when expectancies are imprecise. These results challenge two related commonsense notions: (a) that nonconfirmation of expectancies leads to disappointment, a mildly noxious stimulus condition which raises the probability of subsequent avoidance behavior; and (b) that confirmation leads to a hedonically more pleasant state of affairs which conversely raises the probability of increased approach behavior. It thus appears that a surprising event under certain conditions has the effect of keeping the subject in the presence of the stimulus conditions which produced the event.

The relevance of these findings for a theory of cognitive development is most apparent for Piaget's theory, which places heavy emphasis upon the acquisition of concepts that allow the subject to anticipate correctly important aspects of his physical environment. Knowledge of the latter is generally achieved after prolonged sensorimotor contact between the subject and environmental objects and events. In Piagetian terms, the assimilation of objects or events in the environment presupposes relevant sensori-motor or cognitive structures which, among other things, aid the subject in anticipating the real nature of such objects or events. The failure of assimilation partially indicates that the object or event was incorrectly anticipated. The surprise that normally follows is a manifestation of this failure. However, as argued earlier (Charlesworth, 1963), surprise may not only involve an expressive release of affect, but also have drive qualities and perhaps acquire instrumental value by serving as the mediator through which generalization of curiosity behavior to future surprising events takes place. One of the consequences of curiosity behavior is to produce familiarization with novel stimuli and such familiarization is necessary for accommodation, which can ultimately lead to successful adaptation. The role of surprise then would seem to be important in cognitive development, since it almost invariably accompanies the nonconfirmation of an expected event and can serve to signal the need for a necessary adjustment to take place in the cognitive apparatus.

REFERENCES

Berlyne, D. E. *Conflict, arousal, and curiosity*. New York: McGraw-Hill, 1960.

Berlyne, D. E., & Slater, J. Perceptual curiosity, exploratory behavior, and maze learning. *Journal of Comparative and Physiological Psychology*, 1957, **50**, 228–232.

Butler, R. A. Discrimination learning by rhesus monkeys to visual exploration motivation. *Journal of Comparative and Physiological Psychology*, 1953, **46**, 95–98.

Charlesworth, W. R. The growth of knowledge of the effects of rotation and shaking on the linear order of objects. Unpublished doctoral dissertation, Cornell University, 1962.

Charlesworth, W. R. The role of surprise and novelty in the motivation of curiosity behavior. Paper presented at the meeting of the Society for Research in Child Development, Berkeley, April 1963.

Hunt, J. McV. Motivation inherent in information processing and action. Unpublished manuscript, 1963.

Montgomery, K. C., & Segall, M. Discrimination learning based upon the exploratory drive. *Journal of Comparative and Physiological Psychology*, 1955, **48**, 225–228.

Piaget, J. *The construction of reality in the child*. (Translated by M. Cook). New York: Basic Books, 1954.

Piaget, J., & Inhelder, B. *La genèse de l'idée de hasard chez l'enfant*. Paris: University of France Press, 1951.

III

LANGUAGE ACQUISITION

Charles Clifton, Jr. [1]

In some of the specialized areas within child psychology, one finds a consensus about what kinds of scientific questions can legitimately be asked and a consensus about the proper way of going about answering the questions. The area of language acquisition is not one in which such a consensus is found. Rather, modern child psychologists seem to take a number of incommensurate approaches to the problem of language acquisition. Such a lack of consensus may be surprising when it is realized that the problem of how a child learns language is one of the oldest recognized problems in psychology. The ancient philosophers considered the problem, and those eighteenth-century scientists who can be considered the direct intellectual ancestors of modern child psychologists spent a good deal of their research time collecting data on language acquisition. On somewhat closer examination, however, one finds a good answer to the question

[1] This chapter was written while the author was Assistant Professor in the Institute of Child Behavior and Development at the University of Iowa.

of why psychologists have never settled on one best way of asking and answering questions about language development. The answer is that none of the older approaches has worked very well. The baby biographies written by the eighteenth- and nineteenth-century child psychologists never led to many interesting or secure generalizations about how children acquire language, and neither did the vast amount of normative work that was done in the first half of the twentieth century. Likewise, theories of language acquisition and use (e.g., Skinner, 1957) that stemmed from work on animal and human learning have not shed much light on language development; at best, such theories showed that technical terms, well defined in the field of animal behavior, could have their definitions stretched to include almost anything.

However, one very promising approach to language acquisition and use has developed in the past decade. The present chapter will concentrate on this approach, which stems largely from recent developments in the field of linguistics. These developments will not be discussed in any detail here; rather, a consideration of certain aspects of language acquisition from the new "psycholinguistic" point of view will be emphasized. The student who is ambitious enough to read some of the technical literature in linguistics will find his effort well rewarded. The writings of Noam Chomsky are especially recommended (see Chomsky, 1965). Be warned that the psycholinguistic point of view is in a state of rapid development; there are many questions about language acquisition that have not yet been formulated clearly, much less answered well, and certainly some of the answers that now seem correct will later seem wrong.

From the psycholinguistic point of view, the most interesting (or at least, the most answerable) questions about language acquisition are those that involve the skills of speaking and understanding. This chapter, therefore, will concentrate on how the child learns to speak and understand sentences. Such a concentration will prevent examining some questions about language such as why a child says one thing rather than another and how a child can use language to control and direct his nonverbal behavior. Such questions are very important; after all, speech does serve a purpose. Still, there is a great deal to be learned by studying the form of language and ignoring, for the time being, the function of language.

A few words about the organization of the chapter are in order. The topic of language acquisition has been divided into discussions of the output of the language learner, the input he receives, and the function he uses to get from input to output. (The word "function" is used here in something like its mathematical sense.) In the discussion of output, consideration will be given to what the child knows about language at different points in his development and to the question of how he uses what he knows about language. In the discussion of input, the chapter will consider what little is known about the kinds of experience the child has with language. In the discussion of the function relating input to output, information will be considered about how the child learns a language. A good argument can be made for the point that how a child learns a language is the most important question, and in fact, conclusions about the nature of input or output are interesting only to the extent that they shed light on the process of language acquisition.

Great quantities of normative data about child language are available. One can go to sources such as McCarthy (1954) and learn the mean age at which children can first say a word, the mean length of sentences said by seven-year-olds, the ratio of adverbs to nouns in the speech of four-year-olds, and the like. Such data are necessary, and they are probably invaluable to applied work in language learning. Still, one can immerse himself in these normative data for any length of time and come out having learned little or nothing about the process of language acquisition. These data have not led psychologists to important generalizations.

OUTPUT

Something more must be done than tabulating those characteristics of the utterances made by children that are easily observed and measured. Two complementary suggestions about this "something more" can be made. The first is that the psycholinguist need not arbitrarily choose aspects of utterances to examine. The field of descriptive linguistics (roughly, the science that formulates descriptions of individual languages and of language in general) furnishes the psycholinguist with many secure and far-reaching generalizations about the structure of language. The psycholinguist is well advised to study those aspects of utterances and those aspects of language that cannot be directly observed, but only indirectly inferred, that figure in the generalizations provided by the linguist.

The second suggestion is that the psycholinguist must distinguish between what the child knows about language and the particular utterances he happens to make. It is clear that the particular sentences a language user happens to say or hear are determined not only by his knowledge of the language, but also by the situations in which he finds himself, by how much linguistic and nonlinguistic information he can hold in his mind at one time, etc. It is also clear that adults, and even very young children, continually produce clear utterances that they have never said before, and they can correctly understand sentences they have never heard before. It must be assumed that a person has knowledge about his language that he has not exhibited. It seems that the psycholinguist must aim, not merely at a description of the sentences he hears a child say, but at a description of what the child knows about the language that enables him to say and understand these and many other sentences.

Prelinguistic utterances and early speech

It is commonplace to observe that the infant comes into the world vocalizing. A substantial amount of work has been done in analyzing the vocalizations of the young infant. This work has generally ignored the suggestions related to linguistics that have just been put forward—and probably with good reason. The noises an infant makes in the initial months of life are not linguistic, and they cannot be analyzed as if they were evidence of a developing ability with language.

In the first few weeks, infants' vocalizations are primarily cries. The occurrence of these cries is presumably dependent on something that is happening to the infant, and they may serve to communicate to the mother something about what is happening (see the discussion in Brown, 1958). Noncrying sounds (primarily vowel-like sounds made by vocalizing through a partly open mouth, and consonant-like sounds made in the back of the mouth) make their appearance in the first couple of months. Such sounds are sometimes described as indicating comfort or pleasure. Neither cries nor "pleasure sounds" can be considered much like language. They may serve to communicate, but they have nothing of the structure and regularity that marks human language. They are not random noises, but they probably possess regularities for rather uninteresting reasons. For instance, most of the consonant-like sounds a baby makes are made with the tongue obstructing the vocal tract near the back of the mouth—probably because the tongue of a baby lying on its back tends to drop toward the rear of the mouth.

Something a little more like language appears late in the first half-year of life.[2] This infant "babbling" is marked by greater variety of sounds than were the earlier utterances and does not seem to be so obviously dependent on things that are happening to the infant. One has the impression that the infant is playing with sounds. It cannot be claimed that babbling is language behavior, but psychologists have frequently made the claim that language develops as an elaboration of babbling activity.

Some data suggest that the sounds made as the babbling baby grows older become more and more like the adult sounds in the language the baby hears. It is tempting to think that this change with age is due to the parents selectively rewarding those noises that sound most like their own. However, one becomes doubtful when he observes the tendency of new parents to reward any sound their child makes (or, on some occasions, to reward no sound). Some psychologists (notably O. H. Mowrer, 1952) have made a different suggestion for the babbling drift. Mowrer says that the baby hears his mother making language sounds when she is doing nice things for him, and that through such an association, these sounds gain acquired reward value. Subsequently, when the baby happens to produce an utterance that sounds to him like one of these sounds, his hearing it reinforces the response of making it. Thus, the response is more likely to be made in the future. Gradually, then, the noises the child makes come to be more and more like those of the mother.

A hypothesis like Mowrer's has its attractions. It does tie an aspect of language learning to behavior theory, and it does seem as if it could be extended to cover the whole of language learning. That is, one might claim that a child learns to say grammatical sentences because they are like the sentences he heard his parents say. However, the hypothesis is not above criticism. For one thing, it does not answer the most important question of how the child perceives some of his sounds to be similar to the sounds his mother makes while he perceives other of his sounds to be different. Acoustically, all of the child's sounds are highly distinctive from his parents' sounds. There seem to be no simple physical dimensions on which a sound the parent makes and the child's version of the "same sound" are especially similar. The problem of how the child recognizes simi-

---

[2] The age at which evidence of some bit of grammatical knowledge is observed will usually be mentioned, but these ages should not be taken too seriously. They are very rough estimates based on a small number of children.

larity between his speech and his parents' speech becomes even more acute when the hypothesis is extended to later phases of language learning. The way in which all grammatical utterances are similar to one another, but dissimilar to ungrammatical utterances, is not simple at all. The psychologist who chooses to claim that a child makes utterances that are similar to those that his parents make because the parents' utterances have acquired reward value must explain how the child recognizes some of his utterances to be similar to his parents' utterances. Unless he can explain this, his claim is rather empty.

It is worth considering the possibility that babbling has little to do with later language acquisition beyond exercising the vocal mechanism and allowing the child to learn some relations between his vocal activities and the sounds he produces. It seems likely that the original reason investigators of child language thought babbling to be important was that most human children, and only human children, babble. Likewise, most human children, and only human children, learn language. However, the "if-and-only-if" relationship between babbling and learning language is not perfect. There are children (Lenneberg, 1964) who have learned language (in the sense of being able to understand new, grammatically complex sentences) even though they have never babbled or made any linguistic utterances. Babbling is not necessary for the learning of language. Further, deaf children babble in an apparently normal fashion for their first few months, but are usually seriously retarded in learning language. Babbling is not sufficient for the learning of language. Lenneberg (1967b) summarizes some of these findings in an article reprinted at the end of this chapter.

An additional reason for questioning the notion that language is built out of babbling is that a quantitatively and qualitatively different type of utterance appears at around one year of age when words begin to appear. Quantitatively, one finds such things as a shift in the type of consonants that appear most frequently. Earlier, consonant-like sounds formed in the back of the mouth were the most common, but now consonants formed in the front of the mouth are most common. Qualitatively, one observes the appearance of linguistic structuring in the child's sounds. The prelinguistic utterances did seem to communicate something, but there was no clear pattern of distinctions among the sounds of the utterances. It is as if the child made, on occasion, all the noises his mouth was capable of making, sometimes loudly, sometimes softly. With the appearance of words, however, stable distinctions between classes of sounds appear. The child seems first to make a distinction in his speech between consonants and vowels. When he is saying his word for "mother," he says "ma" or "ba," but does not say "ahm" or "ahb." His word has a consistent consonant-vowel order which indicates that he distinguishes between consonants and vowels. Somewhat later in his development, the child may make a distinction between different consonants, saying "ma" in some situations and "da" in others. Not long after this, a more intricate kind of patterning appears. The child may add a new vowel (perhaps "ĭ") to his speech repertoire. The old distinction between the consonants carries over from words using the old vowel to words using the new one, so that where the child previously had two possible words, "ma" and "da," he now has four, "ma," "da," "mĭ," and "dĭ."

There are fascinating theories, backed up by rather scanty data, about the way in which this sound structuring grows. Leopold (1953–54) discusses one of the most interesting of the theories. The theory states, roughly, that the child neither learns new sounds one at a time, nor gradually becomes more and more able to use a haphazard sample of the sounds he hears. Rather, the child learns distinctions between groups of sounds; that is, he learns attributes of sounds that serve to distinguish one group of sounds from another. For instance, the child who uses the consonants "b" and "d" may learn the distinction between consonants that are made with the vocal cords vibrating and consonants that are made with the vocal cords not vibrating. This single distinction, applied to the two available consonants, will provide the child with a total of four consonants, "b," "p," "d," and "t."

Not enough is known about the development of sound patterning to evaluate the available theories. The topic is open for fruitful research. It is worth noting that the two suggestions about linguistics, made earlier in the chapter, are very relevant to research on the topic. First, linguistics provides the psycholinguist with analyses of language (particularly, ways of classifying and relating different speech sounds) that are applicable to the child's early linguistic behavior. Second, it would be unwise, in research on the topic, to unquestioningly identify what the child is able to say with what the child knows. At the very least, it is possible that the child is able to make consistent distinctions between sounds he hears before he is able to honor these distinctions in his speech.

Earliest sentences

In contrast to the lack of evidence on the acquisition of sound structuring, there is a good deal of recently collected data on the early acquisition of sentence structure. Toward the end of his second year, the child begins putting two words together in a single utterance. These two-word utterances are not haphazard pairings of all the words the child knows. Rather, they have a definite structure; certain word sequences are produced by the child while others are not.

Several workers (e.g., Bellugi & Brown, 1964) have investigated the structure of early sentences. These researchers recorded large numbers of utterances made by a small number of children and applied linguistic techniques of analysis to the utterances in an attempt to describe their structure. They wrote a grammar for each child's language; the grammar consisted of a set of explicit rules that describe what words the child put together in what order to make his sentences. Their endeavor has been remarkably successful, uncovering a striking similarity between children in the types of sentence structure used.

It is possible to describe these young children's grammars informally. The grammars generally make reference to two distinct classes of words. That is, the children studied treat the words they know as if they fall into two classes, and the words in the two classes are used differently in sentences. One class— referred to as the "pivot class"—is composed of a small number of words, each of which occurs with high frequency in the child's speech. The other class—the "open class"—is composed of the remaining words in the child's vocabulary. Most new words that the child learns enter the open class.

The grammars also generally specify that a sentence is composed of a single open-class word (O word) or a combination of an O word and a pivot-class word (P word). For most children, the P word precedes the O word in sentences. Some children seem to have two distinct pivot classes, where the words in one pivot class can precede the O word, and the words in the other pivot class follow the O word. Sentences made up of a single P word, or a P word followed by another P word, are almost never found. Sentences made up of two O words occur, but they occur only infrequently in the first two or three months after a child begins making two-word sentences. They occur more frequently later, but seem to be products of a more elaborate grammar.

The membership of the pivot class and of the open class, are rather heterogeneous with respect to adult parts of speech. For one child, the pivot class might contain adult adjectives, verbs, pronouns, and articles. For another child, the open class might contain adult nouns and adjectives. As an example, Braine (1963a) reported that one child had one pivot class that consisted of "all," "I," "no," "see," "more," "hi," and "other," a second pivot class consisting of "off," "by," "come," and "there" (the last preceded by "on," "in," "up," or "down"), and an open class containing "broke," "bed," "fix," "boot," and a number of other words. The child made utterances like "all broke," "no bed," "no fix," and "boot off."

One thing that has been noticed about the child's two-word utterances and the somewhat longer utterances that appear later is that they often do not include adult "function words," like prepositions, articles, and conjunctions. The child's speech has been called "telegraphic." His speech sounds like the messages one writes in telegrams. Telegraphic is a good description of the child's speech, but it is not an explanation of why his speech sounds as it does. Telegraphic speech does not refer to a process; the child does not start with a full adult sentence, and then lop off the function words in an attempt to keep what he wants to say within his memory or production span.

Braine makes one suggestion toward an explanation of the occurrence of the $P + O$ sentence construction. He says that children learn the position in utterances in which certain words can occur. In the case we are considering, the child learns that his P words can occur in the first position (sometimes, second position) in utterances. The child forms a $P + O$ utterance by putting a word whose position he knows into its position and then by putting another word whose position is not specifically known (an O word) in the other position. Braine presents experimental data indicating that children *can* learn the positions in utterances that words can take. He gathers his evidence in an interesting way, by constructing a simple artificial language and then having his subjects learn the language.

It may well be true that very young children can learn the positions of words in utterances, as Braine says. But this does not mean that they learn such positions when they are learning their natural language. In fact, there is reason to doubt that they do or that such learning forms an important part of learning a natural language. For one thing, it is not likely that the language a child hears has enough positional regularities. In English, just about any word can occur in just about any position in sentences.

If what the child learns accurately reflects what he hears (in terms of the positions in which words can occur), he should not learn that certain words can occur only in certain positions. Rather, he should learn that any word can occur in any position. It might be argued that he notes, and learns, only certain positions that some words can occur in; he notes that some words can occur first in utterances, and ignores the fact that they can also occur later in utterances. He forms his *P* class from these words. However, it would seem that such a process would lead to a haphazard selection of words to put in the *P* class. While the membership of the *P* class is heterogeneous, it is not haphazard. Words that belong to different parts of speech in the adult language do not often fall in different word classes in the child's language. For instance, very seldom do nouns occur both in the *P* class and the *O* class.

McNeill (in Lyons & Wales, 1966) briefly put forward another view. He suggested that the child, at the time he starts learning language, knows such major syntactic relations as "subject of," "predicate of," "modifier of," etc., that appear in all languages. At the start, one child might pick out the relations modifier of (defined as occurring before a noun in the sentence) and predicate of (defined as occurring after the main noun phrase of the sentence).[3] Words that the child notices entering the modifier-of relation form the *P* class; words that enter the predicate-of relation form the *O* class.

As far as it goes, this explanation fits the data. It also accounts for the rather remarkable fact that Russian children (Slobin, in Smith & Miller, 1966), and perhaps Japanese children (McNeill, in Lyons & Wales, 1966), seem to learn a *P* + *O* construction in their first grammar, much as do American children, even though the superficial structure of the language they hear is very different. However, the explanation has its troubles. It is vague. It does not account for how the child recognizes a noun, or a noun phrase, as he must do if he is to recognize the syntactic relations he is presumed to know. And the explanation assumes that the child has a great deal of knowledge about language that he did not acquire through experience. (This point will be considered again in the section on the linguistic input-output func-

---

[3] The phrase, "in the base structure of the sentence," would be more accurate than the phrase, "in the sentence." However, pursuing this distinction would get us into too many (fascinating) linguistic complexities. The interested student would do well to read Postal, in Brown et al., 1964.

tion.) However, the explanation is of a type needed to account for the acquisition of language.

Young children's later grammar

Children's sentences soon become longer. Their grammars become more complex, as does the problem of explaining how they formed the grammar. This chapter will examine only a few aspects of this later grammatical development: the formation of hierarchical structure in three-word sentences, the early development of negative sentences, and the development of patterns of inflections, such as the plural noun suffix and the past-tense verb suffix.

Hierarchical Structure of the Noun Phrase

In a delightful overview of their work, Brown and Bellugi (in Brown et al., 1964) point out two things that happen in the child's developing grammar. For one thing, the child subdivides his vocabulary into additional word classes (beyond the P and O classes). At least at the start, these new classes are formed by successively splitting the P and O classes into finer subclasses. One child might begin with a P class consisting of articles ("a," "the"), a demonstrative pronoun ("that"), a possessive pronoun ("my"), a qualifier ("two"), etc. Several weeks later, the child has split this class into three smaller classes—a class of articles, a class of demonstrative pronouns, and a residual class. He uses the words in these different classes differently in sentences. It has been suggested that a similar process of subdividing old classes into new classes goes on until the classes in the adult grammar are reached. This suggestion is probably too simplified. There do seem to be some instances of words being moved from class to class, especially words that were at one time in different classes being put later into the same class. For instance one child, described by Braine (1963a), used "get" as an O word and "see" as a P word, but both "get" and "see" fall in the class of transitive verbs in the language the child will eventually learn.

The other change that Brown and Bellugi point out is that the child's sentences develop a hierarchical structure. They no longer can be considered simple chains of words. Instead, the sentences can be divided into a small number of parts (immediate constituents), which can in turn be divided into parts until the word is reached. In the speech of the child described by Brown and Bellugi, we find utterances like "That a blue flower," "Where the puzzle go," and "A horsie crying." The first sentence can be divided into the constituents "that" and "a blue flower"; the latter phrase can be broken down into "a" and "blue flower," and so on. The second sentence can be broken down into "where . . . go" and "the puzzle"; the latter phrase can be divided into "the" and "puzzle."

Evidence can be found that word strings like "a blue flower" are indeed units, or constituents, of the child's longer sentence. For instance, some of these presumed constituents occur as complete utterances (sometimes $P + O$ utterances) in the child's speech. Also, the child makes utterances identical to those in which a presumed constituent phrase occurred, except that the phrase is replaced by a single word which we know to be a unit. As an example, we find "that flower," which can be compared to the sentence "That a blue flower" cited earlier. Furthermore, the child sometimes uses pronouns to replace entire noun phrases, as well as to replace single noun words. For instance, he says "Hit ball" and "Get it," as well as "Fix a tricycle" and "Fix it." Also, the child has a revealing tendency to include in the same utterance both a pronoun and the noun or noun phrase for which it stands. For instance, we find "Mommy get it ladder" and "Mommy get it my ladder." Thus, it is quite clear that the sentences a child says in his third year of life already have a moderately complex internal structure. The child does not produce sentences simply by chaining words together.

Early Negative Sentences

Klima and Bellugi (in Lyons & Wales, 1966) have presented a discussion of some aspects of the grammatical development of three children in the third year of life. We will consider the development of negative sentences in these children.

The child's earliest negative sentences can be described as the word "no" or "not" followed by a sentence that, for the child, is grammatical. Less frequently, a negative sentence consists of an affirmative sentence followed by "no" or "not." We find the sentences "No . . . wipe finger," "No the sun shining," and "Not . . . fit" in the speech of Klima and Bellugi's two-year-old children. These sentences do not seem to be like the adult "No, you can't have it" type of sentence, since the child does not put a falling intonation on the "no" in the way an adult does. Also unlike the adult, the child does not produce sentences with the negative element embedded inside. Klima and Bellugi suggest that the child does not even understand sentences with an embedded negative, unless he is prompted. As evidence they furnish the exchange:

Mother: *I'm not sure.*
Child: *Sure.*
Mother: *No, I'm not sure.*

It is interesting to note that Slobin (in Smith & Miller, 1966) observed that Russian children's first negatives are of the same form—e.g., "nyet dam" ("no I-will-give"). This is particularly noteworthy since the adult Russian sentences that the child hears often contain a double negative "nyet ni dam" ("no not I-will-give").

A few months later, the child makes utterances like "No . . . Rusty hat," "I can't catch you," "I don't want it," "He not little, he big," and "I no want envelope." He continues to make negative sentences by adding "no" or "not" to the beginning or the end of a sentence, but he also has some new ways of forming negatives. Particularly, he now can embed some negative elements inside a sentence between the subject nominal and the predicate. The negative element can be "no," "not," "can't," or "don't." The child can also form negative imperatives, such as "Don't bite me yet." Not only can the child produce sentences with embedded negatives, he can understand them, as witness the exchange:

Mother: *Well, I can't change your diaper right now.*
Child: *Why not?*

The child often sounds like he is speaking adult English at this time. However, some things are lacking. For instance, he has no nonnegative auxiliary verbs, like "can," "have," or "do." Also, his negative elements are severely limited in variety. A few months later, though, further changes have occurred. The child is observed to say "I didn't see something," "Cause he won't talk," "This not ice cream," "It's not cold," "I not crying," and "No, it isn't." In addition, he makes affirmative sentences with the modal auxiliaries like "can" and "have." Whereas before we had to consider "can't" a unitary negative element on a par with "no" and "not," now we can consider it the combination of "can" and the contracted "not," as in adult speech. The child now has a more complex and wider system of negatives. The child's language is moving toward adult language in other ways, as in the appearance of sentences like "No, it isn't" pronounced with proper intonation, and in the appearance of indeterminants, such as "I see something."

However, the child is still not speaking adult English. Sentences like "I didn't see something" are still produced by the child; an adult would say "I didn't see anything." The next few months of development of the negative are briefly described by McNeill (in Smith & Miller, 1966). The child picks up more and more of the regularities in adult negatives, but all is not smooth sailing. For one thing, double negatives were not present earlier (except in question sentences, e.g., "Why not cracker not talk?"), but they now appear in full bloom. McNeill presents the observed sentences, "I can't do nothing with no string." The child does not gradually eliminate one type of grammatical error after another in his progression toward the adult language. Rather, the child acquires, one by one, grammatical principles that are behind the regularities in the adult language. Some of these grammatical principles, when added to the child's grammar, will produce utterances that sound less like adult sentences than did earlier utterances. But most of the principles will eventually fit into a grammatical system that allows the child to speak his native language.

Development of Inflections

Adult speakers of English use several inflectional endings in their speech—the third-person-singular verb inflection (jump*s*), the progressive verb inflection (jump*ing*), the past verb inflection (jump*ed*), the plural noun inflection (book*s*), the possessive noun inflection (boy'*s*), and the adjective inflections (*-er, -est*). The way these inflections are pronounced depends on the last sound of the world to which they are added. The plural is pronounced "z" in words like "dog," "s" in words like "book," and "ez" in words like "glass." In addition, some words have more or less unique inflected forms; the plural of "ox" is "oxen" and the past tense of "sing" is "sang." The regular inflectional forms are sometimes called "productive"; we can, and generally do, use them on new words that we learn.

In the utterances we have given as examples of children's speech, inflections (except for the progressive) are not found. In fact, inflections do not appear in children's first grammars (surprisingly, not even in highly inflected languages like Russian). As a rough estimate, inflections begin occurring with moderate frequency about the middle of the third year of life. Rather than trace the order of appearance of the various inflections, let us look at some data that give a more general answer to the question of what is learned in the acquisition of grammar.

Adults apply the productive forms of the inflections to new words they learn. This means that adults have not simply memorized the plural form of each noun, the past tense of each verb, and so on, although they must have done just this for the irregular inflectional forms. Rather, one might say that adults have learned a rule for making singular nouns into plurals, etc., and they apply these rules to new words they learn. We can ask if young children simply memorize pairs of singular and plural nouns, pairs of verb stems and third-person-singular verb forms, etc., or if they learn the rules for adding inflections? In other words, is their use of the inflections productive?

Note that throughout this chapter, the idea has been implicit that children do not simply repeat strings of words that they have memorized, but they continually invent new strings of words, new utterances. These new utterances are formed in accord with the child's grammar. We cannot doubt that this is the case, since children produce too many different utterances, especially too many utterances that seem to have no models in the speech the child has heard. Still it is nice to have direct evidence that the child's utterances are inventions rather than parrotings of utterances he has heard.

Berko (1958) has provided such evidence with respect to inflections. She tested preschool children and first graders for their ability to properly apply inflectional endings to nonsense words. As one task, she showed a child a picture of a birdlike animal, and said "This is a wug." Then she showed the child a picture of two of the animals, and said "Now there is another one. There are two of them. There are two _____ ." As another task, she showed the child a picture of a man with a steaming pitcher on his head. "This is a man who knows how to spow. He is spowing. He did the same thing yesterday. What did he do yesterday? Yesterday he _____ ." The child was encouraged to supply the missing words.

The children were scored for providing the correct form of the regular inflection. There were some differences among the various inflections and among the various forms of the same inflection (for instance, the "z" for the plural inflection was the best, while the "ez" was the worst). There were also age differences for some of the inflections, the older children generally doing better. Still, even the preschool children supplied the correct form of the correct inflection in a high percentage of cases.

By preschool age, children "know rules" for the productive use of inflections. However, inflections appear in their speech at a much earlier age. Ervin (in Lenneberg, 1964) has provided some interesting data about the course of acquisition of the productive inflectional rules. Consider the past-tense inflection of verbs. The first occurrences of past-tense inflections were the irregular inflections on the strong verbs. That is, the children's first inflected forms were words like "came," "went," and "sat." Only later did the regular productive inflections appear. Ervin's surprising finding was that these productive inflections first appeared on the *strong* verbs. The children said "comed," "goed," "sitted" before they said "looked," "walked," "laughed." Actually, it may be that the children applied the productive inflections to all verbs at the same time, but the strong verbs, being more frequent, were observed first by Ervin. Still, the regular inflections, which were not previously practiced a great deal, supplanted the irregular inflections, which had been highly practiced. As suggested before, the child seems to search out the regularities in the language he is learning and follow these regularities as widely as he can.

A comment on the study of linguistic output

This chapter has provided a description of some of the characteristics of the first grammars that children invent and some of the grammatical changes children go through. The descriptions of these characteristics and changes, and the explanations of them, made important use of such linguistic concepts as word class (part of speech), syntactical relation (subject of, predicate of, etc.), and hierarchial structure of sentences. However, the descriptions, which amount to representations of what a child knows about the structure of his language, were inferred almost entirely from the utterances the child was observed to make.

It was argued earlier that this method of inferring the child's knowledge is not sufficient, since what a child knows cannot be equated with what he is observed to do. Certainly, what the child is observed to say is influenced by chance events that occur when we happen to be observing him. Even more, there are limitations on what he can say that are extraneous to what he knows about language—limitations of memory, for instance. Observing speech in a relatively naturalistic situation has limitations as a technique for learning what a person knows about language. Additional techniques must be devised that do not have the same limitations as observing speech does.

Considerable information concerning what an adult knows about his language can be obtained by asking him. One can ask an adult, "Does such-and-such a sentence sound okay?" "Are the two sentences _____ and _____ saying the same thing?" These questions would yield gibberish from a two-year-old child. One comment. Psycholinguists speak of the child and the adult as knowing the grammar of his language and forming utterances in accord with the grammatical rules. They do not mean that the speaker consciously knows the rules. A linguist cannot ask the speaker to write a formal version of his grammar. He cannot, for instance, expect the speaker to tell him that the relative clause "who lost" in the sentence "The boxer who lost retired" is best analyzed as the result of transforming the structure of the sentence "The boxer retired and the boxer lost" into a structure like "The boxer *wh* the boxer lost retired," and then transforming "*wh* the boxer" into "who." Much less can the linguist expect the speaker to provide a set of properly formalized rules describing these grammatical facts. All the psycholinguist can say is that the speaker's utterances have the form and structure described by the formalized linguistic rules. This statement suggests that the utterances have their regular form because the speaker has some linguistic knowledge that is described using grammatical rules. The psycholinguist's task is to provide a psychologically acceptable account of this knowledge and of how it is used in producing and understanding sentences.

One cannot ask a young child direct questions about language. But it is possible to devise experimental techniques that can give information about the child's grammar that cannot be obtained by observing his speech. Berko's study (1958), described earlier, and a paper by Fraser, Bellugi, & Brown (1963), reprinted after the chapter, are instances of the application of such a technique. Fraser, Bellugi, and Brown asked three-year-old children to imitate utterances that were said to them (imitation), to point to pictures that were described by utterances that were said to them (comprehension), and to describe pictures appropriately by choosing utterances the experimenter said to them (production). The sentences involved various grammatical subtleties: the plural inflection, the singular and plural forms of the verb "to be," and the affirmative-negative contrast are examples. The three procedures of imitation, comprehension, and production can all be viewed as different techniques for assessing grammatical knowledge, which we will refer to as "competence." (It might be argued that the imitation procedure does not get at competence, since children can repeat what is said to them without knowing its structure. Actually, it is likely that children must apprehend an utterance's structure in order to repeat it *if* the utterance is long enough that it cannot be remembered as a string of words. The utterances used by Fraser et al. may or may not have all been long enough.) Fraser et al. found that the comprehension technique was a more sensitive indicator of grammatical knowledge than was the production technique, and they found that the imitation technique (subject to the parenthetical comment above) was more sensitive still. Simply observing the child's verbal productions would, therefore, underestimate his grammatical knowledge.

Devising experimental techniques that can be used to assess other facets of grammatical knowledge of younger children is a fascinating challenge, and it is one that is apt to occupy psycholinguists for some time. But we should take a moment to provide a corrective to the second suggestion made at the start of the chapter. The psycholinguist is not simply interested in grammatical competence. He is also interested in the factors that influence what a child says and understands and in the factors that limit the expression of grammatical competence in different settings. He is interested in how competence is used. One can argue that a knowledge of the grammatical competence of the child must come first. The psycholinguist simply does not know what to look at in the complexities of actual verbal performance unless he has a good description of his subject's grammatical competence to serve as a guide.

Advanced grammatical development

The chapter has traced the development of a few of the aspects of children's grammatical knowledge. The claim can be made that the child of four or five years of age knows the basic grammatical system of his native language. Judging from the evidence that we have discussed, and a good deal of similar evidence, the claim is probably valid. However, it does not mean that the child speaks just like an adult.

There are several ways in which the five-year-old's speech differs from the adult's. Although the child uses most of the adult's grammatical devices, he does not use many different grammatical devices or many instances of the same device in a single sentence. Adults can build complex sentences by tucking distorted simple sentences inside other sentences. The sentence "The man—who went to town on the train—when my father did—died not long ago" would not be surprising coming from an adult. But a young child simply does not perform such multiple embedding of sentences in sentences. Also, there are a few advanced grammatical devices that do not occur frequently in the speech of young children. Passive sentences, verb phrases using the "have" auxiliary, conditional sentences, and the like, are rare in the speech of young children (Menyuk, 1963a). In addition, children sometimes fail to follow a grammatical rule that is followed by adults, resulting in sentences in which something is omitted ("I want to go New York") or in which more grammatical elements than necessary are included ("She took it away the hat").

Some experimental techniques have been used in an attempt to determine what grammatical structures are outside the competence of children at around five years of age. Menyuk (1963b) used the technique of determining what types of sentences young children would imitate. She found that there were some sentence types that were seldom imitated correctly by preschool and kindergarten children. Examples of sentence forms that were not often correctly imitated are sentences with the auxiliary verb "have" ("I've already been there"), sentences with the conjunction "so" ("He saw him so he hit him"), and sentences with certain types of nominalizations ("She does the shopping and cooking and baking"). Incidentally, errors were not made on these types of sentences simply because they were long. The correlation between sentence length and number of subjects imitating it correctly was near zero. Apparently errors were made in imitating the sentences because the children did not have control of the grammatical structures of the sentences.

Menyuk (1963b) used another interesting technique for determining grammatical competence. She gave children sentences to imitate that were grammatically deviant in some way. She found that a sizeable number of her subjects spontaneously corrected some of these forms. The children often supplied verb inflections when they were missing, as in "He wash his face." This corrected-imitation technique is a promising one for assessing a child's grammatical knowledge; if a child spontaneously corrects a deviant sentence, he must have some knowledge (though perhaps not verbalizable knowledge) about the way in which the sentence was deviant. However, the technique is not a direct route to grammatical competence; the child may know perfectly well the way in which the sentence is deviant, but may choose not to correct it. Also, the technique comes very close to touching on questions involving how grammatical competence is employed in performance, rather than questions about what is in a child's competence. Questions such as "Does the child actually mishear the deviant sentence as correct, or does he correct it because it is easier for him to produce a grammatically normal sentence" are questions of performance.

Young children have somewhat different grammatical knowledge than do adults. They probably also have different limitations on their ability to employ their grammatical knowledge in speaking and in other tasks such as remembering or understanding sentences. Menyuk's research on imitating sentences can be viewed as an investigation of children's limitations in remembering sentences of different grammatical structures, rather than an investigation of which grammatical structures are within the bounds of a child's grammatical knowledge. The division between studies of linguistic competence and studies of performance involving linguistic knowledge is not always clear, since competence is necessarily investigated by observing performance.

However, some research must be considered an investigation of how linguistic competence is reflected in performance, rather than an investigation of competence per se. Slobin (1966) has conducted such research. The subjects in Slobin's experiment were required to indicate whether a sentence presented to them was true or false with respect to a picture they were shown. Slobin measured the time it took his subjects to indicate their decision. Among other things, he found that it took longer to decide about more grammatically complex sentences than about grammatically simpler sentences. He found few striking age differences, but he did find that the rate with which decision speed increased as age increased was greater for the more complex sentence constructions than for the simpler constructions. As Slobin suggests, this may indicate that the simpler aspects of grammar are stabilized at an earlier age than are the more complex aspects. Additionally, he found that using pictures in which the "actor" and the "victim" were not reversible (e.g., a man eating a watermelon) speeded up reaction time to the passive sentences, especially for younger children. This finding may be traced to the fact that grammatical analysis of passive sentences describing nonreversible pictures is not needed to determine which word is the subject of the sentence and which is the object. All that needs to be done is to pick out the word that makes sense as the subject of the verb and to decide that this is the subject of the sentence.

In later childhood, children become more fluent in using their grammatical knowledge. Additionally they gain new grammatical knowledge. If they go to school, they are even likely to be taught some explicit grammatical rules. However, it seems unlikely that the child acquires any substantial part of his grammatical knowledge through direct tuition. Even when a directly taught rule does seem to influence speech, the rule generally serves as a replacement for some previously learned implicit regularity. For example, when a child is taught not to say "ain't," he simply is given a different rule for changing the form of the verb "to be" preceding negation.

The older child's grammatical competence is close enough to the adult's that questions about further additions to his grammatical knowledge no longer seem to have burning importance. Questions about how competence is employed in the production and understanding of sentences become the central ones. This chapter has touched upon such questions, and they deserve further consideration. Instead of considering them, however, the question of "what kinds of experience with a language allow the child to learn it" will be examined next.

INPUT

If a normal child is exposed to a language, he will learn it. The question that must be asked is, "What beyond mere exposure to a haphazard sample of utterances is needed for language learning?" We can begin answering this question by setting up such subsidiary questions as: "What are some of the ways in which the child's linguistic input does differ from a haphazard sample of utterances? What are some characteristics of linguistic input that facilitate language learning or are even necessary for language learning to occur?"

These questions are important but unanswered. Not until recently have psychologists made systematic surveys of the language environment of the young child. Now, vast quantities of data are available (see Bullowa, Jones, & Bever, in Bellugi & Brown, 1964). But just having the data is not enough. The data must be reduced and analyzed. There are so many observations of mother-child verbal interactions that one does not know where to look first. Psycholinguists have not had many good ideas about how to examine the linguistic input the child receives; even so, a few interesting things are known about the input.

One particularly striking observation is the contrast between the differences in different children's linguistic experiences and the similarities in what they eventually learn about their language. The only child of middle-class parents is apt to have a great deal said to him, and to have attentive adults listening to what he has to say and correcting the way he says it. The seventh child of a non-English speaking immigrant family in a large city is apt to hear most of his early English on the streets from older children who are not particularly interested in him, and they certainly take no pains to correct the linguistic structure of his utterances. Remarkably, both of these children seem to learn the basics of a grammar in their first few years. Admittedly, the grammar that the middle-class child uses will be different from that of a Puerto Rican child in New York. Certainly, their vocabulary and "accent" will be different. Nonetheless, both children have a regularity in the structure of their sentences that can be called "grammatical regularity," and there is no evidence that one child's grammar is less complex than the other's.

The things a child learns about his native language may well be invariant over a very wide range of linguistic experience. Still, not every kind of experience with utterances in a language will serve for the learning of the language. The example has been used of a child in a dark room being hit over the head at five-minute intervals while a tape recorder blared English at him. This child would probably not learn English. Also, the rate of language acquisition will vary with different kinds of linguistic experience. A variety of environmental factors are known to influence speed of language learning. Children from a middle-class home learn language faster than children in an orphanage, although intensive exposure to language will speed up the orphans' learning. In comparison to children with siblings, only children are advanced in their language acquisition and are especially advanced relative to twins.

Other gross environmental differences are known to influence rate of language learning. But we would like to make finer-grained more-analytic statements about what kinds of experience are necessary for, and helpful in, acquiring a language. Let us consider some of the possible types of experience that have been suggested.

One possibility is that children's language learning rests upon exposure to a simplified, grammatically cleaned-up sample of language. The notion is that children will learn the structure of their language faster if it is presented to them in its basic, least complicated form with a minimum of false leads given to them in the form of ungrammatical sentences. The best evidence that is available—and it is none too good—indicates that children of well-educated middle-class parents do not receive a particularly high proportion of fully grammatical utterances. Bever, Fodor, & Weksel (1965) stated that slightly over 40 percent of the mothers' utterances in a nineteen-hour sample of mother-child interactions were ungrammatical. Neither are the children exposed to a particularly simplified version of their language; slightly less than 20 percent of grammatical utterances in the sample were simple declarative sentences. We cannot say whether these percentages are high or low relative to normal adult speech, but at least we can say that exposure to a very highly simplified language sample is unnecessary for language learning. We are not able to say whether exposure to such a simplified sample would speed up language acquisition.

Another possibly helpful experience is that to learn a language children need exposure not only to well-formed utterances in the language, but also to ungrammatical utterances that are identified as being unacceptable. Such exposure could come about through the rejection of, or even correction of, a child's own ill-formed utterances. Brown and Bellugi (in Brown et al., 1964) have discussed the occurrence of one such type of correction. It seems that middle-class parents of young children will, with rather high frequency, imitate what their children say. Not only this, they will expand upon the child's utterance, adding inflectional endings, function words, and the like, to make the utterance well formed. The parents thus furnish their child with information that his utterance was grammatically unacceptable and also with information (assuming that the expansion was appropriate to the situation) on how to make the utterance grammatical.

Giving such information to the child, however, is not the same as ensuring that he use it. What evidence there is about the use of the information in expansions is mixed. Slobin (described by McNeill, in Smith & Miller, 1966) found that children quite frequently tried to imitate their parents' expansions. Furthermore, about half the time, the child's imitation of his parents' expansion was grammatically advanced over the utterances he normally produced. Children do appear to pick up the grammatical improvements their parents make and incorporate them in their own utterances. They may also incorporate the improvements into their grammar. On the other hand, Cazden (1965) took culturally deprived children whose parents expand their speech only infrequently, and she gave them intensive experience in having their ungrammatical utterances expanded. She found that this experience accelerated their language development, but no more than did a comparable amount of verbal stimulation from an adult who did not expand utterances. This evidence suggests that there may be nothing special about parents' expansions of a child's sentences.)

A third possibly helpful experience is that children must have a simple correspondence between some events in their immediate environment and syntactic relations expressed in the sentences they hear. Almost certainly, some correspondence between language and the world is needed if language is to be learned. It is tempting, and perhaps fruitful, to investigate the learning of the internal structure of a language without being directly concerned with the learning of when to use various aspects of language structure. However, the main function of language is to talk about things. The child probably does not learn a natural language as an abstract system, unrelated to what is happening in the world. Still, the hypothesis that the child needs some simple semantic support for his learning of syntactic structure is not a very helpful one. For one thing, psycholinguists have no clear notion of what constitutes simple, as opposed to complex or obscure, semantic support. For another thing, learning of some aspects of language structure does go on without semantic support—for instance, the learning of nonphonemic phonological distinctions, such as the fact that the English "p" sound is exploded in some contexts ("pill"), but not in others ("spill"). The semantic-support hypothesis must be clarified, and the limitations to its applicability must be specified.

Prentice (1966) performed an experimental study on the importance of semantic support in learning the usage of new words. Semantic support, in the form of pictures that could be described by the new words, facilitated learning the meaning of the new words. However, semantic support did not facilitate learning the part of speech of the new word, which was measured as the subject's ability to choose the proper new word to use in a novel sentence. In Prentice's study, simple training to use the new word in several sentences taught the subjects as much about the word's part of speech as did such training plus semantic support.

Braine (1963b) provides us with an instance in which semantic support was not needed for learning the syntax of an artificial language. Although some semantic support may have facilitated learning in Braine's experiment, it must be concluded that children can learn things about the structure of a language in the absence of semantic support. But more work like Prentice's and Braine's is needed before we can specify what aspects of language structure can and cannot be learned without semantic aids.

One final suggestion of a helpful experience is that the child needs to be rewarded for speaking if he is to learn how to speak. On the face of it, such a hypothesis is tempting. Many studies have indicated that reinforcement for some behaviors does increase the frequency of occurrence of those behaviors. As indicated previously in this book, this law of reinforcement applies even to the vocalizations of infants (Rheingold, Gewirtz, & Ross, 1959; Weisberg, 1963, reprinted following the chapter). A child would probably not learn language if nobody ever paid any attention to what he said.

Upon closer examination, though, the reward hypothesis loses some of its charm. Some of the reasons for this will be detailed in the next section. For now let us simply consider the problems involved in describing the child's linguistic input if we are to consider rewards as an important part of the input. How does one identify an instance of a reinforcer? In animal learning, the problem is relatively easy. Psychologists have lists of things that have been shown to serve as reinforcers. If something is not on the list, one can easily run an experiment and see if the new reward increases the frequency of occurrence of a response that it follows. In the case of language learning, the problem of identifying reinforcers is not so easy. Experimental work on social reinforcement has provided us with a short list of events, mostly verbalizations like "that's good," that may serve as reinforcers for speech. But the dedicated reinforcement theorist is not content with restricting himself to this short list when he tabulates the frequency with which rewards are given to the child for speaking. He would claim that many other events could serve as rewards. He may be correct, but in practice it is too easy for the person who wants to find reinforcers to make unjustified, *post hoc* identifications of reinforcers. As an example, Skinner (1957) finds several varieties of self-reinforcement, e.g., ". . . a man talks to himself because of the reinforcement he receives (p. 163)." He also suggests that there is such a phenomenon as reinforcement-in-the-future, as when a writer is presumably reinforced for writing by the reactions readers will have in future years. Elsewhere in his book, Skinner suggests that both replying to a speaker and keeping attentively silent while a speaker talks can serve as reinforcers. Rewards for speaking may in fact be important in language learning, and the reward hypothesis may deserve serious consideration. But if any event, observed or not, is to qualify as a reinforcer, the claim that reinforcement is necessary for language acquisition is empty.

Little positive, useful information about the nature of the linguistic input to the child is available. This may be because the right questions about the nature of the input have not been asked. The reader will note that the questions asked have been suggested by common sense, as were the questions about the possible simplicity of the input or the importance of rewards, or have been suggested by peculiar phenomena observed by casually examining the input, as was the question about adults' expansions. Working within the framework of a particular theory of language acquisition might permit the posing of better questions. It would be possible to examine the linguistic input to see if the events the theory requires to be present are in fact present; at least, it would be possible if the events are less ephemeral than are reinforcers. Let us turn to an examination of theories of language learning. The reader should be warned of one thing, though; those theories that appear promising are not yet well developed enough to have clear implications for what should be observed in linguistic input. The one apparent implication is that a detailed examination of linguistic input is not worth the time it would take.

FUNCTION The question of how a child gets from linguistic input to linguistic output is almost too hard a question to try to answer directly. Psycholinguists have recently tried to answer the question indirectly by first considering what sort of device could, in principle, get from linguistic input to linguistic output. In considering the input-output device, or function, they have been less concerned with making the device conform to known psychological laws of learning and more concerned about making the device capable of getting from input to output. This last problem is hard enough; in this section we will be concerned primarily with the failings of the various attempts to solve it.

Traditional psychological approaches

Let us consider the problem of devising a model of a language learner by first discussing the approaches to the problem that psychologists have traditionally taken. One can identify two main types of traditional psychological theories of language acquisition, imitation theory and reinforcement theory. In their crudest forms, the theories say that children build their linguistic output by imitating what they were given as input, and that children build their output by being reinforced for making the right kinds of output, i.e., speech sounds. We will try to explicate these types of theories, and see where they fall short of being able to explain how the child takes his linguistic input and arrives at his linguistic output.

Consider imitation theories. In a very broad sense, imitation theories must be correct. Children do learn to speak the language that their models speak. If imitating can be equated with behaving like a model, then children's language behavior is imitative. However, when looked at more closely, present versions of imitation theory are not satisfactory. An imitation theory claims that children produce utterances by imitating those utterances, or aspects of those utterances, that they have heard. Let us criticize this claim.

The version that says that children speak by imitating utterances that they have heard is grossly deficient. Children who know a language are able to produce and understand utterances that they have never before experienced. Their knowledge of language is, as mentioned earlier, productive.

The second version, which states that children imitate aspects of those utterances that they hear, deserves a more serious treatment. We will consider the claim in two ways: What might be meant by "aspects," and, is the claim likely to be correct regardless of what is meant by "aspects"? Some psychologists have suggested that the aspects of utterances that are imitated are the possible word sequences; that is, which words can follow which words. Such a suggestion is incorrect; there are simply too many different word sequences to be learned. Miller (1965) has estimated that a speaker of English has the linguistic knowledge to produce about 10^{20} different English sentences, twenty words in length. A child cannot acquire the knowledge necessary to produce these sentences by learning which single words can follow which single words—that is, learning that "red" can follow "the," that "barn" can follow "red," etc. If this is what the child learns, he will produce any number of badly formed utterances, such as "goes down here is not large feet are the happy days . . . ." Some psychologists have suggested that children learn which words can follow which strings of two words, or three words, etc. The utterances a child would be expected to produce under these assumptions are somewhat more like those he actually does produce, but they are not identical in structure. In fact, it turns out that the child would have to learn which words can follow each string of nineteen words. To learn this he must experience every one of the 10^{20} different sentences. This is too much to ask him to do.

The psycholinguist must look beyond word sequences in his

search for the aspects of utterances that children learn. This search is proving more difficult than expected. The aspects of language that must be imitated are quite abstract, quite far removed from the actual utterances and word sequences that are observed. The abstractness of what must be learned is suggested by several observations about language learning. One such observation is that young children regularly produce utterances in which the word order is quite unlike any they could have observed their model saying (e.g., "All gone shoe"). We have every reason to say that these utterances are not haphazard word heaps, but are grammatical in the child's grammar. If the children learned to make such utterances through imitation, they must have been imitating some aspect of language that was more abstract than word order.

Another similar observation is that children seem to learn some aspects of language that are not physically marked in speech. For instance, they learn to pick out the underlying, or logical, subject of sentences. The approximate idea of an underlying subject can be conveyed by the sentences, "John is eager to please" and "John is easy to please." The "John" is the superficial subject of both sentences, but it is the underlying subject of only the first sentence. We can see that the first sentence is related, at least indirectly, to the sentence "John pleases someone," while the second sentence is similarly related to "Someone pleases John." Underlying subjects are not marked by any particular inflection, and they can occur at practically any place in a sentence's word order. The underlying subject of a sentence is rather far abstracted from actual speech.

A final observation that suggests the abstractness of the learned aspects of language is the apparent indifference of what is learned about a language to the particular sample of language presented to a child. Different children learn much the same kinds of things about their language, even though their linguistic inputs seem to have very little in common. Whatever similarities exist between the different inputs, excepting similarities of vocabulary and phonology, are quite abstract. The main similarity is that the languages, of which the inputs are samples, have similar grammars. If the imitation theorist is to maintain that different children learn approximately the same things about language because they imitate the same things in their linguistic input, he is forced to claim that they imitate the grammar of the language. Such a claim is not a very helpful one unless the notion of imitating a grammar is explicated.

If the imitated aspects of utterances are, in fact, as abstract as suggested, then current imitation theories leave the main questions about language learning unanswered. The imitation theorist must answer the questions, "What are the aspects of utterances that are imitated," and "How is the child able to analyze the utterances he hears in such a way that he perceives the aspects he is to imitate?" These questions are the difficult and basic ones. Without answering them, a theorist cannot claim that he has shed much light on the process of language acquisition.

Claiming that current imitation theories are not particularly illuminating is not the same as claiming that they are not correct. Evidence exists, however, that suggests that imitation theories may be incorrect. One kind of evidence comes from the observation that the word order of young children's utterances sometimes deviates systematically from the word order of adults' utterances. It would be a rather perverse imitation theory that claimed that children would not imitate something as obvious as word order, at least in those cases in which adult word order is fairly invariant. Children, however, sometimes fail to retain word order, as when they say "All gone shoe." Another kind of evidence for the incorrectness of imitation theories comes from the observation of children's immediate imitations of adult utterances. One would expect that if children learned more and more about language by imitating more and more of the features of the utterances they heard, then children's immediate imitations of well-formed adult sentences they hear would be grammatically advanced over their nonimitative utterances. The children should pick out of the adults' utterances grammatical features they do not yet have under control and imitate these. In fact, children do not seem to do so, except in their imitations of adults' expansions. Ervin (in Lenneberg, 1964) found that although children frequently tried to imitate an adult utterance that they had just heard, such imitations were not grammatically advanced over the children's own spontaneous utterances.

Neither of these bits of evidence conclusively show that imitation theories of language acquisition must be incorrect. But they do suggest that the psychologist interested in language would be well advised to look elsewhere for an explanation of language learning. One alternative, that has on occasion been considered a supplement to an imitation theory, rather than an alternative, is a reinforcement theory. As was the case with imitation theory, a reinforcement theory must, in some broad sense, be correct.

A child learns a language because knowing it makes good things happen to him. If there were no one to talk to, the child would probably not learn how to talk. But again, as with imitation theory, current reinforcement theories show severe flaws when closely examined.

A reinforcement theory will claim that a child learns those utterances, or aspects of those utterances, for which he is reinforced. A specific reinforcement theory may identify the learning of an utterance with an increase in the probability of that utterance. Reinforcement theory, viewed in this way, is subject to much the same criticisms as was imitation theory. First, we must reject the suggestion that learning a language consists of learning particular utterances through reinforcement. People learn to produce utterances they have never said before. Also, we must reject the suggestion that learning particular word sequences through reinforcement for producing those sequences is the essence of language learning. We reject this suggestion for precisely the same reasons that we used when considering the suggestion that word sequences are learned through imitation. In fact, by following the same line of reasoning as we followed in our consideration of imitation theories, we arrive at the conclusion that whatever aspects of language are learned through reinforcement must be highly abstract.

Reinforcement theorists have developed some tools for dealing with phenomena in which something abstract is learned—for instance, in which the thing that is learned is a class of stimulus-response associations rather than a single association between a particular stimulus and a particular response. The major tool is the theoretical notion of generalization. A person is said to generalize what he has learned to other things, and thus, to show evidence of having learned something abstracted from the particular response, or stimulus-response association, on which he was trained. The principle of generalization, as applied to language learning, indicates that a person who is reinforced for making or understanding some utterances will generalize his knowledge to other utterances. Specifically, a person who has learned, via reinforcement, to make some grammatical utterances, will generalize this learning to other grammatical utterances.

The claim may well be correct. But again, it is not very helpful. It does not answer the questions, "What are the principles of generalization? How does a person know which other sentences are grammatical?" Present generalization theories, either of the nonmediated or the mediated (e.g., Jenkins & Palermo, in Bellugi & Brown, 1964) variety, do not come close to accounting for the type of generalization that is seen in language. As was the case with imitation theory, saying that language is learned through reinforcement is only a minor part of the theoretical game. The difficult part of the game lies in specifying how a child generalizes what he learns, or more generally, how the child learns something that is abstract and not directly represented in his experience.

Criticisms of this sort do not show that reinforcement theories cannot be applied correctly to language learning; they just show that they have not shed much light on the problem. Evidence is available, however, that suggests that reinforcement for speaking is neither necessary nor sufficient for language learning. Such evidence leads one to think that a reinforcement mechanism does not, in fact, underlie language acquisition. The evidence that suggests that reinforcement is not necessary is exemplified in Lenneberg's case of the child who was congenitally unable to vocalize. This child could never have received reinforcement for speaking, yet he appeared to learn to understand English. The evidence that suggests that reinforcement is not sufficient is exemplified by observations made on congenitally deaf children. Such children babble in their early months just like normal children. Presumably they receive a good deal of reinforcement for their babbling, as well as for any later vocalizations. However, they stop babbling rather soon, and in fact, they are retarded in all their language acquisition.

Current approaches

The major implication of our discussion of traditional psychological theories of language learning is that they are not relevant to the most basic problems of language acquisition. The processes of imitation and reinforcement to which these theories point may be active in language learning—and most certainly are active in such aspects of language learning as vocabulary learning and the learning of clichés and idioms. But neither these processes nor any other processes that have been formulated within an associationistic framework come close to accounting for the child's learning of language structure.

As a matter of fact, there is no available theory that provides a satisfactory account of the learning of language structure. However, one promising approach has begun to develop recently. This approach recognizes that a device that can provide a highly structured output (like the language user's knowledge of his language) when it is given a highly unstructured input, having many arbitrary and irrelevant features (like the linguistic input to a child) must be a complex, highly structured device. The approach attributes a sizeable number of information-processing capacities to the device, which is considered in this case to be a model of the language learner.

On a more specific level of analysis, this recent approach seems to claim that the language learner forms implicit hypotheses about the structure of the language to which he is exposed, and he tests these hypotheses against his linguistic input. The approach puts some rather stringent limitations on the types of hypotheses that the language learner will formulate and on the ways in which the hypotheses will be tested. It rules out the possibility that the language learner considers and tests certain hypotheses about language structure that might be consistent with the language data a child has received at some point in time—for instance, the hypotheses that sentence structure depends on the distance from speaker to hearer, or on the absolute level of loudness of the speaker's voice.

It is possible to distinguish two versions of this approach. In one version, the language learner is credited with a number of novel knowledge-acquiring abilities, or inference rules, which may or may not be specific to language. This version may be viewed as an extension of more traditional approaches, since such processes as association formation and stimulus generalization, assumed by traditional approaches, may be viewed as inference rules. The process of association formation may be viewed as the inference rule—"if two events have been contiguous in the past, the present occurrence of one implies the consequent occurrence of the other." Generalization may be viewed as the inference rule—"if event 1 has in the past been contiguous with event 2, an event 'similar' to event 1 implies the consequent occurrence of event 2."

Fodor (in Smith & Miller, 1966) has made some suggestions toward such an approach. He suggests an inference rule that can be described in the following way. Assume that the child has some way of classifying the italicized elements in such utterances as "John *is* eat*ing*," "they *are* play*ing*," "John *has* eat*en*," "the boys *have* see*n*," and "they *have been* play*ing*." The child classes "is," "are," "be" together, and "has," "have" together. The child then notes that whenever a form of "to be" occurs, the suffix "ing" does, and that whenever "to have" occurs, the suffix "en" does.

The inference rule suggested by Fodor allows the language learner to form the hypothesis that the discontinuous elements "to be" and "ing" form a unit (a constituent) on one level of analysis of the structure of an utterance such as "John *is* eati*ng*," as do the discontinuous elements "have" and "en" in an utterance such as "John *has* eat*en*," and further, the second part of the unit (the "ing" or the "en") has been permuted with the following word to form the utterance. The child then subjects the hypothesis to test against other linguistic input data. We should note that the same inference rule is applicable to other linguistic phenomena, such as the dependency between verb and particle in such sentences as "John *phoned* Mary *up*."

The other version of the approach claims not that the language learner has elaborate rules for forming tentative hypotheses from some linguistic input data, but that the language learner has some direct limitations on the kinds of hypotheses he will test. Rather than filling the child with inference rules, this approach fills the child with structural schemata to be applied to the data, that is, knowledge about the ways in which a language can be structured. McNeill (in Smith & Miller, 1966) presents an example of this version. Among the bits of linguistic knowledge he ascribes to the language learner is a knowledge of the basic syntactic relations that can be found in language (such relations as subject of, predicate of, and modifier of, that were defined previously). The language learner, according to McNeill, also knows that a basic sentence must consist of a noun phrase (the subject of the sentence) plus a predicate phrase (the predicate of the sentence). The learner is thus limited to two hypotheses about the basic structure of sentences in the language he is learning: A sentence consists either of a noun phrase followed by a predicate phrase or a predicate phrase followed by a noun phrase. He chooses one of the hypotheses and tests it against his linguistic input data. More commonly the child is not limited to just two possible hypotheses about how some aspects of language structure are expressed. For instance, there are quite a number of hypotheses he could consider about how the relation "modifier of" is expressed in a noun phrase. The point still is that the number of hypotheses about language structure that he will consider is much, much smaller than the number of possible extrapolations from his linguistic input.

Let us consider the value of what psychologists like Fodor and McNeill are doing when they ascribe to the language learner an elaborate set of inference rules or a rather detailed preknowledge of language structure. First, we can notice that their approach is at odds with the tendency of psychological theorists in the recent past to keep the complexity of an organism's presumed capacities to a minimum. However, we can also note that what Fodor and McNeill are doing is different only in complexity, not in principle, from what is more commonly done by psychological theorists. Such theorists generally ascribe to the organisms they study some inference rules and some preknowledge of some aspects of the world's structure. As mentioned earlier, association formation and stimulus generalization can be considered to be inference rules that some psychologists have proposed as basic capacities of organisms. Further, as some psychologists have realized, an organism must be credited with some preknowledge of the ordering of stimuli on physical continua if the organism is to apply the stimulus-generalization inference rule. Moreover, we can note that what Fodor and McNeill are doing is not different at all from what some comparative psychologists have been doing. The ethologists in particular have pointed to highly specific genetically determined capacities of organisms, such as the capacity to be imprinted that is found in many birds. The linguistic information processing capacities suggested by Fodor and McNeill seem to be more elaborate counterparts to the species-specific capacities attributed to some lower organisms.

The language-acquisition theorist must pack his model of the child full of elaborate information-processing abilities if he is to account for the child's ability to acquire a knowledge of his language. The psychologist does worry, however, about ascribing too much to his subject; he remembers the fruitlessness of the once-popular instinct theories that accounted for almost every kind of behavior by postulating a separate instinct for each kind. The psychologist must be able to justify his claim every time he attributes some capacity to an organism. Fortunately, psycholinguists are able to provide some justification for the kinds of abilities they claim that the language learner has.

First, observations made on the young child's learning of language seem consonant with some claims about children's inherent linguistic knowledge or inference rules. For instance, as outlined earlier, the assumption that the child begins learning a language already knowing the major syntactic relations provides an explanation for his formation of the P and O classes. In addition, the child has a tendency to use grammatical patterns that can be applied to his whole language even though these patterns may result in occasional deviations from normal adult usage. Recall the earlier discussion of the child's occasional use of nonnormal word order and the discussion of the child's tendency to use regular inflections in place of the "correct" irregular inflections he used earlier. Such a tendency is consistent with the notion that the child is formulating and testing broad hypotheses.

A second type of justification for the psycholinguist's claim about the language learner's inherent abilities comes from the study of "language universals." Linguists have been collecting evidence that all human languages share some basic features. For instance, all languages seem to draw their phonological contrasts from a small pool of possible phonological contrasts; they all seem to exhibit in one way or another the basic grammatical relations such as "subject of," "modifier of," and they all seem to be describable by grammars of a particular form. The question arises, "Why do all languages that humans speak share these functions?" The answer must appeal to either common experience on the part of all humans or to common language-learning abilities (or, of course, to both). In the case of language, it seems more parsimonious to appeal to shared abilities that are specific enough to lead humans into discovering how the language universals are expressed in their language. It should be mentioned that radical approaches to the problem claim that the knowledge the language learner brings to the task of learning a language is exactly that described in an account of linguistic universals.

A third type of justification for the psycholinguist's claim is exemplified in a study by Lenneberg (1964) (see also Lenneberg, 1967a). The language-learning abilities posited by psycholinguists are unique to man, hence they are genetically determined in a species-specific fashion. Lenneberg provides several arguments for the existence of such a species-specific propensity for learning language, including those arguments we have already presented. He also adds several new arguments, which center on the notion that man has genetically determined abilities that are specific to language behavior. For instance, he points to some cases of an inherited language-specific disability, and he suggests that if such disability may be inherited, language *ability* may also be inherited. He also shows that the ability to learn language is not the simple consequence of a large brain or high intelligence. The ability is more closely associated with one's being human than with one's intelligence, brain weight, brain weight/body weight ratio, or the like.

None of these arguments allows us to say that the case for

elaborate language-specific information-processing abilities has been proved. Much less do they allow us to make any conclusions about any particular suggestions toward the nature of these abilities. However, these arguments do suggest that if the nature of language acquisition is not to remain the mystery it now is, psycholinguists must give serious thought to elaborating their models of the language learner.

SUMMARY   Psycholinguists have spent a good deal of time examining what the young child learns about language; they have spent a small amount of time examining the linguistic experiences the child has; and they have indulged in much speculation about how the child can learn what he does learn, given the kinds of experiences he has.

The examination of what the child learns about language has been fruitful, especially in the area of the learning of grammar. Psycholinguists know many facts about the course of acquiring knowledge of a language. They are also able to make some far-reaching generalizations about the course of acquisition. Among the most important of these generalizations is that the child seems not merely to learn individual facts about the words and sentences in his language, but he learns widely applicable patterns for forming and interpreting sentences in his language.

The examination of the linguistic input of the child has not been so fruitful. Some interesting facts have been turned up, such as the fact that middle-class parents spend a good deal of time expanding and correcting the utterances their children make. But the most far-reaching generalization that seems to be developing out of the work on linguistic input is that the exact nature of the input is not critical for the child's learning of language.

Speculations about the problem of how the child learns a language have, until quite recently, skirted the important and difficult questions about how the language is learned. These older approaches did not make serious attempts to answer the question of how the child is able to project his limited experience with a language onto an ability to produce and understand an unlimited number of sentences in the language. Recent speculative approaches to the problem of language acquisition have recognized that complex abilities must be attributed to a device, such as a language learner, that is able to take a largely arbitrary, unstructured input and arrive at a highly structured output. These recent approaches have made some suggestions about the nature of these abilities, specifically that the abilities are either specialized inference rules or inherent pieces of knowledge about language structure. These approaches are in their infancy and need much development and clarification. However, even now a good deal of justification can be found for them.

BIBLIOGRAPHY

Bellugi, U., & Brown, R. W. (Eds.) The acquisition of language. *Monographs of the Society for Research in Child Development*, 1964, **29**(1, Serial No. 92).

Berko, J. The child's learning of English morphology. *Word*, 1958, **14**, 150–177.

Bever, T. G., Fodor, J. A., & Weksel, W. On the acquisition of syntax: A critique of "contextual generalization." *Psychological Review*, 1965, **72**, 467–482.

Braine, M. D. S. The ontogeny of English phrase structure: The first phase. *Language*, 1963, **39**, 1–13. (a)

Braine, M. D. S. On learning the grammatical order of words. *Psychological Review*, 1963, **70**, 323–348. (b)

Brown, R. W. *Words and things*. Glencoe, Ill.: Free Press, 1958.

Brown, R. W. et al. Language and learning: Special issue. *Harvard Educational Review*, 1964, **34**, No. 2.

Cazden, C. B. Environmental assistance to the child's acquisition of grammar. Unpublished doctoral dissertation, Harvard University, 1965.

Chomsky, N. *Aspects of the theory of syntax*. Cambridge, Mass.: M.I.T. Press, 1965.

Fraser, C., Bellugi, U., & Brown, R. Control of grammar in imitation, comprehension, and production. *Journal of Verbal Learning and Verbal Behavior*, 1963, **2**, 121–135.

Lenneberg, E. H. (Ed.) *New directions in the study of language*. Cambridge, Mass.: M.I.T. Press, 1964.

Lenneberg, E. H. *Biological foundations of language*. New York: Wiley, 1967. (a)

Lenneberg, E. H. The biological foundations of language. *Hospital Practice*, 1967, **2**, 59–67. (b)

Leopold, W. F. Patterning in children's language learning. *Language Learning*, 1953–54, **5**, 1–14.

Lyons, J., & Wales, R. J. (Eds.) *Psycholinguistics papers*. Edinburgh: Edinburgh University Press, 1966.

McCarthy, D. Language development in children. In L. Carmichael (Ed.), *Manual of child psychology*. New York: Wiley, 1954. Pp. 492–630.

Menyuk, P. Syntactic structures in the language of children. *Child Development*, 1963, **34**, 407–422. (a)

Menyuk, P. A preliminary evaluation of grammatical capacity in children. *Journal of Verbal Learning and Verbal Behavior*, 1963, **2**, 429–439. (b)

Miller, G. A. Some preliminaries to psycholinguistics. *American Psychologist*, 1965, **20**, 15–20.

Mowrer, O. H. Speech development in the young child. 1. The autism theory of speech and some clinical applications. *Journal of Speech and Hearing Disorders*, 1952, **17**, 263–268.

Prentice, J. L. Semantics and syntax in word learning. *Journal of Verbal Learning and Verbal Behavior*, 1966, **5**, 279–284.

Rheingold, H. L., Gewirtz, J. L., & Ross, H. W. Social conditioning of vocalizations in the infant. *Journal of Comparative and Physiological Psychology*, 1959, **52**, 68–73.

Skinner, B. F. *Verbal behavior.* New York: Appleton-Century-Crofts, 1957.

Slobin, D. I. Grammatical transformations and sentence comprehension in childhood and adulthood. *Journal of Verbal Learning and Verbal Behavior*, 1966, **5**, 219–227.

Smith, F., & Miller, G. A. (Eds.) *The genesis of language: A psycholinguistic approach.* Cambridge, Mass.: M.I.T. Press, 1966.

Weisberg, P. Social and nonsocial conditioning of infant vocalizations. *Child Development*, 1963, **34**, 377–388.

THE BIOLOGICAL FOUNDATIONS
OF LANGUAGE

Eric H. Lenneberg

An astonishing spurt in the ability to name things occurs at a definite stage in language development It represents the culmination of a process that unfolds very slowly until the child reaches the age of about 18 months, when he has learned to utter between three and 50 words. Then, suddenly and spontaneously, the process begins to gather momentum (Figure 1). There is a burst of activity at 24 to 30 months, so that by the time the child completes his third year, give or take a few months, he has built up a speaking vocabulary of [approximately] a thousand words and probably understands another 2,000 to 3,000 words that he has not yet learned to use.

This "naming explosion" is only one of the extraordinary activities which mark the coming of language, perhaps the most human and least understood form of our behavior. As far as we know, it occurs at about the same age in every healthy child

*From E. H. Lenneberg. The biological foundations of language. Hospital Practice, 1967, 2, 59–67.
(With permission of the author and the Hospital Practice Company.)*

FIG. 1 Data from 10 sample groups of children show sudden jump in vocabulary that consistently occurs around the third birthday.

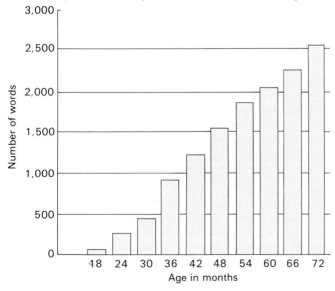

throughout the world. The specific factors responsible, the underlying cerebral mechanisms, are still unknown and promise to remain unknown for some time to come. But investigators are mounting renewed attacks on the problem. Recent studies have served as ground-clearing operations, helping to eliminate or at least reduce many of the confusions of times past and, even more important, indicating directions for the research of the future.

One noteworthy aspect of these studies is a shift of emphasis from the outer to the inner world, from culture to biology. Less attention is being directed to such environmental factors as imitation and conditioning and the approval of parents and rewards and punishments—and more to elements rooted far more deeply in physiological reactions. The primary focus is on the development of language as a biological phenomenon which, like the development of walking and other predominantly innate varieties of neuromotor coordination, proceeds in response to genetically determined changes taking place in the maturing child.

The emergence of this viewpoint illustrates a key fact about research: Discovery often depends on the synthesis of established evidence from many sources as well as on the gathering of brand-new evidence. To be sure, new information about the nature of language and language production has been obtained during the past few years. But valuable insights have also come from the bringing together and analysis of information that has been known to neurologists and other specialists for some time— observations and experimental findings concerning the behavior of normal children, congenitally deaf children, and patients suffering from various language disorders.

As a result, workers in a number of disciplines are becoming aware of the possibilities of applying current knowledge more widely and of the need for new knowledge. There is no doubt that the language education of deaf children may be improved by instituting programs designed to take fuller advantage of the biological capacities they share with hearing children and with hearing teachers. Further progress depends above all on basic studies of the brain and its development, studies which may be expected to provide the information required for more sophisticated theories about the development and evolution of language.

The theories will have to account for a rather subtle course of events. Indeed, there is no better way of indicating the magnitude of the task ahead than to take a closer look at how normal children acquire language. In the beginning nothing spectacular seems to be happening. When the infant is not quiet he is crying or fussing. The first change, which as a rule appears by the sixth to eighth week, consists of cooing, initially characterized by the production of sounds resembling vowels and later of sounds resembling consonants (although spectrograms show they differ acoustically and functionally from true speech sounds).

Further changes follow at a relatively gradual pace. For example, syllable-like babbling generally begins to replace cooing during the sixth month, while the first natural-language feature is observed about two months later in the form of intonations such as those heard in questions and exclamations. A still later step involves the appearance of primitive versions of some phonemes, the 40-odd fundamental speech sounds which in various combinations make up words, as the infant gains an increasing measure of control over his vocal apparatus. By the 12th month or so he is beginning to produce a few sounds acoustically identical to what you might hear in more mature speech

The most striking changes occur from here on, of course, at least as far as readily observed behavior is concerned. The buildup of a working vocabulary starts during the second year of life, and identifying the infant's first word has probably been an established family tradition ever since there were words to identify. Even before the naming-explosion stage he uses words to serve as the equivalent of one-word sentences ("daddy," for example, meaning "here comes daddy!" or "where is daddy?" depending on the intonation); soon he forms two-word sentences and begins to communicate actively with those around him.

As already indicated, the naming explosion itself is one among a number of major developments that proceed spontaneously and at about the same time. The child is also learning the rules for forming questions, negations, past tenses, plurals, and so on. Indeed his progress is so rapid that investigators have difficulty keeping track of it or isolating any single change for detailed analysis. By the age of four the child has managed to master the essentials of his native tongue, the complexity of his utterances being roughly equivalent to that of colloquial adult speech.

Although language comes so easily and naturally that we take it for granted, what lies behind the process is anything but self-evident. The sheer mechanics of speech production demand a fantastically high order of integration, an entire complex of special physiological adaptations. For example, respiration alters in a manner observed during no other form of activity. We inhale somewhat faster than is the case when we are at rest and not talking, and exhale a great deal more slowly—so that the net effect is a sharp reduction in respiratory rate, from some 18 to as few as four to five breaths per minute.

At the same time, respiration becomes much deeper. With every breath we inhale 1,500 to 2,400 cc of air, or about three to five times the average at-rest volume. These changes are all the more remarkable considering our extreme sensitivity to any change in normal breathing. After all, even a moderate amount of hyperventilation is sufficient to produce light-headedness and dizziness. Yet we are able to tolerate the comparatively drastic respiratory adjustments that take place automatically as we talk.

The extra air is used to do a very specific job. Held in the lungs as in a bagpipe, it must be released at precisely controlled rates and divided into precisely measured packets to produce the unique kind of "music" known as speech. Such behavior is based on the workings of elaborate neuromotor mechanisms, the coordinated activity of more than a hundred muscles in the tongue, lips, larynx, thoracic and abdominal walls, and so on. The production of a single phoneme requires that the brain send an appropriate message to each one of these muscles, specifying its state of relaxation or tension, and we are capable of talking at a rate of some 840 phonemes or 120 words per minute—for hours on end if the occasion arises.

All the evidence suggests that the capacities for speech production and related aspects of language acquisition develop according to built-in biological schedules. They appear when the time is ripe and not until then, when a state of what I have called "resonance" exists. The child somehow becomes "excited," in phase with the environment, so that the sounds he hears and has been hearing all along suddenly acquire a peculiar prominence. The change is like the establishment of new sensitivities. He becomes aware in a new way, selecting certain parts of the total auditory input for attention, ignoring others.

A vivid example of the change is provided by observations of children who suffer a total loss of hearing practically overnight, usually following virulent meningeal infection. If the attack occurs before the end of the second year, before the start of accelerated speech learning, the child is in precisely the same position as the congenitally deaf child. He must undergo precisely the same training and progresses to the same limited extent. On the other hand, children who become deaf after as little as a year of speech experience respond much more favorably to training. Even a brief exposure to oral communication, provided it takes place during the resonant period, seems to bring with it an enduring advantage

Language not only appears at a fixed time in the individual's life, it appears at its own pace. Although it seems to be highly sensitive to age, to maturational factors, within limits it appears somewhat more resistant to the impact of environmental factors. Children in orphanages live lives that are deficient linguistically as well as in many other respects; not unexpectedly, tests administered to three-year-olds show that they are frequently well below average in speech development. But the language deficit tends to disappear during subsequent growth, and follow-up tests show that most of them have caught up by the time they are six or seven.

Further insights into the development of language behavior in drastically impoverished environments are furnished by several studies that I conducted some years ago at the Children's Hospital Medical Center in Boston with my associates Irene Nichols, Freda Rebelsky, and Eleanor Rosenberger. In one study we compared the emergence of vocalization during the first three months of life among infants born to normal parents and infants whose parents were both congenitally deaf—and who thus heard far less adult speech and elicited no responses to their own vocalizations. (Deaf mothers cannot easily tell whether or not their infants' facial expressions and gestures are accompanied by sounds.)

There were no significant differences in total amount of vocalization and age of onset. Extensive tape recordings indicate that vowel-like cooing appeared in both groups at about the same time. Moreover, subsequent development continues in normal fashion. We have observed a dozen older children of deaf couples, children who heard only the vocalizations of other adults and their playmates, and in every case they passed without delays through the regular stages from babbling to full command of the language. Incidentally, by their third birthdays or shortly thereafter they were essentially "bilingual," using special sounds and gestures to communicate with their parents, and normal speech for the rest of the world.

The most extreme examples of environmental impoverishment are undoubtedly found among institutionalized mentally retarded children, including microcephalics, patients with phenylketonuria, and so on. In general they live under badly overcrowded conditions, and are comparatively seldom spoken to. Yet considering the circumstances, some children make amazing progress. Although language development is severely limited in the great majority of patients, those who manage to acquire some skill may do surprisingly well. They may not be able to talk, but occasionally they achieve an impressive measure of understanding and show quite clearly that they follow what you say.

Judging by these and other studies language apparently has a kind of self-propelling, driving quality. As a matter of fact it is extremely difficult to suppress its development, even in the most restricted environments encountered. Once the process has been triggered it continues with the pace and rhythm of an organic force until its time is up, until the "switch" that was turned on with the coming of resonance is turned off—at which point there is nothing we can do to extend the period of learning.

Progress in language development usually ceases after the age of 12 or 13, after puberty. One sign of the change may be seen in the learning of a second language. The extent of a foreign accent is directly correlated with the age at which the second language is acquired. At the age of three or four practically every child entering a foreign community learns to speak the new language rapidly and without a trace of an accent. This facility declines with age. The proportion of children who speak the second language with an accent tends to increase, but very slowly, so that by about the age of 12, perhaps 1 percent or 2 percent pronounce words differently from native speakers. A dramatic reversal of form occurs during the early teens, however, when practically every child loses the ability to learn a new language without an accent.

A similar cutoff point exists for language development generally, and we can learn something about this development from studies of children suffering from acquired aphasia. As a rule, the earlier the condition occurs, the more complete the recovery. Cerebral trauma occurring during the period from two to three, the period of most rapid acquisition, may in effect erase all the language the patient has learned. As a result he must start from scratch—which is precisely what he proceeds to do, in almost every case and often at a faster rate than the first time. He runs through each stage of infant vocalization all over again, from babbling on.

There are no "reruns" when aphasia strikes between ages four and 10, patients simply picking up where they left off. Recovery may take place over a period of several years, but is complete in most cases. Puberty again marks the cutoff point. Aphasias which appear after puberty or which have not cleared up by this time usually leave traces in the form of peculiar pauses, searching for words, and other symptoms. Among adults, that is, after the age of 18 or so, complete recovery is the exception rather than the rule, and symptoms that have not disappeared within five months following the aphasic attack are likely to be permanent.

Language development thus runs a definite course on a definite schedule (Figure 2); a critical period extends from about age two to age 12, the beginning and the end of resonance.

So far we have concentrated chiefly on some of the overt changes under way during this period. The problem of understanding language, however, involves going beneath the descriptive level to a consideration of deeper processes. Above all it involves spelling out in as much detail as possible just what it means to say that language is a biological phenomenon and, more specifically, a phenomenon of developmental biology.

For one thing the statement implies an important but limited role for the environment, particularly for parents. Separate studies of actual speech records, done by Martin Braine of the Walter Reed Army Hospital, Roger Brown of Harvard, and Susan Ervin of the University of California, indicate that contrary to former beliefs children do not learn language by parroting what their parents say. Their utterances are truly creative. Phrases such as "daddy allgone," "more up," "hi, milk," etc., represent the chil-

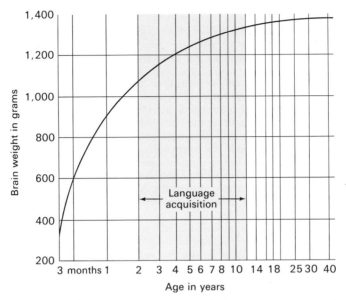

FIG. 2   Period of maximum ability to acquire language appears to end at about the time the normal brain acquires its full weight.

dren's original combinations, not something they have heard and are repeating. Furthermore, we are not their teachers. We do not decide to instruct our offspring in grammar and syntax. This is fortunate because they have their own rules, which we do not know and hence could not teach even if we wanted to.

Children will never learn language unless they hear it, and we fulfill our function simply by talking, the more the better. Beyond that and offering moral support there is little for us to do, because biology takes over. Biology takes over in basically the same fashion as it does when the child metabolizes protein after eating. He uses the proteins but not in ready-made form. They are broken down into polypeptides and amino acids and reassembled according to built-in purposes, purposes embodied in the genetic codes that determine the directions of protein synthesis and serve the needs of his maturing body.

A very close parallel, amounting to far more than a convenient analogy, exists between such reactions and the acquisition of language. The child needs language for survival just as he needs food. The information he receives from us may be regarded as raw material of a sort. It passes via auditory channels into the central nervous system, where it is "absorbed," broken down into its elements, and resynthesized in the achievement of varied and complex language skills. The critical question, of course, is how this processing is accomplished, and at this stage of our ignorance we have clues and hunches rather than answers.

The course of language development somehow seems to be related to a unique characteristic of the human species. Man is born "premature" in a sense that holds true for no other primate. He comes into the world more helpless and remains helpless longer than any other member of the primate order. The weight of his brain at birth is only about a fourth of its adult weight, which means that maturational processes go on long after birth—and that the brain retains some of its "plasticity," its capacity for change and growth, long after birth. There is reason to believe that one of the primary selective values of prolonged cerebral immaturity may be to make language possible.

In this connection the end of resonance may also have special evolutionary significance. Nature must make some sort of compromise between maintaining cerebral plasticity as long as possible and the need for stability, for a kind of "freezing" of developmental possibilities, upon which unvarying adult communication and social cohesion depend. The human group is by far the most complex and demanding that has yet evolved, and language is essential to enable the individual to play his roles in a social context. So it makes sense both that there be ample time for language development and that the process be completed by the age of puberty, when the individual must begin to play his social roles most actively.

As we have already pointed out, language acquisition begins at about the age of two, when the brain has reached some 60 percent of full maturity. This is also a time of rapid progress in walking and other motor skills (Figure 3); indeed, a notable feature of human development is the close synchronization of milestones in the acquisition of such skills and language. Among the most obvious cerebral changes is the increasing involvement of the left hemisphere in language function, which usually becomes well established before the age of 10. The precise significance of cerebral dominance remains unknown. But in general it represents one aspect of prolonged and continuing maturation, reflecting the fact that different parts of the brain are committed at different times in line with programs perhaps specified in genetic codes.

The earliest commitments, and in many ways the most elusive and significant, actually precede the appearance of natural-language features. Infants indicate that they understand some words and simple commands as early as the 12th month, although they may not utter words for another half year or more, and understanding continues to outrun speech production throughout life. I had an opportunity to study an extreme example of this phenomenon in a boy suffering from a congenital neurological deficit of speech articulation, probably due to fetal anoxia. Nine years old when last seen, he was essentially without productive speech. Yet many tests have shown beyond doubt the boy has a full comprehension of spoken language. For example, he follows such instructions as "take the block and put it in the bottle" and answers questions based on stories he has just heard, including questions designed to eliminate visual and other extralinguistic clues.

This case demonstrates the important principle that understanding may not only come before speaking, but that it is in some way simpler and more basic. In other words there is something distinct from speaking, which we may call a knowledge of language —and which takes shape very early in life.

The newborn infant is immersed in sensation, including a rich variety of sounds, and his job is to make sense of them. Perhaps the first and most obvious step is to make a provisional distinction between meaningful sounds that must be heeded and analyzed further, and meaningless sounds that may be ignored. But this is only the beginning of a long series of more and more sophisticated distinctions. For example, as the

FIG. 3 Milestones in motor and language development.

12 Weeks
Baby supports head when in prone position; weight is on elbows; no grasp reflex is present. Crying has diminished, vowel-like cooing has begun and is sometimes sustained for fifteen to twenty seconds.

16 weeks
Head is self-supported, and baby can shake rattle; tonic neck reflex is subsiding. Response to human sounds is more definite; eyes seem to search for speaker. Occasional chuckling sounds are made.

20 weeks
Child can sit with props. Consonantal sounds are beginning to be interspersed with the vowel-like cooing. Acoustically, however, all vocalizations are very different from sounds of mature language.

6 months
Baby bends forward and uses hands for support while sitting; reaching is unilateral. Cooing is changing into babbling with resemblance to single syllables. Most common sounds are "ma," "mu," "da," "di."

8 months
Baby stands holding on and can grasp with thumb opposition. Repetitions of sounds are becoming frequent, intonation patterns distinct, and utterances begin to be used to signal emphasis and emotions.

10 months

Creeping is efficient, and child can take side steps holding on, pull self to standing position. Vocalizations are mixed with sound play like gurgling or bubble blowing; baby tries to imitate sounds, begins to respond differentially to words heard.

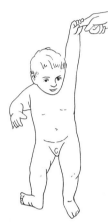

12 months

Child walks when held by one hand, or walks on feet and hands with knees in air, and can seat self on floor. Identical sound sequences are repeated more often, and words ("mamma" or "dadda") are emerging. Definite signs of understanding appear in responses to simple commands.

18 months

Grasp, prehension, and release are fully developed; gait is still stiff. Child can creep downstairs backward. Word repertoire is more than three, less than fifty; understanding is progressing rapidly, but joining of word units into spontaneous two-word phrases is uncommon.

Harvard linguist Roman Jakobson was the first to point out some 25 years ago, the primitive phonemes uttered between the sixth and the 12th months of life are not really clean-cut individual acoustic items. They actually consist of large groups of closely related sounds. In other words, the infant is recognizing and reproducing increasingly subtle acoustic patterns and further subdividing the world of meaningful sounds into classes that will ultimately become what we know as mature phonemes.

This process is also at work during the naming stage. Many of the name-words in early vocabularies have not yet acquired their full "status," their precise adult meanings. Strictly speaking, they are often overgeneralized, standing for groups of objects rather than for particular objects. At one stage all the large deep-voiced objects that enter the infant's field of vision are lumped under the single heading "daddy"; he learns later that the term applies to only one of the objects. Similarly, "truck" may stand for all vehicles, and "bye-bye" for all exits and everything related to them.

Again, it is a matter of recognizing patterns and making increasingly refined distinctions. The process of dividing and subdividing represents a kind of differentiation, and in the last analysis it turns out to be identical to biological differentiation itself—to the complex of stage-by-stage chain reactions whereby a single cell gives rise to hundreds of types or classes of cells. The significance of classifying, creating categories, in language development has been emphasized in basic mathematical studies by Noam Chomsky of the Massachusetts Institute of Technology. Indeed, his research has stirred the imagination of investigators at many laboratories and helped bring about an increase in experimental as well as theoretical studies of language.

One of the major effects of this work has been to stimulate new interest in the truly formidable problem of bringing language to congenitally deaf children. The biological or developmental approach offers considerable encouragement to these patients and to their dedicated teachers. In the first place it is highly probable that their cognitive ability is not defective or inferior to that of hearing children. They may have very little language or none at all by the time they enter a school for the deaf at the age of five or six, but there is every reason to assume that their capacity for reasoning and forming nonverbal concepts has not been adversely affected.

Furthermore, there is reason to believe that the central mechanisms concerned with the essentially automatic development of cognition and language are intact—and that in most cases of sensory deprivation the brain readily accepts information entering through substitute sensory channels. The main qualification here is that the deprivation involve only a single sensory modality. Animal experiments and clinical observations indicate that the loss of two modalities results in severe behavioral disturbances, while the loss of one may have relatively minor central effects. So we may proceed on the basis that as far as the biological apparatus for cognition is concerned, deaf and hearing preschoolers have equal underlying capacities for language development.

A warning is in order here. It is important to point out that this situation apparently holds for a limited period only, the critical period during which the state of resonance exists. While in about three out of four cases a relevant family history or one of the well-known antecedents for congenital deafness (rubella during the first trimester, erythroblastosis fetalis, meningitis, bilateral ear infection, and so on) will alert the parents to the possibility of deafness, in other cases they have no advance warning. An experienced observer can detect deafness as early as the sixth month or so, because the babbling of the affected infant is less varied than that of the hearing infant, and his intonation patterns tend to be inferior. But very commonly the condition is not detected until the end of the first year, and often not until the 18th to 24th month. This is by no means too late, although in general the earlier we recognize the problem the better.

When it comes to special training, prospects are bright for achieving appreciable improvements simply by applying more fully the knowledge we already possess. Schools for the deaf have made notable progress in oral education, in a variety of drills and exercises designed to develop speech as far as possible by promoting proper breathing, lip and tongue articulation, and so on. But there has been a tendency to discourage certain other measures, such as the use of graphics (writing and pictures), partly on the grounds that they might interfere with the achievement of vocal skills.

It so happens that all the available evidence suggests that precisely the opposite is the case. The odds are that graphics will actively facilitate rather than hinder vocal communication. We have emphasized that knowledge of language precedes speech and may exist without speech—and it is this fundamental capacity, rather than subsidiary skills, which must be the primary focus of our educational efforts, which must be fostered and given complete scope for development. That means providing as much language as possible and making the fullest possible use of the visual modality, an especially important point when we consider the limited value of lip-reading. (Hearing adults without formal training do at least as well in lip-reading tests as deaf adults who have been trained for years.)

I am convinced that much can be gained by a more extensive application of graphic techniques. For one thing, the vast majority of deaf individuals cannot produce a page of writing without making at least one grammatical or stylistic mistake, and it seems likely that this difficulty could be eliminated. On a broader scale, the free use of graphics such as notes may be expected to make possible richer, more rapid, and less self-conscious communication with hearing persons.

It may be helpful to consider another serious communication problem, the wide gap between the teacher of the deaf and the physician. The teacher is apt to be isolated from the mainstream of medical investigation and so is not as aware as he might be of recent findings and thinking that could make his work still more productive. On the other hand, the physician, who devotes considerable attention to education for nurses, is often reluctant to take corresponding pains in the case of speech teachers —largely because he does not realize how difficult it is to help deaf children. Part of the solution to this problem calls for a greater involvement of the medical profession and the hospital. Teachers should be included regularly in appropriate seminars and offered more systematic training by physicians in a hospital setting.

From a research standpoint the big task for the future is to understand the detailed anatomy and physiology of language. The task might be less formidable if gross structures of the brain were involved, if language had a reasonably straightforward connection with relative or absolute brain size, for example. Unfortunately this is definitely not the case, a conclusion supported by observations of a rare recessive disease known as nanocephalic dwarfism. Individuals suffering from the condition have normal skeletal proportions, a height of often no more than $2\frac{1}{2}$ feet, and a brain weighing an estimated 400 gm, or about a third of the weight of the normal adult brain. Although these dwarfs are intellectually retarded, they all master the rudiments of language and speak and understand at least as well as a five-year-old child.

It would be difficult indeed to present more striking evidence for the notion that our capacity for language has little to do with the mass or quantity of nervous tissue, with sheer numbers of neurons—and everything to do with how neurons are organized and interact with one another. At this level we know nothing about the shaping or use of language, about the biology of pattern recognition and category formation and naming, but our knowledge of neurophysiology broadly indicates what must be going on.

The brain is a machine where the dynamic changes of developmental processes produce changes of living rhythms. Neurons are not passive receiver-transmitters that "speak only when spoken to," responding only when stimulated. They are constantly on the go, producing spontaneous rhythms. And all our experiences, linguistic and otherwise, are reflected in enduring changes of those rhythms, perhaps analogous to frequency modulation. This process in turn may reflect underlying structural changes on a molecular level, and here, again, we are ignorant.

Relevant biochemical studies are a long way off. We must learn more concerning the basic workings of the brain, the nature of cerebral plasticity and neural coding, and the capacity for categorizing in lower animals, before we become sufficiently sophisticated to conduct research specifically on the neurophysiology of language. Then we shall be coming to grips with the most human thing about human beings, the quality that distinguishes man from all other species.

CONTROL OF GRAMMAR IN IMITATION, COMPREHENSION, AND PRODUCTION[1]

Colin Fraser, Ursula Bellugi, and Roger Brown

"Most writers agree that the child understands the language of others considerably before he actually uses language himself." . . . (McCarthy 1954, p. 520). . . . [This] sentence is certainly an accurate summary of what most writers have written. It is also an accurate summary of what parents believe that they have observed. We will separate out several senses of the thesis, review the relevant evidence, and report some new data bearing on the understanding and production of grammatical features in speech.

The assertion that understanding precedes production can be taken to mean that *some* utterances are ordinarily understood before *any* utterances are produced. There is strong empirical support for this thesis if we are willing to accept the production of an appropriate response as evidence that an utterance has been understood. There are just two kinds of appropriate response that have been commonly reported for children. When an utterance makes reference the child sometimes identifies the referent; when an utterance is intended to be an imperative the child sometimes performs the designated action. Gesell and Thompson (1934), for instance, tested understanding of the questions: "Where is the cup?" "Where is the shoe?" "Where is the box?" by placing the child before a table on which rested a cup, a shoe, and a box and noting his identifying responses. Bühler and Hetzer (1935), in testing the child's understanding of such commands as "Get up" and "Lie down" and "Give that to me," required that the designated actions be performed. Appropriate responses of these two kinds are regularly obtained from normal children before any intelligible speech is heard. Indeed, Lenneberg (1962) has demonstrated linguistic comprehension of a high order in an 8-year-old child who is completely anarthic (speechless). In addition, the chimpanzee Gua, who was raised by Kellogg and Kellogg (1933), could, at the age of 9 months, make appropriate reaction to some 70 utterances though she never learned to speak at all. The Hayeses' chimpanzee, Viki, eventually approximated the sounds of several words but before she could do this she seemed to understand many utterances (Hayes, 1951).

[1] This research was supported by a grant from the National Science Foundation administered through the Center for Communication Sciences, Massachusetts Institute of Technology. The authors are grateful for the advice and assistance given by Dr. Jane Torrey (Connecticut College for Women), Mr. Joseph Mendelson (M.I.T.), and Mr. Sam Anderson (Harvard).

From C. Fraser, U. Bellugi, & R. Brown. Control of grammar in imitation, comprehension, and production. Journal of Verbal Learning and Verbal Behavior, 1963, 2, 121–135. (With permission of the authors and Academic Press, Inc.)

The fact that some utterances usually seem to be understood before any recognizable utterances are produced is a generalization of little significance. The responses that suggest comprehension of an utterance include such very simple actions as orientation of the head, reaching, and grasping. It is not remarkable that some of these responses, those that are congenial to the child or animal, should come under the control of speech stimuli when the organism is not able to perform any of the culturally patterned articulatory movements that constitute speech. Any infant that can clap its hands can appear to its parents to understand "Pat-a-cake"; any animal that can run to its food dish can appear to its owner to understand "Come and get it." Certainly speech can operate as a signal for various nonverbal responses in many organisms that do not produce any speech.

The thesis that understanding precedes production is more interesting in a second form: Particular utterances or features of an utterance are ordinarily understood before the same utterances or features are produced. Our experiment is concerned with this version of the thesis in the case of particular features that are grammatical. Ervin and Miller, in their review of research on the development of language (1963) find that only a few studies have been made which bear, directly or indirectly, on the problem of the development of passive control of grammatical patterns. Neither these studies nor the ordinary observations made by parents provide evidence adequate to establish the thesis that passive control or understanding precedes productive use.

A monograph by Kahane, Kahane, and Saporta (1958) illustrates one sort of evidence. Working from previously published materials on children learning French, English, or German, the authors find that the verbal categories of tense, voice, aspect, and agreement are understood before they are marked in speech. For example, one child is reported to have said "This mine" on a certain occasion and on another occasion "Glenna on bus." There is no verb in either utterance and no marking for tense. However, the parents of the child suggest that the first utterance, really means "This *is* mine" and the second, "Glenna *was* on a bus." The Kahanes and Saporta take the parents' word for it and credit the child with understanding a distinction of tense that he is not yet making. The authors do not go on to say that the child would understand distinctions of tense in the speech of another person but that is a reasonable extension of their position.

How do parents arrive at a gloss for a child's utterance such as "Glenna was on a bus" for "Glenna on bus"? Presumably there was situational support for the linguistic expansion. Perhaps the person named was at home when the child spoke but, on the previous day, had been on a bus. In these circumstances the parents would have said, "Glenna was on a bus" and what the parents would have said is what the child is presumed to have meant. The inference may be correct but it is not appropriate for determining whether understanding does or does not precede expression. When children first begin to combine words, these combinations are "telegraphic" (Brown and Fraser, 1963) and so grammatically incomplete. If whenever a child produces such an incomplete sentence he is to be credited with understanding the complete sentence that an adult would have produced in his circumstances, then the child's understanding must necessarily seem to be in advance of his production. To make an empirical test of the assertion that understanding precedes production one must look for evidence of understanding in the behavior of the child and not simply for the absence of linguistic expression from the child combined with an interpretation by his parents.

Parents, including linguists and psychologists, often see, in their own children, behavior that they take to be evidence of a grammatical understanding that surpasses production. A child who never produces the kind of question that places the verb before the subject may nevertheless appropriately answer "Yes" (or "No") to such a question as "Are you hungry?" Before concluding that the child understands the significance of the verb-subject word order, however, one should try the effect of the single word "hungry" spoken with rising interrogative intonation or even without the intonation. A child who never produces a sentence containing both an indirect and a direct object may nevertheless respond appropriately to: "Bring your game to me." Again, however, one cannot tell whether the grammatical feature has been understood unless appropriate variations are tried. Would the child's response change if one were to say: "Bring me to your game"? . . .

The set of sentences used by Gesell and Thompson in connection with a cup, a shoe, and a box is well designed to test understanding of the substantive words *cup, shoe,* and *box.* In the sentence frame "Where is the _____ ?" they permute the three nouns, and the response pattern reveals whether the variable element has been understood. These sentences do not test understanding of the interrogative pronoun *where* since this word is constant across all sentences. . . . However, there is an occasional exception in the literature that points the way to a test of grammatical comprehension. Gesell and Thompson, for example, have asked children to "Put the block *in* the cup" and have also asked them to "Put the block *over* the cup." By making a function word a variable they obtain evidence on the understanding of such words. . . .

[The purpose of the present study was to test the hypothesis that understanding (comprehension) of language precedes production (use of language). *Comprehension* is measured in this study by the child's ability to correctly identify pictures named by contrasting sentences. Use of language is measured in two ways: (1) *Imitation*—Child must correctly imitate (verbally) two contrasting sentences and (2) *Production*—Child must correctly match the contrasting sentences with the appropriate picture. Production therefore requires both comprehension and imitation.]

OPERATIONS FOR TESTING *IMITATION, COMPREHENSION,* AND *PRODUCTION*

Consider now a concrete problem drawn from those we have devised to test *Comprehension, Imitation,* and *Production.* We begin with a pair of sentences: "The sheep is jumping" and "The sheep are jumping." These two sentences are identical except for the auxiliary verb, which is marked for a singular subject in the first sentence and for a plural subject in the second. . . .

For each of the two sentences there is an appropriate picture (see Figure 1). In both pictures there are two sheep and a small hurdle. In one picture a single sheep jumps while the other looks on; in the other picture both sheep jump. It is necessary to have two sheep in both pictures so that a subject cannot simply match each sentence with its correct picture by noting whether the picture contains one sheep or more than one. . . .

There are three tasks: *I, C,* and *P.* For the *Comprehension* task (*C*) . . . *E* shows the two pictures . . . then speaks one of the sentences and asks *S* to point to the picture

FIG. 1   Pictures illustrating a grammatical contrast. Left, "The sheep is jumping"; right, "The sheep are jumping."

named. . . . *E* then speaks the other sentence and asks *S* to point once more. The *S* is not asked to speak at all; . . . evidence of comprehension is selective pointing.

In the *Imitation* procedure (*I*) no pictures are used. The *E* speaks two sentences that are grammatically equivalent to the two used in *C* (e.g., "The sheep is walking"; "The sheep are walking"). The *S* is then asked to imitate these, one at a time. . . . Since we want to know whether *S* will imitate the features of the sentences that are crucial, . . . we score . . . only *S*'s retention of the contrasting [verbs] *is* and *are*. . . .

In the *Production* procedure (*P*) pictures are once again used [and matched to] a pair of sentences grammatically equivalent to those used in the other tasks ("The sheep is eating"; "The sheep are eating"). The *S* is twice told the [sentences for] the two pictures but not which [sentence] goes with which picture. . . . After repeating the names of the pictures *E* points to one picture at a time and asks *S* to name it. . . . To be scored correct, . . . the contrast has to be appropriately matched with the pictures.

HYPOTHESES

. . . The experimental materials . . . are made up of ten different grammatical contrasts, and these will be called *problems*. The contrast we have described, between the singular and the plural marked by *is* and *are*, is one such problem. Each of the ten problems was administered in all three tasks or procedures.

The . . . prediction that comprehension will be superior to production can be somewhat refined if we think about the psychological operations that would seem to be required for the tasks *I*, *C*, and *P*. For all three tasks *S* must notice and retain the critical difference between the two sentences that make a pair. For the sample sentences . . . the contrast between *is* and *are* must be attended to and identified as a change that matters. . . .

There is reason to expect that the three tasks . . . will show [differences in] difficulty. To perform correctly on *I* it would seem that *S* must not only perceive the contrast between the two sentences but must also have sufficient motor control of speech to produce the difference. To perform correctly on *C*, the *S* must perceive the difference between the sentences and also the difference between the two pictures . . .; he must have motor control of pointing but need not have motor control of the speech contrast. The *P* task requires all the operations of both *I* and *C*. . . . *P*, then, would seem to be more complex than *I* since *P* entails more operations than *I*. *P* would seem to be more complex than *C* since it requires control of speech rather than pointing. . . . *P* should be more difficult than either *I* or *C*.

METHOD

The Imitation-Comprehension-Production (ICP) Test   The test involves 10 grammatical contrasts. A grammatical contrast is always created by the use of two utterances which are identical but for some grammatical feature. Subjects were required to process the grammatical distinctions in each of the three ways described above.

Examples of the 10 grammatical contrasts presented in the ICP Test are listed in Table 1 together with the criteria for scoring them. These 10 problems were selected because previous work (Brown & Fraser, 1963) had shown that complete productive mastery of the contrasts involved was not common in children before about 4 years and because pictorial representations of the differences of reference were possible.

For all utterances, words familiar to young children are used: *cat, dog, mommy, daddy, boat, truck, fall, jump,* etc. For each grammatical contrast there are two utterance-pairs for *I,* two for *C,* and two for *P.* Tasks *C* and *P* involve . . . pictures to illustrate the utterances assigned to these procedures. The Massachusetts Institute of Technology Illustration Service made brightly colored line drawings on 7 $\times$ 5 in. white cards. The two pictures making a pair usually involve the same creatures and things and actions but differ in subject-object relations, in the apparent time of an action, or in the number of creatures performing an action.

Subjects   From a pretest we learned that children 4 years of age or older performed correctly on *I, C,* and *P* with most of the problems. To insure that the performances should not generally be perfect we needed to work with children under 4 years and the pretest suggested that 3 years was the lowest age at which the test procedures would usually be possible. Accordingly, we worked with children whose ages ranged from 37 to 43 months, the mean being 40 months. They were 12 monolingual English-speaking children, 6 boys and 6 girls.

[*Problems*]   Each single problem involved two utterances and both utterances were pronounced twice by *E* on all tasks. . . . For tasks *I* and *C* the posing of a problem necessitates a second pronunciation (e.g., "Show me: 'The sheep are jumping.'") but, for task *P,* the problems can be posed without a second pronunciation (e.g., "What is the name of this picture?"). A second pronunciation was, however, included in the *P* task so as to equate exposure to sentences across tasks.

Procedure   All testing was done in the preschools in small rooms with only the child and two *E*s present. One *E,* who had previously visited the schools to become acquainted with the children, administered instructions and the test materials and encouraged and cajoled when necessary; the other *E* made a . . . record of the child's responses. . . .

Before performing any of the three tasks, the *S* was shown a colored picture-book and encouraged to talk about the pictures. This helped the child to overcome any reluctance to talk and provided a small sample of the child's spontaneous speech. To explain each of the three tasks (*I, C,* and *P*) and to test the *S*'s understanding of each task, *E* always began with the four practice items.

TABLE 1 Sample utterances (Set A) and scoring for the ICP Test

Practice items

The girl with the big hat.	The boy with the blue belt.
The girl playing with the doll.	The bunny eating the carrot.
The cat with the brown face.	The dog with the black tail.
The boy playing with the truck.	The mouse eating the cracker.

1. Mass noun/Count noun.
   Utterances: Some mog/A dap.
   Some pim/A ked.
   Scoring: *Some/A* + any nonsense syllables or appropriate English words.

2. Singular/Plural, marked by inflections.
   Utterances: The boy draws/The boys draw.
   The kitten plays/The kittens play.
   Scoring: Noun without inflection and verb with -s/Noun with -s and verb without inflection.

3. Singular/Plural, marked by *is* and *are*.
   Utterances: The deer is running/The deer are running.
   The sheep is eating/The sheep are eating.
   Scoring: *Is/Are*

4. Present progressive tense/Past tense.
   Utterances: The paint is spilling/The paint spilled.
   The boy is jumping/The boy jumped.
   Scoring: *Is* and verb with *-ing*/No auxillary and verb with *-d*.

5. Present progressive tense/Future tense.
   Utterances: The girl is drinking/The girl will drink.
   The baby is climbing/The baby will climb.
   Scoring: *Is* and verb with *-ing/Will* and verb without inflection.

6. Affirmative/Negative.
   Utterances: The girl is cooking/The girl is not cooking.
   The boy is sitting/The boy is not sitting.
   Scoring: Absence of *not*/Presence of *not,* + some assertion.

7. Singular/Plural, of 3rd-person possessive pronouns.
   Utterances: His wagon/Their wagon.
   Her dog/Their dog.
   Scoring: *His* or *her/Their.*

8. Subject/Object, in the active voice.
   Utterances: The train bumps the car/The car bumps the train.
   The mommy kisses the daddy/The daddy kisses the mommy.
   Scoring: $Noun_1$ + active form of verb + $noun_2$/$Noun_2$ + active form of verb + $noun_1$.

9. Subject/Object, in the passive voice.
   Utterances: The car is bumped by the train/The train is bumped by the car.
   The daddy is kissed by the mommy/The mommy is kissed by the daddy.
   Scoring: $Noun_1$ + verb + *d* + *by* + $noun_2$/$Noun_2$ + verb + *d* + *by* + $noun_1$.

10. Indirect object/Direct object.
    Utterances: The girl shows the cat the dog/The girl shows the dog the cat.
    The boy brings the fish the bird/The boy brings the bird the fish.
    Scoring: Any verb + $noun_1$ + $noun_2$/Any verb + $noun_2$ + $noun_1$.

RESULTS

Scoring   There were two records of each experimental session; one on tape and one written on the scene. The scorers took advantage of the information in both records. . . .

Quantitative findings   Even within the restricted age range represented, there was a [positive] correlation between age and total score. . . . The girls did somewhat better than the boys, but the difference was not significant. . . .

Because all three tasks involve operations of perception, attention and memory, we predicted that the difficulty of the problems would be similar from task to task. . . . [Correlations for the difficulty of problems from task to task indicated that this, in fact, was the case.]

[The results of an analysis of scores on the three tasks] showed that there were significant differences among [them]. . . . The mean number of correct responses of *S*s on *I* was 13.83; on *C,* 10.08; and on *P,* 4.75. In short, [*P* was significantly more difficult than *I* or *C,* and *C* was significantly more difficult than *I.*]

DISCUSSION

How stands the thesis that understanding precedes production in the development of child speech? The thesis is true if by production we mean task *P,* since *C* scores were higher than *P* scores. This outcome suggests that children learn a lot about the referential patterning, the stimulus control of grammatical forms, before they produce these forms.

The thesis that understanding precedes production is false if by production we mean task *I,* since *C* scores were lower than *I* scores. It is very possible, however, that this latter outcome would reverse with still younger children. The longest sentences of the ICP Test were only eight morphemes long which means they were easily within the sentence-programming span of 3-year-old children. However, the much shorter span of children at about 2 : 6 should compel such younger children, in the *I* task, to "reduce" the model sentences of the ICP Test.

SUMMARY

The familiar assertion that, in language development, understanding precedes production was tested for 10 grammatical contrasts with twelve 3-year-old children. Understanding was operationalized as the correct identification of pictures named by contrasting sentences. Production was operationalized in two ways: (a) as the correct imitation of contrasting features in sentences without evidence of understanding; and (b) as the correct production of contrasting features in sentences applied appropriately to pictures. Production, in the second sense, proves to be less advanced than understanding in 3-year-old children. However, production in the sense of imitation proves to be more advanced than understanding in 3-year-olds.

REFERENCES

Brown, R., & Fraser, C. The acquisition of syntax. In C. N. Cofer & B. S. Musgrave (Eds.), *Verbal behavior and learning: Problems and processes; Proceedings.* New York: McGraw-Hill, 1963. Pp. 158–201.

Bühler, C., & Hetzer, H. *Testing children's development from birth to school age.* New York: Farrar & Rinehart, 1935.

Ervin, S. M., & Miller, W. Language development. In H. W. Stevenson (Ed.), *Child Psychology: Sixty-second yearbook of the national society for the study of education.* Chicago: University of Chicago Press, 1963.

Gesell, A. L., & Thompson, H. *Infant behavior; Its genesis and growth.* New York: McGraw-Hill, 1934.

Hayes, C. *The ape in our house.* New York: Harper, 1951.

Kahane, H., Kahane, R., & Saporta, S. *Development of verbal categories in child language.* Bloomington, Ind.: Indiana University Research Center for Anthropology Folklore, Linguistics, 1958.

Kellogg, W. N., & Kellogg, L. A. *The ape and the child; A study of environmental influence upon early behavior.* New York: McGraw-Hill, 1933.

Lenneberg, E. H. Understanding language without ability to speak: A case report. *Journal of Abnormal and Social Psychology,* 1962, **65**, 419–425.

McCarthy, D. Language development in children. In L. Carmichael (Ed.), *Manual of child psychology.* New York: Wiley, 1954. Pp. 492–630.

SOCIAL AND NONSOCIAL CONDITIONING OF INFANT VOCALIZATIONS[1]

Paul Weisberg

Basic to most views on the modification of an infant's early vocalizing are the stimuli afforded by the caretaker's behavior for the control of such social behavior (Lewis, 1959; Miller & Dollard, 1941; Mowrer, 1950). Rheingold, Gewirtz, and Ross (1959) found that an adult's responses contingent on the vocalizing of 3-month-old infants could bring about an increase in that behavior. Subsequently, when the reinforcing stimuli (tactual contact, "tsk" sounds, and smiles) were omitted during two days of extinction, the vocal rate declined to a level about 18 percent above the operant rate. As Rheingold et al. point out, however, the question of whether vocalizing was operantly *conditioned* is equivocal since the reinforcing stimuli, per se, may have acted as social releasers. The possibility exists, then, that response-independent and dependent social events may have both stimulating and reinforcing properties for infant vocal behavior. Moreover, vocalizations may be affected by the presence in the infant's visual environment of a relatively unfamiliar and unresponding adult. That is, an immobile adult may serve as a [cue] for vocal behavior. Finally, if the infant's vocalizing affects any stimulus change in his external environment, then even such physical events (as well as social ones) might reliably strengthen the behavior.

The present investigation attempted to explore these possibilities by testing the effects of a series of short term experimental manipulations on the vocal behavior of infants.

METHOD

Institution and environmental setting

The institution in which the experiment was conducted was an urban Catholic orphan home equipped with fairly modern facilities for the care of children ranging from 2 weeks of age through preschool age. The infants were segregated in wards according to age group. The ward of concern here housed 16 infants of both sexes, with a median age of 3 months. The infants were multiply cared for by full time attendants, by resident "foster mothers," and occasionally by volunteers, but usually one attendant was left in charge of the 16 infants.

[1] This paper is based upon a dissertation submitted to the Department of Psychology, University of Maryland, in partial fulfillment of the requirement for the degree of Doctor of Philosophy. The writer is grateful to Drs. William S. Verplanck and Harriet L. Rheingold for their valuable suggestions and help throughout all phases of the study. Appreciation is extended to Sisters Mary Patricia and Thecla and to the personnel of St. Ann's Infant Asylum, Washington, D.C., where the experiment was carried out.

From P. Weisberg. Social and nonsocial conditioning of infant vocalizations. Child Development, *1963,* **34,** *377–388. (With permission of the author and the Society for Research in Child Development, Inc.)*

Subjects

Thirty-three 3-month-old full term infants, diagnosed as physically healthy, served as Ss. The groups to which the Ss were assigned (to be described below) did not differ significantly on such variables as age, birth weight, pre-experimental weight, and length of time in the institution. The ratio of males to females for each group varied from 5:1 to 3:3.

Procedure

The experiment took place in a small storage room relatively free from distraction by other infants or by the personnel of the orphanage. None of the infants had ever been in this room prior to the experiment. Once an S was ready for testing, that S was carried by E to the experimental room and seated in a canvas swing. . . . E then concealed himself behind a partition in this room and waited 30 sec. before beginning an experimental session. If, within this time an S fell asleep, started to cry or to protest persistently, he was carried back to his crib and another session was attempted after half an hour had elapsed. Two 10-min. sessions were planned daily, but a session was terminated before the full 10 minutes had expired if any of these petulant behaviors appeared during the first 6 min. of a session. Thus every session reported lasted more than 6 min. without a prolonged disturbance by S (76 percent of all sessions ran the full 10 min.). If an S failed to complete two full daily sessions for one reason or another, that S was withdrawn from the experiment; five Ss were dropped following this criterion.

Each response consisted of a "discrete, voiced sound produced by S" (Rheingold, Gewirtz, & Ross, 1959, p. 69) appearing within each respiratory unit. Sounds classified as either "emotional" (protests, crying) or reflexive (coughs, sneezes, and certain digestive outbursts) were excluded. The phonetic topography of the response was not analyzed; the dependent variable was frequency of vocalizations made per min., i.e., rate of responding. . . .

Vocalizations of members of six groups were recorded through eight consecutive days. Either five or six Ss were randomly assigned to each group as they became available; if an S could not complete the experiment, he was replaced by the first available S. The experimental conditions of the fifth and sixth days were the basis for naming the groups. They were: No E present; E present; Noncontingent social stimulation; Noncontingent nonsocial stimulation; Contingent social stimulation; and Contingent nonsocial stimulation. . . . After describing them, the sequences appropriate to each group, each day, will be stated, providing the full experimental procedure.

1. *No E present.* The experimenter (E) remained behind a partition located about 5 ft. to the left of S. The upper part of the partition was transparent and allowed the E to observe all of S's behavior. E stationed himself at an angle which was about 135° from S's foveal line of vision so that, if S turned his head to the left, the chances of seeing E were minimized. E, of course, minimized any auditory or movement cues that might indicate his presence. Under these conditions S oriented towards objects directly in front of himself (including parts of his body) and only occasionally turned to the left or right. S's body size and the construction of the swing prevented him from making large torso movements.

2. *E present.* E seated himself facing S approximately 2 ft. away. E never smiled, frowned, or made rapid jerky movements of the head while in S's presence; he did not open his mouth and maintained a "blank expression" fixating in the

vicinity of *S*'s face. To keep his facial appearance invariant, *E* covertly counted numbers while fixating upon *S*.

3. *Noncontingent social stimulation* *S*s received stimulation on a prearranged schedule from *E* who was seated before them. The stimulation consisted of rubbing *S*'s chin with the thumb and forefinger followed and overlapped by an open-mouthed "toothy" smile and an aspirated "yeah" sound. Each such event lasted for about 2 sec. These events were given randomly four times a minute with the restriction that the interval between one event and the onset of the next be greater than 7 sec. On occasions when social stimulation was not given, *E* reverted to the facial expression described during the "*E* present" condition.

4. *Noncontingent nonsocial stimulation.* A door chime sounded on the same schedule as that followed with noncontingent social stimulation while *E* was seated faced toward *S*. Through successive sessions, the chime sounded 3 ft. to the left or right of *S* in an ABBA sequence.

5. *Contingent social stimulation.* The conditioning operations were performed by presenting the social stimulation described above immediately after each vocalization; that is, the smiles and the like were given contingent upon the infant's vocalizing. Responses made during the presentation of social stimulation were not further reinforced, and, during periods when *S* did not vocalize, *E* maintained the "blank expression."

6. *Contingent nonsocial stimulation.* The chime was sounded by *E* who was seated facing *S* immediately after each response. Vocalizations appearing during the chime's duration did not produce further auditory consequences. Spatial location of the chime also varied in an ABBA fashion from one session to the next.

The sequences through which the various *S*s were run are presented in Table 1.

TABLE 1   Experimental design

	Days			
Group	1 and 2	3 and 4	5 and 6	7 and 8
I (*N* = 6)	No *E*	No *E*	No *E*	No *E*
II (*N* = 5)	No *E*	*E* present	*E* present	*E* present
III (*N* = 5)	No *E*	*E* present	Noncontingent social stimulation	Noncontingent social stimulation
IV (*N* = 6)	No *E*	*E* present	Noncontingent nonsocial stimulation	Noncontingent nonsocial stimulation
V (*N* = 5)	No *E*	*E* present	Contingent social stimulation	Extinction (*E* present)
VI (*N* = 6)	No *E*	*E* present	Contingent nonsocial stimulation	Extinction (*E* present)

Group I controlled for changes in the operant rate of vocalizing with time in the experiment independent of an *E* being present. Group II served as a second control group, and any differences between the rates of groups I and II would indicate whether the presence of a human acted as [a cue for] vocalizations. Groups III and IV were used to determine whether the reinforcing stimuli had eliciting properties and hence to clarify whether any changes in rates observed in groups V and VI could be attributed to reinforcement (namely, social and nonsocial stimulation, respectively), *contingent* upon the occurrence of a response. Groups V and VI were used to show whether the rates of vocalizing shifted upward and downward by the imposition of reinforcement contingencies, and thus whether the behavior could be operantly conditioned.

RESULTS

Control day analysis (Days 1 to 4)

An analysis of . . . *S*s' . . . vocalization . . . for days 1 to 4 . . . revealed . . . that the mean rates for each of the last three days were [significantly] greater than those of day 1. . . . Days 2, 3, and 4 . . . were not significantly different from one another. The increase in rate after the low day 1 rates (mean = .54) probably indicates habituation of initial response to the relatively novel stimuli in the infant's environment. The day 2 rates provide good measures of the infant's vocal behavior when a human is absent from his environment, since the mean for all *S*s on day 2 are close to the mean of the daily rates for just group I (*No E*) on subsequent days of the experiment. . . . Absence of an initial selection bias is suggested by the lack of any significant group differences on these control days and the fact that the days did not discriminate among the groups.

Effect of *E*

Upon the first introduction of *E* on day 3, 17 out of 27 *S*s in groups II to VI (inclusive) increased in their rate over day 2. . . . The median gain for these 17 *S*s was about the same for the 10 *S*s who dropped in rate (medians = +.40 and −.37, respectively). By day 4, nine out of the 17 *S*s whose rates were augmented on day 3 had declined in rate. The changes in mean rate of the six *S*s in group I (*No E*) over this same time span were as follows: three *S*s increased, one *S* decreased, and two *S*s did not change in rate during days 2 to 3; four *S*s increased and two *S*s decreased in rate during days 3 to 4. Thus the presence relative to the absence of an unresponsive, immobile adult in the infant's visual environment is evidently not a releaser or [cue] for vocalizations.

Treatment effects [(Contingent social and nonsocial stimulation)]

. . . The *S*s in group V showed considerable gains in their vocal rates between these two time spans. [This] indicates that social stimulation contingent on the infant's vocalizing acted to reinforce that behavior. However, when the chime was made contingent on vocalizations (i.e., group VI), the over-all rate for this group as well as groups I-IV remained fairly stable. . . .

Performance of socially reinforced *S*s

. . . During social conditioning sessions (days 5 and 6), the median percentage increase based on all *S*s over their operant level merely with *E* present exceeded 282 percent. . . . There seems to be a direct relation between degree of conditioning success and resistance to extinction, with the highly vocal-conditioned infants . . . failing to extinguish. . . .

DISCUSSION

The fact that the group receiving noncontingent social stimulation behaved like those responding under all other conditions except for the socially reinforced group is consistent with the finding of Rheingold et al. (1959) that the vocalization of 3-month-old institutionalized infants can be conditioned by actions of adults.

The present study and that of Rheingold et al. differ in a number of ways. First, in the latter study, the infants' mean operant level (*E* present) was more than four times higher than that found here. The discrepancy is least likely due to subject differences, since both studies were done in the same institution where the caretaking activities have remained invariant over a span of years. More likely, at least three variables (or an interaction among them) may have determined the difference in rates: (a) The infants were observed in different experimental settings. In this study, response of seated *S*s to *E* were made in an unfamiliar room whereas in the Rheingold et al. study, *E* leaned over *S*'s crib. Since the infants were self-nursed in *their crib* (by a propped bottle arrangement), a secondary or conditioned reinforcement (or even a secondary drive stimulus reduction) explanation cannot be ruled out. (b) The length and continuity of experimental sessions differed. Rheingold et al. employed blocks of three 3-min. testing sessions spaced by 2-min. "time out" or "rest" periods. . . . In this study in which "*E* present" sessions were run continuously for 6 to 10 min., the *S*'s intra-sessional response rate was frequently cyclical, suggesting that response recovery was an ongoing process. (c) The relation between the sex of *E* (male in this study and female in Rheingold et al.) in an environment where all caretakers were female is a potentially important difference. While one can only speculate on the unknown dimensions of the human face to which infants respond, it should be pointed out that the greater opportunity for *S*s to respond to "female"-like stimuli (faces, voices, etc.) would thus introduce greater "novelty" of *E* on *S*'s operant level.

The results indicated that the initial presentation of an unresponding human did not serve as a [cue] . . . for vocal behavior. However, the relatively high resistance to extinction rates of the conditioned group suggest that the unresponding adult may have become a discriminative stimulus or, at least, a conditioned reinforcer. Admittedly, the high extinction rates could be due to the fact that not all vocalizing responses were reinforced on a continuous basis so that some of the *S*'s responses could have been conditioned on a very low variable-ratio schedule (effectively, an interval one), thus developing high resistance to extinction. Brackbill (1958) found that several values of intermittent social reinforcement provided by an adult for smiling in 4-month-old infants produced greater resistance to extinction than that resulting from a continuous schedule. In the Rheingold et al. study, however, vocalizations which were socially reinforced either on the average of 72 or 94 percent of the time failed to produce any differential effect both during conditioning and extinction sessions. Since, in the present study the extinction process was not carried to completion, further work is necessary before it can be shown that the details of *E*'s appearance can as stimuli become conditioned reinforcers for infant vocal behavior.

In the Brackbill and the Rheingold et al. studies, an inverse relation of protest (crying) to smiling and vocal behavior was found between conditioning and extinction sessions.

Protest behavior was not directly measured in this study. However, the extinction sessions did not need to be terminated any earlier than any of the other conditions because of persistent protests. During extinction sessions there was, however, a change in the topography of the vocal response. After being emitted by S and then not reinforced by E, the full social response sequence on any one occasion might abruptly shift to pouts and whines only to return to smiles and the like. Both behaviors are mutually exclusive and compete with one another across time, so that, if extinction had been extended the "protest" might have gained in strength, eventually causing E to terminate the session and take the infant out of the situation. Substantiating evidence for this view is reported by Brackbill whose infants, after being extinguished to their operant level and below, refused to fixate to her face—"an occurrence, . . . that was in distinct contrast to S's persistent fixation during conditioning" (Brackbill, 1958, p. 120). The relation between "positive" and "negative" kinds of social behavior may be understood in terms of Estes' (1950) finding that the conditioning of one behavior is a function of the initial strength of all behaviors and of the concurrent extinction of competing reactions.

There remains the question of the unsuccessful attempts to condition vocalizing using a nonsocial stimulus as a reinforcer. Since the noncontingent and contingent nonsocial Ss oriented towards the chime during its initial presentation, it is unlikely that the stimulus was not discriminated. The possibility exists that presenting the chime in the presence of an unresponding adult might facilitate habituation of responses to it. A test of this supposition would be to compare the effects of the chime as either an evoking or reinforcing stimulus when it is given either in the absence or presence of an adult.

The results of this study should not be taken to mean that nonsocial stimuli are necessarily inconsequential for the prediction and control of infant social behavior. These data show only that the particular chime used, under these conditions, in infants of this age, was ineffective. Rheingold, Stanley, and Cooley (1962), Simmons (1962), and Simmons and Lipsitt (1961) have used nonsocial stimuli (lights and chimes) for the maintenance of behavior in older infants. The range of stimuli and subjects investigated must be extended.

SUMMARY

The vocal behavior of institutionalized 3-month-old infants in relation to manipulations in their physical and social environment through eight consecutive days was explored.

The results indicated that, after habituating to an unfamiliar setting devoid of humans, the S's rate of vocalizing did not reliably increase when an unresponding adult was introduced and made part of this environment, i.e., the immobile adult was evidently not a social releaser . . . for vocal behavior. Taking the vocalizing rate in the presence of the unresponsive adult as the operant level, it was found that the behavior could be operantly conditioned by social consequences (the adult briefly touched S's chin and simultaneously smiled at and "talked" to him). Extinction operations subsequently reduced the rate but not to baseline performance. Conditions other than social reinforcement (e.g., presenting the reinforcing stimulus noncontingent upon vocalizing and giving an auditory stimulus in the presence of an unresponding adult both independently of and contingent upon vocalizing) did not seem to control infant vocal behavior.

REFERENCES

Brackbill, Y. Extinction of the smiling response in infants as a function of reinforcement schedule. *Child Development*, 1958, **29**, 115–124.

Estes, W. K. Effects of competing reactions on the conditioning curve for bar pressing. *Journal of Experimental Psychology*, 1950, **40**, 200–205.

Lewis, M. M. *How children learn to speak*. New York: Basic Books, 1959.

Miller, N. E., & Dollard, J. *Social learning and imitation*. New Haven: Yale University Press, 1941.

Mowrer, O. H. *Learning theory and personality dynamics*. New York: Ronald Press, 1950.

Rheingold, H. L., Gewirtz, J. L., & Ross, H. W. Social conditioning of vocalizations in the infant. *Journal of Comparative and Physiological Psychology*, 1959, **52**, 68–73.

Rheingold, H. L., Stanley, W. C., & Cooley, J. A. Method for studying exploratory behavior in infants. *Science*, 1962, **136**, 1054–1055.

Simmons, M. W. Operant discrimination in infants. Unpublished doctoral dissertation, Brown University, 1962.

Simmons, M. W., & Lipsitt, L. P. An operant-discrimination apparatus for infants. *Journal of the Experimental Analysis of Behavior*, 1961, **4**, 233–235.

IV

SEX TYPING, DEPENDENCY, AND AGGRESSION

Eileen Mavis Hetherington

Most cultures expect males and females to exhibit different be- **SEX TYPING**
haviors and to assume different roles in society. "Sex typing" is
the process by which children acquire the motives, values, and
behaviors regarded as characteristically masculine or feminine.

Sex-role standards

Awareness of sex-role standards occurs early, and although the
preschool child's conceptions of masculinity and femininity are
not as clearly delineated as those of older children and adults,
they are similar. These standards are in accord with Parsons'
(1955) classification of the male role as basically instrumental and
the female role as expressive. Males are expected to be powerful,
independent, aggressive, and competent in manipulating the environment, in achievement situations, and in decision making.
In social and sexual relations, they should be competitive, assertive, and dominant. Females are expected to be more dependent,
socially sensitive, and nurturant, but to suppress aggressive and

193

sexual impulses. Expression of fear under stress or affection in warm relationships is regarded as more appropriate for women than men (Bennett & Cohen, 1959; Parsons, 1955). Some writers have attempted to differentiate between the male and female role by stressing the greater demands for competence in the male role. It might be more accurate to say that the areas of competence differ for males and females. Masculine competence is manifested in coping independently and effectively in competitive achievement situations associated with the male's functions as a provider and protector. In contrast, feminine competence is demonstrated in being attractive, loving, and supportive in social relationships, particularly in her role as a wife and mother. Although this may appear to be a rather stereotyped and antiquated concept of the male and female roles, a study by Hartley (1960) has indicated that elementary-school children still view passivity, affection, and nurturance as more characteristic of females, and independence, aggression, and dominance as more characteristic of males. Cross-cultural studies have indicated that these traditional roles tend to prevail not only in the American society but in a wide variety of cultures (D'Andrade, 1966).

Constitutional factors

Current research indicates that both constitutional factors and social learning play important roles in the development of masculinity and femininity. Although in the past psychologists have emphasized the effects of socialization procedures on sex typing, there recently has been a growing interest in the contributions of biological factors to sexual differentiation. This has resulted in a rapid increase in research on sex differences in neonates, since biologically determined patterns of behavior have had less opportunity to be modified through learning in infancy than in later years.

Some of the constitutional factors influencing sex typing may be genetic in origin; some may be due to experiences of the fetus in utero. The effects of these factors are present at birth and continue to be manifested in growing psychological and biological sexual differentiation throughout the course of development.

Many constitutional sex differences, other than those of the reproductive system, are present in infancy. Although male infants tend to be larger, stronger, and to have more advanced muscular development as manifested in such things as head raising, in many other ways the female infant seems to be more mature at birth and to develop more rapidly. Females are mis-carried less frequently, have a lower rate of infant mortality, and are less vulnerable to disease at all ages. As neonates, they are more responsive than are boys to stimulation such as removal of covering blankets, skin exposure, air-jet stimulation to the abdomen, and pain. The areas of the brain involved in speech are more developed at birth in girls than in boys, and girl's basal skin conductance is higher, which again suggests greater neuro-logical maturity. Boys, however, are more active and have a higher basal metabolism rate than girls. This suggests that al-though the female infant is more mature and in some ways more responsive to stimulation, the male infant interacts more violently and actively with his environment.

The relationship between these constitutional factors and later intellectual and personality factors remains an open question. However, if the example is pursued of the contribution of con-stitutional factors to the frequently noted characteristic of greater assertiveness in males than females, interesting speculations arise. It has been found that activity level is higher in male than female neonates; it is a relatively stable behavioral characteristic; and it is highly positively correlated with aggression. Therefore, perhaps activity level is a manifestation of a genetically deter-mined predisposition for assertiveness in males. Certainly marked sex differences in aggression have been noted as early as thirteen months.

A second line of research emphasizes possible effects of pre-natal hormonal changes on the development of sex-typed be-haviors such as aggression.

Young, Goy, & Phoenix (1964) found injecting pregnant monkeys with testosterone during the second quarter of gestation produced pseudohermaphroditic infant female monkeys. These infant female monkeys not only manifested genital alterations, but also social behavior patterns which are characteristic of male monkeys, such as threatening, participation in rough-and-tumble play, less withdrawal in the face of threat or approach by other animals, and more mounting behavior. Although the results of animal studies cannot be directly generalized to those of humans, the possibility has been advanced of a similar phenomenon which would influence the development of assertive masculine be-haviors in humans (Hamburg & Lunde, 1966). It has been sug-gested that changes in androgen level during critical periods in human prenatal development may result in sensitizing circuits in the central nervous system which mediate aggressive behavior, so that the organism is more responsive to aggressive stimuli and more readily learns aggressive patterns of behavior. Thus, it may be that although young girls and boys do not show differences in the concentration of female or male hormones in their bodies, the frequently noted difference in assertiveness in the two sexes may be partially attributed to differential prenatal hormone sensitization.

Such findings indicate that although the child's interaction with his environment may largely determine sex typing, constitutionally determined differences in males and females are present at birth and will predispose the child to respond differentially to social and cultural forces involved in the establishment of gender role.

Developmental patterns

Culturally determined standards for sex roles are communicated earliest and most saliently to the child by his parents; however, as the child grows older and more independent, he is influenced increasingly by forces outside of the home. These external forces include institutions such as the school, church, and social organizations (such as the Boy Scouts) which are formal agents of acculturation, mass media such as books, television, and radio, and significant individuals, other than the parents, with whom the child interacts, such as peers, siblings, and teachers.

The male role is more clearly defined (McKee & Sherriffs, 1957) and more prestigious than the female role (D'Andrade, 1966), and there is more social pressure for boys to adopt standards of masculinity than for girls to adopt feminine standards (Brown, 1958; Hartley, 1959; Lynn, 1961). "Sissies" are rejected, "tomboys" tolerated. Most parents and peers criticize boys for crying in response to frustration, for passivity, and for participation in feminine activities; in contrast, an occasional temper tantrum or participation in a rough-and-tumble game of cowboys and Indians is at least moderately acceptable behavior for girls. However, as children grow older, lack of conformity to sex-role standards will result in rejection for both boys and girls. In view of the greater status and precision of delineation of masculine characteristics, it is not surprising that boys develop an earlier preference for the masculine role than do girls for the feminine role. The most frequently used test of sex-role preference is the "It" test which requires that children tell which item "It," an ambiguous stick figure, would like best in a series of pairs of masculine and feminine items, such as a truck and a doll. Studies (Brown, 1958; Hetherington, 1965) which have utilized the It test have found that girls do indeed prefer masculine items until about the age of ten, when a rapid shift to feminine choices begins. There is some indication that young girls increase rapidly in feminine preferences from age three to four (Hartup & Zook, 1960), but that a shift toward greater masculinity in girls occurs after age four and continues until age ten (Brown, 1957). This might be attributed to the five- to nine-year-old girls' emerging awareness of the greater status and privileges of the male role and her subsequent yielding to social pressure to adopt feminine behaviors. In contrast, most preschool boys have already established and sustain a strong preference for the masculine role.

It is interesting to note that there are different developmental patterns of sex-role preferences in the lower and middle classes. Rabban (1950) found that most lower-class boys showed a strong preference for appropriately sex-typed toys by age four or five, lower-class girls and middle-class boys by about seven, and middle-class girls at age nine were the last to show feminine preferences. These class differences can be attributed to the more rigid delineation of sex roles, less permissiveness for violation of these standards, and more stereotyped masculine or feminine models offered by parents in the lower classes. Most lower-class fathers do not participate in child care or household tasks. Their employment usually involves heavy labor in occupations which are traditionally regarded as exclusively masculine. Their wives' main function is that of household and child care and sexual satisfaction. When lower-class women work, it is frequently in occupations which involve characteristically feminine activities such as cooking, housework, and child care. In contrast, middle-class men are increasingly participating in caring for their children and in household tasks. Fathers change diapers, feed their children, go to PTA meetings, and participate in their children's recreational activities. They may do the family grocery shopping, dry dishes, or occasionally whip up a gourmet delight in the kitchen. The middle-class mother is less acquiescent in her role than is the lower-class mother; she participates actively in family decisions, is involved in many activities outside the home, and if she works, she is likely to be employed in a business or professional occupation which is not regarded as solely feminine.

The tendency to behave in a masculine or feminine manner appears to be a remarkably stable and early developed personality characteristic. A longitudinal study (Kagan & Moss,

1962) conducted at the Fels Institute found sex-typed interests in elementary school were correlated with adult heterosexual behavior. Boys who were interested in typically masculine activities, such as mechanics, gross motor skills, and competitive and aggressive games, and girls who were interested in feminine activities, such as reading, cooking, sewing, and noncompetitive games, were involved in heterosexual activities in adulthood. This stability is more marked for males than for females. In fact, the sex appropriateness of boys' play, even in the preschool years, is highly predictive of adult sex-role interests.

Theories of sex typing

Since sex-typed behaviors occur early, and since the child's initial social interactions are with the parents, most psychological theories of sex typing have assumed that the role of the parents is particularly important in the development of sex typing. However, various theories have tended to emphasize different aspects of the parent-child relationship as being most influential in this process. The aspects of the parent-child relationships that have received the most attention are parental warmth and nurturance toward the child, parental power and control of desired resources, and parental punishment.

The earliest theory that attempted to explain sex typing, and the theory from which most other theories are at least partially derived, is "psychoanalytic theory." In this view, sex typing is only one result of the broader process of identification which also determines the child's self-control, moral values, conscience, and ego ideals. It invokes two types of mechanisms to explain sex typing. The first is anaclitic identification, a preliminary asexual identification based on fear of loss of love; the second is identification with the aggressor, a defensive identification aimed at the avoidance of punishment and castration. Freud (1950) suggests that although both types of identification are important for all children, anaclitic identification is more salient in the development of girls and aggressive identification in boys. Because of their initial helplessness and dependence, both boys and girls form an initial anaclitic bond with the person responsible for the care, feeding, and protection of the child, usually the mother. Later, during the phallic phase, at age three or four, the young boy experiences the Oedipus complex in which he perceives his father as a competitor for his mother's love and fears retaliation from the father in the form of castration. Identification with the father reduces the threat of castration and permits the boy to vicariously sexually enjoy the mother; thus, identification is the process which results in the resolution of the Oedipus complex. It is obvious that fear of castration would be an untenable motive to explain identification in girls since they are already "castrated." Freud consequently assumed that fear of loss of love remains the most important motive in the identification of girls and the complete resolution of the Oedipus complex through aggressive identification does not occur in women. Thus, identification with the aggressor is most important in masculine identification and anaclitic identification in feminine identification.

It should be noted that although Freud regards identification as a process of modeling whereby the child incorporates characteristics of parents, he emphasizes that the child does not necessarily identify with the overt behavior of the parent, but he identifies with the idealized values of the parent's superego. Bronfenbrenner (1960) in his excellent paper on identification states:

> In short, there are three aspects of the parent after which the child may pattern himself, the parent's overt behavior, his motives, or his aspirations for the child. Which aspect of the model is in fact identified with becomes, from our point of view, an empirical question. It seems probable that all three aspects are involved at one time or another. Or it may be that one process, such as anaclitic identification, is more likely to result in the emulation of standards, while another, such as identification with the aggressor, leads to the adoption of parental motives and acts (p. 24).

Considerable controversy has arisen over the utility and necessity of the concept of identification. It has been argued that the behaviors explained by identification can be more parsimoniously dealt with by common forms of learning such as imitation and conditioning based on parental rewards and punishment (Bandura, 1962; Miller & Dollard, 1941; Sanford, 1955). Learning theorists suggest that children are predisposed to imitate and that this proclivity to model will be facilitated by characteristics of the model, such as his warmth, power, and success in obtaining rewards. The research of psychologists who emphasize "social-learning theory" tends to deal with the acquisition of narrow and specific patterns of behavior rather than the child's motivation to acquire the general orientations of the parents. Indeed, Bronfenbrenner (1960) has argued that such a position ignores two important features of identification: that of the motive in the child to become like the parent and the implied introjection of the total pattern rather than specific acts of parental behavior.

When behavior theorists have attempted to explain the motivational system involved in the child's acting like the parents, they have usually based it on the parent's acquired reward value due to the parents' satisfying role as caretakers. If the parent satisfies the child's needs, his presence and approval eventually become rewarding to the child. Through the interaction of the infant's dependence and the parent's nurturance, the child develops a motive to be like the parent in order to avoid loss of parental love and to gain mastery over the environment by emulating the loving, competent parent (Kagan, 1964). Children should acquire the characteristics of warm parents through imitation of parental behaviors and through reinforcements dispensed by the parents for behavior congruent with parental standards. It might be expected that if a father is warm and masculine, and if the child is rewarded for imitating his father, he would develop masculine behavior, and a parallel process between mother and daughter would occur.

Defensive identification does not play a major role in sex typing for most learning theorists, since it would be expected that parental punishment would lead to an avoidance response on the part of the child for the parent and would minimize any tendency to imitate the punitive parent. In contrast to the position that the child, through modeling and reinforcement, becomes sex typed, a more cognitively oriented psychologist (Kohlberg, 1966) has suggested that the child's discrimination and labeling of himself as a male or female precedes, not follows, modeling. Once the child appropriately categorizes himself on the basis of genital differences and differences in size, hair, apparel, social roles, etc., it becomes rewarding to behave like the same-sexed parent and to participate in masculine or feminine activities.

Social-role theorists (Brim, 1958; Cottrell, 1942; Johnson, 1963; Parsons, 1955) have incorporated both the factors of nurturance and rewards and of aggression and punishment into their theories of sex typing. "Role theory" has two unique aspects. The first is the view that the feminine role is basically expressive, and the masculine role is instrumental. The mother's role in the family is one of being loving, supportive, and conciliatory; the father's role is one of mastering the environment and in the control and dispensing of discipline. Although this is similar to Freud's image of the nurturing mother and hostile father there is emphasis on both warmth and aggression in the paternal role. The father, rather than being hostile, is powerful and dominant in his ability to dispense both rewards and punishment.

The second unusual conception in this theory is the function of reciprocal social roles, particularly parent-child roles, in the development of sex-typed behavior. In the process of socialization, the child goes through a series of relationships with other significant people in which he learns about different aspects of his own role and the role of the other person. The most important reciprocal role in the development of masculinity or femininity is the parent-child role. At any stage in development, the child identifies with both the roles of the mother and of himself, thus in the earliest mother-child relationship, the infant internalizes the mother in her role as caretaker and himself in the role of one to be cared for. This subsequently develops into a reciprocal role of the mother as a dispenser of love and himself as an object of love. Again the infant identifies with both roles, he learns how to love and be loved. Early in life, the mother is serving both an instrumental role in caring for the child and an expressive role in loving the child. However, late in the preschool years, as the father participates more decisively in the child's life, the child distinguishes between, and must internalize, not only the expressive role of the mother but also the instrumental role of the father. The early reciprocal-love relationship with the mother serves as the basis on which selective reinforcement for appropriately sex-typed behavior becomes effective. The son first values and identifies with the instrumental role of the father because the mother rewards and encourages him to do so. The theory also indicates that the reciprocal roles between mother and son and father and daughter may be important in sex typing. The older boy learns to act in an instrumental role in relation to the mother's female expressive role; the girl learns how to behave in an appropriately feminine expressive manner through interacting with the father in his instrumental role. This theory, more than the previously discussed theories, suggests the importance of the relationship with the opposite-sexed parent in the acquisition of masculinity and femininity.

Johnson (1963) has extended this reciprocal-role theory and has pointed out that the mother does not respond differentially to male and female children, but that the father does. This differential responsiveness of the father to sons and daughters makes him particularly influential in the development of sex typing in both boys and girls. Some of the research findings which will be reviewed later offer support for this position.)

This brief selective review of a few of the theories of sex typing suggests a difference in emphasis rather than complete divergence of factors considered influential in sex typing. Psychoanalytic theory has focused on both the warmth and punitiveness of the parents, with paternal punitiveness being particularly important in the identification of boys. Social-learning theory has stressed the role of parental nurturance and affection in making the parent an effective model and reinforcer for the child. Role theory has emphasized the importance of maternal warmth and paternal power in dispensing both rewards and punishments.

Parental characteristics

Most research dealing with sex typing and parental behavior has focused on the three parent variables of greatest theoretical concern: warmth, dominance, and aggression. Measures of sex typing have included such widely varied procedures as questionnaire scales, projective measures of masculinity and femininity (such as human figure drawing and doll play) and reports, ratings, and observations of preferences for masculine and feminine toys, games, and interests. In view of the multiplicity of measures utilized in these studies, the consistency of results dealing with these three dimensions of parent behavior is remarkable. However, these relationships between measures of parent characteristics and sex typing in children, although statistically significant, account for only a small portion of the variance. Factors other than parental behaviors obviously influence the development of children's personalities.

Studies of the development of sex typing have used both the differential or correlational method and the experimental method. In the differential method, the researcher seeks out a situation which involves the variables in which he is interested; he does not manipulate the variables. Thus measures of maternal and paternal warmth might be correlated with the amount of time nursery-school boys spend in masculine play activities in a free-play situation. No manipulation of parental warmth would be involved. In contrast, if the experimental method were used, the effects of nurturant or nonnurturant models on the imitation of the models by male subjects might be assessed. The independent variable of warmth or nurturance would be systematically manipulated, with all other variables controlled. The boys' imitative behavior would be the dependent variable. The differential method has the advantages of the naturalism and apparent meaningfulness of the variables and situations measured, but because of the many uncontrolled factors which may be affecting the dependent variables, it can never directly establish cause-and-effect relationships. The experimental method has the asset of greater control and consequent ability to make causal predictions within the laboratory situation. However, it has been criticized as measuring behaviors which are trivial and lack relevance to real-life problems, in the interest of experimental control and precision.

Experimental studies of the effects of models' attributes upon imitation by children are considered relevant to identification and consequently to sex typing. Several assumptions must be made before these laboratory analog experiments can be considered relevant to the development of sex typing. First, it must be assumed that identification and imitation are synonymous, since both encompass the tendency for a person to match the behavior, attitudes, or emotional reactions exhibited by models (Bandura, 1962). Second, there are model characteristics which affect, in a similar manner, the imitation of a wide range of behaviors including sex-typed behaviors. This assumption must be made since most of the studies do not involve behavior directly relevant to sex typing, but measure imitation of such widely divergent and occasionally bizarre model behaviors as striking Bobo dolls, wearing hats with feathers in the back, and making unusual comments and mannerisms. Finally, it must be accepted that simplified, highly controlled, and restricted laboratory manipulations of extremely short duration parallel the phenomena found in intense and sustained complex parent-child relations. It could be argued that a model's giving children M & Ms, praising them, and smiling differs qualitatively from the nurturance and warmth of a loving parent, or that criticism and removal of reward by a stranger is in no way similar to the overwhelming, constant, inescapable threat of a punitive, rejecting parent. The search for experimental control may lead to the violation and distortion of the processes being investigated. However, some support for the generalizability of these laboratory studies is found in the frequent congruence of the results of such experiments and those of more naturalistic studies using the differential method.

There is considerable evidence that warmth or nurturance in the same-sexed parent facilitates identification and appropriate sex-role learning (Bronson, 1959; Helper, 1955; Mussen & Distler, 1959, 1960; Mussen & Rutherford, 1963; Payne & Mussen, 1956; Sears, P. S., 1953) Highly masculine boys perceive their fathers, but not their mothers, as more rewarding and nurturant than do low-masculine boys. In contrast, evidence suggests that warmth in both mothers and fathers increases femininity in girls (Hetherington, 1967a) Evidence from modeling studies confirms that children tend to imitate nurturant more than nonnurturant models, whether the models are strangers (Bandura & Huston, 1961, reprinted following Chapter VI) or parents (Hetherington & Frankie, 1967; Mussen & Parker, 1965).

Evidence for the effects of parental power on identification and sex typing are remarkably consistent. Boys who view their fathers as competent, in control of limit setting, and dominant in dispensing both rewards and punishments, describe themselves as more similar to their fathers and are more masculine than boys who view their fathers as lacking in these characteristics (Hetherington, 1965; Moulton, Liberty, Burnstein, & Altucher, 1966; Mussen & Distler, 1959) Maternal dominance appears to be particularly disruptive of sex typing in boys. In contrast, parental dominance is not related to femininity in girls, although dominance in fathers facilitates girls' cross-sex identification on non–sex-typed traits. Thus, girls with powerful mothers or fathers are equally feminine but those with dominant fathers acquire some of their father's traits which are appropriate to both males and females, such as a good sense of humor, friendliness, etc. Laboratory studies also indicate that children tend to imitate powerful parents and adults (Bandura, Ross, & Ross, 1963b; Hetherington, 1965, reprinted following this chapter).

Families in which the father is absent from home (either permanently due to death, divorce, desertion, or illegitimacy, or for sustained temporary periods due to a father's itinerant occupation or war) might be expected to have an influence on sex typing similar to those found in a mother-dominated home. In such a home, the mother must necessarily assume the instrumental role of decision maker and disciplinarian. Studies have found that boys who were separated from their fathers during their pre-school years are less aggressive, more dependent, and less interested in competitive sports than are boys with fathers present (Hetherington, 1966; Stolz, 1954) In doll play, these boys show play patterns similar to girls and manifest more verbal aggression and less physical aggression than do boys from a normal home situation (Bach, 1946; Sears, P. S., 1951). There is some evidence that separation from the father before age four is more disruptive to sex typing in boys than a later separation (Hetherington, 1966). This is suggestive of a critical period in the preschool years for sex typing which would be in accord with psychoanalytic theory.)

Reports on preadolescent and adolescent boys from father-absent homes have been less consistent than those on younger children. These boys, in contrast to father-present boys, exhibit both more feminine behavior and more compensatory masculine behavior where they behave in an exaggerated masculine fashion.) Biller & Borstelmann (1967), in their review of masculine development, suggest that a masculine sex-role preference develops earlier than a masculine sex-role adoption in boys with fathers absent. The father-absent boys gradually become aware of the greater privileges and status of males in our society and thus prefer the masculine role, but have difficulty in developing an integrated and stable pattern of masculine behavior, since they have no constant paternal model to emulate.)

It is obvious that sex-role models other than the parents are available to children, such as siblings, peers, and other adult males, and that these models may be utilized in place of an absent parent. Children with an older same-sexed sibling exhibit more sex-appropriate behavior than those with an older opposite-sexed sibling (Koch, 1956). In two-child families, teachers rate girls as more feminine and boys as more masculine if the other sibling is of the same sex (Brim, 1958), and more appropriate sex-typed interests are reported by adolescents who recall a greater number of childhood experiences with older members of the same sex (Steimel, 1960).

Father absence appears to be minimally disruptive to the early development of femininity in girls. Preschool and preadolescent girls with absent fathers are reported to be more dependent on their mothers and peers than girls with fathers in the home, but their sex-role preferences, play interests, and behavior are similar at these ages. However, at adolescence a delayed effect of father absence becomes apparent in the heterosexual relations of these girls. Mothers report, and teachers and recreation directors observe, that these girls have a tendency to be either "boy crazy" or abnormally inhibited and shy in relationships with boys. Dating behavior is either accelerated or extremely retarded. At social events, these girls are described as being either inappropriately assertive and provocative or anxious and aloof. Mothers frequently described these daughters as being perfect little ladies not at all interested in boys and sex, or they expressed concern over difficulties in controlling their daughter's possible promiscuity (Hetherington, 1967b). This suggests a latent effect of paternal absence on girls which is manifested at puberty in disrupted emotional relationships with men. It appears that in not undergoing the normal reciprocal-role relationships with a father, these daughters do not learn how to assume the appropriate expressive feminine role in relation to males. The findings of these studies seem to offer considerable support to Johnson's position that the father plays an important role in the sex typing of both boys and girls.

Studies of the role of parental aggression in identification are few and inconsistent. Until recently most support for this position has rested on clinical case studies, anecdotal evidence (Freud, A., 1937), or naturalistic observations such as Bettelheim's concentration-camp studies (1943) in which he reports identification of prisoners with their sadistic guards. In Mussen and Distler's study (1959) of kindergarten boys scoring high and low in masculinity on the It test, it was found that highly masculine boys view their fathers, but not their mothers, as being both more rewarding and more punitive than do low-masculine boys. Parental punishment was not related to sex typing in girls (Mussen & Rutherford, 1963). In contrast, a study of adolescent boys (Bandura & Walters, 1959) found that boys with punitive and nonnurturant fathers did not perceive themselves as emulating or being similar to their fathers. It may well be that if punishment facilitates identification, its effect occurs only when the parent is also nurturant or under extremely restricted conditions.

Sarnoff (1951) has specified three conditions which are essential in identification with the aggressor: a hostile model who directs his aggression toward another person, a victim who is dependent on the aggressive model, and a situation involving stresses and limitations which prevent the victim from escaping the aggression. On the basis of these criteria, identification with an aggressive, powerful parent would seem most likely to occur in a stressful family in which both parents are hostile. Such a situation would give the child no opportunity to escape punishment by identifying with a warm, nondominant parent, and the conflictual family relationship should increase the child's feelings of helplessness and anxiety and consequently his proclivity to defensive identification. A recent study (Hetherington & Frankie, 1967) investigated the effects of parental warmth, dominance, and conflict on imitation of parents by preschool children. The parental measures were obtained from the Structured Family Interaction Test, a procedure that involves parents separately stating how they would deal with various problems in child rearing and subsequently discussing these problems and coming to a mutually agreed upon solution to handling the situations. The measures of dominance and conflict were mainly objective behavioral measures; the measures for warmth-hostility were based upon judges' ratings of the interviews. Measures of dominance included such things as: who changes his position most from his original independent solution to the final joint solution; who speaks first, last, and most; and who passively accepts the spouse's position. Measures of conflict included disagreements and aggressions, simultaneous speech, interruptions, total time spoken (since this is related to difficulty in reaching a compromise solution), and failure to agree.

It was found that while warmth and dominance facilitated imitation in both boys and girls, dominance was more salient for boys and warmth for girls. Boys tend to imitate a dominant father and girls a warm mother. Under the conditions assumed to be most likely to facilitate aggressive identification, we do get imitation of a powerful, hostile parent. Under high conflict, with both parents low in warmth, there is a marked trend for both boys and girls to imitate the dominant parent, whether it is the mother or father. If either the nondominant parent is warm or there is little conflict in the home, there is a trend toward less imitation of the aggressive dominant parent.

Parental characteristics other than warmth, aggression, and power would also be expected to influence the development of sex typing. The masculinity or femininity of the parents and encouragement for adopting appropriately sex-typed behaviors should be particularly important. However, sex typing of parents or encouragement of clearly sex-typed activities is not related to masculinity in boys (Angrilli, 1960; Mussen & Rutherford, 1963; Payne & Mussen, 1956), and femininity in daughters is not related to femininity in mothers, but is related to masculinity in fathers, father's approval of the mother as a model, and reinforcement by the father for participation in feminine activities. Again we see evidence of the importance of the father in sex typing in girls (Hetherington, 1967b; Mussen & Rutherford, 1963).

There is some suggestion in the literature that parental permissiveness for sexual and aggressive behavior in children leads to masculinity and restrictiveness to femininity in both boys and girls (Sears, Rau, & Alpert, 1965). Since permissiveness has been shown to be related to assertiveness, aggression, activity, achievement, and independence (which are masculine characteristics) and restrictiveness to submissiveness, compliance, dependency, politeness, and inhibition of aggression (which are feminine characteristics) (Baldwin, 1949; Levy, 1943; Meyers, 1944; Sears, R. R., 1961; Watson, 1957), these findings are not unexpected.

In summary, the development of sex typing and the parental characteristics influencing this process differ for boys and girls. It has been suggested that sex typing should be more directly related to family characteristics in girls than in boys, since girls are encouraged to remain family oriented, and boys are encouraged to become independent and are thus exposed to more extrafamilial influences and standards. Also, since there is greater clarity in the cultural definition of the male than the female role, it might be expected that cultural stereotypes would be more salient in the development of masculinity, and parental standards and characteristics would be more influential in the development of femininity. The findings do seem to support this position.

The major parental factors influencing sex typing in boys are warmth and dominance of the father. If the father is perceived as nurturant and powerful, boys manifest a high degree of masculinity which is unrelated to the degree of the father's masculinity. This suggests that, rather than imitating specific characteristics of the father when the father is controlling and loving, the son views the masculine role as desirable and becomes motivated to adopt it. Under these conditions, the boy's striving for mastery, competence, and love and the social sanctions reinforcing him for being masculine will lead him to find being masculine gratifying. If the mother is dominant, the boy will tend to sustain his initial anaclitic bond with the mother. In contrast, sex typing in girls is influenced by both parents. Although continued warmth in the mother is necessary to maintain the girl's anaclitic identification with the mother, the reciprocal role relationship with the father seems to be at least as important a factor. A loving masculine father who has a positive and appreciative attitude toward women and who encourages his daughter in feminine activities will nurture femininity in his daughter.

These findings offer considerable evidence in support of a reciprocal-role theory of the development of sex typing in girls. When one considers that the characteristics valued in females, such as physical attractiveness, dependency, suggestibility, and empathy, depend largely on responses and evaluations by others, these results are not surprising. The young girl accepts and values her expressive role by interacting with a warm, masculine, instrumental father who rewards and enjoys her femininity. The relatively greater salience of parental warmth in feminine sex typing and paternal dominance in masculine sex typing is apparent.

The two sex-typed characteristics on which the greatest systematic body of research exists are dependency and aggression. Relatively more work has been focused on aggression, since in its flagrantly antisocial forms, such as juvenile delinquency, aggression has greater obvious impact upon society.

DEPENDENCY AND AGRESSION

Many similar conceptual and theoretical issues are encountered in the study of dependency and aggression, particularly those involving problems of definition, generality, and stability.

Definitions

Definitions of dependency and aggression have fallen into two broad categories: those of motivational constructs involving attributes of generalized drive, or those of behavioral constructs involving observable responses. Neither type of definition is completely satisfactory.

"Dependency" may be defined as a need for reassurance, love, approval, and aid from others (Heathers, 1955) or as "a class of responses that are capable of eliciting positive attending and ministering responses from others" (Bandura & Walters, 1963). Similarly, "aggression" could be defined either as behavior for which "the goal-response is injury of the person toward whom it is directed" (Dollard, Doob, Miller, Mowrer, & Sears, 1939) or as a "response that delivers noxious stimuli to another object" (Buss, 1961). In each case, the first definition involves an assumption of intentionality which must be inferred from the antecedent conditions and context in which the responses are made, while the second definition involves no such assumption. If intentionality is introduced, problems of the reliability and validity of judgments of intent arise, whereas if the results of the subject's actions are focused upon, situations which are obviously not phenomenologically equivalent will receive the same label.

When two children have been quarreling and one child breaks the other's favorite toy, if intent is considered, the act is more likely to be called aggression than it would have been if the children had been playing in a friendly fashion before the incident. If only the destructive end result is considered, the act might be labeled aggression under both circumstances. [The introduction of intent makes it impossible to classify phenotypically identical behaviors consistently as aggressive or dependent, although it differentiates between situations which, from a common sense point of view, would not be considered equivalent. A young child's persistent tugging at his mother's skirt might in some circumstances be called attention-seeking dependency and in others aggression.]

It has been argued that concepts such as aggression or dependency are nothing more than culturally determined quasi-evaluative labels (Bandura & Walters, 1963; Walters & Parke, 1964). Whether such labels are attached to behavior depends on the other characteristics of the individuals involved in the situation, the conditions under which the behavior occurs, and social implications and evaluations of the consequences of the behavior. These situational and evaluative aspects of the labeling process are particularly apparent in relation to age and sex. Thus, different behaviors in young children and in adults, and in males and in females, might be labeled as aggression or dependency, and a label such as dependency would have a more socially unacceptable connotation for males or adults than for females or children. If a man wished to have a car door held open for him, this would probably be classified as dependent behavior. This would not be true if the behavior had been emitted by a woman or a two-year-old child. These definitional problems in aggression and dependency have not been adequately resolved, and they present one of the major difficulties in current research in these areas.

Unidimensionality

If dependency and aggression are regarded either as generalized drives or as personality traits, it might be expected that different manifestations of these traits would be positively correlated and that there would be generality of these traits across situations and over time.

Let us first examine evidence relating to the unidimensionality of dependency. Beller (1957) used nursery-school teachers' ratings to assess the unidimensionality and relationship of dependence and independence. His five measures of dependency, which included seeking help, seeking recognition, seeking attention, seeking physical contact, and seeking to be near others, were highly correlated. Girls were more dependent than boys, particularly in seeking physical contact and nearness to adults. The children were also rated on five indices of independence: taking initiative, overcoming obstacles, persistence, satisfaction from work, and wanting to do things without assistance. Significant correlations among the components of independence were found suggesting that independence may also be considered an acquired drive which is expressed in a multiplicity of behaviors. This study has been criticized on the basis of a possible halo effect in ratings which would increase the likelihood of a finding of unidimensionality. When teachers rate a child on a series of characteristics, early ratings may influence later ratings, or a generally negative attitude toward a child may be reflected in unrealistically unfavorable ratings on all items. Some support for Beller's results were obtained by Crandall, Preston, & Rabson (1960) who also found high positive relationships among three measures of dependency based on observation in a nursery school. Also, support for cross-situational consistency was obtained in high correlations between dependency in nursery school and in the home.

An issue of further interest to Beller was the relation between dependence and independence. Could dependency simply be viewed as a lack of independence? If the bipolarity hypothesis is valid, high negative correlations should be obtained between measures of dependence and independence. Beller obtained only a moderate negative correlation, and subsequent research has found correlations between independence and dependence ranging from negative through zero to positive, depending on the measures used to assess these dimensions and on situational variables. In general, when the measures of independence include both self-reliance and achievement striving, they are not closely related to measures of dependency.

Evidence for generality in dependence and independence is not supported by most other studies. In a carefully designed study, Hartup (1958) found little relation among measures of help seeking, seeking to be near, and reassurance seeking, as assessed by observations in school and in an experimental setting and by teachers' ratings. Sears et al. (1965) found no relation for dependency measures in boys and low relations for girls. The finding of a moderate relation among dependency measures in girls and none in boys is a frequent one except in studies which include negative attention getting as a dependency measure. This measure appears to be more closely related to aggression than dependency. These studies seem to indicate, particularly in boys, that concepts other than a global dependency drive or trait must be invoked to explain the occurrence of dependent behavior.

In contrast, correlations among measures of aggression suggest greater integration of aggressive responses in boys than in girls (Sears et al., 1965), particularly in antisocial forms of aggression such as direct aggression to others and destruction of objects. Sears et al. (1965) cite these findings as evidence for greater influence of situational factors in aggressive behavior in girls and of an integrated aggressive drive in boys. Note that although higher intercorrelations are usually obtained among different measures of aggression than among measures of dependency, these still leave a considerable amount of the variance for which to account.

Before accepting such findings as irrefutable evidence against the possibility of predicting behavior based on relatively stable traits or predispositions of individuals to respond in a specific manner in a variety of situations, alternative explanations must be considered. It may well be that we have not isolated or selected the most valid, stable, and holistic dimensions of personality to investigate. We have selected concepts that are assumed to be valid and meaningful on the basis of current psychological theory. Empirical data often suggest that other concepts have more predictive power. For example, the dimension of activity-passivity appears to be one which is relatively consistent over time and which influences behavior in many situations in a predictable fashion (Kagan & Moss, 1962). Yet most experimenters seek to partial out or control for the effects of activity in order to investigate aggression and dependency. A study by Gewirtz (1956), using a situation where a child painted in the presence of an adult, factor analyzed nine observational measures of child-initiated behavior frequently assumed to be indices of dependency. Two factors emerged. The first involved active direct verbal attempts to gain and maintain the attention of the adult; the second consisted of more passive indirect techniques of attention seeking. It may well be that such factors cut through many of the behaviors which cannot be integrated under more conventional labels. It is also possible that a reasonably circumscribed number of situational dimensions can be identified which will interact with these personality characteristics in a systematic way.

Another difficulty in assessing the unidimensionality of dependency or aggression rests in identifying the phenotypical expression of such drives or traits which are influenced by such things as age, sex, social class, and social learning experiences. This problem is apparent in longitudinal investigations of personality.

[At this point, it must be concluded that the evidence for a holistic trait of dependency or aggression that can be defined without reference to narrow situational variables is at best equivocal.]

Stability of behavior

[Changes in the form of dependent and aggressive behavior occur with age and show a different pattern of development for boys and girls. In general, there is a shift from parents to teachers to peers as objects for dependency, and dependency changes from clinging and hugging to verbal attention seeking and reassurance seeking between the early preschool years and early elementary-school years (Gewirtz, 1954; Heathers, 1955). In aggression, there is a decrease in frequency of aggressive episodes, and a shift from antisocial to prosocial aggression in the same period (Jersild & Markey, 1935; Sears, R. R., 1961).]

[During early childhood years, dependent behavior is manifested more frequently by girls and aggressive behavior by boys. Girls of ages three to nine make more dependent approaches to adults than do boys in free-play situations (Otis & McCandless, 1955). In contrast, boys are more aggressive than girls in the home, in school, with peers, and in fantasy such as doll-play situations. Antisocial forms of aggression such as temper tantrums, quarrels, overt physical aggression, lying, and destructiveness are more frequently found in boys than girls] (Dawe, 1934; Jersild & Markey, 1935; Macfarlane, Allen, & Honzik, 1954).

A classic observational study of aggression in preschool children (Jersild & Markey, 1935) found that nursery-school boys more often instigated and were involved in aggressive altercations than were girls. Some evidence of learning in development of these sex differences is apparent, since at age two screaming, biting, and crying is equally frequent in boys and girls, but by age four girls are involved in fewer physical fights and relatively more verbal altercations and crying than boys. This difference in aggressive behavior is probably a result of the increase in sex typing during these years and of selective reinforcement by peers and adults for overt aggression in boys and girls. These children were observed in kindergarten a year later, and considerable stability of behavior was found from nursery school to kinder-garten. The children who had been most aggressive in the early years were involved in more social conflicts in kindergarten.

Longitudinal investigations of personality, where the same children are studied repeatedly over a period of time, offer an ideal opportunity to assess the developmental stability of dependency and aggression. Kagan & Moss (1960, reprinted after this chapter; 1962) have addressed themselves to this problem in their analyses of the results of the Fels Institute studies of a group of middle-class children from birth to adulthood. These researchers investigated the relations between ratings of behavior in four periods of child development: birth to three years, three to six years, six to ten years, and ten to fourteen years, and ratings of adult behavior. Aggression, dependency, and sex-typed activities were among the behavioral variables studied. The childhood ratings were obtained from interviews and from observations in the home, school, and day camp, and the adult ratings were obtained from interviews when the subjects were between age twenty and thirty. The results of this study indicated: (1) that certain adult behaviors can be predicted on the basis of childhood behaviors, particularly those of the early school years, and (2) that the stability of these behaviors is related to their appropriateness to culturally determined sex-role standards. Thus, intellectual mastery and sex-typed interests are encouraged in both males and females and show great consistency for both sexes from ages six to ten through adulthood. In contrast, childhood sexuality and aggression are predictive of adult sexuality and aggression in males, but not in females, and childhood passivity and dependency are predictive of these adult behaviors in females, but not in males.

Overt aggression and sexuality are congruent with the masculine, but not the feminine role in our culture. These behaviors in girls are subject to disapproval and punishment by parents and peers, but are tacitly encouraged as acceptable behaviors in boys. It is not surprising, therefore, that such things as anger and tantrums in childhood (behavior disorganization) are predictive of ease of anger arousal and direct aggressive relations in adulthood, and that heterosexuality in childhood is related to sexual behavior in adulthood for boys, but not girls. In a similar fashion, passivity and dependency are unacceptable in males, but not females. The differential stability of these behaviors between sexes appears to be a result of variation in reinforcement histories and role models provided for these behaviors for boys and girls.

It might be expected that these sexually incongruent behaviors must lead to some form of substitute or derivative behavior which is more acceptable in adulthood, and indeed, this seems to be the case. Passivity in boys is related to sexual anxiety, social apprehension, and noncompetitiveness in men. Anger and tantrums in girls are related to masculine interests, intellectual competitiveness, and dependency conflict in women. This finding of expression of behaviors in socially approved form, appropriate to a given sex role, is in accord with the results of other studies. These studies have indicated a greater amount of verbal than physical aggression in preschool girls than in boys and more prosocial aggression, such as advocating harsh punishment for transgressions of social prohibitions and tattling, than overt antisocial aggression in girls than in boys. Similarly, preschool boys tend to manifest dependency in the form of instrumental dependency (assistance in the performance of tasks and manipulations) rather than emotional dependency (demands for affection).

Kagan & Moss (1962) conclude:

> It appears that when a childhood behavior is congruent with traditional sex role characteristics, it is likely to be predictive of phenotypically similar behaviors in adulthood. When it conflicts with sex role standards, the relevant motive is more likely to find expression in theoretically consistent substitute behaviors, that are socially more acceptable than the original response. In sum, the individual's desire to mold his overt behavior in concordance with the culture's definition of sex-appropriate responses is a major determinant of the pattern of continuity in his development (p. 269).

Antecedents of dependency

Because of the great complexity and problems in the identification and assessment of child-rearing practices and parent attitudes, the results of studies of the antecedents of dependency and aggression have not always been in agreement; however, some generalizations can be made. The selection of variables to be investigated in any area frequently is determined by theoretical assumptions; thus, in the study of dependency much work has focused on parental nurturance and permissiveness, and in investigations of aggression, work has focused upon frustration and parental punitiveness.

Many theories have assumed that parental nurturance is the most important factor in the development of dependency in children. Learning theorists assume that through the parent's role in caretaking, dependent responses are elicited and reinforced in the child, and the parent acquires secondary reward value through his association with tension reduction. Psychoanalytic theorists assume that dependency is a trait largely determined by libidinal satisfactions, particularly those associated with sucking and feeding experiences in the oral stage of development. On the basis of either theory, it might be expected that a warm, nurturant parent who permits or rewards dependency will have a highly dependent child and that a punitive parent will have a less dependent child. Some support for this position is found in both field and laboratory studies.

Field studies have shown that mothers of preschool children who openly demonstrate affection and reward their children's dependency overtures describe their children as highly dependent (Sears, Maccoby, & Levin, 1957). Similarly a study of aggressive and inhibited adolescent boys suggests that dependency in these boys is related to the amount of participation in caretaking, affection, and reward for dependency by the parents (Bandura, 1960). When children have parents who are nurturant and reinforce dependent behavior, the children are dependent; however, when parents are nurturant, but value independent behavior, it has been found that their children are not dependent. This suggests that parental nurturance leads to the child being responsive to parental reinforcements and values for either dependent or independent behavior. In fact, a large body of research suggests that warmth and nurturance in a parent makes him a generally more effective model and shaper of a wide range of behaviors, including dependency.

Some findings of laboratory studies are congruent with these results. Heathers (1953) had six- to twelve-year-old children walk blindfolded along a narrow plank mounted 8 inches from the floor on springs. His measure of dependency was whether the children accepted or rejected the experimenter's proferred hand when beginning their anxious, unstable walk. Children who took the experimenter's hand had parents who were rated in the Fels Parent Behavior Scale as encouraging dependency and inhibiting the development of independent behaviors and skills appropriate to a child of that age.

In another study (Nelsen, 1960), children were either criticized or commended for making dependent responses in a training session. In a following social-interaction session, it was found that children who had been rewarded for dependency increased their dependent overtures to the reinforcing adult, while those who had been punished decreased in dependent responses.

Unfortunately the effects of parental nurturance are more complex than these studies would indicate. The complexity of predicting the effects of nurturance in the development of dependency is vividly demonstrated in the Levy study of overprotected children. Levy (1943) investigated the effects on children of maternal overprotection defined in terms of: (1) excessive contact manifested in the form of holding, kissing, and touching the child and rarely leaving the child alone; (2) infantilization by assuming caretaking functions, such as dressing or feeding the child, inappropriate for the age; and (3) prevention of independent behavior, encouraging the child not to leave the mother or interact with peers.

These mothers were all regarded as parents who were genuinely fond of their children and who were not using overprotection as a reaction formation to rejection, and these mothers would consequently tend to be nurturant. It might be expected that such maternal practices would reinforce dependency and discourage independent activities. However, the interaction of this factor of overprotection with the permissiveness or restrictiveness of the mother was the key factor in the appearance of dependency in these children. If the mothers were overprotective and were excessively controlling and dominating, these children were dependent. They were described as conforming, polite, passive, neat, and obedient, and the boys were regarded by their peers as sissies. If, on the other hand, the mother was overprotective but indulgent, we found the child was aggressive rather than dependent.

The evidence from these studies suggests that although nurturance is influential in initially making the responses of the mother valued by the child, the parents' subsequent permissiveness and patterns of reinforcement for dependency largely determine the course of the child's development. The lack of a simple relationship between nurturance and dependency becomes even more apparent when we review the literature dealing with intermittent reinforcement, love withdrawal, and punishment. Clinicians have often noted that a child who has been removed from rejecting punitive parents and placed in a warm foster home will continue to yearn for his natural parents for some time and may even run away and attempt to return to his original home. How can this dependence on the apparently nonnurturant parents be explained?

It can be safely assumed that some degree of caretaking is necessary for the survival of the child; therefore, every child has the opportunity to experience some nurturant behavior on the part of his parents. Most children, even when they are rejected by the parents, have either experienced some nurturance which has ceased or have received punishment with intermittent rewards. Few parents are punitive all the time.

Studies consistently have found that nurturance withdrawal or intermittent rewards and punishments for dependent behavior lead to an increase in dependency. Hartup (1958) demonstrated that if a previously nurturant adult withdraws her nurturance by ceasing to talk and respond to a child, the child makes more dependency responses than a child who has been consistently rewarded. This finding is also supported in a study by Gewirtz (1954) who found that an adult who consistently focused his attention on a child elicits less attention-seeking behavior than an adult who remains aloof. In these studies, it must be remembered that the children have probably previously received rewards for dependency responses to other adults. These studies also indicate that children who are highly dependent tend to be more responsive to the withdrawal of nurturance. If there is high habit strength for dependent responses, the impact of rejection or intermittent punishment is greater and results in increased dependency. Such experiments suggest that when rejection takes the form of the withdrawal of rewards and affection rather than consistent punishment, dependency is increased. Field studies also support the position that rejection and withdrawal of love, which may also imply intermittent reinforcement, are positively related to high dependency. Sears et al. (1957) found that maternal rejection led to increased dependency only when the dependent response was also occasionally rewarded.

Although laboratory studies indicate that consistent punishment rapidly leads to the extinction of undesired behavior, this finding is not as clear in field studies. Thus, in the previously cited experimental study by Nelsen (1960), consistent punishment of dependency responses led to a descrease in dependency. It could be argued that, in this study, the children had not really established a dependency relationship with the experimenter. In contrast, two important correlational studies do not yield this result. Bandura (1960), in a study of aggressive and withdrawn boys, found little relation between punishment for dependency and the frequency of dependent behavior although the expression of dependent behavior under severe punishment became less direct. In fact, in aggressive boys there was some indication that punishment increased dependency. This is in agreement with the results of a study on the child-rearing antecedents of aggression and dependency in young children (Sears, Whiting, Nowlis, & Sears, 1953) which found that severe punishment for dependency led to increased dependency in boys, but to inhibition of dependency in girls. The explanation advanced by the experimenters to explain these results involves two assumptions: (1) when a behavior is both rewarded and punished, strength of drive is largely determined by severity of punishment; and (2) girls are more vulnerable than boys to maternal punishment.

If a response is usually rewarded and seldom punished, it remains an instrumental response and never acquires drive properties. If a behavior is too severely punished, it may be completely inhibited. The condition under which maximum dependency should develop is one in which there is sufficient frustration resulting from a moderate level of punishment to establish a dependency drive and an insufficient strength of punishment to result in complete inhibition of dependency responses. Thus, too mild or too severe punishment of a behavior should result in low performance of that behavior.

The second phase of the argument states that since girls are more identified with their mothers than are boys, they will experience punishment of the same objective level of intensity as subjectively more severe. Therefore, maternal punishment is likely to be more effective in inhibiting a response in daughters than in sons.

In summary, although parental nurturance seems to be a necessary antecedent of the initial dependency relationship, other dimensions of the parent-child interaction (such as permissiveness-restrictiveness, rejection, and positive and negative reinforcements for dependent behavior) seem to be important factors in the development of dependency.

Antecedents of aggression

The frustration-aggression hypothesis (Dollard et al., 1939) has been the theoretical focus of a large body of research on aggression. In its original form, it stated that aggression always presupposes the existence of frustration and that frustration inevitably leads to aggression. In subsequent modifications, it was conceded that although aggression was the natural response to frustration, learning experiences could lead to other responses becoming more dominant in the habit family hierarchy related to frustration. However, many psychologists continued to maintain that when aggression does occur, it is always the result of frustration.

The research literature offers little support for the frustration-aggression hypothesis.

Aggression has not been found to be an inevitable consequence of frustration. Laboratory studies have indicated that a great variety of behaviors may occur in response to frustration, depending on personality characteristics and past experiences of the subjects and situational variables in the experimental setting. Aggression, regression, withdrawal, dependency, and constructive and destructive responses have all been made in response to frustration. The role of individual differences in response to frustration is illustrated in a study by Otis & McCandless (1955) which found that dependent children make fewer aggressive responses following frustration than do children with a low need for affection. Since dependent children are more concerned about maintenance of parental love and adult approval, they are less likely to risk censure through behaving in a socially unacceptable fashion. In contrast, aggressive power-oriented children make more aggressive power-assertive responses to frustration. Similarly, because of the sex appropriateness of the behaviors, it might be expected that frustration would more frequently result in dependency in girls and aggression in boys.

A study by Davitz (1952) showed that responses to frustration can be altered by direct training. Children were observed in a free-play situation, and the frequency of their cooperative and aggressive responses was recorded. One-half of the children were then given a series of training trials where they received approval for responding cooperatively and constructively in a competitive situation; one-half received approval for competitive aggressive responses. All the children subsequently underwent a frustration manipulation in which a sucker they had been given was taken away from them and an exciting movie they had been viewing was terminated just before the climax. The children then were observed again in a free-play situation. The children who had been trained in cooperative behavior responded in a constructive way following frustration; the children who had been trained in aggression responded more aggressively. It appears that frustration is an emotionally arousing state which activates the child to make a variety of responses determined by his personality and past learning experiences. The finding that frustration frequently leads to aggression probably attests to the success of aggression as a mechanism for removing the source of the interference with goal-directed activity that was the basis of the frustration.

Frustration has not been demonstrated to be an essential

antecedent of aggression. Aggression may be an instrumental response which serves as a means of attaining a goal, but which is not involved with an emotionally arousing state such as frustration or anger. Aggression may occur in the absence of frustration, in response to the behavior of models and experienced or anticipated rewards or punishments.

There is ample evidence that positive reinforcement in the form of active encouragement or permissiveness leads to an increase in aggressive responses. The role of permissiveness is twofold: (1) it allows the child to perform aggressive acts more frequently, and (2) the nonintervention by others may be interpreted by the child as implicit approval of his aggressive behavior. In the previously cited study by Bandura (1960), it was found that parents of aggressive children rewarded and encouraged their son's aggression toward siblings and peers, but were punitive and nonpermissive with the son's aggressive responses toward the parents. This differential reinforcement is apparent in the son's subsequent discrimination between objects for his aggression. He is aggressive with peers and resistant with teachers, but not aggressive toward his parents. The parents' restrictiveness and punitiveness effectively inhibit the child's aggressive behavior in the home while their reinforcements increase aggression outside the home. Children thus learn to emit or inhibit aggressive responses in different situations on the basis of differential reinforcement.

Children not only discriminate between situations in which to be aggressive, but generalize from one aggressive response and from one situation to another if there are no additional inhibiting factors present. Thus in a permissive experimental situation, such as that utilized by Lovaas (1961), children who were reinforced for verbal aggression toward two dolls increased in verbal aggression; those reinforced for nonaggressive responses increased in these responses. In the subsequent free-play situation with a ball cage and striking doll, children reinforced for verbal aggression also showed an increase in nonverbal aggression. The children generalized their responses from the original training situation to the free-play situation and from one class of responses to another. This study is significant not only for demonstrating the role of positive reinforcement in the acquisition and generalization of aggressive responses, but also in showing the mediating function of language in the performance of other aggressive acts. This mediating role of language has often been utilized in applied problems such as training fighting men to be aggressive by having them shout "I'm a killer! I'm a killer" in hand-to-hand combat drill, or encouraging a tearful child to swallow a noxious medicine by saying "He's a brave boy."

Studies of the effects of punishment on aggressive behavior have focused on three different aspects of the punishment: (1) punishment as frustration, (2) the agent of punishment as an aggressive model, and (3) punishment as inhibition. Unfortunately, it has been methodologically impossible to isolate the effects of these three factors. When a parent punishes a child, he is frustrating the child by interfering with a goal, and he is behaving aggressively and is thus offering the child an aggressive model to imitate. In addition, the parent anticipates that fear of the punishment will inhibit the child's unacceptable activity.

Many differential studies, such as that by Eron, Walder, Toigo, & Lefkowitz (1963) reprinted following the chapter, suggest that severe punishment in the home is associated with low aggression toward parents, but high aggression in other situations where the child has less fear of punishment, such as with peers or in fantasy situations.

In the study of antecedents of dependency and aggression (Sears et al., 1953) discussed earlier, the same relationship was found between punishment for aggression and aggressive behavior as between punishment for dependency and dependent behavior. Girls who were severely punished for aggressive behavior showed little aggression; in contrast, boys showed a positive relation between amount of punishment and amount of aggression in nursery school. The same explanation of more severely experienced punishment by girls due to identification with the mother is invoked to explain the sex differences in aggression.

Sears speculates that severe punishment for aggression leads both to frustration with resulting increase in aggressive drive and to inhibition of aggression based on fear of the punishment. The highly punished child would thus have a high drive level of aggression, but would only express his aggression in a permissive situation where he anticipates little punishment. Children who are highly punished for aggression show little aggression in the home, but show more aggression in a permissive doll-play situation than less-severely punished children; this finding seems to support Sears' premise. However, the same results might be interpreted without reference to frustration by saying that the punitive parent offers a model of aggressive behavior to the child and that the child will emit this behavior in a situation where he has little anxiety about punishment.

The results of experimental studies of the effects of punishment and modeling upon aggressive behavior appear to be in agreement with findings of field studies. In the only experimental study (Hollenberg & Sperry, 1951) on the effects of punishment on aggression, two groups of children participated in four doll-play sessions. Experimental subjects were criticized for making aggressive responses only during the second session; control subjects were never criticized. The aggressive responses of the experimental subjects decreased markedly in the third session, following the negative reinforcement of the second session. The aggressive responses of the control subjects increased steadily over the four sessions; this is a frequent finding in doll-play studies usually attributed to a lessening of the child's inhibition due to the experimenter's permissiveness. The effects of the criticism on the experimental children was short-lived, however, since by the fourth session, there were no significant differences in the number of aggressive responses in the two groups.

In contrast to the dearth of experimental studies dealing with punishment of aggressive responses, there is a systematic group of studies dealing with the effects of modeling on aggression. These studies have consistently found that following observation of a live or filmed aggressive model, children make more frequent and intense aggressive responses in a permissive-play situation. Bandura & Walters (1963) suggest that two different processes are involved in the imitation of aggressive behavior. The first is the accurate reproduction of the model's novel behavior; the second is a reduction of the inhibitions which permit the child to perform aggressive responses which are already in his repertoire.

Individual difference variables in both the model and subject, and variables such as the chances for detection or the consequences of his aggressive behavior to the model, have been shown to influence the imitation of aggression. Children are more likely to imitate a warm or powerful model and a model who has been rewarded rather than punished for his aggression. Sex of model and sex of subject seem to be particularly influential factors in the imitation of aggressive responses. Bandura, Ross, & Ross (1961, 1963a) found that although boys exhibit more overall imitative and nonimitative aggression than girls, the sexes did not differ in the amount of imitative verbal aggression manifested. This is congruent with the findings of other studies which have reported that boys show more physical and antisocial aggression than girls, but that girls show as much verbal and prosocial aggression. These studies also found that an aggressive male model elicited more aggressive responses, and a nonaggressive male model elicited more nonaggressive responses than did the equivalent female models. This suggests that the effectiveness of a model in eliciting imitative responses depends on the sex appropriateness of the behavior for both the model and the child. Since physical aggression is more congruent with the male role, we find less modeling of this behavior when either the model or imitator is female. Although parallel studies on the effect of sex of model and child on imitation of dependency responses have not been done, it might be speculated that more imitation of dependent behaviors would be obtained with a female model and subject.

In a recent study, Bandura (1965) had boys and girls observe a filmed aggressive model who received reward, punishment, or no consequences for his aggressive behavior. Children in the rewarded or no-consequences group were significantly more aggressive in a subsequent play session than the children who had viewed the model being punished; however, this difference was mainly due to the differences among conditions for girls. In the next step in the study, in an effort to free the children from inhibiting aggressive responses, the children were reinforced by juice or sticker pictures for each imitative response they could make. The introduction of these incentives almost eliminated the differences between previous reinforcement groups, but girls still emitted fewer matching aggressive responses than did boys. It is suggested that the greater difficulty in disinhibiting girls is attributable to the differing reinforcement histories for aggression of boys and girls. Boys and girls may be equally aware of the aggressive responses made by the model, but girls are less likely to reproduce such responses because they have been discouraged from doing so in the past. It has been found (Sears et al., 1957) that aggression is the form of behavior for which parents most clearly have different attitudes and disciplinary practices for boys and girls. Boys, more often than girls, are permitted to express aggression toward their parents and peers and are actively encouraged to fight back in disagreements.

Increases in aggression are apparent, not only when parents and other adults administer reinforcements, but also when peers are the models or reinforcing agents. A study by Hicks (1965) investigated the relative effectiveness of filmed peer and adult male and female models as transmitters of aggressive behaviors to preschool boys and girls. It was found that children imitate aggressive responses of both adults and peers; however, a shift in effectiveness of a given model occurs with time. Children who viewed an aggressive male peer model showed the most immediate imitative aggression, but a retest six months later indicated that the adult male model had the greatest long-term effect. This study is important, not only for demonstrating that peers serve as effective aggressive models, but also in showing that caution must be used in generalizing from immediate to long-term effects of modeling.

The important role of peers in shaping aggression is clearly substantiated in a recent observational study of nursery-school children by Patterson, Littman, & Bricker (1967) which demonstrated that the responses of peers can serve either to reinforce or extinguish aggressive responses in children. The aggressive behaviors studied included bodily attack, attack with an object, verbal or symbolic threats, demands or derogations, and invasion of territory or infringement of property, such as taking away toys. When aggression was followed by a reinforcing response by the victim, such as crying, defensive posturing, passive protests, or yielding of toys, the aggressor in subsequent assertion had a high probability of performing the same aggressive act toward the same victim. In contrast, if the behavior was followed by negative reinforcement, such as teacher intervention, the victim telling the teacher, recovering his property, or retaliating, or by hitting the aggressor, then on subsequent aggressive acts, the aggressor had a high probability of either shifting victims or altering the form of his aggression.

In this study, another peer behavior which was found to increase aggressiveness in initially nonassertive children was victimization. Children who are frequently victimized by peers have more opportunities to counterattack their aggressors than children who are seldom victimized. When a counterattack occurs, there is a high probability (median 69 percent) of the attack being successful and thus of the victim being reinforced for his counteraggression. This study found a striking association between the frequency with which children were victimized by aggressive acts of peers, the frequency of their successful counterattacks, and increases in their aggressive behavior.

Other studies, discussed in Chapter V, have demonstrated that the effectiveness of peers as reinforcers or models increases with age. As the child grows older and more independent of parents, the acceptability of his behavior to his peer group becomes more influential. Approval by peers in the form of group acceptance and popularity serves as a powerful reinforcer for school-aged children. In general, popularity and acceptability in elementary-school children is related to conformity to sex-typed behaviors. Docility, neatness, warmth, lack of assertiveness in girls and daring, leadership, assertiveness, and athletic ability in boys are related to popularity (Tuddenham, 1951, 1952).

The social acceptability by peers of aggressive and dependent behaviors varies with social class. In a study by Pope (1953) of a group of upper-middle- and a group of lower-upper- and lower-lower-class early adolescents, it was found that both groups regard "the little lady" pattern of behavior (comprised of friendliness, conformity, goodness, and tidiness) as most desirable in girls. However, divergent standards were present for boys in the lower and higher socioeconomic classes. Popular lower-class boys were frequently belligerent, domineering, and aggressive. These traits were unacceptable to the higher-class boys. Power and assertiveness in the higher-class boys were acceptable in the form of skill in competitive sports and intellectual achievement, but not in fighting or bossiness. The sissy characterized by passivity, dependency, and conformity was unacceptable to both groups of boys. Thus, reinforcement in the form of approval and acceptance from peers might be expected to differentially reinforce aggressiveness in boys and girls and to reinforce the acceptability of various forms of assertive behavior in lower- and higher-class boys.

In summary, the most important antecedents of aggression appear to be the presence of an aggressive model, permissiveness, and reinforcement either by adults or peers for aggressive behavior. Frustration stimulates the organism to make a variety of responses including aggression, and it is a possible, but not inevitable, antecedent of aggressive behavior.

SUMMARY   Sex typing occurs early and is an influential force in shaping personality development. The acquisition of appropriate masculine and feminine attitudes, values, and behaviors is based upon the interaction of constitutional factors and social-learning experiences. The pattern of development of sex typing, the effects of child-rearing practices, and the relationship of sex-typed behaviors with other personality characteristics differ for boys and girls. This is particularly apparent in the growth of dependency and aggression which are highly sex-typed behaviors.

If a behavior is appropriate for a given sex, it tends to appear in a relatively direct form and to remain stable throughout the course of development. If it is sexually inappropriate, it may be manifested in indirect or derivative behaviors and is less developmentally consistent. Thus aggression is more direct, integrated, and stable in boys as is dependency in girls.

Although socialization practices and parental behaviors are salient forces in shaping dependency and aggression, other less-intensively studied variables such as biological and situational factors also play an influential role in their development.

BIBLIOGRAPHY

Angrilli, A. F. The psychosexual identification of preschool boys. *Journal of Genetic Psychology,* 1960, **97,** 329–340.

Bach, G. R. Father-fantasies and father-typing in father-separated children. *Child Development,* 1946, **17,** 63–80.

Baldwin, A. L. The effect of home environment on nursery school behavior. *Child Development,* 1949, **20,** 49–61.

Bandura, A. Relationship of family patterns to child behavior disorders. Progress Report, U.S.P.H. Research Grant M-1734, Stanford University, 1960.

Bandura, A. Social learning through imitation. In M. R. Jones (Ed.), *Nebraska symposium on motivation.* Lincoln: University of Nebraska Press, 1962. Pp. 211–269.

Bandura, A. Influence of model's reinforcement contingencies on the acquisition of imitative responses. *Journal of Personality and Social Psychology,* 1965, **1,** 589–595.

Bandura, A., & Huston, A. C. Identification as a process of incidental learning. *Journal of Abnormal and Social Psychology,* 1961, **63,** 311–318.

Bandura, A., Ross, D., & Ross, S. A. Transmission of aggression through imitation of aggressive models. *Journal of Abnormal and Social Psychology,* 1961, **63,** 575–582.

Bandura, A., Ross, D., & Ross, S. A. Imitation of film-mediated aggressive models. *Journal of Abnormal and Social Psychology,* 1963, **66,** 3–11. (a)

Bandura, A., Ross, D., & Ross, S. A. A comparative test of the status envy, social power, and secondary reinforcement theories of identificatory learning. *Journal of Abnormal and Social Psychology,* 1963, **67,** 527–534. (b)

Bandura, A., & Walters, R. H. *Adolescent aggression.* New York: Ronald Press, 1959.

Bandura, A., & Walters, R. H. *Social learning and personality development.* New York: Holt, 1963.

Beller, E. K. Dependency and autonomous achievement-striving related to orality and anality in early childhood. *Child Development,* 1957, **28,** 287–315.

Bennett, E. M., & Cohen, L. R. Men and women: Personality patterns and contrasts. *Genetic Psychology Monographs,* 1959, **59,** 101–155.

Bettelheim, B. Individual and mass behavior in extreme situations. *Journal of Abnormal and Social Psychology,* 1943, **38,** 417–452.

Biller, H. B., & Borstelmann, L. J. Masculine development: An integrative review. *Merrill-Palmer Quarterly*, 1967, **13**, 253–294.

Brim, O. G. Family structure and sex role learning by children: A further analysis of Helen Koch's data. *Sociometry*, 1958, **21**, 1–16.

Bronfenbrenner, U. Freudian theories of identification and their derivatives. *Child Development*, 1960, **31**, 15–40.

Bronson, W. C. Dimensions of ego and infantile identification. *Journal of Personality*, 1959, **27**, 532–545.

Brown, D. G. Masculinity-femininity development in children. *Journal of Consulting Psychology*, 1957, **21**, 197–202.

Brown, D. G. Sex role development in a changing culture. *Psychological Bulletin*, 1958, **55**, 232–242.

Buss, A. H. *The psychology of aggression*. New York: Wiley, 1961.

Cottrell, L. S., Jr. The adjustment of the individual to his age and sex roles. *American Sociological Review*, 1942, **7**, 617–620.

Crandall, V. J., Preston, A., & Rabson, A. Maternal reactions and the development of independence and achievement in young children. *Child Development*, 1960, **31**, 243–251.

D'Andrade, R. G. Sex differences and cultural institutions. In E. E. Maccoby (Ed.), *The development of sex differences*. Stanford, Calif.: Stanford University Press, 1966. Pp. 174–204.

Davitz, J. R. The effects of previous training on postfrustration behavior. *Journal of Abnormal and Social Psychology*, 1952, **47**, 309–315.

Dawe, H. C. An analysis of two hundred quarrels of preschool children. *Child Development*, 1934, **5**, 139–157.

Dollard, J., Doob, L. W., Miller, N. E., Mowrer, O. H., & Sears, R. R. *Frustration and aggression*. New Haven: Yale University Press, 1939.

Eron, L. D., Walder, L. O., Toigo, R., & Lefkowitz, M. M. Social class, parental punishment for aggression, and child aggression. *Child Development*, 1963, **34**, 849–867.

Freud, A. *The ego and the mechanisms of defense*. London: Hogarth, 1937.

Freud, S. Some psychological consequences of the anatomical distinction between the sexes. In *Collected papers of Sigmund Freud*. Vol. 5. London: Hogarth, 1950. Pp. 186–197.

Gewirtz, J. L. Three determinants of attention-seeking in young children. *Monographs of the Society for Research in Child Development*, 1954, **19**(2, Serial No. 59).

Gewirtz, J. L. A factor analysis of some attention-seeking behaviors of young children. *Child Development*, 1956, **27**, 17–36.

Hamburg, D. A., & Lunde, D. T. Sex hormones in the development of sex differences in human behavior. In E. E. Maccoby (Ed.), *The development of sex differences*. Stanford, Calif.: Stanford University Press, 1966. Pp. 1–24.

Hartley, R. E. Sex-role pressures and the socialization of the male child. *Psychological Reports*, 1959, **5**, 457–468.

Hartley, R. E. Children's concepts of male and female roles. *Merrill-Palmer Quarterly*, 1960, **6**, 83–91.

Hartup, W. W. Nurturance and nurturance-withdrawal in relation to the dependency behavior of preschool children. *Child Development,* 1958, **29**, 191–201.

Hartup, W. W., & Zook, E. A. Sex-role preferences in three- and four-year-old children. *Journal of Consulting Psychology,* 1960, **24**, 420–426.

Heathers, G. Emotional dependence and independence in a physical threat situation. *Child Development,* 1953, **24**, 169–179.

Heathers, G. Emotional dependence and independence in nursery school play. *Journal of Genetic Psychology,* 1955, **87**, 37–57.

Helper, M. M. Learning theory and the self concept. *Journal of Abnormal and Social Psychology,* 1955, **51**, 184–194.

Hetherington, E. M. A developmental study of the effects of sex of the dominant parent on sex-role preference, identification, and imitation in children. *Journal of Personality and Social Psychology,* 1965, **2**, 188–194.

Hetherington, E. M. Effects of paternal absence on sex-typed behaviors in Negro and white preadolescent males. *Journal of Personality and Social Psychology,* 1966, **4**, 87–91.

Hetherington, E. M. The effects of familial variables on sex typing, on parent-child similarity and on imitation in children. In J. P. Hill (Ed.), *Minnesota symposia on child psychology.* Vol. 1. Minneapolis: University of Minnesota Press, 1967. Pp. 82–107. (a)

Hetherington, E. M. Effects of paternal absence on sex typed behaviors in girls. Unpublished manuscript, 1967. (b)

Hetherington, E. M., & Frankie, G. Effects of parental dominance, warmth, and conflict on imitation in children. *Journal of Personality and Social Psychology,* 1967, **6**, 119–125.

Hicks, D. J. Imitation and retention of film-mediated aggressive peer and adult models. *Journal of Personality and Social Psychology,* 1965, **2**, 97–100.

Hollenberg, E., & Sperry, M. Some antecedents of aggression and effects of frustration in doll play. *Personality,* 1951, **1**, 32–43.

Jersild, A. T., & Markey, F. V. Conflicts between preschool children. *Child Development Monographs,* 1935, No. 21.

Johnson, M. Sex role learning in the nuclear family. *Child Development,* 1963, **34**, 319–333.

Kagan, J. Acquisition and significance of sex typing and sex role identity. In M. L. Hoffman & L. W. Hoffman (Eds.), *Review of child development research.* Vol. 1. New York: Russell Sage Foundation, 1964. Pp. 137–167.

Kagan, J., & Moss, H. A. The stability of passive and dependent behavior from childhood through adulthood. *Child Development,* 1960, **31**, 577–591.

Kagan, J., & Moss, H. A. *Birth to maturity: A study in psychological development.* New York: Wiley, 1962.

Koch, H. L. Sissiness and tomboyishness in relation to sibling characteristics. *Journal of Genetic Psychology,* 1956, **88**, 231–244.

Kohlberg, L. A cognitive-developmental analysis of children's sex-role concepts and attitudes. In E. E. Maccoby (Ed.), *The development of sex differences.* Stanford, Calif.: Stanford University Press, 1966. Pp. 82–173.

Levy, D. M. *Maternal overprotection.* New York: Columbia University Press, 1943.

Lovaas, O. I. Interaction between verbal and nonverbal behavior. *Child Development,* 1961, **32**, 329–336.

Lynn, D. B. Sex differences in identification development. *Sociometry,* 1961, **24**, 372–383.

Macfarlane, J. W., Allen, L., & Honzik, M. P. A developmental study of the behavior problems of normal children between 21 months and 14 years. In *University of California Publications in Child Development,* 1954, No. 2.

McKee, J. P., & Sherriffs, A. C. The differential evaluation of males and females. *Journal of Personality,* 1957, **25**, 356–371.

Meyers, C. E. The effect of conflicting authority on the child. *University of Iowa Studies in Child Welfare,* 1944, **20**, No. 409.

Miller, N. E., & Dollard, J. *Social learning and imitation.* New Haven: Yale University Press, 1941.

Moulton, R. W., Liberty, P. G., Burnstein, E., & Altucher, N. Patterning of parental affection and disciplinary dominance as a determinant of guilt and sex typing. *Journal of Personality and Social Psychology,* 1966, **4**, 356–363.

Mussen, P. H., & Distler, L. Masculinity identification and father-son relationships. *Journal of Abnormal and Social Psychology,* 1959, **59**, 350–356.

Mussen, P. H., & Distler, L. Child rearing antecedents of masculine identification in kindergarten boys. *Child Development,* 1960, **31**, 89–100.

Mussen, P. H., & Parker, A. L. Mother nurturance and girls' incidental imitative learning. *Journal of Personality and Social Psychology,* 1965, **2**, 94–97.

Mussen, P. H., & Rutherford, E. Parent-child relations and parental personality in relation to young children's sex role preferences. *Child Development,* 1963, **34**, 589–607.

Nelsen, E. A. The effects of reward and punishment of dependency on subsequent dependency. Unpublished manuscript, Stanford University, 1960.

Otis, N. B., & McCandless, B. R. Responses to repeated frustrations of young children differentiated according to need area. *Journal of Abnormal and Social Psychology,* 1955, **50**, 349–353.

Parsons, T. Family structure and the socialization of the child. In T. Parsons & R. F. Bales (Eds.), *Family, socialization, and interaction process.* Glencoe, Ill.: Free Press, 1955. Pp. 35–131.

Patterson, G. R., Littman, R. A., & Bricker, W. Assertive behavior in children: A step toward a theory of aggression. *Monographs of the Society for Research in Child Development,* 1967, **32**(5, Serial No. 113).

Payne, D. E., & Mussen, P. H. Parent-child relations and father identification among adolescent boys. *Journal of Abnormal and Social Psychology,* 1956, **52,** 358–362.

Pope, B. Socio-economic contrasts in children's peer culture prestige values. *Genetic Psychology Monographs,* 1953, **48,** 157–220.

Rabban, M. Sex role identification in young children in two diverse social groups. *Genetic Psychology Monographs,* 1950, **42,** 81–158.

Sanford, N. The dynamics of identification. *Psychological Review,* 1955, **62,** 106–118.

Sarnoff, I. Identification with the aggressor: Some personality correlates of anti-Semitism among Jews. *Journal of Personality,* 1951, **20,** 199–218.

Sears, P. S. Doll play aggression in normal young children: Influence of sex, age, sibling status, father's absence. *Psychological Monographs,* 1951, **65**(6, Whole No. 323).

Sears, P. S. Child-rearing factors related to playing of sex-typed roles. *American Psychologist,* 1953, **38,** 431. (Abstract)

Sears, R. R. Relation of early socialization experiences to aggression in middle childhood. *Journal of Abnormal and Social Psychology,* 1961, **63,** 466–492.

Sears, R. R., Maccoby, E. E., & Levin, H. *Patterns of child rearing.* New York: Harper & Row, 1957.

Sears, R. R., Rau, L., & Alpert, R. *Identification and child rearing.* Stanford, Calif.: Stanford University Press, 1965.

Sears, R. R., Whiting, J. W. M., Nowlis, V., & Sears, P. S. Some child-rearing antecedents of aggression and dependency in young children. *Genetic Psychology Monographs,* 1953, **47,** 135–234.

Steimel, R. J. Childhood experiences and masculinity-femininity scores. *Journal of Counseling Psychology,* 1960, **7,** 212–217.

Stolz, L. M. *Father relations of war-born children.* Stanford, Calif.: Stanford University Press, 1954.

Tuddenham, R. D. Studies in reputation: III. Correlates of popularity among elementary-school children. *Journal of Educational Psychology,* 1951, **42,** 257–276.

Tuddenham, R. D. Studies in reputation: I. Sex and grade differences in school children's evaluations of their peers. II. The diagnosis of social adjustment. *Psychological Monographs,* 1952, **66**(1, Whole No. 333).

Walters, R. H., & Parke, R. D. Social motivation, dependency, and susceptibility to social influence. In L. Berkowitz (Ed.), *Advances in experimental social psychology.* Vol. 1. New York: Academic Press, 1964. Pp. 231–276.

Watson, G. Some personality differences in children related to strict or permissive parental discipline. *Journal of Psychology,* 1957, **44,** 227–249.

Young, W. C., Goy, R. W., & Phoenix, C. H. Hormones and sexual behavior. *Science,* 1964, **143,** 212–218.

A DEVELOPMENTAL STUDY OF THE EFFECTS OF SEX OF THE DOMINANT PARENT ON SEX-ROLE PREFERENCE, IDENTIFICATION, AND IMITATION IN CHILDREN

E. Mavis Hetherington

Most theories of identification agree that identification is based on a process or processes whereby the child through imitation, modeling, or introjection acquires traits, characteristics, and values similar to the parent. In normal development the boy is assumed to identify with the father, and the girl with the mother which results in the preference for and adoption of appropriate sex-role behavior. Psychoanalytic theory has stressed the role of fear of punishment and identification with the aggressor, while learning theory has stressed the facilitating effects of reward in promoting identification. A third theory (Parsons, 1955) has emphasized the importance of total parental power in the development of identification. According to Parsons, the child identifies with the parent because he is powerful in his ability to dispense both rewards and punishments. Several recent experiments support the position that parental power or dominance plays a major role in identification (Hetherington & Brackbill, 1963; Mussen & Distler, 1959).

In identifying with parents, children may acquire traits and values which are particularly characteristic of either male or female roles in our society. This would be directly related to the formation of sex-role preferences. They may also imitate parental behaviors which are not sex typed but which are equally appropriate in males and females. It would be expected that the rate of development and type of sex-role preference would be related not only to parental behavior but also to social pressures to conform, and the status of a given sex in the culture. Parent-child similarity in traits which are not sex typed should have fewer extra familial social sanctions bearing on them and therefore should be more directly and consistently related to reinforcements and imitative models provided by the parents. Since the child has relatively few social contacts outside the family in the preschool years it would be expected that identification on both sex-typed and non-sex-typed measures would be closely related to family power structure in 4- and 5-year-old children. However, in older children sex-typed behaviors should be increasingly influenced by social norms. Boys will be encouraged by peers and adults outside the family to develop masculine sex-role preferences and girls feminine sex-role preferences and these preferences should therefore be less directly related to parental dominance in older than in younger children. It would also be predicted that because of the greater prestige and privileges of males in our culture,

From E. M. Hetherington. A developmental study of the effects of sex of the dominant parent on sex-role preference, identification, and imitation in children. Journal of Personality and Social Psychology, *1965, 2, 188–194. (With permission of the author and the American Psychological Association, Inc.)*

girls will be slower and less consistent in developing appropriate sex-role preferences than boys (Brown, 1956, 1958). In contrast parent-child similarity on non-sex-typed traits should be closely related to parental dominance in both preschool and school aged boys and girls. This similarity would be expected to increase with age as identification is more fully established.

If children identify with the dominant parent and this parent is the same sex as the child this should facilitate the development of normal sex-role preferences. If the dominant parent is the opposite sex of the child this should strengthen cross-sex identification and may retard the development of normal sex-role preferences. This disruption in identification and sex-role preferences should be particularly marked in boys from mother-dominant homes since the acquiescing father supplies a socially inappropriate model for the son. In contrast, girls from father-dominant homes at least have parental models whose power relationships are appropriate for their culturally defined sex roles. Although it could be argued that a dominant mother does not provide a normal sex-role model for girls, maternal dominance may not preclude the mother having other feminine traits with which a daughter will identify.

If imitation is involved in identification, children's performance on an experimental task involving imitation of the parents and a measure of parent-child personality similarity should be positively related. Past research (Bandura, 1962; McDavid, 1959) suggests that although children tend to imitate the most powerful model there is a greater readiness for both boys and girls to imitate a male model. Thus children should imitate and have personality traits similar to the most dominant parent, particularly if it is the father. The findings of McDavid also suggest that girls will imitate increasingly with age while boys will imitate less.

The present study investigated the effects of parental dominance on sex-role preferences, parent-child trait similarity, and imitation of boys and girls of three different age levels.

METHOD

Subjects

Subjects were three groups of 36 boys and 36 girls ages 4–5, 6–8, and 9–11 enrolled in nursery schools or in elementary schools in a public-school system. Half of the boys and girls in each group came from mother-dominant homes and half from father-dominant homes.

Experimenters

Half of the subjects in each condition were run by male experimenters and half by female experimenters. Since no experimenter differences were found in a preliminary analysis of the data, this variable was not considered in the final analysis.

Parental dominance measure

The parental dominance measure was adapted from a procedure by Farina (1960). Farina's problem situations were modified to make them more suitable for all age levels in the present study. Each parent was seen individually in a quiet room in his own home. He was read 12 hypothetical problem situations involving child behavior and asked how he would handle them when he was by himself. Both parents were then brought together and asked to arrive at a compatible solution on handling these children's problems. The discussion of each problem continued until both parents said the terminating signal, "agreed." The experimenter participated only minimally in the discussion in order to clarify scoring responses. All interviews were tape-recorded and scored later.

The scoring procedure was identical with that used by Farina (1960) which involved seven indices of parental dominance. If six of the seven indices indicated paternal dominance the family was classified as father dominant; if six of the indices indicated maternal dominance the family was classified as mother dominant. A total of 326 couples were run in order to obtain the 108 mother-dominant and 108 father-dominant families for the study.

Procedure

The study was comprised of three procedures: the It Scale for Children (ITSC; Brown, 1956), a parent-child similarity task, and an imitation task.

ITSC

The ITSC, a projective test of sex-role preference, was administered to each subject at school. In this test the child is presented with a drawing of an ambiguous child figure referred to as "It," and is asked to choose what It would like in a series of 36 picture cards of objects and figures identified with masculine or feminine roles. Scores can range from 0, exclusively feminine choices, to 84, exclusively masculine choices. It is assumed that "the child will project himself or herself into the It-figure on the basis of his or her own sex-role preference, and will attribute to It the child's own role preference (Brown, 1956, p. 5)."

Parent-child similarity measure

A list of 130 adjectives was given to 10 advanced education students who were asked to categorize the adjectives as more characteristic of males, or females, or as neutral (equally applicable to both sexes). They were also asked to check whether each adjective was descriptive of the behavior of children or adults or both. Forty adjectives which had been rated as neutral by 90 percent of the judges and as descriptive of both adults and children by all were included in the final list (e.g., friendly, honest, imaginative, humorous, pleasant, capable, etc.). These adjectives appeared to give a broad view of non-sex-typed personality traits.

Parents were asked to give the name of someone who knew them well enough to rate them on the adjective check list. Different raters were used for each parent. The lists were sent to the raters with assurances of the confidentiality of the responses and were returned by mail to the experimenter. If the list was not returned in 2 weeks, raters were contacted by phone. Eleven of the raters refused to cooperate and others suggested by the parents were substituted. Children were rated on the same list by their teachers. In an attempt to control for response bias raters were asked to mark 15 adjectives which were most like the ratee X, 15 which were most unlike the ratee 0, and to leave 10 blank.

The procedure was repeated on 45 of the families 1 month later. The test-retest reliabilities were .82 for ratings of mothers, .86 for fathers, and .79 for children.

Similarity scores were based on the number of identical responses in the mother and child, and father and child lists. Two blanks, X-X or O-O pairings on an item were scored as similar.

Imitation task

Each child was run in his home on the imitation task twice, once with each parent as a model. The child was instructed that he and his parent were participating in a study attempting to evaluate what things people think are prettiest. While the child watched, the parent, who had been coached before the experimental session, was asked to indicate by pointing and naming which picture in each of 20 pairs of pictures he thought was prettiest. The parent repeated this procedure three times consistently selecting the predetermined prettiest pictures. The child then went through the series once selecting the pictures he thought were prettiest. One month later the same procedure was repeated with the other parent and a second series of pictures. Order of presentation of list and parent models was balanced for male and female children. An imitation measure of number of similiar responses was derived for mother-child and father-child.

RESULTS

Separate [data] analyses . . . were run on ITSC scores, parent-child similarity measures, and parent-child imitation scores. . . .

Sex-role preference

. . . As was expected, parental dominance influenced sex-role preference. More appropriate sex-role preferences occurred when the father is dominant than when the mother is dominant. [The results] indicated that the differences in sex-role preferences for girls from mother- and father-dominant homes were nonsignificant; however these differences for boys were significant at all ages. Mother dominance was related to less masculine sex-role preferences in boys.

As predicted, girls were later in developing feminine sex-role preferences than were boys in masculine sex-role preferences. Boys at age 4–5 had already developed a preference for the masculine role which continued and increased slightly but nonsignificantly through ages 9–11. In contrast, girls showed a significant increase in preference for the feminine role in the age 9–11 group. . . .

Parent-child similarity

. . . [The] mother-child and father-child similarity measures obtained from the adjective check list ratings by friends and teachers . . . indicate[d] that 4- and 5-year-old children obtained lower parent-child similarity ratings than the two older groups who did not differ from one another.

Dominance played an important role in parent-child similarity. Children tended to be more similar to the dominant parent than the passive parent. Mother dominance appeared to inhibit father-child similarity. This similarity was lower than mother-child similarity in father-dominant homes. The disrupted identification of boys was again particularly marked in mother-dominant homes. In father-dominant homes the boy identified significantly more with the father than the mother; however in mother-dominant homes this relation was reversed. In fact, the mother-son similarity in mother-dominant homes did not differ from the father-son similarity in father-dominant homes.

In contrast, girls in father-dominant homes identified equally strongly with both parents. Also their mother-daughter similarity did not differ from that in mother-dominant homes. On the other hand, girls in mother-dominant homes identified notably more with mother than father. The father-daughter similarity scores in mother-dominant homes were significantly lower than similarity scores in any other group. . . .

Parent-child imitation

. . . [The data on the] child's imitation of the parent, as in sex-role preferences and parent-child similarity [indicated] parental dominance was a significant factor. Children of both sexes imitated the dominant parent more than the passive parent. The prediction that children would imitate the father more than the mother was not confirmed. There were no significant differences between imitation of the dominant mothers and fathers, or between passive mothers and fathers. As was expected on the basis of past research, girls imitated more than boys; however no differential trends with age for the two sexes were found. . . .

Relations among measures

The ITSC scores, father-child and mother-child similarity measures, and father-child and mother-child imitation scores were correlated separately for boys and girls in mother- and father-dominant homes for each age group. The results suggest that these measures are meaningful . . . only for older girls from father-dominant homes. In this group, girls who imitate their mother are rated as being similar to them on the adjective check list . . . and have feminine sex-role preferences . . . . When they have masculine sex-role preferences they are rated as similar to their fathers. . . . It appears that in homes where parents serve as culturally appropriate sex-role models with the father more dominant than the mother, girls' feminine sex-role preferences are closely related to imitation of the mother and similarity to the parents on other traits which are not sexually defined.

In contrast, there are few systematic or meaningful relationships for girls from mother-dominant homes or for boys from either mother- or father-dominant homes. There was a tendency for parent-child imitation to be related to parent-child similarity in these groups, but there was little relationship between sex-role preference and the other measures. In fact, for boys there were no significant correlations between the ITSC and any other measures at any age.

DISCUSSION

The results appear to support partially a theory of identification based on parental power. Parental dominance influenced children in imitation of parents, sex-role preferences, and similarity to parents in non-sex-typed traits. Inversions of the normal parental dominance pattern were related to more disruption in the identification of boys than of girls. Boys from mother-dominant homes acquired non-sex-typed traits like the mother and also more feminine sex-role preferences than boys from father-dominant homes. Contrary to expectations these differences in sex-role preferences were present at ages 4–5 and were sustained through ages 9–11. The predicted decrease in the relationship between sex-role preference and parental dominance with age did not occur. It appears that later social pressures on boys to acquire masculine preferences do not adequately counteract the early developed more feminine preferences of boys in mother-dominant homes. The prediction of an increasing similarity of the child and dominant parent on non-sex-typed traits with age is supported. This similarity is significantly less in 4- and 5-year-olds than in older children. Since the period from 3 to 6 years is considered to be a critical formative one in which identification is rapidly changing and growing, this increase in similarity following the preschool years might be anticipated. After this marked increase in identification, a stabilizing of identification on non-sex-typed traits appears to occur early in the school aged years.

It was surprising that girls from mother- and father-dominant homes showed no difference in sex-role preference at any age, since it might be assumed that a dominant mother offers her daughter a rather "unfeminine" role model. However, it should be remembered that the measure of maternal dominance in this study was one of dominance relative to the spouse and not to other members of her own sex. Thus a mother could be more dominant than a passive husband and still not be dominant or "unfeminine" relative to other women. The significance of parental dominance relative to other members of the same sex remains to be investigated. It is possible that since the feminine role in our culture is less well defined, less highly valued (Lynn, 1959; McKee & Sherriffs, 1957), and later acquired than the male role, these factors attenuate any differences due to maternal dominance.

It could be argued that lack of appropriate paternal dominance rather than the presence of maternal dominance led to the obtained findings. If boys and girls initially both identify with the mother, the socially appropriate sex-role behavior of paternal dominance may be necessary to facilitate the shift in identification models for the boy. Since normal identification for girls involves sustaining and intensifying the mother-child relationship, father dominance may contribute only to cross-sex identification and do little to disrupt the girls' primary identification. Social pressures may also encourage the child to identify with the like-sexed parent unless his behavior is culturally inappropriate. Since the feminine role is less well defined than the masculine role, either dominant or passive behavior in mothers may be regarded as more acceptable than passivity in fathers. Evidence for this is provided not only by the different results for boys and girls on the ITSC, but also by the parent-child similarity on traits not influenced by sex typing. Paternal dominance facilitated cross-sex identification in girls but did not disturb like-sex identification. Thus the mother-daughter and father-daughter similarity in father-dominant homes, and mother-daughter similarity in mother-dominant homes did not differ significantly. However, neither the sons nor daughters in mother-dominant homes identified with the passive father.

This interpretation of the role of dominance in identification appears to be consistent with the psychoanalytic stress on the great importance of "identification with the aggressor" in boys' identification, and its lesser importance in the identification of girls.

REFERENCES

Bandura, A. Social learning through imitation. In M. R. Jones (Ed.), *Nebraska symposium on motivation.* Lincoln: University of Nebraska Press, 1962. Pp. 211–269.

Brown, D. G. Sex-role preference in young children. *Psychological Monographs,* 1956, **70**(14, Whole No. 421).

Brown, D. G. Sex role development in a changing culture. *Psychological Bulletin,* 1958, **55**, 232–242.

Farina, A. Patterns of role dominance and conflict in parents of schizophrenic patients. *Journal of Abnormal and Social Psychology,* 1960, **61**, 31–38.

Hetherington, E. M., & Brackbill, Y. Etiology and covariation of obstinacy, orderliness and parsimony in young children. *Child Development,* 1963, **34**, 919–943.

Lynn, D. B. A note on sex differences in the development of masculine and feminine identification. *Psychological Review,* 1959, **66**, 126–135.

McDavid, J. W. Imitative behavior in preschool children. *Psychological Monographs,* 1959, **73**(16, Whole No, 486).

McKee, J. P., & Sherriffs, A. C. The differential evaluation of males and females. *Journal of Personality,* 1957, **25**, 356–371.

Mussen, P. H., & Distler, L. Masculinity, identification, and father-son relationships. *Journal of Abnormal and Social Psychology,* 1959, **59**, 350–356.

Parsons, T. Family structure and the socialization of the child. In T. Parsons & R. F. Bales (Eds.), *Family, socialization, and interaction process.* Glencoe, Ill.: Free Press, 1955. Pp. 35–131.

THE STABILITY OF PASSIVE AND DEPENDENT BEHAVIOR FROM CHILDHOOD THROUGH ADULTHOOD[1]

Jerome Kagan and Howard A. Moss

A basic assumption of developmental theory is that adult behaviors are often established in early childhood. Although retrospective reports obtained from the verbal protocols of adults support this assumption, it has been difficult to produce a more objective demonstration of the long term stability of childhood behavior patterns. This unhappy state of affairs is a consequence of the expense and difficulty associated with collecting long term longitudinal information on a large sample of children. Only extensive, longitudinal research programs, as exemplified by the Berkeley Growth Study or the Fels Research Institute, can furnish the answers to this developmental problem.

This paper presents one set of results which have emerged from a recent study of a group of "normal" adults from the Fels longitudinal research population for whom extensive information was available from birth through adolescence. The findings deal specifically with the long term stability of passive and dependent behavior in the face of situations which are frustrating and/or demand problem solving activity. This particular behavioral variable was chosen for initial analysis because theoretical essays on personality development emphasize that the early dependence of the child on the parent is of the utmost importance in shaping his future personality. That is, the development of a variety of adult motives and behaviors are based on the quality and intensity of the dependent relationship with the mother and mother-substitute figures. Further, psychological symptoms are theoretically attributed to inconsistency in the gratification of the child's dependent overtures and/or to denial or inhibition of dependent motives or behavior.

In addition to the longitudinal material, each subject was recently assessed during early adulthood by means of both interview and test procedures. The adult assessment was focused on the behavioral variables of dependency, aggression, achievement, and sexuality and on the degree of conflict and type of defensive responses associated with behavioral strivings in these areas. It was anticipated that there might be important

[1] This research was supported, in part, by research grant M-1260 from the National Institute of Mental Health, United States Public Health Service. Parts of this paper were presented at the annual meeting of the Midwestern Psychological Association in Chicago, May 1959.

From J. Kagan & H. A. Moss. The stability of passive and dependent behavior from childhood through adulthood. Child Development, *1960,* **31,** *577–591. (With permission of the authors and the Society for Research in Child Development, Inc.)*

239

sex differences with respect to occurrence of these behaviors, and the assessment procedures were designed to detect these potential sex differences.

METHOD

Sample

The subjects (*S*s) in this analysis were 27 male and 27 female Caucasian adults born between 1930 and 1939 who had recently been through a comprehensive assessment program which included an average of five hours of tape recorded interview and a variety of test procedures. The *S*s were between 20 and 29 years of age at the time of the assessment. In addition, these *S*s had fairly complete longitudinal records from 3 to 10 years of age. The *S*s were predominantly middle class but came from a variety of vocational backgrounds including agricultural, skilled labor, tradesmen, and professional groups. The religious affiliations of the group included 43 Protestants, 10 Catholics and 1 Jewish subject. The mean Wechsler-Bellevue IQ of the group was 120 with an IQ range of 97 to 142.

Interview variables: Adult assessment

Each *S* was interviewed by the senior author for approximately five hours over two to three sessions. *The interviewer had absolutely no knowledge of any of the longitudinal information on the Ss.* Since these *S*s had been studied by psychologists for over 20 years, rapport was usually excellent, and defensive and evasive answers were infrequent. Following the interviews, each *S* was rated (7-point scale) on 59 variables. Six of these adult interview variables dealt specifically with passive and dependent behavior; abridged definitions of these variables follow:

Degree to which dependent gratifications were sought in choice of vocation. This variable assessed the degree to which security was an important aspect of job choice, the degree to which the subject looked to his employer for gratification of his dependent needs, reluctance to shift jobs because of temporary loss of security. For nonworking women, emphasis was placed on her attitudes about the importance of security in her husband's job.

Degree of dependent behavior toward a love object. This variable assessed the degree to which the subject sought advice and emotional support from a love object (sweetheart, husband, wife), degree to which the subject looked for stability and wisdom in a love object, degree to which responsibility for decision making was given to love object.

Degree of dependent behavior with parents. This variable assessed the degree to which the subject looked for advice, support, emotional encouragement, and nurturance from one or both parents.

Degree of dependent behavior toward nonparental figures. This variable assessed the degree to which the subject sought advice, emotional support, and nurturance from nonparental figures who were not love objects, e.g., friends, relatives, and teachers.

Tendency to display behavioral withdrawal in the face of anticipated failure. This variable assessed the frequency and consistency with which *S* tended to withdraw from tasks and situations which he thought were difficult to master and in which failure was anticipated.

Degree of conflict over dependent behavior. This variable assessed the degree to which the subject avoided placing himself in dependent positions, his derogation of dependent behavior in self and others, and his emphasis on the value and importance of independent behavior.

A random sample of 32 taped interviews were independently studied and rated. The interrater reliabilities for the six dependency variables ranged from .63 to .82 with an average coefficient of .74.

Procedure for evaluation of childhood behavior

The junior author, who had no knowledge of the adult psychological status of the Ss, evaluated narrative reports based on direct observation of the child in a variety of situations. Summaries of interviews with the child and the mothers were also available. The observation reports were based on (a) semiannual visits to the home in which a staff member observed the child interact with mother and siblings for a two to four hour period, (b) semiannual or annual observations of the child in the Fels experimental nursery school and day camp settings, (c) interviews with the child, and (d) observations of the child in the classroom. After studying this material, the psychologist rated each child for a comprehensive set of variables (7-point scale). The rater studied the material for each S for ages 3 to 6 and made his ratings. Following a period of interpolated work, he then studied all the material for each S for ages 6 to 10 and again made the ratings. A period of approximately six months intervened between the evaluation of the material for any one child for ages 3 to 6 and 6 to 10. The rater felt that retroactive inhibition was sufficiently intense to mask any halo effect of the preschool ratings upon the later ratings made for 6 to 10 years of age. That is, the amount of material studied and the large number of variables rated militated against the recall of specific ratings over such a long period of time. In addition, the high degree of interrater reliability for these ratings supports the above statement. Independent ratings of the four childhood dependency variables by a second psychologist produced satisfactory interrater reliabilities. . . . The four childhood variables which involved passive and dependent behavior were defined as follows:

Tendency to behave in a passive manner when faced with environmental obstacles or stress (rated for ages 3 to 6 and 6 to 10). This variable assessed the degree to which the child was behaviorally passive in the face of external frustrations and failed to make any active mastery attempts to obtain desired goal objects following frustration. The rating of a passive behavioral reaction emphasized withdrawal from the frustration but included whining, crying, and soliciting help.

Tendency to seek support, nurturance, and assistance from female adults when under stress: general dependence (rated for age 3 to 6). This variable assessed the S's behavioral tendency to obtain assistance, nurturance, or affection from mother and other female adults when confronted with a threat to his well-being, a problem, or loss of a desired goal object. Dependent behavior included seeking out adults when faced with a problem or personal injury, reluctance to start a task without help or encouragement, seeking assistance of others, seeking affection from and close contact with female adults.

Tendency to seek affection and emotional support from female adults (rated for ages 6 to 10). This variable assessed the degree to which the child sought affection or emotional encouragement from mother or mother substitute figures. Evidence included kissing, holding hands, clinging, seeking encouragement or proximity to female adults.

Tendency to seek instrumental assistance from female adults (rated for ages 6 to 10). This variable assessed the degree to which the child sought instrumental help with specific problems from mother, teachers, or other female authority figures. Instrumental dependent acts included seeking help with tasks, seeking help when physically threatened.

Tachistoscopic perception

After the interviews and interview ratings were completed, each adult S was seen for a variety of test procedures, one of which was a tachistoscopic perception task. A series of 14 scenes were drawn to suggest action in the areas of dependency, aggression, sexuality, and physical danger. Three motivationally neutral, control pictures were also included.[2] For nine of the 14 pictures, separate pairs of illustrations were made for males and females so that the sex of the central figure was the same as the sex of the subject. The pictures were black and white line drawings with minimal background details. A brief description of the three dependency pictures follows:

1.   A young adult in the foreground (male for male Ss and female for female Ss) is on his knees clutching the waist of a figure of the same age but of opposite sex who is standing and looking forward. The figure on the floor is looking up at the face of the standing figure.
2.   A young adult in the foreground (male for male Ss and female for female Ss) has his arms extended in an imploring gesture toward an adult of the same sex who is standing in the background with his back to the figure in the foreground.
3.   A young adult (male for male Ss and female for female Ss) is seated on a chair with head buried in the abdomen of an adult of the opposite sex who is standing and comforting the seated figure.

The 14 pictures were presented seven times at seven different exposure speeds and in six different orders. The seven speeds ranged from .01 to 1.0 second. The pictures were shown initially at the fastest exposure (.01 second), and each succeeding series was presented at a slower exposure speed. All exposures were above threshold and all Ss reported seeing something at each exposure. The S sat in a light proof room, 22 in. from a flash-opal milk glass screen. The image was projected from the back of the screen, and the field was constantly illuminated by a 35 mm. projector (30 ft.-candles at the screen). The subject was told to state for each picture (a) the sex of each figure, (b) the approximate ages of each figure, and (c) what each figure on the picture was doing. The S was given three practice pictures to adapt him to the task and its requirements, and the entire protocol was electrically recorded and transcribed verbatim.

The protocols were scored for recognition threshold for each picture. Recognition threshold was defined as the first series at which the picture was described accurately and all succeeding trials were accurately described. The distribution of recognition thresholds differed among the 14 pictures and were markedly skewed either to the low or high end of the scale. Thus, the distribution of recognition thresholds for each picture was divided at the median into early and late recognition groups for statistical operations.

RESULTS

Stability of dependent behavior

. . . The major result is that passive and dependent behaviors were fairly stable for females but not for males. For girls the ratings of passivity during ages 6 to 10 correlated significantly with the adult ratings of a dependent orientation in vocational choice, dependency on love object, dependency on parents, and withdrawal to failure.

[2] Photostats of the 14 stimuli are available upon request.

Childhood passivity was inversely correlated with adult conflict over dependent behavior. That is, females who were passive as children were apt to accept their dependent behavior in adulthood and show minimal anxiety over their dependent motives. Only dependent behavior toward nonparental figures failed to show a significant, positive correlation with the childhood ratings of passivity. Similarly, the childhood ratings of both instrumental and emotional dependency on female adults, for girls aged 6–10, predicted adult ratings of dependency on love object, dependency on parents, and withdrawal to anticipated failure situations.

For the men there were only two significant correlations between the childhood dependency ratings and those based on the adult interview. Boys who were high on instrumental dependency for ages 6 to 10 were high on dependent behavior towards nonparental figures in adulthood. Second, emotional dependence during ages 6 to 10 was positively correlated with adult withdrawal to failure.

Of the 18 correlations between each of the three childhood variables for ages 6 to 10 and the six adult variables, 60 percent were significant in the expected direction for females, while only 9 percent were significant for the men. . . .

The correlations among the passive and dependency variables between ages 3 to 6 and 6 to 10 were generally more consistent for girls than for boys. That is, for girls the correlations among passivity and general dependence for ages 3 to 6 and the three variables for ages 6 to 10 were all consistently high. For boys the stability of the passivity rating for ages 3 to 6 and 6 to 10 was quite high. However, the relationships between passivity for 3 to 6 and the two dependency behaviors for 6 to 10 were not as high as they were for girls. This finding suggests that overt seeking of affection and/or instrumental aid in school age boys begins to be dissociated from a passive withdrawal reaction to problem situations.

The intercorrelations among the adult dependency variables were generally positive for both sexes. Dependency on parents and dependency on love objects were each associated with withdrawal to failure and negatively related to conflict over dependency. It is interesting to note that women who are dependent on their parents tended to be dependent on their love object but not on friends or authority figures. Men, on the other hand, who were dependent on their parents tended to be dependent on friends and authority figures rather than on a love object. Dependency on parents and friends usually involves instrumental aid with problems, while dependency on a love object more often included the soliciting of emotional support and affection. . . . Thus, male dependent behavior is apt to emphasize the seeking of instrumental assistance with problems, while females are likely to seek affection and emotional support in addition to instrumental aid.

It is important to note that passive and dependent behavior for ages 6 to 10 showed a better relation to adult dependent behavior than the ratings for 3 to 6 years of age. This finding indicates that important age changes occur between ages 3 and 10 and that behavior displayed during the first few years of school is a better index of adult functioning than the earlier preschool behavior patterns.

Tachistoscopic perception of dependent pictures

There were significant sex differences in recognition threshold for the three dependency pictures with the females recognizing all three pictures earlier than the males. The scene that depicted a person imploring a same sexed adult (picture 2) yielded the most significant sex difference. . . .

The aggressive pictures, on the other hand, produced opposite results, for the females recognized two of the four aggression pictures significantly later than the men. . . . There were no significant sex differences for the sex, physical danger, or three neutral scenes.

There was not a highly consistent relationship between recognition threshold for the dependent scenes and the interview ratings of dependency conflict. Only recognition of the scene that illustrated a man on his knees in front of a woman (picture 1) showed a relation to dependency conflict, and this held only for males. The males who were above the median in recognition threshold for this scene (late recognition) were rated as more conflicted over dependent behavior than males who recognized this picture early. . . . For the females, recognition threshold for the dependency pictures showed no significant relation to ratings of dependency conflict.

DISCUSSION

The results support a basic hypothesis of developmental theory which states that the acquisition of certain adult response patterns begins in early childhood. The differential stability of passive-dependent behavior for men and women is probably the result of several factors. However, one set of processes which may contribute to this phenomenon is derived from the commonly accepted hypothesis that passive and dependent behavior is less punished in females than in males. Further, females are often encouraged to be passive while men are expected to be independent and autonomous in the face of frustration. Parental and peer group punishment for passive and dependent behavior should result in some inhibition of this behavior in males. Thus, we would not expect this class of behavior to be as stable for men as for women. Studies of both overt behavior and fantasy (Hattwick, 1937; Kagan, 1959; Sanford, Adkins, Miller, & Cobb, 1943; Watson, 1959; Whitehouse, 1949) . . . indicate that dependent responses are more frequent for girls than for boys. Further, the sex stereotypes presented by communication media fit this description. The analysis of children's books by Child, Potter, and Levine (1946) indicated that girls are portrayed as passive while boys are presented as independent and heroic. Finally, a study of the likes and dislikes of 10-year-old children (Tyler, 1955) confirms the belief that girls accept passive behavior as more appropriate for their sex role than do boys.

The present tachistoscopic threshold data support the notion that men are more conflicted over dependent behavior than women. It will be recalled that the women recognized all three scenes depicting dependent behavior much earlier than the men. This finding suggests that the tendency to perceive dependent behavior in adults is much weaker in men than it is in women. . . .

Detailed analysis of the 54 cases indicates that there was a greater proportion of men, than women, who shifted from high dependency during childhood to independent behavior as adults. The women tended to be either dependent or independent for both childhood and adulthood. For example, in comparing emotional dependence for ages 6 to 10 with adult dependency on parents, not one female showed a major shift from high dependency in childhood to low dependency in adulthood. For the men, however,

20 percent were rated very dependent during the ages 6 to 10 and very independent in adulthood.

The authors do not suggest that passive and dependent behavior in girls is rigidly fixed at school age and that change is a rare or unusual phenomenon. It must be kept in mind that the social milieu of these particular subjects remained rather constant throughout their lives. Their familial and extrafamilial environments were not disrupted to any marked degree. The parents and peers of these *S*s retained their same values, their reference groups remained constant, and, in most cases, their geographical travel was limited. Thus, the degree of behavioral stability obtained for these females might not hold for populations that are more mobile or transient, for different ethnic or class samples, or for people subjected to major traumata during adolescence and early adulthood. . . .

Although case history material can never prove an hypothesis, it often facilitates scientific communication by placing some flesh on the skeleton of a correlation matrix. The following case material is presented to give the reader a clearer picture of the material upon which our childhood evaluations were based and to illustrate dramatically the degree of constancy of behavioral passivity for two specific individuals.

Case A   Miss A is a 21-year-old, unmarried woman, who was in her senior year in an eastern college. She was one of the most independent women in our sample and one who showed a strong reaction against dependent behavior in a wide variety of situations. As an adult she was described as a woman with a very strong need for recognition by others combined with a striving for achievement-related goals. She had a strong desire to nurture others and often sought out situations in which she could give advice, support, and encouragement to peers. Miss A stated during the interview that she liked to keep her personal problems to herself. She did not like to discuss her personal problems because she felt that this behavior made her appear "helpless and weak." Statements like this indicate very strong conflict and anxiety over being in a passive-dependent position with other people. She was trying to sever any semblance of a dependent relation with her mother and derogated the latter because the mother seemed to be dependent upon her for companionship. Miss A sometimes felt lonely but said that she fights these feelings and tries to be able to live with them, for she does not like to admit that she needs friends or companionship. Her relationship with men seems to be consistent with the above pattern, for she tends to withdraw from heterosexual relationships that become too intense. Miss A said that she does not like men [who] make demands upon her, and she avoids men who attempt to place her in a passive role or position.

The following material represents selected verbatim excerpts from the longitudinal material on this subject.

Age 3 years, 4 months: Summary of Fels Nursery School Observations. S seems to be able to control and channel her behavior so that she got done just what she wanted to get done. In this activity she was very independent and capable. She was very social but also had a streak of aloof self-sufficiency, and she always made her individuality felt. She was what might be called a strong personality, often very intense, quite stubborn. . . . Her most outstanding characteristic was her consistent independence and integrity. In spite of the fact that she imitated and followed certain boys, she seemed to do this very much from her own choice, and she never lost the flavor of her individuality. She was capable of being social and seemed to enjoy contacts but at all times she was her own master. She would often withdraw from play and go on in her own direction at any time that she wished. . . . She was independent with adults and at times negativistic just to be devilish. She seemed somewhat self-conscious and had some cute little tricks. . . . In all, she could be characterized best by being called "tough minded." She shows determination and will, originality and spark, curiosity and interest in factual detail. She likes to quibble and argue, to verbalize, to construct, to accomplish. She is an individualist, independent and stubborn.

Age 5 years, 4 months: Fels Nursery School Observation. S seems to be vigorous, ruthless, competitive, highly sensual young woman, but one felt quite often that antagonism toward others was simply a direct response to their behavior. . . . She has grown far more social and also popular with an increasingly large crowd of special friends in a gang. She could be, when she chose, quite a successful leader, forging ahead and organizing a group on a hike, directing them and arranging things, and particularly keeping order in a fair sharing of the tools in the carpentry shop. . . . Many of S's conflicts with the adult world seemed a direct imitation of a certain boy. She needed a chance to grumble, would scornfully refuse any adult suggestions or orders, would usually go officially ahead to carry them out. She was quite demanding, often shouting an order to an assistant. . . . With her other work the same drive for strong achievement was also evident, sticking to anything until it was finished, whatever the group stimuli. S still had real trouble in fine motor coordination, would growl as she worked, "I'm doing this as well as I can steer my pencil." For all her teeth gritted effort, the final results would still be relatively crude. She was very skilled in the use of puzzles and interested in the problems of designs and the way things fit together. She scorned any of the ready-made designs for the Christmas tree decorations.

Age 7 years: Observation in Fels Day Camp. S came accompanied by one friend. S did not seem overwhelmed by the large proportion of adults around, but in her sturdy self-sufficient manner went ahead with her own activities. Her friend was at first rather shy and withdrawn and S, with her usual confident bullying and bossing of the adults, tended to take the girl under her wing and make sure she had a good time. S remains an exceptionally eager, imperturbable young woman. On a number of small issues she did insist on her own way, on just how long she would stay in the gym and play before lunch, but was quite reasonable about making compromises. She chose a rather difficult necklace to make and got quite mad when it didn't work out well. She kept doggedly with it, very self-sufficient, and continuing all on her own after getting some initial advice. . . . Her major effort was put on self-appointed tasks, to be able to master jumping over the horse at the gym where she took numerous tumbles until she succeeded. In spite of her distractability and preference for the apparatus she did set herself to learning the new skills required there.

Age 9 years: Report from Teacher. S is one of the most responsible children in the group. . . . She is self-reliant, independent, and knows how to plan her time well. She enters all games with enthusiasm, is very well coordinated, is full of personality and "joie de vivre."

Case B   Miss B is a 23-year-old, unmarried woman, who is working and living with her parents. She was one of the most overtly dependent women in the sample. During the interview she was very dependent on the interviewer for structure and was rather mild and meek. Her most typical reaction to failure or stressful situations is to deny or withdraw and she says quite blithely, "I'm not a worrier." She is very sensitive to the opinions of other people and usually conforms with their expectations for her. She accepts her passive-dependent role with authority people and with love objects. S tends to be very dependent on peers for advice, likes being close to the family, and tends to see herself as inadequate in the face of problem situations.

Following are selected excerpts from her longitudinal records:

Age 2 years, 6 months: Fels Nursery School Observation. At the first day of nursery school, S seemed rather frightened and very reluctant to leave her mother this morning. The mother had to carry her and hold her in the car until the door was shut. For the first few miles she cried and then suddenly stopped and began to take an interest in the various animals and objects. She cried when she reached the nursery school but stopped as soon as she left the other children. On the second day of nursery school she cried again but seemed much less frightened and more angry. During the nursery school she stood watching the other children and at one point ran to another girl and stood beside her. The other little girl paid no attention, and S trailed after her. S wandered around and, when the teacher went to the house, S rushed to follow her and stood around the teacher. S tagged after another little girl all morning. During the nursery school two-week period she was timid and tense.

Age 3 years: Fels Nursery School Summary. At first, S was timid and tense and was gathered under the wing of another peer and her cohorts. From then on she was "at home" with the group. She followed another girl's lead and joined in the activities the other girl organized. On days when this girl was absent she was at loose ends and tended to return to her original dependence on an adult. Several weeks after her nursery school stay she visited the school one morning for several hours. She was a little apprehensive at first but made no real protest. She stood around not joining in the play until an adult suggested an activity.

Age 4 years: Fels Nursery School Summary. S cried the first day of nursery school after she saw another girl cry. She stayed close to the teacher the first few days and watched the other children with a worried expression on her face. Indoors she chose small blocks or color cubes to play with. In the yard S was very cautious about trying out the apparatus, particularly when there was any balancing involved. She has a high, whining nasal voice, and several letter substitutions made her speech rather difficult to understand. She was quite complying with adult requests. Frequently, she appealed to adults for help in conflicts, such as getting a turn to slide, which is a situation she could have handled for herself.

Age 6 years: Visit to the School. S is retiring, quiet, and shy. She doesn't show the enthusiasm that most of the children in the class do. She seems content. . . . She goes to the teacher for suggestions and skips to her seat jubilantly with a word of approval from the teacher. S recites a bit timidly in front of the whole class but accepts the teacher's support and gets through successfully. Her voice is a little soft and her enunciation is not clear. S volunteers information a bit tentatively and without enthusiasm. The teacher reports that S is about the brightest of the average group. S is not a leader but she is very sweet and cooperative and is never any trouble.

Age 6 years, 6 months: Summary of Fels Day Camp Observations. S was outclassed in almost every respect in this group but fluttered happily about after the others doing the best she could. She occasionally withdrew or grew silent but, when encouraged by an adult, she soon recovered. She was not insensitive and did not seem to have her security disturbed more than momentarily. She seems to feel a great confidence and trust in adults and could always be bought off or led along. She lacked initiative in almost every way. She could not go ahead on any craft project nor could she assert herself socially. She needed help and encouragement, hung about the adults, not exposing herself to the center of the group. She is essentially a conformist and wanted only to do what was right. She got into no mischief and had little sense of fun. She was happiest when settled into a situation that was approved and guided by an adult, and at these times she would proddle along very happily. Her main interests lay in conforming to any plans laid by adults and working on simple handcrafts. She was rather unsure in her accomplishments. She was often physically apprehensive.

Age 7 years, 6 months: Summary of Fels Day Camp Observations. The most characteristic aspect of S's day camp behavior was her ability, high conformity, and social reticence. She did not participate in social activities to any extent and was generally ignored by the other children. She clung to adults, wanted to assist them when possible, and wanted their approval and comforting in all her activities. She seemed to be somewhat apprehensive of physical contacts, especially if they became at all rough. She was apprehensive about almost any physical danger. Her actual physical ability was not particularly poor, and, when she was put into athletic situations, she did surprisingly well. Her general lack of physical participation seems not to be due to poor ability as much as to lack of motivation and apprehension.

Age 8 years: Visit to the School. S is always anxious to do what is right all of the time. She is not a discipline problem. *S* shows no interest in physical activities. Initially, she is lost at school work and takes some time to adjust to new work. *S* was pretty tentative in her first attempt to get the teacher's attention and held up her paper hesitantly. She was very pleased when the teacher came to her. She was uncertain about the problems although they had similar ones before.

Age 8 years, 8 months: Fels Day Camp Summary. S is a small, dark looking girl, bent over, with thick dark hair and a tired face. Her voice is high but with no force; her hands hanging limp at the wrists. Much of this lack of force seemed related to her personality, and at the races she surprised us by doing remarkably well. *S* obeyed adults implicitly and wanted to have their sanction for even small acts which the group had already been given permission for. She has a rather cringing, servile manner. This clinging around adults was particularly marked the first day when she ate her lunch with them.

Age 9 years, 8 months: Fels Day Camp Summary. S is a rather pathetic looking little girl. Rather thin, droopy eyed, clammy handed, somehow reminiscent of an orphan in an old melodrama. She seems nearer to seven or eight than her actual age and with a kind of naiveté and unsureness about all she did. She was an exceedingly compliant child in taking the tests, even the reading tests which she obviously disliked, without a murmur.

SUMMARY

This paper summarized some results from a larger investigation of the stability of behavior in a group of subjects who were part of the Fels Research Institute's longitudinal population. This report dealt specifically with the long term stability of passive and dependent behavior from childhood through adulthood.

The *S*s were 27 males and 27 females for whom extensive longitudinal information was available from birth through adolescence. One psychologist studied narrative reports based on observations of the child in various settings and rated each child on four variables describing types of passive and dependent behavior for ages 3 to 6 and ages 6 to 10. A second psychologist, who had no knowledge of the childhood data, interviewed each *S* in adulthood and rated each *S* on six variables related to aspects of adult passive and dependent behavior. In addition, each adult *S* was administered a tachistoscopic perception task in which scenes illustrating dependent activity were presented at seven different exposure speeds.

The results revealed that passive and dependent behaviors were quite stable for women, but minimally stable for men. Over 60 percent of the correlations between the childhood (ages 6 to 10) and adult ratings of dependency were statistically significant for females, while only 9 percent were significant for men. . . .

It was suggested that environmental disapproval and punishment of dependent behavior in young males led to inhibition of and conflict over dependency in the growing boy. The social acceptance of passive and dependent behavior in females would be expected to result in greater stability for this class of responses for women than for men. The fact that females recognized the tachistoscopically presented dependency scenes earlier than the men was interpreted as support for this explanation.

Case history material for two female subjects was presented to illustrate the type of information utilized in this study.

REFERENCES

Child, I. L., Potter, E. H., & Levine, E. M. Children's textbooks and personality development: An exploration in the social psychology of education. *Psychological Monographs,* 1946, **60**(3, Whole No. 279).

Hattwick, L. A. Sex differences in behavior of nursery school children. *Child Development,* 1937, **8**, 343–355.

Kagan, J. The stability of TAT fantasy and stimulus ambiguity. *Journal of Consulting Psychology,* 1959, **23**, 266–271.

Sanford, R. N., Adkins, M. M., Miller, R. B., & Cobb, E. A. Physique, personality and scholarship: A cooperative study of school children. *Monographs of the Society for Research in Child Development,* 1943, **8**(1, Serial No. 34).

Tyler, L. E. The development of "vocational interests": I. The organization of likes and dislikes in ten-year-old children. *Journal of Genetic Psychology,* 1955, **86**, 33–44.

Watson, R. I. *Psychology of the child.* New York: Wiley, 1959.

Whitehouse, E. Norms for certain aspects of the Thematic Apperception Test on a group of nine and ten year old children. *Personality,* 1949, **1**, 12–15.

SOCIAL CLASS, PARENTAL PUNISHMENT FOR AGGRESSION, AND CHILD AGGRESSION[1]

Leonard D. Eron, Leopold O. Walder, Romolo Toigo, and Monroe M. Lefkowitz

According to behavior theory (Child, 1954; Dollard, Doob, Miller, Mowrer, & Sears, 1939), punishment for aggression should result in the learning of anxiety about its consequences and therefore have an inhibiting effect on the expression of aggression. Thus, it would be predicted that increased punishment for aggression will lead to reduced frequency of aggressive behavior, especially when the situations in which the behavior is punished and later evoked are similar. While carefully controlled laboratory studies with animals (Seward, 1946) and preschoolers (Hollenberg & Sperry, 1951) and questionnaire studies of college students (Doob & Sears, 1939) have in general confirmed this view, survey studies of the childrearing antecedents of aggressive behavior have on the whole yielded opposite findings. It has been monotonously reported in the latter studies (e.g., Bandura & Walters, 1959; Glueck & Glueck, 1950; Sears, Maccoby, & Levin, 1957) that increased punishment for aggression by socializing agents is related to increased aggression on the part of the child. These findings have been called into question because usually (except for Bandura and Walters' study with adolescents) the same informant is utilized in both antecedent and consequent measures (Eron, Banta, Walder, & Laulicht, 1961). Indeed a seven-year follow-up study by Sears (1961) did show an inverse relation between punishment and aggression when he used different informants for these two measures.[2]

Another regular finding is that children from lower class backgrounds tend to be more aggressive than children of upper class origins (Goldstein, 1955; McKee & Leader, 1955; Stoltz & Smith, 1959). An allied finding is that punishment for aggression tends to be more severe among middle class children than lower class children (Davis, 1943),

[1] The program of research on which this report is based has been generously supported by Grant M-1726, National Institutes of Health, U.S. Department of Health, Education, and Welfare. The Columbia County Tuberculosis and Health Association, Inc., has over the years also made regular financial contributions to this program for which we are grateful. We would like to thank the IBM Watson Scientific Computing Laboratory at Columbia University for making computer time available without charge. Our greatest debt of gratitude is to the children, parents, and educators of Columbia County, New York, who have steadfastly supported this research from its inception in 1956.

[2] In this study Sears reassessed 42 percent of his original sample and predicted from self-ratings of aggressive attitude, rather than mothers' reports (as in the initial investigation), to the original childrearing data obtained from the mother. The author justifies his use of an attitude scale as a measure of overt behavior thus: "the reading of a statement would arouse an imaginal representation of the act or feeling described and . . . marking the scale would be by response generalization an affirmation or rejection of that representation" (p. 471).

From L. D. Eron, L. O. Walder, R. Toigo, & M. M. Lefkowitz. Social class, parental punishment for aggression, and child aggression. Child Development, 1963, 34, 849–867. (With permission of the authors and the Society for Research in Child Development, Inc.)

although this has been questioned by Maccoby and Gibbs (1954). In addition, psychological punishment has been reported as more characteristic of socialization practices of middle class parents and physical punishment of lower class parents (Allinsmith, 1960). However, no pattern of punishment can be the exclusive property of any one class and overlapping patterns of punishment no doubt exist from one social class to another (Littman, Moore, & Pierce-Jones, 1957). Is it the differential modes of punishment which supposedly exist in different classes which is the crucial factor in accounting for more aggression in one class than another or is there something else about social class which has to be invoked as an explanatory principle? For direct aggression, at least as experienced by children in their projective story completions, Allinsmith (1960) demonstrated that parental discipline in itself, independent of social class membership, was of overriding importance, while social class alone had no relation to direct expression of aggression in story completions. Do the same relations hold when aggressive behavior is measured by other than projective techniques?

In the present research it has been possible to study the aggressive behavior of a large sample of children of varied socioeconomic backgrounds and to relate this behavior to social class and punishment habits of mother and father and then to examine the interaction between social class and punishment in relation to aggressive behavior. It is emphasized that the aggression measure, the father data, and the mother data were all obtained independently from different informants.

PROCEDURE

Subjects

The subjects were 206 girls, 245 boys, each of their mothers, and each of their fathers. These children were drawn from the entire population of children enrolled in the third grade in the spring of 1960 in a semirural county in New York's Hudson River Valley who were being studied in a larger investigation of the psychosocial antecedents of aggressive behavior. The current sample included every child in the larger pool ($N = 865$) who was from an intact family, who was in attendance at all three testing sessions conducted in the classroom a week apart, and whose mother and father both contributed scorable personal interviews (less 10 lost randomly in an IBM editing routine).

Measures

The aggression score for each child was derived from a peer-rating procedure in the form of a "Guess-Who" in which each child rated every other child in his class on a series of 10 items having to do with specific aggressive behaviors.[3] The derivation, reliability, and validity of this instrument have been described elsewhere (Walder, Abelson, Eron, Banta, & Laulicht, 1961).

---

[3] The aggressive items comprising this scale are: (1) Who does not obey the teacher? (2) Who often says, "Give me that"? (3) Who gives dirty looks or sticks out their tongue at other children? (4) Who makes up stories and lies to get other children into trouble? (5) Who does things that bother others? (6) Who starts a fight over nothing? (7) Who pushes or shoves children? (8) Who is always getting into trouble? (9) Who says mean things? (10) Who takes other children's things without asking?

Parent measures were derived from a 286-item objective, precoded, personal interview, administered usually in the respondent's home but occasionally in the researcher's office.[4] The mechanics of the interviewing procedure is described in more detail in Walder, Eron, Lefkowitz, and Toigo (1962). The punishment scale consisted of responses to 24 items. These had to do with the likely response of a parent to four kinds of aggressive behavior on the part of the child (two dealing with aggression toward the respondent and two with aggression toward other children). Two specific punishments from each of three levels of intensity[5] were assigned to each of the four items, giving 24 punishments in all. Each item received a weighted score (3 for high; 2 for medium; 1 for low intensity) if the respondent agreed that he would likely administer that punishment for the given behavior. The sum of the scores for all 24 items was the total punishment score used in the current analyses. The items (which are listed with their intensity ratings in Table 1) were administered in block format, i.e., all six punishments for a given aggressive act were in a unit. . . .

Occupation of father which was classified according to the Census Bureau classification (1950) of 10 categories of occupation was used as a measure of social class. Research has shown that the single occupational classification is as meaningful an index to social class as any combination of factors (Kahl & Davis, 1955; Lawson & Boek, 1960). The cutting points for the three status levels which were determined automatically by the computer so as to cut this sample into the closest approximation of equal thirds placed 0 and 1 classifications in the upper class; 2, 3, and 4 in the middle class; and 5 to 9 in the lower or working class.

RESULTS

Punishment

When punishment scores by mother, father, and mother plus father are categorized into three levels of intensity . . . it is apparent that there is a strong relation between punishment for aggression and the appearance of that behavior in school as rated by peers . . . : the more severely punished children being rated more aggressive in school. The effect of mother's punishment seems more pronounced than that of father's punishment. When . . . relating both mother's punishment and father's punishment . . . to school aggression as rated by peers, . . . there [is an] effect only for

---

[4] The Rip Van Winkle Child-Rearing Questionnaire, Guide to the Questionnaire, and the Interview Manual have been deposited as Document number 7660 with the ADI Auxiliary Publications Project, Photoduplication Service, Library of Congress, Washington 25, D.C.

[5] Intensity of the punishment had been determined in previous studies. Originally, as reported in Eron, Banta, Walder, & Laulicht (1961), parental punishment for specific aggressive behaviors (corresponding to items in which the child was rated in the classroom) were recorded verbatim by the interviewer and later rated on a 7-point scale of intensity by three judges with very good agreement. A second study was then successful in translating responses from the open-ended questions to an objective format. Approximately 30 parents (of third graders of the year preceding this sample) were asked to judge 40 punishments (selected from those obtained in the previous study) along a 9-point scale from harshness to mildness, using Thurstone's method of equal appearing intervals. The median scale values were calculated, and all 40 punishments were ordered in terms of these values. It was possible to distinguish clearly three categories of intensity of punishment. At each cutting point approximately 10 punishments were deleted so that any punishment in a given category had very little chance of having a true value in any other category. The items selected finally were those with the most agreement among parents.

TABLE 1   Items in punishment scale

	Mean intensity value
If NAME were rude to you, would you:	
Tell him: "I will give you something you like if you act differently"?	1.4
Wash out his mouth with soap?	7.7
Remind NAME of what others will think of him?	4.6
Say: "Get on that chair and don't move until you apologize"?	5.7
Tell NAME that young men (ladies) don't do this sort of thing?	3.4
Spank NAME until he cries?	7.8
If you saw NAME grab things from another child, would you:	
Tell him that young men (ladies) don't do this sort of thing?	3.4
Say: "I would like to be proud of you"?	3.5
Make NAME apologize?	5.8
Tell NAME you don't love him?	7.7
Point out how some close friend of his behaves better than NAME does?	4.9
Not let him play with his friends for two days?	7.7
If NAME got very mad at you, would you:	
Get very angry at him?	4.4
Slap him in the face?	7.9
Say: "That isn't a nice thing to do"?	3.5
Tell NAME you don't love him?	7.7
Tell NAME in a nice way how to act differently?	2.8
Send him to another room where he would be alone and without toys?	6.0
If you heard NAME say mean things to another child, would you:	
Tell him in a nice way to act differently?	2.8
Say: "Get on that chair and don't move until you apologize"?	5.7
Not let NAME play with his friends for two days?	7.7
Point out how some close friend of his behaves better than NAME does?	4.9
Wash out his mouth with soap?	7.7
Say: "I would like to be proud of you"?	3.5

mothers of boys. . . . However, when boys' and girls' scores are added together, there is [an] effect for both mother's and father's punishment. . . . There is a steady increase in aggression score as you go from children of mothers and fathers who are both low punishers to mothers and fathers who are both high punishers. However, when mother is a moderate punisher, boys tend to be less aggressive than when mother is a minimal or severe punisher regardless of father's punishment. . . . Two additional factors are apparent from these [data]. Boys get much higher scores than girls on the aggression measure and girls are punished less severely. This probably accounts for the increased strength of relation when boys and girls are pooled in one group.

. . . Very few parents report that the father alone takes responsibility for the child's discipline.[6] . . . However, . . . whether mother alone or mother plus father are the chief disciplinarians, the relation of the punishment of either mother or father to aggression is the same.

[6] This information was taken in response to the following question: "Who takes responsibility for NAME's discipline?" (1) father mostly (2) both (3) mother mostly (4) neither.

Social status

. . . Children whose fathers have higher status jobs obtain higher aggression scores than children of fathers with lower status jobs . . . [This is statistically significant for boys only.]

Social status [and] punishment

. . . [The] effects of father's punishment and occupational status on child's aggression yielded interesting findings . . . , especially for boys. When father's punishment is [classified by] occupational level, there is a significant effect for his punishment on boy's aggression score. . . . It seems . . . that high status boys who are severely punished for aggression are by far the most aggressive. Although girls show . . . effect[s] only for punishment, the high status girls who are severely punished are also the most aggressive of all girls. When all subjects are combined, the effects of both occupational status and punishment, as well as the interaction between them, show up in even more striking manner.

However, when mother's severity of punishment is [classified] by father's occupation, the only significant effects are for punishment, for both boys . . . and girls. . . . The effect of mother's punishment is overriding. Social class does not contribute anything significant.

Since the effect of punishment is so clearly related to the social class position of the socializing agents, especially as measured by father's occupational status, it was considered desirable to see if there are actually different patterns of punishment for aggression from one status to another. . . . There is [in fact], a differing intensity of punishment for aggression according to occupational level for fathers of girls, so that lower status girls are punished more severely by their fathers for aggression than are upper status girls. . . . The mean punishment scores by mothers of girls, according to father's occupation, are in the same direction, although there is no significant difference in score among the different occupational levels. There are also no significant differences for boys among mean punishment scores at each occupational level.

. . . The punishment scores [were] partitioned into punishment for aggression against peers and punishment for aggression against parents. Comparisons on mean score were made among the three occupational levels. . . . Parents of all occupational levels punish equally severely for [aggression against parents.] However, for aggression against the child's peers, there are important differences according to occupational status. . . . Girls of high status are punished significantly less severely by their parents for aggression against peers than are girls of low status. . . . Boys of middle status mothers are less severely punished for aggression against other children than boys of either high or low status mothers. . . . For mother and father combined there is [also] a difference with the middle status boys less severely punished than either the high or low status boys for aggression against other children. . . .

DISCUSSION

It is apparent from the results that punishment for aggression and social class as determined by father's occupation are both important factors in the child's aggression as rated by his peers in school. As for the first variable, the more these third grade children are punished for aggression by their parents, the more aggressive they tend to be as rated by their peers. This supports the finding of Sears, Maccoby, and Levin (1957) in their study of kindergarten children when both antecedent and consequent measures were obtained from the same informant (the mother). It is contrary to Sears' (1961) later finding when his subjects reached middle childhood (age 12) and rated themselves on aggressive attitude. At this age there was an inverse relation between these ratings and the punishment practices reported by the parents when the children were 5 years old.[7] Sears ascribed this shift from a positive to a negative relation between aggression and punishment for it to the supposition that, ''during the intervening years, the inhibitory effect of the punishment had an opportunity to be influential; no longer was the punishment for aggression simply a goad to frustration—it reduced the tendency to express the punished forms of behavior (p. 477).'' Apparently from our data by age 8 this shift has not yet occurred. Or else the difference in result may be accounted for by the different measurement operations of aggression in the three studies. Sears' earlier measure was ratings made by psychologists of verbatim accounts of mothers' punishment practices as given in individual recorded interviews. His later measure was self-rating of aggressive attitude. The measure used in the current study is of actual specific aggressive behaviors rated by the child's peers.

There is one interesting exception to the monotonous finding with our various samples of a positive relation between increasing punitiveness and increasing aggression, and that is the result with mothers of boys, where the relationship is apparently curvilinear. Those mothers who are in the medium punishment group have boys who are less aggressive than those with either low or high punishment. This result is one indication supporting behavior theory. Boys who are minimally punished at home for aggression tend to be more aggressive than those who are moderately punished for aggression. However, when they are maximally punished for this behavior, the instigating effect of the punishment (frustration) seems to overcome the inhibiting effect (anxiety) and the boys are very aggressive. . . . However, this is not what would have been predicted from the conflict hypothesis (McKee, 1949) which states that moderate punishment should lead to increased conflict between the tendency to aggression and anxiety inhibiting the expression of aggression, which in turn heightens the drive level and thus evokes increased aggressive behavior, and that very severe punishment should lead to generalized inhibition of aggressive behavior in many situations.

One interesting finding, when considering either mothers' or fathers' reports, is that the father is rarely credited with being the chief disciplinarian. Usually both parents or the mother alone take responsibility for the child's discipline. However, regardless of whether or not he is solely responsible for the child's discipline, father's punishment severity is related to aggression as rated by the child's peers. Possibly it is necessary to distinguish between delegated authority and absolute authority. Thus, even in those instances when the mother is seen as taking chief responsibility for child's discipline, there will be many cases where she is acting as a surrogate for the father. It is quite possible that for many mothers the capacity to discipline the children is derived from the moral authority of the father (as both she and her children perceive it). Hence, the father's style of discipline may be quite important in defining the limits of the mother's disciplinary activity, even though he may be physically out of the house most of the day. On the other hand, perhaps mother sets the patterns. This research design does not yield an answer.

---

[7] It should be noted that, although Sears reports this in his discussion, the relation does not reach significance.

Predictions improve when they are made from both punishment and father's occupation considered jointly. For example, father's punishment intensity by itself shows no significant relation to aggression of boys as rated by peers. However, when social class is controlled, a significant relation emerges. There is an interaction between social class and punishment, with boys of high status who are punished severely by their fathers being far and away the most aggressive. However, the effect of mother's punishment is not thus related to occupational status of the family. This may explain why Allinsmith (1960) found the effect of punishment to be independent of social class. She used only mothers' reports. Also, of course, the criterion measure of aggression is different. Allinsmith used a projective measure as reported in story endings made up by the subjects, and ours was a measure of reputation for aggression as rated by the subject's peers.

Our general finding that high status children are rated as more aggressive by their peers than low status children is contrary to most past results. The same is true for the finding that lower status girls are punished more severely for aggression against children than upper status girls and that children from all classes, both boys and girls, are punished equally severely for aggression towards parents. Much has been published by Davis (1941, 1943, 1948) suggesting that lower class parents encourage and reward aggression while middle class parents are less tolerant. Duvall (1946) writes that lower class children are much less likely to be punished for the overt expression of aggression, since in some neighborhoods it is necessary for the preservation of life. One of the few contrary findings is that of Maccoby and Gibbs (1954) who found middle class parents more permissive than lower class parents. They worked with nursery school children while the others worked with older groups of preadolescents. Maccoby and Gibbs explained the contradictory findings on the basis of this difference in age. Our data would indicate that even up to age 9 what differences do appear in socialization practices of parents of different classes are not in the direction of more leniency toward aggression on the part of lower class parents. In this respect, our findings, obtained in a semirural county, agree with those of Maccoby and Gibbs whose subjects were from a highly urban area. Lower class children tend to be less aggressive in school than upper class children and to be punished more severely, especially girls, for aggression against other children, while there is no difference among classes in punishment for aggression toward parents.

Further, we have no evidence that upper status parents use more psychological punishment and lower class parents more physical punishment. If anything, it would seem that upper class mothers use more physical punishment for aggression against other children and lower class fathers use more psychological punishment for aggression against both other children and themselves. The difference in these results from those of Allinsmith (1960) may perhaps be due to the difference in measurement operations. Allinsmith used ratings of recorded interviews, and the current measure is a simple count of "yes" responses to four questions having to do with the likelihood of a parent using a specific punishment for a specific behavior. Other reasons for differences include geographical and urban-rural differences in the samples.

However, all results reported here tend to suggest that some traditional notions about the differential distribution of socialization practices and child behaviors among various social classes may be in need of revision. It has been pointed out by Bronfenbrenner (1958) that the gap between social classes has been narrowing over the past quarter of a century with middle class parents becoming more permissive and lower class parents more conforming and restrictive. These data contribute additional evidence of the similarity in patterns of punishment at the present time among different social class levels. But this is not to say that social class membership is an unimportant influence on aggressive behavior of children since there is an interaction between social class and intensity of punishment, although no type of punishment is exclusively characteristic of any class. It may indeed strike the reader that we have substantiated some important class differences, e.g., lower class girls are punished more severely by parents for aggression against children than upper class girls and at the same time lower class girls are rated as less aggressive by their peers than are upper class girls (the latter is not significant). Also middle class boys are punished least for aggression against other children (not significant) and are rated as least aggressive by their peers.[8] However, this does not tell us anything about the relation between punishment for aggression and aggressive behavior in individual boys and girls. The reader is referred to the controversy over the interpretation of ecological correlations which has appeared in the literature recently (Duncan & Davis, 1953; Lazarsfeld & Menzel, 1961; Robinson, 1950). Our best information on the basis of the data presented here is that there is a positive relation between punishment for aggression by parents and the appearance of that behavior in school and that this relation is exaggerated by social class membership, with children of high status who are punished most severely being most aggressive as rated by their peers in school. Finally, it should be pointed out that our earlier assertions. (Eron et al., 1961) in regard to the importance of obtaining parallel data from mothers and fathers independently about socialization practices have certainly been substantiated by these results.

SUMMARY

Third grade children in a semirural county ($N = 451$) were rated for aggressive behavior by their classmates. Concurrently, the mother and father of each subject were interviewed individually to obtain information about punishment practices and social class position (as measured by father's occupation). Relations among these three sources of information were evaluated by [statistical analyses] with the following results:

1. With increased punishment for aggression at home there is increased aggression in school. This holds for mothers and fathers, boys and girls. The only exception is that with mothers there is a tendency for moderately punished boys to be less aggressive in school than those minimally punished for aggression. However, those boys who are severely punished by their mothers are the most aggressive.
2. Mother's and father's punishment for aggression are additive rather than interactive and generally operate in the same way regardless of which parent is chiefly responsible for the child's discipline.
3. With an increase in social position, as measured by father's occupation, children (especially boys) are rated as more aggressive in school.
4. Relations to the criterion are strongest when both social class and punishment are considered simultaneously, especially for fathers, and there is a significant interaction between social class and punishment for aggression in predicting . . . aggression in school.
5. Children of all social status levels are punished equally severely for aggression against parents; upper class girls tend to be punished less severely for aggression against peers than lower class girls.

---

[8] These results with lower class girls and middle class boys appear to be contradictory in their implications for reinforcement theory.

6.   There is no difference among classes in the differential use of psychological and physical punishment as measured here.

These results would indicate: (a) Although punishment for aggression and social status are by themselves good and fair predictors, respectively, to an independent measure of aggression, for the best predictions to the criterion both should be considered simultaneously. (b) Whatever differences exist in aggressive behavior among different classes are not due to the differential application of punishments by parents consistently from class to class.

REFERENCES

Allinsmith, B. B. Expressive styles. II. Directness with which anger is expressed. In D. R. Miller & G. E. Swanson, *Inner conflict and defense.* New York: Holt, 1960.

Bandura, A., & Walters, R. H. *Adolescent aggression.* New York: Ronald Press, 1959.

Bronfenbrenner, U. Socialization and social class through time and space. In E. E. Maccoby, T. M. Newcomb, & E. L. Hartley (Eds.), *Readings in social psychology.* New York: Holt, 1958. Pp. 400–424.

Child, I. L. Socialization. In G. Lindzey (Ed.), *Handbook of social psychology.* Vol. 2. New York: Addison-Wesley, 1954. Pp. 655–692.

Davis, A. American status systems and the socialization of the child. *American Sociological Review,* 1941, **6**, 345–354.

Davis, A. Child training and social class. In R. G. Barker, J. S. Kounin, & H. F. Wright (Eds.), *Child behavior and development.* New York: McGraw-Hill, 1943. Pp. 607–619.

Davis, A. *Social-class influences upon learning.* Cambridge, Mass.: Harvard University Press, 1948.

Dollard, J., Doob, L. W., Miller, N. E., Mowrer, O. H., & Sears, R. R. *Frustration and aggression.* New Haven: Yale University Press, 1939.

Doob, L. W., & Sears, R. R. Factors determining substitute behavior and the overt expression of aggression. *Journal of Abnormal and Social Psychology,* 1939, **34**, 293–313.

Duncan, O. D., & Davis, B. An alternative to ecological correlation. *American Sociological Review,* 1953, **18**, 665–666.

Duvall, E. N. Conceptions of parenthood. *American Journal of Sociology,* 1946, **52**, 193–203.

Eron, L. D., Banta, T. J., Walder, L. O., & Laulicht, J. H. Comparison of data obtained from mothers and fathers on childrearing practices and their relation to child aggression. *Child Development,* 1961, **32**, 457–472.

Glueck, S., & Glueck, E. *Unravelling juvenile delinquency.* Cambridge, Mass.: Harvard University Press, 1950.

Goldstein, A. Aggression and hostility in the elementary school in low socio-economic areas. *Understanding the Child,* 1955, **24**, 20–21.

Hollenberg, E. H., & Sperry, M. S. Some antecedents of aggression and effects of frustration in doll play. *Personality,* 1951, **1**, 32–43.

Kahl, J. A., & Davis, J. A. A comparison of indexes of socio-economic status. *American Sociological Review,* 1955, **20**, 317–325.

Lawson, E. D., & Boek, W. E. Correlations of indexes of families' socio-economic status. *Sociological Forces,* 1960, **39**, 149–152.

Lazarsfeld, P. F., & Menzel, H. On the relation between individual and collective properties. In A. Etzioni (Ed.), *Complex organization.* New York: Holt, 1961. Pp. 422–440.

Littman, R. A., Moore, R. C. A., & Pierce-Jones, J. Social class differences in child rearing: A third community for comparison with Chicago and Newton. *American Sociological Review,* 1957, **22**, 694–704.

Maccoby, E. E., Gibbs, P. K., et al. Methods of child rearing in two social classes. In W. E. Martin & C. B. Stendler (Eds.), *Readings in child development.* New York: Harcourt, Brace, 1954. Pp. 380–396.

McKee, J. P. The relationship between maternal behavior and the aggressive behavior of young children. Unpublished doctoral dissertation, State University of Iowa, 1949.

McKee, J. P., & Leader, F. B. The relationship of socio-economic status and aggression to the competitive behavior of preschool children. *Child Development,* 1955, **26**, 135–142.

Robinson, W. S. Ecological correlations and the behavior of individuals. *American Sociological Review,* 1950, **15**, 351–357.

Sears, R. R. Relation of early socialization experiences to aggression in middle childhood. *Journal of Abnormal and Social Psychology,* 1961, **63**, 466–492.

Sears, R. R., Maccoby, E. E., & Levin, H. *Patterns of child rearing.* New York: Harper & Row, 1957.

Seward, J. P. Aggressive behavior in the rat: IV. Submission as determined by conditioning, extinction, and disuse. *Journal of Comparative Psychology,* 1946, **39**, 51–76.

Stoltz, R. E., & Smith, M. D. Some effects of socio-economic, age and sex factors on children's responses to the Rosenzweig Picture-Frustration Study. *Journal of Clinical Psychology,* 1959, **15**, 200–203.

United States Bureau of Census. *1950 census of population: Classified index of occupations and industries.* Washington, D.C., 1950.

Walder, L. O., Abelson, R. P., Eron, L. D., Banta, T. J., & Laulicht, J. H. Development of a peer-rating measure of aggression. *Psychological Reports,* 1961, **9**, 497–556. (Monograph Supplement 4-V9)

Walder, L. O., Eron, L. D., Lefkowitz, M. M., & Toigo, R. Relationships of home and school aggression measures of third grade children. Unpublished manuscript, 1962.

V

PEER RELATIONS

Willard W. Hartup

Children are responsive to the behavior of their peers before the termination of babyhood. Observation of infants reared together in institutions or of babies brought together strictly for experimental purposes both confirm that peer influences on behavior are evident in infancy. At first, responsiveness to other babies consists of little more than orienting to the movements or sounds of other infants. By five months, however, most infants respond to the crying of other babies, and after this point, the complexity of infant-infant interactions increases markedly.

During the last half of the first year, contacts between babies are likely to consist of behaviors that are similar to the infant's approaches to play materials. That is, social behavior consists mainly of exploration, visual attending, and "hanging on." Fighting, principally over toys, is common during the first half of the second year. During the latter part of the second year, however, toys actually serve to facilitate positive social contact. Individual differences among babies in their responsiveness to peers have been noted by all investigators working in this area. The general

261

sequence in the development of age-mate interaction has been described in the results of several studies (e.g., Maudry & Nekula, 1939).

The determinants of these changes in age-mate interaction during infancy are largely unknown. Undoubtedly, the emergence of social behavior is correlated with changes occurring in perceptual and motor behavior, cognitive functioning, and emotional behavior. Recent evidence from comparative studies suggests that the early development of peer interactions in human infants is not unlike the pattern with which age-mate interaction develops in other species. Harlow & Harlow (1965), for example, found a four-stage sequence with which the age-mate affectional system develops in infant rhesus monkeys. First to appear was a "reflex stage," during which attending to other infants and following them were typical. Succeeding stages consisted of an "exploration stage," during which manipulation of other babies was common, and an "interactive stage" which was marked by vigorous roughhousing. At approximately one year of age, an "aggressive stage" occurred, during which social contact included aversive wrestling, biting, and squeezing.

The importance to the child's total development of early contact with peers is a matter of conjecture. Few human children are reared under conditions in which contact with other children (either siblings or nonrelated peers) is absent. Numerous one-child families live in remote places, but the social development of children reared under such conditions has not been described in the scientific literature. Such cases, however, would yield evidence that would have to be interpreted cautiously, since living completely apart from organized social groups is usually accompanied by various forms of environmental deprivation and genetic anomalies.

Other evidence suggests that early contact with peers may contribute importantly to the child's socialization. Several studies have shown that peer contact can serve a compensatory function when contact with parents or parent surrogates is inadequate. This evidence provides a basis for inferring that peer contacts are, indeed, of major significance to the child's personality and social development.

One group of compensatory studies has involved the rhesus monkey. Harlow & Harlow (1965) found that when infant monkeys are reared with no mother or with an artificial "mother" constructed of cloth and wire mesh, those animals who have contact with age mates appear to be similar to animals reared in the wild insofar as their later social behavior is concerned. On the other hand, complete isolation from other monkeys (from both mother and from peers) produces severe and long-lasting deficits in the young monkey's social behavior.

One experiment of nature, involving human infants, has yielded similar results. Freud & Dann (1951) carefully observed a group of six Jewish children who had lived in close contact with one another after their parents were killed in German concentration camps during World War II. The period of peer contact lasted from the time that the children were a few months old until they were about four years of age. When brought to England, these children showed many bizarre reactions to adults. On the other hand, their behavior toward each other was characterized by affection, proximity seeking, and helpfulness. The fact that the children were not psychotic or totally deficient in their social adjustment suggests that the close peer contacts they had experienced during their first several years served to offset the consequences of the disruption and violence that had occurred during that time. It is possible, of course, that there would have been little additional damage to these children even if peer contact had been absent, but this is difficult to believe.

Clearly, much potential lies in peer relations for furthering the development of social and personal competence in children. In most life situations, the impact of the peer culture occurs in conjunction with the impact of the adult culture. Thus, contact with peers has an additive or interactive effect on the child's development. Early childhood usually is a time when adult influences are paramount in the shaping of the child's behavior. It is probably not appropriate, however, to regard either adult influences or peer influences—one versus the other—as more important to the child's development after this period. If peers have any influence at all on the child's acquisition of the standards which govern behavior in social settings (norms), then the influence of peers is vital. Such is the case regardless of how much the child might also be learning from parents or teachers.

Thus, the crucial problem is not simply whether children are influenced by their peers; of greater significance is the discovery of those factors that determine the manner and extent to which the child will respond to the behavior of his age mates. It is important to remember, however, that individual differences among children in responsiveness to peer influences are marked. Also, even though an individual child may be generally disposed to imitate his peers or to yield to their persuasions, such responsiveness is likely to vary considerably from situation to situation. In other words, while there may be some cross-situational generality in children's responsiveness to peers, there is also considerable situational specificity in yielding to peer influences. Indeed, one cannot predict children's yielding behavior without knowing something about the larger cultural context, the peer exerting the pressure, and the salience of the task for the child.

PRESCHOOL YEARS **Patterns of peer interaction**

Given these considerations, research has shown that important and pervasive changes occur during the child's early years in the way he interacts with age mates. Most of the pertinent data are derived from studies of children enrolled in nursery schools. Relatively little is known about children's interactions with each other during the preschool years as these occur at home, in the neighborhood, or in other social gatherings. Nevertheless, some of the more important trends revealed in research findings can probably be generalized rather widely.

It has long been known that the amount and nature of social participation changes extensively during the preschool years. Mildred Parten, in a classic series of studies conducted during the late 1920s, found that as nursery-school children become older, they engage more frequently in associative and cooperative activities with age mates and less frequently in solitary play, onlooker behavior, and isolated play. More recent investigators have found that such interactions are infused with behaviors that carry weight as social reinforcers or social rewards. Charlesworth & Hartup (1967) studied the occurrence of four types of positive social reinforcers as these took place during the peer interactions of nursery-school children. Included were: giving positive attention and approval, giving affection and personal acceptance, submitting to the demands of other children, and giving tangible objects to others. These behaviors occurred significantly more frequently in the interactions of four-year-olds than in the play of three-year-olds. The findings also showed that giving such social rewards to others was associated with receiving them, and most children who supplied frequent reinforcement to other children tended to direct their positive behaviors to relatively many children.

Needless to say, the behaviors observed by Charlesworth and Hartup do not include all of the peer interactions that sustain or maintain behavior (i.e., that carry reinforcing value). Almost any social act can acquire reinforcing value, even aggressive behavior, depending on the learning history of the individual child. It is also clear that some behaviors carry weight as reinforcers for certain types of activity, but not for others. For example, some of the types of peer reinforcement that sustain aggressive behavior are undoubtedly different from the peer-group responses that sustain dependent activity. Thus, the child's learning history appears to determine the incentive value of particular peer behaviors which, to some extent, is specific to the kind of behavior in question.

As previously discussed in Chapter IV, Patterson, Littman, & Bricker (1967) were able to demonstrate that specific reactions of the peer group serve to reinforce aggressive acts in nursery-school children. The reader will recall that when aggression was followed by passivity, crying, or defensiveness, the attacking child would tend to aggress again toward his initial victim. On the other hand, counteraggression tended to change the aggressor's behavior. Either he changed his response toward the victim, chose a new victim, or both. It would appear possible then that within the totality of children's interactions, certain classes of behaviors that sustain particular responses by the recipient—in this case, aggression—can be identified. Although these same peer actions may also sustain other behavior classes (e.g., dependency), the results help to clarify the particular peer interactions that are pertinent to children's aggression. The results also show that some social environments provide unexpectedly high rates of positive peer reinforcement for antisocial behavior.

All social groups do not provide the same types of peer reinforcement in the same quantities. Attention giving and other positive reinforcers occur with sharply different frequencies in various nursery-school classrooms, and they also vary in accordance with the kinds of activity taking place within the classroom. For example, dramatic play is associated with much more frequent peer reinforcement than table activities. It appears, then, that the ecology of children's peer groups is an important determinant of the kinds of interaction that are shown in the group. Additional data, obtained with preadolescent boys, confirm the findings with nursery-school children (Gump, Schoggen, & Redl, 1957). Among boys attending a summer camp, it was found that vigorous interactions with peers (e.g., assertiveness, frustration attempts, and attack) occurred more frequently during swimming periods than during crafts periods. Helping behaviors, however, occurred more frequently during the latter activity. Here, then, is further evidence concerning a major characteristic of peer interaction: Children's behavior toward age mates and the consequences of such behavior are functionally related to the situation.

Some additional social behaviors that change with increasing age include the following: (1) Dependency directed toward peers, relative to dependency directed toward adults, increases from age two to age five; (2) Sympathy and altruism increase slowly during this period; (3) Ascendance increases during this period and appears to stabilize during middle childhood; (4) Competition, particularly in response to instructions emphasizing comparative evaluation of performance, increases sharply during the preschool years; (5) Quarreling decreases, but quarrels are likely to last longer; (6) Aggressive activity increases somewhat, but tends to decline after the nursery-school years.

Qualitative changes in peer interaction, however, must not be minimized in this accounting of quantitative changes. In the case of aggressive activity, it is relatively clear that age changes in total aggression differ according to the child's sex. The lesser aggressiveness of girls is more apparent at age six than at age three. Further, physical aggression, along with crying and screaming, tends to decline during early childhood, and there is some evidence to show that verbal aggression increases during this period.

Thus, a child's peers come to elicit a variety of responses during the nursery-school years. But peer behavior also seems to exert some very specific forms of social control over the behavior of individual children. Reinforcing control has already been mentioned. Peers also influence the individual child in a variety of other ways. They serve as models for the child and as sources of "contagious" influence.

Two recent studies illustrate the manner in which peers function as models during early childhood. As indicated in the previous chapter, Hicks (1965) was able to show that nursery-school children reproduce the aggressive actions of other children whose behavior has been displayed through the medium of a movie film. In evaluating the results of this study, it is important to recognize that the peer-modeling effects were found with respect to the specific behaviors shown by the model (e.g., striking a Bobo doll). It is not known whether exposure to the peer models produced generalized effects wherein other forms of aggression became more pronounced.[1] Neither is it known whether the film-

---

[1] Studies using aggressive adult models suggest that this may be the case.

mediated peer modeling produced more aggressiveness in the setting of the nursery school; this last issue is an important one and can be raised with respect to almost all of the research in the field of peer influences. Research workers have created ingenious life-like situations for the study of various forms of peer influences; little has been done, however, to test the generalizability of these influences. It is imperative, therefore, that caution be used in considering how widely the results of peer-influence studies, including studies of peer modeling, may be generalized.

Another study (Hartup & Coates, 1967, reprinted following the chapter) shows that peer models can affect the prosocial behavior of the young child. Young children were exposed to another nursery-school-aged child who displayed an unusually high level of "sharing behavior." Modeling effects were clearly apparent. That is, those children who had an opportunity to observe a sharing peer model subsequently shared more of their materials than did children who had had no opportunity to observe a model.

Although the young child is influenceable through peer reinforcement and peer modeling, he is not as sensitive to normative influence as are older children. That is, young children's peer groups are not bound together by the complex network of shared standards, values, and rules that operate within peer groups of older children. Young children certainly comply with rules, but primarily such compliance is to rules imposed by authority figures. The young child's peer group itself tends to generate relatively few standards for guiding conduct. Thus, the period is one of "social egocentrism," according to Piaget. Overall there is less compliance, conformity, and yielding to be found among young children with respect to peer-produced social norms than among older children.

It should be made clear, though, that norm sharing is not totally absent in young children's groups; such collectives do generate certain primitive norms. For example, two-year-olds who have been reared in Israeli "kibbutzim" have been observed to distinguish clearly the in-group from various out-groups ("we" versus "they"), to defend each other when quarrels occur with an out-group child, and to have, as one of their common interests, an investment in role-playing activities (Faigin, 1958). Traditions such as a spontaneous consensus about seating arrangements, agreement concerning the ownership of objects, and the development of certain simple rituals and ceremonies are also evident in groups of young children. These standards of conduct, however, appear to be less binding and are applied less consistently than the codes and rules developed by children in preadolescent or adolescent groups.

It is also true that young children's behavior in ordinary conformity or yielding tasks is very difficult to predict. In one study, kindergarten children were asked to choose a line from among a group of comparison lines that would match the length of a standard line (Hunt & Synnerdahl, 1959). The subjects' choices were given after exposure to false judgments from peer confederates. One hundred and eighty judgments were obtained from ten children, and it was found that only 12 percent were in the same direction as the false judgments. These results contrast sharply with results obtained for older children, as will be seen in a later section of this chapter.

Status in the peer group

Even though responsiveness to peer influences is not especially pervasive in groups of young children, such groups are structured in ways that are similar to groups of older children. That is, young children differentiate their companions according to whether they "like" them and can respond reliably to "Guess Who" types of inquiry (e.g., "Who is the child who is always mean to the other children?"). Direct questioning of young children shows that their groups possess a hierarchical structure. Some children are popular, others are less popular or rejected; some children are leaders, in the sense that they are particularly successful in influencing the behavior of their fellows. Such structuring has been found by observing group interaction, as well as by sociometric questioning of the type mentioned above.

Over time, how stable are the structures found in young children's groups? It is sometimes thought that the friendships and associations of young children are extremely ephemeral, in fact, that they change radically from day to day. Recent evidence contradicts this notion. Sociometric techniques have been improved a great deal during recent years. The invention of the "picture sociometric test" is one major technological advance. Each child is interviewed individually, and he is presented with an array of pictures showing all of the children in his group. After carefully naming the pictures, the child is then asked to make choices concerning his friends and his enemies. The use of an individualized test, with pictures, apparently minimizes the contaminating effects on the results of what the child was doing immediately before the test. On the basis of data derived from such tests, stability coefficients ranging between .41 and .76 have been found for several different subgroups of nursery-school children who were tested and retested at twenty-day intervals (McCandless & Marshall, 1957). More recently, it has been reported by one group of investigators (Hartup, Glazer, & Charlesworth, 1967) that such scores were correlated, on a test-retest basis, at a magnitude of .68 when the test interval was five months. The foregoing findings indicate both that sociometric tests are reasonably reliable (they provide *consistent* measures of social status) and that status itself is a reasonably stable phenomenon.

It should be emphasized that the sociometric tests, on which the foregoing findings were based, consisted of positive choices. That is, the sociometric score consisted of the number of times that a child was chosen as a "liked" peer by the other members of the group. The small amount of existing evidence that concerns social rejection in groups of young children suggests that being disliked is far less stable than being liked. One reason for this may be that the behaviors manifested by disliked children are less consistently reinforced by the environment (both adults and peers), and this acts to lessen the stability of rejection scores over time.

The purpose of most sociometric studies has been to assess the degree to which a child's peers wish to have some positive, friendly contact with him. These may be considered as studies of social acceptance or popularity. Sociometric tests are also used to assess the extent to which a child is ignored by the peer group, is disliked by it, is respected, is seen as a "powerful" person, or is seen as a leader. The fact that investigators have used such varied criteria in their sociometric studies points up the fact that social status is a multidimensional, rather than a unidimensional, aspect of group structure. The reader should, therefore, attend closely to the particular sociometric criterion that is involved in each of the studies mentioned in the following pages.

The behavior of popular and unpopular children is not markedly different when nursery-school children are contrasted with older children. Large quantities of data concerning the correlates of sociometric status are available in the literature of child psychology. Following is a brief summary that pulls together the results of many studies.

First, it is relatively clear that popular preschool children are more friendly, sociable, outgoing, altruistic, and positively reinforcing to their peers than are less popular children. It should be pointed out that lack of friendliness is only associated with low acceptance; it has not been found to be associated with high rejection. This finding underscores the necessity of carefully considering the type of sociometric measures used in any given study of peer relations. Low popularity must not be equated with social rejection. The child who is not popular, in the sense that he receives few positive sociometric choices, may simply be ignored by his fellows. On the other hand, some other children who also receive few choices, may be actively rejected. To recapitulate: Popular children are outgoing and friendly, but rejected children are not necessarily unsociable nor unfriendly. It has also been found that accepted children are generally socially appropriate in their behavior, that they comply to both peer and adult requests, and that they are generally cooperative. In short, popular young children appear to be well on the way toward the internalization of appropriate social standards. The reader should note that the relation between compliance and popularity is positive. This should not be interpreted to mean that the popular child is submissive or conformity prone. On the contrary, the data suggest that he is simply an effective mediator in his social group and responsive to the needs and wants of others.

The popular preschool child is also likely to be dependent, but on peers rather than heavily on adults. They are also likely to manifest dependent behavior of a socially mature type (such as the seeking of help or approval) rather than in immature ways (such as seeking affection, showing off, and so forth). Thus, with respect to dependency, the popular child appears to differ qualitatively from the less popular child, rather than quantitatively. The same appears to be true with respect to aggressiveness. Popular children are not necessarily less aggressive than non-popular children. On the other hand, they appear to be more direct and reality oriented in their aggression than nonpopular children. Here once again, however, it is necessary to distinguish between the sociometric dimensions of acceptance and rejection. The above findings hold only for social acceptance. When a young child's social status is measured in terms of the frequency with which he is disliked, different results emerge. Disliked children are clearly more aggressive, in terms of total amount, than are children who are not disliked.

The foregoing paragraphs summarize characteristics which research has shown to differentiate popular from nonpopular preschool children. Other factors, including IQ, social class, birth order, and personality adjustment play a role in determining the older child's status with his peers, but these variables have not been extensively explored in relation to the popularity of young children.

Turning now to the peer interactions of children in middle childhood, the following two topics will be emphasized: group behavior and peer influences on individual children. Some research with adolescents will be discussed in this section, but the principal stress will be on findings obtained with children between the ages of six and thirteen. **MIDDLE CHILDHOOD**

Considerable continuity exists in peer interaction between the preschool years and middle childhood, but the latter period is sharply different in several important ways. First, patterns of interaction and preference become more stable in middle childhood. Second, norms become a much more salient feature of group behavior. Finally, responsiveness to peer influences in the form of conformity, suggestibility, and modeling all become much more common than in early childhood.

Group behavior

Peer groups emerge and function under a variety of conditions. Implicit in the concept of "group" is the notion of interaction. That is, groups are composed of individuals who communicate with one another. But groups, as opposed to conglomerations of individuals, also possess common goals, values, or norms. Furthermore, all groups sooner or later develop a hierarchical structure. In some instances, individual children can be brought together (as in a schoolroom), and group norms and a social structure can be imposed from external sources. This is what every teacher does when special-project groups are constituted. Other groups, however, develop spontaneously. The attributes of communication, norms, and structure are important features of group behavior in any setting, regardless of how the group originated.

Group Formation

The formation of informal peer groups has been described by numerous investigators. Sherif, Harvey, White, Hood, & Sherif (1961) have described this process with great clarity, using groups of preadolescent boys as subjects. The Sherif study was conducted under naturalistic conditions, but experimental manipulations were also imposed. Thus, the results yield a clear picture of some of the factors that influence group formation. This type of methodology is particularly desirable and appropriate in studies of peer-group interaction, but is used too infrequently.

In the Sherif study, 22 fifth-graders were taken to a summer camp. Two matched subgroups of eleven boys each were constituted from this sample. Neither group knew of the other group's presence in camp during the initial phases of the experiment. The children were carefully observed by the counselors (who were really participant observers). A variety of observational and sociometric data were secured. Each of these groups became cohesive units within a few days. A hierarchical structure became visible, leadership positions became clearly defined, and social-status levels became polarized. Although there was a positive relation between leadership and popularity, it is important to note that this correlation was not perfect. Group norms developed within a short period. Each group selected certain activities that it valued and places in camp that were considered special. When the presence of the other group was finally detected, the number of norms increased. Group names, codes of conduct, badges, and so forth were adopted. Thus, an initially conglomerate set of individuals, when brought together with a common purpose (camping activity), developed into a cohesive and structured society.

A second purpose of this study was to examine the consequences of bringing the two groups into contact under conditions of competition and frustration. A series of contests was arranged with the outcomes rigged so that neither group was more successful than the other. That is, sometimes one group was successful while the other failed, and at other times, the outcome of the competition was reversed. This intergroup competition increased the amount of hostility manifested between groups. In general, the solidarity of each group was intensified by the conflict, although temporary disruption in in-group cohesiveness was also apparent at times when a group failed in the competition.

To some extent, the organization of each of the groups changed after the competitions began. Those boys who were skillful in sports tended to rise in status. This finding underscores one very important point—leadership tends, in part, to be a function of the situation or the values that are operative in a group at a given moment. While some individual children seem to be leaders in many different situations and in many different peer groups, it is still the case that leadership, in some degree, is situationally determined. As soon as a leader's behavior becomes tangential or inappropriate to the group's main activities, a new leader will emerge. The results of the study (Sherif et al., 1961) are extremely clear on this point.

One of the main outcomes of this second phase of the Sherif experiment is the finding that competition and conflict in intergroup relations tend to increase intergroup hostility. Such results have obvious practical, as well as theoretical, significance. There are particularly important implications here for those who work with children's groups and for those who would use group experience as a mechanism for reducing ethnic and other social tensions.

A final phase of this study relates specifically to the reduction of intergroup hostility. If intragroup cohesiveness is enhanced by the existence of a common goal, then cooperative goal-directed activity should act to reduce the conflict between two hostile groups. In the present experiment, the investigators contrived several instances in which both groups had to work together on high-incentive tasks (e.g., restoring the water supply and fixing the food truck). These experiences did, in fact, reduce the hostility between the groups, and friendship choices across groups began to occur.

The norms endorsed by preadolescent and adolescent groups vary widely. No broad-scale taxonomic attempt to describe the norms of United States children's groups has ever been made. Existing data suggest that group loyalty is one pervasive norm, and in adolescent groups, there is considerable emphasis on emancipation from the home and the assumption of adult-like roles. Ordinarily, appropriate sex-typed behavior is valued in most children's groups. To a considerable extent, however, group norms vary as a function of factors such as social class, ethnicity, and the subculture. Values, goals, and aspirations tend to vary in particular. Recent work by Sherif & Sherif (1964), though, shows that peer-group loyalty, excellence in sports, and emancipation from the adult culture are norms held by adolescent peer groups in virtually every socioeconomic segment of United States culture.

Influences on Group Functioning

Some of the factors that influence group behavior have already been mentioned. For example, the situation itself, including the types of activities in which the group engages, is a powerful influence on the selection of leaders, the polarization of social-status positions, and the types of interaction that occur between the group members. The adult supervisors of children's groups are also important determinants of peer interaction. In a series of well-known studies, Lewin, Lippitt, & White (1939) found that "authoritarian" leadership generally produced disharmony and disruption in group functioning as compared to what was called "democratic" leadership. The climate created by a sort of dicta-torial adult leadership was either aggressive or apathetic; work tended to be sporadic in the leader's absence; in both authori-tarian and "laissez faire" climates, hostility was relatively fre-quent. The authoritarian groups tended to be less cohesive al-though peer dependence and friendly overtures did not vary as a function of adult-leadership style.

These studies are important because they make the general point that the style of adult leadership is one important situa-tional influence on the functioning of children's groups. There is some question, however, as to whether we can say that au-thoritarian leadership inevitably leads to the kinds of group be-havior found in the study. The leader-experimenters selected in this study were pretty much committed to a democratic phi-losophy (even though they played various leadership roles in rotation), and the children all came from essentially democratic homes. It may be that a "benevolent dictator" would not create the aggressive or apathetic social climates recorded in these data. Thus, there are a number of ways in which these studies can and should be extended. In the meantime it is clear that the type of adult supervision provided for children's groups is, in general, an important determinant of the kinds of interaction taking place in such groups.

Other research (Kipnis, 1958) shows that the type of leader-ship that is imposed on children's groups affects the results of the sanctions that the leader uses. For example, it was found that when rewards constituted the mechanism being used to change behavior, participatory ("democratic") leadership produced more change than a lecture procedure. Conversely, when punishment for noncompliance was the technique employed, the lecture method produced more change than participatory leadership.

Other studies have focused directly on cooperation and com-petition as factors affecting intragroup behavior. With grade-school children, it has usually been found that assignment to cooperative tasks produces more frequent instances of friendly conversation, offers of assistance, and sharing of materials than does assignment to competitive tasks. The effects of competition are more variable. It will be recalled from the study of Sherif et al. (1961) that competition (in spite of temporary disruption of group solidarity) actually increased cohesiveness within each of the peer groups studied. Another team of investigators (Phillips & D'Amico, 1956) has found, however, that it is difficult to predict the outcome of competitive experience with respect to group cohesiveness. Whether a group's cohesiveness changes under competition seems to be dependent upon whether the group itself decides to distribute its labor so that equitable rewards result from the competitive experience. If so, cohesiveness remains at its initial level or actually increases. If the group does not respond to competition in this manner, then solidarity is likely to be disrupted. Thus, the manner in which a group itself adjusts to competition is one factor in determining the effects of such experience on intragroup relations.

Other situational influences on group behavior include the size of the group, the composition of the group, patterns of reinforcement to which the group is exposed, and the expectations possessed by group members concerning the results of group action. Research concerning these factors is too extensive to be reviewed in detail here, but the following paragraphs summarize some of the relevant findings.

Interpersonal behavior is clearly different in large groups of children as compared to small groups. The leaders in larger groups must be more skillful; consensus is harder to reach; the members feel that their own opinions are less important; and general cohesiveness is likely to be lower. When the group's purpose is to exert persuasive influence on one of its members, this influence is likely to vary as a curvilinear function of the group's size. Research with children is not extensive on this point, but generally such influence increases as the group's size varies from two to about seven or eight, at which point an asymptote is reached.

Groups made up of friends are likely to reach closure on discussion problems faster than do groups composed of nonfriends. In group-study sessions, nonfriends are more likely to behave in an independent nonreciprocating manner. Hence, while groups of friends are sometimes more productive when working together than when working alone, this difference is less apparent when study groups are comprised of nonfriends. Homogeneity in attitudes and personal biases also tends to promote greater spontaneity in group discussion, more talk, and fewer disagreements than when a group is composed of children holding diverse viewpoints.

Reinforcement conditions can affect the quality of a group's behavior. That is, contingencies of extrinsic reinforcement act to determine the nature of the interaction taking place in the group. Azrin & Lindsley's (1956) study of two-child groups (dyads) dramatically illustrates this point. In this experiment, reinforcement was contingently dispensed to the subjects whenever they simultaneously placed a stylus in designated holes on a board. In this study, social "cooperation" was the type of response necessary for solution of the experimental problem. The reinforcement consisted of candy and was given to each child after every correct cooperative response. The experimenter provided reinforcement for cooperation for at least fifteen minutes, after which, an extinction period was introduced. The findings revealed sharp increases in cooperative responding during the acquisition phase and a decrease after the extinction procedure was introduced. Weingold & Webster (1964) found, in an extension of this study, that punishment (losing a point during the "game") hastened the extinction of cooperative responding.

Situational factors sometimes affect group behavior differently, according to the types of children composing the group. For instance, the effects of different leadership styles may depend on the ability of the children or personality factors. One example of research that shows an interaction between situational and subject factors in group behavior is provided by Lott & Lott (1966). These investigators found that the group's cohesiveness was positively related to output on a verbal-learning task providing that the group was composed of high-IQ children. Those who were placed in cohesive groups did better than those placed in noncohesive groups. For less bright children, there was a tendency for the children placed in noncohesive groups to outperform those placed in cohesive groups. The results suggest that when a task is easy (as this one would have been for bright children), interaction in a close-knit group adds an incentive which enhances each child's performance. On the other hand, such incentives may disrupt performance when the task is more difficult, as would have been the case for the less bright children. There are myriad ways in which personal factors can interact with situational factors to affect group behavior. This one example shows that the milieu in which the group functions, including the cohesiveness of the group, affects behavior to an extent that depends on the types of children making up the group. Indeed, prediction of group behavior in childhood is a complex rather than a simple matter.

Several studies show how expectations and past experience affect the functioning of children's groups. Again, important interactions are present. For example, information concerning what one's partner expects to obtain during a bargaining task seems to heighten the number of equalitarian decisions reached, providing that the subjects are friends (Morgan & Sawyer, 1967). Pairs of nonfriends, on the other hand, are almost always equalitarian in the decisions they reach (i.e., they will not permit their partners to get away with anything). But nonfriends reach their equalitarian decisions faster when they know what their opponents expect than when this information is not available. Thus, among friends, foreknowledge affects the type of decision made in bargaining tasks; among nonfriends, foreknowledge affects the speed with which the decision is reached.

Past group experience also affects the behavior of children working together. Goldberg & Maccoby (1965) studied second-grade children who had previously participated in group tower building. Some of the subjects had participated in four different groups; others had worked for four sessions in the same group. When all of the subjects were transferred to a final group for testing, the output of those children who had worked in one group was superior to the output of children who had worked in four different groups. Of course, this study permitted the children who worked in different groups to have only one work session in each group. Consequently, we do not know if longer experience in many different groups would have produced debilitating effects on performance. But other results from this study suggest that children require some period of time working with one group of partners to develop the easy-going, equalitarian, cooperative techniques required for effective group performance. Without this opportunity, individual performance is variable and not as effective as when opportunity for repeated association with one group of partners is provided.

Status in the Peer Group

Turning now to status in groups of preadolescents and adolescents, we find that the behavioral characteristics associated with high status do not differ markedly from those that characterize popular younger children. Friendliness, for example, is associated with acceptance during middle childhood and in adolescence just as among nursery-school children. It is interesting, however, that friendliness (sociability) is more closely related to popularity during adolescence than it is to what can be called "prestige."

Undoubtedly, the relation between friendliness and social acceptance is reciprocally caused. That is, friendliness may make the child salient in his peer group and enhance his attractiveness, but it is probably also true that positive endorsement by the peer group motivates the child to be outgoing and friendly. It is also possible that attributes such as intelligence and good internalization of social standards enhance both sociability and popularity. The fact that friendliness and popularity are correlated tells us relatively little about the causal factors involved in this relation. The data do establish that these traits covary, and it is important to know this. On the other hand, those persons who are interested in "what causes what" are left somewhat up in the air by findings such as these.

Research with elementary-school-age children also reveals that there is a relation between popularity and certain forms of dependency and aggression. Immature dependence (e.g., negative attention getting, showing off, and the like) is negatively associated with being liked by the peer group, and indirect aggression also characterizes the less popular child. On the other hand, "mature" dependent overtures are actually shown more frequently by popular children than their less popular peers; the same is also true of direct physical aggression. Thus, once again, we see that the relation between many personality attributes and popularity is not a simple one.

Anxiety and adjustment are also related to popularity. Most investigators who have employed paper-and-pencil tests of anxiety, such as the Children's Manifest Anxiety Scale, report low negative correlations between anxiety and popularity among children in the intermediate grades of elementary school. In at least one study (Hill, 1963) important sex differences have been revealed in the relation between anxiety and popularity. These sex differences involve popularity with opposite-sex peers rather than same-sex peers. Specifically, boys tended to prefer low-anxious girls (who are somewhat more masculine in behavior than their high-anxious counterparts), whereas girls tended to prefer high-anxious boys (who are somewhat more feminine than low-anxious boys). It should be pointed out that these subjects were elementary-school children who ordinarily choose same-sex peers on sociometric tests more frequently than opposite-sex peers. Consequently, it is interesting that, when compelled to make choices from among children of the opposite sex, Hill's subjects tended to select those children whose behavior most closely resembled the child's own sex.

Self-esteem also bears a relation to popularity, although the relation is not a simple linear one. Specifically, Reese (1961) reported that children whose self-concepts were moderately positive were more acceptable to their peers than either children with low or with high self-concepts. Data are lacking, but children with low and high self-concepts may be unpopular for different reasons. The child with inordinately low self-esteem may possess a variety of socially undesirable characteristics such as being less bright, less successful academically, less sociable, and so on. On the other hand, the child who evaluates himself very highly may be rejected because he behaves in ways which antagonize his peers, such as being overconfident and snobbish. Further research is needed in order to clarify these results. Nevertheless, we already know that self-esteem is not related to popularity in a simple fashion.

A large body of evidence suggests that bright children are more popular than less bright children. This conclusion is based on two types of studies: (1) investigations in which IQ data have been correlated with sociometric data in unselected populations of school children, and (2) research focusing on the social relations of gifted children, on the one hand, and retarded children on the other. Many of the studies with ordinary school children are difficult to interpret because popularity is related to both IQ and social class, and, further, because IQ and social class are correlated with each other. Consequently, the correlation between IQ and popularity could be due to an independent relation between social class and peer acceptance. One recent study (Roff & Sells, 1965, reprinted at the end of this chapter) has supplied evidence which clarifies this issue. A large population of Minnesota schoolchildren was divided into four socioeconomic groups. This was accomplished on the basis of census records. Then IQs of popular and nonpopular children were compared at each social-class level. The results showed clearly that the popular children were brighter than the nonpopular children when social class was held constant. The mean differences in IQ between popular and nonpopular children varied from twelve to twenty points. Thus, there seems to be unequivocal evidence that the relation between IQ and popularity is positive.

Surprisingly, the contribution made by social class to a child's peer status is not clearly elucidated in research. Perhaps the best study of this problem is by Grossman & Wrighter (1948). These investigators divided a group of sixth-graders into three IQ levels. It was found at each level that there was a positive association between the child's socioeconomic background (as measured by the father's occupation) and the popularity of the child. There is a need for more data on this particular question, however, than currently exist.

Academic success is positively correlated with acceptance and so are athletic skill, strength, and attractive physical appearance. To some extent, school grades are more highly associated with prestige (i.e., social power) than they are with popularity. All of the research in this area suggests that the child who possesses a wide variety of culturally approved attributes is likely to enjoy higher status in his peer group than the child who is less well endowed.

Once again, we must be cautious concerning the manner in which these data are interpreted. Preadolescents and adolescents who are not bright, attractive, and athletic may not be accepted for these reasons, but a lack of acceptance (for some other reason) may actually depress performance in school, lower self-esteem, and so forth. It is difficult, however, to account for the relation between social class and popularity in this manner. This relation is undoubtedly mediated by values and behaviors associated with social class, and these have not been well documented in research. That is, social class does not cause behavior, as such; only factors associated with socioeconomic background do. There is some evidence that competiveness and participation in school activities are valued more highly by upper-class adolescents than by middle- and lower-class adolescents. It is class differences such as these that may play key roles in determining the relation between socioeconomic background and popularity that has been reported in research.

Success experiences also play a role in determining peer status. In one experimental study (Flanders & Havumaki, 1960), one-half of the students in one simulated class received attention and praise from the teacher-experimenter, while the other half was largely ignored. In another class, the teacher directed praise and attention to the group as a whole. It was found that the individual recipients of praise in class 1 received a disproportionate number of positive sociometric choices as compared to the more-or-less even distribution of such choices in class 2. Other investigators have reported that school failure is associated with low peer status. These findings, of course, could be generated by the many complex factors associated with such failure rather than by the failure experience itself.

Merely experiencing success in the company of other children will enhance the social attractiveness of those same children. Lott & Lott (1960) divided a sample of elementary-school children into small groups for the purpose of playing a "rocket game." One-half of the children obtained rewards for successful performance, while the remainder of the subjects did not. Afterward, socio-metric data revealed that the children who had experienced success singled out the other members of their play group as preferred companions more frequently than did the subjects who had played the game in nonrewarded groups. It would appear that the attraction between individuals, which is the basis for status in the peer group, is a product of both the rewards a child receives from others and the degree to which other children have received reinforcement in his presence.

As mentioned earlier, "leadership" refers to the capacity to influence the behavior of other people. To some extent, leader-ship can be considered as a personality attribute. Some children seem to possess social power and to be respected or admired in many different peer groups. The specific situation, however, also determines the designation of leaders. Thus, it is necessary to consider situational sources of variance in any analysis of leadership behavior in children's groups.

These two considerations with respect to leadership are both emphasized in a survey study of adolescents' perceptions of social power that was conducted by Rosen, Levinger, & Lippitt (1961). First, a high degree of consensus existed among these students concerning traits that were believed to characterize leaders. These traits included helpfulness, fairness, sociability, expertness, fearlessness, and physical strength. The subjects rank ordered these traits in the order given. Next, the subjects were asked to rank order these same six traits with respect to their importance in several specific social situations. The initial rank ordering (as given above) prevailed when the hypothetical social situation consisted of such events as organizing a party or con-ducting a meeting. The order shifted markedly, however, if the reference situation consisted of dissuading an angry crowd or training a group of commandos. In these social situations, fear-lessness and physical strength were placed much higher in the rank ordering than they were with respect to the other social situations. Thus, in adolescents' perceptions of social power, there is a limited degree of cross-situational generality in those characteristics that are believed to distinguish the high-power child. Equally important is the finding that the nature of the social situation itself makes a great deal of difference in the designation of leaders in children's groups.

Leadership qualities are associated with many of the same traits that characterize the popular child. Leaders are high in sociability, have good social and emotional adjustment, and are likely to have positive self-concepts. Leaders are high in the instigation of direct social-influence attempts and are also sources of "contagious" influence. Aggressiveness is characteristic of male leaders, but is not consistently related to leadership in girls. One investigation showed, however, that aggressiveness is a characteristic of leaders depending on their intellectual ability. Zander & Van Egmond (1958) found that among low-IQ boys, leaders were more aggressive than nonleaders; among high-IQ boys, aggressiveness did not differentiate leaders from nonleaders.

Leaders of children's groups are generally aware of their status in the group. This is revealed by the fact that there is a high correlation between self-ratings and other children's ratings of social power. In some studies, leadership has been shown to be correlated with willingness to "follow," but studies of social behavior in boys' camps suggest that leaders tend to resist the direct influence attempts of their less powerful peers. Thus, overall, leaders in children's groups tend to be sociable, assertive, and bright; they are able to hold their own in social interchange, but are usually not ruthless and socially insensitive. In fact, observations usually show that once a leader's actions begin to disenchant or distress the members of an informal peer group, a change in leadership takes place.

Influences on the individual child

Peer influence in the form of conformity, suggestion, modeling, persuasion, and behavior contagion increases during middle childhood. Much of the research in this area has consisted of laboratory studies in which experimenters have simulated real-life social-influence situations. Experimental procedures are usually ingenious, but it is important to remember that we are still largely ignorant concerning the extent to which experimental results may be generalized to informal peer groups or to more formal groups such as those found in schools and other community institutions. The research concerning the forms of peer influence mentioned above is of two general types: Some studies deal with situational correlates; others emphasize personality factors as these affect the child's susceptibility to the influence of his peers.

Age Changes

The most explicit theoretical base from which to predict age differences in children's responsiveness to peer pressures has been formulated by Piaget. In one of his early volumes, *The Moral Judgment of the Child* (1932), Piaget postulated that the child's responsiveness to peers passes through three major stages. The first is an egocentric stage which lasts until the child is approximately six. During this period, the child's level of cognitive functioning and his lack of extensive interaction with peers produce a rather casual and indifferent attitude toward rules or norms emanating from the peer culture. At this time, children may be responsive to social pressures, but usually the pressures are of an absolutistic sort, such as those emanating from adults. Play is essentially egocentric. The child is unable to imagine himself in another person's shoes, and full social intercourse with age mates is lacking.

A second stage, which lasts until about the eleventh year, is marked by extreme conformity and responsiveness to peer influences; solidarity in peer relationships is marked. At this time, conformity to peer pressures is almost its own raison d'être. The child sees social rules as coercive and binding.

A third stage begins when the child understands that social rules develop from group consensus. The idea that rule application is not invariant is fully grasped. During early adolescence, when social norms are understood as emanating from the initiative of the individual children composing the peer group, there is a lessening of the universal conformity to peer influences that characterizes middle childhood. In short, Piaget's theory suggests that conformity to peer influences is a curvilinear function of age from the preschool years through late adolescence.

Research concerning age changes in conformity is extensive but fragmented. Although there are many studies, few span the entire period mentioned above. Making comparisons across studies is hampered by the fact that different experimenters have used different procedures for measuring conformity and for selecting subjects. Nevertheless, a consistent picture of age differences in conformity to peer influences emerges when one examines this literature as a whole. The evidence unmistakably confirms the hypotheses suggested by Piaget's theories.

We have already reported that preschool children do not consistently conform to peer norms. However, Berenda (1950) reported that children between the ages of seven and thirteen readily yield to group norms in conformity situations. Berenda used a kind of "prestige" conformity situation, in that the influence source in her studies consisted of the eight brightest children in the subjects' classes. Age differences were relatively slight, but there was somewhat less responsiveness to peer influences among the eleven- to thirteen-year-olds than among the seven- to ten-year-olds. McConnell (1963) found that yielding to false peer judgments concerning the similarity of geometric figures was relatively high between the ages of six and thirteen, but progressively declined between fourteen and eighteen. In a series of studies done in Texas, Iscoe, Williams, & Harvey (1963, 1964) found that conformity in a click-counting task increased between ages seven and twelve (for Caucasian children) and declined thereafter for girls, remaining high for boys until fifteen. For Negro children, conformity increased between ages seven and nine, declining after that.

Perhaps the most comprehensive study of age differences in yielding to peer pressures was completed by Costanzo & Shaw (1966); this study is reprinted following the chapter. Here, subjects ranged in age between seven and twenty-one years. Conformity was relatively low among children between seven and nine; it was highest among children between eleven and thirteen; and it was low once more for subjects between nineteen and twenty-one years of age.

The overall pattern in the findings is remarkably clear. Conformity to peer norms increases during middle childhood, peaking during preadolescence. The timing of this peak has varied from one set of research results to another. In the studies of Texas Negro children, this peak period occurred as early as nine, whereas in other studies, it occurred as late as fifteen. As will be shown in later sections of this chapter, conformity is subject to many different situational influences. That is, conformity may vary according to the type of problem used to measure yielding, the attractiveness of the influence source, the background of the subjects, and so forth. These influences could be responsible for the inconsistencies across studies. Far more important is the fact that the general pattern of the findings is quite consistent. That is, middle childhood (just as Piaget suggested) is the period at which the child is most susceptible to the attitudes, values, and judgments of his peers.)

Factors Affecting Peer Influences on the Individual Child

Some of the other factors which affect the child's yielding to peer norms are reviewed in the following paragraphs. One major theme in this discussion will be that conformity is quite variable, being high for a particular child in some situations and low in others. There is one study (Stukát, 1958) in which the structure of conformity behavior was explored in subjects between nine years of age and adulthood. The subjects were given a very large battery of conformity tests ranging from body sway to perceptual co-judge tasks. Resulting factor analyses indicated the presence of two general factors. One consisted entirely of conformity or yielding in tasks in which adults constituted the source of social influence. Nevertheless, all of the task scores loading highly on this factor involved what can be called "hypnotizability," i.e., all the tests involved responsiveness to monotonous and repetitive verbal or motoric suggestions. A second factor ("secondary suggestibility") was comprised of more conventional yielding tests. The influence source in some of the tests was an adult, but in others it consisted of a peer. The emergence of this second factor suggests that influenceability by peers is embedded in a more general tendency to copy the behavior of other people. That is, there is something of a generalized tendency to conform in children. Still, situational effects are apparent in many different types of conformity behavior. We now turn our attention to some of these.

Sex differences have been found in many studies of peer conformity. The usual finding is that females are more responsive to peer influences than males. This is consistent with research results in other areas in which it has been shown that females are more dependent, have higher needs for social approval, and the like. It should be pointed out that the nature of the peer pressure may affect the magnitude of this sex difference or determine whether it is found at all. For example, in one study (Patel & Gordon, 1960), greater conformity was shown by ninth-grade girls than by boys of the same age. The conformity situation involved a low-prestige influence source (bogus norms representing the performance of students a year behind the subject in school). This sex difference disappeared among twelfth-grade students. On the other hand, when a high-prestige source was employed (more advanced students), the sex difference was clearly apparent among high-school students at all grade levels. Other investigators, who have used instructions in their experiments which emphasize the desirability of doing well (i.e., achievement was stressed), have actually produced greater conformity to peer pressures among boys than among girls. It is well known that appeals to task mastery are more potent in influencing the behavior of males than of females. Females, on the other hand, seem to be particularly responsive to conditions arousing needs for social approval. Thus, the context in which peer influence is exerted has an important modifying effect on sex differences in conformity behavior.

Similar complexities mark the relation between birth order and peer conformity. Studies with both children and adults have shown that, in general, first-born individuals are more conforming than later-born individuals. This is in line with data which show first borns to be more affiliative, dependent, and socially anxious than later borns. It has been hypothesized that these differences between first- and later-born individuals derive from differences in early socialization. There is also some tendency for first-born individuals to manifest higher achievement motivation than later-borns. Thus, when peer conformity is studied under instructions that stress individual achievement, the peer norms are likely to be ignored and lesser conformity noted in first borns than in later borns. Only in situations where the instructions are relatively neutral, or where affiliation and group consensus is stressed, is the tendency found for first-born subjects to be more conforming than later borns (e.g., Becker, Lerner, & Carroll, 1966). Once again, it is clearly evident that personality variables tend to interact with situational variables in determining the extent to which the individual child is influenced by his peers.

The relation between conformity to peer pressures and the child's social orientation appears to change between early and middle childhood. Young children who comply to peer demands during nursery-school play are likely to be spontaneous, attention seeking, friendly, empathic, easy going, less rigid, and less perfectionistic than less compliant children (Crandall, Orleans, Preston, & Rabson, 1958). Thus, at this time, peer compliance seems to be one attribute shared by outer-directed socially effective children. But the position of peer compliance in the general personality structure seems to change during middle childhood. Observations of elementary-school-aged children who were attending day camps showed that peer-compliant children tended to be nonaggressive, passive, nonassertive, suggestible, and reliant on others for making decisions. A transformation seems to occur between the early- and middle-childhood years such that peer compliance emerges during the latter time in a cluster of traits that suggests low ego strength, inferiority, and "conformity proneness." The determinants of this transformation are not well understood. Longitudinal study of compliance to peer pressures is badly needed. On the other hand, it appears that an out-going type of yielding to peer pressures during early childhood may function as a precursor to effective peer relations later. In other words, there may be a time for "giving in" to peers, but it also appears necessary for the child to shift to a more independent mode for interacting with others as he moves through the elementary-school years, even though the latter period is marked by considerable general conformity to peer pressures.

High yielding to peer influences by older children and adolescents appears to be correlated with traits such as introversion, submissiveness, and lack of self-sufficiency, attributes that characterize adults who are "conformity prone." Other studies have identified more specific personality characteristics that distinguish the conforming child from his more independent age mate. McDavid (1959), for example, studied two groups of adolescent boys: one that was identified as being primarily concerned with the content of messages in interpersonal communication and another that was identified as more concerned with the source of such messages. Conformity proved to be greater among the source-oriented group. Further, when yielding to false norms occurred, it was more likely to be a total capitulation to the false norm among the source-oriented subjects. There was relatively more compromising, or finding a middle ground, among those subjects identified as message oriented. In studies of younger boys, conformity to peer pressures has also been linked to dependency.

It is clear that personality factors, such as dependency or source orientation, interact with situational factors in determining conformity to peer influences. Wilson (1960) distinguished two groups of boys: one was concerned with being socially accomodative, while the other was composed of individuals who were particularly concerned with the accuracy of information received in interpersonal messages. The influence source consisted of a peer who was either liked or disliked by the subject. Overall, the accomodative subjects did not conform to the peer influence more than did the information-oriented subjects. On the other hand, there was a greater tendency for the accomodative subjects to change their opinions in the face of peer pressure when the influence source was liked than when he was disliked; this difference was not found for the information-oriented subjects. Thus, the attractiveness of the pressure source seems to interact with the subject's own personality in determining conformity behavior. Consequently, personality factors alone do not furnish a firm basis for precisely predicting the performance of children and adolescents in peer-influence situations.

What situational factors are particularly important in predicting peer conformity? There are many adult studies that have examined the effects of such variables as perceived competence of the source, attractiveness of the influence source, difficulty of the task, and the like. In some respects, the few studies in this area that have been conducted with children confirm the adult research. In other instances, however, the evidence is too scattered to draw firm conclusions. We do not know that children conform more to peer influences when the task is difficult than they do when the task is easy. Berenda's research suggests that this is so, in that those subjects tended to yield to peer norms more when longer lines were judged than when short lines were judged and they yielded more when the difference between comparison lines was small than when the difference was relatively large. Thus, yielding seemed to be more frequent under conditions of high task difficulty than under low task difficulty. But in a conformity task that involved counting clicks (delivered to the subject over earphones), Iscoe et al. (1963) found that the subjects conformed to peer influences more on easy tasks than on difficult ones. To complicate the picture still further, Mc-David's results showed that the effects of task difficulty depended on the personality of the subject. Specifically, those adolescents who were concerned with the content of interpersonal messages, as opposed to those who were concerned with the message source, tended to yield more readily as task difficulty increased. Clearly, the nature of the task is relevant to predictions concerning the child's influenceability by his peers. But to date, this important area of research has not yielded definitive results.

As indicated previously, the attractiveness of the influence source is an important factor in predicting peer conformity. The competence of the source also influences the amount of conformity, as shown in an excellent study of fifth-grade children by Gelfand (1962). In this study, which is reprinted following the chapter, the subject's evaluations of the influence source were manipulated experimentally. That is, one-half of the subjects took a series of tests in the company of another child (the experimenter's confederate). The children were subsequently told that the subject had performed very poorly, but that the confederate had done extremely well. The remainder of the subjects were given feedback designed to create the reverse impression. That is, the confederate appeared to fail, while the subject appeared to succeed. In a post-training persuasibility test, the subjects yielded more to the judgments of successful peers than to the judgments of unsuccessful ones. This study also reveals that the subject's own typical level of self-esteem is another determinant of peer conformity. Thus, the prestige and the competence of the influence source have much to do with a child being influenced by his peers. Naturalistic studies also show that competent children tend to initiate more influence attempts during peer interaction than less competent children, and they are more successful in their influence attempts.

The child's status in his peer group also has something to do with how readily he will be influenced by his peers. Those who occupy middle-status positions in the peer group appear to be most vulnerable or most willing to be influenced by the opinions and attitudes of their peers. For example, in the previously mentioned study by Wilson, middle-status boys yielded more than either high-status or low-status boys. Other research suggests that children who are close to the highest status position in the group, but who have not quite reached the most favored position, are the most readily influenced of all. In general, though, middle status in the peer group appears to distinguish children who are particularly open to pressure for conformity from their peers.

Now we briefly turn to a consideration of some additional forms of peer influence on the behavior of children. It has already been mentioned that peer models affect such diverse behaviors as aggression and altruism. Other investigators have demonstrated that peer modeling can modify problem-solving behavior, patterns of self-reward, and resistance to temptation. Relatively little is known about the factors that make some models potent sources of influence and others less so. A recent study by Clark (1965) shows that reinforcement of the model is one such factor. Children were more likely to copy solutions to a discrimination task displayed by models who were rewarded than by models who were not rewarded. The study by Hartup & Coates (1967) shows that both the child's previous interactions with the model and his history of interaction in the peer group affect his susceptibility to peer modeling. Specifically, it was found that children who had a long-term history of positive interaction with their peers copied rewarding models more readily than models who were not rewarding. On the other hand, the children who had had little positive interaction with their playmates tended to imitate nonrewarding children more readily than rewarding children. It would appear, then, that children need to have had some level of minimum interaction with other children in order for copying the behavior of rewarding peers to acquire reinforcing value.

The effects of direct peer reinforcement also depend on the child's past history with the child who gives him reinforcement. A series of studies with both preschool and elementary-school children (e.g., Hartup, 1964) suggests that friendship is one determinant of the effectiveness of peer reinforcement. For example, in simple operant tasks, praise is given by one preschool child to another preschool child. This approval is more effective when given by a nonfriend (someone that the child does not like) than when given by a friend. The task performance of older children has been tested when peer reinforcement is given either by children who are popular, unpopular, or by "isolates" (those rarely chosen as either liked or disliked). The results suggest that performance improves more when the approval is given by an unpopular child than when given by either a popular child or an isolate. Other findings suggest that peer reinforcement is more potent when the reinforcing agent is either older or younger than the subject, rather than when he is the same age.

At the moment, researchers have not isolated the factors responsible for the diverse effects of peer reinforcement. Taken together, the results mentioned above suggest that conditions that are somewhat strange to the child or that are a little different from his usual interactions with peers, enhance the effectiveness of peer reinforcement. It may be that when positive feedback from peers occurs in an unexpected setting, it is more potent than when such reinforcement occurs in a setting where it is expected. These experiments, of course, have involved tasks that differ considerably from those activities which precipitate the exchange of approval and disapproval in informal peer groups. Research now underway, in which the consequences of both positive and negative reinforcement are being studied in naturalistic situations, will determine the extent to which these intriguing experimental findings may be generalized to other situations.

The research presented in this chapter is unusually diverse. Some studies have emphasized the factors that affect the formation of children's groups; others concern the child's status in such groups; still others have dealt with the manner in which peers contribute to the socialization of the child. There is little research that involves study of the same problem with groups that vary widely in age. Age trends are fairly well documented in the area of peer conformity, but the factors that influence the formation of informal peer groups have not been studied intensively in groups of children other than preadolescents.

Thus, it is not possible at this time to present a truly integrated picture of the social development of children as it takes place among age mates. And yet, the literature concerning peer relations that has accumulated during the past fifty years contains much information which is of both theoretical and practical significance. The person who works with children in settings where interpersonal tension is rife can hardly fail to derive useful information from those studies that have dealt with competition and conflict in intergroup relations. Similarly, the person who is interested in enhancing the child's acquisition of appropriate social standards cannot fail to learn something from the literature on peer conformity. Much remains to be learned in this important area of child psychology. There is adequate information already in existence upon which future studies can be built. There is also more consistency in present findings than one might suspect. One general statement must stand as the conclusion to this chapter. The prediction of peer influences and group behavior in childhood is a complex process. It must take into account the child's previous socialization history, aspects of his ability and personality, the characteristics of the children with whom he is interacting, and the situation in which peer interaction takes place. Both research and application in this area must be multivariate, rather than univariate, in character.

SUMMARY

Azrin, N. H., & Lindsley, O. R. The reinforcement of cooperation between children. *Journal of Abnormal and Social Psychology,* 1956, **52,** 100–102.

Becker, S. W., Lerner, M. J., & Carroll, J. Conformity as a function of birth order and type of group pressure: A verification. *Journal of Personality and Social Psychology,* 1966, **3,** 242–244.

BIBLIOGRAPHY

Berenda, R. W. *The influence of the group on the judgments of children.* New York: King's Crown, 1950.

Charlesworth, R., & Hartup, W. W. Positive social reinforcement in the nursery school peer group. *Child Development,* 1967, **38,** 993–1002.

Clark, B. S. The acquisition and extinction of peer imitation in children. *Psychonomic Science,* 1965, **2,** 147–148.

Costanzo, P. R., & Shaw, M. E. Conformity as a function of age level. *Child Development,* 1966, **37,** 967–975.

Crandall, V. J., Orleans, S., Preston, A., & Rabson, A. The development of social compliance in young children. *Child Development,* 1958, **29,** 429–443.

Faigin, H. Social behavior of young children in the kibbutz. *Journal of Abnormal and Social Psychology,* 1958, **56,** 117–129.

Flanders, N. A., & Havumaki, S. The effect of teacher-pupil contacts involving praise on the sociometric choices of students. *Journal of Educational Psychology,* 1960, **51,** 65–68.

Freud, A., & Dann, S. An experiment in group upbringing. In R. S. Eissler, A. Freud, H. Hartman, & E. Kris (Eds.), *The psychoanalytic study of the child.* Vol. 6. New York: International Universities Press, 1951. Pp. 127–168.

Gelfand, D. M. The influence of self-esteem on rate of verbal conditioning and social matching behavior. *Journal of Abnormal and Social Psychology,* 1962, **65,** 259–265.

Goldberg, M. H., & Maccoby, E. E. Children's acquisition of skill in performing a group task under two conditions of group formation. *Journal of Personality and Social Psychology,* 1965, **2,** 898–902.

Grossmann, B., & Wrighter, J. The relationship between selection-rejection and intelligence, social status, and personality amongst sixth-grade children. *Sociometry,* 1948, **11,** 346–355.

Gump, P., Schoggen, P., & Redl, F. The camp milieu and its immediate effects. *Journal of Social Issues,* 1957, **13,** 40–46.

Harlow, H. F., & Harlow, M. K. The affectional systems. In A. M. Schrier, H. F. Harlow, & F. Stollnitz (Eds.), *Behavior of nonhuman primates: Modern research trends.* Vol. 2. New York: Academic Press, 1965. Pp. 287–334.

Hartup, W. W. Friendship status and the effectiveness of peers as reinforcing agents. *Journal of Experimental Child Psychology,* 1964, **1,** 154–162.

Hartup, W. W., & Coates, B. Imitation of a peer as a function of reinforcement from the peer group and rewardingness of the model. *Child Development,* 1967, **38,** 1003–1016.

Hartup, W. W., Glazer, J. A., & Charlesworth, R. Peer reinforcement and sociometric status. *Child Development,* 1967, **38,** 1017–1024.

Hicks, D. J. Imitation and retention of film-mediated aggressive peer and adult models. *Journal of Personality and Social Psychology,* 1965, **2,** 97–100.

Hill, K. T. Relation of test anxiety, defensiveness, and intelligence to sociometric status. *Child Development*, 1963, **34**, 767–776.

Hunt, R. G., & Synnerdahl, V. Social influence among kindergarten children. *Sociology and Social Research*, 1959, **43**, 171–174.

Iscoe, I., Williams, M., & Harvey, J. Modification of children's judgments by a simulated group technique: A normative developmental study. *Child Development*, 1963, **34**, 963–978.

Iscoe, I., Williams, M., & Harvey, J. Age, intelligence, and sex as variables in the conformity behavior of Negro and white children. *Child Development*, 1964, **35**, 451–460.

Kipnis, D. The effects of leadership style and leadership power upon the inducement of an attitude change. *Journal of Abnormal and Social Psychology*, 1958, **57**, 173–180.

Lewin, K., Lippitt, R., & White, R. K. Patterns of aggressive behavior in experimentally created "social climates." *Journal of Social Psychology*, 1939, **10**, 271–299.

Lott, A. J., & Lott, B. E. Group cohesiveness and individual learning. *Journal of Educational Psychology*, 1966, **57**, 61–73.

Lott, B. E., & Lott, A. J. The formation of positive attitudes towards group members. *Journal of Abnormal and Social Psychology*, 1960, **61**, 297–300.

McCandless, B. R., & Marshall, H. R. A picture sociometric technique for preschool children and its relation to teacher judgments of friendship. *Child Development*, 1957, **28**, 139–148.

McConnell, T. R. Suggestibility in children as a function of chronological age. *Journal of Abnormal and Social Psychology*, 1963, **67**, 286–289.

McDavid, J. Jr. Personality and situational determinants of conformity. *Journal of Abnormal and Social Psychology*, 1959, **58**, 241–246.

Maudry, M., & Nekula, M. Social relations between children of the same age during the first two years of life. *Journal of Genetic Psychology*, 1939, **54**, 193–215.

Morgan, W. R., & Sawyer, J. Bargaining, expectations and the preference for equality over equity. *Journal of Personality and Social Psychology*, 1967, **6**, 139–149.

Parten, M. B. Social participation among pre-school children. *Journal of Abnormal and Social Psychology*, 1932–33, **24**, 243–269.

Patel, A. S., & Gordon, J. E. Some personal and situational determinants of yielding to influence. *Journal of Abnormal and Social Psychology*, 1960, **61**, 411–418.

Patterson, G. R., Littman, R. A., & Bricker, W. Assertive behavior in children: A step toward a theory of aggression. *Monographs of the Society for Research in Child Development*, 1967, **32**(5, Serial No. 113).

Phillips, B. N., & D'Amico, L. A. Effects of cooperation and competition on the cohesiveness of small face-to-face groups. *Journal of Educational Psychology*, 1956, **47**, 65–70.

Piaget, J. *The moral judgment of the child.* (Translated by M. Gabain.) Glencoe, Ill.: Free Press, 1948.

Reese, H. W. Relationships between self-acceptance and sociometric choices. *Journal of Abnormal and Social Psychology,* 1961, **62,** 472–474.

Roff, M., & Sells, S. B. Relations between intelligence and sociometric status in groups differing in sex and socio-economic background. *Psychological Reports,* 1965, **16,** 511–516.

Rosen, S., Levinger, G., & Lippitt, R. Perceived sources of social power. *Journal of Abnormal and Social Psychology,* 1961, **62,** 439–441.

Sherif, M., Harvey, O. J., White, B. J., Hood, W. R., & Sherif, C. W. *Intergroup conflict and cooperation: The robbers cave experiment.* Norman, Okla.: University of Oklahoma Press, 1961.

Sherif, M., & Sherif, C. W. *Reference groups.* New York: Harper & Row, 1964.

Stukát, K. G. *Suggestibility: A factorial and experimental analysis.* Stockholm: Almqvist and Wiksell, 1958.

Weingold, H. P., & Webster, R. L. Effects of punishment on a cooperative behavior in children. *Child Development,* 1964, **35,** 1211–1216.

Wilson, R. S. Personality patterns, source attractiveness, and conformity. *Journal of Personality,* 1960, **28,** 186–199.

Zander, A., & Van Egmond, E. Relationship of intelligence and social power to the interpersonal behavior of children. *Journal of Educational Psychology,* 1958, **49,** 257–268.

IMITATION OF A PEER AS A FUNCTION OF REINFORCEMENT FROM THE PEER GROUP AND REWARDINGNESS OF THE MODEL[1]

Willard W. Hartup and Brian Coates

Considerable research has been generated by the hypothesis that rewarding models are imitated to a greater extent than nonrewarding models. This hypothesis figures prominently in several general theories of identification, including the theory of anaclitic identification developed by Freud (1914), the secondary reinforcement interpretation of imitation by Mowrer (1950, 1960), and the extension of these theories formulated by Sears (1957) and Sears, Rau, and Alpert (1965).

The formulation developed by Mowrer is particularly specific concerning the mechanisms underlying imitation. Mowrer suggested that rewards given to S by a model increase the secondary reinforcing value (for S) of behaviors manifested by the model. When S reproduces these behaviors, the proprioceptive feedback from the imitative acts is presumed, as a consequence of stimulus generalization, to be secondarily reinforcing. This secondary reinforcement predisposes S to reproduce the behavior of the model. Although Mowrer originally provided this theory as an explanation for the imitation of verbal behavior, the theory has since been extended to account for all imitative acts (Mowrer, 1960; Sears, 1957). . . .

Experimental evidence concerning this hypothesis has been provided by Bandura and Huston (1961), who found that preschool Ss who had received social rewards from the model during two 15-minute play periods reproduced "incidental" verbal and motor responses displayed by the model to a greater extent than Ss experiencing nonrewarding interaction. These two groups, however, did not differ significantly in duplicating the model's choices in a discrimination task. Next, Bandura, Ross, and Ross (1963) reported that nursery school children more frequently imitated models from whom they received social and material rewards than models with whom they competed for such rewards. Mischel and Grusec (1966) found that the rewardingness of the model facilitated imitation, but this effect depended on the type of behavior being modeled ("aversive" or "neutral") and whether imitation was measured in terms of "rehearsal" or "transmission." More recently, Grusec (1966) reported that the model's rewardingness influenced children's imitation of self-criticism, depending on whether the model had previously used withdrawal of love, as opposed to withdrawal of material rewards.

[1] This study was completed with the assistance of a stipend awarded to Brian Coates from grant 5-T01-MHO-6668, National Institute of Mental Health. The authors are particularly grateful to Rosalind Charlesworth for her help and to the collaborating nursery school teachers.

From W. W. Hartup & B. Coates. Imitation of a peer as a function of reinforcement from the peer group and rewardingness of the model. Child Development, 1967, 38, 1003–1016. (With permission of the authors and the Society for Research in Child Development, Inc.)

Other evidence pertinent to the secondary reinforcement theory of imitation is provided by Rosenblith (1959), who reported that the attentiveness of the experimenter-model, as compared to attention withdrawal, enhanced imitation, but only in girls. Rosenhan and White (1967) reported no effect of the prior relation existing between S and model on the imitation of altruistic behavior, except that boys whose relations with the model were "negative" showed greater continuity in amount of imitation from model-present to model-absent conditions than boys whose relations with the model were positive or boys who had no prior relations with the model.

Stein and Wright (1964) reported that nurturance by an adult model affected imitation in preschool children, depending on the extent of change in the manifestation of dependency by the child during the experimental session. The Ss who responded to withdrawal of nurturance or to isolation with *increased* dependency and Ss who responded to continuous nurturance from E with *decreased* dependency imitated the model to a greater extent than Ss whose changes in dependency were in directions opposite to those mentioned. Lastly, Kobasigawa (1965) reported that adult models who had previously dispensed social rewards and were then observed to undergo a frustration experience elicited no greater emotionality in first-grade boys than models not dispensing social reinforcement. . . .

The main purpose of this experiment was to study one likely source of variation in the effect of the model's rewardingness on imitation—S's general history of reinforcement from persons resembling the model. The study was based on the hypothesis that the effects of exposure to a rewarding model, as compared to a nonrewarding model, depend on the nature of S's previous experience with people who are like the model. Peers were selected as the class of models to be used. Nursery school children were believed to be appropriate Ss because, even in nursery school groups, the range of reward frequencies exchanged among them is large. . . .

The behaviors modeled in the experiment consisted of an altruistic response plus a group of verbal and motoric actions "incidental" to the altruistic act. Since the study involved peers as models and altruistic behavior as the major dependent variable, it accomplishes two secondary purposes: (a) it contributes to the slowly growing literature concerning the influence of peer models on the socialization of the child (e.g., Bandura & Kupers, 1964; Clark, 1965; Grosser, Polansky, & Lippitt, 1951; Hicks, 1965), and (b) it adds to the sparse evidence concerning imitation as a determinant of altruism (Rosenhan & White, 1967).

METHOD

Subjects

The pool from which Ss were drawn consisted of 64 children enrolled in four groups at the Laboratory Nursery School of the University of Minnesota. This pool included all children enrolled both at the time observations were conducted in the peer group and during a later experimental period. The Ss were 56 children from this pool. Excluded were two children who were receiving psychotherapy, two children who refused to participate, two children whose models failed to carry out the prescribed procedure, and two who were dropped to yield equal cell frequencies. These Ss ranged in age from 3–9 through 5–4, with a mean age of 4–6.

Experimental design

The experimental design consisted of the following groups:

Frequent reinforcement from peers (FR):
    Rewarding peer model (RM) ($N = 12$)
    Nonrewarding peer model (NRM) ($N = 12$)
Infrequent reinforcement from peers (IR):
    Rewarding peer model (RM) ($N = 12$)
    Nonrewarding peer model (NRM) ($N = 12$)
No model (control) ($N = 8$)

Assignment of subjects

The initial step in the assignment of Ss was the measurement of reinforcement frequencies occurring in the nursery school peer group. For this purpose, observations were conducted extending over a 5-week period.[1] Briefly, the observations produced twelve 3-minute samples of each child's behavior, recorded in running account form by observers stationed in the nursery school. These records contained information concerning the child's activity, persons in his vicinity, and accounts of the interaction occurring between the child and other persons.

The 3-minute protocols were then rated by two judges. The records were screened for instances in which the child dispensed or received "generalized social reinforcers" (Skinner, 1953). Four types of positive social reinforcers were tabulated: (a) attention and approval (e.g., attending, offering praise, smiling and laughing, offering guidance or suggestions); (b) affection and personal acceptance (both physical and verbal); (c) submission (e.g., passive acceptance of another child's demands, sharing, compromise); (d) tokens (tangible objects).

A total of 161 protocols were rated by both raters. The ratio of agreements concerning the occurrence of social reinforcement divided by agreements plus disagreements was .77.

It was possible to compute the total number of reinforcements dispensed by each child to his peers and the number received. The latter score was assumed to be an index of the total frequency of positive reinforcement the child received from the peer group.[2] It was on the basis of these scores, which ranged from 0 to 55, that the children were divided into two groups: those above the median, for their own nursery school class, in number of reinforcements received (frequent reinforcement group) and those below (infrequent reinforcement group). The mean number of reinforcers received from peers in the FR group was 24.9, while the mean for the IR group was 9.0.

---

[1] A detailed description of the observational procedure can be found in Charlesworth & Hartup (1967).

[2] The extent to which the total number of positive reinforcements received serves as an index of total social interaction is not known. It was possible to compute correlations between receipt of positive and receipt of negative reinforcements for Ss in two of the preschool groups. These correlations were .43 ($p < .10$) and .51 ($p < .05$). Incidents of nonreinforcing contacts among peers were numerous but were not tabulated.

The children in each of the two reinforcement groups were then randomly assigned to model conditions: rewarding peer model (RM) or nonrewarding peer model (NRM). The observational records for each S assigned to group RM were searched for the name of the like-sex peer who had given S the most frequent reinforcement during the observations. This peer was designated as S's model. The RM Ss had received a mean of 5.4 reinforcements from their models during the 36 minutes of observation. Next, a list was prepared for each S in group NRM consisting of all like-sex children in the class who had never been observed to furnish S with reinforcement. One child, randomly selected from this list, was designated as S's model. The mean reinforcements given to the NRM Ss by their models had, of course, been zero. . . .

One boy and one girl from each preschool class were required to start the testing by serving as "first" models. These children were randomly selected. If this selection did not make it possible to test all of the children in that preschool class in sequence, substitute first models were picked. Those children designated as first models completed the experimental task prior to being trained as models. This group of eight children (two from each preschool class) thus comprised a no-model control group (C).

Procedure

No-Model Condition

The S was brought to a laboratory room which contained three hats (maroon, green, and yellow) hung on pegs, three feathers (white, yellow, and orange) placed on a chair, three pencils (black, brown, and green) also hung on pegs, and a table containing a stack of dittoed mazes (simple one-turn puzzles) and three bowls. One bowl, placed in front of the child, was a receptacle for trinkets released by a dispensing device. The other bowls were placed to S's left and right . . . ; one was designated as belonging to a preschool child (not known to S) whose picture was attached, the other was designated as S's bowl. The following instructions were given:

We have a game for you today. It is a puzzle game and these are the puzzles. (E displays puzzles.) The way you play this game is to draw a line from one flower to another flower, like this. (E demonstrates.) Now you can do some. (S [is] helped to complete two or three of the puzzles.) There is one other thing that I want to tell you about the game. Whenever you are doing a good job on the puzzle, some little cats will come out of the machine back there. They will come down this chute and fall into this bowl. Whenever some cats come down the chute I want you to put them in one of these other bowls. Either put them over here in Alec's bowl (Kathy's for female Ss) or over here in your bowl. Alec is another boy in the nursery school. Now remember, whenever you are doing a good job on the puzzle, some little cats will come out of the machine into this bowl here and you are to put them in one of these two bowls, either in Alec's bowl or your bowl, your bowl or Alec's bowl. Do you understand? I have to do some work so I will sit in here.

Nothing further was said concerning whether S could keep the trinkets in his bowl at the conclusion of the session. The E then went into an adjoining room, left the door ajar, and seated himself out of sight. S was told to proceed, and after each maze was completed six trinkets were ejected through the chute. The session consisted of ten mazes, each followed by the dispensing and allocation of six trinkets. If S failed to pick up the trinkets, E urged him to do so by saying, "Put the cats in the bowls; in Alec's bowl or your bowl, your bowl or Alec's bowl."

Model Conditions

Training the model   Each child designated as a model was brought to the laboratory several days after he had participated as *S*. He was reminded of the earlier session, given an opportunity to complete two mazes, and asked to help *E* by demonstrating the game for another child from his class. The *E* stressed that it was necessary to play the game in a particular way. First, *M* was told that he should go to the hats, pick out the green one (color alternated across *S*s), attach the white feather (also alternated) to the hole in the hat, and put the hat on his head. Next, he was told to select the black pencil (color also alternated), to seat himself at the table, and begin work on the puzzles. Then *M* was instructed to pick up the six trinkets ejected after each maze, place them in a row on the table, and to pick them up one at a time, placing all but the last one in Alec's (or Kathy's) bowl. The *M* was also instructed to repeat the words "One for Alec" each time a trinket was placed in "Alec's bowl." The *E* stressed that only the last trinket should be placed in *M*'s own bowl. This procedure was practiced, with *E* coaching and sometimes demonstrating, until *M* was able to perform the task with consistent accuracy. The *M* accompanied *E* to the nursery school for the purpose of inviting *S* to play the game.

Experimental session   When the children arrived in the laboratory, *E* described the game using the instructions given above. He also explained that the children would take turns and that *M* would be first. The *S* was seated so as to face *M* at a 90° angle and was told that he should try not to bother *M*. The *E* entered the adjoining room, leaving the door partly open. Then *M* was told to proceed. If *M* failed to respond or engaged in distracting behavior, *E* prompted him from the other room. In no case, however, were mistakes in allocating trinkets corrected. Such mistakes were made by only two *M*s whose *S*s were subsequently excluded from the experiment.

After ten mazes, the children were told it was time for *S* to play the game. The *M* was invited to wait in the adjoining room with *E*, and the instructions were repeated briefly to *S*. When everyone had reached his appropriate spot, *S* was told to begin.

Response measures

The following information was recorded by *E* (observing through a small one-way window): (a) whether or not *S* chose a hat, a feather, and/or a pencil and the colors of these objects; (b) whether or not *S* lined up the trinkets and whether the trinkets were placed in the bowls one at a time or in groups; (c) frequency with which *S* reproduced the verbalization of *M*; and (d) the particular bowl chosen for allocation of each trinket.

The response measures derived from these records included: (a) presence-absence of imitative hat, feather, and pencil choices; (b) presence-absence of "line up" behavior on each trial (ranging from 0 to 10 over entire session); (c) presence-absence of imitative verbalization (ranging from 0 to 6 on each trial); (d) number of trinkets placed in the "other's" bowl (ranging from 0 to 6 on each trial); (e) latency of the first nonaltruistic choice—the number of trinkets placed in "other's" bowl before placement of the first trinket in *S*'s own bowl (ranging from 0 to 7 on each trial). . . .

RESULTS

Effect of model

To assess the effects of observing a model on altruistic behavior, [an] . . . analysis . . . was conducted on the data for all five of the groups in the experiment. . . . [The results revealed that] observation of the model produced significantly more altruism than occurred when no opportunity to observe a model was provided (see Table 1).

Observing the model also affected the frequency of "incidental" behaviors. Statistical analysis was not performed, but it can be seen in Table 2 that no verbalization or "line up" behavior occurred in [the control] group . . . , although appreciable amounts were displayed by Ss who had observed a model.

Effects of peer reinforcement and rewardingness of model

The "giving to other" scores for Ss who observed models were subjected to [statistical] analysis. . . . [Comparisons were made of the frequency of reinforcement from peers (FR vs. IR), . . . the type of peer model (RM vs. NRM), and . . . the first five trials vs. the second five trials.] Mean scores for each subgroup may be seen in Table 1.

The analysis revealed a significant effect of trial blocks . . . indicating fewer altruistic responses were made during the second block of five trials than during the first. . . . There was a significant interaction between reinforcement from peers and type of model in the data for the first five trials . . . , but not for the second. During the first trials, Ss who had received frequent reinforcement from their peers imitated a rewarding peer model more frequently than a nonrewarding model. . . . On the other hand, Ss who were observed to receive infrequent peer reinforcement imitated a nonrewarding model more frequently than a rewarding model. . . . Additional contrasts made on the data for the first five trials revealed: (a) among Ss who observed a rewarding model, those with a history of frequent peer reinforcement did not differ significantly from those with a history of infrequent reinforcement . . . ; (b) among those who observed a nonrewarding model, Ss who had received infrequent reinforcement from the peer group imitated significantly more than those who had received frequent peer reinforcement. . . .

TABLE 1   Mean "giving to other" scores in blocks of five trials by reinforcement condition and type of peer model

Group	Trial block	
	1	2
Frequent reinforcement:		
Rewarding model	21.00	19.25
Nonrewarding model	13.42	13.83
Infrequent reinforcement:		
Rewarding model	17.50	17.08
Nonrewarding model	22.83	18.58
No model	5.63	3.75

TABLE 2   Mean number of "incidental" behaviors according to reinforcement condition and type of peer model

Group	Verbalization (total)	Line-up responses (total)
Frequent reinforcement:		
Rewarding model	36.83	4.50
Nonrewarding model	7.58	1.67
Infrequent reinforcement:		
Rewarding model	21.08	3.92
Nonrewarding model	18.00	3.92
No model	0.00	0.00

Analysis of imitative verbalization scores was [also] conducted. . . . As can be seen from Table 2, Ss who observed a rewarding model reproduced the model's verbal behaviors [significantly] more frequently than Ss who observed nonrewarding models. . . . "Line up" scores [did not produce any significant effect.] The data concerning the child's behavior with hats, feathers, and pencils were analyzed [with no significant effects]. . . . With respect to these particular incidental behaviors, then, the experimental conditions failed to influence differentially the child's imitative behavior.

DISCUSSION

Effects of model

Observation of altruistic models increased the frequency of altruistic behavior of the Ss, a finding which confirms the results of Rosenhan and White (1967). . . .

Can it be assumed that the behavior displayed by the model was construed by S as "altruism"? It is true that S was not told explicitly that he would be able to keep the trinkets in his own bowl and that those in the other child's bowl were to be given away. Nevertheless, in postsession interviews with ten Ss, all ten thought they could keep the trinkets in their own bowl, and seven thought the trinkets in the second bowl would be given to the child whose picture was attached to the bowl. Consequently, the assumption that the experiment involved imitative effects on altruism is tenable.

Among Ss who observed a model, those showing imitative altruism tended to imitate other components of the altruistic response sequence. . . . The peer reinforcement history tended to have significant effects on behavior which was central in the altruistic response sequence (frequency of "giving to other"). Borderline effects of peer reinforcement were found with respect to imitative verbalization, and no effects were obtained with respect to less central actions ("lining up" behavior or choices of hat, feather, and pencil). . . . It is also possible that the treatment effects did not generalize to "lining up" scores and hat, feather, and pencil choices because these behaviors occurred much less frequently than trinket sorting or verbalization.

Effects of peer reinforcement

The relation between rewardingness of the peer model and imitative altruism was positive when S was reinforced frequently by the peer group but negative when reinforcement was infrequent. . . .

It is concluded that the results support Mowrer's secondary reinforcement theory of imitation when S's history includes relatively frequent reinforcement from persons resembling the model. For infrequently reinforced Ss, the influence of model rewardingness did not diminish; rather, nonrewarding models proved to be more efficacious than rewarding ones.

One explanation for these results is based on the assumption that children who receive little reinforcement are also anxious when placed in contact with other children. For them, exposure to a nonrewarding model may arouse discomfort or anxiety, adding motivation to perform the actions which the situation elicits (including, in the present instance, imitation). Exposure of such children to a rewarding model, however, could result in anxiety reduction, thereby lowering S's motivation for imitative behavior.

This argument implies a dual theory of peer imitation: (a) when reinforcement from peers is frequent, matching the behavior of a rewarding model has greater incentive value than matching a nonrewarding model (the Mowrer hypothesis); (b) when peer reinforcement is not frequent, a nonrewarding model sustains or increases anxiety, whereas the presence of a rewarding model reduces such motivation for imitation. . . .

It is also possible to consider the present results in terms of perceived similarity. It is known that, in the peer group, the correlation between "giving reinforcement to others" and "getting reinforcement from others" is positive and high (Charlesworth & Hartup, 1967). Thus, it is possible that FR-RM Ss perceive themselves to be similar to the model (both give as well as receive frequent reinforcements) as do IR-NRM Ss (both receive and give few reinforcements). On the other hand, perceived similarity would not be great in the other two experimental groups, FR-NRM and IR-RM. Earlier studies have shown that if S perceives himself as similar to M, conformity is enhanced (e.g., Stotland & Patchen, 1961) as well as imitation (Maccoby, 1959; Rosekrans, 1967). The perceived similarity (or reduced dissimilarity) existing for frequently reinforced Ss with rewarding models and for infrequently reinforced Ss with nonrewarding models would thus account for the greater amounts of imitation shown by these two groups than by the other groups in the experiment.

The present study helps to clarify the influence of the model's rewardingness on imitation. The generality of the results needs to be assessed in further research and theoretical implications explored. It appears, however, that the child's socialization history contributes importantly to the effects on imitation of rewards from the model.

REFERENCES

Bandura, A., & Huston, A. C. Identification as a process of incidental learning. *Journal of Abnormal and Social Psychology,* 1961, **63**, 311–318.

Bandura, A., & Kupers, C. J. Transmission of patterns of self-reinforcement through modeling. *Journal of Abnormal and Social Psychology,* 1964, **69**, 1–9.

Bandura, A., Ross, D., & Ross, S. A. A comparative test of the status envy, social power, and secondary reinforcement theories of identificatory learning. *Journal of Abnormal and Social Psychology,* 1963, **67**, 527–534.

Charlesworth, R., & Hartup, W. W. Positive social reinforcement in the nursery school peer group. *Child Development,* 1967, **38**, 993–1002.

Clark, B. S. The acquisition and extinction of peer imitation in children. *Psychonomic Science,* 1965, **2**, 147–148.

Freud, S. On narcissism: An introduction (1914). In J. D. Sutherland (Ed.), *Collected papers of Sigmund Freud.* Vol. 4. London: Hogarth, 1957. Pp. 30–60.

Grosser, D., Polansky, N., & Lippitt, R. A laboratory study of behavioral contagion. *Human Relations,* 1951, **4**, 115–142.

Grusec, J. Some antecedents of self-criticism. *Journal of Personality and Social Psychology,* 1966, **4**, 244–252.

Hicks, D. J. Imitation and retention of film-mediated aggressive peer and adult models. *Journal of Personality and Social Psychology,* 1965, **2**, 97–100.

Kobasigawa, A. Observation of failure in another person as a determinant of amplitude and speed of a simple motor response. *Journal of Personality and Social Psychology,* 1965, **1**, 626–630.

Maccoby, E. E. Role-taking in childhood and its consequences for social learning. *Child Development,* 1959, **30**, 239–252.

Mischel, W., & Grusec, J. Determinants of the rehearsal and transmission of neutral and aversive behaviors. *Journal of Personality and Social Psychology,* 1966, **3**, 197–205.

Mowrer, O. H. Identification: A link between learning theory and psychotherapy. In *Learning theory and personality dynamics.* New York: Ronald Press, 1950. Pp. 69–94.

Mowrer, O. H. *Learning theory and the symbolic processes.* New York: Wiley, 1960.

Rosekrans, M. A. Imitation in children as a function of perceived similarity to a social model and vicarious reinforcement. *Journal of Personality and Social Psychology,* 1967, **7**, 307–315.

Rosenblith, J. F. Learning by imitation in kindergarten children. *Child Development,* 1959, **30**, 69–80.

Rosenhan, D., & White, G. M. Observation and rehearsal as determinants of prosocial behavior. *Journal of Personality and Social Psychology,* 1967, **5**, 424–431.

Sears, R. R. Identification as a form of behavioral development. In D. B. Harris (Ed.), *The concept of development.* Minneapolis: University of Minnesota Press, 1957. Pp. 149–161.

Sears, R. R., Rau, L., & Alpert, R. *Identification and child rearing.* Stanford, Calif.: Stanford University Press, 1965.

Skinner, B. F. *Science and human behavior.* New York: Macmillan, 1953.

Stein, A. H., & Wright, J. C. Imitative learning under conditions of nurturance and nurturance withdrawal. *Child Development,* 1964, **35**, 927–938.

Stotland, E., & Patchen, M. Identification and change in prejudice and in authoritarianism. *Journal of Abnormal and Social Psychology,* 1961, **62**, 265–274.

RELATIONS BETWEEN INTELLIGENCE AND SOCIOMETRIC STATUS IN GROUPS DIFFERING IN SEX AND SOCIO-ECONOMIC BACKGROUND[1]

Merrill Roff and S. B. Sells

This study was part of a larger research program which has as its major objective the systematic exploration of both short-term and long-term correlations among potentially relevant variables and peer status during childhood, on a very large sample of children in two states. This project grew out of an earlier set of studies comparing factors operating during childhood with adult outcome (Roff, 1956, 1957, 1960, 1961, 1963). In this series childhood peer status emerged as a significant predictor of young adult adjustment level. These studies used information abstracted from child guidance records as predictors and young adult information from military service records of the same individuals as criteria.

Earlier reports in the present series have presented information concerning the correlations between siblings in choice status as an indication of the degree of family resemblance (Sells & Roff, 1964a), of birth order of both boys and girls in relation to peer status (Sells & Roff, 1964b), and of estimation problems (Sells & Roff, 1964c). The present study explores in a multivariate rather than a bivariate manner some of the factors operating in the already known relationship between childhood choice status and IQ. This relationship is further analyzed with a separation by sex and by socio-economic background.

The earliest study combining intelligence and sociometric status which we have found is that of Almack (1922). . . . He reported positive correlations between the IQs of . . . children and [the IQs] of the children they chose [as their friends.]

The earliest study comparing IQ and choice status directly for a grade school sample is that of Hardy (1937). . . . Choices of desired associates were obtained during an interview. Intelligence was appraised by the Stanford-Binet. A correlation of .37 was reported between number of choices received and IQ. Later studies essentially similar to this one commonly obtained correlational values of this general magnitude (Bonney, 1942, 1943, 1944, 1946; Davis, 1957; Gallagher & Crowder, 1956; Johnson, 1950; McGahan, 1940). On the other hand, Jennings (1943), in a study of adolescent girls in a training school, found a correlation of only .04 between IQ and choices received. This result is not typical of those obtained with unselected public school samples.

[1]A report of Cooperative Research Project No. 1351, Contract No. OE-2-10-051, Cooperative Research Branch, U.S. Office of Education.

From M. Roff & S. B. Sells. *Relations between intelligence and sociometric status in groups differing in sex and socio-economic background.* Psychological Reports, *1965,16, 511–516.*

Two studies have gone beyond this gross correlational approach. One of these, by Grossmann and Wrighter (1948), employing a sample of four 6th grade classes in a university community, compared the relationships between intelligence and sociometric status using a three-interval breakdown of intelligence levels. They concluded that "intelligence did make a difference up to a certain point—normal intelligence—but beyond that it did not materially affect the selection-rejection score" (1948, p. 354). This study is somewhat unsatisfactory since the middle intelligence group was defined so broadly as to leave few cases for the upper and lower groups. It is of interest since an hypothesis of a differential relation between intelligence level and sociometric status is stated.

The second of these studies, by Porterfield and Schlichting (1961), compared reading achievement scores . . . with various pupil characteristics, including sociometric scores. Their sample was drawn from 6th grade pupils . . . drawn about equally from schools of high, middle, and low SES. As would be expected from the studies of intelligence, they found a firm relationship between this achievement test and sociometric status. When results by socio-economic levels were examined, they found a relationship between achievement scores and social acceptability status in the high and middle group, but the relation between test scores and social acceptability was not significant in the low SES schools, although it was in the expected direction. This is similar to the Grossmann and Wrighter study in suggesting that the relationship between an intellectual variable and sociometric status is different at various levels, but data are opposing in the reported level at which the difference occurred. . . . In the absence of clearer support from the literature than is afforded by the studies reviewed here, we simply analyzed the material to see what we would find. There was no compelling reason to hypothesize that a difference would occur at any point in the scale, or that no difference would appear at any level.

PROCEDURE

The sample was part of the total project sample of around 37,000 pupils of both sexes in the 3rd, 4th, 5th, and 6th grades from cities in Texas and Minnesota. This sample included 4th grade children of both sexes from all schools in one city (2,800 cases). The 4th grade in this city was employed because these children had been given the Lorge-Thorndike Intelligence Test during the school year, and because this city was the largest one in the study for which results were available for the entire city.

Sociometric information was obtained using pre-printed mark-sense cards. Within each class, choices were made separately of boys by boys and of girls by girls. This was done in the belief that at this age level the same-sex peer group is of major importance. Rosters on which each name on the list was numbered were prepared and furnished to each child at the time of the administration. The pupils nominated four individuals, by number, whom they liked most, and two whom they liked least, and blacked in the appropriate spaces on the mark-sense cards. . . . The student choices were converted to standard scores. Separate standard scores were computed for Like-most, Like-least, and a combination of the two (Like-most minus Like-least) for each child.

Socio-economic level was determined on a census tract basis, making use of a combination of adult income and education from the 1960 census values. Separate classifications of census tracts on these two criteria gave highly similar results. The entire set of schools in the city was then divided into quartiles on a basis of area in which each was located. Other information indicates that this classification of schools would correspond very closely to that made with the use of any other relevant indices of socio-economic status, of which there are many. The difference between the upper and lower socio-economic levels on the Lorge-Thorndike Intelligence Test was approximately the same in IQ points as the difference between highest and lowest socio-economic levels of the Stanford-Binet when these were classified according to occupational level of father (McNemar, 1942). The differences found here are greater than those reported by Anderson (1962) for the Lorge-Thorndike Test for a partial sample from Syracuse, New York; there SES was estimated on the basis of the Sims Social Class Identification Scale.

At each of our four SES levels, the group of "high" girls and "high" boys was defined as consisting of all those with standard scores 1 *SD* or more above the mean on the Like-most minus Like-least composite. A corresponding group of "low" girls and "low" boys was defined as consisting of those with a Like-most minus Like-least standard score 1 *SD* below the mean. When the mean IQ for each of these groups was computed, the values shown in . . . Figure 1 were obtained. . . .

FIG. 1   The IQ and choice status of (*a*) girls and (*b*) boys in relation to socio-economic background.

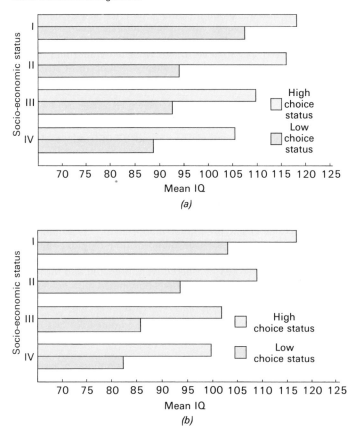

(a)

(b)

There was a consistent sex difference of about 5 IQ points in favor of the girls at all four socio-economic levels and for the total groups. This did not affect the general pattern of differences between high and low choice groups at the different socio-economic levels. Inspection of Figure 1 shows the same pattern of results for girls and for boys at different socio-economic levels. At all four levels the differences between the high and low groups for both sexes are about the same.

In terms of IQ points, there is a difference of about 15 to 20 points between the high and low choice status groups at various socio-economic levels. The only exception to this is in the top socio-economic group where the differences for girls and boys are only 11.5 and 14.3 points, respectively. The smaller standard deviations of these groups suggest that the test may not have had sufficient ceiling for these groups.

This finding is in line with the impressions obtained from earlier work with childhood case histories. A child of either sex with an IQ of 80 in a low socio-economic group is at a real social disadvantage. Similarly, a child with an IQ of 100 in an upper socio-economic group is also at a disadvantage. An intelligence level above the average of the peer group is an asset in a wide variety of groups.

REFERENCES

Almack, J. C. The influence of intelligence on the selection of associates. *School and Society,* 1922, **16**, 529–530.

Anderson, W. F. Relation of Lorge-Thorndike Intelligence Test scores of public school pupils to the socio-economic status of their parents. *Journal of Experimental Education,* 1962, **31**, 73–76.

Bonney, M. E. A study of social status on the second grade level. *Journal of Genetic Psychology,* 1942, **60**, 271–305.

Bonney, M. E. The relative stability of social, intellectual and academic status in grades II to IV, and the inter-relationships between these various forms of growth. *Journal of Educational Psychology,* 1943, **34**, 88–102.

Bonney, M. E. Relationship between social success, family size, socio-economic home background, and intelligence among school children in grades III to V. *Sociometry,* 1944, **7**, 26–39.

Bonney, M. E. A sociometric study of the relationship of some factors to mutual friendships on the elementary, secondary, and college levels. *Sociometry,* 1946, **9**, 21–47.

Davis, J. A. Correlates of sociometric status among peers. *Journal of Educational Research,* 1957, **50**, 561–569.

Gallagher, J. J., & Crowder, T. The adjustment of gifted children in the regular classroom. *Exceptional Children,* 1957, **23**, 306–319.

Grossmann, B., & Wrighter, J. The relationship between selection-rejection and intelligence, social status, and personality amongst sixth grade children. *Sociometry,* 1948, **11**, 346–355.

Hardy, M. C. Social recognition at the elementary school age. *Journal of Social Psychology,* 1937, **8**, 365–384.

Jennings, H. H. *Leadership and isolation.* New York: Longmans, 1943.

Johnson, G. O. A study of the social position of mentally handicapped children in the regular grades. *American Journal of Mental Deficiency,* 1950, **55**, 60–89.

McGahan, F. E. Factors associated with leadership ability of the elementary school child. Unpublished master's thesis, North Texas State Teachers College, 1940.

McNemar, Q. *The revision of the Stanford-Binet Scale.* New York: Houghton Mifflin, 1942.

Porterfield, O. V., & Schlichting, H. F. Peer status and reading achievement. *Journal of Educational Research,* 1961, **54**, 291–297.

Roff, M. *Preservice personality problems and subsequent adjustments to military service; Gross outcome in relation to acceptance-rejection at induction and military service.* Randolph AFB, Texas, School of Aviation Medicine, USAF, 1956. (Rep. No. 55–138.)

Roff, M. *Preservice personality problems and subsequent adjustments to military service; The prediction of psychoneurotic reactions.* Randolph AFB, Texas, School of Aviation Medicine, USAF, 1957. (Rep. No. 57–136.)

Roff, M. Relation between certain preservice factors and psychoneurosis during military duty. *U.S. Armed Forces Medical Journal,* 1960, **11**, 152–160.

Roff, M. Childhood social interactions and young adult bad conduct. *Journal of Abnormal and Social Psychology,* 1961, **63**, 333–337.

Roff, M. Childhood social interaction and young adult psychosis. *Journal of Clinical Psychology,* 1963, **19**, 152–157.

Sells, S. B., & Roff, M. Family influence as reflected in peer acceptance-rejection resemblance of siblings as compared with random sets of school children. *American Psychologist,* 1964, **19**, 454. (Abstract) (a)

Sells, S. B., & Roff, M. Peer acceptance-rejection and birth order. *Psychology in School,* 1964, **1**, 156–162. (b)

Sells, S. B., & Roff, M. Problems in the estimation of peer rejection in the early grades. *Psychology in School,* 1964, **1**, 256–262. (c)

CONFORMITY AS A FUNCTION OF AGE LEVEL[1]

Philip R. Costanzo and Marvin E. Shaw

It is generally assumed that conformity behavior is the result of developmental processes (Berg & Bass, 1961). However, the nature and consequences of these developmental processes have not been fully explored, and the theories concerning the relation between ontogenetic level and conformity are often in disagreement. The stimulus for the present study is derived from the work of Piaget (1954). He proposed that social development progresses through an orderly sequence of stages. Implicit in his analysis of the way the child learns the "rules of the game" is the hypothesis that the relation between age and conformity to rules (norms) is curvilinear. That is, at an early age the child is uninfluenced by rules but gradually begins to follow them until at about age 11–12 the rules are internalized and utilized completely. After this stage, the individual begins to express individual modes of response by creating and codifying certain of his own rules. Since conformity is the act of behaving in accordance with social rules or norms, it follows that conformity behavior should increase with increasing age until the child reaches the stage at which rules are internalized, and decrease thereafter.

Experimental studies of the relation between age and conformity typically have dealt with only limited age ranges. The evidence relative to the above hypothesis is therefore less than adequate, but, with a few exceptions, it appears to support the hypothesis. Marple (1933) found that high school students were more likely to conform to majority or expert opinion than either college students or adults. Similarly, Patel and Gordon (1960) found that conformity decreased from the tenth to the twelfth grade, although there were some reversals with high-prestige suggestions. These findings led Campbell (1961) to conclude that "The older a person is, the more established his dispositions, and therefore the less conformant he is" (Campbell, 1961, p. 114). However, both Marple (1933) and Patel and Gordon (1960) limited their sample to postadolescent age groups. Their results are therefore consistent with both Campbell's conclusion and our hypothesis.

Berenda (1950) reports evidence that appears to be contrary to our hypothesis. She conducted four experiments, two of which involved a single subject exposed to erroneous judgments of length of lines. In both studies, subjects in the 7–10 age group conformed more than did subjects in the 10–13 age group. However, there are some aspects of Berenda's study that may account for this seeming contradiction. In the

[1] This report is based upon a master's thesis submitted to the University of Florida by Philip R. Costanzo in partial fulfillment of the requirements for the degree of Master of Arts. The authors wish to thank Dr. J. B. Hodges and Dr. Donald Hartsough for making available the students and facilities of the P. K. Yonge Laboratory School.

From P. R. Costanzo & M. E. Shaw. Conformity as a function of age level. Child Development, *1966,* **37,** *967–975. (With permission of the authors and the Society for Research in Child Development, Inc.)*

first experiment, pressure was exerted by the eight brightest children in the class, whereas in the second experiment, pressure was exerted by the teacher. Thus, in both experiments subjects were exposed to pressure from high-status persons. It may well be that age differences in conformity to prestige suggestions follow a different pattern than age differences in conformity to peer suggestions. In this connection, it might be worth noting that Berenda found statistically reliable differences between age groups only when social pressure was exerted by the teacher.

A more recent study (Iscoe, Williams, & Harvey, 1963) presents results that are consistent with our hypothesis for females but not for males. These investigators studied four age groups (7-, 9-, 12-, and 15-year-old subjects) in a simulated conformity situation in which the task was to count the number of metronome clicks in a series. Maximum conformity occurred in the 12-year group for females, but in the 15-year group for males, although the difference between the 12-year and the 15-year male groups was not significant.

Thus, despite some inconsistent data, the evidence generally supports the hypothesis. Theoretical arguments in support of the hypothesis are also compelling. Until the child has had an opportunity to learn both the norms of his group and that conformity brings rewards, there is no logical reason to expect him to conform. Therefore, one would expect at least an initial increase in conformity with age. With increased age, many additional variables come into play. For example, it has been shown that lesser conformity is associated with (a) higher education (Tuddenham, 1959), (b) higher status (Crutchfield, 1955; Kelley & Volkart, 1952; Tuddenham, 1959), and (c) greater competence (Crutchfield, 1955; Tuddenham, 1959). Since all of these variables covary with age, it follows that, after an initial increase in conformity as a result of learning, conformity will decrease with age. These arguments are consistent with the hypothesis, but the age at which the shift from increasing to decreasing conformity occurs is not specified.

The present research was designed to measure directly the relation between age level and conformity. Based upon the considerations outlined above, it was expected that conformity, defined as a response to social pressure from peers, can best be represented by a two-stage theory of development. It was hypothesized that conformity increases with age in the preadolescent period to an asymptotic level in adolescence and then decreases in postadolescence through early adulthood.

METHOD

Subjects

The subjects were 72 students from the P. K. Yonge Laboratory School at the University of Florida and 24 undergraduates at the same university. The admissions policies at the laboratory school virtually insure that subjects in different age groups are similar with respect to general intelligence and socioeconomic level. Half of the subjects were male and half were female.

Experimental design

. . . Twenty-four subjects, 12 male and 12 female, were assigned to each [of four] age group[s]. Group I subjects ranged in age from 7 to 9 years; Group II subjects ranged from 11 to 13 years; Group III subjects ranged from 15 to 17 years; and Group IV subjects ranged from 19 to 21 years.

Materials and apparatus

The apparatus used was similar to that described by Crutchfield (1955). It consisted of five booths arranged in a semicircle. The center booth was occupied by the experimenter (E). It contained [an] opaque projector for projecting the stimuli on a screen in front of the booths, and master panels of lights and switches. The subjects (Ss) occupied the four side booths and faced the projection screen which was approximately 10 feet from each booth.

Each subject booth contained a panel of twenty lights arranged in four rows of five lights each, with five mercury switches placed below the fourth row of lights. Each of these switches, when turned on, activated the light immediately above it in the fourth row and a corresponding light on the master response panel in E's booth. The lights in the other three rows on the S's panel were controlled by master switches in E's booth, although the procedure was such that each S believed these lights reflected the responses of other Ss. In the present experiment, only three of the five lights in each row were utilized.

The stimulus materials were patterned after those used by Asch (1958). Twelve stimulus cards were prepared, each containing three comparison lines and a standard line. One of the three comparison lines was the same length as the standard, one was $\frac{1}{4}$-inch shorter than the standard, and the third was $\frac{1}{4}$-inch longer than the standard. The S's task was to choose the line which matched the standard in length.

Procedure

The experimental sessions were conducted in a room located at the school from which the Ss were drawn. Four Ss, all from a given age group and of the same sex, were run in each experimental session. The order in which the groups were run was random within the limits imposed by scheduling difficulties.

When Ss reported at the scheduled time, they were asked to select one of the four subject booths and be seated. The nature of the task and the manner of responding were explained in detail. The Ss were told that the order of responding would be random and that each S was to respond when E called out the number in his cubicle. Talking was prohibited. After the general instructions were given, E went to each booth and answered any questions that Ss posed concerning procedure. At this time, each person was assigned the number "4." When E was sure that everyone understood the instructions, five practice trials were administered to insure that Ss understood and were able to perform the task. Following the practice trials, each stimulus card was presented twice in a predetermined order. Erroneous responses were signaled by E for Ss 1, 2, and 3 on 16 of the 24 trials. The conformity score for each S was the number of times his response agreed with the erroneous responses on these 16 critical trials. Therefore, the score for any given subject could range from zero to 16.

At the end of the experimental session, each S was asked the following question: "Did you find that some of your answers were different from the others, and if so, what do you think the reason for this was?"

RESULTS

Before reporting the main results, it may be noted that on the preexperimental, non-pressure trials only two errors were made on a total of 480 judgments. This result indicates that the errors made under pressure conditions cannot be attributed to the difficulty of the task.

The results of pressure on conformity behavior under the various experimental conditions are presented graphically in Figure 1. . . . The only significant effect was that produced by the age variable. . . . As can be seen in Figure 1, conformity was least for Group I (ages 7–9), increased to a maximum for Group II (ages 11–13), and decreased again for Group III (ages 15–17) and Group IV (ages 19–21). Females conformed more than males at all age levels, although differences were not statistically significant.

It is perhaps worth noting that conformity as a function of age was also examined for each age level. The pattern of conformity was essentially the same as that shown in Figure 1, although the curve was not as smooth. Maximum conformity occurred at age 12.

The responses to the postexperimental question indicated that all Ss perceived some discrepancy between their responses and those of the other Ss in the group. The reasons given for these discrepancies were classified as either "internal" (that is, self-attributed reasons) or "external" (that is, other-attributed reasons). For example, "I must be going blind; I was wrong most of the time" was classified as internal, whereas "I think the other guys were crazy" was classified as external. These classifications were made by four graduate students in psychology who showed 100 percent agreement. Since the two classes are reciprocally related, only the internally attributing responses were considered. The 7–9 age group gave 6 internally attributing responses, the 11–13 age group gave 17, the 15–17 age group gave 13, and the 19–21 age group gave 11. The distributions of internal-external responses among age groups differed significantly . . . . This pattern corresponds closely to the pattern of conformity behavior (cf. Figures 1 and 2), suggesting that Ss who blame themselves when their behavior is discrepant from that of their peers are more likely to conform to group pressure than Ss who place the blame on others.

FIG. 1   Mean conformity as a function of age.

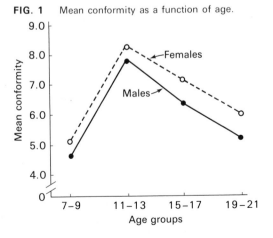

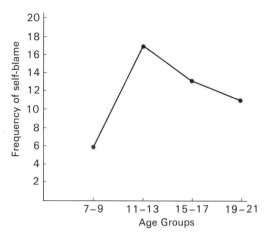

FIG. 2   Frequency of self-blame responses as a function of age.

In order to test this suggestion more directly, a [correlation] was computed between conformity and internal-external classification of subjects. This showed a highly significant relation (.87). To clarify further the relations among age, blame attribution, and conformity, an index of correlation was computed between age and conformity [which] yielded a [significant] value of .57. . . . The results indicate, therefore, that both the tendency to blame one's self and the tendency to conform to peers increase with age during the preadolescent period and decrease thereafter—at least through early adulthood.

DISCUSSION

The results of this study lend decisive support to the hypothesis that conformity to pressure from peers is a nonlinear function of age. The developmental function (see Figure 1) representing the mean number of conforming responses in each of the composite age groups supports the hypothesis that, from the preadolescent to the adolescent period of development, the amount of conformity to external social pressure increases, whereas conformity decreases after adolescence and through early adulthood.

Essentially, it appears that the development of conforming behavior patterns runs parallel with the socialization process. That is, the child in his early development is probably not fully aware of the social pressure to conform to certain standards adopted by his peers. Thus, the effect of a unanimously wrong majority is not extremely threatening to the younger child, and hence the lower percentage of conformity in the 7–9 age group in this experiment. On the other hand, with the onset of pubescence, the child becomes acutely aware of his social peers and relies upon them for many of his external behavior patterns (that is, ways of dress, "code" between buddies, clubs, "gang age," etc.). Therefore, the child at the pubescent stage displays much uncertainty with his own judgments and mirrors the behavior of his peers. By the postadolescent and early adulthood stages, the individual has learned that there are both situations which call for conformity and those which call for individual action. Thus, he becomes more confident about his own judgments despite the disagreement of a unanimous majority. However, since the individual in this postadolescent and young adult stage has experienced socialization, and since he has at some earlier time experienced the penalties of nonconformity, he does not attain the degree of individuality of judgment that is evident in the presocialization stage.

This interpretation is also consistent with the results of the analysis of the responses to the postexperimental question. It will be recalled that the pattern of internal attribution of responsibility for discrepant responses paralleled the conformity pattern.

Finally, it should be noted that the results of this experiment are generally consistent with those reported by Iscoe et al. (1963) but are in disagreement with Campbell's (1961) hypothesis concerning the relation of age and conformity and with results reported by Berenda (1950). The reasons for the failure to support Campbell's hypothesis are quite clear. His formulation was based upon the results of studies (Marple, 1933; Patel & Gordon, 1960) using high school students and adults as subjects, thus representing only the postadolescent period. The reasons for the discrepancy between our results and those reported by Berenda are not so obvious. As noted . . . above, however, there were some significant differences in the experimental situations.

Probably the most important differences were in the nature of the social pressure. It will be recalled that in Berenda's experiments pressure was exerted by high-status persons: the eight brightest children in the class or the teacher. It was suggested that age differences in conformity might vary, depending upon whether the social pressure emanates from higher-status persons or from peers. One might suspect that younger children are relatively more influenced by high-status persons than by peers, whereas older children are relatively more influenced by peers. In fact, data concerning the typical adolescent reaction to authority figures are consistent with this hypothesis. If this line of reasoning is correct, the differences between the results of the present study and the results of the Berenda study can be accounted for by the differences in kind of social pressure. On the other hand, if this reasoning is correct, it means that our hypothesis of a bi-directional, two-stage relation between age and conformity is valid only for situations involving pressure from peers.

REFERENCES

Asch, S. E. Effects of group pressure on the modification and distortion of judgments. In E. E. Maccoby, T. M. Newcomb, & E. L. Hartley (Eds.), *Readings in social psychology.* New York: Holt, 1958. Pp. 174–183.

Berenda, R. W. *The influence of the group on the judgments of children.* New York: King's Crown, 1950.

Berg, I. A., & Bass, B. M. (Eds.) *Conformity and deviation.* New York: Harper, 1961.

Campbell, D. T. Conformity in psychology's theories of acquired behavioral dispositions. In I. A. Berg & B. M. Bass (Eds.), *Conformity and deviation.* New York: Harper, 1961. Pp. 101–142.

Crutchfield, R. S. Conformity and character. *American Psychologist,* 1955, **10**, 191–198.

Iscoe, I., Williams, M., & Harvey, J. Modification of children's judgments by a simulated group technique: A normative developmental study. *Child Development,* 1963, **34**, 963–978.

Kelley, H. H., & Volkart, E. H. The resistance to change of group-anchored attitudes. *American Sociological Review,* 1952, **17**, 453–465.

Marple, C. H. The comparative susceptibility of three age levels to the suggestion of group versus expert opinion. *Journal of Social Psychology,* 1933, **4**, 176–186.

Patel, A. S., & Gordon, J. E. Some personal and situational determinants of yielding to influence. *Journal of Abnormal and Social Psychology,* 1960, **61**, 411–418.

Piaget, J. *The moral judgment of the child.* New York: Basic Books, 1954.

Tuddenham, R. D. Correlates of yielding to a distorted group norm. *Journal of Personality,* 1959, **27**, 272–284.

THE INFLUENCE OF SELF-ESTEEM ON RATE OF VERBAL CONDITIONING AND SOCIAL MATCHING BEHAVIOR[1]

Donna M. Gelfand[2]

Recent years have witnessed an increasing interest in determining personality correlates of responsiveness to social influence processes. One variable which has received a good deal of research attention has been self-esteem, typically defined as a person's characteristic evaluations of himself and his accomplishments. Low self-esteem is characterized by feelings of personal inadequacy, guilt, shyness, and social inhibitions; high esteem reflects feelings of self-confidence and satisfaction (Hovland, Janis, & Kelley, 1953).

A person's characteristic self-esteem is believed to be a function of his reinforcement history (Cohen, 1959; Lesser & Abelson, 1959; Sears, 1942). The high esteem individual has presumably had a past history of chiefly positive reinforcement for his efforts, while a low esteem person has met with negative reinforcement in a variety of situations. It has been hypothesized that self-esteem is negatively related to social suggestibility on the assumption that low self-esteem and high persuasibility stem from the same type of previous experience, i.e., negatively reinforced instances of disagreement or discrepancy (Lesser & Abelson, 1959). Research done to date generally provides support for this theory (Hovland & Janis, 1959).

Since investigators interested in self-esteem have primarily been social psychologists, persuasibility measures such as opinion change (Janis & Field, 1959) and matching behavior (Abelson & Lesser, 1959) have been extensively studied. However, other measures usually employed by experimental psychologists (e.g., verbal learning) have not been investigated as they might relate to persuasibility and self-esteem. Furthermore, except for one or two studies (deCharms & Rosenbaum, 1960), measures of self-esteem have been largely response inferred (e.g., global ratings or personality questionnaires) rather than experimentally manipulated.

The purpose of the present study was to investigate the effects of both response inferred and of experimentally manipulated self-esteem upon social suggestibility as measured by a picture preference test involving matching behavior, and a measure

[1] This article is based on a dissertation submitted to the Department of Psychology of Stanford University in partial fulfillment of the requirements for the Ph.D. degree.

[2] The author is greatly indebted to Albert Bandura for his advice and assistance in carrying out this research and in preparation of the manuscript for publication.

From D. M. Gelfand. The influence of self-esteem on rate of verbal conditioning and social matching behavior. Journal of Abnormal and Social Psychology, *1962,* **65,** *259–265. (With permission of the author and the American Psychological Association.)*

traditionally used more by experimental psychologists, verbal operant conditioning. Children were assigned to high and low self-esteem groups on the basis of their scores on a self-concept questionnaire, and equal numbers of subjects from each group were then exposed either to a success or a failure experience designed to manipulate self-esteem. Following the esteem manipulation, subjects participated in a picture preference task with an experimental confederate and the subjects' tendency to match the behavior of the confederate was measured. Finally, subjects were administered a verbal conditioning task in which their responsivity to the experimenter's verbal reinforcement was measured.

Experimental hypotheses were derived from the theory proposed by Hovland, Janis, and their associates, that self-esteem and persuasibility are inversely related. It was predicted that in relation to high self-esteem subjects (high rated esteem subjects who succeeded), subjects low in self-esteem (low rated esteem subjects who failed) would be more inclined to match picture preference choices of the confederate and to condition reinforced verbal responses to a higher level. No predictions were advanced concerning performances of subjects whose experimentally mediated experiences contradicted their customary esteem expectations, i.e., subjects high in rated esteem who failed and subjects low in rated esteem who succeeded.

METHOD

Subjects

Subjects were 60 fifth grade public school children, 30 of whom were males and 30 females. Sixty additional children served as experimental confederates. Since there is some evidence that females are generally more persuasible than males (Hovland & Janis, 1959), subjects of both sexes were included in the study to check this finding.

Design and procedure

. . . Subjects were first administered a self-concept test developed by Sears (1960). The test consisted of 100 questionnaire items covering 10 different areas of competence presumed important in children's self-evaluations. Subjects were asked to rate their ability on a five-point scale on each item. Self-esteem scores were the average of the subjects' self-ratings over the 100 items. On the basis of their test scores, subjects were dichotomized at the median into high and low self-esteem groups. One-third of each group was then randomly assigned to an experimental success manipulation designed to heighten self-esteem, one-third to a failure condition designed to lower self-esteem, while one-third constituted the control group which did not experience the experimental manipulations.

Experimental manipulations

Failure condition   Subjects were run in pairs in which one served as the experimental subject, while the other acted as an unwitting confederate. Subjects participated in four tasks in which the experimenter controlled results so that the confederate's performance was consistently better than the subject's.

The first task consisted of a 261-item arithmetic test involving addition, subtraction, and multiplication subtests, and was presented as a test of "arithmetic reasoning ability.'' In order to heighten the apparent importance of the test, it was prominently labeled Standard Arithmetic Reasoning Ability Test. Subjects were allowed 3 minutes to work on each subtest, and after 9 minutes, the experimenter ostensibly scored the tests and reported that the confederate completed twice as many problems correctly as did the subject. To emphasize further the success of the confederate, subjects were asked to record each other's scores on all tasks.

For the second task, subjects were asked to participate in a ''test of physical power.'' Test apparatus consisted of a large, black box (16'' × 17'' × 23'') with a stirrup-type handle anchored on one side, a meter on another side, and a cord by which the experimenter could control the meter reading on a third side. The subject and the confederate were asked to take two turns each; while the subject was pulling, the confederate called out the meter reading and vice versa. Players received tied scores on this task because pretesting showed that having the confederate best on all four tasks made subjects withdrawn or unduly upset.

The third task involved the use of materials from the Wisconsin Card Sort materials and was presented as a test of ''problem solving ability.'' The task was arranged so the subject and the confederate could not see each other's sorts nor could they determine the correct criteria. Subjects were asked to sort the cards twice, and each time the confederate apparently achieved the solution much more quickly than did the subject.

The final task was a test of ''hand-eye coordination.'' The equipment consisted of a miniature bowling alley (36'' × 12'' × 6'') with a runway at the end of which were three upright, doweled targets. The target area was screened from view by a fiberboard shield so the players had no way of knowing whether or not they struck a target. As a sign to the subjects that they had hit a target, a doweled marker dropped. The targets, however, were controlled with strings by the experimenter who was positioned at the side of the apparatus. The confederate and the subject each had two turns at bowling, and the confederate again won, receiving twice as high a score as the subject.

To further emphasize the differences in ability between the confederate and the subject, the experimenter instructed them to total scores obtained on all four tasks in order to establish the winner. The experimenter then congratulated the confederate on being the winner. For a detailed discussion of instruction and procedure see Gelfand (1961).

Success and control conditions   Experimental procedures in the success condition were identical to those described above, except the subject rather than the confederate was the successful partner. Control group subjects did not participate in experimental manipulations, performing only the two criterion tasks.

Dependent variables

Two different criterion tasks were employed in this study. The first was a picture preference test consisting of 20 pairs of pictures representing a wide variety of subject matter and mounted on 11'' × 14'' white cardboard cards. A large pool of pictures was pretested on 60 fifth grade children and pairs of pictures were selected in which one picture was preferred by a three-to-one margin. The confederate was previously informed that this was actually a test to see whether children would follow a leader and that he would serve as leader. The confederate had first choice on each item and was asked to pick the picture the experimenter indicated for each pair. The experimenter held each card by one hand nearest the picture to be chosen. In each case, the confederate chose the picture less preferred by the pretest sample. To increase social pressure on the subject, the experimenter expressed agreement with the confederate's choices by saying "Good" after the confederate's response on each of the first five items. The score on this test was the number of unpopular pictures chosen by the subject.

Following the picture preference task, the experimenter remarked that the subject and the confederate had worked together on a number of tests and that now they would perform different activities. The confederate was given a neutral task (crossing out letters in a text) while the experimenter administered a modified Taffel (1955) verbal conditioning procedure to the subject. The subject was presented with 1 series of 100 3" × 5" white index cards on each of which was printed a verb in the past tense and the same six pronouns: I, We, He, You, She, and They. The subject was instructed to choose one of the pronouns on each card and say it aloud together with the verb.

The first block of 20 trials was used as a measure of operant level, and no reinforcement was given. For the following four blocks of 20 items each, the experimenter reinforced the subject's use of We and They with approving remarks such as, "That's a good one" or "Good one." The score on the conditioning series was the difference in number of We and They responses produced between operant level and the fourth reinforced block.

At the conclusion of the experimental session, the child who had previously experienced failure was given a success experience on the coordination task to heighten his feelings of self-esteem and thus counteract the reaction induced by the experimental failure condition.

RESULTS

Effectiveness of esteem manipulation

As a check on the effectiveness of the esteem manipulation, subjects rated their performance before and after each task on a five-point rating scale ranging from 1—Very good to 5—Not very good. A [statistical] . . . test . . . revealed no significant differences in initial self-ratings between Success and Failure groups . . . , but differences between groups were highly significant on final ratings. . . . The results clearly indicate that the experimental manipulations were successful in altering self-esteem so that subjects in the Success group rated themselves more favorably while subjects who failed evaluated themselves less favorably.

Additional evidence concerning the effectiveness of the esteem manipulations was provided by a check list completed by the experimenter on the subjects' behavior during the conditioning task. Subjects were rated on "anxiety" versus "confidence" behaviors. Behavior considered indicative of anxiety included speech regression, manual-oral contact, frequent sighing, reduction in response speed, drop in voice level, etc. Confident behavior included speaking in a loud, clear voice, increased speed in responding, and absence of fidgeting. In contrast to the High esteem-Success group which displayed 1 anxiety sign and 18 confidence signs, the Low esteem-Failure group yielded 18 anxiety and 5 confidence signs. Although these data were not analyzed statistically, it seems apparent that the Low esteem-Failure group exhibited considerably more overt anxiety than did the High esteem-Success or any other treatment group.

Matching behavior on preference task

The first dependent variable measured was the number of imitative responses made by subjects in the picture preference task. . . . An analysis . . . performed on these data . . . [revealed that the variance of preference] test scores was greater for Control subjects than for Success or Failure subjects. With this restriction, [the] effect [of] experimental esteem manipulation proved significant. Subjects who experienced failure gave significantly more imitative responses than did subjects who experienced success. Neither initial self-esteem nor the interaction between initial and experimentally manipulated esteem significantly affected picture preference scores. . . .

Failure subjects were significantly more persuasible on the picture preference task than were Success subjects regardless of initial esteem level. Also, Control subjects high in self-esteem were more persuasible than were High esteem-Success subjects. . . .

Verbal conditioning rate

The second dependent variable measured was the number of reinforced responses produced in the verbal conditioning task. An analysis . . . performed on the 20-trial operant series revealed that the treatment groups did not initially differ significantly in production of the reinforced class of responses. Neither initial esteem, . . . experimental manipulations, . . . nor the interaction . . . significantly affected operant level of production of We and They responses.

An analysis . . . of the conditioning data . . . [indicated that] the variance of High esteem-Success subjects' scores was small while variance of scores for Control subjects was considerably larger. . . . Initially low esteem subjects who experienced success were significantly more conditionable than were initially low esteem subjects who experienced failure. Conversely, initially high esteem subjects who experienced failure conditioned to a significantly higher degree than did initially high esteem subjects in the Success condition. Control subjects initially low in esteem were significantly more conditionable than were High esteem-Success subjects. . . .

Contrary to the majority of previous findings by Hovland, Janis, and their associates (1959), male and female subjects did not differ significantly in their performance on any of the experimental measures.

DISCUSSION

The significant group differences in persuasibility found in this study partially confirm the Hovland and Janis hypothesis that self-esteem and persuasibility are negatively correlated. An inverse relationship between self-esteem and persuasibility was obtained on both dependent measures, but it was experimentally manipulated esteem which affected scores on the picture preference task while the interaction between rated and manipulated esteem was the variable related to verbal conditioning scores. The High esteem-Success group proved least suggestible on both criterion tasks as predicted, and the high suggestibility of the Low esteem-Failure subjects on the picture preference task also followed prediction. However, the minimal responsivity of the Low esteem-Failure group on the conditioning task clearly contradicted the experimental hypotheses.

Differences in relative persuasibility of groups between the two criterion tasks may have been due to any or all of a number of factors:
1. The persuasion source was a peer, the confederate, in the picture preference task while the experimenter served as persuasive agent in the conditioning situation.
2. The status of the source was varied in the preference task while status remained relatively constant for the experimenter as source.
3. The preference measure was temporally closer to the experimental esteem manipulation than was the conditioning measure.
4. The measures differed in complexity. The subject chose between many alternatives in the conditioning task while only two alternatives existed in the preference test—to follow or not to follow the confederate in making a choice.

The influence of the first three of these factors can only be surmised, but there is some experimental evidence concerning operation of the fourth factor. Several experimenters have reported the finding that high anxiety facilitates learning simple tasks, but interferes with performance on complex tasks (Montague, 1953; Sarason, Davidson, Lighthall, Waite, & Ruebush, 1960; Taylor & Spence, 1952). The experimenters' ratings of subjects' behavior during the conditioning task provide some evidence that treatment groups differed in overt manifestations of anxiety. Groups which displayed moderate amounts of "anxiety" *and* "confidence" behavior (Low esteem-Success and High esteem-Failure) received the highest conditioning scores, while the Low esteem-Failure group which appeared the most anxious scored relatively low in conditioning. Since a high level of anxiety interferes with learning complex tasks (Taylor & Spence, 1952), there is reason to believe that the conditioning performance of the Low esteem-Failure group was affected by their anxiety and tension. Conversely, the high level of performance of Low esteem-Failure subjects on the relatively simple preference task could also be due to their high anxiety which facilitates performance on simple tasks. Although evidence for facilitating and interfering effects of anxiety is mostly indirect in this study, the available data are consistent with this formulation. . . .

deCharms and Rosenbaum's (1960) findings that rated, but not manipulated self-esteem was associated with matching behavior are at variance with results of the present study. This discrepancy in findings may be due to differences in potency of experimental manipulations. deCharms and Rosenbaum's esteem manipulation was relatively superficial in nature, in that adult subjects were simply instructed that they were either high or low in leadership potential. In contrast, the manipulations in the present experiment involved several tasks performed by young children who tended to be highly competitive with each other. Since a series of success or failure experiences was involved, the cumulative effects were very powerful. Differences in subjects' ages may also have contributed to the discrepancy in results obtained in the two studies. Adults may be more influenced by internal norms based on an extensive reinforcement history, while children may be more dependent on external feedback concerning the adequacy of their performance.

Finally, the results of the present study may partially explain the finding of Kanfer and Karas (1959) that prior success and failure experiences did not affect verbal conditioning performance. Such negative results might be due to an unassessed interaction effect between initial self-esteem and experimental manipulations. When initial, rated self-esteem is not considered, conditioning data from the present experiment yield results similar to those obtained by Kanfer and Karas. Since success and failure interact with initial self-esteem to affect social suggestibility, it is clear that a study utilizing only one type of esteem measure may produce somewhat misleading results. Therefore, both rated and manipulated esteem should be considered in designing future suggestibility studies.

SUMMARY

The present study was designed to investigate the effects of response inferred and of experimentally manipulated self-esteem upon social suggestibility in children. Experimental hypotheses were derived from Hovland and Janis' (1959) theory that self-esteem and persuasibility are inversely related.

A personality inventory measure of self-esteem was administered to subjects who were assigned to high and low initial esteem groups on the basis of their test scores. Equal numbers of subjects from each group were then exposed either to an experimental success manipulation designed to heighten esteem or to a failure condition designed to lower esteem. Social suggestibility was measured by a picture preference task and a verbal operant conditioning procedure.

Results obtained were as follows:
1. Subjects who experienced failure exhibited significantly more matching responses on the picture preference task than did subjects who experienced success. Matching behavior, however, was not influenced by rated self-esteem.
2. A highly significant interaction was obtained between rated and experimentally manipulated self-esteem on performance in the conditioning procedure. Subjects exposed to experiences inconsistent with their customary self-evaluations (High esteem-Failure and Low esteem-Success groups) showed significantly more verbal conditioning than did subjects whose experiences were consistent with their self-attitudes (High esteem-Success and Low esteem-Failure groups).

Overall results were generally in accord with the theory that self-esteem and persuasibility are negatively correlated.

REFERENCES

Abelson, R. P., & Lesser, G. S. The measurement of persuasibility in children. In C. I. Hovland & I. L. Janis (Eds.), *Personality and persuasibility*. New Haven: Yale University Press, 1959. Pp. 141–166.

Cohen, A. R. Some implications of self-esteem for social influence. In C. I. Hovland & I. L. Janis (Eds.), *Personality and persuasibility*. New Haven: Yale University Press, 1959. Pp. 102–120.

deCharms, R., & Rosenbaum, M. E. Status variables and matching behavior. *Journal of Personality*, 1960, **28**, 492–502.

Gelfand, D. M. The influence of self-esteem on rate of conditioning and social matching behavior. Unpublished doctoral dissertation, Stanford University, 1961.

Hovland, C. I., & Janis, I. L. (Eds.) *Personality and persuasibility*. New Haven: Yale University Press, 1959.

Hovland, C. I., Janis, I. L., & Kelley, H. H. *Communication and persuasion*. Princeton: Princeton University Press, 1953.

Janis, I. L., & Field, P. B. Sex differences and personality factors related to persuasibility. In C. I. Hovland & I. L. Janis (Eds.), *Personality and persuasibility.* New Haven: Yale University Press, 1959. Pp. 55–68.

Kanfer, F. H., & Karas, S. C. Prior experimenter-subject interaction and verbal conditioning. *Psychological Reports,* 1959, **5**, 345–353.

Lesser, G. S., & Abelson, R. P. Personality correlates of persuasibility in children. In C. I. Hovland & I. L. Janis (Eds.), *Personality and persuasibility.* New Haven: Yale University Press, 1959. Pp. 187–206.

Montague, E. K. The role of anxiety in serial rote learning. *Journal of Experimental Psychology,* 1953, **45**, 91–96.

Sarason, S. B., Davidson, K. S., Lighthall, F. F., Waite, R. R., & Ruebush, B. K. *Anxiety in elementary school children.* New York: Wiley, 1960.

Sears, P. S. The pursuit of self-esteem: The middle childhood years. Paper presented at the meeting of the American Psychological Association, Chicago, September, 1960.

Sears, R. R. Success and failure: A study of motility. In Q. McNemar & M. A. Merrill (Eds.), *Studies in personality.* New York: McGraw-Hill, 1942. Pp. 235–258.

Taffel, C. Anxiety and the conditioning of verbal behavior. *Journal of Abnormal and Social Psychology,* 1955, **51**, 496–501.

Taylor, J. A., & Spence, K. W. The relationship of anxiety level to performance in serial learning. *Journal of Experimental Psychology,* 1952, **44**, 61–64.

VI

LEARNING AND REINFORCEMENT EFFECTS

Harold W. Stevenson [1]

This chapter is an introduction to the study of children's learning. Although learning has been one of the core areas of psychology for many years, only recently has the study of children's learning received a great deal of attention. To understand why this is true, one must look briefly into the history of experimental psychology. When psychologists first ventured into the scientific investigation of the learning process, they were acutely aware of the importance of imposing appropriate controls on their experimental subjects, both in the laboratory and in their everyday lives. Because it seemed to be so much more difficult to control the environment and physiological state of young human beings than of lower animals, the animal laboratory became the principal locus of research on the learning process.

Some early investigators did use children as subjects; and if

[1] This chapter was written while the author was in residence as a Fellow at the Center for Advanced Study in the Behavioral Sciences, Palo Alto, California, supported in part by Special Fellowship HD-35961 from the National Institute of Child Health and Human Development, U.S. Public Health Service.

one looks at their studies, it is obvious that children were not only interesting and cooperative subjects, but also their behavior was both lawful and consistent. It is not clear why it took other psychologists so long to realize this. At any rate, the pace of research on children's learning began to accelerate about twenty years ago, and during these two decades a large amount of information has been accumulated.

Because so many studies are available, it is necessary to be highly selective in including topics in this chapter. In making these selections, three criteria were considered: general interest, importance for understanding children's behavior, and definitiveness of the data. Many possible worthwhile topics have been omitted because they are of interest primarily to the specialist within the field of learning, or because they contribute more to knowledge about learning in general than about children's behavior.

The chapter begins with a discussion of learning as represented by studies of classical and operant conditioning and then attempts to show how the variables that are important in influencing the behavior of young children must be extended and modified in experimental work if the behavior of older children is to be understood. Age in isolation is not a meaningful variable, but as the child grows older he acquires skills, such as the use of language, and has experiences, such as those occurring as he becomes socialized; these skills and experiences have pervasive effects on the rate and manner in which the child will learn.

STUDIES OF CONDITIONING

Learning in the newborn

One of the first questions asked about children's learning is, "How early can learning occur?" This is an important question, for theories of personality, such as psychoanalytic theories, propose that the earliest experiences of the infant can have profound effects on later personality development. If it were shown that the newborn baby is already capable of learning, the position that very early experiences could have significant effects on later behavior would be strengthened.

The primary method employed in studies of early learning has been the conditioned response. Both classical and operant methods, and variants of each, have been used. In classical conditioning studies, an unconditioned stimulus, such as a light or a sound, is presented to the baby before the insertion of a nipple into its mouth. After a series of trials, the nipple is omitted, and the baby is observed to see whether sucking has become a conditioned response to the presentation of the conditioned stimulus, the light. In operant conditioning, a base-line measure is obtained of the frequency with which the baby makes a particular response; following this, each of these responses is reinforced for a specified number of times; a measure is then taken to see if the frequency of such responses has increased significantly.

Several decades ago it would have been necessary to conclude that the human infant is incapable of learning before the age of two months, for repeated attempts to develop conditioned responses in neonates resulted in either failure or methodological impasses. An example of the latter is seen in a study by Wickens & Wickens (1940), who worked with three groups of newborns. During the training trials, an experimental group was presented with the sound of a buzzer as the conditioned stimulus and a shock to the foot as the unconditioned stimulus. In one control group the neonates were presented only with the buzzer during these trials, and in another, only the shock. The test trials were the same for all babies; on these trials only the buzzer was presented.

Successful conditioning was demonstrated in the experimental group; when the shock was omitted on test trials, the babies retracted their foot to the sound of the buzzer—a response they had not made to the buzzer at the beginning of the conditioning trials. Unexpectedly, similar results were found for the group that had been presented only with the shock during the training trials. These infants also retracted their foot to the sound of the buzzer during the test trials. How can these results be interpreted? Possibly, the shock had sensitized the babies so that practically any stimulus could elicit foot retraction. Or the shock may have constituted a change in the stimulus situation, and therefore, the effective conditioned stimulus was a change in stimulation rather than the appearance of a particular stimulus. At any rate, attempts to interpret these results were so confusing that it seemed nearly impossible to design a study that could provide a critical test of the conditionability of neonates.

There the matter rested for nearly twenty years. Some work was done in the Soviet Union, but interest in the problem was minimal until Papoušek, a Czech pediatrician, published his studies of conditioned head turning in the neonate. Papoušek (1967) obtained firm evidence that the neonate can be conditioned, while in earlier studies the results were equivocal. The major differences appear to be that the earlier studies had used noxious stimuli, such as shock, or unstable responses, such as sucking. On the other hand, Papoušek, as indicated in an earlier chapter, used head turning to milk reinforcement in a modified classical-operant conditioning procedure. A tone was sounded, and if the baby turned his head to the left, milk was offered to him. If the baby did not turn his head, the assistant touched the left corner of his mouth with the nipple, and if this was ineffective in eliciting head turning, the baby's head was turned to the left and the nipple placed in his mouth. Ten trials a day were given until the baby made five consecutive positive responses in a daily session, that is, until the baby turned his head in the correct direction in five consecutive presentations of the conditioned stimulus (tone).

This procedure was used with three groups of infants, with average ages of 3, 86, and 142 days at the beginning of the study. On the average, the babies in the youngest group reached criterion on the eighteenth experimental day. There were, however, wide individual differences in the rate with which neonates could be conditioned. Some required as few as seven days, while others required more than a month of training. As might be expected, the older infants required notably fewer average numbers of days to reach criterion than did the newborns. The oldest group reached criterion on the third experimental day, and the middle group, on the fourth.

Since the publication of Papoušek's studies, other investigators have reported successful conditioning within the first weeks of life. The article by Siqueland & Lipsitt (1966) that accompanies this chapter is an example of the application of conditioning procedures to the study of conditioned discrimination of auditory stimuli. As will be seen, these investigators provided further evidence that newborns can be conditioned. In addition, they found that newborns were capable of responding differentially to two stimuli, one of which was accompanied by reinforcement.

Habituation

In line with the studies of conditioning, studies of habituation also have offered evidence that the behavior of the newborn can be modified through repeated experience. The reader will recall from the discussion in Chapter II that habituation is demonstrated if a stimulus which is initially effective in suppressing a particular response ceases to be effective after a series of presentations. It still is not clear whether habituation is a form of

learning or whether it is dependent upon a more basic physiological process such as neural adaptation. The important factor
for the present discussion is that habituation offers additional
evidence that environmental events may have predictable effects
on early behavior.

A typical study of habituation was reported by Engen & Lipsitt
(1965). Infants one to six days old were observed until the infant
appeared to be asleep, with no gross motor activity and regular
patterns of breathing. An odorant, such as anise, then was placed
in front of the infant's nostrils. The introduction of this stimulus
resulted in an increase in motor activity. The odorant was removed, and after the infant again became quiet, the odorant was
re-presented. The average number of responses to the odorant
decreased with successive presentations, indicating that habituation had occurred. When habituation had occurred to an odorant
which was a mixture of two substances, movement increased
again when only one of the two substances was presented. The
reappearance of movement to one of the substances offers some
evidence that the decrement in response was not a result of
sensory fatigue. Although the authors interpret their results as
examples of learning, additional studies will be needed before
other interpretations can be rejected with confidence.

Conditioning with older infants

Studies with older infants have used the same techniques used
with neonates, but the broader repertoire of behavior in older
infants makes it possible to work with a richer variety of responses. An example of a study with implications for children's
later development and for child-care practices is the Rheingold,
Gewirtz, & Ross (1959) study of the conditioning of vocalizations
in three-month-olds. The purpose of this study was to determine
whether the frequency of vocalization could be increased by
reinforcement and then decreased by the withdrawal of reinforcement.

Three-month-olds generally have a moderate rate of vocalization, and through observation, a base rate of vocalization can be
established. After obtaining the base rate for each infant, Rheingold et al. responded to each vocalization with a complex of social
acts, including smiling, making "tssk" sounds, and touching the
baby's abdomen. The experiment was conducted in 9 three-
minute sessions, daily over six days, with two separate samples
of babies. By the end of the second day of conditioning, the

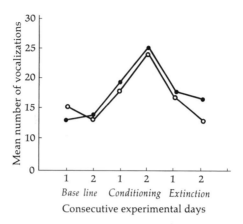

FIGURE 1 *The mean number of vocalizations made by the two groups of subjects on the six days in the Rheingold, Gewirtz, & Ross (1959) study of conditioning of infants' vocalizations.*

frequency of vocalization was nearly twice the base-line rate. When vocalization was no longer reinforced, there was a consistent decline in vocalization to approximately the base-rate level. The results, as can be seen in Figure 1, are very similar for each sample of infants.

At first glance, the study appears to offer clear evidence of conditioning, but as often happens, an alternative interpretation of the increase and subsequent decrease in vocalization is possible. The form of reinforcement used in the study may have had an arousing effect on the infants so that frequency of vocalization was a function of level of arousal rather than a product of learning. The more the infants vocalized, the more frequently the adult responded to them, and thus, the more aroused they may have become. To rule out the possibility that the increase in vocalization was a result of arousal, it would be necessary to demonstrate that "noncontingent" reinforcement would not have a similar effect.[2] In the present case, then, infants should be responded to in the same manner embodied in the presentation of contingent reinforcement, but the time and frequency of the adult's

[2]Noncontingent reinforcement is distinguished from contingent reinforcement in the following way. In noncontingent reinforcement, the delivery of reinforcement does not depend on the subject's making a particular response; in contingent reinforcement, it does. Thus, the time and frequency of noncontingent reinforcement can be determined before the experiment begins. Contingent reinforcement, on the other hand, cannot be delivered until the subject makes the appropriate response.

response should be independent of the child's vocalizing. If the frequency of vocalization does not increase with this treatment, it can be concluded that the increase found with contingent reinforcement *was* a result of learning.

Weisberg (1963) replicated the conditions of the Rheingold study, but included a group for which reinforcement was not contingent upon vocalization; and he also included groups in which a nonsocial stimulus (chime) was used as a contingent and as a noncontingent reinforcer. In addition, to rule out the possibility that simply seeing an adult might be arousing, a group was tested in the presence of a nonresponsive adult. Successful conditioning and extinction were found only in the group for which social reinforcement was contingent upon vocalization (see Weisberg's article at the end of Chapter III). The Rheingold results, therefore, must represent conditioning, and such conditioning seems to be dependent upon contingent reinforcement with social stimuli.

These studies demonstrate a simple but important point for anyone who wishes to modify the behavior of infants and children. General attentiveness, as represented by noncontingent reinforcement, was not effective in producing an increase in vocalization. Only when the reinforcement *followed* the desired response in a consistent fashion was an increase obtained. Thus, although attentiveness by the adult may be an important factor in maintaining general responsiveness in the infant, its effectiveness as a means of producing behavioral change seems to be restricted to its occurring after the desired response has been performed. Many other studies with animals and humans offer additional support for such a contention.

Behavior modification

Some of the most dramatic applications of the preceding point are found in studies of behavior modification. In these studies, an explicit attempt is made to change some aspects of the child's behavior through the systematic application of reinforcement. Before such a study is undertaken, two important decisions have to be made: first, what change in behavior is desired, and second, what type of stimulus will function effectively as a reinforcer for the particular child being studied. The first is usually the easier decision. The success of many studies of behavior modification appears to be attributable not only to the systematic control of the outcomes of behavior, but also to remarkably astute analyses of the effective conditions of reinforcement. The types of stimuli that may be effective as reinforcers differ greatly for different children. For some, it may be adult approval, for others, seashells, and for still others, French fried potatoes. In extraordinary cases, where the child is severely disturbed and his behavior has serious effects on his health, the cessation of noxious stimuli, such as electric shock applied to the child's feet, has been used as the reinforcing stimulus. Behavior modification has achieved success in so many different cases that it rapidly has become a popular method of treating psychological problems.

The work by Brown & Elliott (1965), with a group of preschool boys, is a good example of how operant procedures have been applied in behavior modification. In this study, an attempt was made to reduce aggressive behavior and to increase cooperative behavior during the boys' free-play periods in nursery school. During a pretreatment period, observations were made to obtain base rates of physical and verbal aggression. Then the teachers who acted as the agents of treatment were given the following instructions:

> Briefly, we will try to ignore aggression and reward cooperative and peaceful behavior. Of course if someone is using a hammer on another's head we would step in, but just to separate the two and leave. It will be difficult at first because we tend to watch and be quiet when nothing bad is happening and now our attention will as much as possible be directed toward cooperative, or non-aggressive behavior. It would be good to let the most aggressive boys see that the others are getting the attention if it is possible. A pat on the head, 'That's good Mike,' 'Hello Chris and Mark, how are you today?' 'Look what Eric made,' etc. may have more rewarding power than we think. On the other hand, it is just as important during this week to have no reprimands, no 'Say you're sorry,' 'Aren't you sorry?' Not that these aren't useful ways of teaching proper behavior, but they will only cloud the effects of our other manner of treatment. It would be best not even to look at a shove or small fight if we are sure no harm is being done; as I mentioned before, if it is necessary we should just separate the children and leave (p. 105).

The procedure was effective in reducing the average number of aggressive acts. There was a daily average of 41.2 instances of physical aggression within the group before the experimental period and 26.0 afterwards. The decline in verbal aggression, from a mean of 22.8 to 17.4, was less marked, but was significant statistically. The teachers, as do other adults, had difficulty in restraining themselves from responding to the aggressive acts. The interest and concern over children's aggressive behavior that adults commonly have may function as a source of reinforcement for aggressive responses and thereby increase, rather than decrease, children's tendencies to be aggressive.

Among the most interesting studies of the use of behavior modification with clinical subjects have been those of Lovaas and his coworkers. Lovaas has chosen to work with some of the most intractable forms of behavior and with some of the most difficult types of children. In an article which is reproduced after this chapter, Lovaas, Berberich, Perloff, & Schaeffer (1966) describe efforts to teach 2 six-year-old schizophrenic boys imitative speech. The behavior of these boys was severely impoverished, and initially they were incapable of any form of speech. Since the desired behavior was not present, it was necessary, through a series of increasingly demanding steps, to produce this behavior. Lovaas describes how this was accomplished, and how, gradually, the production of speech appeared to become rewarding in itself. It is toward this goal, the ultimate production and elaboration of responses without the use of external reinforcers, that work with clinical groups often is directed.

Variables influencing performance

Establishing the fact that conditioning occurs is one step; next, efforts must be made to determine the conditions resulting in the most effective performance. Because of the difficulties in obtaining young infants for study, most of the research on variables influencing performance in studies of conditioning has been conducted with older children on tasks involving simple instrumental motor responses. Several of the variables related to conditioning will be discussed in this section.

Drive Level

It is usually impossible or undesirable to withhold such things as food and water from children. Therefore, it is somewhat more difficult to study the effects of drive on the performance of children than of animals, but several methods of varying drive level have been used successfully. These include depriving children of social stimuli for short periods, introducing mild frustration by withholding rewards, and selecting children who differ in level of anxiety.

A study by Gewirtz & Baer (1958) illustrates how deprivation and satiation may influence the rate of conditioning. Before performing the experimental task, one group of preschool children was subjected to twenty minutes of social isolation by being left alone in an empty room, while another group was praised periodically for twenty minutes while they performed a simple task. A third group (control) was given no preliminary experience. The experimental task involved dropping marbles into two holes of a container. After establishing a base line of response, social reinforcement in the form of supportive comments ("good," "fine") was given every fifth time the children dropped a marble into the hole that had been preferred least during the last minute of the base-line period. It was assumed that supportive statements would be more effective as reinforcing agents following isolation than following praise. The results supported this assumption. The increase between the base-line and experimental periods in the number of responses to the nonpreferred hole was greatest following deprivation and least following satiation, with an intermediate value being obtained for the control group. Isolation thus enhanced the effectiveness of social stimuli as reinforcers of a simple motor response.

Frustration has been studied on the assumption that an increase in frustration is accompanied by an increase in drive. A common method for inducing frustration has been to omit reinforcement on certain trials while continuing to reinforce responses on other trials. A typical study was reported by Penney (1960). Children were tested on an apparatus equipped with two levers, and their task was to pull the first lever to its terminus and then to repeat the act with the second lever. Pulling the first lever sometimes resulted in the delivery of reinforcement and sometimes it did not. The second lever always yielded reinforcement. The average speed with which the second lever was pulled was greater following nonreinforcement than following reinforcement on the first lever. Nonreinforcement in the context of a series of reinforced trials apparently was frustrating, and the frustration resulted in more vigorous response to the second lever.

A final example is a study on the effects of anxiety on escape conditioning (Penney & McCann, 1962). Anxiety was assumed to act as an irrelevant drive that energized all existing habits. In the lever-pulling task, which involves a well-learned response, highly anxious children should have faster response speeds than children with lower levels of anxiety. Third- and fourth-graders were selected on the basis of their scores on an anxiety questionnaire to form high- and low-anxious groups. In the experimental task, a loud unpleasant tone could be terminated only by pulling the lever through its full excursion. As predicted, high-anxious children had faster response speeds than those with lower levels of anxiety.

Increases in drive, whether produced by deprivation, frustration, or by selecting anxious children as subjects, thus seem to have similar effects on the performance of simple motor responses. In the studies discussed, an increase in drive consistently resulted in more efficient and effective responses. It should be noted, however, that these conclusions apply primarily to simple motor responses, such as are required in studies of conditioning. When the responses are more complex or are subject to competition from other responses, as would be the case in problem-solving tasks, an increase in drive has been found to have a disruptive rather than a facilitative effect on performance.

Delay of Reward

A number of explanations have been offered for the finding that a delay in the delivery of reinforcement retards the rate of conditioning. One of the more convincing explanations was tested in a study by Rieber (1961) on a lever-pulling task with kindergarten children. It was assumed that a delay in reinforcement increases the possibility that responses incompatible with the execution of the instrumental response will become associated with a conditioned stimulus. For example, while waiting for the delivery of the reward, the children might look at the reward box. On subsequent trials they might tend, therefore, to look at the reward box when the signal appeared rather than to pull the lever. In this study, the children either were reinforced immediately after their responses, or there was a twelve-second delay between response and reward. There were two delayed reinforcement groups. In one, the conditioned stimulus (a light) remained visible during the delay period, and in the other, the stimulus terminated with the completion of the child's response. The probability that competing responses would be conditioned to the light (and subsequently would be elicited by the light) was assumed to be greater when the light remained on during the delay interval than when it was terminated by the child's response. As predicted, starting speed was fastest with immediate reinforcement and slowest when the signal remained on during the delay interval.

Although this, and many other studies, have found deleterious effects on performance of simple motor tasks with a delay of reinforcement, the results from studies with more complex tasks frequently have not found such effects. This is especially true when older children are used as subjects. Presumably, older children are capable of bridging the gap between the time of response and the delivery of reinforcement by some form of self-instruction, thereby reducing the effects of delayed reinforcement.

Stimulus Familiarization

There is a common saying that familiarity breeds contempt; in conditioning, familiarity does not necessarily lead to contempt, but it may lead to poorer performance. The effect appears to be attributable to habituation. In line with our earlier discussion, repeated presentation of any stimulus, including a conditioned stimulus, should result in habituation. Cantor & Cantor (1965) have studied the problem with young children. The subjects were given 40 three-second exposures to either a red or a green light. Both the red and green lights were used in the experimental task, and the subjects were required to press a red button when the red light appeared and a green button when a green light appeared. Response speeds were faster for the novel than for the familiar stimulus. Familiarity had reduced the effectiveness of the stimulus as an elicitor of response.

The studies of familiarization and satiation indicate that prior experience may reduce effectiveness of stimuli as elicitors and reinforcers of performance. Both of these phenomena appear to be useful in interpreting the results of a study by Stevenson, Keen, & Knights (1963) on the effectiveness of parents and strangers as reinforcing agents. Parents may observe that other adults frequently induce their children to work harder and have a greater impact on their children's behavior than they do themselves. Since, by definition, children are more familiar with their parents and have received more praise from their parents than from a stranger, it might be expected that because of familiarization, parental requests would be less effective in eliciting responses, and that because of satiation, parental praise would be less effective as a reinforcer of their performance in certain tasks. The results of the Stevenson et al. study were in line with these expectations; the rate at which preschool children responded in a marble-dropping task similar to that used by Gewirtz and Baer generally was lower when the children were tested by one of their parents than when they were tested by a strange adult. The rate of response actually decreased across the six minutes of the task when social reinforcement was delivered by their parents; but when supportive comments were made by a stranger, an increase in rate was observed.

Schedules of Reinforcement

Investigators interested in operant conditioning have given a great deal of attention to the effects of different schedules of reinforcement on conditioning. An early and important discovery was that the strength of the conditioned response is greater under intermittent than under continuous reinforcement. Response strength typically has been assessed by determining the number of nonreinforced trials that are required to extinguish the response.

A study by Kass & Wilson (1966) offers an interesting example of how different schedules of reinforcement can produce quite different effects on children's behavior. The apparatus was a simulated slot machine. The children were told they could win pennies by operating the machine and that they could play as long as they wished. One-half of the children were reinforced on one-third of the trials, and the other half were reinforced on every trial. The number of training trials also differed; some children were given three trials before the extinction trials began, and others were given nine, twenty-one, forty-five, or sixty trials. As can be seen in Figure 2, the mean number of responses made during extinction was consistently higher for the groups that had received intermittent reinforcement. A second finding is also immediately apparent; the number of responses made during extinction decreased as the number of training trials increased. These results provide support for a discrimination hypothesis of extinction, which states that the rate of extinction is dependent upon the degree to which the subject is able to discriminate between the training and extinction periods. This discrimination should be easier when all responses have been reinforced during the training trials and when there has been a large number of training trials, than it is when reinforcement is intermittent or smaller amounts of training have been provided.

Adults are often advised by psychologists to be consistent in the way they interact with children. The basis for this advice is relatively clear. Inconsistency results in frustration and in greater

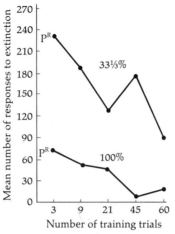

FIGURE 2   *The mean number of reponses to ex-tinction as a function of percentage of reinforcement and number of training trials in the study by Kass & Wilson (1966).*

persistence on the part of the child. If the child finds that tantrums never lead to reward, tantrums will be extinguished; but if the parent at times succumbs to his child's wailing (intermittent reinforcement), the child will repeat the act many times before giving it up as a means of controlling parental responses.

Developmental changes

The previous studies might lead to the conclusion that classical and operant conditioning offer a means of explaining a good deal of children's behavior. The principles are explicit, simple, and appear to be widely applicable. Some psychologists, in fact, have attempted to describe the process of behavioral development in terms of conditioning (e.g., Bijou & Baer, 1961, 1965). When young children or simple responses are involved, conditioning descriptions are persuasive, and with a convincing consistency, are validated by experimental data. In the preceding paragraphs, however, it has been noted that the variables may have different effects with complex tasks or older children. In such cases, the principles of conditioning begin to lose some of their power as explanatory devices. There will be many more examples, in subsequent sections of this chapter, of the difficulties in a conditioning or stimulus-response approach to understanding children's behavior. Although the principles of conditioning eventually may be extended to encompass such findings, presently they remain as potential sources of explanation whose limits of applicability still are to be demonstrated.

Some of the problems that a stimulus-response approach to learning faces are encountered in developmental studies, where response characteristics of children at one age are displaced by other quite different forms of behavior at later ages. Two examples will illustrate the types of problems that arise. The first is a developmental study of the effects of reinforcement and non-reinforcement of a single response (Stevenson & Weir, 1961). The data were obtained from a three-choice task in which two of the choices were never reinforced. Children indicated their choices by pressing a button; marbles, which later could be exchanged for a prize, were used as reinforcers. An analysis was made of the proportion of subjects who repeated their response following the *first* reinforcement or nonreinforcement of the preceding response. The subjects were children of ages three, five, seven, and nine years. According to traditional reinforcement concepts, reinforcement should increase the tendency to repeat the reinforced response on the subsequent trial, and nonreinforcement should reduce this tendency. The behavior of the three-year-olds can be readily accounted for in these terms. Over 80 percent of the three-year-olds repeated the response after reinforcement and fewer than 50 percent did so after nonreinforcement. By age nine, however, nearly 80 percent of the children *changed* their response after reinforcement and nearly all changed their response after nonreinforcement. Between these two ages, there was a systematic increase in the percentage of children changing response after each type of event. It appears that the older children were utilizing a strategy to direct their response, while the younger children were more dependent upon the outcomes of what they had done. The nine-year-olds performed as if they were applying a win-shift lose-shift strategy by which they were attempting to assess the characteristics of the situation before settling on the choice of a particular stimulus. Introducing the term "strategy" implies a mentalism unacceptable to the reinforcement theorist. But is there a simpler way to explain these results?

A second example is a developmental study of discrimination learning by Graham, Ernhart, Craft, & Berman (1964). Children between the ages of 2 and $4\frac{1}{2}$ were presented pairs of stimuli, each pair consisting of a common stimulus and a second stimulus larger or smaller than the first. Choices of the common stimulus were reinforced consistently for one-half of the children, while for the other half, responses to the relation between the stimuli were reinforced (i.e., choices of the larger stimulus in each pair were reinforced). If it is assumed that the probability of the children's choosing a particular stimulus is dependent upon the frequency with which the choice is reinforced, it would be predicted that learning would proceed more rapidly for the group that was reinforced consistently for the choices of the common stimulus. The results indicated the opposite effect; it was much easier at all ages for the children to learn the relational problem. In fact, performance on the relational problem was maximal by the age of three. To interpret these findings, it appears to be necessary to posit that responding to relations among stimuli is a primitive mode of response, one that is characteristic of young children and that is more influential in determining their rate of learning than is the schedule of reinforcement. This position is very similar to that espoused by the Gestalt psychologists who discussed learning in terms of the perceptual organization of stimuli—a position strongly opposed by reinforcement theorists.

At this point a new concept should be introduced—"verbal mediation." Perhaps what was being reinforced in the last example was not the overt response of picking up a particular stimulus, but an implicit verbal response, such as, "Pick up the big one." It is a commonly accepted fact that words have a directive influence on adult behavior. For example, in following directions in a strange city, the adult rehearses to himself, "Turn right at the gasoline station, go for two blocks, and then turn left for six blocks." In such a case, the environment has an influence on behavior primarily in its providing the context for applying the directions and for verifying their correctness, but the words determine the responses that will be made. Verbal mediation occurs when an external stimulus elicits an implicit (or explicit) verbal response, and the motor act is conditioned to the stimuli produced by the evocation of this verbal response. The verbal response acts as a "mediator" between the external stimulus and the motor act. The concept of verbal mediation has been used in discussing children's performance in many types of tasks, and some of these will be discussed in the following section.

VERBAL MEDIATION   One of the most important accomplishments during childhood is the acquisition of language. For the infant, words have no significance other than as sounds; gradually, meaning becomes attached to the sounds, and eventually the child is able to form words himself. Several additional steps are necessary, however, before words can be used as mediators of response. Even after the child acquires words, he frequently appears to be unable to use them effectively as a means of guiding his response. Verbal mediation typically cannot be demonstrated experimentally until the child is about five or six years old, and even then, the mediation process often is less effective than at later ages.

Transposition

Studies of transposition offer a good example of how verbal mediation has been used in explaining children's performance. In the commonly used two-choice transposition problem, subjects are trained to respond, for example, to the larger of two stimuli. In the test trials, the smaller of the original pair is replaced by a third, still larger stimulus (see Figure 3). Will the subjects choose the stimulus that led to reinforcement, or will they choose the larger stimulus in the test pair? Generally, animals of different species and humans of different ages transpose; that is, they choose the stimulus in the test set that has the same relation to this set that the reinforced stimulus had to the training set (i.e., they chose the larger of the two stimuli). This tendency toward relational response was used by the Gestalt psychologists as

FIGURE 3 *The transposition problem. In this example, subjects must pick the larger of the two squares during the training trials. On "near" tests of transposition, the previously positive stimulus is retained, and a new larger stimulus replaces the previously smaller stimulus. In tests of "far" transposition, two more remote stimuli are used. In both types of test trials, a choice of the larger stimulus provides evidence for transposition. The left-right relation of the smaller and larger stimuli would differ for different subjects on the test trials and would be random across the training trials for each subject.*

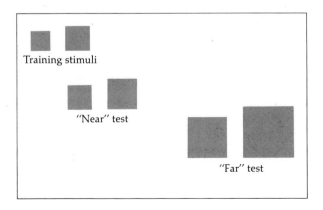

further support of their view that learning is a result of developing an understanding of the relations that exist among stimuli. This view runs into difficulty, however, when the test stimuli are not adjacent to the training pair ("near" test). When the stimuli are further removed on the stimulus dimension ("far" test), work with animals has shown that transposition tends not to occur; the subjects either respond randomly or choose the stimulus nearer the training pair (the smaller stimulus).

Spence (1937), a leading exponent of the stimulus-response approach, proposed a theoretical model that was capable of predicting both findings: transposition on near tests and a decreased frequency of transposition with more remote sets. The details of the model do not need to be discussed here other than to indicate that they involve an interaction between gradients of stimulus generalization derived from the positive and negative stimuli of the training pair. What is important is that the model offers an S-R interpretation of transposition.

Now, how does all of this apply to the behavior of children? Kuenne (1946), a student of Spence, was interested in this question. She made the assumption that young preverbal children would perform in a manner similar to that predicted for lower animals, and that the behavior of both animals and preverbal children was controlled by the same types of mechanisms. Older children, however, were assumed to be capable of verbal mediation. She assumed that older children spontaneously apply verbal labels to the stimuli and would learn a response, such as "Pick the big one," during the course of the training trials. The test stimuli should elicit this mediator, and consequently, children should choose the larger stimulus regardless of the differences in absolute size of the training and test sets. In other words, it was predicted that older children would show a high frequency of transposition on both near and far tests, but that younger children would show a lower frequency of transposition on the far than on the near tests.

The stimuli were squares of different sizes, and the subjects were preschool children with mental ages (MA) of three, four, five, and six years. As can be seen in Figure 4, the results supported the predictions. Transposition was at a high level across all MA levels for the near set of stimuli, but decreased for the far set as MA decreased. The children's verbalizations provided additional support for Kuenne's position. Practically none of the three-year-olds were able to verbalize the size relation that existed within the pairs of stimuli, and nearly all of the five- and

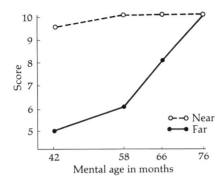

FIGURE 4 *The incidence of transposition as a function of mental age for "near" and "far" tests of transposition in the study by Kuenne (1946).*

six-year-olds were able to verbalize the principle either spontaneously or upon questioning.

Although the results of this study supported the predictions that were made, it is necessary to point out that in many studies, neither the original Spence model nor the modifications suggested by Kuenne prove to be capable of providing a straightforward explanation of the results. For example, a study by Johnson & Zara (1960) indicates the types of problems this approach encounters when slight modifications are made in the training procedure. By using *two* sets of training stimuli, Johnson and Zara were able to get three- and four-year-olds to perform in much the same manner as the older children did in the study by Kuenne.

Paired-associate learning

Learning to associate one stimulus with another is a common event in everyday life. For example, we engage in paired-associate learning in learning to speak English. For each object and each act, we must learn the appropriate English word. This round, colored object is an "orange;" moving one's hand in this way is to "wave." The rate of learning is expedited if the object elicits an association that aids us in recalling the word, or it is impaired if the association results in our making another, incorrect response. In both cases the intervening association is acting as a mediator between the stimulus (object) and the response (word).

Nikkel & Palermo (1965) have provided experimental evidence that such processes occur in children. The design of the study is a bit complicated. Stimuli were constructed according to the following pattern: Word A was assumed to evoke the implicit response B, which in turn was assumed to lead to response C. The A-B stimuli were words selected from wo.·d-association norms that had high associative strength, such as "boy-girl." Training was given on the B-C association, "girl-var." After this had been learned, the children were presented the A-C pair, "boy-var." It was assumed that learning "boy-var" would be facilitated by the fact that "boy" would evoke the implicit response, "girl," and that this response would act as a mediator between "boy-var." Since "girl-var" had already been learned, it should be easier, therefore, to learn the associate "boy-var." Interference can be produced in such a list by arranging pairs of stimuli so that the mediator elicits the incorrect association. For example, "carpet-rug" are high frequency associates, as are "eagle-bird." If, in the first stage of the study, "rug" is associated with "dit" and "bird" with "pon," and in the second stage, "carpet" with "pon" and "eagle" with "dit," the sequence "carpet-rug-dit" would tend to be evoked by the word "carpet," and this should interfere with learning the correct association, "carpet-pon." Lists of stimuli were constructed in the manners described above. The results gave clear evidence of facilitation and interference, depending on how the sequences of pairs were constructed. It appeared, therefore, that the hypothesized mediational processes had been operative.

So what does this all mean? It means that with the acquisition of language, it becomes possible for the human being to utilize words as a means of directing response rather than relying on environmental events. The significance of this accomplishment is seen in the use of instructions. In the Kuenne study, for example, the older children might have been told, "Pick the big one," and by using this instruction these children could have responded correctly on the first trial. Whether the younger children uniformly would have benefited by this instruction is questionable, for, as Kuenne found, they are less effective in using verbal mediators. This discussion is relevant to the common complaint that young children are unable to follow instructions. Their inability may be due, not to obstinacy or perversity, but to the fact that they have not yet reached the age where their behavior is readily influenced by verbal mediation. It is especially important when working with young children to realize that although they know the words and can produce them, they may be unable to use them effectively as a means for guiding responses.

[There are many indications that experience in learning results in more efficient learning of later problems. Readiness programs, such as those related to reading, have capitalized on this fact.] By knowing how to attend to relevant cues, what to expect in level of difficulty, and how to employ the most informative strategies, the child is able to respond to new problems with an ease and effectiveness that would be impossible without previous experience. In having learned how to learn, the child has developed what is called a "learning set." The results of studies on learning set emphasize the importance of learning academic skills, independent of subject matter. In the long run, knowing *how* to learn may be as important as remembering *what* has been learned, as far as academic achievement is concerned. This aspect of learning is discussed in more detail in Chapter VII.

LEARNING SET

[Common sense would predict that children will learn faster if they are working for an incentive of high value than if they are working for an incentive of low value.] But, as sometimes happens, common-sense predictions are not supported. The evidence for this assertion comes from studies of discrimination learning by children in which objects of different value have been used as incentives. The study by Miller & Estes (1961), which is reprinted following this chapter, is a good example of how a monetary incentive of high value may result in no more rapid learning than an incentive of low value. In some ways this study tests the limits of what can be done, at least within the funds available in most research budgets, for some of the subjects received as much as 50 cents for each correct response. Nevertheless, as will be seen, these subjects learned no more rapidly than those who received only 1 cent. Furthermore, both of these groups learned more slowly than a third group of subjects who received only a signal light indicating that their choice had been correct.

INCENTIVES AND LEARNING

How can such unexpected findings be interpreted? As the authors point out, one factor may be the children's level of motivation. Nine-year-old middle-class boys, such as the boys used in this study, typically enter the experimental situation with a strong motivation to perform well. Since their level of motivation is already so high, it is very difficult to increase motivation further through the use of material incentives. What might happen, then, if the children were from lower social classes? These children may have a lower level of motivation to attain success in formal learning tasks, and at the same time, they may be more desirous of obtaining material incentives. Terrell, Durkin, & Wiesley (1959) included lower-class children in a study of discrimination learning involving a two-choice size discrimination. Each correct response was reinforced either with a piece of candy or by the flash of a signal light. The lower-class children learned more rapidly when they were reinforced with candy. These results, then, fall in line with common sense if a slight but critical correction is made in our assumptions. The effectiveness of an incentive is determined not by its objective value, but by the child's level and source of motivation.

PUNISHMENT   Thus far, no mention has been made of the role of punishment in learning. Many institutions in society and many individuals operate on the assumption that punishment will reduce the tendency to repeat an incorrect or undesired response, just as its counterpart, reward, will increase the tendency to make the approved response. The number of "repeaters" in prisons is one of many indications that punishment may be less effective as an incentive than is commonly assumed.

Research on punishment with children meets with obvious problems; parents and teachers, as well as researchers themselves, are reluctant to allow severe forms of punishment to be used with children. Only one study has been published in recent years that deals with this question. Nelson, Reid, & Travers (1965) gave elementary-school children a strong electric shock for incorrect responses on a form of paired-associate learning, or the experimenters merely informed them that they were "right" or "wrong." Despite the fact that the shock was so strong that it sometimes produced tears, rate of learning did not differ significantly among the various conditions. Shock appeared to be useful only as a source of information, and the results indicated that this information could be imparted as satisfactorily by telling the children they were wrong as by shocking them. Needless to say, this is one study that probably will not be repeated on ethical and humanitarian grounds, however interesting it is theoretically.

It is not unreasonable, however, to use mild forms of punishment in studies with children. For example, children may be given a reward for a correct response, and a reward may be taken away for an incorrect response. A study by Brackbill & O'Hara (1958) illustrates how such a procedure may influence children's learning. Kindergarten boys were given fifteen pieces of candy before the experiment began. Some were told that each time they made a correct choice they would find another piece of candy, but that each time they made an incorrect choice, they would have to return a piece to the experimenter. Another group was not required to return the candy following incorrect choices. The rate at which the first group (who had to give up candy) learned a three-choice discrimination problem was significantly faster than that of the second group.

Several possible interpretations may be offered of how learning was facilitated by this form of punishment. Knowing that an object may be taken away may enhance its value. On the other hand, a mild form of punishment may result in the child's paying closer attention. The results of other studies, with both animals and humans, indicate the importance of the latter point. It appears that punishment is effective if it results in the child's paying closer attention (1) to the situation and (2) to the responses he is making. However, in complex learning situations strong forms of punishment appear to have little effect other than as a source of information, or may have negative effects. Two of the most frequently cited negative effects of punishment are its tendencies to produce emotion and to result in generalized inhibition. In the first case, learning will be impeded because, as has been discussed earlier, a high level of emotion (such as anxiety) interferes with learning in complex tasks or in tasks that do not involve responses that are already well learned. An indication of what is meant by generalized inhibition is seen in the cowering behavior of animals that have been severely punished. In such cases, punishment may have been effective in getting the subjects to inhibit certain responses, but at the same time the inhibition has become generalized and thereby has reduced the possibility of the subjects to learn effectively in other situations.[3]

CONCEPT LEARNING

The structure of a concept-learning task is quite different from that of the conditioning or discrimination-learning task. Since the same stimuli are not necessarily encountered more than once, it is extraordinarily difficult to achieve a high score on a concept-learning task by learning simple stimulus-response relations. A child must learn a generalized idea of classes of objects, those in one class being correct and those in another class being incorrect. The performances of older children in transposition prob-

[3]Nevertheless, it should be pointed out that in many less complex situations the inhibition of response produced by punishment may be the most efficient means of controlling behavior. For example, punishment may be the most effective, and in some cases the only way, in which a young child may learn not to insert his finger in an electric outlet or not to run out into the street.

lems and in the acquisition of learning sets are examples of concept learning that already have been discussed.

Much of the research with children has been devoted to delineating developmental changes in concept learning and the relation of concept learning to intelligence. At the descriptive level, the results are in line with what would be expected: Older and brighter children learn concepts more rapidly than younger or duller children. What is interesting about the research, however, is that the studies do give us some notion of the processes that underlie these differences. An illustrative set of studies are those by Osler and her associates dealing with the concept learning of bright and average children of different ages.

In an initial study (Osler & Fivel, 1961), children were presented a two-choice discrimination problem in which correct responses depended upon the subjects' isolating the concept "bird," "animal," or "living thing." The materials were cards bearing colored pictures of two objects. One picture represented an example of the concept; the other picture represented an object not belonging to the concept category. Since 900 cards were prepared for the study, it was unlikely that the subject could reach a level of consistently correct responses solely on the basis of trial and error. The three concepts were assumed to be of increasing levels of difficulty, and different children were tested with each concept.

The children were six-, ten-, and fourteen-year-olds; one-half had above-average IQs (mean IQ of 121), and one-half had average IQs (mean IQ of 101). The older and brighter children at each age learned the concepts more rapidly, but there were no differences in the rate with which the three concepts were learned. But was the learning a sudden or gradual process? If it was a sudden process, it could be assumed that the children had been trying out many different hypotheses, and having found one that led to reinforcement, they adopted it for the remaining trials. Performance on the ten trials preceding criterion were analyzed for each child. Those whose percentage of correct responses fell below the median were classed as sudden learners and those above the median as gradual learners. The incidence of sudden learning was a function of IQ, but not of age or concept. It was inferred, therefore, that one of the characteristics of bright children is that they are better able to develop hypotheses than are children of average levels of intelligence.

If this inference is correct, stimuli that are likely to elicit a large number of irrelevant hypotheses should result in bright subjects' performing more poorly than they would if the stimuli permitted a more restricted number of hypotheses. This possibility was tested by Osler & Trautman (1961) with samples of children of the same age and IQ levels used in the first study. The concept to be learned was "two;" that is, the children were required to distinguish cards with two elements from those that contained one, or more than two, elements. The concept was represented either by dots or by pictures of common objects. It was assumed that the irrelevant cues contained in the pictures would facilitate the formation of a large number of hypotheses. If this occurred, it might tend to retard the development of the simpler but correct hypothesis of "two." As predicted, the bright children had more difficulty in learning the discrimination when the stimuli were objects than when they were dots, but the average children learned each with equal ease. Thus, being able to develop hypotheses may not always lead to rapid success, especially if the hypotheses tend to be more complex than the situation demands.

Another possible difference between bright and average children is that the bright children may be better able to define problems. In the two previous studies the bright subjects learned more rapidly than the average subjects, but the instructions were nonspecific. That is, the child was not told explicitly what he was to do, other than to get as many marbles as he could. What would happen if the children were given a more precise indication of how they should respond? To answer this question, Osler & Weiss (1962) repeated the Osler & Fivel study (1961), but told one-half of the children: "If you look at the pictures carefully, you will see that there is something in the pictures like an idea that will tell you which one to choose to get a marble." The earlier results were replicated for the subjects who were given the nonspecific instructions, but differences in the performance of the bright and average subjects disappeared under the explicit instructions. As expected, the explicit instructions helped the average children, but resulted in no improvement in the performance of the bright children. The bright children apparently were able to define the task without additional cues from the experimenter.

It was stated at the beginning of this section that concept-learning problems were difficult because the subjects would not necessarily encounter the same stimuli on more than one trial. But can elementary-school children solve a problem in which the cues change? White (1965) sought to answer this question. In a study in which ever-changing cues were used, White describes how fourth- and fifth-grade children solve such a discrimination problem. The children's ability to learn when both positive and negative cues change from trial to trial poses serious questions for a theory postulating that learning is a result of approach and avoidance tendencies resulting from reinforcement and nonreinforcement.

The area of concept learning has been briefly introduced in this chapter. This topic will be developed further in Chapter VII, where emphasis is given to the whole area of conceptual development.

OBSERVATIONAL LEARNING

The research discussed thus far has involved the active participation of the subject in the performance of the task. This type of learning is of great importance in producing behavioral change; a baby cannot learn to walk and a child cannot learn to speak without performing the necessary acts himself. But we know that learning can also occur through observation and imitation of the behavior of others. In fact, an important part of children's learning occurs as they observe peers and adults interacting with other people and objects in their environment. Children can, for example, learn how to solve many types of problems and learn how to behave in different social settings by observing the behavior of others.

For many types of behavior, observation is as effective as, or more effective than, active participation. A study by Wilson (1958) illustrates this point. One group of preschool children was given a standard two-choice discrimination problem in which choices of one of the objects yielded reward. Another group was given preliminary experience in learning to imitate the choices of an adult. In this phase, the adult consistently chose one of two identical objects, always responding on the basis of the relative position of the objects. In the second phase, the objects used in the discrimination problem were introduced, and the model consistently chose the reinforcing object for eight trials. The adult then left the room. The children continued to choose the correct object in the absence of the adult. They were much more effective than were the children who had participated in the discrimination-learning task without an adult model. Thus, even though the children had not been instructed to imitate the adult's behavior, they not only learned to imitate, but also learned the nature of the critical cues in doing so.

A much more elaborate series of responses were involved in the study by Bandura & Huston (1961) which is the last reprinted

study following this chapter. A two-choice discrimination problem was used in this study, but the adult exhibited a variety of
verbal, motor, and aggressive responses in the course of his performance. The degree to which children imitated these responses
and the influence of prior interaction with the adult on their
imitation are discussed in this article.

If children learn by observing the behavior of others, then
what about the violence and aggression they see while watching
television? Could this have an influence on their everyday behavior? Many believe that it does, and their position is given
support by the results of a number of experimental studies, some
of which are reported in previous chapters. For example, Bandura, Ross, & Ross (1963) showed that following mild frustration,
children, especially boys, who had seen aggression displayed in
real life or in films showed a much higher incidence of aggression
than did children who had not witnessed such acts. Children's
aggression was measured by determining the numbers and types
of responses they made when they were put in a situation containing the types of materials they had seen in the demonstration.
The basic study was repeated by Hicks (1965). The reader will
recall that in the Hicks study, children were shown a film in
which a model exhibited a wide range of verbal and physical
aggression. Different films were made in which the model was
a male or a female adult or a male or a female peer. The male
peer had the greatest immediate influence as a model for imitative
aggression, but the adult male had the most lasting effect, as seen
in aggression displayed by the children after a six-month interval.

Different experimental conditions must play an important role
in determining the degree to which children are capable of learning by observation. Verbalization has been found to be an important variable in facilitating other types of learning. Bandura,
Grusec, & Menlove (1966) asked whether verbalization also
would be of help in observational learning. Children were shown
a short film in which an adult displayed a series of novel patterns
of behavior and used play materials in unusual ways. Some subjects were instructed to verbalize the content of the observed
behavior, while others were allowed to watch the film without
describing its contents. When the children later were asked to
demonstrate all the model's responses they could recall, those
who had verbalized received a significantly higher score than the
passive observers. Translating actions into words appears, therefore, to have a general facilitating effect on learning.

The consequences of the model's acts also may influence later performance of the observer. Bruning (1965) tested kindergarten children in a lever-pulling task similar to that used in the studies discussed earlier. For thirty trials, the subjects received either one or five pieces of candy as a reward each time they pulled the lever. For the next thirty trials, the reward conditions either (1) remained the same or (2) were reversed, i.e., those who had received one piece of candy now received five and vice versa. The children performed the task alone, or they observed another child perform during the first thirty trials and then performed themselves during the last thirty trials. The speed with which the children pulled the lever was faster with the lower level of incentive, and a shift from a high to a low level produced increased speeds of response. The results were the same whether the child was an observer or a performer during the first set of trials. Level of reward had an influence on the performance of the participant and exerted comparable effects on the subsequent performance of an observer who was present in the situation.

Finally, Baer & Sherman (1964) have shown that reinforcement of imitation may generalize to the imitation of responses that are never reinforced. In other words, if imitation of a particular response leads to reinforcement, the child may imitate other responses, even though they are not reinforced themselves. The study used a talking puppet. Preschool children were introduced to the puppet who then engaged them in conversation and induced them to imitate such behavior as head nodding, mouthing, and making strange sounds. The puppet praised the children liberally for imitating its performance, and in the course of subsequent interactions, began pressing a bar. A similar bar was in front of the child. Nearly two-thirds of the children imitated the puppet's bar pressing, even though no comment was made about this act. When the puppet ceased praising the children for their other imitative responses, the frequency with which the children pressed the bar decreased. It seems, therefore, that children can learn by doing and they can learn by observing. But the consequences of response have an important influence on the degree to which learning will occur in either case.

SUMMARY These, then, are some of the things we know about how children learn. The study of children's learning is obviously a complex field of investigation. It is complex not only because of the great variety of possible influences on learning, but also because given variables have different effects, depending upon the developmental status of the child, his background of experience, intellectual level, and motivational and personality characteristics. As the studies that have been discussed and those you are about to read have shown, the complexities are not insuperable—so long as the requisite controls are exerted and attention is paid to the characteristics of the subjects under study. Because the complexities yield to analysis, the study of children's learning is a challenging and productive area in child psychology.

BIBLIOGRAPHY

Baer, D. M., & Sherman, J. A. Reinforcement control of generalized imitation in young children. *Journal of Experimental Child Psychology,* 1964, 1, 37–49.

Bandura, A., Grusec, J. E., & Menlove, F. L. Observational learning as a function of symbolization and incentive set. *Child Development,* 1966, 37, 499–506.

Bandura, A., & Huston, A. C. Identification as a process of incidental learning. *Journal of Abnormal and Social Psychology,* 1961, 63, 311–318.

Bandura, A., Ross, D., & Ross, S. A. Imitation of film-mediated aggressive models. *Journal of Abnormal and Social Psychology,* 1963, 66, 3–11.

Bijou, S. W., & Baer, D. M. *Child development.* Vol. 1. *A systematic and empirical theory.* New York: Appleton-Century-Crofts, 1961.

Bijou, S. W., & Baer, D. M. *Child development.* Vol. 2. *Universal stage of infancy.* New York: Appleton-Century-Crofts, 1965.

Brackbill, Y., & O'Hara, J. The relative effectiveness of reward and punishment for discrimination learning in children. *Journal of Comparative and Physiological Psychology,* 1958, 51, 747–751.

Brown, P., & Elliott, R. Control of aggression in a nursery school class. *Journal of Experimental Child Psychology,* 1965, 2, 103–107.

Bruning, J. L. Direct and vicarious effects of a shift in magnitude of reward on performance. *Journal of Personality and Social Psychology,* 1965, 2, 278–282.

Cantor, G. N., & Cantor, J. H. Discriminative reaction time performance in preschool children as related to stimulus familiarization. *Journal of Experimental Child Psychology,* 1965, 2, 1–9.

Engen, T., & Lipsitt, L. P. Decrement and recovery of responses to olfactory stimuli in the human neonate. *Journal of Comparative and Physiological Psychology,* 1965, 59, 312–316.

Gewirtz, J. L., & Baer, D. M. Deprivation and satiation of social reinforcers as drive conditions. *Journal of Abnormal and Social Psychology,* 1958, 57, 165–172.

Graham, F. K., Ernhart, C. B., Craft, M., & Berman, P. W. Learning of relative and absolute size concepts in preschool children. *Journal of Experimental Child Psychology,* 1964, 1, 26–36.

Hicks, D. J. Imitation and retention of film-mediated aggressive peer and adult models. *Journal of Personality and Social Psychology,* 1965, 2, 97–100.

Johnson, R. C., & Zara, R. C. Relational learning in young children.

Journal of Comparative and Physiological Psychology, 1960, **53**, 594–597.

Kass, N., & Wilson, H. Resistance to extinction as a function of percentage of reinforcement, number of training trials, and conditioned reinforcement. *Journal of Experimental Psychology,* 1966, **71**, 355–357.

Kuenne, M. R. Experimental investigation of the relation of language to transposition behavior in young children. *Journal of Experimental Psychology,* 1946, **36**, 471–490.

Lovaas, O. I., Berberich, J. P., Perloff, B. F., & Schaeffer, B. Acquisition of imitative speech by schizophrenic children. *Science,* 1966, **151**, 705–707.

Miller, L. B., & Estes, B. W. Monetary reward and motivation in discrimination learning. *Journal of Experimental Psychology,* 1961, **61**, 501–504.

Nelson, F. B., Reid, I. E., & Travers, R. M. W. Effect of electric shock as a reinforcer of the behavior of children. *Psychological Reports,* 1965, **16**, 123–126.

Nikkel, N., & Palermo, D. S. Effects of mediated associations in paired-associate learning in children. *Journal of Experimental Child Psychology,* 1965, **2**, 92–102.

Osler, S. F., & Fivel, M. W. Concept attainment: I. The role of age and intelligence in concept attainment by induction. *Journal of Experimental Psychology,* 1961, **62**, 1–8.

Osler, S. F., & Trautman, G. E. Concept attainment: II. Effect of stimulus complexity upon concept attainment at two levels of intelligence. *Journal of Experimental Psychology,* 1961, **62**, 9–13.

Osler, S. F., & Weiss, S. R. Studies in concept attainment: III. Effect of instructions at two levels of intelligence. *Journal of Experimental Psychology,* 1962, **63**, 528–533.

Papoušek, H. Experimental studies of appetitional behavior in human newborns and infants. In H. W. Stevenson, E. H. Hess, & H. L. Rheingold (Eds.), *Early behavior: Comparative and developmental approaches.* New York: Wiley, 1967. Pp. 249–277.

Penney, R. K. The effects of non-reinforcement on response strength as a function of number of previous reinforcements. *Canadian Journal of Psychology,* 1960, **14**, 206–215.

Penney, R. K., & McCann, B. The instrumental escape conditioning of anxious and nonanxious children. *Journal of Abnormal and Social Psychology,* 1962, **65**, 351–354.

Rheingold, H. L., Gewirtz, J. L., & Ross, H. W. Social conditioning of vocalizations in the infant. *Journal of Comparative and Physiological Psychology,* 1959, **52**, 68–73.

Rieber, M. The effect of CS presence during delay of reward on the speed of an instrumental response. *Journal of Experimental Psychology,* 1961, **61**, 290–294.

Siqueland, E. R., & Lipsitt, L. P. Conditioned head-turning in human newborns. *Journal of Experimental Child Psychology,* 1966, **3**, 356–376.

Spence, K. W. The differential response in animals to stimuli varying within a single dimension. *Psychological Review,* 1937, **44**, 430–444.

Stevenson, H. W., Keen, R., & Knights, R. M. Parents and strangers as reinforcing agents for children's performance. *Journal of Abnormal and Social Psychology,* 1963, **67**, 183–186.

Stevenson, H. W., & Weir, M. W. Developmental changes in the effects of reinforcement and nonreinforcement of a single response. *Child Development,* 1961, **32**, 1–5.

Terrell, G., Jr., Durkin, K., & Wiesley, M. Social class and the nature of the incentive in discrimination learning. *Journal of Abnormal and Social Psychology,* 1959, **59**, 270–272.

Weisberg, P. Social and nonsocial conditioning of infant vocalizations. *Child Development,* 1963, **34**, 377–388.

White, S. H. Discrimination learning with ever-changing positive and negative cues. *Journal of Experimental Child Psychology,* 1965, **2**, 154–162.

Wickens, D. D., & Wickens, C. A study of conditioning in the neonate. *Journal of Experimental Psychology,* 1940, **26**, 94–102.

Wilson, W. C. Imitation and the learning of incidental cues by preschool children. *Child Development,* 1958, **29**, 393–397.

CONDITIONED HEAD-TURNING IN HUMAN NEWBORNS[1]

Einar R. Siqueland and Lewis P. Lipsitt

Recent conditioning studies with human newborns (Papoušek, 1961; Lipsitt & Kaye, 1964) suggest that, with increasing refinement of experimental techniques, analyses of learning processes are now possible in young organisms whose immature neuro-muscular status has been a barrier previously to extensive behavioral study. Such investigations have shown that certain behavior patterns of human newborns can be viewed as learning phenomena, and traditional learning concepts such as reinforcement, conditioning, and extinction are useful in the analysis of infant behavior. It was the purpose of the present studies to explore the usefulness of a special form of instrumental conditioning in newborns. As yet there has been little experimental data clearly demonstrating that some environmental events may act as reinforcing stimuli to shape or selectively strengthen responses in the behavioral repertoire of the newborn (Lipsitt, 1963). The present study sought to increase the probability of occurrence, through reinforcement consequences, of an elicited response in the behavior repertoire of the newborn. Thus, the present procedure capitalized upon a response which at the outset is an elicited response, but which gains in response-strength through reinforcement of that elicitation. The response selected for study was that of head-turning to tactile stimulation of the face.

A number of investigations have focused on parameters of head movement in infants as an unconditioned response (e.g., Pratt, Nelson, & Sun, 1930; Gentry & Aldrich, 1948; Prechtl, 1958; Blauvelt & McKenna, 1961; Peiper, 1963; Turkewitz, Gordon, & Birch, 1965). These investigators have studied the influence of such parameters as duration and intensity of stimulus, deprivational state, arousal level, age of infant, and medication of mother during delivery. Prechtl (1958) has provided the most complete description of head movement in the human newborn.

Clinical observations of the initial feeding interactions between the mother and newborn (Gunther, 1959; Blauvelt & McKenna, 1961) have also resulted in the observation that the head-turning response may serve an important function in the early feeding history of the infant and also in speculation as to the role of learning on subsequent behavior in the feeding situation. Such observations suggest there may be conditions under which environmental consequences of this response alter the likelihood of the

[1]This research was supported by grant No. NB 04268 (National Institute of Health) to Lewis P. Lipsitt for the study of sensory discrimination and learning in infants. These studies were conducted while the first author was a Postdoctoral Fellow of the United States Public Health Service. We wish to thank the staff of the Providence Lying-In Hospital for their continued encouragement and cooperation.

From E. R. Siqueland & L. P. Lipsitt. Conditioned head-turning in human newborns. Journal of Experimental Child Psychology, 1966, 3, 356–376. (With permission of the authors and the Academic Press Inc.)

response. Gewirtz (1961) has in fact suggested that instrumental or operant learning concepts are useful in understanding behavior of young organisms in which specific components of unconditioned responses are shaped or strengthened by environmental consequences functioning as reinforcers.

The focus of the present investigation was to evaluate the cumulative effect of reinforcement operations on the response of ipsilateral [turning toward] head movements to tactile stimulation of the face. These experiments investigated whether, under certain reinforcement conditions, the likelihood of this response in newborns can be altered, a response which is considered by many to be in fact a reflex. The first experiment studied the effect of experimentally pairing reinforcement with the occurrence of ipsilateral head movements to tactile stimulation. The effect of reinforcement parameters on probability of response occurrence over successive presentations of the tactile stimulus was assessed; thus the data were evaluated for evidence of instrumental conditioning in the first days of human life.

EXPERIMENT 1

Subjects and design

The Ss were 36 full-term newborns, 14 males and 22 females, tested between 40 and 93 hours (median 73) after birth at the Providence Lying-In Hospital. The Ss, selected from a population of awake infants, were all bottle-fed, and were studied in the morning between 8:00–9:15 and between 10:30–12:00. The Ss were assigned to two deprivation groups on the basis of time from previous feeding when brought to the laboratory. All infants in this hospital are routinely fed at intervals of 4 hours. Thus, time from previous feeding reflects an approximation of the naturally occurring food deprivation of this population. Group L (low hunger) was brought to the laboratory 30 to 90 minutes (median 60) after feeding, and Group H (high hunger) was tested 120 to 180 minutes (median 150) after feeding. Both deprivation groups were subdivided further by random assignment of infants to experimental and control groups (L-E, L-C, H-E, and H-C).

Apparatus

All testing procedures were accomplished in a stabilimeter crib described previously by Lipsitt and DeLucia (1960). Breathing was monitored by an . . . infant pneumograph strapped around the abdomen. Respiration and general body activity were recorded continously during experimental sessions on a . . . polygraph. The respiration and activity measures enabled E to visually monitor the general status of infants during conditioning, but these data were not subjected to further analysis. A manually operated event marker was used to record presentation of auditory and tactile stimulation and to designate observation periods on the polygraph record. Auditory stimuli were presented from an . . . audio-oscillator and a 10-watt amplifier, connected to an 8-inch . . . speaker placed approximately 10 inches above S's head.

Experimental procedure

Infants were brought individually from the nursery to the laboratory by a nurse who assisted in experimental procedures. Swaddling with arms positioned on the chest prevented the infant's arms and hands from touching the face during testing. Testing began approximately 4 minutes after Ss were placed supine in the experimental crib with head positioned in a head cushion molded of linen.

During training all four groups received tactile stimulation on each of 30 trials involving a 5-second presentation of buzzer (a low frequency square wave tone, approximately 80 db with a fundamental component of 23 cps). The buzzer was introduced for two reasons: (a) as an experimental arousal stimulus in an attempt to deal with the general problem of rapidly fluctuating states of wakefulness in the human newborn, and (b) to deal with the possibility that increased frequency of anticipatory responses to buzzer might occur through reinforcement. The tactile stimulus was presented for 3 seconds to the S's left cheek 2 seconds after buzzer onset and coincided with the last 3 seconds of buzzer. The tactile stimulus consisted of three light strokes of E's finger moving vertically on the infant's left cheek a distance of 2.5 cm., beginning approximately 1.5 cm. from the corner of the lips. The response was the occurrence of an ipsilateral head rotation on each trial. A trial was defined as the 6-second time interval beginning with onset of buzzer. Two observers (E and an experimentally naive nurse) independently scored Ss for occurrence or absence of a perceptible ipsilateral head movement on each trial.

All Ss received 30 training trials with a 30-second intertrial interval. After training, all infants received at least 12, but not more than 30, extinction trials. Extinction trials were terminated when Ss met an extinction criterion of four successive trials without occurrence of a response. Training for the experimental groups consisted of a 2-second presentation of a 5 percent dextrose solution via nipple contingent upon response occurrence on each trial. Control Ss were matched trial for trial with experimental Ss on reinforcements over training trials, but dextrose presentation always occurred 8–10 seconds after termination of the tactile stimulus. Thus, these Ss were never reinforced by chance for turning to tactile stimulation but controlled for effects of arousal level and sensitization over trials.

Results and discussion

Agreement between observers in scoring occurrence of perceptible head-turn responses was high (number of agreements minus number of disagreements, divided by total number of observations), ranging from .89 to 1.0 over individual Ss, with a mean agreement ratio of .97 (median .97) for the 36 infants. On the few trials in which the two observers disagreed, no response was inferred.

The measure of performance in this experiment was the percent occurrence of left-turn responses over training and extinction trials. The mean percent response for each of the four subgroups is presented in Table 1 in blocks of three trials for the ten blocks of training trials and four blocks of extinction trials. Figure 1 summarizes these results by comparing the experimental group (N = 18) and the control group (N = 18), deprivation disregarded, over training and extinction trials. The training and extinction data, presented in Table 1, were treated separately by [statistical] analyses. . . .

[The results indicated] that the procedure of pairing reinforcement with the response of turning to tactile stimulation resulted in more responding by experimental Ss than control Ss during training and extinction. The fact that the control group, who received the same number of dextrose presentations during training, failed to show similar response increments indicates that this increased probability of response for the ex-

TABLE 1   Percent of head-turning over training and extinction of experimental and control groups under two levels of deprivation (three-trial blocks)

Median hours since feeding	Training										Extinct			
	1	2	3	4	5	6	7	8	9	10	1	2	3	4
$2\frac{1}{2}$	Exp. 30	44	58	63	67	55	63	89	85	89	85	70	52	67
	Con. 30	26	41	22	18	41	30	15	33	22	26	22	07	15
1	Exp. 30	44	41	55	63	59	52	70	72	78	70	55	70	44
	Con. 37	15	30	26	41	22	15	15	30	18	15	18	30	07

perimental group was not attributable to simple arousal effects of dextrose presentation. In contrast to the relatively stable base rate of response for the control Ss, experimental Ss demonstrated a reliable [increase in responses] over the ten blocks of training trials, shifting in probability of response occurrence from .30 to .83. Of 17 infants in the experimental group who shifted between the first and tenth blocks, all showed [a significant] increase . . . , whereas 6 of 7 Ss that shifted in the control group showed a decrease. A similar analysis of the shifts by these two groups between the first block of training trials and the first extinction block showed that 15 of 16 experimental Ss who shifted, increased [significantly] in response probability . . . , whereas 7 of the 9 control Ss who changed, decreased in response.

The analysis of the extinction data indicates that the pairing of reinforcement with left-turn responses for the experimental groups resulted in more responding for these groups as compared with the control groups after termination of reinforcement. . . . The experimental groups were observed to further decrease in responding over subsequent extinction trials with 15 of 18 infants meeting the extinction criterion within 30 trials. . . .

FIG. 1   Mean percent responses to eliciting stimulus during training and extinction trials for experimental and control groups (Experiment 1).

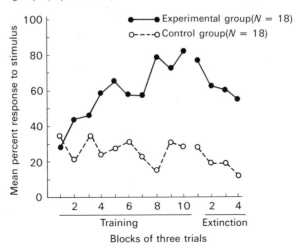

A more general problem for experimental investigations with newborns is the rapid fluctuation in sleep-awake cycle during the first days of life. Behavioral effects of experimental procedures, even of brief duration, may be confounded by rapid shifts in arousal of the S. In the present experiments, the use of an auditory stimulus preceding and overlapping the tactile stimulus reflects an attempt to maintain a more stable base line of arousal for the duration of the experimental procedure.

In the present experiment, there were no reliable differences between experimental and control Ss in the occurrence of responses to buzzer alone (i.e., left-turn responses during the 2-second interval between onset of auditory stimulus and presentation of the tactile stimulus). The primary experimental effect was an increase in ipsilateral responding to tactile stimulation as a result of pairing reinforcement with the occurrence of the turning response. These results suggest that the effect of the reinforcement procedure was to produce stable responding in the presence of a stimulus which normally functioned as a "relatively weak eliciting stimulus." Results similar to these were obtained by Lipsitt, Kaye and Bosack (1966), who demonstrated conditioning of the sucking response under a procedure where the CS was a rubber tube which functioned as a weak eliciting stimulus for the sucking response. On the basis of a demonstrated increase in sucking to the tube after reinforcement trials, . . . it was concluded that "a nonoptimizing sucking stimulus can be transformed into a more effective elicitor of sucking through pairing with it of a suitable reinforcing agent. . . ." (Lipsitt, 1965).

EXPERIMENT 2

[A second] experiment was designed to assess the experimental effect of pairing reinforcement differentially with two responses for individual Ss. It was assumed that experimental evidence for differential changes in probability of response occurrence for reinforced and nonreinforced head-turning responses would represent learned differentiation in human newborns.

Subjects and design

The Ss were 40 full-term infants, 19 males and 21 females, tested 120 to 180 minutes after feeding. They were selected from newborns ranging from 24 to 112 hours of age. . . . Infants were assigned to two groups on the basis of their age at time of testing, Group Y (younger, tested 24–48 hours from birth; median 36 hours), and Group O (older, tested 64–112 hours from birth; median 80.5 hours). Both age groups were subdivided further by random assignment of Ss to experimental and control groups (Groups Y-E, Y-C, O-E, and O-C).

Experimental procedures

The apparatus and pre-experimental preparations with Ss were identical to those used in the first experiment. . . .

The procedure of presenting tactile stimulation to infants overlapping the last 3 seconds of a 5-second auditory stimulus was continued in the present experiment with the following modifications. On alternate trials the tactile stimulus was presented to the right or left cheek of the infant. For individual Ss right- and left-sided stimulation were consistently paired with distinctive auditory stimuli (labeled "buzzer" and "tone" in this experiment). The buzzer was identical to that in the first experiment. . . . This single alternation procedure of presenting right- and left-sided tactile stimulation to infants paired with buzzer and tone was maintained over experimental trials. The order of stimulus presentation and pairing of the two auditory stimuli with loci of tactile stimulation were counterbalanced across Ss within each of the four subgroups.

The response measure was the occurrence or absence of an ipsilateral head rotation on each trial (i.e., left rotation to left-sided stimulation and right turn to right-sided stimulation). . . . The reinforcing stimulus (i.e., 2-second presentation of dextrose solution) was identical to that used in the previous experiment.

All four groups received 6 base-line, 48 training, and 36 extinction trials, 1 trial every 30 seconds. For experimental Ss during training trials, response to one of the two eliciting stimuli was reinforced (R^{s+} [dextrose]), but response to the other stimulus was not followed by reinforcement (R^{s-}).

Control Ss were matched with individual experimental Ss on total number of reinforcements over training trials, but presentation of the dextrose solution, 8–10 seconds after tactile stimulation, was not contingent upon head-rotation responses. . . .

Results and discussion

. . . These results [indicate] that experimental Ss as compared with control Ss demonstrated a [significantly] higher total incidence of R^{s+} over training. [In addition, both experimental and control groups decreased in R^{s-} occurrence over training.] . . .

[An] analysis of R^{s+} [and R^{s-}] occurrence over extinction trials [indicated a reliable age effect, i.e.,] older infants were responding more than the younger infants during extinction. . . . It is [also] clear that the experimental group had a higher probability of R^{s+} occurrence than the control group during extinction. . . . These data show that training altered natural response preferences in the neonate. The results also demonstrate learned discrimination as a function of differential reinforcement of the two responses. . . . Ipsilateral head movement to right- and left-sided stimulation (the two loci of tactile stimulation paired with distinctive auditory stimuli) clearly reflected the effects of differential reinforcement.

Turkewitz et al. (1965) have reported evidence of right turn bias in newborns (i.e., higher probability of ipsilateral turns to right-sided stimulation than ipsilateral turns to left-sided stimulation). Although the experimental parameters of stimulation were quite different in the present experiment, a similar effect was observed in the base-line response measures of the 40 infants tested. These infants made significantly more right turns to right-sided stimulation than left turns to left-sided stimulation. . . . The mean percentages of ipsilateral turns to right-sided and left-sided stimulation were 40 and 32, respectively. In addition, it was found that although the two age groups did not differ in total number of ipsilateral responses to stimulation during base line, they did differ significantly with respect to a right-sided bias. . . .

EXPERIMENT 3

In this experiment the two auditory stimuli served experimentally as the positive and negative cues for reinforcement. Initially, ipsilateral turns to right-sided stimulation

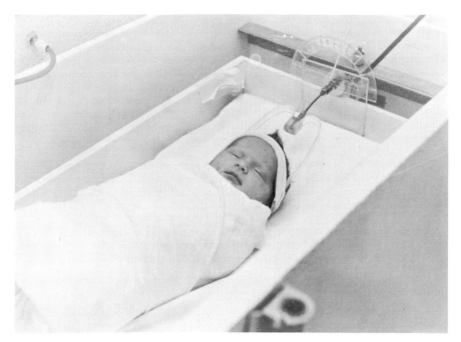

FIG. 2 Neonate with headpiece attached for recording head-turning responses.

in the presence of one auditory stimulus were reinforced while ipsilateral turns to right-sided stimulation in the presence of the other were not. In a subsequent stage, the relation of reinforcement to the auditory stimuli was reversed so that turning to the previously reinforced cue was now nonreinforced and vice versa.

Apparatus

Modification of a head-turning apparatus previously described in a study with 4-month-old infants (Siqueland, 1964) provided instrumentation and automatic recording of head movements with newborns. The present apparatus consisted of a light-weight plastic headpiece connecting [to] a . . . circuit by means of a flexible shaft. A photograph of the head apparatus is shown in Figure 2. The photograph shows the flexible plastic headpiece resting on the infant's temples, held in position by an adjustable, elastic headband. . . .

Subjects and design

The *S*s were two groups of eight infants, 6 males and 10 females, 48 to 116 hours of age. They were tested approximately 2–3 hours after previous feeding. In this experiment tactile stimulation to the right side was presented in the presence of buzzer or tone on alternate trials, and right turns to the tactile stimulus were differentially reinforced in the presence of the two auditory stimuli. The infants were randomly assigned to two groups. For half (Group 1), tone was the positive stimulus (S^+, turning right to right-sided stimulation in presence of tone being paired with reinforcement), while buzzer was the negative stimulus (S^-, turning right to right-sided stimulation in the presence of buzzer not followed by reinforcement). For the other half (Group 2), the buzzer functioned as S^+ and the tone as S^-. Subsequent to original training, reversal training was presented to both groups.

Results and discussion

These [data] indicated that the primary experimental effect during original training was to increase the probability of response occurrence to the positive stimulus over training trials, . . . while responding in the presence of the negative stimulus showed negligible change. . . . By contrast, the primary experimental effect during reversal was a decrease in response occurrence in the presence of S^- (the positive stimulus during original training) over trials, . . . while S^+ responding . . . showed no significant change over reversal trials. . . .

The evidence of auditory discrimination in this experiment reflects primarily an increased probability of ipsilateral head movements to the positive stimulus, while probability of ipsilateral head movements to the negative stimulus showed negligible change. . . .

The present data provide evidence of an acquired auditory discrimination in the first days of human life. The newborn infants' responding to the positive and negative stimuli clearly reflect the effects of the discrimination training procedures employed in this experiment.

GENERAL DISCUSSION

These experiments show that, under certain experimental conditions, environmental events can function as reinforcing stimuli to shape or selectively strengthen components of "unconditioned responses." The results indicate that presentation of dextrose via nipple can function as a positive reinforcing stimulus for head movement responses in human newborns. Bilateral head movements, of the amplitude observed and quantified in these studies, were brought under the control of instrumental reinforcement contingencies. It is suggested that the rapid acquisition effects demonstrated in these experiments may reflect the immediate temporal relationship between response occurrence and the reinforcing event. Head rotations of a specified response class were followed immediately by presentation of a stimulus event which provided infants with both oral-tactile and taste stimulation.

In the first experiment the effect of reinforcement was to produce stable responding to a stimulus (tactual stimulation of cheek) which functioned initially as a "low-level elicitor" of the to-be-reinforced response class. For control Ss response habituation (response decrement below base line) occurred over successive presentations of the eliciting stimulus. For experimental Ss, reinforcement resulted in a reliable acquisition effect, and termination of reinforcement resulted in extinction. . . .

Our second experiment suggests a type of learned discrimination in newborns in that responding to two different eliciting stimuli, in the context of differential reinforcement, was brought under control of these reinforcement contingencies. Individual infants demonstrated not only a decrement in the nonreinforced response (habituation), but also showed increased occurrence of the reinforced response (acquisition). Reliable extinction effects were demonstrated after termination of reinforcement.

Evidence of an acquired stimulus discrimination was seen in the last experiment. When response to a tactile stimulus was differentially reinforced in the presence of two auditory stimuli, newborns showed increased responding to tactile stimulation in the presence of the positive auditory cue, but response to the same tactile stimulus in the presence of the negative auditory cue did not change.

Possibly the type of learning experiences provided for newborns in the normal feeding situation may not be too different from the experimental prototypes investigated in these experiments. . . . The breast-fed infant may demonstrate a higher probability of ipsilateral turning to tactile stimulation when held in feeding position at the mother's breast than when lying supine on the mother's lap. This suggests that infants may readily learn to turn differentially to the tactile stimulus when it is presented in the context of complex visual and postural cues signaling that reinforcement or nonreinforcement will follow occurrence of the turning response.

It is difficult to specify clearly the type of learning processes involved in these experiments. The distinction between respondents and operants as labels for response classes in the newborn become somewhat blurred and may be cumbersome and arbitrary. Furthermore, in the immature organism there may be interactions between these response classes (Bijou & Baer, 1961, pp. 71–73). It was observed in the course of these experiments that marked increases in spontaneous turning responses occurred during the intertrial intervals after a few trials of reinforced responding. A similar observation has been reported by Papoušek (1965). The only quantitative data on this observed increase in intertrial turning was provided by the third experiment. Examination of the analog records indicated that infants showed a marked increase in spontaneous turning over the first blocks of training trials, reaching asymptote by the fourth and fifth blocks of trails. They subsequently showed a gradual decrease in spontaneous turning over the last five blocks of training trials. It is not possible to determine from these results whether the observed increase in spontaneous head movements reflected a general arousal effect or whether it specifically reflects the reinforcement of the response class.

It is clear from these results that head turning to tactile stimulation in newborn infants may be influenced by environmental events which function as reinforcers. It is suggested also that some environmental stimuli may under certain conditions have complex functions for the human newborn's behavior and very early in the history of the organism begin to reflect interactions between eliciting and learned cue functions.

REFERENCES

Bijou, S. W., & Baer, D. M. *Child development*. Vol. 1. *A systematic and empirical theory*. New York: Appleton-Century-Crofts, 1961.

Blauvelt, H., & McKenna, J. Mother-neonate interaction: Capacity of the human newborn for orientation. In B. M. Foss (Ed.), *Determinants of infant behavior*. New York: Wiley, 1961. Pp. 3–29.

Gentry, E. F., & Aldrich, C. A. Rooting reflex in newborn infant; Incidence and effect of sleep on it. *American Journal of Diseases in Children*, 1948, **75**, 528–539.

Gewirtz, J. L. A learning analysis of the effects of normal stimulation privation and deprivation on the acquisition of social motivation and attachment. In B. M. Foss (Ed.), *Determinants of infant behavior*. New York: Wiley, 1961. Pp. 213–290.

Gunther, M. Infant behavior at the breast. In B. M. Foss (Ed.), *Determinants of infant behavior*. New York: Wiley, 1961. Pp. 37–39.

Lipsitt, L. P. Learning in the first year of life. In L. P. Lipsitt & C. C. Spiker (Eds.), *Advances in child development and behavior.* Vol. 1. New York: Academic Press, 1963. Pp. 147–195.

Lipsitt, L. P. Learning processes of human newborns. *Merrill-Palmer Quarterly,* 1966, **12**, 45–71.

Lipsitt, L. P., & DeLucia, C. A. An apparatus for the measurement of specific response and general activity in the human neonate. *American Journal of Psychology,* 1960, **73**, 630–632.

Lipsitt, L. P., & Kaye, H. Conditioned sucking in the human newborn. *Psychonomic Science,* 1964, **1**, 29–30.

Lipsitt, L. P., Kaye, H., & Bosack, T. Enhancement of neonatal sucking through reinforcement. *Journal of Experimental Child Psychology,* 1966, **4**, 163–168.

Papoušek, H. Conditioned head rotation reflexes in infants in the first months of life. *Acta Paedopsychiatrica,* 1961, **50,** 565–576.

Papoušek, H. Experimental appetitional behavior in human newborns and infants. Reported at Social Science Research Council Conference on Learned and Non-Learned Behavior in Immature Organisms, Stillwater, Minn., June, 1965.

Peiper, A. Cerebral function in infancy and childhood. (Translated by B. Nagler & H. Nagler.) New York: Consultants Bureau, 1963.

Pratt, K. C., Nelson, A. K., & Sun, K. H. The behavior of the newborn infant. *Ohio State University Studies, Contributions in Psychology,* No. 10, 1930.

Prechtl, H. F. R. The directed head turning response and allied movements in the human baby. *Behavior,* 1958, **13**, 212–242.

Siqueland, E. R. Operant conditioning of head turning in four-month infants. *Psychonomic Science,* 1964, **1**, 223–224.

Turkewitz, G., Gordon, E. W., Birch, H. G. Head turning in the human neonate: Effect of prandial condition and lateral preference. *Journal of Comparative and Physiological Psychology,* 1965, **59**, 189–192.

ACQUISITION OF IMITATIVE SPEECH
BY SCHIZOPHRENIC CHILDREN[1]

O. Ivar Lovaas, John P. Berberich, Bernard F. Perloff, and Benson Schaeffer

With the great majority of children, the problem of teaching speech never arises. Speech develops within each child's particular environment without parents and teachers having to know a great deal about how it occurs. Yet, in some children, because of deviations in organic structure or prior experience, speech fails to develop. Children with the diagnosis of childhood schizophrenia, especially autistic children, often show little in the way of speech development (Rimland, 1964). The literature on childhood schizophrenia suggests two conclusions regarding speech in such children: first, that the usual treatment setting (psychotherapy) in which these children are placed might not be conducive to speech development (Brown, 1960); and second, that a child failing to develop speech by the age of 5 years remains withdrawn and does not improve clinically (Brown, 1960). That is, the presence or absence of speech is an important prognostic indicator. It is perhaps obvious that a child who can speak can engage in a much more therapeutic interchange with his environment than the child who has no speech.

The failure of some children to develop speech as a "natural" consequence of growing up poses the need for an increased knowledge of how language is acquired. A procedure for the development of speech in previously mute children would not only be of practical importance but might also illuminate the development of speech in normal children. Although several theoretical attempts have been made to account for language development, the empirical basis for these theoretical formulations is probably inadequate. In fact, there are no published, systematic studies on how to go about developing speech in a person who has never spoken. We now outline a procedure by which speech can be made to occur. Undoubtedly there are or will be other ways by which speech can be acquired. Furthermore, our procedure centers on the acquisition of only one aspect of speech, the acquisition of vocal responses. The development of speech also requires the acquisition of a context for the occurrence of such responses ("meaning").

Casual observation suggests that normal children acquire words by hearing speech; that is, children learn to speak by imitation. The mute schizophrenic children with whom we worked were not imitative. Thus the establishment of imitation in these children appeared to be the most beneficial and practical starting point for building

[1] Study supported by grants from Margaret Sabl of Los Angeles. We express appreciation to James Q. Simmons and the staff at the Children's Unit, Neuropsychiatric Institute, University of California, Los Angeles.

speech. The first step in creating speech, then, was to establish conditions in which imitation of vocal sounds would be learned.

The method that we eventually found most feasible for establishing verbal imitation involved a discrimination training procedure. Early in training the child was rewarded only if he emitted a sound within a certain time after an adult had emitted a sound. Next he was rewarded only if the sound he emitted within the prescribed interval resembled the adult's sound. Toward the end of training, he was rewarded only if his vocalization very closely matched the adult's vocalization—that is, if it was, in effect, imitative. Thus verbal imitation was taught through the development of a series of increasingly fine discriminations.

The first two children exposed to this program are discussed here. Chuck and Billy were 6-year-old in-patients at the Neuropsychiatric Institute at UCLA. These children were selected for the program because they did not speak. At the onset of the program, vocal behavior in both children was restricted to occasional vowel productions with no discernible communicative intent. These vowel sounds occurred infrequently, except when the children were tantrumous, and did not resemble the pre-speech babbling of infants. In addition, the children evidenced no appropriate play (for example, they would spin toys or mouth them). They engaged in a considerable amount of self-stimulatory behavior such as rocking and twirling. They did not initiate social contacts and became tantrumous when such contact was initiated by others. They evidenced occasional self-destructive behavior (biting self, head-banging, and so forth). Symbolic rewards such as social approval were inoperative, so biological rewards such as food were substituted. In short, they were profoundly schizophrenic.

Training was conducted 6 days a week, 7 hours a day, with a 15-minute rest period accompanying each hour of training. During the training sessions the child and the adult sat facing each other, their heads about 30 cm apart. The adult physically prevented the child from leaving the training situation by holding the child's legs between his own legs. Rewards, in the form of single spoonsful of the child's meal, were delivered immediately after correct responses. Punishment (spanking, shouting by the adult) was delivered for inattentive, self-destructive, and tantrumous behavior which interfered with the training, and most of these behaviors were thereby suppressed within 1 week. Incorrect vocal behavior was never punished.

Four distinct steps were required to establish verbal imitation. In step 1, the child was rewarded for all vocalizations. We frequently would fondle the children and we avoided aversive stimulation. This was done in order to increase the frequency of vocal responses. During this stage in training the child was also rewarded for visually fixating on the adult's mouth. When the child reached an achievement level of about one verbal response every 5 seconds and was visually fixating on the adult's mouth more than 50 percent of the time, step 2 of training was introduced.

Step 2 marked our initial attempt to bring the child's verbal behavior under our verbal control in such a manner that our speech would ultimately stimulate speech in the child. Mastery of this second step involved acquisition of a temporal discrimination by the child. The adult emitted a vocal response—for example, "baby"—about once on the average of every 10th second. The child was rewarded only if he vocalized within 6 seconds after the adult's vocalization. However, any vocal response of the child would be rewarded in that time interval. Step 3 was introduced when the frequency of the child's vocal responses within the 6-second interval was three times what it had been initially.

Step 3 was structurally similar to the preceding step, but it included the additional requirement that the child actually match the adult's vocalization before receiving the reward. In this and in following steps the adult selected the verbalization to be placed in imitative training from a pool of possible verbalizations that had met one or more of the following criteria. First, we selected vocal behaviors that could be prompted, that is, vocal behaviors that could be elicited by a cue prior to any experimental training, such as by manually moving the child through the behavior.

An example of training with the use of a prompt is afforded in teaching the sound ''b.'' The training would proceed in three stages: (1) the adult emitted ''b'' and simultaneously prompted the child to emit ''b'' by holding the child's lips closed with his fingers and quickly removing them when the child exhaled; (2) the prompt would be gradually faded, by the adult's moving his fingers away from the child's mouth, to his cheek, and finally gently touching the child's jaw; (3) the adult emitted the vocalization ''b'' only, withholding all prompts. The rate of fading was determined by the child; the sooner the child's verbal behavior came under control of the adult's without the use of the prompt, the better. The second criterion for selection of words or sounds in the early stages of training centered on their concomitant visual components (which we exaggerated when we pronounced them), such as those of the labial consonant ''m'' and of open-mouthed vowels like ''a.'' We selected such sounds after having previously found that the children could discriminate words with visual components more easily than those with only auditory components (the guttural consonants, ''k'' and ''g,'' proved extremely difficult and, like ''l'' and ''s,'' were mastered later than other sounds). Third, we selected for training sounds which the child emitted most frequently in step 1.

Step 4 was a recycling of step 3, with the addition of a new sound. We selected a sound that was very different from those presented in step 3, so that the child could discriminate between the new and old sounds more easily. To make certain that the child was in fact imitating, we randomly interspersed the sounds of step 3 with the sound of step 4, in a randomized ratio of about 1 to 3. This random presentation ''forced'' (or enabled) the child to discriminate the particular sounds involved, in order to be rewarded. There was no requirement placed upon the child in step 3 to discriminate specific aspects such as vowels, consonants, and order of the adult's speech; a child might master step 3 without attending to the specific properties of the adult's speech. Each new introduction of sounds and words required increasingly fine discrimination by the child and hence provided evidence that the child was in fact matching the adult's speech. All steps beyond step 4 consisted of replications of step 3, but new sounds, words, and phrases were used. In each new step the previously mastered words and sounds were rehearsed on a randomized ratio of 1 to 3. The next step was introduced when the child had mastered the previous steps—that is, when he had made ten consecutive correct replications of the adult's utterances.

One hour of each day's training was tape-recorded. Two independent observers scored the child's correct vocal responses from these sessions. A correct response was defined as a reconizable reproduction of the adult's utterance. The observers showed better than 90 percent agreement over sessions. When the child's correct responses are plotted against days of training, and the resulting function is positively accelerated, it can be said that the child has learned to imitate.

The results of the first 26 days of imitation training, starting from introduction of step 3, have been plotted for Billy (Figure 1). The abscissa denotes training days. The words and sounds are printed in lowercase letters on the days they were introduced and in capital letters on the days they were mastered. It can be seen that as training progressed the rate of mastery increased. Billy took several days to learn a single word during the first 2 weeks of the program, but a single day to master several words during the last 2 weeks. Chuck's performance was very similar to Billy's.

After 26 days of training both children had learned to imitate new words with such ease and rapidity that merely adding verbal responses to their imitative repertoire seemed pointless. Hence the children were then introduced to the second part of the language training program, wherein they were taught to use language appropriately.

The imitation training took place in a rather complex environment, with many events happening concurrently. We hypothesized that it was the reward, given for imitative behavior, which was crucial to the learning. To test this hypothesis, the adult uttered the sounds as during the training and the children received the same number of

FIG. 1 Acquisition of verbal imitation by Billy. The abscissa denotes training days. Words and sounds are printed in lowercase letters on the days they were introduced and in capital letters on the days they were mastered.

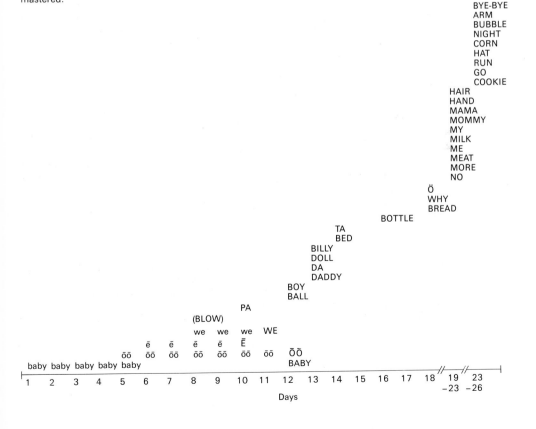

rewards as before. However, the rewards were contingent upon time elapsed since the last reward, regardless of the child's behavior.

The data show a deterioration in imitation behavior whenever rewards are shifted from response-contingent to time-contingent delivery. It is concluded, therefore, that reward immediately following correct, imitative behavior (and withholding of reward following incorrect responding) is a crucial variable in maintaining imitative behavior in these children. The same finding has been reported by Baer and Sherman (1964) who worked with imitative behavior in normal children.

Since the child was rewarded whenever he responded like the adult, *similarity* was consistently associated with food. Because of such association, similarity should become symbolic of reward. In other words, imitative behavior, being symbolic of reward, should eventually provide its own reward (Baer and Sherman, 1964). To test this hypothesis, both children were exposed to Norwegian words which they were unable to reproduce perfectly when first presented. The adult simply stated the Norwegian word and the child always attempted to repeat it; no extrinsic rewards were delivered. However, occasionally the child was presented with English words which the adult rewarded when correctly imitated. This procedure was necessary to maintain the hypothesized symbolic (learned) reward function of imitation.

The children improved in the imitation of the Norwegian words over time. It is as if they were rewarded for correct behavior. In view of the data pointing to the need for rewards in maintaining imitative behavior, and in the absence of extrinsic rewards, we would argue that the reward was intrinsic and a function of the prior imitation training. There is one implication of this finding which is of particular interest for therapeutic reasons: children may be able to acquire new behaviors on their own. (This finding contrasts with the frequent stereotype of a conditioning product, namely, that of an automaton unable to function independently.)

Currently, three new schizophrenic children are undergoing the same speech training program as Billy and Chuck. After 3 days of training, one of these children achieved a level of imitative behavior similar to that shown by Billy and Chuck after 26 days. It should be pointed out that schizophrenic children are a very heterogeneous group with respect to their speech histories and symptomatology in general, and that Billy and Chuck had failed in development to a profound degree. Insofar as one works with such a diverse population, it is likely that numerous procedures could be helpful in establishing speech.

REFERENCES

Baer, D. M., & Sherman, J. A. Reinforcement control of generalized imitation in young children. *Journal of Experimental Child Psychology,* 1964, **1**, 37–49.

Brown, J. L. Prognosis from presenting symptoms of preschool children with atypical development. *American Journal of Orthopsychiatry,* 1960, **30**, 382–390.

Rimland, B. *Infantile autism.* New York: Appleton-Century-Crofts, 1964.

MONETARY REWARD AND MOTIVATION IN DISCRIMINATION LEARNING[1]

Louise Brightwell Miller and Betsy Worth Estes

A number of comparative studies have shown that amount of reinforcement is an effective variable in certain classical and instrumental conditioning situations. Experimental attempts to generalize this finding to discrimination tasks have produced conflicting results. Evidence on human *S*s is particularly limited and also inconsistent (Cantor & Hottel, 1955; Terrell & Kennedy, 1957).

For decisive effects with human *S*s rather large differences in amount might be necessary because knowledge of results may provide a basic incentive level sufficient to mask small accretions. No-difference results might also be attributable to the possibility that motivation was already at asymptote (Muenzinger, 1934). Moreover, an interaction between motivation and incentive might be expected.

This study represents an attempt to measure the effects of a 50 to 1 differential in monetary reward on human discrimination learning. Motivation was measured by ''[need for] Achievement'' (n Ach) scores. High n Ach scorers have been shown to be better learners (Lowell, 1952) and better performers (Atkinson & Reitman, 1956; Lowell, 1952).

METHOD

Design . . . The general procedure consisted of obtaining n Ach scores and dividing them at the median. Equal numbers of high and low scorers, drawn at random from the original group, then received the different reward levels during discrimination learning. All three incentive groups were informed of success by a red light. The KOR group [knowledge of results group] received no additional reward. The 1¢ group and the 50¢ group received the appropriate amounts for each correct choice, and forfeited the same amounts for each error. There were 24 *S*s in each incentive group, a total of 72.

A preliminary experiment was performed to determine whether the forfeiture of money for errors would constitute a different reward situation from that of reward with no corresponding penalty. [An] analysis [of the data] indicated no difference between the two methods.

[1] Based on a study submitted by LBM in partial fulfillment of the requirements for a Ph.D. degree from the University of Kentucky. Sincere appreciation is due James S. Calvin for invaluable advice and criticism in planning the experiment. This research was supported in part by a grant from the University of Kentucky Faculty Research Fund to BWE.

From L. B. Miller & B. W. Estes. Monetary reward and motivation in discrimination learning. Journal of Experimental Psychology, *1961,* **61**, *501–504. (With permission of the authors and the American Psychological Association.)*

Since Meyer (1951) has shown that range of rewards is an effective variable, the different incentive levels were offered at separate schools. Because of this deliberate confounding of schools with incentive, matching with respect to socioeconomic status was necessary particularly for the main comparison between the 1¢ and 50¢ groups. Schools were selected on the basis of a recent study by Sparks (Sparks & Ray, 1957). Mean occupational status of fathers of experimental Ss, using the same index (Warner, Meeker, & Eells, 1949) was exactly the same in the 1¢ and 50¢ groups.

Subjects   The Ss were males only, taken from the third and fourth grades of the public schools. All Ss were between CA 9–0 and 9–11.

n Ach scores   The method of obtaining n Ach scores was patterned after an experiment by Winterbottom (1953). Eight written stories were obtained from a group of 35–40 boys at each school. Printed themes were presented consecutively. For example, the first suggestion read, ''Tell a story about a mother and her son. They look worried.'' All eight stories were written in one session, with 4 min. allowed for each story.

The scoring method was modified from that described by McClelland, Atkinson, Clark, and Lowell (1953, Ch. 2, 24). Only two of the suggested categories were used: Achievement-Imagery and Achievement-Thema. Each of these, if present, contributed one point to each story score.

Discrimination task   The Ss were asked to discriminate between two line drawings of faces, which were presented side by side on a card (Figure 1). The two faces were identical in all respects except the height and spacing of the eyebrows. Two stimulus cards were used, presenting reverse positions of the two faces. Duplicates were used as needed.

Apparatus   The apparatus was designed for tachistoscopic presentation of stimuli and automatic delivery of reward. On S's side were (from top to bottom): a red signal lamp, viewing window, money slot, tin cup for coins, and selection switch. On E's side a hinged door in the top permitted insertion of cards into the tachistoscope. Below the door were placed: slot for insertion of coins, switch for presetting correct choice, starter switch, red signal lamp, and timer. An incorrect choice merely stopped the timer and removed the card from view. Correct selection lighted red signal lamps on both sides and in the money groups activated a solenoid which released the coin.

FIG. 1   Stimulus card with high eye-brows on the left.

Instructions and procedure Each *S* was tested individually. The task was presented as one of learning to tell twins apart, Bill from his brother, and to choose Bill every time. Practice was given with a sample pair of square faces, in which the nose of one was larger and higher. Almost all *S*s recognized this exaggerated difference immediately. Those who did not were shown the difference. The cards were presented in random order with each face appearing equally often on the left and right. The face selected by each *S* on the first trial was rewarded, and was considered correct thereafter. In the money groups, *S* was loaned 10 coins at the beginning, and was told that after the session he would be allowed to keep all that he had received, minus these 10.

Choice was forced after 2 sec. The noncorrection procedure was used. Criterion was 16 consecutive correct choices. Trials were massed and sessions terminated after 100. In addition to errors, a record was kept of the time interval between presentation of the stimulus and selection by *S*. Both errors and time were recorded manually.

RESULTS

Overall results are presented in Table 1. Incentive was a significant source of [difference between the groups]. . . . There was no difference between the 50¢ and 1¢ groups, but both these groups made *more* errors than did the KOR group. [Analysis of the data] showed the difference between the means of the two money groups combined and the KOR group to be significant at better than the .01 level. Of 37 *S*s who reached criterion performance, 15 were in the KOR group, 10 in the 1¢ group, and 12 in the 50¢ group. These differences, however, are not statistically significant.

[n Ach . . . scores were also . . . significantly different for the three groups. . . .] More errors were made by low n Ach *S*s. . . The number of *S*s who learned to criterion was significantly larger in the high n Ach group. Of the total, 26 were high n Ach *S*s and 11 were low. . . .

[An] analysis . . . of [the] time scores did not reveal any significant variation, and it can be seen from Table 1 that time scores of the six treatment groups were approximately the same.

TABLE 1   Mean error and time scores of six treatment groups

Incentive	Errors			Time (sec.)		
	High n Ach	Low n Ach	Total	High n Ach	Low n Ach	Total
Knowledge	17.5	24.3	20.9	2.56	2.54	2.55
1 cent	27.6	37.4	32.5	2.10	2.09	2.10
50 cents	27.7	40.3	34.0	2.58	2.32	2.45
Total	24.3	34.0		2.42	2.32	

DISCUSSION

The no-difference results repeatedly found in comparative studies of incentive variation in visual discrimination are further substantiated by these results on human *S*s. If reward was effective at all, it would be difficult to account for the lack of superiority in the 50¢ group, unless there was some systematic difference which produced better learners in the 1¢ group. But the two money groups did not differ in socioeconomic status; median n Ach scores were the same; mean IQs based on available group scores differed by only 2 points. Correlation between IQ and number of correct trials proved to be low (.19).

The clear inferiority of the reward groups was an unexpected result, unaccountable for by theory or previous empirical evidence. The implication that monetary incentive had a detrimental effect cannot be substantiated from this study alone, although observations made during the experiment suggested that preoccupation with the money (counting, gloating, worrying) constituted a sort of interpolated task.

On the other hand, any incentive effect—whether facilitating or detrimental—might be expected to interact with motivation. Yet significantly poorer learning with money was the case for both high and low n Ach Ss. The statistical analysis revealed no significant interaction between n Ach and incentive, . . . although it appears from inspection that the two poorest groups were low n Ach Ss who received money.

Motivation effects are apparent, in that low n Ach Ss made significantly more errors than high n Ach Ss. The relationship between n Ach and IQ does not appear important. . . . This result extends the generality of the n Ach score as a measure of the need to achieve on a discrimination task.

It is interesting that of those Ss who learned, less than half were able to verbalize the relevant cue. Among the statements made by these Ss were: "Bill's mouth is straighter;" "Bill's nose is littler;" "Bill had the most teeth." None of these differences actually existed, of course, yet these Ss had made at least 16 successive correct choices, the chance probability of which is so small as to be negligible. They had learned to discriminate without identifying the locus of difference. There were no significant differences in errors or trials for Ss who could identify the relevant cue, as compared with those who could not.

SUMMARY

An experiment was performed to investigate the effects of different levels of monetary incentive and n Achievement on the acquisition of a visual discrimination habit. Groups of 9-yr. [-old] boys learned to discriminate between drawings of faces which differed only in the height and spacing of the eyebrows. Pictures were presented tachistoscopically for 2-sec. intervals. The Ss received after each correct choice: 50¢, 1¢, or only knowledge of results.

The major results were: (a) There was no difference in number of errors made by Ss rewarded with 50¢ pieces and those given pennies. (b) Groups who received money made significantly *more* errors than those receiving only knowledge. (c) Low n Ach Ss made significantly more errors than high n Ach Ss. (d) There were no significant differences among experimental groups in time required to respond. These results were interpreted as substantiating the no-difference results repeatedly found in comparative studies of incentive variation on discrimination learning.

REFERENCES

Atkinson, J. W., & Reitman, W. R. Performance as a function of motive strength and expectancy of goal-attainment. *Journal of Abnormal and Social Psychology*, 1956, **53**, 361–366.

Cantor, G. N., & Hottel, J. V. Discrimination learning in mental defectives as a function of magnitude of food reward and intelligence level. *American Journal of Mental Deficiency,* 1955, **60**, 380–384.

Lowell, E. L. The effect of need for achievement on learning and speed of performance. *Journal of Psychology,* 1952, **33**, 31–40.

McClelland, D. C., Atkinson, J. W., Clark, R. A., & Lowell, E. L. *The achievement motive.* New York: Appleton-Century-Crofts, 1953.

Meyer, D. R. The effects of differential rewards on discrimination reversal learning by monkeys. *Journal of Experimental Psychology,* 1951, **41**, 268–274.

Muenzinger, K. F. Motivation in learning. I. Electric shock for correct response in the visual discrimination habit. *Journal of Comparative Psychology,* 1934, **17**, 267–277.

Sparks, P. E., & Ray, L. C. An evaluation of two methods of teaching reading. *Elementary School Journal,* 1957, **57**, 386–390.

Terrell, G., Jr., & Kennedy, W. A. Discrimination learning and transposition in children as a function of the nature of the reward. *Journal of Experimental Psychology,* 1957, **53**, 257–260.

Warner, W. L., Meeker, M., & Eells, K. *Social class in America: A manual of procedure for the measurement of social status.* Chicago: Science Research Associates, 1949.

Winterbottom, M. The relation of childhood training in independence to achievement motivation. Unpublished doctoral dissertation, University of Michigan, 1953.

IDENTIFICATION AS A PROCESS
OF INCIDENTAL LEARNING[1]

Albert Bandura and Aletha C. Huston

Although part of a child's socialization takes place through direct training, much of a child's behavior repertoire is believed to be acquired through identification with the important adults in his life. This process, variously described in behavior theory as "vicarious" learning (Logan, Olmsted, Rosner, Schwartz, & Stevens, 1955), observational learning (Maccoby & Wilson, 1957; Warden, Fjeld, & Koch, 1940), and role taking (Maccoby, 1959; Sears, Maccoby, & Levin, 1957) appears to be more a result of active imitation by the child of attitudes and patterns of behavior that the parents have never directly attempted to teach than of direct reward and punishment of instrumental responses.

While elaborate developmental theories have been proposed to explain this phenomenon, the process subsumed under the term "identification" may be accounted for in terms of incidental learning, that is, learning that apparently takes place in the absence of an induced set or intent to learn the specific behaviors or activities in question (McGeoch & Irion, 1952).

During the parents' social training of a child, the range of cues employed by a child is likely to include both those that the parents consider immediately relevant and other cues of parental behavior which the child has had ample opportunities to observe and to learn even though he has not been instructed to do so. Thus, for example, when a parent punishes a child physically for having aggressed toward peers, the intended outcome of the training is that the child should refrain from hitting others. Concurrent with the intentional learning, however, a certain amount of incidental learning may be expected to occur through imitation, since the child is provided, in the form of the parent's behavior, with an example of how to aggress toward others, and this incidental learning may guide the child's behavior in later social interactions.

The use of incidental cues by both human and animal subjects while performing nonimitative learning tasks is well documented by research (Easterbrook, 1959). In addition, studies of imitation and learning of incidental cues by Church (1957) and Wilson (1958) have demonstrated that subjects learn certain incidental environmental cues while imitating the discrimination behavior of a model and that the incidental learning guides the subjects' discrimination responses in the absence of the model.

[1] This investigation was supported in part by Research Grant M-1734 from the National Institute of Health, United States Public Health Service, and the Lewis S. Haas Child Development Research Fund, Stanford University.

From A. Bandura & A. C. Huston. Identification as a process of incidental learning. Journal of Abnormal and Social Psychology, *1961, **63**, 311–318. (With permission of the authors and the American Psychological Association.)*

The purpose of the experiment reported in this paper is to demonstrate that subjects imitate not only discrimination responses but also other behaviors performed by the model.

The incidental learning paradigm was employed in the present study with an important change in procedure in order to create a situation similar to that encountered in learning through identification. Subjects performed an orienting task but, unlike most incidental learning studies, the experimenter performed the diverting task as well and the extent to which the subjects patterned their behavior after that of the experimenter-model was measured.

The main hypothesis tested is that nursery school children, while learning a two-choice discrimination problem, also learn to imitate certain of the experimenter's behaviors which are totally irrelevant to the successful performance of the orienting task.

One may expect, on the basis of theories of identification (Bronfenbrenner, 1960), that the presence of affection and nurturance in the adult-child interaction promotes incidental imitative learning, a view to which empirical studies of the correlates of strong and weak identification lend some indirect support. Boys whose fathers are highly rewarding and affectionate have been found to adopt the father-role in doll play activities (Sears, 1953), to show father-son similarity in response to items on a personality questionnaire (Payne & Mussen, 1956), and to display masculine behaviors (Mussen & Distler, 1959, 1960) to a greater extent than boys whose fathers are relatively cold and unrewarding.

One interpretation of the relationship between nurturance and identification is that affectional rewards increase the secondary reinforcing properties of the model and, thus, predispose the imitator to reproduce the behavior of the model for the satisfaction these cues provide (Mowrer, 1950). Once the parental characteristics have acquired such reward value for the child, conditional withdrawal of positive reinforcers is believed to create additional instigation for the child to perform behaviors resembling that of the parent model, i.e., if the child can reproduce the parent's rewarding behavior he can, thus, reward himself (Sears, 1957; Whiting & Child, 1953). In line with this theory of identification in terms of secondary reward, it is predicted that children who experience a warm, rewarding interaction with the experimenter-model should reproduce significantly more of the behaviors performed by the model than do children who experience a relatively distant and cold relationship.

METHOD

Subjects

The subjects were 24 boys and 24 girls enrolled in the Stanford University Nursery School. They ranged in age from 45 to 61 months, with a mean age of 53 months. The junior author played the role of the model for all 48 children, and two other female experimenters shared in the task of conducting the study.[2]

[2] The authors wish to express their appreciation to Alice Beach and Mary Lou Funkhouser for their assistance in collecting the data, and to Ruth Barclay and Claire Korn for their help with the behavior observations.

General procedure

Forty subjects were matched individually on the basis of sex and ratings of dependency behavior, and subdivided randomly in terms of a nurturant-nonnurturant condition yielding two experimental groups of 20 subjects each. A small control group comprising 8 subjects was also studied.

In the first phase of the experiment half the experimental and control subjects experienced two nurturant rewarding play sessions with the model while the remaining subjects experienced a cold nonnurturant relationship. For the second phase of the experiment subjects performed a diverting two-choice discrimination problem with the model who exhibited fairly explicit, although functionless, behavior during the discrimination trials, and the extent to which the subjects reproduced the model's behavior was measured. The experimental and control procedures differed only in the patterns of behavior displayed by the model.

Matching variable

Dependency was selected as a matching variable since, on the basis of the theories of identification, dependency would be expected to facilitate imitative learning. There is some evidence, for example, that dependent subjects are strongly oriented toward gaining social rewards in the form of attention and approval (Cairns, 1959; Endsley & Hartup, 1960), and one means of obtaining these rewards is to imitate the behavior of others (Sears, Maccoby, & Levin, 1957). Moreover, such children do not have the habit of responding independently; consequently they are apt to be more dependent on, and therefore more attentive to, the cues produced by the behavior of others (Jakubczak & Walters, 1959; Kagan & Mussen, 1956).

Measures of subjects' dependency behavior were obtained through observations of their social interactions in the nursery school. The observers recorded subjects' behavior using a combined time-sampling and behavior-unit observation method. Each child was observed for twelve 10-minute observation sessions distributed over a period of approximately 10 weeks; each observation session was divided into 30-second intervals, thus yielding a total of 240 behavior units.

The children were observed in a predetermined order that was varied randomly to insure that each child would be seen under approximately comparable conditions. In order to provide an estimate of reliability of the ratings, 234 observation sessions (4,680 behavior units) were recorded simultaneously but independently by both observers.

The subjects' emotional dependency was assessed in terms of the frequency of behaviors that were aimed at securing a nurturant response from others. The following four specific categories of dependency behavior were scored: seeking help and assistance, seeking praise and approval, seeking physical contact, and seeking proximity and company of others.

The dependency scores were obtained by summing the observations made of these four different types of behaviors and, on the basis of these scores, the subjects were paired and assigned at random to the two experimental conditions.

Experimental conditions

In the *nonnurturant* condition, the model brought the subject to the experimental room and after instructing the child to play with the toys that were spread on the floor, busied herself with paper work at a desk in the far corner of the room. During this period the model avoided any interaction with the child.

In contrast, during the *nurturant* sessions the model sat on the floor close to the subject. She responded readily to the child's bids for help and attention, and in other ways fostered a consistently warm, and rewarding interaction.

These experimental social interactions, which preceded the imitation learning, consisted of two 15-minute sessions separated by an interval of approximately 5 days.

Diverting task

A two-choice discrimination problem, similar to the one employed by Miller and Dollard (1941) in experiments of matching behavior, was used as the diverting task which occupied the subjects' attention while at the same time permitting opportunities for the subjects to observe behavior performed by the model in the absence of any instructions to observe or to reproduce the responses resembling that of the model.

The apparatus consisted of two small boxes, identical in color (red sides, yellow lid) and size ($6'' \times 8'' \times 10''$). The hinged lid of each box was lined with rubber stripping so as to eliminate any auditory cues during the placement of the rewards which consisted of small multicolor pictures of animals and flowers. The boxes were placed on small chairs approximately 5 feet apart and 8 feet from the starting point.

At the end of the second social interaction session the experimenter entered the room with the test apparatus and instructed the model and the subject that they were going to play a game in which the experimenter would hide a picture sticker in one of the boxes and that the object of the game was to guess which box contained the sticker.

The model and the subject then left the room and after the experimenter placed two stickers in the designated box, they were recalled to the starting point in the experimental room and the model was asked to take the first turn. During the model's trial, the subject remained at the starting point where he could observe the model's behavior.

Although initially it was planned to follow the procedure used by Miller and Dollard (1941) in which one of two boxes was loaded with two rewards and the child made his choice immediately following the leader's trial, this procedure had to be modified when it became evident during pretesting that approximately 40 percent of the subjects invariably chose the opposite box from the model even though the nonimitative response was consistently unrewarded. McDavid (1959), in a . . . study of imitative behavior in preschool children, encountered similar difficulties in that 44 percent of his subjects did not learn to imitate the leader even though the subjects were not informed as to whether the leader was or was not rewarded.

In order to overcome this stereotyped nonimitation, the experimenter placed two rewards in a single box, but following the model's trial the model and the subject left the room and were recalled almost immediately (the intratrial interval was approximately 5 seconds), thus creating the impression that the boxes were reloaded. After the subject completed his trial, the model and the subject left the room. The experimenter recorded the subject's behavior and reloaded the boxes for the second trial. The noncorrection method was used throughout. This procedure was continued until the subject met the learning criterion of four successive imitative discrimination responses, or until 30 acquisition trials had been completed. The slight modification in procedure proved to be effective as evidenced by the fact that only 9 of the 48 children failed to meet the criterion.

In order to eliminate any position habit, the right-left placements of the reward were varied from trial to trial in a fixed irregular order. This sequence was randomly determined except for the limitation that no more than two successive rewards could occur in the same position.

The number of trials to criterion was the measure of the subjects' imitation behavior on the discrimination task.

Although the establishment of imitative choice responses was, in itself, of some theoretical interest, the discrimination problem was intended primarily as an orienting or distraction task. Thus, on each discrimination trial, the model exhibited certain verbal, motor, and aggressive behaviors which were totally irrelevant to the performance of the task to which the subject's attention was directed. At the starting point, for example, the model remarked, "Here I go," and then marched slowly toward the box containing the stickers repeating, "March, march, march." On the lid of each box was a small rubber doll which the model knocked off aggressively when she reached the designated box. She then paused briefly, remarked, "Open the box," removed one sticker and pasted it on a pastoral scene that hung on the wall immediately behind the boxes. The model terminated the trial by replacing the doll on the lid of the container. The model and the subject then left the room briefly. After being recalled to the experimental room the subject took his turn, and the number of the model's behaviors reproduced by the subject was recorded.

Control group

In addition to the two experimental groups, a control group, consisting of eight subjects, comparable to the experimental groups in terms of sex distribution, dependency ratings, and nurturant-nonnurturant experiences was studied. Since the model performed highly novel patterns of responses unlikely to occur independently of the observation of the behavior of the model, it was decided to assign most of the available subjects to the experimental groups and only a small number of subjects to the control group.

The reasons for the inclusion of a control group were twofold. On the one hand, it provided a check on whether the subjects' behavior reflected genuine imitative learning or merely the chance occurrence of behaviors high in the subjects' response hierarchies. Second, it was of interest to determine whether the subjects would adopt certain aspects of the model's behavior that involved considerable delay in reward. With the controls, therefore, the model walked to the box, choosing a highly circuitous route along the sides of the experimental room; instead of aggressing toward the doll, the model lifted it gently off the container and she left the doll on the floor at the completion of a trial. While walking to the boxes the model repeated, "Walk, walk, walk."

Imitation scores

On each trial the subjects' performances were scored in terms of the following imitation response categories: selects box chosen by the model; marches; repeats the phrases, "Here I go," "March, march," "Open box," or "Walk, walk;" aggresses toward the doll; replaces doll on box; imitates the circuitous route to the box.

Some subjects made a verbal response in the appropriate context (for example, at the starting point, on the way to the box, before raising the lid of the container) but did not repeat the model's exact words. These verbal responses were also scored and interpreted as partially imitative behavior.

In order to provide an estimate of the reliability of the experimenter's scoring, the performances of 19 subjects were scored independently by two judges who alternated in observing the experimental sessions through a one-way mirror from an adjoining observation room.

RESULTS

Reliability of observations of dependency behavior [and imitation scores]

The reliability of the observers' behavior ratings was estimated by means of an index of agreement based on the ratio of twice the number of agreements over the combined ratings of the two observers multiplied by 100. . . . The interobserver reliabilities for the dependency categories considered separately were as follows: Positive attention seeking, 84 percent; help seeking, 72 percent; seeking physical contact, 84 percent; and seeking proximity, 75 percent.

[In imitation] . . . (Table 1) . . . the subjects' behavior was scored with high reliability and, even in the letter response category, the scoring discrepancies arose primarily from the experimenter's lack of opportunity to observe some of the behaviors in question rather than from differences of interpretation, for example, when the subject made appropriate mouth movements but emitted no sound while marching toward the containers. This partial imitation of the model's verbalizations could not be readily observed by the experimenter (who was at the starting point) but was clearly evident to the rater in the observation room.

Incidental imitation of model's behavior

Since the data disclosed no significant sex differences, the imitation scores for the male and female subgroups were combined in the statistical analyses.

Ninety percent of the subjects in the experimental groups adopted the model's aggressive behavior, 45 percent imitated the marching, and 28 percent reproduced the model's verbalizations. In contrast, none of the control subjects behaved aggressively,[3]

[3]One subject in the control group hit the doll off the box on one trial only.

TABLE 1   Scorer reliability of imitative responses

Response category	Percentage agreement
Aggression	98
Marching	73
Imitative verbal behavior	80
Partially imitative verbal behavior	83
Other imitative responses	50
Replaces doll	99
Circuitous route	96

marched or verbalized, while 75 percent of the controls and none of the experimental subjects imitated the circuitous route to the containers. Except for replacing the doll on the box, which was performed by most of the experimental and control subjects, there was no overlap in the imitative behavior displayed by the two groups (see Table 2).

While the control subjects replaced the doll on the box slightly more often than the subjects in the experimental group, this difference . . . was not statistically significant. . . . Evidently the response of replacing things, undoubtedly overtrained by parents, is so well established that it occurs independently of the behavior of the model. Since this was clearly a nonimitative response, it was not included in the subsequent analyses.

TABLE 2   Amount of imitative behavior displayed by subjects in the experimental and control groups

Response category	Experimental Subjects N = 40		Control Subjects N = 8	
	Percentage imitating	Mean per trial	Percentage imitating	Mean per trial
Behaviors of experimental model				
Marching	45	.23	0	0
Verbal responses	28	.10	0	0
Aggression	90	.64	13	.01
Other imitative responses	18	.03	0	0
Partially imitative verbal behavior	43	.11	0	0
Replacing doll	90	.60	75	.77
Behaviors of control model				
Circuitous route	0	0	75	.58
Verbal responses	0	0	13	.10

Note.   The mean number of trials for subjects in the experimental group (13.52) and in the control group (15.25) did not differ significantly.

To the extent that behavior of the sort evoked in this study may be considered an elementary prototype of identification, the results presented in Table 2 add support to the interpretation of identification as a process of incidental imitative learning.

Effects of nurturance on imitation

In order to make comparable the imitation scores for the subjects who varied somewhat in the number of trials to criterion, the total imitative responses in a given response category were divided by the number of trials. . . . The predicted facilitating effect of social rewards on imitation was essentially confirmed. . . . Subjects who experienced the rewarding interaction with the model marched and verbalized imitatively, and reproduced other responses resembling that of the model to a greater extent than did the subjects who experienced the relatively cold and distant relationship. Aggression, interestingly, was readily imitated by subjects regardless of the quality of the model-child relationship.

Imitation of discrimination responses

[An] . . . analysis . . . of the trial scores failed to show any significant effects of nurturance or sex of imitator on the imitation of discrimination responses, . . . nor did the two groups of experimental subjects differ significantly in the number of trials in which they imitated the model's choice or in the number of trials to the first imitative discrimination response.

While nurturance did not seem to influence the actual choices the subjects made, it nevertheless affected their predecision behavior. A number of the children displayed considerable conflictful vacillation, often running back and forth between the boxes, prior to making their choice. In the analysis of these data, the vacillation scores were divided by the total number of trials, and [these . . . differences were analyzed]. . . . The results . . . revealed that the subjects in the nurturant condition exhibited [significantly] more conflictful behavior than subjects in the nonnurturant group. . . . This finding is particularly noteworthy considering that one has to counteract a strong nonimitation bias in getting preschool children to follow a leader in a two-choice discrimination problem as evidenced by McDavid's (1959) findings as well as those of the present study (i.e., 75 percent of the subjects made nonimitative choices on the first trial).

Dependency and imitation

Correlations between the ratings of dependency behavior and the measures of imitation were calculated separately for the nurturant and nonnurturant experimental subgroups, and where the correlation coefficients did not differ significantly the data were combined. The expected positive relationship between dependency and imitation was only partially supported. High dependent subjects expressed [significantly] more . . . imitative verbal behavior . . . (.60) . . . and exhibited more predecision conflict on the discrimination task . . . (.26) . . . than did subjects who were rated low on dependency.

Dependency and total imitation of nonaggressive responses were positively related for boys . . . (.31) but negatively correlated for girls . . . (−.46). These correlations, however, are not statistically significant. Nor was there any significant relationship between dependency and imitation of aggression . . . (.20) or discrimination responses . . . (−.03).

DISCUSSION

The results of this study generally substantiate the hypotheses that children display a good deal of social learning of an incidental imitative sort, and that nurturance is one condition facilitating such imitative learning.

The extent to which the model's behavior had come to influence and control the behavior of subjects is well illustrated by their marching, and by their choice of the circuitous route to the containers. Evidence from the pretesting and from the subjects' behavior during the early discrimination trials revealed that dashing toward the boxes was the dominant response, and that the delay produced by marching or by taking an indirect route that more than doubled the distance to the boxes was clearly incompatible with the subjects' eagerness to get to the containers. Nevertheless, many subjects dutifully followed the example set by the model.

Even more striking was the subjects' imitation of responses performed unwittingly by the model. On one trial with a control subject, for example, the model began to replace the doll on the box at the completion of the trial when suddenly, startled by the realization of the mistake, she quickly replaced the doll on the floor. Sure enough, on the next trial, the subject took the circuitous route, removed the doll gently off the box and, after disposing of the sticker, raised the doll, and then quickly replaced it on the floor reproducing the model's startled reaction as well!

The results for the influence of nurturance on imitation of verbal behavior are in accord with Mowrer's (1950) autism theory of word learning. Moreover, the obtained significant effect of nurturance on the production of partially imitative verbal responses indicates that nurturance not only facilitates imitation of the specific behaviors displayed by a model but also increases the probability of responses of a whole response class (for example, verbal behavior). These data are essentially in agreement with those of Milner (1951), who found that mothers of children receiving high reading readiness scores were more verbal and affectionately demonstrative in the interactions with their children than were the mothers of subjects in the low reading ability group.

That the incidental cues of the model's behavior may have taken on positive valence and were consequently reproduced by subjects for the mere satisfaction of performing them, is suggested by the fact that children in the nurturant condition not only marched to the containers but also marched in and out of the experimental room and marched about in the anteroom repeating, ''March, march, march,'' etc., while waiting for the next trial. While certain personality patterns may be, thus, incidentally acquired, the stability and persistence of these behaviors in the absence of direct rewards by external agents remains to be studied.

A response cannot be readily imitated unless its components are within the subjects behavior repertoire. The fact that gross motor responses are usually more highly developed than verbal skills in young children may explain why subjects reproduced the model's marching . . . and aggression . . . to a significantly greater extent than they did her verbal behavior. Indeed several subjects imitated the motor component of speech by performing the appropriate mouth movements but emitted no sound. The greater saliency of the model's motor responses might also be a possible explanation of the obtained differences.

"Identification with the aggressor" (Freud, 1937) or "defensive identification" (Mowrer, 1950), whereby a child presumably transforms himself from object to agent of aggression by adopting the attributes of an aggressive, punitive model so as to allay anxiety, is widely accepted as an explanation of the imitative learning of aggression. The results of the present study, and those of a second experiment now in progress, suggest that the mere observation of aggressive models, regardless of the quality of the model-child relationship, is a sufficient condition for producing imitative aggression in children. A comparative study of subjects' imitation of aggressive models who are feared, who are liked and esteemed, or who are more or less neutral figures would throw some light on whether or not a more parsimonious theory than the one involved in "identification with the aggressor" can explain the modeling process.

Although the results from the present study provide evidence that nurturance promotes incidental imitative learning, the combination of nurturance followed by its withdrawal would be expected, according to the secondary reinforcement theory of imitation, to furnish stronger incentive than nurturance alone for subjects to reproduce a model's behavior. It is also possible that dependency may be essentially unrelated to imitation under conditions of consistent nurturance, but may emerge as a variable facilitating imitation under conditions where social reinforcers are temporarily withdrawn.

The experiment reported in this paper focused on immediate imitation in the presence of the model. A more crucial test of the transmission of behavior through the process of social imitation involves the generalization of imitative responses to new situations in which the model is absent. A study of this type, involving the delayed imitation of both male and female aggressive models, is currently under way.

SUMMARY

The present study was primarily designed to test the hypotheses that children would learn to imitate behavior exhibited by an experimenter-model, and that a nurturant interaction between the model and the child would enhance the secondary reward properties of the model and thus facilitate such imitative learning.

Forty-eight preschool children performed a diverting two-choice discrimination problem with a model who displayed fairly explicit, although functionless, behaviors during the trials. With the experimental subjects the model marched, emitted specific verbal responses, and aggressed toward dolls located on the discrimination boxes; with the controls the model walked to the boxes choosing a highly circuitous route and behaved in a nonaggressive fashion. Half the subjects in the experimental and control groups experienced a rewarding interaction with the model prior to the imitative learning while the remaining subjects experienced a cold and nonnurturant relationship.

The following results were obtained:
1. The experimental and the control subjects not only reproduced behaviors resembling that of their model but also, except for one response category, did not overlap in the types of imitative responses they displayed.
2. The predicted facilitating effect of social rewards on imitation was also confirmed,

the only exception being for aggression, which was readily imitated by the subjects regardless of the quality of the model-child relationship.

3. Although nurturance was not found to influence the rate of imitative discrimination learning, subjects in the nurturant condition exhibited significantly more predecision conflict behavior than did subjects in the nonnurturant group.

REFERENCES

Bronfenbrenner, U. Freudian theories of identification and their derivatives. *Child Development,* 1960, **31**, 15–40.

Cairns, R. B. The influence of dependency-anxiety on the effectiveness of social reinforcers. Unpublished doctoral dissertation, Stanford University, 1959.

Church, R. M. Transmission of learned behavior between rats. *Journal of Abnormal and Social Psychology,* 1957, **54**, 163–165.

Easterbrook, J. A. The effect of emotion on cue utilization and the organization of behavior. *Psychological Review,* 1959, **66**, 183–201.

Endsley, R. C., & Hartup, W. W. Dependency and performance by preschool children on a socially reinforced task. *American Psychologist,* 1960, **15**, 399. (Abstract)

Freud, A. *The ego and the mechanisms of defense.* London: Hogarth, 1937.

Jakubczak, L. F., & Walters, R. H. Suggestibility as dependency behavior. *Journal of Abnormal and Social Psychology,* 1959, **59**, 102–107.

Kagan, J., & Mussen, P. H. Dependency themes on the TAT and group conformity. *Journal of Consulting Psychology,* 1956, **20**, 29–32.

Logan, F., Olmsted, D. L., Rosner, B. S., Schwartz, R. D., & Stevens, C. M. *Behavior theory and social science.* New Haven: Yale University Press, 1955.

Maccoby, E. E. Role-taking in childhood and its consequences for social learning. *Child Development,* 1959, **30**, 239–252.

Maccoby, E. E., & Wilson, W. C. Identification and observational learning from films. *Journal of Abnormal and Social Psychology,* 1957, **55**, 76–87.

McDavid, J. W. Imitative behavior in preschool children. *Psychological Monographs,* 1959, **73**(16, Whole No. 486).

McGeoch, J. A., & Irion, A. L. *The psychology of human learning.* New York: Longmans, 1952.

Miller, N. E., & Dollard, J. *Social learning and imitation.* New Haven: Yale University Press, 1941.

Milner, E. A study of the relationship between reading readiness in grade one school children and patterns of parent-child interaction. *Child Development,* 1951, **22**, 95–112.

Mowrer, O. H. Identification: A link between learning theory and psychotherapy. In O. H. Mowrer (Ed.), *Learning theory and personality dynamics.* New York: Ronald Press, 1950. Pp. 573–616.

Mussen, P. H., & Distler, L. Masculinity, identification, and father-son relationships. *Journal of Abnormal and Social Psychology,* 1959, **59**, 350–356.

Mussen, P. H., & Distler, L. Child-rearing antecedents of masculine identification in kindergarten boys. *Child Development,* 1960, **31**, 89–100.

Payne, D. E., & Mussen, P. H. Parent-child relations and father identification among adolescent boys. *Journal of Abnormal and Social Psychology,* 1956, **52**, 358–362.

Sears, P. S. Child-rearing factors related to playing of sex-typed roles. *American Psychologist,* 1953, **8**, 431. (Abstract)

Sears, R. R. Identification as a form of behavioral development. In D. B. Harris (Ed.), *The concept of development.* Minneapolis: University of Minnesota Press, 1957. Pp. 149–161.

Sears, R. R., Maccoby, E. E., & Levin, H. *Patterns of child rearing.* Evanston, Ill.: Harper & Row, 1957.

Warden, C. J., Fjeld, H. A., & Koch, A. M. Imitative behavior in cebus and rhesus monkeys. *Journal of Genetic Psychology,* 1940, **56**, 311–322.

Whiting, J. W. M., & Child, I. L. *Child training and personality.* New Haven: Yale University Press, 1953.

Wilson, W. C. Imitation and the learning of incidental cues by preschool children. *Child Development,* 1958, **29**, 393–397.

VII

CONCEPTUAL DEVELOPMENT

Harry Osser

There has been a rapid growth of interest in the study of conceptual development, particularly in the past decade or so. This phenomenon relates almost entirely to the stimulation provided by the empirical research and the theorizing of the Swiss psychologist Jean Piaget, who for a period of about forty years has been concerned with describing and explaining the course of human conceptual growth.

Researchers who have worked in the mainstream of American psychology, namely behaviorism, have not evidenced much curiosity about the *development* of conceptual behavior. This lack of interest is traceable, in part, to the common behaviorist assumption that the governing laws are the same for *all* behaviors and *all* organisms, whether the behaviors are simple or complex or whether the organisms are high or low on the phylogenetic scale. This position does not lead naturally to a concern for developmental processes; and in fact, research on conceptual behavior from the behaviorist viewpoint has not been as prolific as research on the development of learning, perception, or other "classical" areas. Another problem has been that conceptual behaviors are relatively inaccessible to observation, so that the behaviorist has had to devise techniques to externalize and therefore objectify them. Not every behaviorist has chosen to avoid research on conceptual development; in fact, Harlow (1959) and Kendler & Kendler (1962), among others, have made important contributions in this area. This chapter will focus upon a few basic issues and the research of some of the most prominent contributors.

In order to understand the complexities involved in studying the child's development of concepts, consider the enormous range of concepts in the adult's repertoire, such as "red," "science," "large," "triangularity," "soft," "energy," "chair," "intelligence," "ugliness," "matter," and "life." The list could properly include many thousands of different concepts. The central problem for the developmental psychologist is to demonstrate how the child acquires the concepts available to the adult.

What is a concept? A "concept" can be thought of as a class of objects or events that have been integrated by virtue of one or more common elements which they share. The concept of "human being" is presumably developed for each one of us out of our encounters with others. From this experience, we distill an essence which we designate by using the verbal description "human being." It is obvious that human beings differ over a wide range of physical and psychological characteristics: some are short; some are tall; some are white; some are black; some are thin; some are fat; some are young; some are old; some are male; others are female. Yet we have little difficulty in deciding whether or not a particular stimulus configuration is classifiable as a human being.

What is the basis for grouping objects or events into discrete classes? Classification behavior depends upon the similarity among the objects or events in the group. On what basis do we judge that two or more objects are similar? The general criterion of similarity refers to physical and/or psychological properties shared by a group of objects. After inspecting the contents of a rather specialized store, we might conclude that all the objects in it are classifiable as "chairs." This judgment could relate to the fact that all the objects share the following physical characteristics: (1) legs, (2) a back rest, and (3) a surface for sitting on. Here the concept "chair" is defined by these three attributes. (This is a narrow definition, for it excludes the possibility of defining objects as members of the category "chair" if they have only two of the three attributes.)

The members of the category "chair" in the above example shared certain physical similarities; other concepts are defined by the "functional" similarities among their members. For example, there is very little physical similarity between an orange, a banana, a pear, and a pineapple; yet they all meet the criterial demands of the concept "fruit." What these objects share are certain psychological characteristics, or in other words, their function is similar. It is of course true that members of the category of "banana" share some physical characteristics. This leads to the point that concepts are organized in hierarchies with the most generalized concept on the top, so that an individual banana is a member of the class "banana," but this class is a member of the larger class "fruit," and "fruit" is a member of the even larger class "food." This is another way of saying that an object can be a member of many different classes. The adult comprehends an enormously intricate network of interrelated classifications.

To return to the question "What are concepts?", one way of answering this is to specify the psychological processes that are involved in the development of concepts. These processes include: (1) the differentiation of the properties of the environment, (2) the grouping of selected properties on the basis of similarity, and (3) the classification of the groups into a hierarchy of categories.

A concept is an economical way of dealing with the environment. Typically we do not have to recapitulate all our past encounters with human beings in order to identify a human being. Once the concept "human being" has been acquired, it is almost impossible to forget it. Another way of viewing the functional properties of a concept is to consider the behavior of a person toward a really novel object. He inspects it very carefully with as many of his senses as possible. This inspection procedure may be very prolonged. If objects were not categorized (i.e., by forming concepts), every slightly novel object (virtually every object) would have to be responded to in the painstaking fashion referred to above. This would mean that a new response would have to be affixed to every stimulus in the environment. If this were the case, over a lifetime very little significant learning could be accomplished. A concept, then, can be briefly defined as the imposition of a particular system of regularity on nature. It functions to reduce the complexity of the environment.

There are essentially two current approaches to the study of conceptual development. Each is derived from a distinct tradition which differs with respect to both theory and methodology. The first approach to be discussed is that of the neobehaviorist, and the second approach is that of Piagetian cognitive psychology. A discussion of the similarities and differences between these two positions will be delayed until some representative research has been examined.

NEOBEHAVIORIST APPROACH   An assumption shared by neobehaviorist researchers is that discrimination is significantly involved in concept formation and that it functions by directing attention to the relevant features of a stimulus as well as by permitting the neglect of irrelevant features. A further assumption is that reinforcement is the agent by which discriminative responses develop.

Learning sets

Harlow (1959) has made an important contribution to the neobehaviorist approach to the study of conceptual processes through his work on a special type of learning which he calls "learning set." For Harlow, discrimination plays an essential role in learning set, and consequently in concept formation. His position is that learning set is the process underlying concept formation; it may be defined as the discrimination process which involves the elimination of both responses and response tendencies that are inappropriate to a particular learning situation.

Harlow employs several ingenious techniques in his research, e.g., one of his procedures is to present his experimental subject (typically a rhesus monkey) with an extended series of discrimination problems. In each problem the monkey is presented with two stimulus objects, say a cube and a small cylinder, one of which (the positive stimulus) covers a piece of food. If the monkey reaches out for the positive stimulus, he receives the reward. If, on the other hand, he selects the negative stimulus, he does not get a reward. After a fixed number of trials, a new pair of stimulus objects are introduced where again the experimenter has previously selected one to be the positive stimulus. The monkeys eventually work their way through several hundred such discrimination problems.

The results of such experiments demonstrate that although each discrimination task is different, the monkeys do not have to start afresh in each successive problem. In fact, they improve their performance on successive tasks. The quality of their performance is clearly revealed by the choices made by them on the second trial of each problem. On the first trial there is no information available to the monkeys that would permit them to select the positive stimulus. If the monkey chose the negative stimulus on the first trial, he would (after going through a long series of similar tasks) tend to respond correctly on the second trial and continue to respond successfully until the end of that particular block of trials. The subjects learned to respond appropriately after having received the cue provided by the first trial of a new problem. In general, the older the monkey, the greater was the likelihood that he would quickly adopt this particular strategy.

Harlow interprets these results as supportive evidence that a learning-how-to-learn ability develops when a subject works his way through a series of similar problems, or in other words, the subject develops a learning set. It is clear that learning set is a special case of transfer of training, where the transfer is between numerous problems drawn from one class of problems.

Concept formation, according to Harlow, is basically a process of broad stimulus generalization, which is achieved by extensive training on a wide range of problems within one class, i.e., concept formation derives from the process of learning-set formation.

The discrimination learning-set procedure has been used in various studies with young children. Stevenson & Swartz (1958) compared the performance of normal and retarded groups of children on a series of object-discrimination tasks. The results of their study showed that the intellectual level of the subjects was clearly related to their responses on the discrimination problems. The normal subjects found the tasks quite simple, whereas the retarded group performed significantly more poorly on them. Stevenson and Swartz noted that successful children typically named or commented about the stimulus, whereas unsuccessful children made irrelevant verbal responses. This finding is very similar to that of Kendler, Kendler, & Learnard (1962) discussed later in this chapter.

A more recent study by Harter (1965) illustrates how learning-set studies are conducted and offers a demonstration of how learning set and intelligence are related. The subjects were presented 10 four-trial discrimination problems a day until over 90 percent of their responses were correct on five successive problems. All of the problems consisted of learning to choose one of a pair of objects. The objects were pieces of "junk" such as an irregularly shaped piece of metal and a strip of cloth, each mounted on a wooden block. The experimenter, out of the child's view, hid a marble under one of the objects. The particular object in each pair that was "correct" was determined at random by the experimenter before beginning the study. The child's task was to find the marble. He was told that he should look under a block to see if he could find the marble and that if he found enough, he could win a prize. The child made his choice, and then the experimenter rearranged the objects, and the child was allowed to make another choice. Each time, the marble was hidden under the same object. Two more trials were given, and then a new pair of objects was introduced.

During the first few problems the child had no basis, other than trial and error, for knowing under which block the marble had been hidden. Gradually, he learned the marble was hidden consistently under one of the objects. Eventually, he should learn that if he did not find the marble on the first trial, he should look under the second object on the remaining trials.

Nine groups of children from three mental-age levels (five, seven, and nine years) and from three levels of IQ (70, 100, 130) were included in the study. For example, there were three groups of children with mental ages of five years—those with IQs of 70, 100, and 130. This means, of course, that the chronological ages of the groups differed, since IQ is defined as mental age divided by chronological age. Learning sets were developed more rapidly at the higher *levels* of intellectual development, as measured by MA, and at the higher *rates* of intellectual development, as measured by IQ. Chronological age, independent of mental age, was not related to the speed with which learning sets were developed. None of the subjects required more than seven days of training to reach criterion. Interestingly, however, only 38 percent of the subjects could verbalize the basis of solving the problem when they were questioned at the end of the test. At least to the degree that their answers represented what actually had occurred, it must be concluded that the majority solved the problem on a nonverbal basis.

These results suggest that a significant difference between bright and dull children is the degree to which they are capable of benefiting from prior experience. The ease with which bright children learn new problems may be due, in part, to their greater ability to apply in new situations what they have learned in other contexts.

Mediation theory

Psychologists who work within the neobehaviorist tradition have adapted basic S-R theory so that they may integrate certain complex behaviors, such as concept formation, into their theories.

An example of such adaptation is present in the work of the Kendlers and their associates (e.g., Kendler, 1963, reprinted following this chapter). The learning model utilized is a mediation model. An earlier behaviorist model, Thorndike's single-unit S-R model, viewed learning simply as the change in the strength of an association bond between an external stimulus and an observable response. The model was a single unit because it required no assumptions to be made about events which might intervene between the stimulus and the response.

A mediation model, by contrast, postulates that the stimulus and the response are terminal points in a more complicated chain of events. The external stimulus (S), according to this view, evokes an implicit response (r) which embodies the discrimination of the stimulus by the learner. The occurrence of the implicit response (r) changes the incoming stimulation by providing an implicit stimulus (s) to which the overt response (R) becomes associated. The mediating response is significant in that it *produces* the stimuli for further responses. Therefore, the formula which designates the single-unit model is S-R; the mediation model is described by the sequence S-r-s-R.

Reversal learning

One variation in the learning-set experiment has been introduced through the development of the technique called "reversal learning," which relates fundamentally to the transfer from an initial discrimination to a subsequent one; i.e., the subject has to learn to do the opposite of what he previously did. This technique has been used in a program of research that was designed to elucidate the role of mediation processes in concept formation and in order to test the adequacy of the single-unit model of learning against the mediation model (Kendler, 1963).

Kendler & Kendler (1962) argue that conceptual behavior can be understood only if mediation processes are understood, and in order to discover how these processes develop in children, they have reduced the obvious complexities of the process of concept formation to some very simple operations that have the virtue of easy experimental manipulation. They expect that by simplifying the process, the origins of these operations can be studied in young children. The Kendlers have studied the development of mediation by using the reversal-learning technique. For example, in the initial discrimination task, two stimuli are presented which differ in two dimensions, but only one of the

dimensions is relevant to correct responding. For the purpose
of examining transfer effects, a second discrimination task is
presented. Although incorporating the same or similar stimuli
as the first task, the second discrimination task requires a shift
in response. There are two types of shift. The first, called a
"reversal shift," requires the subject to respond to a different
aspect of the previously relevant dimension. The second type is
the "nonreversal shift." For this type of shift, the subject is required to respond to the previously irrelevant dimension. For
example, if the subject is trained first on stimuli that differ both
with respect to brightness (black versus white) and size (large
versus small), and he is rewarded for his responses to black only,
a reversal shift would consist of his learning to respond to white,
and a nonreversal shift would consist of his learning to respond to small, the dimension that was previously irrelevant
(see Figure 1).

   The viewpoint that stresses the role of mediators in complex
psychological processes would predict that reversal shifts are
easier to make than nonreversal shifts, as in a reversal shift both
the initial dimension and the mediated response are still relevant,
and only the overt response has to be changed. In the nonreversal
shift, however, the mediated response is no longer relevant, so

FIGURE 1   *Examples of a reversal and a nonreversal shift. (After Kendler &
Kendler, 1962)*

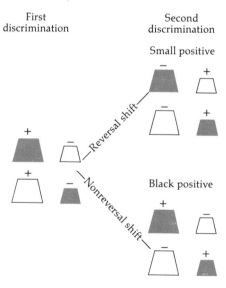

both a new mediator and a new overt response have to be acquired, which makes such a shift more difficult than a reversal shift.

It is clear from this line of argument that organisms that operate with mediators will acquire a reversal shift more easily than a nonreversal shift. In fact, the Kendlers assume that a mediator is defined by such behavior. Rats, for example, have been found to acquire nonreversal shifts more easily than reversal shifts (Kelleher, 1956), whereas college students behave in the opposite way (Kendler & D'Amato, 1955). These results support the mediational viewpoint.

These observed differences between college-student and rat performance on reversal-learning tasks led to a number of such studies of young children. It was discovered that children between three and four years of age behaved predominantly like rats, i.e., they were nonmediators (Kendler, Kendler, & Wells, 1960). Children in the age range of five to seven years divide equally into mediators and nonmediators (Kendler & Kendler, 1959). In another study (Kendler, Kendler, & Learnard, 1962), children from three to ten years of age were tested to further illuminate this developmental process. The procedure was modified to permit the children to choose whether they would behave mediationally or not. It was assumed that those who chose the reversal shifts were mediators. The results showed that at three years, 37.5 percent mediated; at four years, 50 percent; at six years, 50 percent; and at ten years, 62.5 percent mediated.

There were three styles of responding, rather than two. These styles were mediation, nonmediation, and inconsistency. One of the most interesting differences that emerged from this experiment arose from information obtained after the experiment was formally concluded. Each child was asked to talk about the task, and it was discovered that the children who used mediation also used verbalizations that were more closely relevant to their previous behavior than did the children in the two other groups; e.g., if a mediator was rewarded for "size," he tended to talk about this dimension.

In a subsequent experiment, an attempt was made to obtain further information on the role of verbalization in a mediation experiment (Kendler & Kendler, 1962). Children of four and seven years of age were presented with another variation of the reversal-shift problem. In an initial task they learned to discriminate between a pair of stimuli that differed simultaneously in size and brightness. During the time spent learning the discrimination, one-third of each age group was encouraged to verbalize the relevant dimension, another third verbalized the irrelevant dimension, and the remaining children were not encouraged to verbalize at all.

The results showed that for both age groups, the effects of relevant verbalization were superior to those of irrelevant verbalization in aiding the child to deal with the reversal-shift problem. The four-year-olds' performance on the reversal-shift task was facilitated by their learning relevant verbalization and hindered if they learned the irrelevant verbal labels; however, the effects were small. Among the seven-year-olds, those in the relevant-verbalization group performed quite similarly to those in the nonverbalization group. Irrelevant labels on the other hand yielded gross interference, such that the seven-year-olds in this group performed slightly worse than the four-year-old children in the nonverbalization group. Other results favored the older children; for example, those in the relevant-verbalization and nonverbalization groups performed better than the younger children in the relevant-verbalization group.

One interpretation of these findings is that the older group made more use of verbalizations than the younger group, so that providing them with relevant mediating responses did not ensure that they would be used. The importance of this point is expressed by the Kendlers when they suggest that the development of mediational processes is closely related to the development of the ability to associate words with actions. This point will be further analyzed in a later discussion of the role of language in the development of concepts. We will now turn to the second dominant approach to research on conceptual development.

THE PIAGETIAN APPROACH

One of the basic problems in biology is to explain how structures evolve so that organisms can adapt to their environments. This biological question has been posed by Piaget in his analysis of the nature of conceptual development. He concludes that intellectual structures (e.g., concepts) develop in the individual in order to support his adjustment to the demands of the environment. The individual's adaptation is achieved partly by a process of assimilation and partly by the complementary process of accommodation.

"Assimilation" refers to the psychological process by which the individual modifies his environment to his needs; "accommodation" is the process by which the individual has to adapt his behaviors to the environment. The following example illustrates the relationship between these two processes. A child who has learned to turn handles to open doors will, on being presented with a new type of door-opening device, have to develop a new sequence of hand movements in order to open the door; that is, he will have to accommodate to the environment. However, once the child has learned the new responses, this new mode of adapting to the environment will be integrated with the class of door-opening behaviors available to him; in other words, he will have assimilated the new experiences. When the child is faced with a similar problem, he will be able to recall the appropriate sequence of behaviors.

Whenever the child is faced with a "problem," he is, in Piagetian terms, in a state of "disequilibrium;" he is not adapted to his environment. When this disequilibrium occurs, the dual processes of accommodation and assimilation are focused upon the specific problem. If it is resolved, equilibrium is not only restored, but it is reestablished at a higher level than before. The individual is better adapted to his environment than he was previously. Children over time gradually become capable of dealing with broader and broader ranges of problems as they acquire more and more complex strategies of processing environmental information.

Stages of conceptual development

In examining the child's development of such real concepts as "number," "time," and "space," Piaget has observed that the adaptive modes of immature versus mature human beings are distinctly different (Piaget, 1947, 1952, 1954, 1956; Inhelder & Piaget, 1958; see also Flavell, 1963). On the basis of studies of what he considers to be the laws under which knowledge develops and changes, Piaget has formulated a "stage" theory of conceptual development in which each stage reflects the direction and course of mental development. As the child passes from one stage of development to another, information-processing strategies that were developed in earlier stages become integrated with strategies developed at later stages.

The order of succession of the stages of development is constant; the age of attainment of a particular stage, however, will vary among individual children as a function of many growth and experiential factors. As the child develops conceptually, Piaget views him as progressing through three major stages (sensorimotor, preoperational, and operational); these stages are further broken down into a number of substages. This schema can be outlined as follows:

Sensorimotor stage (birth to two years)
Preoperational stage
  1. Preconceptual thought (two to four years)
  2. Intuitive thought (four to seven years)
Operational stage
  1. Concrete-operational thought (seven to eleven years)
  2. Formal-operational thought (eleven to sixteen years)

Sensorimotor Stage (Birth to Two Years)

At birth the infant has available a variety of simple sensorimotor organizations, such as sucking, grasping, and looking. More complicated behavior occurs a few weeks later when the infant begins to coordinate some of these reflexive responses. For example, looking will be coordinated with arm movements so that a new behavior, namely hand watching, emerges. At a later stage of development the infant achieves a high-order coordination between various motor activities and what he perceives so that he appears to act intentionally on the environment. He will kick his feet in order to make a mobile above his crib move.

In the first ten months after birth, the child develops a variety of elementary schemas. A "schema" is defined as a behavior applicable to many different objects. Sucking behavior in the young infant is reflexive in origin, but in the course of repeating routines, the infant groups together various kinds of stimulation, e.g., visual and tactile, and a schema emerges. This permits the child to build up a more complex response than a simple reflex, for now his sucking behavior is applicable in different situations. The infant with a well-developed sucking schema will open his mouth one way at the sight of a bottle and another way at the sight of a spoon (Piaget, 1956).

In the course of coordinating his actions with what he perceives and through repeated contacts with his environment, the infant develops "object permanence." For an adult, an object is not changed when its position is changed or when the level of illumination on it varies. The object is independent of the adult's experience of it. This is not the case for the young infant. Piaget claims that the infant constructs the concept of the permanent object during the sensorimotor period. The reader will recall from the discussion in Chapter II that Piaget offers the following observations as support for this viewpoint. He notes that at an early stage of development, the infant demonstrates no attempts to search for an object hidden from his view, nor does he appear to be interested in looking for a vanished object. However, with further experience, he behaves as though he realizes that a hidden object still exists, as he now looks for it after he has seen it hidden.

The behavioral basis for the development of object permanence resides in the fact that the infant is now capable of some internal representation of the external world. He has begun to experience the world as an orderly and coherent environment that is provided by the development of object constancy. The child, during the stage of sensorimotor development, has in fact acquired some elementary operations of intelligence. The quality of his adaptive behavior has increased as a function of the nature of his grasp of object permanence, the development of a number of sensorimotor schemas, and the resulting repertoire of actions. Sensorimotor intelligence continues to develop after two years of age and is exemplified in the older child's exploration of new objects and substances.

Preoperational Stage

This stage is subdivided into two principal substages.

1 *Preconceptual thought (two to four years)* One of the major advances made by the child during this substage is that the child's adaptations to the environment are now beginning to be mediated by signs and symbols, particularly words and images. The child develops imagery and is primarily concerned with imitation and play behavior. He develops the ability to defer his imitation; i.e., he can imitate the behavior of absent people. This suggests that his memory is developing, presumably letting him internally represent features of the environment which are not immediately present to his perceptual apparatus. This extends the child's control over his environment, but he is still a very long way from operating on the environment in an adult-like fashion.

At this stage, the child's reasoning is preconceptual rather than conceptual (in the adult sense). Whereas the adult can reason both inductively and deductively, the child makes no distinction between the general and the particular. He does not know whether the moon he sees from time to time through the trees is the same moon or a series of different moons.

2 *Intuitive thought (four to seven years)* ⌊This substage indicates the halfway point between preconceptual thought and the more advanced stage of concrete-operational thought.⌉ The child's thinking at this point can be exemplified by the following situation (Piaget, 1952). A child is presented with two small glass containers A_1 and A_2 which have identical dimensions. He is asked to place one bead in each container alternately until both are filled. Then the contents of container A_2 are emptied into a taller but thinner glass B. The child in the intuitive-thought stage thinks that the amount of beads has changed, even though he will admit that no beads were removed or added. The child usually says that there are more beads in B, since it is taller than A_1. He appears to be focusing his attention upon one aspect of the situation, either height or width. To resolve the problem, the child has to take into account both aspects simultaneously. (This is an example of a "conservation" problem; this type of problem will be discussed in more detail in a later section of the chapter.) During the later stage of operational thought, the child develops the ability to reason with respect to both relations at the same time, and thus he deduces the fact that the quantity of beads remains the same even when the dimensions of the container change.

⌊Another significant difference between the stages of intuitive thought and operational thought relates to the ways in which children at these stages form classes.⌉ The cardinal properties of number (e.g., $3 = 1 + 1 + 1$) involve the ability to classify and combine classes. Piaget (1947) placed twenty wooden beads in a box (all of the beads made up class B). A few of the beads were white (subclass A_1) and the remainder were brown (subclass A_2). The question to be asked was at what age a child should be capable of understanding the logical operation $A_1 + A_2 = B$. Piaget found that when he asked the children whether there were more wooden beads or more brown beads, they typically replied that there were more brown beads and added "since there are only three white ones." Apparently, the child at this age (up to seven years) can focus his attention on either the whole class B (he acknowledges, when asked, that the beads are all wooden), or the subclasses A_1 and A_2; he cannot grasp both simultaneously. The resolution of this kind of problem occurs when the child is at the stage of concrete-operational thought.

Operational Stage

The stage of operational thought, which is divided into two substages, marks the advent of rational activity in the child. It is during this stage that children demonstrate their grasp of inductive and deductive logic.

1 *Concrete-operational thought* (*seven to eleven years*) The thought processes of the child during this period are concrete in the sense that they deal only with objects that can be handled or imagined in concrete form and not with more abstract material, such as hypotheses or purely verbal propositions. In discussing the nature of concrete operations, it is necessary to outline four specific operations (essentially properties of logical thought) which are available to the child at this stage of development:

COMBINATIVITY is the operation that permits the child to form classes and superclasses and put them in a hierarchical arrangement (e.g., the class of brown wooden beads combined with the class of white wooden beads forms the more general class of wooden beads).

REVERSIBILITY consists of the operation whereby a superclass (animals) can be broken into its original components (dogs, cats, monkeys, etc.).

ASSOCIATIVITY refers to the operation where the same result may be obtained by combining units in different ways (e.g., two 6-inch sticks and one 24-inch stick can be put together in several ways to obtain a yard measure).

IDENTITY is an operation whereby combining an element with its opposite annuls it (e.g., 1 pint of water minus 1 pint of water equals no water).

The difference between the thought of a child at the stage of intuitive thought and that of the child who has these four operations available may be demonstrated by reconsidering their likely responses to the previously discussed conservation problem. At the intuitive-thought stage, the child alternately focuses on the height feature and the width feature of the containers. During the concrete-operational stage, however, the child can focus simultaneously on both features, thereby deducing conservation. When asked for an explanation, the child at this stage of concrete operations indicates in his verbalizations that he has been able to bring to bear on the problem several concrete operations. He points out that the quantities of beads in both glasses are the same and argues that if the beads were put back into the other glass from which they had been taken, the beads would be the same height again (the operation of reversibility). The child at this stage might also comment that the quantities of beads are the same now because they were the same at the beginning (the operation of identity).

2 *Formal-operational thought (eleven to sixteen years)* The substage of formal operations marks the emergence of the ability to solve problems at a level that transcends concrete experience. Formal thinking marks the completion of the child's emancipation from reliance on direct perception and action. In contrast to the concrete action-oriented thought of the child, the adolescent thinker is liberated from the here-and-now and can develop theories about anything that concerns him.

An example of this ability is contained in the following problem of "seriation" where three terms are presented as propositions. "A is bigger than C; A is smaller than B; who is the smallest of the three?" When this problem is presented to a seven-year-old in a concrete form, i.e., by asking him to arrange three dolls placed in front of him according to their size, it is clearly a simple task for him. Nevertheless, the seven-year-old cannot handle the aforementioned verbal equivalent of this concrete task. By contrast, the child in the early part of the formal-operation period is able to deal with both forms of this problem successfully (Piaget, 1952).

A second example of the difference between the behavior of the child at the stage of concrete operations and one at the stage of formal operations comes from Inhelder and Piaget's (1958) account of the child's acquisition of the law of floating bodies. In this experiment the child was presented with a series of objects, and was asked to classify them according to whether or not they floated on water. He was then asked to give reasons for his classifications. Next the subject experimented with the objects, and finally he was asked to summarize his observations and to invent a law to cover the phenomena.

The law to be found was that objects float if their density, or specific gravity, is less than that of water. Children in the late stage of concrete operations exhibited a behavior that reflected their incomplete development of the concept of specific gravity. They sometimes assessed the specific gravity of some objects correctly and sometimes they did not. When the children were asked to provide a law to explain why some objects floated and others sank, they were unable to do so. However, children at the stage of formal operations not only were able to classify objects appropriately, but could also offer explanations that clearly demonstrated their understanding of the law of floating bodies. To relate the weight of a body to the weight of an equal body of water is to employ the "hypo-thetico-deductive method," for the situation has no empirical correlate, as only the total volume of the water in the recepta-cle is observed. The point is that the formal-operational ado-lescent can make "logical" experiments, not merely factual ones. He has available the tools of propositional logic which enable him to test the validity of statements by reference to their purely logical properties, rather than to their corre-spondence with the concrete empirical world. In other words, the adolescent is able to deal with the form of a proposition as well as its content.

Piaget (1947) points out that concrete reasoning concerns internalized actions that have become capable of combination or reversal, whereas formal reasoning consists of reflecting on operations or on their results; it is a case of "operating on operations." At the stage for formal-operational thought, the adolescent is able to manipulate intellectually the content of a hypothetical situation and can systematically evaluate a lengthy set of alternative possibilities.

To briefly summarize Piaget's stage theory of conceptual de-velopment, it is an attempt to describe the ontogenetic develop-ment of the child's adaptation to his environment from infancy to maturity. The sensorimotor stage of development sees the first combination of perceptual experiences that leads to the develop-ment of the concept of object permanence. This, in turn, is funda-mental to the development of the concepts of time, space, and causality. During the preoperational stage, there is further elab-oration of the child's conceptual life as he begins to use language, concrete imagery, and symbolic play. In the operational stage, the individual extends the world of empirical reality by repre-senting the world not only as it is, but also as it could possibly be. In this final stage of development, abstract logic is available to the individual in dealing with problems of environmental adjustment.

Conservation

The concept of conservation is one of the basic themes around which Piaget has organized much of his research and thinking about conceptual development. "Conservation" refers to the fact that, despite certain alterations in the perceivable features of an object, the object has not been essentially changed. For very young children, pouring a pint of milk from a bottle into a shallow pan often leads them to judge that there is less milk in the pan than there was in the bottle. The previously discussed situation with the containers of beads is another example of a conservation problem. For very young children, the solution of conservation problems is impossible because they have not yet developed the use of the logical operations of reversibility and identity.

Piaget has studied the conservation of weight, volume, quantity, etc., and has experimented with "continuous" substances, such as water and clay, as well as with "discontinuous" substances, such as beads and shells. He has concluded that there are three stages of development in the acquisition of the concept of conservation. The first stage is the period of "nonconservation" when the child's thinking is perceptually dominated so that his attention is centered exclusively on one dimension of the situation. This period coincides with the preoperational stage. The second stage is a "transitional" period where the child appears to be a conserver under some conditions and a nonconserver when these conditions are slightly changed. This generally occurs toward the end of the preoperational stage. The final stage is that of "conservation." For some types of conservation this stage coincides with the early part of the period of concrete-operational thought. The successful conserver not only resolves the conservation task, but can also support his decisions by argument.

One of the current theoretical problems associated with Piaget's research and hypothesizing is the role of experience in the development of conservation behavior. Many experimenters have attempted to hasten the process of normal development from nonconservation to conservation (e.g., Beilin & Franklin, 1962; Wohlwill & Lowe, 1962). The success in such endeavors has been limited (see Wallach, 1963). Piaget would have predicted this general result, for he stresses the role of the child, rather than external agents, as being primarily responsible for conceptual development.

The lack of general success of the training experiments may

be attributed to a number of different factors, including the obvious factor of the content of the training. An original approach to the problem of training has been developed by Sigel, Roeper, & Hooper (1966), who chose to train children on some of the skills that Piaget has maintained are crucial to the development of the concept of conservation. The question posed by these researchers was, "Can conservation be induced in the child?" To answer this question, they constructed teaching situations to enable children to attend to the fact that objects have multiple characteristics (operation of "multiple classification"), that characteristics can be combined in various ways to produce new categories (operation of "multiple relations"), and finally that categories of objects can be reorganized and brought back to the original (operation of "reversibility").

The outcome of the training procedures used by Sigel et al. was clear. As can be seen from their study, which is reprinted following this chapter, the subjects who received special training on the three criterial operations increased their ability to perform correctly in a number of different conservation tasks. Furthermore, the children showed an increase in their ability to verbalize the operations underlying the tasks and the critical dimensions involved in the test situations. The control group showed no changes either in conservation ability or verbalization skills.

Interestingly, Sigel et al. do not claim that these results demonstrate that conservation skills are ordinarily directly taught. Instead, they imply that children with the necessary logical skills may well discover the concept of conservation by themselves. Some indirect support for this interpretation derives from their own experiment in which the experimental subjects were not actually taught to conserve directly. Although the Sigel, Roeper, and Hooper study provides the clearest evidence that the development of the concept of conservation can be accelerated through manipulation of the child's environment (training), the experimenters nevertheless stress the possibility that their success might well be related to their subjects being at the transitional stage of such development. It is entirely possible that their training procedures might not have been successful if the children had been "nonconservers."

An earlier study (Smedslund, 1961) attempted an evaluation of the notion that the concept of conservation has to be constructed spontaneously by the child if it is to have any degree of permanence. Smedslund worked with a group of children who had been "taught" to conserve and with another group who had already been conserving at the beginning of the study. In order to test the stability of the conservation concept, he showed them two balls of Plasticine that were equal in weight when placed upon the balance scale. He then changed the shape of one of the balls and surreptitiously removed some of the Plasticine from it. Next he asked the children to predict whether or not the reshaped ball would weigh the same as the unaltered one. The children who had been "taught" to conserve in the experimental training situation quickly reverted to nonconservation. The "spontaneous" conservers, however, tended to protest that something had happened, and they voluntarily offered the argument that if the balls had weighed the same originally, they should continue to be equal despite the change in appearance. These research results emphasize the "self-motivational" factors involved in conceptual development. Piaget has argued that the child achieves his conceptual growth largely through his spontaneous actions rather than by external directive.

While major importance has been attached to the role of self-regulation or equilibration (i.e., whenever there is disequilibrium, a state of need results which in turn leads to attempts on the part of the individual to reduce the need and thereby reestablish the state of equilibrium), Piaget (1964) has suggested that at least three other variables are involved in the child's transition from one stage of conceptual development to another: (1) "Maturation" refers to the increasing elaboration of central nervous system processes; (2) "Experience" consists of the child's encounters with his physical environment; and (3) "Social transmission" involves a subcategory of experience, namely, human encounters in formal or informal educational settings.

Research findings in the Piagetian system have typically been described according to stages of development indicating approximate relationships between age and stage. For Piaget, age and stage are not synonymous. If they were, he could accurately be described as belonging to the "maturational" camp, which is clearly not the case. While Piaget considers experience to be of fundamental importance in the explanation of conceptual development, he has not interested himself in the analysis of the *specific* characteristics of experience that might explain individual differences in rate of conceptual growth. One possible strategy that could lead to the determination of the precise details of the process of conceptual formation is to use the training experiments (such as Sigel et al., 1966) for this purpose, as it is likely that they will reveal the specific skills necessary for the development of a particular concept.

The preceding discussions of representative studies on the neo-behaviorist and Piagetian approaches to conceptual development provide some basis for comparison of these approaches. To begin with, the methods of studying behavior differ. The neobehaviorists select rigorous procedures and try to handle each child in a highly similar manner. By contrast, Piaget uses a clinical method which permits him to approach an individual child with great flexibility. These differences in approach are understandable when reference is made to the basic purposes of the research. The neobehaviorists select novel stimuli in order to control for the past experiences of the children; i.e., they want to eliminate the effects of individual differences in development. The main purpose of this type of approach is to be able to manipulate the experimental stimuli in such a way that the child's resultant behavior can be explained as a function of antecedent operations such as reinforcement, amount of practice, type of practice, etc. Piaget, on the other hand, arranges his experimental situations to direct the child to reveal his conceptual processes. This program permits a considerable latitude in examining the child and is based upon the premise that using standardized procedures induces the risk of missing unexpected and perhaps significant features of the child's thinking processes.

The two approaches also differ with respect to the role of learning in conceptual development. The neobehaviorist models (e.g., Harlow, 1959; Kendler & Kendler, 1962) attempt to explain development by reference to experience and reinforcement. Piaget (1964), while agreeing that experience is vital to conceptual development, suggests that other factors such as maturation and, even more importantly, equilibration are implicated in development. In fact, Piaget rejects the argument that external reinforcement is important. He does not, however, consider reinforcement of any kind unimportant. Piaget appears to be willing to equate his term "equilibration" to internal reinforcement.

One basic problem for the early behaviorists was to account for the fact that responses that were not originally associated with stimuli could nevertheless be evoked by them. The first attempts to deal with this problem used the concepts of "stimulus generalization" and "response generalization." These explanatory concepts work quite well if transfer clearly depends upon the physical similarity between the stimuli and responses. The concepts appear less applicable, however, when used to explain problem solving where a principle is transferred from one physically dissimilar situation to another. Neobehaviorists have attempted to solve these transfer problems by postulating a hypothetical mediation process (i.e., implicit behavior) that could render physically dissimilar situations equivalent by virtue of constituting the common organismic response evoked by each situation. Piaget has taken quite a different approach to mediating events; instead of defining them in terms of stimuli and responses, he defines them as "structures," "schemas," "operations," etc.

Piaget confronts the behavioristically oriented researcher with a mass of incompletely developed theoretical formulations, but he also provides the richest available fund of empirical observations on the processes of conceptual development.

ROLE OF LANGUAGE IN CONCEPT FORMATION The role of language in the development of conceptual behavior is by no means a new topic. It has recently been rediscovered, however, and several experimenters (e.g., Bruner, 1964; Bruner, Olver, & Greenfield, 1966; Furth, 1964) have become interested in discovering the impact of language on concept formation. While it is clear from some studies (e.g., Kendler, Kendler, & Learnard, 1962; Stevenson & Swartz, 1958) that relevant verbalizations by the learner aid him in various tasks, it also seems to be the case that some concepts do not depend upon language usage (Harlow, 1959). Harlow has demonstrated in his work on the discrimination learning of monkeys that these animals eventually acquire the "oddity" concept; they learn to respond to the one odd object in a trio of objects where two are identical, even though they obviously do not verbalize.

Furth (1964), in reviewing the research literature on concept formation in deaf children, argues that conceptual development is not simply a function of language development. He acknowledges, however, the probability that the possession of language increases the efficiency of the user to resolve certain problems. Furth's position is that the role of language in conceptual development has been exaggerated. To provide evidence for this position, he has carried out a series of studies contrasting the conceptual abilities of groups of deaf and of hearing subjects. Furth's research is based upon the assumption that deaf children are basically languageless individuals, as the sign language used by them is a very impoverished form of speech.

In one study (Furth, 1961), three nonverbal concept-learning tasks were administered to 180 deaf children and 180 hearing children (ages seven to twelve years). Two of the tasks (sameness and symmetry) were selected because they did not give advantage to the hearing children. The third task (opposition) was chosen because performance on it would likely be aided by a child's having language available.

The results of this study, reprinted at the end of this chapter, supported Furth's predictions. There were no differences between the hearing and deaf children on the sameness and symmetry tasks, but there were significant differences between the two groups on the opposition tasks.

Vygotsky (1962) has also been interested in the role of language in conceptual development. One of his experiments was concerned with an investigation of how nonsense syllables can gradually acquire meaning. The materials used in this study consisted of twenty-two wooden blocks varying in color, shape, height, and size. On the underside of each block (unknown to the child) was written one of four nonsense words: "lag," "bik," "mur," and "cev." Regardless of color or shape, "lag" was written on all tall, large blocks; "bik" on all flat, large blocks; "mur" on all tall, small blocks; and "cev" on all flat, small blocks. Vygotsky's procedure was to place the blocks randomly in front of the child. He turned up one of the blocks and read its name to the child who was then asked to pick out the blocks that he thought belonged to the same group. When the child had finished, the experimenter then turned up one of the blocks that had been incorrectly selected for the group and pointed out that the block was of a different kind from the original sample block. The child made a new attempt to sort the blocks. When the child had completed his sorting, the experimenter would turn up another wrongly placed block. Eventually the child discovered that the nonsense words referred to specific characteristics of the blocks so that the words finally came to stand for definite kinds of blocks.

One value of Vygotsky's procedure is that the child's reasoning processes are reflected in the manner in which he sorts the blocks. Using this procedure, three stages of concept formation were isolated:

Stage 1 The child sorts the blocks into unorganized heaps.
TYPE A   The sorting is done by trial and error.
TYPE B   The child groups blocks that are spatially close together.

Stage 2 A "complex" is formed by the child. He may add a block to the first block because it is the same color. A third block may be added to the group because it is the same shape as the first block, etc. This attempt at classification is, of course, ineffectual because it does not abstract the common attributes of the group that the child is supposed to be forming.

Stage 3   The child achieves true classificatory behavior. At this stage, if it is pointed out to the child that his grouping is incorrect, he will often remark that the criterion of classification is not color, etc., and he will begin to sort all over again using another criterion. [One of the significant differences between the unsuccessful performances of children at stages 1 and 2 and the successful performance of children at stage 3 appears to be the *use* the children at stage 3 make of "verbal labels" (nonsense words) for classificatory purposes and, additionally, the child's verbalizations of the attributes of the blocks.]

Vygotsky's classification task is quite complicated for young children. Although he does not specify the age correlates for each stage of behavior, it is very likely that the child who is at stage 3 according to Vygotsky's schema is classifiable, in Piagetian terms, as being at the stage of concrete-operational thought (at least seven years old).

How would a deaf child fare on such a complex task as that described above? Oléron (1953), who has worked with deaf children, has discovered that they are able to develop concepts of shape, size, and color. Furth (1961), as previously discussed, demonstrated that deaf children are able to deal with the concepts of sameness and symmetry. Together these results support Furth's view that there is not a one-to-one relationship between concept formation and the availability of language. However, from Furth and others, there is evidence which clearly shows that language plays an important part in the development of complex concepts. For example, Oléron found that whereas hearing children had no great difficulty in forming class concepts which depended upon the mental manipulation of *several* attributes of phenomena simultaneously, this was not true for deaf children. It seems reasonable to speculate, then, that while various kinds of conceptual/classificatory behaviors can be carried on without language, as these behaviors become increasingly complex, an abstract language becomes important.

Still another approach to conceptual development is that of Bruner (1964) reprinted after this chapter. He has been interested in the ontogenesis of the representation of experience; i.e., the procedures that are used to store and recall experience. Bruner has suggested that conceptual growth depends upon the emergence of two forms of competence, namely, "representation" and "integration" of experience. He argues that children have to acquire procedures for representing the recurrent regularities in their environment in order to be able to process information economically with respect to immediate problems. They must also learn to integrate acts of information processing into higher-order cognitive structures to deal with long-range problem solving.

Bruner describes the emergence of three modes of representation during the child's development (enactive, iconic, and symbolic). These three stages of development complement Piaget's three major stages of conceptual development.

Enactive representation   This mode refers to representing events through appropriate motor responses, i.e., by muscle imagery such as tieing shoelaces. For adults, the enactive mode represents motor skills, but for children, it is the initial means of representing objects.

Iconic representation   This mode of representation is action free and depends upon visual-spatial imagery. Here images stand for perceptual events in the same way that a picture stands for the object pictured.

Symbolic representation   A child at this stage can translate his experience into symbol systems. By using these symbol systems (e.g., language) as cognitive instruments, he is able to transcend his immediate experience. The child is now able to transform the regularities of his experience with far greater flexibility and power than before.

The successive emergence of action, image, and word as the vehicles of representing experience bear a close correspondence to Piaget's preoperational, concrete-operational, and formal-operational stages of conceptual development.

From the studies that have been reviewed above, it would seem that when language is crucial to concept formation, the mere possession of language is not enough; it is necessary to develop the parallel ability to use language in a relevant manner.

SUMMARY

One of the basic problems in research on conceptual development concerns the nature of the mechanisms that support the child's acquisition of a wide range of basic concepts and their organization into a hierarchical system. The neobehaviorists' and the Piagetians' approaches to this problem are the two dominant ones in contemporary research. They differ in their theoretical analyses of the processes underlying concept formation and in their use of particular research methods.

The neobehaviorist position interprets concept formation as being a result of discrimination learning and associated broad stimulus generalization. For purposes of precise experimental control, the concepts to be learned in such research are simple and artificial.

The second position is exemplified in the research of Piaget where the process of concept formation is related to the development of appropriate "intellectual structures" or "information-processing strategies." Piaget has investigated the acquisition of "natural" concepts such as the development of the concept of conservation (the knowledge that altering the shape of an object does not necessarily entail a change in it).

There are some possibilities for integrating the neobehaviorist and Piagetian approaches, e.g., by utilizing the rigorous techniques of the neobehaviorists in a fine-grained analysis of the experiential sources of complex conceptual behaviors.

Another current problem concerns the role of language in concept formation. Furth's research with deaf children's conceptual behavior suggests that language is not a necessity, at least for some kinds of conceptual performance. Other researchers, however, have argued that the symbolic function of language is essential to complex conceptual behavior.

BIBLIOGRAPHY   Beilin, H., & Franklin, I. C. Logical operations in area and length measurement: Age and training effects. *Child Development*, 1962, **33**, 607–618.

Bruner, J. S. The course of cognitive growth. *American Psychologist*, 1964, **19**, 1–15.

Bruner, J. S., Olver, R. R., & Greenfield, P. M. *Studies in cognitive growth.* New York: Wiley, 1966.

Flavell, J. H. *The developmental psychology of Jean Piaget.* Princeton, N.J.: Van Nostrand, 1963.

Furth, H. G. The influence of language on the development of concept formation in deaf children. *Journal of Abnormal and Social Psychology*, 1961, **63**, 386–389.

Furth, H. G. Research with the deaf: Implications for language and cognition. *Psychological Bulletin*, 1964, **62**, 145–164.

Harlow, H. F. The development of learning in the rhesus monkey. *American Scientist*, 1959, **47**, 459–479.

Harter, S. Discrimination learning set in children as a function of IQ and MA. *Journal of Experimental Child Psychology*, 1965, **2**, 31–43.

Inhelder, B., & Piaget, J. *The growth of logical thinking.* (Translated by A. Parsons & S. Milgram.) New York: Basic Books, 1958.

Kelleher, R. T. Discrimination learning as a function of reversal and nonreversal shifts. *Journal of Experimental Psychology*, 1956, **51**, 379–384.

Kendler, H. H., & D'Amato, M. F. A comparison of reversal and nonreversal shifts in human concept formation behavior. *Journal of Experimental Psychology*, 1955, **49**, 165–174.

Kendler, H. H., & Kendler, T. S. Vertical and horizontal processes in problem solving. *Psychological Review*, 1962, **69**, 1–16.

Kendler, T. S. Development of mediating responses in children. In J. C. Wright & J. Kagan (Eds.), Basic cognitive processes in children. *Monographs of the Society for Research in Child Development*, 1963, **28** (2, Serial No. 86). Pp. 33–48.

Kendler, T. S., & Kendler, H. H. Reversal and nonreversal shifts in kindergarten children. *Journal of Experimental Psychology*, 1959, **58**, 56–60.

Kendler, T. S., Kendler, H. H., & Learnard, B. Mediated responses to size and brightness as a function of age. *American Journal of Psychology*, 1962, **75**, 571–586.

Kendler, T. S., Kendler, H. H., & Wells, D. Reversal and nonreversal shifts in nursery school children. *Journal of Comparative and Physiological Psychology*, 1960, **53**, 83–88.

Oléron, P. Conceptual thinking of the deaf. *American Annals of the Deaf*, 1953, **98**, 304–310.

Piaget, J. *The psychology of intelligence.* (Translated by M. Piercy & D. E. Berlyne.) London: Routledge, 1947.

Piaget, J. *The child's conception of number.* (Translated by C. Gattegno & F. M. Hodgson.) New York: Humanities Press, 1952.

Piaget, J. *The construction of reality in the child.* (Translated by M. Cook.) New York: Basic Books, 1954.

Piaget, J. *The origins of intelligence in the child.* (Translated by M. Cook.) New York: International Universities Press, 1956.

Piaget, J. Cognitive development in children. In R. E. Ripple & V. N. Rockcastle (Eds.), *Piaget rediscovered.* Ithaca: Cornell University, 1964. Pp. 6–48.

Sigel, I. E., Roeper, A., & Hooper, F. H. A training procedure for acquisition of Piaget's conservation of quantity: A pilot study and its replication. *British Journal of Educational Psychology*, 1966, **36**, 301–311.

Smedslund, J. The acquisition of conservation of substance and weight in children: III. Extinction of conservation of weight acquired "normally" and by means of empirical controls on a balance scale. *Scandinavian Journal of Psychology*, 1961, **2**, 85–87.

Stevenson, H. W. Piaget, behavior theory, and intelligence. In W. Kessen & C. Kuhlmann (Eds.), Thought in the young child. *Monographs of the Society for Research in Child Development*, 1962, **27** (2, Serial No. 83). Pp. 113–126.

Stevenson, H. W., & Swartz, J. D. Learning set in children as a function of intellectual level. *Journal of Comparative and Physiological Psychology*, 1958, **51**, 755–757.

Vygotsky, L. S. *Thought and language.* (Translated by E. Hanfmann & G. Vakar.) Cambridge, Mass.: M.I.T. Press, 1962.

Wallach, M. A. Research on children's thinking. In H. W. Stevenson (Ed.), *Child psychology. Sixty-second yearbook of the national society for the study of education.* Chicago: University of Chicago Press, 1963.

Wohlwill, J. F., & Lowe, R. C. Experimental analysis of the development of the conservation of number. *Child Development,* 1962, **33**, 153–167.

DEVELOPMENT OF MEDIATING RESPONSES IN CHILDREN[1]

Tracy S. Kendler

Learning theory and general behavior theory have, for the most part, shown little concern with developmental research. This is not to be taken as reflecting a lack of interest in children. There is an honorable, but spotty, tradition of experimental studies that used children as subjects dating back to Watson and his famous Albert. But the use of children does not automatically make the research developmental, especially if the emphasis is on the generality of behavior principles across species or across age levels within any one species.

Perhaps this indifference arises because developmental research appears to be more concerned with finding *differences* between age groups than in finding general laws of behavior applicable to all age groups. Learning theory, on the other hand, commits the investigator to studying general processes that relate the organism to its environment through its past history. "The organism," which may range from amoeba to homo sapiens, is often either a white rat or a pigeon. The use of these animals is not due to any particular interest in the species but rather to some very important advantages they provide to the researcher. For example, their past histories and motivational states can be manipulated or controlled at will and there are few ethical limitations imposed on the tasks they may be required to perform. Though he may restrict his research to some convenient laboratory organism, the behavior theorist implicitly assumes that at least some aspect of his findings are common to a wide range of organisms, usually including mankind. Within this tradition investigators who use human beings as subjects, and are explicit about the species, are often more interested in demonstrating the universality of the behavioral laws derived from animal experiments than in obtaining differences that might appear to reduce their generality.

If a discipline like comparative or developmental psychology is as much interested in differences as in similarities, then its finding may supply the ammunition for an attack on the vital assumption of the generality of behavioral laws. This is possible, but it is not necessarily so. If the principles generated by research with laboratory animals are applicable to higher level human behavior, then research directed at understanding the changes that take place with increasing maturity can extend the range and the vitality of behavior theory. If some of the knowledge derived from learning experiments can give direction to developmental research and can help to explain and organize its findings, behavior theorists may yet convert a potential enemy into a valuable ally. . . .

[1] The research described in this paper is supported by a grant from the National Science Foundation.

From T. S. Kendler. Development of mediating responses in children. Monographs of the Society for Research in Child Development, *1963, 28(2, Serial No. 86). Pp. 33–48. (With permission of the author and the Society for Research in Child Development, Inc.)*

The mediated response is one of the mechanisms most often used to find a common theme between simple and complex behavior within this theoretical framework. The mediator is a response, or series of responses, which intercede between the external stimulus and the overt response to provide stimulation that influences the eventual course of behavior. These responses may be overt, but they are usually presumed to be covert. The mediated response is not an original idea. All theories of thinking, motor or central, behaviorist or phenomenological, dealing in the second-signal system or using computer models, postulate internal processes that intervene between the presentation of the problem and its solution, between the input and output, or between the stimulus and the response. The differences arise in the model used to generate hypotheses about the nature of this internal process and in the methods used to validate these hypotheses. Watson, who coordinated thinking with subvocal talking, used conditioning as his model and sought verification by direct measurement of the muscles of speech. The contemporary behaviorist approach allows for a wider range of mediating responses and for the possibility of treating them as theoretical constructs rather than as directly observable behavior. The schema is exemplified in the research to be described in this paper.

The research started with a general interest in the mediating process and has become more and more concerned with how the process develops in children. This development has been studied in two interrelated ways. One way is primarily comparative. It consists of presenting a similar experimental situation to different species and to different age levels to study the uncontrolled changes that occur as a function of the differences among subjects. The other way employs the experimental method to discover and manipulate the variables that appear to be related to these ''natural'' developmental changes in order to determine how they come about and consequently render them subject to experimental control.

We have experimented in two areas that are generally conceded to be part of that area variously called cognitive process, thinking, or problem solution. One of the areas is *concept formation* or *abstraction.* The other is *inference,* defined as the spontaneous integration of discretely acquired habits to solve a problem. These processes have been reduced to some very simple operations in order to study them at their inception in young children. The operations are so simple that there may be some disagreement about their continuity with the high level process that they presume to study. The prepared reply to such potential objection is that there is no known way of reliably determining, on an a priori basis, the proper level of analysis for scientific research. It is only by its fruits that we shall know it.

CONCEPT FORMATION

The experimental paradigm used in the investigation of concept formation is based on procedures developed by Buss (1953) and Kendler and D'Amato (1955). It consists essentially of studying mediation by means of the transfer demonstrated from an initial to a subsequent discrimination. The initial discrimination presents stimuli that differ simultaneously on at least two dimensions, only one of which is relevant. After criterion is reached, another discrimination is presented that utilizes the same or similar stimuli but requires a shift in response. One type of shift, called a *reversal shift,* requires the subject to continue to respond to the previously relevant dimension but in an opposite way. In another type of shift, called a *nonreversal shift,* the subject is required to respond to the previously irrelevant dimension. . . Comparisons between these two types of shifts are of particular interest because theories based on single-unit versus mediated S-R connections yield opposed predictions about their relative efficiency. A single-unit theory assumes a direct association between the external stimulus and the overt response and would predict a reversal shift to be more difficult than a nonreversal shift. This is because reversal shift requires the replacement of a response that has previously been consistently reinforced with a response that has previously been consistently extinguished. In a nonreversal shift previous training has reinforced responses to the newly positive and negative stimuli equally often. Strengthening one of these associations does not require as much extinction of its competitor as in a reversal shift and should, therefore, be acquired more easily. Kelleher (1956) confirmed the prediction that, for rats, a reversal shift was more difficult than a nonreversal shift.

A theory that includes a mediating link (or links) between the external stimulus and the overt response leads to a different prediction. . . . In a reversal shift, the initial dimension maintains its relevance, hence, so does the mediated response. Only the overt response needs to be changed, and since the experimental situation provides only one alternative overt response, the problem presents no great difficulty. In a nonreversal shift the previously acquired mediation is no longer relevant, consequently both the mediating and the overt response must be replaced, making the task more difficult than a reversal shift. It is therefore to be expected that for subjects who mediate, a reversal shift will be acquired more easily than a nonreversal shift. Experiments by Buss (1953), Kendler and D'Amato (1955), and Harrow and Friedman (1958), using a more complex variation of the reversal-nonreversal technique with college students, confirmed the prediction of the mediational analysis. Unlike rats, college students learn a reversal shift more easily than a nonreversal shift.

This discontinuity between rats and adult humans led to two investigations with young children to determine whether their behavior, in this type of situation, was more consistent with the single-unit or the mediational formulation. The results suggested that children between 3 and 4 years of age respond predominantly in the single-unit manner (Kendler, Kendler, & Wells, 1960) and that children between 5 and 7 years of age divide about evenly, with half mediating and half not (Kendler & Kendler, 1959). What seemed to be implied was a developmental process in which very young children's behavior is governed by a relatively primitive, single-unit S-R process. Increasing maturity leads to increases in the proportion of children whose performance is determined by some mediating system of responses.

A recent investigation of the shift behavior of children from five age levels (3, 4, 6, 8, and 10 years) provided a direct test of these developmental implications (Kendler et al., 1962). Previous procedures were modified to allow each subject to choose whether or not he would behave mediationally. This was accomplished in the following way. For their initial discrimination (Series I) the children were presented, in random alternation, with two pairs of stimulus cards. One pair consisted of a large black square (LB) and a small white square (SW). The other pair consisted of a large white square (LW) and a small black square (SB). Each concept (L, B, S, W) was correct for one-fourth of the subjects.

For the purpose of illustration let us take a child for whom black was the correct concept and size was irrelevant. For him all responses to SB or LB were rewarded with a marble. If he responded to SW or LW, he had to return a marble to the experimenter. After he reached the criterion of nine out of ten successive correct responses, a second discrimination (Series II) was presented that involved only one of the stimulus pairs, e.g., LB and SW, and the reward pattern was reversed. Now only responses to SW were rewarded, and he was again run to a criterion of nine out of ten successive correct responses. The child could reach criterion in this series by responding to the whiteness, in which case he was categorized as a *reversal* subject since he was responding in a reverse way to the original concept. Such a child is, by virtue of the previous analysis, presumed to have made relevant mediating responses in the first discrimination which either led to other relevant mediators or continued to be relevant in the second discrimination, thus requiring a shift only in the overt response.

A child could also reach criterion in Series II by responding to the smallness of SW. Such a choice would be expected from nonmediators since during Series I responses to small were rewarded half of the time, while responses to whiteness were never rewarded. Such a child would, therefore, respond more readily to a stimulus from the previously irrelevant dimension (S) than to the incorrect stimulus of the previously relevant dimension (W) and would consequently be categorized as a nonreversal subject.

The last possibility is that the child learned to respond to both the smallness and the whiteness. A single-unit analysis would predict this result for nonmediating children who take a relatively long time to learn Series II since each reinforcement should increase the habit strength of both stimulus components. As the trials increase, the difference in the excitatory strengths of white and small should decrease and ultimately disappear. Such children, for reasons that will soon be clear, were categorized as *inconsistent*.

In order to determine on which of the three possible bases Series II was learned, it was followed immediately by a third series. During this last series both pairs of stimuli were again shown in random alternation. The pair that had not been used in Series II, which is LW and SB in our illustration, served as the test pair. With this pair the child could respond either to the whiteness or to the smallness but not to both simultaneously. The test pair was presented ten times and either choice was rewarded. On the basis of his choices to this pair the child was classified as one of the three categories just described. The function of the other pair, which maintained its previous reinforcement pattern, was to keep the child responding as he did in Series II.

The results for each category are presented in Figure I. The prediction, based on theoretical analysis and previous results, was that the percentage of children who reversed (mediated) would be below 50 between the ages of 3 and 4 (Kendler, Kendler, & Wells, 1960), rise to about 50 between 5 and 7 (Kendler & Kendler, 1959), and then continue to increase with increasing age until some relatively high asymptote was reached. The results, which are in good agreement with the prediction, serve to confirm the general developmental implications of previous studies.

It was expected, of course, that the percentage of nonmediators would decrease with age. There seemed no a priori reason for making a discrimination between the nonreversal and inconsistent children, and so the decrease was expected in both categories. The results show a sharp and steady decrease for the inconsistent category. There was, however, no perceptible trend in the nonreversal group.

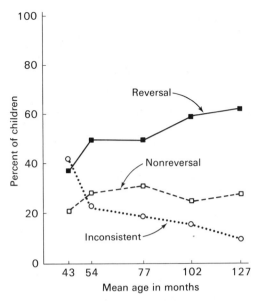

FIG. 1   Percentage of children in each choice category as a function of chronological age.

Despite the need for explanation of the performance of the nonreversal group, to which we shall return presently, it seems reasonable to conclude that the results of this experiment bear out the implication that there is a transition in the course of human development from unmediated, single-unit behavior to mediated behavior, at least with reference to size and brightness concepts. They also suggest that the proportion of children who have made this transition increases in a gradual and lawful manner. It remains for further research to determine whether the same or similar relationships will obtain with other concepts.

In addition to these results there were some *ad hoc* observations about the verbal behavior of the children that provide interesting suggestions about the nature of the mediation process and its development. These verbalizations should not be regarded as demonstrative of confirmed relationships. They should be regarded as empirically derived suggestions that require further experimental verification.

After the children had completed Series III, they were shown the stimulus pair used in Series II and asked a series of questions to find out whether they could or would give a correct verbal report of what they had been doing and whether there would be any relationship between this after-the-act verbal behavior and mediated choices in Series III. Table 1 presents these results arranged in three categories that are illustrated as follows. If a child had been responding to brightness in the test pair and described the "winner" as white (or black), he was grouped with those who *verbalized the correct dimension*. If he said "the square one" or "that one," or merely pointed without saying anything at all, he was placed with the *no relevant verbalization* group.

TABLE 1   Percentage of subjects giving various descriptions as a function of their choices in Series III

Kind of choice	Verbalized correct dimension	Verbalized incorrect dimension	No relevant verbalization
Reversal	84.8	7.6	7.6
Nonreversal	66.7	25.6	7.7
Inconsistent	57.7*		42.3

*If the behavior was categorized as inconsistent neither dimension could be considered correct. Therefore, mentions of either dimension were combined and placed between the two columns to indicate their special character.

Despite the pressure on the child to respond generated by E's persistent questions, with the stimulus cards in full view, 42 percent of the inconsistent children failed to produce any relevant verbalization. If verbalization is important for the mediating process, then it would follow that nonmediators would be relatively inarticulate. By the same token, mediating (reversal) children should produce a relatively large proportion of verbal comment that was relevant to their previous performance. The data in Table 1 support this expectation. If the pattern is clear for the reversal and inconsistent children, the nonreversal children present more complications. Two statements may be made about this group. First, an overwhelming proportion produced descriptions of the stimuli in terms of at least one of the manipulation dimensions. The proportion for the nonreversal group was just as large as that for the reversal group, suggesting that, under pressure to do so, the nonmediators could verbally describe the stimuli as well as the mediators. However, the verbalizations of nonreversal children were less frequently relevant to their previous behavior than were those of reversal children.

One tentative way to tie these observations together, and simultaneously throw further light on the fact that the proportion of nonreversal children did not decrease with age, is to propose that reversal, nonreversal, and inconsistent choice behavior represent a three-stage hierarchy of development. Reversal choice reflects the highest level where covert verbal responses occur during training and mediate choice behavior. Nonreversal choice constitutes an intermediate level, at which covert verbal responses can occur and sometimes do, but either occur rather late in the learning or they do not necessarily or readily mediate choice behavior. The most primitive level is characterized by little or no covert response and is manifested in inconsistent choice behavior. With increasing CA more and more children reach the highest level (i.e., reversal) and fewer and fewer are left at the lowest level (i.e., inconsistent), but at each age tested the proportion in transition between the two extreme levels (i.e., nonreversals) tends to be constant.

Such an analysis would lead to the expectation that the proportion of children who verbalized correctly would increase with age; the proportion of children whose verbalizations were absent or irrelevant would decrease with age; and the incorrect dimension category would not change. Figure 2 presents the verbalization data in terms of chronological age. The data demonstrate considerable correspondence between expectation and results and show a striking similarity to the choice behavior presented in Figure 1, a similarity that occurs despite the fact that the children who comprise each set of parallel developmental trends are not identical. For example, the "verbalized-correct-dimensions" results of Figure 2, which parallel the "reversal-choice" trend of Figure 1, included 67 percent of the nonreversal children as well as 85 percent of the reversal children. Thus, although these results do not point to a perfect relationship between verbal and choice behavior, the similarity of trends certainly suggests that the development of the mediational process is intimately related to the development of the ability to relate words to actions.

There is one more suggestive result yielded by the verbalization data that may help to explain (a) the high proportion of nonreversal children who verbalized correctly, (b) why the reversal results approached such a low asymptote, and (c) the lack of a decrease in the nonreversal category even at the ripe old age of 10. Some children described the "winner" accurately by mentioning both dimensions, e.g., "The big, white one." When this tendency was sorted out by age, it was found that the percentage of children who accurately described *both dimensions* was zero at age 3 and increased gradually to 25 at age 10, implying, reasonably enough, that there is a developmental aspect to the number of simultaneous mediating responses a child can handle. It also implies that at the upper age levels a nonreversal response to situations as simple as Series II may not necessarily denote a primitive process. Instead it may represent the ability to integrate more than one mediating response. This is another way of saying that the task may have been too easy for the older children and that consequently they complicated it for themselves. It may be that the failure of the reversal curve to rise above 62 percent and the nonreversal curve to drop below 28 percent at age 10 is due to a perennial difficulty in developmental research: devising one task that is easy enough for the lower end of the scale and yet difficult enough to pose the proper challenge at the upper end. Although in the present instance the task was clearly capable of differentiating among the various age levels tested, it may be that the differences at the upper age levels were attenuated.

FIG. 2   Percentage of children in each verbalization category as a function of chronological age.

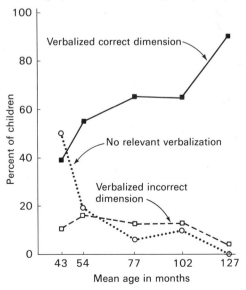

Thus far, the data derived from a comparative type of analysis show a measurable transition from a lower to a higher level behavioral process as a function of increasing chronological age. They also suggest that this development is somehow related to language. The relationship is probably not simple. Even the youngest children had a vocabulary sufficient for describing the simple concepts used. Moreover, one of the early experiments had demonstrated that with simple instructions all of the children could interpose relevant verbal comment between the presentation of the stimuli and their overt choice. It is clear that, if the overt behavior of the younger children is not influenced by mediating verbal discriminators, it is not because they are incapable of making these responses. This leaves two alternatives. One is that, although they are capable of doing so, they nevertheless do not, in the ordinary course of events, make such responses. The other is that they do make some verbal responses, but these responses, for some reason, do not serve as mediators. In order to explore some of these issues another experiment was performed which manipulated overt verbal mediation to ascertain its effect on the reversal shift behavior of 4- and 7-year-old children. Note that, while this study has developmental implications, it is more experimental in nature.

The same stimuli were used as in the study previously described, but they were presented differently. The initial discrimination used only one pair of discriminanda, thus rendering both stimulus dimensions relevant. Under these circumstances a child could be required to describe the correct stimulus according to either one of its two components. For example, if LB was correct, the child could be instructed to use either "large" or "black" to describe the correct stimulus. In the second discrimination both pair of stimuli were presented and all children learned a reversal shift. Only one dimension was relevant. For some children the reversal was on the size dimension, and for some it was on the brightness dimension. In this way the verbalization during the initial discrimination was rendered relevant or irrelevant according to the experimental group to which the child had been randomly assigned. For example, if the child had learned to describe the correct stimulus (LB) as "large," he would be rewarded in the second discrimination for response to SB and SW (small) if he was in the relevant group. If he was in the irrelevant group, he was rewarded for responses to SW and LW (white). A control group with no verbalization completed the design.

The first question to be asked is whether such overt verbalization, intervening between stimulus and response, affects the acquisition of the reversal shift. The answer is clear: it does. For both age groups relevant verbalization produced significantly faster shifts than irrelevant verbalization. These results add credence to the mediating response model used to explain reversal-nonreversal shift behavior. They also provide a technique for exploring the interaction between verbal and other developmental variables.

TABLE 2 Mean number of trials to criterion on reversal shift for each verbalization condition at two age levels

Age	Verbalization condition		
	Relevant	Irrelevant	None
4 years	16.1	30.4	22.2
7 years	8.3	35.6	8.8

Another question this research was designed to answer was whether the utilization of verbal mediators differs with age as has been suggested by Luria (1957). That is, will the difference between the reversal shift behavior of younger and older children be reduced or eliminated when both are provided with the same verbal response, or is there another ingredient, associated with development, which is necessary before words exercise control over overt behavior?

Table 2 presents the results analyzed separately for each age group. It can be seen that the effects were somewhat different for the two age levels. As expected, when there was no verbalization the 4-year-olds took significantly more trials to reverse than the 7-year-olds. Relevant verbalization did not facilitate the shift for the older children, presumably because they did not require instruction about verbalization to supply relevant mediation. They were able to supply it themselves. The responsiveness of the older children to verbal labels is seen, however, in the sharp increase in learning difficulty produced by irrelevant verbalization.

The 4-year-olds, on the other hand, profited from relevant verbalization and, like the older children, were hindered by irrelevant verbalization. This suggests that, although they are not likely to supply their own mediators, they can use their own words in this capacity when language responses are required. . . .

Although it is clear that we have much to learn, some general conclusions can be drawn from these several studies. In this simple situation, which straddles the boundary between discrimination learning and concept formation, it seems that the single-unit S-R model adequately explains the behavior of the majority of children below 5 or 6 years of age. It does not explain the behavior of the majority of the older children. Invoking the theoretical construct of the mediating response can account for the more mature behavior within the S-R framework. This approach has the advantage of providing for continuity between the laws governing the behavior of younger and older children, since it attributes the observed developmental changes to a new and important system of responses, probably bound up with the development of language, rather than to a different set of behavioral laws. It is not sufficient, however, to point to an explanatory mechanism. After recognizing its potential it becomes necessary to show when and how it functions. The study of mediating responses in children can provide information about the nature and development of mediating processes at their source. Such information can serve to enlarge the scope of behavior theory until it can encompass human problem solving. . . .

CONCLUSIONS

Some interesting developmental changes occurring between early and middle childhood have emerged from applying an S-R learning theory approach to problem solving in children. Analyses of these changes in terms of a very broad conception of behavior theory has shown that the behavior of very young children is dependent on environmental cues, with which relatively simple S-R connections are formed and to which the laws of learning derived from simpler species are applicable. Older children's behavior, if it is to be dealt with in an S-R framework, must be conceptualized in terms of chains of responses in which some of the links are or become covert. It is proposed that a combined developmental-experimental approach can provide an understanding of how this transition occurs by studying it at its inception.

REFERENCES

Buss, A. H. Rigidity as a function of reversal and nonreversal shifts in the learning of successive discriminations. *Journal of Experimental Psychology,* 1953, **45**, 75–81.

Harrow, M., & Friedman, G. B. Comparing reversal and nonreversal shifts in concept formation with partial reinforcement controlled. *Journal of Experimental Psychology,* 1958, **55**, 592–598.

Kelleher, R. T. Discrimination learning as a function of reversal and nonreversal shifts. *Journal of Experimental Psychology,* 1956, **51**, 379–384.

Kendler, H. H., & D'Amato, M. F. A comparison of reversal shifts and nonreversal shifts in human concept formation behavior. *Journal of Experimental Psychology,* 1955, **49**, 165–174.

Kendler, T. S., & Kendler, H. H. Reversal and nonreversal shifts in kindergarten children. *Journal of Experimental Psychology,* 1959, **58**, 56–60.

Kendler, T. S., Kendler, H. H., & Learnard, B. Mediated responses to size and brightness as a function of age. *American Journal of Psychology,* 1962, **75**, 571–586.

Kendler, T. S., Kendler, H. H., & Wells, D. Reversal and nonreversal shifts in nursery school children. *Journal of Comparative and Physiological Psychology,* 1960, **53**, 83–88.

Luria, A. R. The role of language in the formation of temporary connections. In B. Simon (Ed.), *Psychology in the Soviet Union.* Stanford, Calif.: Stanford University Press, 1957. Pp. 115–129.

A TRAINING PROCEDURE FOR ACQUISITION OF PIAGET'S CONSERVATION OF QUANTITY: A PILOT STUDY AND ITS REPLICATION[1]

Irving E. Sigel, Annemarie Roeper, and Frank H. Hooper

INTRODUCTION

Conservation is defined by Flavell (1963, p. 245) as "the cognition that certain properties (quantity, number, length, etc.) remain invariant (are conserved) in the face of certain transformations (displacing objects or object parts in space, sectioning an object into pieces, changing shape, etc.)." This process is considered by Piaget as "a necessary condition for all rational activity" (Piaget, 1952, p. 3). On the basis of extensive studies, Piaget identifies three stages of development for each type of conservation: stage 1, in which no conservation is found, and child focuses in this instance on irrelevancies; stage 2, a transitional period, in which the child is dominated by perceptual appearances and in which conservation may or may not appear; stage 3, the stage of natural conservation, in which the child readily and logically demonstrates understanding of invariant properties in the face of transformations. The stages are presumed to be fixed and invariant, irrespective of the properties under study. There is an additional developmental sequence which exists across the different quantity subclasses. Conservation of substance appears at about 8 to 10 years of age, preceding conservation of weight which is apparent between the ages of 10 to 12. Functional acquisition of volume occurs after the age of 12. The invariant sequence of the development of substance, weight, and volume conservation has generally been verified, with certain qualifications, in a number of studies by Elkind (1961a, 1961b, 1961c), Kooistra (1963), Lovell (1961), and Smedslund (1961a, 1961b, 1961c, 1961d, 1961e, 1961f).

Can conservation be induced in the child? Piaget (1952) holds that for conservation to appear the child must be able to perform the following operations: multiple classification, multiple relationality, atomism, reversibility, and seriation. We contend that conservation can be induced if the training procedures embody these prerequisite operations.

PREVIOUS TRAINING RESEARCH

The majority of previous attempts at conservation modification or acceleration have dealt with areas other than quantity concepts. These include number conservation, Wohlwill (1960), Wohlwill and Lowe (1962), and area conservation, Beilin and Franklin

[1] A partial report of this study was read at the Conference on "New Media in Education, Business and Industry," Wayne State University, Detroit, Michigan, January, 1965.

From I. E. Sigel, A. Roeper, & F. H. Hooper. *A training procedure for acquisition of Piaget's conservation of quantity: A pilot study and its replication.* British Journal of Educational Psychology, *1966*, **36**, *301–311*. (*With permission of the authors and the* British Journal of Educational Psychology.)

428 PERSPECTIVES IN CHILD PSYCHOLOGY

(1962). Training results in these studies have essentially been negative. Piagetian concept acquisition has not proved amenable to laboratory training techniques based upon traditional learning approaches, e.g., see Flavell (1963, pp. 370–379). The studies which have attempted to induce conservation generally provide no information as to the child's ability to employ any or all of the prerequisite operations. They merely indicate the extent to which the child can conserve (Bruner, 1964; Smedslund, 1961a). Further, these investigators shed no light on the relationship between the mental operations, e.g., multiple classification and conservation.

Piaget assigns a clearly subordinate role to language as a necessary condition in the development of conservation, holding that changes in cognitive structure are not accomplished via verbal enrichment or sophistication. Bruner, however, contends that acquisition of conservation is related to linguistic experiences. He reported a study by Frank who tested the Bruner hypothesis that "improvement in language should aid this type (conservation) of problem solving" (Bruner, 1964, p. 5). Activation of language would enable the child to be less dominated by perceptual forces in the setting, less inhibited in utilizing symbolic processes, and consequently, be able to deal with the conservation problem. Frank, using subjects age 4 to 7, tested the children on the classic paradigm of conservation of continuous quantity (liquid), in one case with the materials in full view, and for several conditions in which the beakers are screened. In the latter condition the child is asked to verbalize. Increases in conservation responses occurred under the screened conditions and the older subjects maintained correct responses in post-test and transfer task situations. These results are offered by Bruner as support for the significance of verbalization in conservation acquisition (Bruner, 1964, pp. 6–7). . . .

Another set of studies involving the acquisition of the conservation of weight has been reported by Smedslund (1961a, 1961b, 1961c, 1961d, 1961e, 1961f). Working with children from 5 to 7, Smedslund attempted to train children to conserve weight by employing two training procedures. In one situation he reinforced trials in the conservation of matter. He altered the form of one of the balls of clay and asked the child to predict which one would weigh more. The child's prediction was tested directly by placing the object on a scale in the child's presence. A second procedure was to add or subtract pieces of Plasticine and show the child the relative effect of these actions. The assumption in this latter approach was that if the addition-subtraction schema were exercised, the child would more easily acquire conservation of weight. The results for this study were essentially negative.

One experiment in this series by Smedslund is of considerable interest in that it provides exciting possibilities for inducing conservation by the creation of cognitive conflict, i.e., competing cognitive systems. Smedslund reasoned that creation of such conflict would induce cognitive reorganization. Two kinds of transformations were employed, i.e., deformation by changing the shape, and addition and subtraction of quantity. Thus, if the child was inclined to think that flattening out a piece of clay increased its size, and that subtracting a piece of it would decrease its size, the experimenter would employ both actions at the same time and ask the child whether the transformed and subtracted item was the same or less than the standard. Presentation of two conflicting approaches is presumed to give the subject a situation in which he has to pause and decide between the conflicting possibilities. Of all the conditions Smedslund employed to induce conservation, the conflict paradigm was the most successful.

A recent study by Gruen (1964) compared verbal pre-training on number conservation, in combination with direct reinforced practice, against a verbal cognitive conflict paradigm drawn from Smedslund's approach. Although training effects were generally small, a significant difference between verbal conflict training and control groups was demonstrated. In addition, Beilin (1965) found a verbal-rule instruction method to be effective in the inducement of length and number conservation. Tests on an area generalization task revealed a notable absence of any transfer effects.

It may be that facilitating as cognitive conflict is, it may have to be more intensive as well as extensive. In Smedslund's studies only five of thirteen subjects manifested changes in conservation ability. Why not all, in view of their common exposure to the training? Our contention is that conservation can be induced only by training the child in the prerequisites to such mental operations. Such training may, in fact, induce conflict since it exposes the child to experiences which force him to reorganize cognitively.

The potential role of operational reversibility in mediating conservation development is indicated by Eifermann and Etzion (1964) for adult subjects, and by Wallach and Sprott (1964) for young children. The latter study utilized a reversibility training approach very similar to that found in the final sessions of the present enrichment program. Experimental training groups of 6–7-year-old children were found to differ significantly from controls on discontinuous quantity conservation and numerical correspondence responses.

RATIONALE FOR PROPOSED TRAINING PROGRAM

To conserve, the child must be able to emancipate himself from the perceptual demands of the situation, to know that the size or shape of the items can be changed, i.e., be transformed, and still not lose every one of the initial attributes, and to acknowledge that objects are multidimensional. Given that the child learns that objects can be classified and reclassified on the basis of any one of the single attributes, he is now in a position to learn that objects can be classified and reclassified on the basis of two or more attributes. Combining two or more dimensions of objects signifies the beginning of multiplicative relations, an operation that leads to the creation of a large array of classes. Since objects have a large number of possible class memberships, classifications are, to a degree, relative. The creation of classes becomes dependent on the criteria selected as bases for classification. An interesting by-product of this is the awareness that class membership of an item may be defined by the individual, since it is he who decides what attributes to use.

The above operations are presumed to be critical for the acquisition of conservation. What about the schemas? Piaget proposes the schema of atomism, the awareness that objects are made up of minute particles. The transformations are said to relocate these particles in space without changing their number. It is our contention that such knowledge is unnecessary for the level of comprehension of conservation under discussion here.

In summary, then, we conclude that conservation is possible only when the mental operations of *multiple classification, multiple relationality,* and *reversibility* are present as the cognitive structure basic to adequate conservation performance. The goal of our program was to train children in these operations.

PLAN OF THE INVESTIGATION

Subjects

Ten children ranging in age from 4.9 to 5, were divided in two groups of five and comprise the pilot sample. One group was designated Training Group and the other Control. . . . The mean Stanford-Binet IQs were 149 for the T group and 152 for the C group. . . .

Conservation tasks

Each of the ten children was given conservation tasks of continuous quantity (Plasticine) for substance, weight, and volume, and one conservation of liquid substance. The tests were administered in the classical way. A child passed a conservation task when he could indicate that at least in two of the three transformations the two items were still identical in terms of the property under discussion. Post-tests were administered two weeks after the training period.

Teaching procedures

. . . The children were told that they were going to do some work, and nothing was said about the relationship between the work . . . and the testing experiences.

On the basis of the theoretical position presented earlier, the training focused on multiple labeling which was followed by multiple classification and multiplicative relations. Finally, reversibility was introduced. In Table 1 we have a verbatim account of the teacher introducing an object, in this case a banana, and the encouragement toward labeling. This is followed by another object, an orange. This same procedure is followed. Having focused on the characteristics of each, the teacher presents two similar objects and asks the children to label differences between the tangerine and the orange. Having identified the difference, she now proceeds to discuss similarities.

We assume that directing the children's attention to the similarities, as well as the differences of objects, facilitates perception of comparison and distinction. . . . Having ascertained and verbalized apparent similarities such as shape and color, the teacher introduces another basis of classification, in this particular case, functional attributes. Having worked with the two different objects, yet of the same general class, she now introduces the original banana, which is different, and focuses on similarities again. The process of naming the additional attributes, searching for class labels, and defining criteria of class membership goes on until the group, under the teacher's guidance and stimulation, has exhausted the possibilities. Following this, the children were introduced to the idea of multiplicative relations in which two criteria are co-ordinated as a basis of classification, e.g., "Can you think of two things that you are at the same time?" Starting with the personal, that is the egocentric, the teacher moved to non-personal objects.

Reversibility was the final operation to be introduced. The children were given a constant number of pennies, which were divided amongst them. The goal here is to demonstrate that irrespective of how the pennies are divided or arranged on the table, the total remains the same and can be recombined to form a pile equal to the original one.

TABLE 1 Portion of verbatim transcript of a training session dealing with multiple attributes of objects

Teacher:	Can you tell me what this is, Mary?
Mary:	A banana.
Teacher:	What else can you tell me about it?
Mary:	It's straight.
Teacher:	It's straight. What else?
Mary:	It has a peel.
Teacher:	It has a peel. . . . Tom, what can you tell me about it?
Tom:	Ummm . . . It has some dark lines on it.
Teacher:	Uh-huh.
Tom:	It has some green on it.
Teacher:	What can you do with it?
Tom:	You can eat it!
Teacher:	That's right! . . . Now let's see . . .
Children:	. . . I love bananas!
Teacher:	What is this?
Children:	An orange.
Teacher:	Is it really an orange?
Children:	Uh-huh. . . . Yes.
Teacher:	Look at it closely.
Child:	It's an artificial one.
Teacher:	Oh, that's right, it's an artificial one . . . But, what else can you tell me about it?
Children:	You can eat it . . . It is round . . .
Teacher:	Uh-huh.
Children:	. . . Orange.
Teacher:	That's right!
Child:	It has a stem.
Teacher:	Now, look at this one . . . What's this?
Children:	An orange . . . orange.
Teacher:	And what can you do with it?
Children:	You can eat it . . . and it's round . . .
Teacher:	It is round . . .
Child:	It has a peel . . .
Teacher:	It has a peel . . . Now, look at these two things. Are they the same?
Children:	No.
Teacher:	What's different?
Children:	This one . . . this one here is pressed in on the side a little . . . this one is lighter.
Teacher:	Do you know what this really is? This is a tangerine . . . and this is an orange. Now tell me in what ways they are alike.
Children:	This is smaller and that's bigger.
Teacher:	I said, "In what way are they alike?"
Children:	They are both round . . . they both have a stem . . . both orange.
Teacher:	They both have a stem, both round, both orange: Anything else alike about them?
Child:	They're both fat.
Teacher:	Uh-huh. What can you do with them?
Children:	We can eat them . . .
Teacher:	We can eat them . . . Now, tell me, what's the same about all these things?
Child:	These are round, but this isn't.
Teacher:	I said, what is the same about them, not what's different about them.
Children:	They're both round . . . they're round . . . they're round . . . and they are both artificial.
Teacher:	They're all artificial, and, . . . are they all round?
Child:	No.
Teacher:	What about the banana?
Child:	It's straight.

TABLE 1   Portion of verbatim transcript of a training session dealing with multiple attributes of objects (*continued*)

Teacher:	But, . . . tell me something else that's the same about all of these things.
Child:	. . . They have . . . all have a peel.
Teacher:	That's right, too, but what can you do with all of them?
Children:	You can eat them!
Teacher:	That's right! That's the same about every one of them. Do you have a name for all of them?
Children:	Yes!
Teacher:	What?
Child:	A banana.
Teacher:	A banana? No, . . . is there something that you can call all of them?
Children:	Fruit . . . fruit.
Teacher:	And what's the same about all fruit?
Children:	They are all round except bananas.
Teacher:	No, . . . why do you call all of these things fruit?
Children:	Because you can eat them.
Teacher:	You can eat them.
Children:	And they are food.
Teacher:	And they are food. If I had a piece of bread here, would that be fruit too?
Children:	No.
Teacher:	Why not?
Children:	Because it is not sweet . . . not round . . .
Teacher:	Because it is not sweet. I think that's a good reason . . . and, you eat bread too?
Children:	Yes.
Teacher:	But it is still not a fruit . . . right?
Children:	Yes.
Teacher:	Now, can you tell me again what this is? We talked about it yesterday.
Child:	A pencil.
Teacher:	What else can you tell me about it?
Children:	It's round. . . . You said you were going to put it in . . .
Teacher:	That's right . . . Ah . . . Tom, what is this?
Tom:	Chalk.
Teacher:	What else can you tell me about it?
Tom:	It's white.
Teacher:	Gail, tell me, what's the same about these two things?
Gail:	They're both round.
Teacher:	What else?
Gail:	. . . Ummm . . .
Teacher:	John, tell me, what's the same about these two things?
John:	. . . Both write.
Teacher:	That's right! There are two things that are the same about it. Tell me what they are?
John:	Well . . . I don't know . . .
Teacher:	What are they, Mary?
Mary:	They're round and they write.
Teacher:	Very good!

The opportunity to use language and language formulas, and to provide schemas in the context of learning particular information was deliberate. We also believe that opportunities for cognitive reorganization were provided, in that the children learn two or more attributes of an object which can be combined to define another class. Thus, through structural teaching involving verbalization and demonstrations, we sought to bring to the children's attention the fact that objects have multiple characteristics (multiple classification), that these can be combined in various ways to produce new categories (multiple relations), and that categories of objects can be reorganized and brought back to the original (reversibility). . . .

INITIAL RESULTS

. . . Each child in the Training Group was able to solve correctly at least one more conservation task in the post-testing than in the pre-testing session. . . . For the Control Group children, two out of the three were unable to solve any of the conservation tasks on the pre-training tests and were also unable to solve any of the tasks on the post-training testing. . . .

In discussing the findings, we must keep in mind that the children are of comparable IQ, chronological age, social status, and educational level. The answers to the differences in the abilities to resolve the conservation tasks cannot be attributed to any of these variables.

RESULTS OF REPLICATION STUDY

The results of the first training session were sufficiently encouraging to warrant a replication. In the selection of the second sample, we made certain that none of the ten children could conserve. The children were assigned randomly to the Training and Control Groups, the average ages were 4.3 and 4.5, respectively, and mean Stanford-Binet IQ scores were identical, 143.8. Identical testing and training procedures, as described in the first situation, were used. . . .

In the pre-test, not one child was capable of conserving. In the post-test, we find that four of the five children were able at least to conserve one or more properties. It is particularly interesting to note that Child 5 was able to conserve weight but not substance or liquid substance. Beyond the objective pass-fail considerations, the training subjects revealed a heightened awareness and verbal sophistication within the post-test setting. Thus, the children not only increased in their ability to conserve correctly, but also showed an increase in their ability to verbalize the underlying operations and the salient dimensions of the criterion test situation. The Control Group showed no change in conservation ability or verbalization skills.

DISCUSSION AND CONCLUSION

How can we explain these particular findings? The only significant difference in the educational experience of the Training and Control Groups was the training session during the five-week period. These findings indicate that given training in such operations as multiple classification and reversibility, conservation, at some level, has a greater probability of appearing.

We do have the single case of the child in the first Control Group who showed a change over the course of the five-week period. This may be due to the child's already exhibited ability to conserve which was highlighted by the experimental situation. Yet, we find no such phenomenon in the second Control Group, e.g., no conservation in the pre-test, none in the post-test. This strongly supports the contention that the child who can conserve is in the process of demonstrating it in more situations. If we discount, then, the child Martha in the Training Group, and Em in the Control Group, who had shown pre-test conservation, we find that the children in the first Training Group who had no conservation did acquire conservation ability, whereas this was not the case in the Control Group. The children who show no such ability are able to solve conservation problems *only* after the training experiences. This suggests that the testing situation may not be an influence unless some ability to profit from the experience is present. Combining the two samples, eight training and seven control subjects indicated pre-test non-conservation. There were no post-test successes for any of the seven control subjects. In contrast, of the eight training subjects, five conserved substance, three conserved liquid substance, five conserved weight, and one subject succeeded on the volume task. Pass-fail contingency comparisons show differences between training and control performances on the substance and weight cases. . . .

The sequence of development, described by Piaget and confirmed by Elkind, Kooistra, Lovell, and Smedslund, appears in this study. . . . The degree to which the enrichment experiences were assimilated by the Training Group is reflected in the type of response given to the inquiry questions in the post-training session. The children verbalized their explanations in an articulate way, employing statements of reversibility, for example, as explanations. During the post-testing session, in response to the question, "Do I have more or less, or the same amount of clay?" the answer was much more complex than in the pre-training session. The child answered, "This piece is the same as this piece (points to the shape-transformed stimuli), it looks the same, it is the same. It is the same clay, it is turned into a ball just like that (points to the comparison stimuli), then you changed it into something else. It looks the same, the same amount of clay." What is of interest in this case is that the explanations are at levels expected as a consequence of training experience. The children who did not have any training showed little change in verbalization patterns from initial to post-training test situations. Even when giving the wrong answer, the Training Group was more articulate and fluent than the Control Group.

The results demonstrated in the ability to articulate as well as in the ability to answer the questions correctly are to be explained primarily as a function of the training experience. Such a conclusion is warranted on theoretical as well as empirical grounds. Reading the transcripts, it becomes readily apparent that the children become sensitized to the multiplicity of attributes of objects and to the possibility of coordinating combinations of attributes. They seem to be encouraged by such an experience to make inferences, that is, to view objects in terms of their classificatory relationships to other objects. The encouragement to verbalize their ideas about objects and to direct attention to the multidimensionality of objects may have played an important part in the child's assimilation of this new knowledge. Such encouragement to verbalize, in conjunction with the prerequisite operations, may combine to provide the appropriate experiences necessary for the child to acquire conservation. In this sense, Bruner's emphasis upon the verbal aspect of the situation may well be correct.

The quantitative and qualitive analyses of the results of this study provide support for the basic hypothesis that training programs focusing on prerequisites for relevant cognitive operations influence the resultant cognitive structures. This modification of cognitive structure, directed by such a training procedure, provides for the emergence of new sets of abilities and demonstrates the interdependence of cognitive stages and precursors. On the basis of this position, conservation *per se* need not be taught directly. Possessing the necessary prerequisites, children may "discover" conservation as a principle and apply it to substance, weight, and volume. Increased affirmation of their competence in a specific area could be obtained through extended practice. They already have the necessary logical structure, in this instance, to master conservation of continuous quantity. Children having experience with conservation of continuous quantity could then be exposed to discontinuous quantities, number, etc. In this way, progress toward comprehensive logical thought can be developed. Insofar as stage placement within a given quantity conservation type is concerned, the present training subjects were probably at a transitionary or intuitive level. It appears reasonable that transitionary stage individuals would derive the greatest benefit from the training experiences. Unfortunately, no attempt was made to determine stage location in this study.

REFERENCES

Beilin, H. Learning and operational convergence in logical thought development. *Journal of Experimental Child Psychology,* 1965, **2**, 317–339.

Beilin, H., & Franklin, I. C. Logical operations in area and length measurement: Age and training effects. *Child Development,* 1962, **33**, 607–618.

Bruner, J. S. The course of cognitive growth. *American Psychologist,* 1964, **19**, 1–15.

Eifermann, R. R., & Etzion, D. Awareness of reversibility: Its effect on performance of converse arithmetical operations. *British Journal of Educational Psychology,* 1964, **34**, 151–157.

Elkind, D. The development of quantitative thinking: A systematic replication of Piaget's studies. *Journal of Genetic Psychology,* 1961, **98**, 37–46. (a)

Elkind, D. Children's discovery of the conservation of mass, weight, and volume: Piaget's replication study II. *Journal of Genetic Psychology,* 1961, **98**, 219–227. (b)

Elkind, D. Quantity conceptions in junior and senior high school students. *Child Development,* 1961, **32**, 551–560. (c)

Flavell, J. H. *Developmental psychology of Jean Piaget.* Princeton, N.J.: Van Nostrand, 1963.

Gruen, G. E. Experience affecting the development of number conservation in children. Unpublished doctoral dissertation, University of Illinois, 1964.

Hunt, J. McV. *Intelligence and experience.* New York: Ronald Press, 1961.

Kooistra, W. Developmental trends in the attainment of conservation, transitivity, and relativism in the thinking of children: A replication and extension of Piaget's ontogenetic formulations. Unpublished doctoral dissertation, Wayne State University, 1963.

Lovell, K. *The growth of basic mathematical and scientific concepts in children.* New York: Philosophical Library, 1961.

Piaget, J. *The child's conception of number.* (Translated by G. Gattegno & F. M. Hodgson.) London: Routledge, 1952.

Smedslund, J. The acquisition of conservation of substance and weight in children. I. Introduction. *Scandinavian Journal of Psychology,* 1961, **2**, 11–20. (a)

Smedslund, J. The acquisition of conservation of substance and weight in children. II. External reinforcement of conservation of weight and of the operations of addition and subtraction. *Scandinavian Journal of Psychology,* 1961, **2**, 71–84. (b)

Smedslund, J. The acquisition of conservation of substance and weight in children. III. Extinction of conservation of weight acquired 'normally' and by means of empirical controls on a balance. *Scandinavian Journal of Psychology,* 1961, **2**, 85–87. (c)

Smedslund, J. The acquisition of conservation of substance and weight in children. IV. Attempt at extinction of the visual components of the weight concept. *Scandinavian Journal of Psychology,* 1961, **2**, 153–155. (d)

Smedslund, J. The acquisition of conservation of substance and weight in children. V. Practice in conflict situations without external reinforcement. *Scandinavian Journal of Psychology,* 1961, **2**, 156–160. (e)

Smedslund, J. The acquisition of conservation of substance and weight in children. VI. Practice on continuous versus discontinuous material in problem situations without external reinforcement. *Scandinavian Journal of Psychology,* 1961, **2**, 203–210. (f)

Wallach, L., & Sprott, R. L. Inducing number conservation in children. *Child Development,* 1964, **35**, 1057–1071.

Wohlwill, J. F. A study on the development of the number concept by scalogram analysis. *Journal of Genetic Psychology,* 1960, **97**, 345–377.

Wohlwill, J. F., & Lowe, R. C. Experimental analysis of the development of the conservation of number. *Child Development,* 1962, **33**, 153–167.

THE INFLUENCE OF LANGUAGE ON THE DEVELOPMENT OF CONCEPT FORMATION IN DEAF CHILDREN[1]

Hans G. Furth[2]

Attempts to appraise the contribution of language[3] in the development of thinking are made difficult by the fact that ordinarily language and thinking develop together. However, children born with profound deafness, or afflicted with it at a very early age, do not learn ordinary language as the usual by-product of living; through them we may study the influence of language deficiency on the development of cognitive functions and clarify the role of language in cognition. There appears to be wide agreement that the average deaf person is inferior to hearing persons in all activities requiring thinking in abstract terms (Levine, 1950). Ewing and Stanton (1943), Templin (1950), Myklebust and Brutten (1953), and Oléron (1953) among others have held that the "conceptual retardation" of deaf people is intrinsically related to their lack of language experience.

The purpose of this study is to demonstrate that the capacity of deaf people to deal with conceptual tasks may not in fact be generally retarded or impaired. Cognitive capacity, it is proposed, develops naturally with living, whether or not spoken language is part of the child's experience, and the role of language is restricted and extrinsic: e.g., familiarity with certain words may increase the efficiency with which the solution of certain problems may be reached. It follows that deaf children should not differ from hearing children in their performance on conceptual learning tasks where it can be assumed that specific language experience does not favor the hearing child. However, on conceptual tasks where one has reason to assume that specific language familiarity gives the hearing child an advantage, deaf children should be inferior to hearing children.

Following a lead of Levy and Cuddy (1956), three concept learning tasks, differing in relation to the language repertoire of the two samples, were chosen to measure the basic cognitive potential of the children and establish norms for various age groups.

[1]This report is based on a Ph.D. dissertation submitted to the University of Portland, and part of this paper was read at the APA convention, Chicago, 1960. This investigation was supported by a fellowship, MF 9902, from the National Institutes of Health, United States Public Health Service.

[2]The writer is deeply indebted to Nissim Levy for his guidance and critical review of the manuscript.

[3]The meaning of language in this article is restricted to the ordinary spoken language of a society.

From H. G. Furth. The influence of language on the development of concept formation in deaf children. Journal of Abnormal and Social Psychology, *1961, 63, 386–389. (With permission of the author and the American Psychological Association.)*

The tasks were nonverbal and consisted of the operational attainment of a concept or a principle according to which a subject's choice could be consistently correct. For the first two tasks the correct principle or concept could be assumed to be as familiar or unfamiliar to the deaf as to the hearing children. The idea of "same," involved in the first task, is so primitive that workers with deaf children report that there is no deaf child in school who does not have at least some gesture for this idea. On the basis of Levy and Ridderheim's (1958) study, partially replicated here, it seems that hearing children before the age of 12 do not have the concept of "symmetry" readily available and, therefore, also should have no advantage over the deaf children on the Symmetry task.

The concept of "opposition," however, should be quite familiar to hearing children beyond 6 years old, as a study by Kreezer and Dallenbach (1929) showed. Our language employs many dimensions in terms of opposites: hot-cold, good-bad, long-short. As a rule a child learns the words denoting extremes before he learns the words characterizing the dimension as such. In such linguistic contexts a child becomes naturally acquainted with the concept of opposition and when he has reached the age of 6 can readily grasp the meaning of the word "opposite." In distinction from the hearing child, the deaf child, without the benefit of this specific language experience, finds it relatively difficult to learn the concept of opposite for one dimension and then generalize the concept to other dimensions. Teachers of the deaf report that their pupils are being "taught" the meaning of "opposite" when they are in the intermediate grades or about 14 years old.

METHOD

Subjects

All pupils aged 7–12 years from the three schools for the deaf located in one state, with an additional 44 subjects from a neighboring state, made up the deaf sample. Excluded were those few who did not have an early hearing loss of at least 50 decibels in the better ear. There were 30 subjects in each of the six age groups. Since the majority of the deaf sample consisted of practically all deaf children of the desired age living in the state at one time, it can be reasonably assumed that a relatively unbiased and representative sample of deaf children was achieved. The hearing sample consisted of 180 subjects randomly selected from five different grade schools and classified into six age groups, 7–12 years, of 30 subjects each. The hearing sample had an equal number of boys and girls; however, the deaf sample at ages 7, 9, and 12 showed a slight imbalance in favor of boys.

The procedure of matching the hearing and deaf group only on age and sex and permitting other possibly pertinent variables to vary randomly was judged superior to an attempted control of IQ, institutional education, etc. With regard to IQ in particular, it is known that tests, standardized on a hearing sample and based on an average experiential and educational background, are of questionable value with deaf children. The deaf group had a somewhat lower overall socioeconomic rating than the particular hearing sample used in this study. In the light of the reported relationship between the intelligence of children and parental occupation (Terman & Merrill, 1937), the somewhat uneven socioeconomic distribution in the two samples would bias the results, if at all, against the deaf and, therefore, against the main hypothesis.

Tasks

The three tasks employed in the study were these:

1. *Sameness task*   This task consisted of a series of 40 different pairs of round tin covers with two simple figures drawn on each cover. The two figures on one of the covers were identical, on the other the two were different. Under the cover with the identical figures a checker was placed indicating to the child the correct choice. The criterion for success was 10 consecutive correct choices. The trials were terminated after the criterion was reached, or with the first error after Trial 30. A modified stimulus presentation apparatus was used on this and the following task.

2. *Symmetry task*   Forty different pairs of 7 $\times$ 9 inch cards were prepared for this task and simple figures were drawn in heavy black ink on a white background. On one card of each pair the figure to be rewarded was a symmetrical one, while on the other it was asymmetrical. The procedure and criterion were the same as those used with the Sameness task.

3. *Opposition task*   This task was in two parts. (a) Opposition Acquisition: From a set of eight wooden discs ranging in diameter from .5 inch to 2.25 inches and hidden from the subject's view, four were selected in a fixed order and randomly thrown on the table in front of the child. The experimenter either pointed to the largest or to the smallest disc. If the experimenter picked the largest, the subject's task was to discover that he had to pick the smallest; if the experimenter picked the smallest, the subject had to pick the largest. Subjects were given a maximum of 36 trials. The criterion was six consecutive correct choices. (b) Opposition Transfer: One uncorrected trial was given only to those subjects who succeeded on Opposition Acquisition, on each of the following six Transfer dimensions: Volume, Length, Number, Brightness, Position, and Texture. While the experimenter pointed to the stimulus on one extreme of the continuum of four or five stimuli, the child showed transfer of concept by pointing to the opposite extreme.

The performance of the two groups was compared in terms of the proportion of subjects reaching the criterion. Other methods of measuring performance yielded similar trends and are not reported here except in the case of Opposition Acquisition. For Opposition Transfer the total number of nontransferred responses was used for computational purposes.

RESULTS

. . . The comparative results for the Sameness and Symmetry tasks were fairly similar. The hearing group showed no superiority over the deaf; on the contrary, there was a tendency for the younger deaf children to surpass the hearing children of comparable age. Also, the overall comparisons for all ages combined on the Symmetry task was significantly in favor of the deaf group.

Both groups showed a significant change of proportional success with age. . . . While this change was consistently in a positive direction for the hearing children, the 11-year-old deaf group reversed the trend for the deaf sample. . . .

Hearing children were significantly superior to deaf children on the Opposition Acquistion task . . . at each age level. . . .

. . . The relevant data for the Transfer test . . . indicated that the hearing children were superior, the degree of superiority varying with age.

DISCUSSION

The facilitative influence of language was highlighted in the present study when one considers that the same deaf children who demonstrated their equality on the Sameness and Symmetry tasks were consistently below the same hearing children on the Opposition task. On the two former problems, the deaf children in the lower age range were actually superior, perhaps because of their less sophisticated approach to the problem situation. Insofar as the problem required the attainment of one simple concept, the hearing child's greater store of available categories may have been distracting.

Regarding the developmental trend in the hearing group, the findings on the Symmetry task are in excellent agreement with the results of Levy and Ridderheim (1958) on an entirely different sample. The drop in the relative performance of the 11- and 12-year-old deaf group is somewhat puzzling, if it is not a sampling artifact.

Successful performance on these concept learning tasks, it should be understood, is related to but in no way identified with the knowledge of the concept or of the word. Although both deaf and hearing children at the youngest age level knew the word or the concept of sameness, only a few of them succeeded on the Sameness task. At the other extreme, neither deaf nor hearing 7-year-old children were familiar with the word "symmetry," yet a few 7-year-old children succeeded on that particular task.

SUMMARY

Contrary to widely accepted conclusions that deaf people are inferior in conceptual thinking and the theories proposed to link conceptual inferiority and language retardation, the present study suggested that the influence of language on concept formation is extrinsic and specific. According to this view, language experience may increase the efficiency of concept formation in a certain situation, but is not a necessary prerequisite for the development of the basic capacity to abstract and generalize.

To test this assumption, 180 deaf and 180 hearing subjects, 30 subjects for each age group from 7 to 12 years, were given three nonverbal concept learning tasks differing with respect to the relevance of the language experience of the two samples. With regard to the Sameness and Symmetry task, the groups were assumed to be equivalent in relevant language experience. In contrast, concerning Opposition Acquisition and Transfer, specific language experience was assumed to give hearing children an advantage over the deaf. Accordingly, it was predicted that the hearing subjects would not be superior to the deaf subjects in their performance on the Sameness and Symmetry tasks, yet would be superior on Opposition Acquisition and Transfer problems. The results confirmed the experimental predictions and gave support to the proposed theory.

REFERENCES

Ewing, A. S. G., & Stanton, D. A. G. A study of children with defective hearing. *Teacher of the Deaf*, 1943, **41**.

Kreezer, G., & Dallenbach, K. M. Learning the relation of opposition. *American Journal of Psychology*, 1929, **41**, 432–441.

Levine, E. Psychological testing of the deaf. In *Rehabilitation of the deaf and the hard of hearing*. Washington, D.C.: Federal Security Agency, Office of Vocational Rehabilitation, 1950.

Levy, N. M., & Cuddy, J. M. Concept learning in the educationally retarded child of normal intelligence. *Journal of Consulting Psychology*, 1956, **20**, 445–448.

Levy, N. M., & Ridderheim, D. S. A developmental study of the concept of symmetry. Paper presented at the meeting of the Eastern Psychological Association, Philadelphia, April 1958.

Myklebust, H. R., & Brutten, M. A study of the visual perception of deaf children: *Acta Oto-Laryngologica.* Stockholm, 1953, Supplementum 105.

Oléron, P. Conceptual thinking of the deaf. *American Annals of the Deaf,* 1953, **98**, 304–310.

Templin, M. C. *The development of reasoning in children with normal and defective hearing.* Minneapolis: University of Minnesota Press, 1950.

Terman, L. M., & Merrill, M. A. *Measuring intelligence.* Boston: Houghton Mifflin, 1937.

THE COURSE OF COGNITIVE GROWTH

Jerome S. Bruner[1]

[This paper shall] take the view . . . that the development of human intellectual functioning from infancy . . . is shaped by a series of technological advances in the use of mind. Growth depends upon the mastery of techniques and cannot be understood without reference to such mastery. These techniques are not, in the main, inventions of the individuals who are ''growing up;'' they are, rather, skills transmitted . . . by the culture—language being a prime example. Cognitive growth, then, is in a major way from the outside in as well as from the inside out.

Two matters will concern us. The first has to do with the techniques . . . that aid growing [humans] . . . to represent in a manageable way the recurrent features of the complex environments in which they live. It is fruitful . . . to distinguish three systems of processing information by which human beings construct models of their world: through action, through imagery, and through language. A second concern is with integration, the means whereby acts are organized into higher-order ensembles, making possible the use of larger and larger units of information for the solution of particular problems.

Let me first elucidate these two theoretical matters, and then turn to an examination of the research upon which they are based, much of it from the Center for Cognitive Studies at Harvard.

On the occasion of the One Hundredth Anniversary of the publication of Darwin's *The Origin of Species,* Washburn and Howell (1960) presented a paper at the Chicago Centennial celebration containing the following passage:

It would now appear . . . that the large size of the brain of certain hominids was a relatively late development and that the brain evolved due to new selection pressures *after* bipedalism and consequent upon the use of tools. The tool-using, ground-living, hunting way of life created the large human brain rather than a large brained man discovering certain new ways of life. [We] believe this conclusion is the most important result of the recent fossil hominid discoveries and is one which carries far-reaching implications for the interpretation of human behavior and its origins. . . . The important point is that size of brain, insofar as it can be measured by cranial capacity, has increased some threefold subsequent to the use and manufacture of implements. . . . The uniqueness of modern man is seen as the result of a technical-social life which tripled the size of the brain, reduced the face, and modified many other structures of the body [p. 49 f.].

This implies that the principal change in man over a long period of years—perhaps 500,000—has been . . . by linking himself with new, external implementation systems rather than by any conspicuous change in morphology. . . .

[1]The assistance of R. R. Olver and Mrs. Blythe Clinchy in the preparation of this paper is gratefully acknowledged.

From J. S. Bruner. The course of cognitive growth. American Psychologist, *1964, 19, 1–15.*
(With permission of the author and the American Psychological Association.)

Any implement system, to be effective, must produce an appropriate internal counterpart, an appropriate skill necessary for organizing sensorimotor acts, for organizing percepts, and for organizing our thoughts in a way that matches them to the requirements of implement systems. These internal skills . . . are slowly selected in evolution. In the deepest sense, then, man can be described as a species that has become specialized by the use of technological implements. . . . We move, perceive, and think in a fashion that depends upon techniques rather than upon wired-in arrangements in our nervous system.

Where representation of the environment is concerned, it too depends upon techniques that are learned—and these are precisely the techniques that serve to amplify our motor acts, our perceptions, and our . . . [reasoning] activities. We know and respond to recurrent regularities in our environment by skilled and patterned acts, [through] . . . imagery, . . . perceptual organization, and . . . [language]. In short, the capacities that have been shaped by our evolution as tool users are the ones that we rely upon in the primary task of representation. . . .

As for integration, it is a truism that there are very few single or simple adult acts that cannot be performed by a young child. In short, any more highly skilled activity can be decomposed into simpler components, each of which can be carried out by a less skilled operator. What higher skills require is that the component operations be combined. Maturation consists of an orchestration of these components into an integrated sequence. The "distractability," so-called, of much early behavior may reflect each act's lack of imbeddedness in what Miller, Galanter, and Pribram (1960) speak of as "plans." These integrated plans, in turn, reflect the routines and subroutines that one learns in the course of mastering the patterned nature of a social environment. So that integration, too, depends upon patterns that come from the outside in. . . .

If we are to benefit from contact with recurrent regularities in the environment, we must represent them in some manner. To dismiss this problem as "mere memory" is to misunderstand it. For the most important thing about memory is not storage of past experience, but rather the retrieval of what is relevant in some usable form. This depends upon how past experience is coded and processed so that it may indeed be relevant and usable in the present when needed. The end product of such a system of coding and processing is what we may speak of as a representation.

I shall call the three modes of representation mentioned earlier enactive representation [action], iconic representation [imagery], and symbolic representation [language]. Their appearance in the life of the child is in that order, each depending upon the previous one for its development, yet all of them remaining more or less intact throughout life. . . . By enactive representation I mean a mode of representing past events through appropriate motor response. We cannot, for example, give an adequate description of familiar sidewalks or floors over which we habitually walk, nor do we have much of an image of what they are like. Yet we get about them without tripping or even looking much. Such segments of our environment— bicycle riding, tying knots, aspects of driving—get represented in our muscles, so to speak. Iconic representation summarizes events by the selective organization of percepts and of images, by the spatial, temporal, and qualitative structures of the perceptual field and their transformed images. Images "stand for" perceptual events in the close but conventionally selective way that a picture stands for the object pictured. Finally, a symbol system represents things by design features that include remoteness and arbitrariness. A word neither points directly to its referent here and now, nor does it resemble it as a picture. The lexeme "Philadelphia" looks no more like the city so designated than does a nonsense syllable. The other property of language that is crucial is its productiveness in combination, far beyond what can be done with images or acts. . . .

An example or two of enactive representation underlines its importance in infancy and in disturbed functioning, while illustrating its limitations. Piaget (1954) provides us with an observation from the closing weeks of the first year of life. The child is playing with a rattle in his crib. The rattle drops over the side. The child moves his clenched hand before his face, opens it, looks for the rattle. Not finding it there, he moves his hand, closed again, back to the edge of the crib, shakes it with movements like those he uses in shaking the rattle. Thereupon he moves his closed hand back toward his face, opens it, and looks. Again no rattle; and so he tries again. In several months, the child has benefited from experience to the degree that the rattle and action become separated. Whereas earlier he would not show signs of missing the rattle when it was removed unless he had begun reaching for it, now he cries and searches when the rattle is presented for a moment and hidden by a cover. He no longer repeats a movement to restore the rattle. In place of representation by action alone—where "existence" is defined by . . . present action—it is now defined by an image that persists autonomously.

A second example is provided by the results of injury to the occipital and temporal cortex in man (Hanfmann, Rickers-Ovsiankina, & Goldstein, 1944). A patient is presented with a hard-boiled egg intact in its shell, and asked what it is. Holding it in his hand, he is embarrassed, for he cannot name it. He makes a motion as if to throw it and halts himself. Then he brings it to his mouth as if to bite it and stops before he gets there. He brings it to his ear and shakes it gently. He is puzzled. The experimenter takes the egg from him and cracks it on the table, handing it back. The patient then begins to peel the egg and announces what it is. He cannot identify objects without reference to the action he directs toward them.

The disadvantages of such a system are illustrated by Emerson's (1931) experiment in which children are told to place a ring on a board with seven rows and six columns of pegs, copying the position of a ring put on an identical board by the experimenter. Children ranging from 3 to 12 were examined in this experiment and in an extension of it carried out by Werner (1948). The child's board could be placed in various positions relative to the experimenter's: right next to it, 90 degrees rotated away from it, 180 degrees rotated, placed face to face with it so that the child has to turn full around to make his placement, etc. The older the child, the better his performance. But the younger children could do about as well as the oldest so long as they did not have to change their own position vis-à-vis the experimenter's board in order to make a match on their own board. The more they had to turn, the more difficult the task. They were clearly depending upon their bodily orientation toward the experimenter's board to guide them. When this orientation is disturbed by having to turn, they lose the position on the board. Older children succeed even when they must turn, either by the use of imagery that is invariant across bodily displacements, or, later, by specifying column and row of the experimenter's ring and carrying the symbolized self-instruction back to their own board. It is a limited world, the world of enactive representation.

We know little about the conditions necessary for the growth of imagery and iconic representation, or to what extent parental or environmental intervention affects it during the earliest years. In ordinary adult learning a certain amount of motoric skill and practice seems to be a necessary precondition for the development of a simultaneous image to represent the sequence of acts involved. If an adult subject is made to choose a path through a complex bank of toggle switches, he does not form an image of the path, according to Mandler (1962), until he has mastered and overpracticed the task by successive manipulation. Then, finally, he reports that an image of the path has developed and that he is now using it rather than groping his way through.

Our main concern in what follows is not with the growth of iconic representation, but with the transition from it to symbolic representation. For it is in the development of symbolic representation that one finds, perhaps, the greatest thicket of psychological problems. The puzzle begins when the child first achieves the use of productive grammar, usually late in the second year of life. Toward the end of the second year, the child is master of the single-word, agrammatical utterance, the so-called holophrase. In the months following, there occurs a profound change in the use of language. Two classes of words appear—a pivot class and an open class—and the child launches forth on his career in combinatorial talking and, perhaps, thinking. Whereas before, lexemes like *allgone* and *mummy* and *sticky* and *bye-bye* were used singly, now, for example, *allgone* becomes a pivot word and is used in combination. Mother washes jam off the child's hands; he says *allgone sticky*. In the next days, if his speech is carefully followed (Braine, 1963), it will be apparent that he is trying out the limits of the pivot combinations, and one will even find constructions that have an extraordinary capacity for representing complex sequences—like *allgone bye-bye* after a visitor has departed. A recent and ingenious observation by Weir (1962) on her $2\frac{1}{2}$-year-old son, recording his speech . . . after he was in bed with lights out, indicates that at this stage there is a great deal of . . . play with words in which the child is exploring the limits of grammatical productiveness.

In effect, language provides a means, not only for representing experience, but also for transforming it. As Chomsky (1957) and Miller (1962) have both made clear in the last few years, the transformational rules of grammar provide a syntactic means of reworking the "realities" one has encountered. Not only . . . did the dog bite the man, but the man was bitten by the dog and perhaps the man was not bitten by the dog or was the man not bitten by the dog. The range of reworking that is made possible even by the three transformations of the passive, the negative, and the query is very striking indeed. . . .

Once the child has succeeded in internalizing language . . . it becomes possible for him to represent and systematically transform the regularities of experience with far greater flexibility and power than before. . . .

. . . We turn now to some new experiments designed to shed some light on the nature of representation and particularly upon the transition from its iconic to its symbolic form.

Let me begin with an experiment by Bruner and Kenney (in Bruner et al., 1966) on the manner in which children between 5 and 7 handle a double classification matrix. The materials of the experiment are nine plastic glasses, arranged so that they vary

⊔⊔⊔⊔⊔⊔⊔ Scale in inches
0 1 2 3 4 5 6

FIG. 1   Array of glasses used in study of matrix ordering (Bruner & Kenney, in Bruner et al., 1966).

in 3 degrees of diameter and 3 degrees of height. They are set before the child initially, as in Figure 1, on a 3 × 3 grid marked on a large piece of cardboard. To acquaint the child with the matrix, we first remove one, then two, and then three glasses from the matrix, asking the child to replace them. We also ask the children to describe how the glasses in the columns and rows are alike and how they differ. Then the glasses are scrambled and we ask the child to make something like what was there before by placing the glasses on the same grid that was used when the task was introduced. Now we scramble the glasses once more, but this time we place the glass that was formerly in the southwest corner of the grid in the southeast corner (it is the shortest, thinnest glass) and ask the child if he can make something like what was there before, leaving the one glass where we have just put it. That is the experiment.

The results can be quickly told. To begin with, there is no difference between ages 5, 6, and 7 either in terms of ability to replace glasses taken from the matrix or in building a matrix once it has been scrambled (but without the transposed glass). Virtually all the children succeed. Interestingly enough, *all* the children rebuild the matrix to match the original, almost as if they were copying what was there before. The only difference is that the older children are quicker.

Now compare the performance of the three ages in constructing the matrix with a single member transposed. Most of the 7-year-olds succeed in the transposed task, but hardly any of the youngest children. . . . The youngest children seem to be dominated by an image of the original matrix. They try to put the transposed glass "back where it belongs," to rotate the cardboard so that "it will be like before," and sometimes they will start placing a few glasses neighboring the transposed glass correctly only to revert to the original arrangement. In several instances, 5- or 6-year-olds will simply try to reconstitute the old matrix, building right over the transposed glass. The 7-year-old, on the other hand, is more likely to pause, to treat the transposition as a problem, to talk to himself about "where this should go." The relation of place and size is for him a problem that requires reckoning, not simply copying. . . .

The findings of this experiment suggest two things. First, that children who use iconic representation are more highly sensitized to the spatial-qualitative organization of experience and less to the ordering principles governing such organization. They can recognize and reproduce, but cannot produce new structures based on rule. And second, there is a suspicion that the language they bring to bear on the task is insufficient as a tool for ordering. . . .

Piaget and Inhelder (1962) have shown that if children between ages 4 and 7 are presented two identical beakers which they judge equally full of water, they will no longer consider the water equal if the contents of one of the beakers is now poured into a beaker that is either wider or thinner than the original. If the second beaker is thinner, they will say it has more to drink because the water is higher; if the second beaker is wider, they will say it has less because the water is lower. Comparable results can be obtained by pouring the contents of one glass into several smaller beakers. In Geneva terms, the child is not yet able to conserve liquid volume across transformations in its appearance. Consider how this behavior can be altered.

Françoise Frank (in Bruner et al., 1966) first did the classic conservation tests to determine which children exhibited conservation and which did not. Her subjects were 4, 5, 6, and 7 years old. She then went on to other procedures, among which was the following. Two standard beakers are partly filled so that the child judges them to contain equal amounts of water. A wider beaker of the same height is introduced and the three beakers are now, except for their tops, hidden by a screen. The experimenter pours from a standard beaker into the wider beaker. The child, without seeing the water, is asked which has more to drink, or do they have the same amount, the standard or the wider beaker. . . . In comparison with the unscreened pre-test, there is a striking increase in correct equality judgments. Correct responses jump from 0 percent to 50 percent among the 4s, from 20 percent to 90 percent among the 5s, and from 50 percent to 100 percent among the 6s. With the screen present, most children justify their correct judgment by noting that "It's the same water," or "You only poured it."

Now the screen is removed. All the 4-year-olds change their minds. The perceptual display overwhelms them and they decide that the wider beaker has less water. But virtually all of the 5-year-olds stick to their judgment, often invoking the difference between appearance and reality—"It looks like more to drink, but it is only the same because it is the same water and it was only poured from there to there," to quote one typical 5-year-old. And all of the 6s and all the 7s stick to their judgment. Now, some minutes later, Frank does a post-test on the children using a tall thin beaker along with the standard ones, and no screen, of course. The 4s are unaffected by their prior experience: None of them is able to grasp the idea of invariant quantity in the new task. With the 5s, instead of 20 percent showing conservation, as in the pretest, 70 percent do. With both 6s and 7s conservation increases from 50 percent to 90 percent. I should mention that control groups doing just a pre-test and post-test show no significant improvement in performance. . . . It is plain that if a child is to succeed in the conservation task, he must have some internalized verbal formula that shields him from the overpowering appearance of the visual displays much as in the Frank experiment. . . .

Consider now another experiment by Bruner and Kenney (in Bruner et al., 1966) also designed to explore the border between iconic and symbolic representation. Children aged 5, 6, and 7 were asked to say which of two glasses in a pair was fuller and which emptier. "Fullness" is an interesting concept to work with, for it involves in its very definition a ratio or proportion between the volume of a container and the volume of a substance contained. It is difficult for the iconically oriented child to see a half-full barrel and a half-filled thimble as equally full, since the former looms larger in every one of the attributes that might be perceptually associated with volume. It is like the old riddle of which is heavier, a pound of lead or a pound of feathers. To make a correct judgment of fullness or emptiness, the child must use a symbolic operation, somewhat like computing a ratio, and resist the temptation to use perceptual appearance . . . . Figure 2 contains the 11 pairs of glasses used, and they were selected with a certain malice aforethought.

FIG. 2   Eleven pairs of glasses to be judged in terms of which glass is fuller and which emptier (Bruner & Kenney, in Bruner et al., 1966).

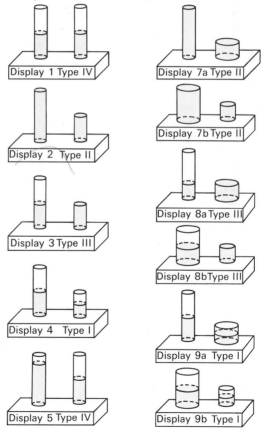

Display 1 Type IV

Display 2 Type II

Display 3 Type III

Display 4   Type I

Display 5 Type IV

Display 7a Type II

Display 7b Type II

Display 8a Type III

Display 8b Type III

Display 9a Type I

Display 9b Type I

Scale in inches
0 1 2 3 4 5 6

There are four types of pairs. In Type I (Displays 4, 9a, and 9b), the glasses are of unequal volume, but equally, though fractionally, full. In Type II (Displays 2, 7a, and 7b) again the glasses are of unequal volume, but they are completely full. Type III (Displays 3, 8a, and 8b) consists of two glasses of unequal volume, one filled and the other part filled. Type IV consists of identical glasses, in one case equally filled, in another unequally (Displays 1 and 5).

All the children in the age range we have studied use pretty much the same criteria for judging *fullness,* and these criteria are based on directly observable sensory indices rather than upon proportion. That glass is judged fuller that has the greater apparent volume of water, and the favored indication of greater volume is water level; or where that is equated, then width of glass will do; and when width and water level are the same, then height of glass will prevail. But now consider the judgments made by the three age groups with respect to which glass in each pair is *emptier.* The older children have developed an interesting consistency based on an appreciation of the complementary relation of filled and empty space—albeit an incorrect one. For them "emptier" means the glass that has the largest apparent volume of unfilled space, just as "fuller" meant the glass that had the largest volume of filled space. In consequence, their responses seem logically contradictory. For the glass that is judged fuller also turns out to be the glass that is judged emptier—given a large glass and a small glass, both half full. The younger children, on the other hand, equate emptiness with "littleness:" That glass is emptier that gives the impression of being smaller in volume of liquid. . . . Consider only the errors. The glass with the larger volume of empty

FIG. 3   Percentage of children at three ages who make contradictory and plain errors in judging which of two glasses is fuller and which emptier. (A contradictory error is calling the same glass both fuller or emptier or calling them equally full but not equally empty or vice versa. A plain error is calling one glass fuller and the other emptier, but incorrectly.) From Bruner & Kenney (in Bruner et al., 1966).

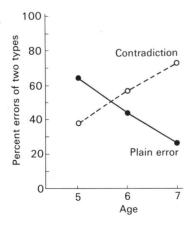

space is called emptier by 27 percent of the erring 5-year-olds, by 53 percent of the erring 6-year-olds, and by 72 percent of erring 7-year-olds. But the glass with the smallest volume of water is called emptier by 73 percent of the 5-year-olds who err, 47 percent of the 6s, and only 28 percent of the 7s. When the children are asked for their reasons for judging one glass as emptier, there is further confirmation: Most of the younger children justify it by pointing to "littleness" or "less water" or some other aspect of diminutiveness. And most of the older children justify their judgments of emptiness by reference to the amount of empty space in the vessel.

The result of all this is, of course, that the "logical structure" of the older children seems to go increasingly awry. But surely, though Figure 3 shows that contradictory errors steadily increase with age (calling the same glass fuller and emptier or equally full but not equally empty or vice versa), the contradiction is a by-product of the method of dealing with attributes. How shall we interpret these findings? Let me suggest that what is involved is a translation difficulty in going from the perceptual or iconic realm to the symbolic. If you ask children of this age whether something can be fuller and also emptier, they will smile and think that you are playing riddles. They are aware of the contrastive nature of the two terms. Indeed, even the very young child has a good working language for the two poles of the contrast: "all gone" for completely empty and "spill" or "tippy top" for completely full. Recall, too, that from 5 to 7, there is perfect performance in judging which of two identical beakers is fuller and emptier. The difference between the younger and the older child is in the number of attributes that are being attended to in situations involving fullness and emptiness: The younger child is attending to one—the volume of water; the older to two—the volume of filled space and the volume of empty space. The young child is applying a single contrast pair—full-empty—to a single feature of the situation. The older child can attend to two features, but he does not yet have the means for relating them to a third, the volume of the container per se. To do so involves being able to deal with a relation in the perceptual field that does not have a "point-at-able" or ostensive definition. Once the third term is introduced—the volume of the glass—then the symbolic concept of proportion can come to "stand for" something that is not present perceptually. The older child is on the way to achieving the insight, in spite of his contradictions. And, interestingly enough, if we count the number of children who justify their judgments of fuller and emptier by pointing to *several* rather than a single attribute, we find that the proportion triples in both cases between age 5 and age 7. The older child, it would seem, is ordering his perceptual world in such a way that, shortly, he will be able to apply concepts of relationship that are not dependent upon simple ostensive definition. As he moves toward this more powerful "technology of reckoning," he is led into errors that seem to be contradictory. What is particularly telltale is the fact, for example, that in the Type III displays, younger children sometimes seem to find the judgment easier than older children—pointing to the fuller by placing their finger on the rim of the full member and pointing to the emptier with the remark that "It is not to the top." The older child (and virtually never the younger one) gets all involved in the judgment of "fuller by apparent filled volume" and then equally involved in the judgment of "emptier by apparent empty volume" and such are his efforts that he fails to note his contradiction when dealing with a pair like Display 8b. . . .

We have said that cognitive growth consists in part in the development of systems of representation as means for dealing with information. The growing child begins with a strong reliance upon learned action patterns to represent the world around him.

In time, there is added to this technology a means for simultanizing regularities in experience into images that stand for events in the way that pictures do. And to this is finally added a technology of translating experience into a symbol system that can be operated upon by rules of transformation that greatly increase the possible range of problem solving. One of the effects of this development, or possibly one of its causes, is the power for organizing acts of information processing into more integrated and long-range problem solving efforts. To this matter we turn next.

Consider in rapid succession three related experiments. All of them point, I think, to the same conclusion.

The first is by Huttenlocher (in Bruner et al., 1966), a strikingly simple study, performed with children between the ages of 6 and 12. Two light switches are before the child; each can be in one of two positions. A light bulb is also visible. The child is asked to tell, on the basis of turning only one switch, what turns the light on. There are four ways in which the presentations are made. In the first, the light is off initially and when the child turns a switch, the light comes on. In the second, the light is on and when the child turns a switch, it goes off. In the third, the light is on and when the child turns a switch, it stays on. In the fourth and final condition, the light is off and when the child turns a switch, it stays off. Now what is intriguing about this arrangement is that there are different numbers of inductive steps required to make a correct inference in each task. The simplest condition is the off-on case. The position to which the switch has just been moved is responsible for the light going on. Intermediate difficulty should be experienced with the on-off condition. In the on-off case, two connected inferences are required: The present position achieved is rejected and the original position of the switch that has been turned is responsible for lighting the bulb. An even larger number of consecutive acts is required for success in the on-on case: The present position of the turned switch is rejected, the original position as well and the present position of the *other* switch is responsible. The off-off case requires four steps: rejecting the present position of the turned switch, its original

FIG. 4 The proportion of children at different ages who use connected questions in a Twenty-Questions game (Mosher, 1962).

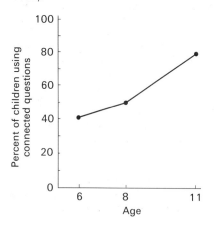

position, and the present position of the other switch, finally accepting the alternative position of the unturned switch. The natures of the individual steps are all the same. Success in the more complex cases depends upon being able to integrate them consecutively.

Huttenlocher's results show that the 6-year-olds are just as capable as their elders of performing the elementary operation involved in the one-step case: the on-off display. They, like the 9s and 12s, make nearly perfect scores. But in general, the more inferential steps the 6-year-old must make, the poorer his performance. By age 12, on the other hand, there is an insignificant difference between the tasks requiring one, two, three, or four connected inferences.

An experiment by Mosher (1962) underlines the same point. He was concerned with the strategies used by children from 6 to 11 for getting information in the game of Twenty Questions. They were to find out by "yes-no" questions what caused a car to go off the road and hit a tree. One may distinguish between connected constraint-locating questions ("Was it night-time?" followed up appropriately) and direct hypothesis-testing questions ("Did a bee fly in the window and sting the man on the eye and make him go off the road and hit the tree?"). From 6 to 11, more and more children use constraint-locating, connected questioning [see Figure 4]. Let me quote from Mosher's account.

We have asked children . . . after they have played their games, to tell us which of two questions they would rather have the answer to, if they were playing the games again—one of them a typical constraint-seeking question ("Was there anything wrong with the man?") and the other a typical discrete test of an hypothesis ("Did the man have a heart attack?"). All the eleven-year-olds and all the eight-year-olds choose the constraint-seeking question, but only 29 percent of the six-year-olds do [p. 6].

The questions of the younger children are all one-step substitutes for direct sense experience. They are looking for knowledge by single questions that provide the answer in a finished form. When they succeed they do so by a lucky question that hits an immediate, perceptible cause. When the older child receives a "yes" answer to one of his constraint-locating questions, he most often follows up by asking another. When, on the rare occasions that a younger child asks a constraint question and it is answered "yes," he almost invariably follows it up with a specific question to test a concrete hypothesis. The older child can accrete his information in a structure governed by consecutive inference. The younger child cannot.

Potter's (in Bruner et al., 1966) study of the development of perceptual recognition bears on the same point. Ordinary colored photographs of familiar scenes are presented to children between 6 and 12, the pictures coming gradually into focus. Let me sum up one part of the results very briefly. Six-year-olds produce an abundance of hypotheses. But they rarely try to match new hypotheses to previous ones. "There is a big tower in the middle and a road over there and a big ice cream cone through the middle of the tower and a pumpkin on top." It is like a random collage. The 9-year-old's torrent of hypotheses, on the other hand, shows a sense of consistency about what is likely to appear with what. . . . Something is seen as a merry-go-round, and the child then restricts later hypotheses to the other things to be found in an amusement park. The adolescent operates under even more highly organized sequential constraints: He occasionally develops his initial hypotheses from what is implied by the properties of the picture. . . . "It is red and shiny and metallic: It must be a coffee-pot."

Once such constraints are established, the order of hypotheses reflects even more the need to build up a consistent world of objects—even to the point of failing to recognize things that do not fit it.

What shall we make of these three sets of findings—that older children are able to cumulate information by asking questions in a directed sequence leading to a final goal, and that they are capable of recognizing visual displays in a manner . . . that transcends momentary and isolated bits of information? Several points seem apparent. The first is that as children mature, they are able to use indirect information . . . other than the act of pointing to what is immediately present. They seem . . . to make . . . reference to states and constraints that are not given by the immediate situation, to go beyond the information given. Second, . . . they seem to be able to cumulate information into a structure that can be operated upon by rules that transcend simple association by similarity and contiguity. In the case of Twenty Questions, the rule is best described as implication—that knowing one thing implies certain other things and eliminates still others. In the experiments with the light switches, it is that if the present state does not produce the effect, then there is a system for tracing back to the other states that cause the light to go on. . . . The rule is that a piece of information from one part of the display implies what other parts might be. The child, in sum, is translating redundancy into a manipulable model of the environment that is governed by rules of implication. It is this model of the environment that permits him to go beyond the information before him. . . .

. . . Such a system of processing environmental events depends upon the translation of experience into symbolic form. Such a translation is necessary in order for there to be the kind of remoteness of reference as is required when one deals with indirect information. . . . Hockett (1959), in describing the design features of language, includes this feature as crucial. He is referring to human speech as a system of communication. The same point can be made about language as an instrument of thought. That humans have the *capacity* for using speech in this way is only part of the point. What is critical is that the capacity is *not* used until it is coupled with the technology of language in the cognitive operations of the child. . . .

My major concern has been to examine afresh the nature of intellectual growth. . . . It seems to me that growth depends upon the emergence of two forms of competence. Children, as they grow, must acquire ways of representing the recurrent regularities in their environment, and they must transcend the momentary by developing ways of linking past to present to future—representation and integration. I have suggested that we can conceive of growth in both of these domains as the emergence of new technologies for the unlocking and amplification of human intellectual powers. Like the growth of technology, the growth of intellect is not smoothly monotonic. Rather, it moves forward in spurts as innovations are adopted. . . .

. . . Our attention has been directed largely to the transition between iconic and symbolic representation. In children between 4 and 12 language comes to play an increasingly powerful role as an implement of knowing. Through simple experiments, I have tried to show how language shapes, augments, and even supercedes the child's earlier modes of processing information. . . .

What of the integration of intellectual activity into more coherent and interconnected acts? It has been the fashion, since Freud, to see delay of gratification as the principal dynamism behind this development. . . . Without intending to question the depth of this insight, let me suggest that delay of immediate gratification, the ability to go beyond the moment, also depends upon techniques, and again they are techniques of representation. . . .

Once language becomes a medium for the translation of experience, there is a progressive release from immediacy. For language . . . has the . . . features of remoteness and arbitrariness: It permits productive, combinatorial operations in the *absence* of what is represented. With this achievement, the child can delay gratification by virtue of representing to himself what lies beyond the present, what other possibilities exist beyond the clue that is under his nose. . . .

REFERENCES

Braine, M. D. S. On learning the grammatical order of words. *Psychological Review,* 1963, **70,** 323–348.

Bruner, J. S., Olver, R. R., & Greenfield, P. M. *Studies in cognitive growth.* New York: Wiley, 1966.

Chomsky, N. *Syntactic structures.* S'Gravenhage, Netherlands: Mouton, 1957.

Emerson, L. L. The effect of bodily orientation upon the young child's memory for position of objects. *Child Development,* 1931, **2,** 125–142.

Hanfmann, E., Rickers-Ovsiankina, M., & Goldstein, K. Case Lanuti: Extreme concretization of behavior due to damage of the brain cortex. *Psychological Monographs,* 1944, **57**(4, Whole No. 264).

Hockett, C. F. Animal "languages" and human language. In J. N. Spuhler (Ed.), *The evolution of man's capacity for culture.* Detroit: Wayne State University Press, 1959. Pp. 32–39.

Mandler, G. From association to structure. *Psychological Review,* 1962, **69,** 415–426.

Miller, G. A. Some psychological studies of grammar. *American Psychologist,* 1962, **17,** 748–762.

Miller, G. A., Galanter, E., & Pribram, K. H. *Plans and the structure of behavior.* New York: Holt, 1960.

Mosher, F. A. Strategies for information gathering. Paper presented at the meeting of the Eastern Psychological Association, Atlantic City, N.J., April, 1962.

Piaget, J. *The construction of reality in the child.* (Translated by M. Cook). New York: Basic Books, 1954.

Piaget, J., & Inhelder, B. *Le développement des quantités physiques chez l'enfant.* (2nd rev.) Neuchâtel, Switzerland: Delachaux & Niestlé, 1962.

Washburn, S. L., & Howell, F. C. Human evolution and culture. In S. Tax (Ed.), *The evolution of man.* Vol. 2. Chicago: University of Chicago Press, 1960. Pp. 33–56.

Weir, R. H. *Language in the crib.* The Hague: Mouton, 1962.

Werner, H. *Comparative psychology of mental development.* (Rev. ed.) Chicago: Follett, 1948.

AUTHOR INDEX

Page references in *italics* indicate entire chapter or article by author.

Crowder, T., 304, 307
Crutchfield, R. S., 310–311, 314
Cuddy, J. M., 436, 439

Dallenbach, K. M., 437, 439
D'Amato, M. F., 397, 415, 418–419, 426
D'Amico, L. A., 275, 293
D'Andrade, R. G., 194, 196, 228
Dann, S., 263, 292
Darwin, C., 441
Davidson, K. S., 321, 323
Davis, A., 250, 256, 258
Davis, B., 257–258
Davis, J. A., 252, 258, 304, 307
Davitz, J. R., 220, 228
Dawe, H. C., 213, 228
de Charms, R., 316, 321–322
DeLucia, C. A., 357, 365
Distler, L., 204, 206, 230, 232, 238, 377, 386
Dollard, J., 185, 191, 199, 209, 219, 228, 230, 250, 258, 379, 386
Doob, L. W., 209, 228, 250, 258
Duncan, O. D., 257–258
Durkin, K., 346, 355
Duvall, E. N., 256, 258

Easterbrook, J. A., 376, 386
Eells, K., 372, 375
Eifermann, R. R., 429, 435
Eissler, R. S., 292
Elkind, D., 96, 427, 434–435
Elliott, R., 332, 353
Emerson, L. L., 443, 453
Emerson, P. E., 17, 29–31, 33, 59–60
Endsley, R. C., 378, 386
Engen, T., 329, 353
Ernhart, C. B., 339, 353
Eron, L. D., 222, 228, *250–259*
Ervin, S. M., 142, 155, 169, 178, 184
Escalona, S. K., 54, 60, 84–85, 95
Estes, B. W., 345, 354, *371–375*
Estes, W. K., 190–191
Etzel, B. C., 21, 32
Etzion, D., 429, 435
Etzioni, A., 258
Ewing, A. S. G., 436, 439

Faigin, H., 267, 292
Fainstat, T. D., 35, 42
Fantz, R. L., 43, 47, 49–50, 79–81, 84, 87, 96, 109–111, 117
Farina, A., 233–234, 238
Farris, E. J., 40, 42
Ferreia, A. J., 11–12, 32
Field, P. B., 316, 323
Fivel, M. W., 348–349, 354
Fjeld, H. A., 376, 387
Flanders, N. A., 280, 292
Flavell, J. H., 96, 399, 414, 427–428, 435
Fodor, J. A., 149, 158–160, 163
Foss, B. M., 33, 73, 364
Frank, F., 428, 446
Frankie, G., 204, 206–207, 229
Franklin, I. C., 406, 414, 427, 435
Fraser, C., 143–144, 163, *177–184*
Fraser, F. C., 35, 42
Freud, A., 206, 228, 263, 292, 385–386
Freud, S., 198–200, 228, 295, 303, 452
Friedman, G. B., 419, 426
Furth, H. G., 410–412, 414, *436–440*

Gabain, M., 293
Galanter, E., 442, 453
Gallagher, J. J., 304, 307
Gattegno, C., 415, 435
Gelfand, D. M., 289, 292, *316–323*
Gentry, E. F., 356, 364
Gesell, A. L., 177, 179, 184
Gewirtz, J. L., 21, 23, 32, 63, 73, 114, 117, 151, 164, 185–186, 189, 191, 211–213, 218, 228, 329–330, 333, 336, 353–354, 357, 364
Gibbs, P. K., 251, 256, 258
Gibson, E. J., 81–82, 84, 96, 99, 101–102, 107, 109–110
Gibson, J. J., 107, 110
Glazer, J. A., 269, 292
Goldberg, M. H., 277, 292
Goldstein, A., 250, 258
Goldstein, K., 443, 453
Gorbman, A., 42
Gordon, E. W., 356, 365
Gordon, J. E., 285, 293, 309, 314–315

SUBJECT INDEX